PORTUGUESE COCHIN AND THE MARITIME TRADE OF INDIA 1500-1663

SOUTH ASIA INSTITUTE, NEW DELHI BRANCH
HEIDELBERG UNIVERSITY
SOUTH ASIAN STUDIES NO. XXXIX

Portuguese Cochin and the Maritime Trade of India 1500-1663

PIUS MALEKANDATHIL

MANOHAR
2026

First published 2001
POD reprint 2021, 2022, 2023, 2024, 2025
Reprinted 2026

ISBN 978-81-7304-406-9

Published by
Ajay Kumar Jain *for*
Manohar Publishers & Distributors
4753/23 Ansari Road, Daryaganj
New Delhi 110 002

Printed at
Replika Press Pvt. Ltd.

Contents

Illustrations

Foreword

Cochin was an exceptional bridgehead of the Portuguese seaborne empire. Unlike Goa and Malacca which were conquered with brute force, the Portuguese stronghold in Cochin was acquired by diplomacy. The king of Cochin became a faithful ally of the Portuguese because this served his own interest as he had to defend his realm against his rival, the Zamorin of Calicut. The king of Cochin was an exceptional one, because his power was mainly based on the control of many temples in the hinterland. His ritual sovereignty had real benefits not only because he could derive income from these temples, but because he had access to pepper-producing areas. He also controlled an exceptional port which owed its origin to a flood in the fourteenth century which had opened a new passage from the lagoon into the sea at Cochin while at the same time silting up the ancient port of Cranganore (Muziris). Many small rivers flowing into the lagoon created a magnificent network connecting Cochin with its hinterland. But there was a rival network connecting this hinterland via the ghat routes to Tamilnadu whose traders used to bring essential commodities to the pepper country and could take along pepper on their return journey.

This is the setting in which the drama unfolds which has been portrayed in this book. In the first act (1500-20) the Portuguese prosper. They fix the price of pepper at a fairly low level and secure an adequate supply by providing subsidies to the king and several of his underlings so as to guarantee a flow of pepper from the hinterland while at the same time patrolling the coast in order to ward off interlopers. The fixed price seems to have been an incentive rather than a disincentive in this initial period, because it was stable and predictable. The export to Lisbon increased rapidly. At the same time the Portuguese were able to lay the foundations of a thriving municipality at Cochin.

The second act of the drama (1520-50) which is outlined in the first part of the fourth chapter shows the beginnings of ominous developments. The royal pepper trade declines abruptly while the private trade of the settled Portuguese traders married to local women (*casados*) increases and influential Muslim traders of Cochin who had cooperated with the Portuguese so far leave Cochin and side with the Zamorin. This happened because the Portugese ships attacked Muslim ships indiscriminately in the 1520s. The *casados* had settled in Cochin in increasing numbers (from 160 in 1527 to 500 in 1551). They were naturally more interested in their own profit than in that of the Portuguese crown. The Cochin municipality gained in substance and influence due to the new residents who were also joined by New Christians (Jews) who came to Cochin which was still free from the inquisition.

The third act (1551-98) is characterized by two contrasting trends: In the religious field the Portuguese crown imposes more rigorous controls whereas it liberalizes trade to some extent. The inquisition comes to Cochin and harasses the

New Christians. The native St. Thomas Christians are now pressed to adopt Latin rites and revolt against this. They divert much of the pepper which they grow to the ghat route and this affects the official pepper trade from Cochin to Lisbon. The Portuguese crown which is cash-strapped for several reasons offers contracts to European merchants so as to revive the dwindling pepper trade. In the meantime the Asian trade of the *casados* thrives. They convert Cochin into a major emporium. Their privilege of paying an exceptionally low rate of customs duties to the king of Cochin (3.65 per cent) contributes to the rise of this emporium. Moreover, the proud Portuguese *armada* which used to patrol the coast is now converted into a municipal navy financed by the *casados* for the protection of their farflung Asian trading network.

The third act closes in 1598 when the Portuguese crown once more assumes the direct control of the pepper trade. But instead of a revival of the prosperous years of the early sixteenth century, this only means a short interlude which ends in a complete disaster.

The fourth act (1599-1612) witnesses a brief increase of the pepper export from Cochin to Lisbon, but at the same time the Dutch and the British appear in the Indian Ocean and challenge the Portuguese seaborne empire. The king of Cochin gets more and more alienated and looks for other European allies. Finally the Portuguese decide in 1612 to close the direct route from Cochin to Lisbon and to concentrate on the Goa-Lisbon route. This leads to a large scale exodus of the *casados* who prefer to settle down in other Asian ports.

The fifth act (1613-63) which ends with the conquest of Cochin by the Dutch shows the slow decay of this proud emporium. All kinds of halfhearted measures are introduced in order to revive the pepper trade. Those *casados* who still live in Cochin are invited in 1628 to send their own ships directly to Lisbon, in addition a Portuguese India Company is formed by officials in Lisbon in 1629 who are inspired by the British and Dutch East India companies, but most of the capital of this Portuguese company has to be contributed by the crown. This venture is not profitable and is terminated in 1634.

The fall of Ormuz in 1622 and of Malacca in 1641 not only affected the Portuguese seaborne empire in general but also the *casados* of Cochin who had plied an active trade with those centres. The *casados* had in many ways defied the control of the Portuguese crown, but they had also benefited from Portugese sea power and had often lent substantial amounts of money to the crown. After the demise of the Portuguese empire they blended with the network of intra-Asian trade, but they could no longer lay claim to maritime power.

In this brief outline of the drama presented in this book some *dramatis personae* who entered the stage now and then have not been mentioned here so far. These are the Italian and German merchants who concluded pepper contracts with the Portuguese crown, distributed the pepper throughout Europe and also provided essential commodities such as silver and copper for export to India. The author has found a great deal of sources which throw new light on the activities of those merchants. They sent their own agents to India who reported to their masters at home. These accounts are very valuable because they present views independent of the official Portuguese position. The relations of the Portuguese crown with those merchants were not always very harmonious. Portuguese kings were often profligate and spent more money than they could afford, thus they badly needed the capital of those merchants. But whenever the kings felt that they could make more money by cutting out those middlemen, they refused to enter into contracts with them. After the death of Manuel most Portuguese kings used to treat their empire as an estate from which they could derive rents without making investments. For the investment they turned to European merchants and also to the *casados.* The present thesis provides a great deal of evidence for this state of affairs.

Another unfortunate pattern which is well illustrated by the thesis is the growth of Portuguese intolerance and highhandedness which spoiled the relations with influential elements of Indian society which were initially not averse to cooperation with the Portuguese. A particular case in point are the relations with the St. Thomas Christians who initially perceived the Portuguese as Christian brethren but were sorely disappointed when they were pressed to adopt Latin rites. The diversion of the pepper they grew via the ghat route was a severe blow to Portuguese interests. The inveterate hatred of the Muslims also harmed Portuguese trade. The Arab traders who had controlled the trade of the Arabian Sea before the Portuguese appeared on the scene were obviously opposed to them, but the Muslims were not a monolithic community and the traders among them were eager to adjust to the Portuguese system. This was certainly true of Cochin in the period before 1520.

The Portuguese seaborne empire has attracted many historians and some of the features of this empire which have been touched upon in this book have already been treated elsewhere. But in making Cochin the focus of his study and presenting a great deal of new source material, the author has made an extremely valuable contribution to historical scholarship in this field.

Heidelberg DIETMAR ROTHERMUND
April 1998

Acknowledgements

This research work was made possible with the help and encouragement of several persons and the fellowships awarded by a number of international agencies. The work on this theme was begun with the help of a research Fellowship granted to me for one year by Instituto Camões, Lisbon, which enabled me to work in the Archives of Portugal and Rome. On my return to Kerala, a three-year fellowship was granted by Commissão Nacional para as comemorações dos Descobrimentos Portugueses, Lisbon for conducting further research in India, which was again followed by a grant from the same institution to visit the archives of Portugal in the final stages of my research. Meanwhile, the Max Müller Bhavan (Goethe Institute) of Madras had given me a scholarship to learn the German language to enable me to consult the relevant German documents. In 1996 I was awarded an UGC-sponsored DAAD fellowship (Deutscher Akademischer Austauschdienst, Bonn, under the Indo-German Exchange Programme) for twenty-eight months for conducting research in Germany, and to work in European archives as well as libraries. I wish to place on record my indebtedness to these institutions.

I would like to express my gratitude in a very special way, to Deutscher Akademischer Austauschdienst, Bonn, for the Fellowship which enabled me to finish this work. DAAD also helped me to register at the Heidelberg University, Germany under the 'Sandwich Programme' and to conduct research under Dietmar Rothermund of Südasien Institute. I am deeply indebted to Christa Klaus and S. Conradi of DAAD office, Bonn who were very prompt and extremely helpful in providing facilities and means for conducting research in the various archives of Germany and other parts of Europe. I recall with gratitude the prompt help given to me by the Directors and Staff of the various archives and libraries of Lisbon, Evora, Rome, Munich, Augsburg, Bremen, Aachen, Heidelberg, Dillingen/Donau, Vienna, Goa, Madras, Pondicherry and Kerala.

I wish to express my sincere thanks to K.S. Mathew, my Ph.D. supervisor, and Head of the History Department at Pondicherry University. It is he, who introduced me to the history of trade, and as the ideal supervisor, with encouraging and inspiring guidance, he instilled in me a keen desire and confidence to undertake this research. At every stage, he has been a source of reference and inspiration. I have special debt of gratitude to Dietmar Rothermund, an erudite scholar on Indo-European economic history, of Südasien Institute, Heidelberg University, Germany, who guided my research for two years in Germany. It is with great pleasure and deep gratitude that I recall his scholarly guidance which made me see the theme in its wider Indo-European context. Rothermund took pains to go through the first and the final drafts of my thesis and has been of immense help at all levels of my research in Heidelberg. I express sincere thanks to him and Manfred Hake for having included this work as a volume in the South Asian Series of Heidelberg University. My debts are also due to Tilman Frasch and other staff of the Department of History of Südasien Institute, Heidelberg University and its Librarians, who were extremely kind and helpful in providing all the required facilities for my work. It is with deep gratitude that I recall the immense help and prompt service which I received from both the teaching and non-teaching staff of the Department of History, Pondicherry University. I would like to mention gratefully the advice and guidance drawn from conversations with eminent scholars such as Luis Filipe Thomaz, R. Hildebrandt, Wolfgang Knabe, Teotonio de Soua, A.R. Kulkarni and Ranabir Chakravarti. Moreover, Luis Filipe Thomaz, R. Hildebrandt and Wolfgang Knabe allowed me to make use of their rare personal collections. I am very grateful for the help of my Portuguese friends, João Manuel de Almeida Teles e Cunha and Jose Alberto Rodrigues da Silva Tavim, who introduced me to some interesting Portuguese documents and themes. I recall with gratitude the teachers and the various institutions who helped me to learn different languages, essential for consulting the relevant documents. I pay obeisance to Fr. George Padinjarekutt and late Fr. John Kunnappilly who taught me the Latin and Sanskrit languages respectively, in the seminaries, which were a great help all through my research. I place on record my indebtedness to Fr. Cajetan Coelho, my teacher of the Dutch language at the Department of History, Pondicherry University, the teachers of l'Alliance Française, Pondicherry who gave me lessons in the French Language, the teachers of Faculdade de Letras, Universidade de Lisboa, who taught me Portuguese, and the teachers of Goethe Institute, Pune as well as Bremen (Germany), where I learnt German. I acknowledge my debt also to the Faculdade de Ciencias Sociais e Humanas da Universidade Nova de Lisboa for giving me special permission to attend the Portuguese palaeography course offered by the university.

I am greatly indebted to H. Nischk, the cartographer of the Department of Geography of the Südasien Institute, Heidelberg University,Germany, who designed the maps of this work. I wish to record my special thanks to Archbishop Dom Jose Policarp (the Patriarch of Lisbon) and Pe. Manuel Clemente of the Seminario dos Olivais, Lisbon, as well as to Abbot Franziskus, P. Suitbert Jaspers and Bro. Joseph of Benediktinerabtei, Heidelberg for the help and the arrangements made for my stay in Portugal and Germany. I am very grateful to Mar George Punnakkottil, the Bishop of Kothamangalam and Mar Joseph Pallickaparambil, the Bishop of Palai, for their encouragement and moral support. My special thanks are due to the Manager and the Principal of St. Thomas College, Palai, Kerala, for giving me the necessary permission to take duty leave and undertake this research. I remember with special gratitude, the immense and timely help rendered by Shri P.J. Joseph, the Education Minister of Kerala who did the needful to help me utilize leave provisions and benefits of the UGC granted to DAAD Fellows. I remember with immense gratitude Mathias and Margaret Frenz who helped me immensely during my research in Germany. My gratitude is also due to all my well-wishers and friends who helped me in one way or other.

Heidelberg
September 1998

PIUS MALEKANDATHIL

Abbreviations

ANTT	Arquivo Nacional da Torre do Tombo, Lisboa.
AHU	Arquivo Historico Ultramarino, Lisboa.
BNL	Biblioteca Nacional de Lisboa.
BA	Biblioteca da Ajuda.
BPE	Biblioteca Publica e Arquivo Distrital de Evora.
FA	Fürstlich und Gräflich Fugger'sches Familien und Stiftungs Archive, Dillingen/Donau, Germany.
HAG	The Historical Archives of Goa.
IESHR	Indian Economic and Social History Review.

CHAPTER I

Introduction

Scholars of pre-industrial cities maintain that cities were first created by the exercise of power by some groups over others, to extract agricultural surplus and provide services to a particular geographically defined society. Later,.other settlements may have been planted within that society as a means of furthering political control, and for creating and expropriating surplus. The cities which the Europeans founded outside their own continent were developed with a view to extracting those products which they could not acquire in Europe. These goods were largely agricultural, and grown very often in a climate not found in Europe. The great demand for these commodities in Europe made it necessary for the colonizers to exercise control in the processes of extraction and distribution. The requirements of colonization demanded many unequivocally urban functions. Most important among them was the need for a port, to allow export of colonial wares and also the import of commodities from Europe. When the colonists established themselves with the help of a port, governmental centres and garrisons became necessary, which led to an increase in the density of urban life, as numerous suppliers, retailers and craftsmen arrived to serve such institutions.

1. CONCEPTUAL FRAME

The colonial city is usually considered as a port and a fort. Here the ports are meant not as mere centres of exchange; they also become tools for sponging and extracting surplus from the production centres. The colonists could not have thrived without the help of a port-city. It provided the door for penetration into the surrounding economies. The structure and functions of the colonial cities are designed to serve the colonizers and are basically parasitical and extractive.[1]

The port is the main dynamic force and the central organizing principle in port-cities and the specialized function of the port determines the character, the morphology, the structure and functioning of the port-city settlements. Settlements in port cities are comparable to those which arise when particular specialized functions are called for, such as caravan cities, mining cities and ceremonial cities. The port-city has its own specific characteristics derived from the maritime functions of exchange, enterprise and transport. It has its settlement apart from the surrounding regions and from the other urban settlements and these determine its physical, economic and social configurations.[2]

Another important feature of the port city is that its economic life is linked with two or more marketing systems. Foreland implies those areas of the overseas world with which the port is immediately linked through its shipping, trade and passenger traffic, and represent the external dimension. These are the major overseas markets to which hinterland products are carried and the places from which goods are imported for consumption and further distribution throughout the hinterland.[3] Hinterland, on the other hand, represents the internal dimensions including productive and consumptive activities. It is the organized and developed land spaces which are connected with a port by means of transport lines and which receive or ship goods through that port.[4] The hinterland comprises more economic units than geographical regions, supplying the city with commodities to be taken to overseas markets as well as for local consumption. The hinterland is at the same time a market for the foreign commodities imported to the port.[5] The colonial port cities are instituted to extract the surplus of the hinterland by trading only with the mother country. The role of the port-cities is understandable only by analysing the various networks by which the hinterlands are incorporated into the foreland.[6]

The colonists used the city to further extend the boundaries of their society, by transportation (initially shipping), to incorporate other territories and peoples overseas. Thus the colonial city, as a cultural artifact, becomes an instrument of colonization. It is also explained as a spearhead of economic, political and cultural penetration, following which the structural organization and re-organization of the colonized society or territory takes place.[7]

The unique features of the colonial port city are apparently three: 1. The economic, social and political power is principally in the hands of a non-indigenous minority; while the rights of the colonized are either nil or very restricted. 2. This minority is superior in terms of military, technological and economic resources and as a result in social organization. 3. The colonized majority is racially, culturally and religiously different from the colonists who are culturally European, and by religion, Christian.[8] Another striking feature of the colonial city is the emergence of a new settlement as separate from, but close to, the existing one. The new settlement is relatively European and maintains some distance from the existing native part of the city. Other features like the relative absence of females and of European women, the consequent creation of a mixed-race population, the presence of a bachelor chummery, male troops, high rates of venereal diseases, special provision of hospitals, vast areas of space laid out for recreational use and the like are unique to colonial cities. Even the church and its institutions are made instruments of colonization and social control. In short, colonial cities are those extractive and parasitical urban centres created by the colonists in order to serve their interests.[9]

The port-cities are viewed as the very essence of colonial life. Without these port-towns, colonial penetration would have been impossible.[10] Against this backdrop, the role of Cochin in the maritime trade of India is taken up for study in this work.

2. REVIEW OF LITERATURE

It seems pertinent here to review some of the works which are related to the subject under study. Though many general works on the Portuguese in Goa or on the administrative and political history of Portuguese Asia are available, only a very few deal with the Portuguese in Cochin, the first capital of the *Estado da India*; even fewer for the socio-economic history of this city.

The significant general works which give some account of Cochin are *The Rise of Portuguese Power in India, 1497-1550* written by R.S. Whiteway[11] and *The Portuguese in India* written in 2 volumes (volume I deals with the period from 1481 to 1571 and volume II with the period from 1571 to 1894) by F.C. Danvers (1833-1906).[12] To this general category, one could add C.R. Boxer's *The Portuguese Sea-borne Empire, 1415-1825.*[13] These general accounts are standard works for Portuguese Asia; but the developments in Cochin are mentioned only at random. Even these, though they supply lot of material to work with, do not explain the inner logic behind many incidents in Cochin for which one would have to look elsewhere. The value of these general accounts lie in the fact that they form a vague and scattered matrix out of which one could reconstruct a significant portion of the history of Cochin.

The Portuguese phase in Kerala history is dealt with in several standard works like *History of Kerala* by K.P. Padmanabha Menon,[14] *Medieval Kerala* by P.K.S. Raja,[15] *A Survey of Kerala History* by A. Sreedhara Menon,[16] *The Kunjalis, Admirals of Calicut* by O.K. Nambiar,[17] *Mamale de Cananor* by Genevieve Bouchon.[18] The first three works treat this phase in a very superficial way without making critical study of the Portuguese sources; while the last two works deal mostly with the rival figures of the Portuguese and their activities. A highly esteemed work on the Portuguese presence in Malabar was produced by K.M. Panikkar first under the title *Malabar and the Portuguese*[19] and later incorporated into *A History of Kerala 1498-1801.*[20] Though it is a very good work, it is mostly political and administrative, rather than economic history. Two very significant works on the economic history of Portuguese Malabar are *Portuguese Trade with India in the Sixteenth Century* by K.S. Mathew[21] and *Twilight of the Pepper Empire* by A.R. Disney.[22] But the first work confines itself to a period from 1500 to 1530; while the second work dwells only on the trade of the early seventeenth century. Though these two works deal also in relative detail with the export-import trade in Cochin, they do not go deep into the economic life of Cochin.

Several works like *The Land of the Perumals or Cochin* by Francis Day,[23] *The Cochin State Manual* by C. Achyuta Menon,[24] *Kochi Rajya Charitram* by K.P. Padmanabha Menon,[25] *Castes and Tribes of Cochin* by L.K. Ananthakrishna Iyer [26] deal with the history of Cochin. The first three authors treat Cochin as a political unit and narrate the political and administrative history of the kingdom of Cochin; Ananthakrishna Iyer has dwelt on the castes and tribes of the kingdom of Cochin. A notable work on the port of Cochin has been written by Robert Bristow under the title *Cochin Saga.*[27] But this deals mainly with the British phase and is less scientific. An attempt is made to study the town of Fort Cochin by K.L .Bernard,[28] however this work is superficial and unscientific. *A Translation of a Record, Grandhavari in the State Archives*[29] which dwells more on the genealogy of the kings of Cochin, and *Padapattu*[30] which deals mainly with the Portuguese-Dutch war in Cochin in 1660s are good native sources for corroborative study.

Gervasis J. Mulakara has made a study of the history of the Diocese of Cochin.[31] This helps one to understand the various ecclesiastical institutions of the Portuguese city of Cochin, but ignores other urban institutions, and covers only a very short period, i.e. up to 1558. The accounts of the Jews of Cochin during the Portuguese period are given in the works of Mosseh Pereyra de Paiva[32] (*Notisias dos Judeus de Cochim, mandadas por Mosseh Pereyra de Paiva*), David Mandelbaum[33] (*The Jewish Way of Life in Cochin*), J.B. Segal[34] (*A History of the Jews of Cochin*) and Thomas A. Timberg[35] (*Jews in India*). These authors confine themselves only to the history of the Jews of Cochin and ignore other social groups in the native as well as Portuguese parts of the city of Cochin.

A good introduction to the urban space of Cochin is given in A.M. Mundadan's article, 'The Town of Cochin and the Portuguese'.[36] The initial phase of Cochin is studied by Jean Aubin in his article 'L'apprentissage de L'Inde: Cochin 1503-1504'.[37] However these two works do not go deep into the historical changes and economic activities in Cochin. A valuable work which is very much useful for any study of Cochin is *Emergence of Cochin in the Pre-Industrial Era: A Study of Portuguese Cochin* edited by K.S. Mathew and Afzal Ahmad.[38] It is mainly a collection of primary documents related to Cochin, dealing more with the city administration. It deals very little with the economic aspect of its history. The articles written by R.O.W. Goertz under the same title 'The Portuguese in Cochin' in *Indica*[39] and in *Studia*[40] give lot of information about the trade in Cochin. But these deal primarily with the private trade and smuggling of spices that became common in Cochin by the 1540s. Sanjay Subrahmanyam covers rather a long period of trade in Cochin in his article 'Cochin in Decline, 1600-1650: Myth and Manipulation in the *Estado da India*'[41] and in his book *The Political Economy of Commerce: Southern India 1500-1650.*[42] He dwells more on the trade of the *casados* and ignores other mercantile groups and many social as well as economic changes in Cochin. A recent doctoral thesis, '*O Estado Português da India: da Rendição de Ormuz à Perda de Cochin, 1622-1663*' of Maria Manuela Sobral Blanco[43] submitted at the Faculdade de Letras de Universidade de Lisboa (1992) deals with the final phase of Cochin and shows how the destruction of the caravan route along with the loss of Ormuz effected the downfall of Cochin. But this study deals mainly with the *Estado da India* and with regard to Cochin, it covers only very short period, i.e. from 1622-63.

A scientific, critical and holistic study of the city of Cochin, the first base and headquarters of the Portuguese in Asia, and its commercial relations is a must, at least now, when the world celebrates the five hundredth anniversary of the arrival in India of the Portuguese under Vasco da Gama.

3. THE IDENTITY OF THE AREA OF STUDY

It is very important to identify the area of study, as the name Cochin denotes different geographical units. Cochin is understood as, first, the present city corporation of Cochin which comprises the present Ernakulam mainland, Cochin proper, the islands of Venduruthy, Wellington, Bolgatty, Vaipin and Gundur, secondly, the former kingdom of Cochin, and thirdly, the town of Cochin in which was located the port and which was also the capital of the kingdom of Cochin. During the period under study, this town of Cochin was also understood as being two geographical and urban entities: Native Cochin (*Cochim de Cima* or the present Mattancherry area) and Portuguese Cochin (the city of *Santa Cruz* or the present Fort Cochin area).

The focal area of our study is both the towns of Cochin with special emphasis on Portuguese Cochin. The role of the Portuguese city of *Santa Cruz* in the maritime trade of India is analysed against the native urban background.

4. ANALYTICAL FRAME

When preparations are being made all over the world for celebrating the fifth centenary of Vasco da Gama's arrival in India, scholars wonder how a small nation like Portugal with limited manpower and limited economic resources could have established a large far-flung politico-commercial empire touching the four continents of the world. The emergence of this small Iberian nation into a world-power is a puzzling phenomenon in world history, which requires deeper researches into developments outside the mother country. An answer to this riddle is proposed by studying Cochin, the first colonial base of the Portuguese in Asia. The central purpose of this study is to see how Cochin rose up from a small fishing village into an international trade centre as well as a port-city and what role did Cochin, the first political headquarters of the Portuguese Government in the East (till 1530), and later the commercial capital of the Portuguese trade empire till 1663, play in organizing the maritime trade of India, and also how far its trade contributed to the build-up of the universal empire of the Lusitanians.

This study is confined to the Portuguese phase of Cochin and so the '*terminus a quo*' is 1500 when the first Portuguese, Pedro Alvares Cabral reached Cochin and the '*terminus ad quem*' is the year 1663, when the Dutch occupied the city after defeating the Portuguese. Though the period from 1500 to 1663 is quite long, it has been chosen for a variety of reasons. This 163-year Portuguese phase thematically forms one unit of study. A fragmentary study confined to particular years would not give us a holistic view of the changes over time and would not serve the purpose for which this study has been conducted. The pattern of trade at various periods was different and the export-trade-index of Cochin always fluctuated with upward and downward trends depending on local conditions and native factors, an assessment of which would be impossible without taking the entire Portuguese period into account. The indigenous co-operation was never unconditional or static, the changes in which have had long-term repercussions that affected the entire Portuguese phase.

The first chapter, being introductory, is an attempt to review the conceptual frame and the existing literature related to the topic. It states the central purpose and identifies the geographical area of the study. It also puts forward the problem that is to be analysed in the succeeding chapters. Mention is made regarding the method of study and the nature of sources consulted, giving details about the principal archives and libraries visited for the collection of data.

The second chapter tries to analyse the general condition of Cochin in the pre-Portuguese period. It also attempts to see when it did emerge as a port and how far the emergence of this new port affected the existing economic and political life of Malabar. At this point, it is necessary to highlight the reactions of various political powers to the emerging port and its initial trade activities. The chapter also proposes to study the initial traders, the various countries with which Cochin had commercial relationship, as well as the nature and pattern of settlement in the city that developed around this port. It is necessary to examine the factors that accounted for the state formation in Cochin and the general political conditions that prompted the native king, later, to offer protection and a part of the city of Cochin to the Portuguese. An attempt is made to examine the important hinterlands that supplied spices and other commodities to the port of Cochin and where they were located. This chapter investigates the principal pepper producers and the important land routes that connected the hinterland with the port of Cochin. It traces the principal riverine routes that were used to penetrate into the hinterland and the major markets which were located in the hinterland.

The third chapter dwells on the urban phenomenon in Cochin. It also examines the circumstances which compelled the Portuguese to land in Cochin and the reasons why Cochin was chosen as the principal base for the Portuguese establishments in the East. An attempt is made to study the location of the port, the Manuel Fort, the Portuguese part of the city as well as its native counterpart in Cochin. Discussions on the juridical establishment of the urban unit of Santa Cruz of Cochin, its demographic structure, and the administration of the city as well as the role of the municipal council in the administration of the city are also included in this chapter. The important economic activities in the city of Santa Cruz, and how far the ship-building activities in Cochin were necessary for maintaining regular ships for the *carreira* service are also considered here. Special attention is given to look at the social life in Cochin and see how the urban society was stratified. The important educational institutions, the structure and function of *Misericordia,* hospitals and other social welfare institutions in Cochin are examined bringing out their role in the urban life. It is equally important to examine the important ecclesiastical institutions in the city of Santa Cruz and see how far the activities of the Franciscans, the Jesuits, the Dominicans and the Augustinians affected the socio-religious life of the city. Along with this, the chapter examines how far the establishment of the bishopric of Cochin with jurisdiction over the entire south-eastern India, was utilized in order to realize the Portuguese policy of socio-economic penetration. It also examines how far the institution of the Inquisition set up in Cochin, affected the socio-economic activities of the various religious groups.

Chapter four is devoted to finding answers to the questions related to the nature of the Intra-Asian trade in Cochin during the period between 1500 and 1570. An attempt is made to trace the main features of the local as well as intra-local trade that centred around Cochin and the volume of illegal pepper-trade conducted through the ghat routes that ran from the hinterland of Cochin. The chapter also tries to see how the intra-Asian trade emanating from Cochin, which had so far been mono-polized by the Muslim merchants, slowly passed into the hands of Portuguese entrepreneurs and how the latter organized themselves into a lobbying group known as 'the Cochin group' and were opposing state trade and state intervention in commerce. The trade in Cochin was never a monolithic phenomenon; on the contrary it included several strands and layers. This chapter examines the main features of the various layers of licensed trade and also the illicit trade conducted in Cochin. It also tries to see how the voyages were converted into a trade system, and to what degree the ships with *cartazes* were used for licensed trade. The chapter also looks into the commercial arrangements made by the *casados,* almost parallel to those of the *Estado*; it further examines the patrons, partners and associates of the *casados* in their illegal trade transactions, including smuggling of spices. In this connection, a mention is made about the way in which the estranged Muslim merchants of Cochin resorted to the so-called corsair activities as an alternative means of trade.

The fifth chapter treats the important features of the Indo-European trade, conducted in Cochin, during the period between 1500 and 1570. The initial thirty-five years of Portuguese establishment in Cochin witnessed flourishing trade via the Cape route with the Atlantic port of Lisbon and its satellite trade house in Antwerp. It is necessary to examine the factors that could be held responsible for this and the role of the fortress-*armada* system; the fixation of permanent prices for the various spices, and the amount of cooperation extended by various native groups are therefore analysed in this context. A mention is made of the reasons why the Portuguese crown was compelled to make the Germans and the Italians participate in Indian trade and the degree of involvement of the Germans and Italians in the commercial activities of Cochin. The volume and commodities of export and import are also discussed. The important features of the export trade for the period between 1535 and 1570 are analysed separately. It seeks answers to the questions as why the royal monopoly was relaxed, why was private trade viewed as an exigency of the time, and how far were the tensions in the hinterland associated with the diminishing supply of spices in Cochin. It also examines how far the developments in Cochin favoured the revival of the Levantine trade, how far the international changes affected the trade in Cochin, and how far the changes in the trade pattern of Cochin influenced the changing international scenario.

The sixth chapter seeks answers to the questions on the nature of the intra-Asian trade conducted in Cochin during the period between 1570 and 1663. It chiefly examines the circumstances that led to the thriving of private trade during this period and the volume of intra-Asian trade. The chapter also tries to see the development of a 'mixed economy phenomenon' in Cochin, in which the Portuguese officers and also the ordinary *casados*, while co-operating with the official Cape-route-trade, had built up a private empire of their own. The reasons for the apparent decline of European as well as Intra-Asian trade in the seventeenth century are also analysed. The analysis tries to see how far the Dutch blockade in the eastern space of Indian Ocean as well as the tensions in the hinterland and the consequent estrangement of the principal pepper cultivators followed by the diversion of spices to places other than Cochin, affected the private trade of the *casados.* The impact of the fall of Ormuz on the private traders of Cochin is also analysed in this chapter.

The seventh chapter looks at the ups and downs in the Indo-European trade during the period between 1570 and 1663. It tries to look into the reasons why the royal monopoly was given up. An attempt is made to trace the nature of the contract trade carried out for twenty-eight years (1570-98), as well as the principal European contractors engaged in trade with Cochin. The seventeenth-century kings of Cochin turned out to be more assertive. It is necessary to see how far this affected the Indo-European trade of the Portuguese in Cochin and how far the Portuguese succeeded in bringing them to a cooperative endeavour. Attempts are also made to examine the circumstances that led to the establishment of Portuguese India Company and to see how far the Company administration succeeded in improving the export-trade of Cochin. The circumstances in which trade contracts were made with the *casado* traders of Cochin for exporting spices to Lisbon on regular basis, and the extent to which this arrangement turned out to be successful are also briefly discussed here.

An attempt is made in the concluding chapter, to bring out the role played by Cochin in organizing the maritime trade of India and to see how far Cochin's trade was utilized by the Lusitanians as a means of extracting the surplus for their own empire building.

The select bibliography falls into two parts: the first part gives a list of the primary sources, while the second part mentions the secondary sources including studies both in periodicals and other publications in both European and local languages.

5. METHODOLOGY AND SOURCES

The methodology employed in this study is primarily analytical and descriptive. The basic data for the study have been collected from the various sources (both published as well as unpublished), available in archives and libraries of Europe and India. The important archives and libraries consulted in Europe are Arquivo Nacional da Torre do Tombo (Lisboa), Arquivo Historico Ultramarino (Lisboa), Biblioteca Nacional de Lisboa, Biblioteca da Ajuda (Lisboa), Filmoteca Ultramarina Portuguesa (Lisboa), Biblioteca da Academia das Ciencias (Lisboa), Biblioteca de Sociedade de Geografia (Lisboa), Biblioteca Publica e Arquivo distrital de Evora, Stadtarchiv-Augsburg, Stadtbibliothek-Augsburg, Stadtbibliothek-Nürnberg, Fürstlich und Gräflich Fugger'sches Familien und Stiftungs Archiv-Dillingen/Donau, Fürstlich Waldburg-Zeilschen Archiv, Leutkirch, Nationalbibliothek-Vienna, Archivum Romanum Societatis Jesu-Rome and the Vatican Library. The Indian archival repositories consulted for this work include the Padroado (Diocesan) Archives of Cochin, the Kerala State Archives, Regional Office (Ernakulam), the Tamilnadu State Archives (Egmore, Madras), the Archives of the Madurai Province of the Society of Jesus (Shembaganur, Kodaikanal) and the Historical Archives of Goa (Panjim).

In the process of analysis, this documentary evidence is corroborated with the help of inscriptions and the studies on Portuguese numismatics as well as through conducting field studies in areas related to this theme. The graphs and diagrams are drawn on the basis of the data supplied in the text, for which references are given in the notes of respective chapters.

NOTES

1. Anthony D. King, 'Colonial Cities: Global Pivots of Change', in *Colonial Cities: Essays on Urbanism in a Colonial Context*, edited by Robert Ross and Gerard J. Telkamp, Leiden, 1985, p. 8; Robert Ross and Gerard J. Telkamp (eds.), *Colonial Cities: Essays on Urbanism in a Colonial Context*, pp. 1-4.
2. Frank Broeze (ed.), *Brides of the Sea: Port Cities of Asia from 16th-20th Centuries,*

Australia, 1989, p. 11; Frank Broeze, Peter Reeves and Kenneth McPherson, 'Port Cities in the Indian Ocean Region 1815-1939: Functional and Methodological Issues', A Paper presented at the *Second International Conference on Indian Ocean Studies*, held in Perth, 5-12 December 1984, p. 8; P. Reeves, Frank Broeze and McPherson, 'Studying the Asian Port City', in *Brides of the Sea: Port Cities of Asia from 16th -20th Centuries*, p. 40; P. Reeves, K. McPherson and F. Broeze, 'Port Cities: The Conceptual Problems', A Paper presented in the *Australian Historical Association*, Sydney, 1982, pp. 3-5.

3. G.G. Weigned, 'Some Elements in the Study of Port Geography', *Geographical Review*, XL, VIII, April, 1958, pp. 185-200.
4. Ibid., pp. 192-3.
5. Atiya Habeeb Kidwai, 'Conceptual and Methodological Issues: Ports, Port-Cities and Port-Hinterlands', in *Ports and their Hinterlands in India 1700-1950*, edited by Indu Banga, New Delhi, 1992, pp. 15-19; Frank Broeze, 'The External Dynamics of Port-City Morphology: Bombay 1815-1914', in *Ports and their Hinterlands in India*, pp. 250-2.
6. The port links the hinterland with the foreland. Foreland is defined as those areas of the overseas world with which the port-city is immediately linked through its shipping, trade and passenger traffic. See for details Atiya Habeeb Kidwai, op. cit., pp. 22-3.
7. Anthony D. King, op. cit., pp. 8-13.
8. Ibid., pp. 9-10; see also G. Balandier, 'The Colonial Situation: A Theoretical Approach', in *Social Changes: The Colonial Situation*, edited by Immanuel Wallerstein, New York, 1966, pp. 34-61.
9. Anthony D. King, op. cit., pp. 10-21.
10. How far the port cities of Bombay and Madras were utilized for colonial penetration was excellently explained in the works of Dick Kooiman and Susan Lewandowski. See Dick Kooiman, 'Bombay: From Fishing Village to Colonial Port-City 1662-1947', in *Colonial Cities: Essays on Urbanism in a Colonial Context*, edited by Robert Ross and Gerard J. Telkamp, pp. 227 ff. Susan Lewandowski, 'Urban Growth and Municipal Development in the Colonial City of Madras, 1800-1900', *Journal of Asian Studies*, 1975, pp. 342-60.
11. R.S. Whiteway, *The Rise of Portuguese Power in India*, New Delhi, 1989.
12. F.C. Danvers, *The Portuguese in India*, 2 vols., New Delhi, 1988.
13. C.R. Boxer, *The Portuguese Sea-borne Empire, 1415-1825*, London, 1969.
14. K.P. Padmanabha Menon, *History of Kerala*, 4 vols., New Delhi, 1982.
15. P.K.S. Raja, *Medieval Kerala*, Calicut, 1966.
16. A. Sreedhara Menon, *A Survey of Kerala History*, Kottayam, 1967.
17. O.K. Nambiar, *The Kunjalis: Admirals of Calicut*, London, 1963.
18. Genevieve Bouchon, *Mamale de Cananor-Un adversaire de l'Indie Portugais (1507-1528)*, Paris, 1975.
19. K.M. Panikkar, *Malabar and the Portuguese*, Bombay, 1929.
20. K.M. Panikkar, *A History of Kerala 1498-1801*, Annamalainagar, 1960.
21. K.S. Mathew, *Portuguese Trade with India in the Sixteenth Century*, Delhi, 1983.
22. A.R. Disney, *Twilight of Pepper Empire: Portuguese Trade in South West India in the Early Seventeenth Century*, Cambridge, 1978.
23. Francis Day, *The Land of the Perumals or Cochin: Its Past and its Present*, New Delhi, 1990.
24. C. Achyuta Menon, *The Cochin State Manual*, Ernakulam, 1911.
25. K.P. Padmanabha Menon, *Kochi Rajya Charitram*, Kozhikode, 1989.
26. L.K. Ananthakrishna Iyer, *Castes and Tribes of Cochin*, Cochin, 1909.

27. Robert Bristow, *Cochin Saga*, Cochin, 1967.
28. K.L. Bernard, *History of Fort Cochin*, Cochin, 1991.
29. *A Translation of a Record, Grandhavari in the State Archives*, Trivandrum, 1973.
30. Ulloor Parameswara Aiyyar (ed.), *Padappattu*, Trivandrum, 1924.
31. Gervasis J. Mulakara, *History of the Diocese of Cochin: European Missionaries in Cochin 1292-1558*, vol. I, Rome, 1986.
32. Mosseh Pereyra de Paiva, *Notisias dos Judeus de Cochim, mandadas por Mosseh Pereyra de Paiva*, introduction by Moses Bensabat Amzalak, Lisbon, 1923.
33. David Mandelbaum, 'The Jewish Way of Life in Cochin', in *Jewish Social Studies*, vol. I, 4, 1939, pp. 423-60.
34. J.B. Segal, 'White and Black Jews at Cochin, the Story of a Controversy', in *Journal of the Royal Asiatic Society of Great Britain and Ireland*, 2, 1983, pp. 228-52; see also *A History of the Jews of Cochin*, London, 1993.
35. Thomas A. Timberg (ed.), *Jews in India*, Delhi, 1986.
36. A.M. Mundadan, 'The Town of Cochin and the Portuguese', in *II Seminario Internacional de Historia Indo-Portuguesa, Actas*, ed. by Luis de Albuquerque and Inacio Guerreiro, Lisbon, 1985, pp. 251-63.
37. Jean Aubin, 'L'apprentissage de L'Inde: Cochin 1503-1504', in *Moyen Orient & Océan Indien, XVIe-XIXe. S.*, IV, Paris, 1987, pp. 1-20.
38. K.S. Mathew and Afzal Ahmad, *Emergence of Cochin in the Pre-Industrial Era: A Study of Portuguese Cochin*, Pondicherry, 1990.
39. R.O.W. Goertz, 'The Portuguese in Cochin in the Mid-Sixteenth Century', in *Indica*, vol. 23, nos.1 & 2, 1986, pp. 63-78.
40. R.O.W. Goertz, 'The Portuguese in Cochin in the Mid-Sixteenth Century', in *Studia*, 49, 1989, pp. 5-38. Though the two articles of R.O.W. Goertz have the same title, there is substantial difference in the contents.
41. Sanjay Subrahmanyam, 'Cochin in Decline, 1600-1650: Myth and Manipulation in the Estado da India', in *Portuguese Asia: Aspects in History and Economic History (Sixteenth and Seventeenth Centuries)*, edited by Roderich Ptak, Stuttgart, 1987, pp. 59-85.
42. Sanjay Subrahmanyam, *The Political Economy of Commerce: Southern India 1500-1650*, New York, 1990.
43. Maria Manuela Sobral Blanco, 'O Estado da India: Da Rendição de Ormuz á Perda de Cochim: 1622-1663', vol. I, Unpublished Doctoral Dissertation in History submitted to the Faculdade de Letras de Universidade de Lisboa, 1992.

CHAPTER II

Native Cochin and the Hinterland

Significant changes appeared in the exhange systems of the Indian Ocean after the port of Cochin was established. As early as the beginning of the fifteenth century, Cochin had attracted long-distance traders from China, Arabia and Persia and had emerged as an important trading centre. In and around this port, there developed eventually a city, which was later called native Cochin and which became the seat of the kingdom of Cochin as well as the habitat for native merchant groups. The trade activities of this port and the jurisdictional rights which the Perumpadappu kings exercised over various and scattered temples of Malabar played a key role in the state formation of Cochin. The state was ruled by the senior-most member of the royal family, which was divided into five branches. Besides the kingdom of Cochin, many kingdoms of central Kerala such as Porcad, Thekkenkur, Vadakkenkur, Kizhumalainadu, Alengad, Parur, Cranganore, all noted for their large-scale spice-production, had been carved out in to the hinterland of Cochin. Later the Portuguese offering monetary rewards to the rulers of these kingdoms, tried to closely integrate and incorporate the hinterland with the port of Cochin. The Vembanadu lake into which the different land routes and the seven riverine routes merged, facilitated the easy transportation of commodities from the hinterland to Cochin. There were also some satellite markets such as Erumely, Kanjirappilly, Erattupetta, Thodupuzha, Kothamangalam and Chalakudy which were located in the interior. These maintained commercial links both with the port of Cochin through the land and riverine routes as well as with the ports of Tamilnadu through the Ghat route. The flow of spices in both directions varied on the basis of prices offered as well as on the basis of tensions and conflicts that erupted in the hinterland. This chapter deals primarily with the native part of Cochin and the various parts of the spice-growing hinterland which Cochin enviously retained till the middle of the seventeenth century.

1. EMERGENCE OF COCHIN

I. THE EARLY PHASE OF COCHIN

The emergence of Cochin as a port is attributed to the great geophysical changes that occurred because of the flood in the river Periyar in 1341. The floods swept down the river Periyar, and while one branch of it silted up the harbour of Cranganore (the old Muziris), the other branch which flows into Verapoly and merges into the Vembanadu lake, opened wide the entrance from the sea to the lagoons and thereby brought into existence the harbour of Cochin.[1] As a result of the natural convulsions, and the interaction between the flood water and the sea, besides the wide outlet made into the sea, a vast strip of land—about more than thirteen miles long by three miles broad—known as Puthu Vaippu between Cochin and Cranganore and along the sea was also created.[2] The geographical changes which affected Cochin, Vaipin and Cranganore were commemorated by the Puthu Vaippu Era from the date of Vaipin's formation in 1341.[3] This new era was recognized mainly by the St. Thomas Christians of Njarakkal church in the Vaipin island.[4]

The newly-created water passage provided safe anchorage and good shelter for ships. Eventually it came to be called *Kochi*, which is believed to have been a contraction of the word *Kochazhi*, meaning small or new harbour in order to distinguish it from the large or old harbour of Cranganore.[5] Merchant ships engaged in coastal trade and long-distance commerce began to frequent this port and by the beginning of the fifteenth century, it came to occupy a prominent position in the trade map of Malabar coast.

The fact that trade does not exist in a political vacuum and that rulers are always eager to participate in the gains from trade can be deduced from the political developments that took place during this period.[6] The ruler of *Perumpadappu* realizing the possibility of making capital out of the situation, in 1405 shifted his residence from Mahodayapuram to the Calvethy region of Cochin.[7] *Perumpadappu swarupam* had its headquarters in Vanneri from where they had been compelled to move to Mahodayapuram a long time previously on account of the military expeditions of the Zamorin.[8] It may be recalled that the *swarupam* already possessed a palace at Mahodayapuram. But later, the *swarupam* abandoned it and shifted his capital to Cochin, which, besides the fact that it was situated outside the immediate orbit of the Zamorin's conquest, offered considerable income by way of customs duties.[9]

The Zamorin, who had continuously chased the king of the *Perumpadappu swarupam* from Vanneri to Mahodayapuram and later threatened him even in Cochin, was the ruler of Calicut or Vikramapuram (as sometimes called in Malayalam). It was only after the transfer of the royal residence of the Zamorin from Nediyirappu in Ernad to Calicut, that he undertook a grand expansionist policy.[10] By the time Ibn Batuta visited Calicut in 1343, a visit which corresponds almost to the emergence of the port of Cochin, Calicut had become the most important port of Malabar.[11] It was the income from the port of Calicut, to which traders from China, Java, Ceylon, Maldives, Yemen, and Persia brought commodities,[12] which helped the Zamorin to carry out his conquests and military expeditions that threatened Malabar. The situation was such that it seemed as if a political power with a sound economic basis or fed by a strong port would be able to challenge the supremacy of Calicut. Behind the transfer of the capital of the *Perumpadappu swarupam* to the newly emerged port site of Cochin, there seems to have been the desire to build on the gains from trade, a strong state that could check the Zamorin's expansionism.

However, this tract of land (which comprises the present towns of Cochin, i.e. Fort Cochin or Portuguese Cochin and Mattancherry or native Cochin), to which the king of *Perumpadappu swarupam* had moved in 1405, originally belonged to the king of Edappally. Edappally or Rapolim was a small kingdom, which included Edappally proper, Punithura and Tripunithura[13] and had been ruled by *Nampoothiri* Brahmins of *Elangallur swarupam*.[14] At the end of the fourteenth century or at the beginning of the fifteenth century, the king of Edappally had presented this tongue of land of Cochin as a gift to the ruling king of *Perumpadappu swarupam* who

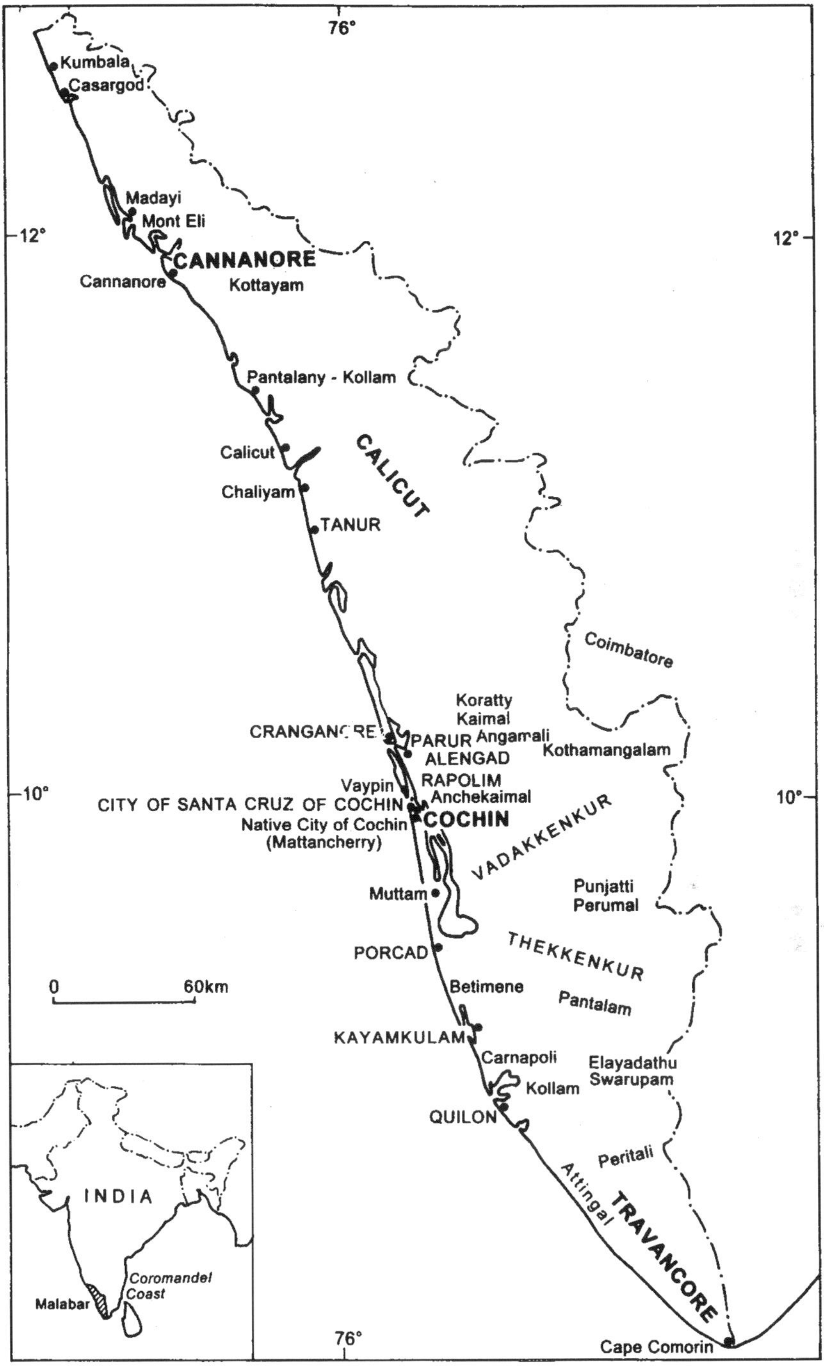

Cartography: H. Nischk

The Map of Malabar in the Sixteenth and Seventeenth Centuries. The Map is designed by H. Nischk, the cartographer of the Department of Geography, South Asian Institute of Heidelberg University, Germany on the basis of the details furnished by the author.

happened to be his son.[15] But later when Cochin developed into a flourishing port and acquired economic importance, the successors of the Edappally king wanted to regain it from the *Perumpadappu swarupam*. This led to constant rivalry and fighting between the two, for years together. Moreover, the rulers of Edappally used to provide a base for the Zamorin's military operations against Cochin[16] and the Zamorin, in turn, used to champion the cause of Edappally.[17] However, the *Perumpadappu* kings who had better financial resources through their participation in the gains of trade were the victors in these wars and able to maintain their hold over Cochin.

With the establishment of a considerable strong power at the port site, security and safety required for the development of trade were guaranteed. As a result, merchants and traders from various countries began to flock to this port. By 1409, the commercial activities were vibrant and perceptible enough as to invite the great Cheng Ho mission sent by the Ming dynasty of China.[18] Ma Huan, who accompanied Cheng Ho wrote in 1409: 'there were five classes of people in Cochin. The noble caste with a thread over their shoulders (*Nampoothiris*) formed the first class, while Mohammedans occupied the second position. *Chetties*, *Kolings* and *Mukkuvas* held the other positions respectively'.[19] It is here important to note that out of these five classes, three, viz., Mohammedans, *Chetties* and *Kolings* (*Kelings* derived from Kalinga) were merchant groups. *Chetties* were the capitalists and the leading merchant community. They bought pepper from the farmers and sold it to foreign ships that frequented Cochin. *Kolings* were the commission agents.[20]

These three merchant groups were not original natives of Cochin and their presence in Cochin suggests that this port had, by this time, opened doors to merchant groups from other emporia and ports of Asia making possible long-distance-movement of commodities. The *Chetties*, with a strong base in the ports of Coromandel, were great merchants, owners of ships, and used to trade with Cambay, Dabul and Chaul in areca, coconuts, pepper, *jagra* and palm sugar.[21] *Kolings*, often referred to as *Kelings*, were traders from the Coromandel coast, Pegu and Malacca.[22] Their involvement in the Cochin trade indicates that this port had been incorporated into the exchange systems of South East Asia. Ma Huan's mention of Muslims and their important position (second) in the social hierarchy deserves special attention as they were, during this period, associated with the trade activities of the Persian gulf and the ports of the Red Sea. As spices were available at a cheaper rate in Cochin, ships from Arabia and Persia used to cast anchor off this port frequently.[23]

With the arrival of Cheng Ho, the trade relationship between Cochin and China flourished actively and articles of tribute were sent to China,[24] in 1436, to reinforce this commercial bond. Fei Hsin writes, 'the commodities brought from China for trade in Cochin included coloured satins, white silk, blue and white porcelain-ware, gold and silver'.[25] Chinese junks, carried back spices such as pepper and ginger as well as some precious substances such as ivory, pearl, coral, and the like. The fact that several items used in this part are given the epithet '*cheena*' such as *cheenachatti* (a household utensil almost like a frying-pan), *cheenavala* (fishing net), *cheenavedi* (used for fireworks) shows that they were of Chinese origin and speaks for the long Chinese contacts with this region.[26]

Ma Huan, while speaking about the trade transactions at the port of Cochin, mentions that pepper was sold at five *tales* the *P'o-ho*, which is 400 *cattis* of Chinese weight. The coin was a gold piece, called *fanam* weighing one *candareen*; there was also a little silver coin called a *ta-urh*, which was used for making small purchases in the market. Fifteen *ta-urhs* made a *fanam.*[27] Fei Hsin, who visited Cochin in 1436 testifies to the fact of wide circulation and the use of coins in the trade transactions of this port.[28] However, by the end of the fifteenth century, most of the coins used in mercantile transactions were not issued by the king of Cochin, as he was deprived of the right to strike coins by the Zamorin.[29]

It is also quite possible that the shrewd old merchants of Cranganore especially the St. Thomas Christians, and later, Jews, read the signs of the times and shifted to Cochin as this gateway became an important economic centre.[30] In 1503 Francisco de Albuquerque referred to a Christian merchant guild, called *Korram*, which was very active in Cochin and conducted organized trade.[31] In the letter, based on the report from Pedro Alvarez Cabral and written by D. Manuel (1501) to Ferdinand and Isabella of Spain, the Portuguese king says that in the city of Cochin there were many ships and he learned that two merchants of this city alone had as many as fifty ships.[32] Fei Hsin says that in Cochin, wealthy people had put up broad godowns for storing pepper.[33] The presence of mecantile organizations almost like guilds, large numbers of ships and storing facilities for buying pepper at harvest time or when the prices were low show that the trade in Cochin had taken on an organized shape after 1430. The overseas traders, who previously had to accept the prices dictated by the local merchants because of the monsoon, which determined the movement of ships and specified the maximum time-limit for their stay in a port, might have played a significant role in organizing the trade of this port. Ma Huan's mention of trade in pearl and other precious stones and cutting and polishing of coral into beads by skilled workmen is suggestive of the emergence of production in the secondary sector, as well.[34]

The natural result of these developments was the genesis of an urban centre in and around the port of Cochin. While referring to Cochin, Nicolo Conti says that it was a city of five miles in circumference.[35] But it seems that the area mentioned by Nicolo Conti might not be the core area of the city, but the zone under the influence of the urban phenomena of Cochin. It must be mentioned that though Cochin raised a serious challenge to the port of Calicut, it could not rise up to the level of the Zamorin's port all through the pre-Portuguese phase.

II. THE PORT OF COCHIN AND THE POLITICAL ECONOMY OF MALABAR

It seems that there existed two inter-related phenomena in the history of the pre-Portuguese Malabar. On the one hand, there existed a port hierarchy in which, from among the various nodal points along its coast, one port would emerge and act for a definite period of time as the central port. Others would become minor satellite ports revolving round this principal and pivotal port.[36] Thus the prime and pivotal position occupied in the ancient period, by Muziris (Cranganore) was taken over by Quilon in the early medieval period, which later was assumed by Calicut during the period till sixteenth century.[37] With the advent of the Portuguese, this prime position was taken over by Cochin. On the other hand these economic centres or trade centres for spices became the major units of political life in Malabar. The more intense the economic life was, the more vibrant were the political activities in these trade centres. So it was quite natural that the movement of Cochin into the orbit of economic activities had its repercussions in the political scenario, as well. The emergence of the port of Cochin not only drove a wedge into the then existing hinterland geography and framework of port hierarchy, but also carved out a considerable space of spice growing hinterland for its commercial development. Many of the political changes of this period were related, in one way or another, to Cochin through its newly-acquired economic importance.

Perumpadappu swarupam or the rulers of the Cochin kingdom trace their origin back to the last Kulasekharas' sister, who was married to a Nampoothiri of Perumpadappu.[38] This has to be seen against the peculiar custom that prevailed among the Nampoothiri Brahmins of Kerala where only the first-born married the Brahmin ladies while the younger sons of Brahmins used to marry ladies from non-Brahmin high castes such as the Kshatriyas (who were relatively very few) and the Nairs. It seems that the founder of *Perumpadappu swarupam* was a younger son of a Brahmin and the matrilineal rights as well as the caste, took predominance over patrilineal caste and rights. This must have been the reason why the king of Cochin was considered not a Brahmin; but as a Kshatriya by birth,[39] into which category the Perumpadappu kings fell because of the link with the last Perumal (the Kulasekhara ruler). The full official designation of the kings of Cochin in vernacular was '*Perumpadappu Gangadhara Vira Kerala Trikkovil Adhikarikal*'[40] and as this title indicates, he exercised jurisdiction over a large number of temples in Kerala, irrespective of all considerations of political boundaries.[41] It was a time when the state was defined not merely by geographical boundaries. The jurisdiction over temples scattered all over Kerala played a major role in the state formation. It seems that the Brahmin link must have also given some added reasons to the Perumpadappu kings to exercise control over diverse temples.[42] Perhaps it might have been because of the vast spiritual power which the king of Cochin wielded, that Tomé Pires called him the 'Pope of the country'.[43] In fact, this moral and religious authority exercised by him more than compensated for his lack of political power and stature.

The royal family was divided into five branches or *tavazhis*, viz., Mutta, Elaya, Palluruthi, Muringur and Chazhur. Each branch had its own seat and crown lands for its support, as well as its own retainers and militia. But the right of succession to the throne was common to all; the eldest male member of all the five branches taken together, was made the king of Cochin.[44] The internal dissensions among these family branches or *tavazhis* gave the Zamorin great opportunities to interfere in the affairs of Cochin. In most cases, the custom of *Perumpadappu Mooppil* or religious recluse, which was instituted to ensure sound governance, was a major source of discord in the royal family of Cochin. According to this custom, if the ruling chief grew too old or was otherwise too feeble to govern the country in troublesome times, he abandoned the throne and led the life of a religious recluse, so that the administration of the country could be entrusted to the rightful heir or to the next eldest member of his own branch of the family. In the latter case, the governance was carried out as in a regency, where the regent was bound on the death of the retired chief, not only to make way for the rightful heir, but also to retire from the world and become a religious recluse. This arrangement was made to prevent him from using the power and prestige that he might have gained while he was acting as *de facto* ruler of the state against the rightful heir.[45] But as this practice touched the very core of power, it created enormous dissensions among the members of royal family. In several of the Zamorin's wars one or more branches of the royal family were on his side against the ruling head of Cochin. The Zamorin took advantage of these dissensions to consolidate his power and dominion as well as to extend the economic sphere of influence of Calicut.

Already with the development of trade in Calicut, the Zamorin began to undertake an expansionist policy and the men and money supplied by the wealthy Arab merchants always helped to turn the tide of the events in his favour. The first target was Tirunavai (which was situated on the banks of the river Bharatapuzha in the territory of the Valluvanadu ruler) where the famous pan-Kerala assembly, often called the festival of *Mamankam* was held once in every twelve years under the chairmanship of the Valluvanadu ruler. Tirunavai was politically important and the right to preside over the *Mamankam* was viewed and coveted enviously by the rulers of Kerala. So it was quite natural that the avaricious eyes of the Zamorin fell first on this prestigious place. By conquering this territory of Tirunavai, the Zamorin acquired the time-honoured privilege of presiding over the *Mamankam.*[46] With this conquest he assumed the cultural leadership of Kerala with an already established economic and political supremacy. After having brought the neighbouring principalities of Nilambur, Manjeri, Malappuram and Kottakkal under his suzerainty, the Zamorin turned to Cochin, where the growing port had already attached to itself some of the areas in the pepper-producing hinterland that belonged to Calicut. The dissensions between the *Mutta tavazhi* and *Elaya tavazhi*, to which the ruling king belonged, gave the Zamorin a chance to interfere in the politics of Cochin. Thus, the Zamorin, by the end of the fifteenth century, took active interest in the affairs of Cochin. He supported the *Mutta tavazhi* and in the war that broke out by the end of the fifteenth century, the Zamorin came out victorious. His nominee from this *tavazhi* was made the king of Cochin.[47] But the other results of this war were drastically harmful to Cochin. The kingdom of Cochin was narrowed down to the island of Vaipin and of Cochin[48] and its king was deprived of the right to strike coins or to roof his palace with tiles.[49] The ultimate economic result of this intervention was that the Zamorin got the opportunity he needed, to control the activities of the port of Cochin. He succeeded in getting all the pepper and merchandise of Cochin re-directed to Calicut port.[50] In the agreement that was made between the Zamorin and the ruling chief of Cochin, an agreement largely influenced by the Muslim merchants of Calicut, it was stipulated that the merchants from the St. Thomas Christian community should be driven out from Cochin.[51] All other merchants were enticed away from this port to Calicut by the Zamorin with the help of the Arab traders.[52] Thus the Zamorin succeeded in forcing the developing port of Cochin, the source of power for the *Perumpadappu* kings, into the inferior position of a satellite port of Calicut.

Though the political position of the king of Cochin, by the end of fifteenth century, was no better than that of other innumerable petty chieftains of Malabar of that time, he had one advantage: that he possessed a very good natural harbour which could at any time transform his stature and role. Moreover, the port of Cochin was the main window for the spice-growing hinterland scattered in the kingdoms of Parur, Mangattu (Alengad), Porcad (Chembakasserry) Vadakkenkur, Thekkenkur, Kizhumalainadu, the realm of Anchekaimal, etc. Most of these kingdoms were located around the Vembanadu lagoon. In the fifteenth century, Cranganore was linked more with Calicut than with Cochin. The kingdom of Edappally, though was bordering on this lagoon, also paid allegiance to Calicut. Thus, though the political supremacy of the Zamorin was on the whole an accepted fact, vague signs of economic division of the spice-hinterlands between Cochin and Calicut had already appeared. Most of the kingdoms which were politically neutral found Cochin near, and accessible because of the lagoon systems. Commodities from these kingdoms found their way to the port of Cochin from where a good portion was again taken to Calicut, as well. The overseas trade in the entire Indian Ocean region, by the end of fifteenth century, was monopolized by Arab traders, who were patronized and intimately connected with the Zamorin of Calicut,[53] who wanted to nip in the bud, the rising popularity of Cochin port. So the king of Cochin had to look for another overseas trading group, with whom Cochin could carry on independent trade and with the help of whom foreign ships could be made to frequent Cochin.

III. SETTLEMENT PATTERN IN NATIVE COCHIN

The freedom of trade in the port of Cochin attracted merchants from different parts of the world, as we have already seen, to this nodal point where they settled down as the monsoon wind system which controlled their trade made their stay—either temporary or permanent—inevitable. Initially this was for a temporary period; later it became permanent. As settlement of various merchant groups in the port area became a common feature, urban phenomena and street-based settlement pattern appeared in Cochin.[54] It began to house a heterogenous population including representatives of all the seafaring communities of the Indian Ocean region. The rights, customs and culture of these foreigners were respected and they were allowed not only to settle down and set up their own stations and colonies but also to be administered by their own chiefs and law codes, in Cochin, resembling a state of extra-territoriality. The only obligation on the part of the foreigners was that they should respect the religious feelings of the natives.[55]

The settlement pattern of Cochin was of such a nature that members of each group could enjoy and exercise the varied rights of extra-territoriality. The palace of the king was in Calvethy area, not far from the port.[56] The royal presence in the port area not only provided a common political umbrella but also effected an economic co-ordination of various port mechanisms. The urban population was distributed into various segregated groups of single communities. People belonging to a particular caste would congregate on one street. New castes would demarcate a particular street for themselves.[57] Besides the caste factor, religious considerations and professional interests also played a key role in this settlement distribution. The Mohammedan merchants had better houses surrounded with stone walls and a city of their own,[58] which extended up to Calvethy.[59] Amaravati was inhabited by *Chetties* and Goldsmiths.[60] The Konkanis and the St. Thomas Christians occupied particular portions of the town along the street. The Jews, who came later were allotted space adjacent to the palace.[61] The degree of relationship with, and the involvement of various merchants and service groups in port activities determined their nearness to the port. The service staff was near the warehouses; then came the merchants' city divided according to faith and origin. Brahmins and Nairs were in the estates. The low castes and the untouchables were on the coast, well out of the sight of Brahmins and Nairs.[62] Just as in any pre-colonial city of Malabar, in Cochin also, neither the merchants nor the ruler had built large establishments on the water-front or the seaside. As Fei Hsin says, the sea shore was occupied by villages, most probably inhabited by lower castes or *Mukkuvas.*[63] The process of urban expansion left the water-front behind and started from the port (Calvethy area) to the hinterland. This town that developed at the hinterland end of the port was the native Cochin (Mattancherry). It was also called *Cochin de cima* (upper Cochin) during the Portuguese period.[64] The present day Mattancherry area, which corresponds to the old native Cochin, even today preserves the old settlement pattern, even though the numerical strength of various communities and castes has undergone much change.[65]

The seaside, which was left vacant, was later given to the newly-arrived Portuguese: they settled at the water-front and expanded more along the seaside, as they had come from across the sea and their power was based on the Ocean.[66] The urban unit that developed at the water-front became the city of Santa Cruz or Portuguese Cochin, which today is known as Fort Cochin.

IV. THE EARLY PHASE OF PORTUGUESE SETTLEMENT AND THE ROLE OF NATIVE COCHIN

Receiving the royal standard from Dom Manuel (the king of Portugal) in the cathedral of Lisbon,[67] Vasco da Gama started his journey from Belem on 9 July 1497.[68] This expedition of four ships (*S. Gabriel, S.Raphel, Berrio* and the provision ship)[69] under Vasco da Gama was 'in search of Christians and spices'.[70] They reached Capocate (two leagues from Calicut) on 20 May 1498.[71] The Portuguese in Calicut found themselves 'pigmis' in stature in contrast to the Mohammedan traders who had better commercial links and political influence. They could impress neither the king nor the market and they found it difficult to sell Portuguese commodities.[72] The Mohammedan traders, who had monopolized the Calicut trade, were on the defensive and their intrigues and machinations succeeded to a certain extent, in keeping the Portuguese away from the market of Calicut.[73] But, because of the prompt help extended by the Kolathiri raja, Vasco da Gama was successful in shipping sufficient cargo from Cannanore, worth sixty times the cost of the expedition.[74] Though the initial response from India was not very promising, it sounded like a big beginning in Europe: The king of Portugal, Dom Manuel assumed rather a high sounding title: 'Lord of the Conquest, the Navigation and Commerce of Ethiopia, Arabia, Persia and India.'[75]

Meanwhile, preparations had started in Lisbon for assembling a new fleet to sail to India. This fleet consisted of thirteen vessels and twelve hundred men. The captains were chosen with care to impress the rulers of India regarding the greatness of Portugal, so members of noble families were given command of many of these ships. This was the first commercial fleet to sail for India. One of these ships belonged to Bartolomeo Marchioni, a Florentine and to other Italian merchants. Another ship was provided by a Portuguese nobleman. The rest was financed by the crown.[76] The chief command of this new fleet and this great endeavour was given to Pedro Alvarez Cabral.[77] Cabral was given a diplomatic mission and was asked not to do any injury to any of the ships which he might come across in Calicut and the route between Calicut and Anjedive, even though they might be from Mecca.[78] He was asked to establish peace and friendship with the Zamorin. The initial relationship with the Zamorin was cordial so that Cabral could load two of the ships with spices. The friendship that developed between the Portuguese and the Zamorin as well as the size of the ships the Portuguese used for loading spices prompted the Mohammedan traders to hide the merchandise for their advantage.[79]

The hoarding of spices led to an artificial shortage, as a result of which the Portuguese had to keep waiting even after three months.[80] On the other hand, the spice hoarded and transferred from the market was secretly shipped in vessels destined for Mecca.[81] The Zamorin, to whom the Portuguese complained about this incident, allowed the latter to conduct a search in Mohammedan ships for merchandise. The search, which the Portuguese conducted on 16 December 1500, in a Mohammedan vessel and its consequent capture led to great uproar and revolt by the Mohammedans against the Portuguese. The disturbed mob killed the Portuguese factor and along with him fifty people were lost, either dead or captured.[82] This was followed by inhuman vengeance and brutality: massacring of the innocents, capturing and burning down of the ships and bombarding of the city.[83] For the first time, the Indian Ocean was turned into a battlefield. The Portuguese found themselves encountered by enemies rather than competitors in this disturbed milieu. In this hostile and belligerent atmosphere, they were eagerly looking for a helping hand, or at least some quarter of land on the coast, where they could ensure indigenous assistance and a regular supply of spices.

Finding no other land to occupy, Pedro Alvarez Cabral, as led by Gaspar da Gama came to Cochin on 24 December 1500.[84] Meanwhile, the king of Cochin, who was waiting for an opportunity to overthrow the hegemony of the Zamorin, found in the newly-arrived traders, potency and strength to regain his lost power and to assert himself. The king of Cochin welcomed the Portuguese whole-heartedly and did everything possible to help load their ships with spices.[85] With the co-operation of the native ruler, all seven ships were entirely laden in nine days with spices namely, cloves, cinnamon, nutmeg and pepper. The king, also sent another fourteen small boats of spices as a gift, without any kind of exchange.[86] A treaty of peace and friendship was concluded between the king and Cabral. Moreover, the native ruler gave Cabral a specific portion of the port area and the land adjacent to it for the establishment of a Portuguese factory. For security reasons, the then reigning king, Unni Goda Varma Koil Tirumulpad, allowed them a guard and permitted them to sleep within the walls of his palace.[87] This was the stepping-stone to a long-term alliance and friendship between the two.

The Portuguese fleet under João da Nova came to Cochin in 1501, after having sunk five large vessels and nine *parãos* of Calicut. The king of Cochin fearing that the Mohammedans might kill them, provided accommodation for them in his palace, giving them a guard of Nairs for their protection. Further, when João da Nova had difficulty in buying spices for want of cash, the king of Cochin stood as surety and supplied pepper and other spices to be taken to Portugal.[88]

Meanwhile in 1502, the Zamorin sent a letter to the king of Cochin asking him not to entertain the Portuguese further. But the king explained his inability to violate the peace and trade treaty concluded with the Portuguese.[89] In November 1502, Vasco da Gama came to India with a great fleet of twenty vessels. He moved to Cochin, after having bombarded the city of Calicut and annihilated the Arab merchant fleet. The king of Cochin along with a large number of attendants and six elephants went to the waterside to receive him.[90] One of the major achievements of Vasco da Gama's second voyage was that after talks with the king and later with local merchants, at the suggestion of the king, he could establish a fixed price for the spices.[91] The king was given the responsibility to make spices available at the prices already fixed.

After the departure of Vasco da Gama, the Zamorin attacked Cochin demanding the surrender of the Portuguese factors, who were under the protection of the king. But the ruler of Cochin refused to comply with this demand. Even the members of the king's council and the royal family pleaded with him to expel the Portuguese to avoid war. But the king preferred taking arms rather than any breach of alliance. In the fierce fighting that followed the three ablest princes of the royal family were killed (other losses being much beyond quantification).[92] Vicente Sodre, who was supposed to fight against the Zamorin, evaded the situation under the pretext of patrolling the Red Sea. With the death of the gallant princes and annihilation of the army, the king with his family and the Portuguese took refuge in the *Sanketam* of Elankunnapuzha temple in Vaipin.[93] Though the Zamorin dared not violate the sacrosanctum, he certainly burnt down the city of Cochin.[94] It must be mentioned here that the Portuguese commercial endeavour did acquire some roots in Indian soil, mainly because of the losses and sacrifices faced by the king of Cochin and his loyal subjects of native Cochin.

Against this background of continuous attack from the Zamorin, the Albuquerques were sent to India in 1503.[95] Though Francisco de Albuquerque reinstated the king on the throne and severely attacked Edappally, which was the base for the Zamorin's operations, the war atmosphere continued.[96] Before the departure of the Albuquerques to Portugal, they requested the king for permission to erect a fort at Cochin for the protection of the Portuguese factory. The king not only granted permission but also undertook the work at his own expense.[97] The war which continued up to 1504 took a decisive turn when a large-scale military operation of the Zamorin was foiled by the valiant and timely action of Duarte Pacheco assisted by native soldiers sent from native Cochin.[98]

By the time Francisco de Almeida, the first viceroy, arrived at Cochin in 1505, the king of Cochin had abdicated and become a religious recluse. As the two senior princes, who were next in succession, were supporting the Zamorin, the retiring king had appointed as regent, his surviving nephew, Unnirama Koil Tirumulpad, alias Rama Varma.[99] Though this arrangement was temporary and Rama Varma, had to become a religious recluse later, after the death of Goda Varma, according to the practice of *Perumpadappu Mooppil*, Almeida, in order to ensure a pro-Portuguese ruler on the throne and thus royal assistance, suppressed this age-old practice and crowned him solemnly as the king. Moreover he presented the golden crown sent by D. Manuel and gave him an annuity (*copa*) of 640 *cruzados.*[100]

This money, which the Portuguese continued to give to the kings of Cochin under the name of *copas*, was paid partly as the assessment on the land handed over to the Portuguese for constructing the fort and as compensation for the death of the three princes in the fight against the Zamorin in defence of the Portuguese.[101] Meanwhile Almeida, who had come with explicit orders to establish the headquarters of Portuguese India in Cochin, constructed a strong fortress in Cochin in place of the earlier wooden structure. This fortified area in the Portuguese colony was made the first seat of the governmental activities of the Lusitanians.[102] With this, the Portuguese part of Cochin began to take on a unique administrative, jurisdictional and urban shape quite different from that of native Cochin.

However, native Cochin continued to be the main vehicle for the integration of various elements of indigenous assistance with Portuguese Cochin. In the initial phase of establishment, when the Portuguese were confronted with lack of personnel and lack of funds, it was the native city that came to their rescue. The king of Cochin either gave them loans or supplied commodities on credit, so that the amount which the Portuguese owed to the native ruler rose to 10,000 *cruzados* in 1513.[103] Besides financial assistance and political protection amounting to a certain degree of 'patronage' extended by the king of Cochin, there were other areas of co-operation from the native Cochin. Any organized enterprise of large scale commercial operations at that time required an elaborate system of spy networks, wider commercial links with solid capital, and an adequate fighting force. Unfortunately, in the first decade of the sixteenth century, the Portuguese seemed to lack in these three areas. Often, they had to look often to native Cochin for timely help. It was mainly the Nampoothiri Brahmins, linked closely to the kingdom of Cochin, who assisted them as spy-workers.[104] The Nairs and the St. Thomas Christians from native Cochin and the neighbouring principalities formed an important part of the fighting force that waged wars for the Portuguese.[105] The Mohammedan merchants of native Cochin, who had a large number of personnel as well as huge capital resources and partnership links, supplied commodities to the Portuguese, when the latter did not have enough means and personnel to penetrate into the production centres.[106] It seems that it was only because of this varied assistance, which the Portuguese received from the people of native Cochin, especially in first decade of the sixteenth century, that they were able to establish solid commercial and political bases for their empire in Asia.

2. THE HINTERLAND OF COCHIN

I. THE PRINCIPAL SPICE HINTERLANDS

No city stands on its own, and the study of a city takes one to the interior land space which feeds the city. This is all the more true of Cochin, whose ups and downs depended heavily on its relationship with the hinterland. Right from the beginning,

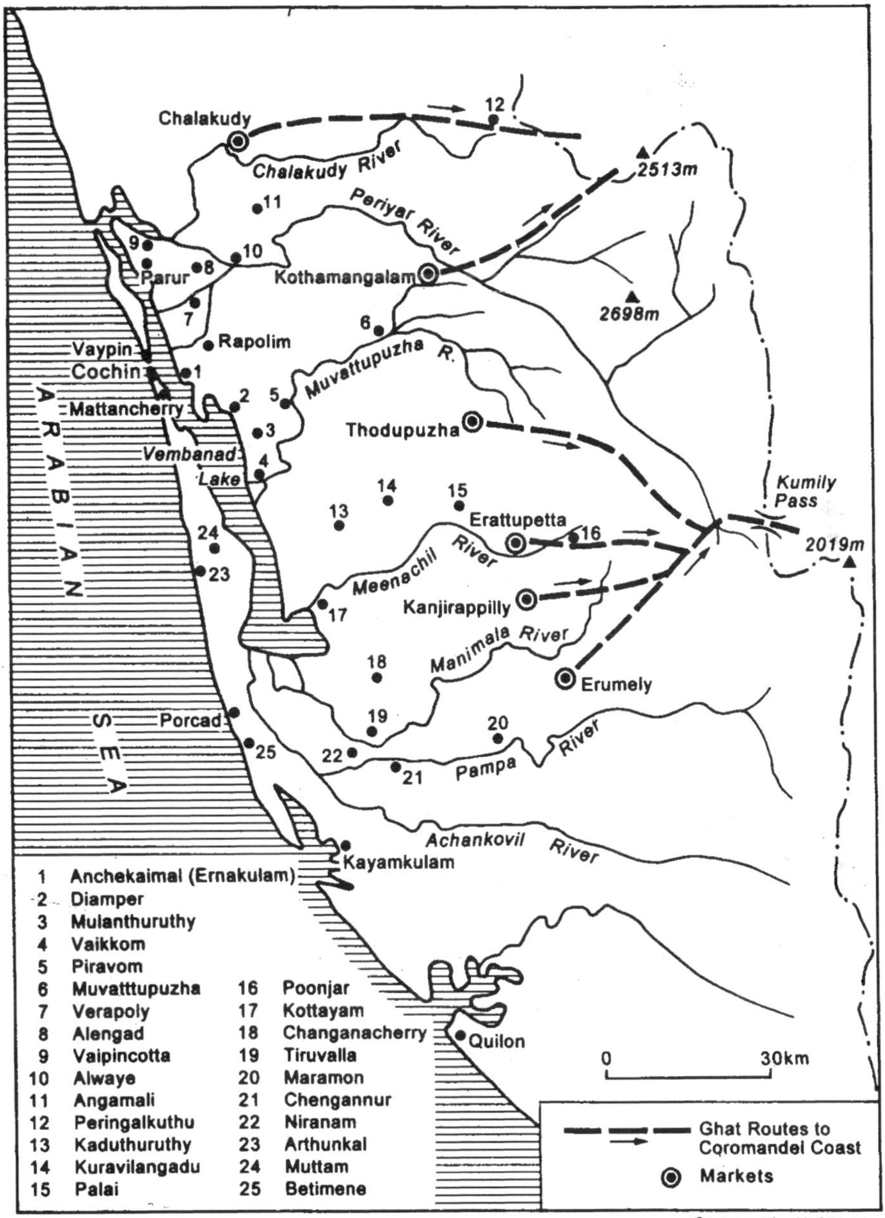

Cartography: H. Nischk

The Map of the Hinterland of Cochin: 1500-1663. The Map is designed by H. Nischk, the cartographer of the Department of Geography, South Asian Institute of Heidelberg University, Germany on the basis of the details furnished by the author.

the land of Cochin did not produce anything (except coconuts) significantly worthy of trade. Most of the commodities that were transacted in the port came from interior land. With the high demand for pepper and ginger, for which the foreign vessels began to frequent Cochin, this port had to look more and more to the production centres lying inland, to ensure a regular supply. Eventually, the economic life of the port of Cochin necessitated the carving out of large spice-growing land spaces scattered in central Kerala for its commercial activities. The attempt to convert the various spice-growing inland areas into the hinterland of Cochin was a gradual one and was carried out through diverse strategies.

Hinterland can be described as organized and developed land spaces which are connected with a port by means of transport lines, and which receive or send goods through that port.[107] Port hinterland is often considered as an economic rather than a geographical region. There are cases when a port does not necessarily have exclusive claim to any part of its hinterland and an inland area may be the hinterland of several ports. The port is the window of the hinterland to the sea as well as a window from the sea to the land.[108] The hinterland could also be conceived in terms of the area from which the city draws material for the construction of its buildings, factories, houses and streets.[109] It is that area from which the port obtains its goods for export overseas and to which it distributes the imported goods.[110]

The Portuguese made use of every possible means to integrate the distant and remote spice hinterlands with the port of Cochin. The kingdoms of Cochin, Cranganore, Parur, Alengad, Porcad, Vadakkenkur and Thekkenkur were brought within the economic orbit of Cochin and were made the principal hinterlands for this port.

According to Jan Kieniewicz, there were three areas of intensive pepper-growing in Kerala between the fifteenth and nineteenth centuries. 1. The area situated in the south, in the regions of Attingal and Peritaly. 2. The area that existed in the north in the Chirakkal and Kottayam regions of Malabar. 3. The lands in the central part of Kerala, which formed the hinterland of Cochin and which were of the greatest importance all through this period. Pepper cultivation was concentrated in these three regions on a large scale, not only because of the rich and properly irrigated soil, but also because of the proximity of transport routes.[111] The area of central part was demarcated by the river Periyar to the north, a plane on lake Vembanadu to the west and the Achenkovil river to the south[112] and formed the main hinterland of Cochin. The lands of Kothamangalam, Aragosha (Arakuzha), Porrota (Piravom) and Palaya (Pala) were the most productive centres of pepper-cultivation.[113] The inscriptions kept in the churches of St. Thomas Christians and the various Portuguese accounts help us to locate the various important spice-growing centres of this period and to trace the land and riverine routes that connected these regions to the port of Cochin.

Out of the various and diverse inland spaces or hinterlands, the kingdom of Cochin stood in the central zone. It was only fifty-two leagues (52 x 4 = 208 miles) in circumference.[114] The treaty of peace and friendship concluded between the king of Cochin and Pedro Alvarez Cabral in 1500 opened up for the Portuguese traders not only the port, but also the very kingdom of Perumpadappu as the hinterland.[115] In 1502, D. Manuel wrote a personal letter to the king of Cochin expressing his gratitude.[116] The interior parts of the kingdom of Cochin served as the basic hinterland of this port and the annual amount of 640 *cruzados*, which the Portuguese continued to give to the king of Cochin as *copa*, later included the remuneration for ensuring a regular supply of spices to the port of Cochin.[117] Vasco da Gama in 1502 fixed the prices of the spices in Cochin at one thousand and twenty-four *reais* per quintal.[118] As a result, the chance of cheating the cultivators by the traders in the name of fluctuations in the market was reduced. Though it led to underpricing of the commodity, it equally helped to maintain uniform prices in this part of the hinterland. The trade routes of the kingdom of Cochin intersected at three junctions: Bardela (Vaduthala), Castello (south of the island of Venduruthy) and Cochin de Cima (Mattancherry). The small peddling traders who were carrying commodities to and from Cochin had to pay taxes at the customs houses of these places.[119] The taxes collected in Castello and Mattancherry (except Vaduthala which was in the Vadakkenkur kingdom), as taxes for the entry into and exit from the kingdom, were an additional source of income to the king of Cochin, in addition to the export and import duties levied by the king at the port.

Another important spice-growing centre was the kingdom of Cranganore which lay between Chetwayi and the kingdom of Cochin.[120] It had a heterogenous population consisting of Mohammedans, Jews, Hindus and St. Thomas Christians.[121] The kings of Cranganore owed their allegiance either to the Zamorin or to the Perumpadappu kings.[122] But during the early years of our study, the king of Cranganore was related to the king of Cochin who also received a part of the revenue of Cranganore (temples)[123] and their relationship was on the whole cordial. However, by about 1614 to 1615, when this kingdom was annexed by the Zamorin, it ceased to be an active feeding centre for Cochin.[124] As much of the pepper from here was taken to Calicut, D. Francisco de Almeida wrote in 1508 to the king of Portugal to erect a fort in Cranganore.[125] In 1536, during the governorship of Nuno da Cunha, a strong fortress was built here to divert the pepper trade to Cochin.[126] Since this fortress was located between the warring kingdoms of Cochin and Calicut, it played a significant role in carving out hinterlands for the port of Cochin.[127] The Portuguese also sought the help of the bishop Mar Jacome Abuna to persuade his subjects, the St. Thomas Christians of Cranganore, and other areas who possessed the monopoly of pepper cultivation to sell their pepper directly to the Portuguese.[128] The bishop even took them directly to the Portuguese factory in Cochin, not once but several times. This initiative from the religious leader of the pepper cultivators played a very important role in integrating the pepper-growing areas of Cranganore with Cochin.[129] As most of the cultivators in Cranganore were St. Thomas Christians,[130] attempts were also made in the first half of the sixteenth century to placate them through financial help for the maintenance of their church.[131] Moreover, by 1545, a college was instituted in Cranganore only for the training of the seminarians of the St. Thomas Christians.[132] Though the genuine intention behind these religious favours should not be wrongly interpreted, the economic effect shows that these actions played a considerable role in incorporating significant portions of this kingdom into the orbit of the port of Cochin. From Cranganore came a lot of pepper, wild cinnamon, raw hides, wood, sandalwood, *angelins*, etc.[133]

The kingdom of Alengad or Mangatte was another hinterland of Cochin and its ruler belonged to the Nair caste and was often called Mangatte Kaimal.[134] The Portuguese documents of the period between 1550 and 1575, state that the ruler of Alengad was also designated as Chyrama (Cheraman).[135] Antonio Bocarro gives a detailed description about this land. Situated on the side of the river (Periyar) the kingdom of Alengad had only a small land space. The king had sixteen thousand soldiers and was almost a subject of the king of Cochin. The kingdom was thickly populated and a good number of them were St. Thomas Christians and they lived more near their farms than in the bazaars. People could travel and sleep safely anywhere in the kingdom and the king used to take very rigorous and strict measures against robbers and criminals. The customs duty was comparatively little and the maximum tax rate did not even reach two *reais*.[136] The Archbishop D. Alexis Meneses, who visited the churches of the St. Thomas Christians to win their co-operation, also came to Alengad in the troublesome days following the synod of Diamper (1599).[137] The visits were made to ensure the collaboration of the pepper cultivators of Alengad and to retain them as strong supporters of the Portuguese religious and commercial policies.

Mangatte Kaimal in his letter to the king of Portugal speaks about the various services he rendered to the kings of Cochin and Portugal.[138] In 1548, he was actively involved in the war fought by the Portuguese and the king of Cochin against Vadakkenkur and the Zamorin.[139] It is significant that in the war against Calicut, the rulers of the hinterlands always stood by the king of Cochin, who was the owner of the port, thus giving us the impression that though they were politically and geographically different, they formed one integral economic unit. For the regular supply of pepper to Cochin, the Mangatte Kaimal used to receive 72,000 *reais* per year.[140]

Parur, another hinterland of Cochin, was situated near Cranganore.[141] Diogo Gonçalves writes: 'the ruler of Parur was of Brahmin caste and he is almost a subject of the king of Cochin with the obligation of sending twelve thousand Nairs for Cochin in the war against the Zamorin'.[142] In 1546, we read about the Portuguese who were making visits to the king of Parur with a view to procuring spices.[143] In the war of 1548, the king of Parur joined forces with Cochin against Calicut and Vadakkenkur.[144] During the visit of Dom Alexis Meneses, the St. Thomas Christians of Parur showed great rebellious spirit, but their co-operation was purchased with strenuous efforts.[145] At the beginning of the seventeenth century, the ruler of Parur turned out to be a friend of the Zamorin and was often at war with Cochin, as testified by Antonio Bocarro.[146] But this was only a temporary estrangement, because the Portuguese won him back.[147] For the continuous support and supply of the goods to the port, the ruler of Parur used to get an annual amount of 72,000 *reais*.[148]

Though the ruler of Rapolim or the king of Edappally was an enemy of the king of Cochin, a major portion of its produce went to the port of Cochin. As we have already seen, Edappally was ruled by Nampoothiri Brahmins called *Lamgualu Nambiadiri* (*Elangallur Nampiyathiri*).[149] Edappally was politically associated with the rulers of Calicut, who often came down to this place for performing their coronation ceremonies.[150] By the 1540s, many Portuguese, who were engaged in clandestine commercial activities, used to procure pepper for their trade from Edappally.[151] Salvador de Leão speaks of the promise which the king of Edappally made to supply *angelins* (for ship-building), and pepper, to the king of Portugal.[152] At the entrance of the kingdom of Edappally there was a customs house to collect taxes on the commodities taken to and from Cochin.[153]

The kingdom of Porcad (Purakkad) was ruled by *Chembachere Nampiartiri* (*Chempakasserry Nampiyathiri*) belonging to Brahmin caste.[154] It consisted of the present Ambalapuzha and Kuttanadu taluks. The economic life of Porcad was linked to the commercial activities of the port of Cochin. The king of Porcad was very tolerant and benevolent towards the cultivator-group, the St. Thomas Christians. He even built a church for them in Kudamaloor.[155] The ruler of this kingdom was paid an annual amount of 72,000 *reais* for his services towards promoting the trade of Cochin.[156] The customs house of the kingdom of Porcad was situated in Qeygeyra (Kayalkara) where the entry and exit taxes were collected.[157]

Another significant hinterland of Cochin was Bembalanaru (Vembolinad) that extended from Valiaperumpulley (Valiaperumpuzha near Ashtamudi lake) up to the river Urupulley (Muvattupuzha). During the period of our study it was already divided into Tecamcurru (Thekkenkur) and Barecamcurru (Vadakkenkur) kingdoms.[158] The kingdom of Thekkenkur consisted of the modern taluks of Changancherry, Kanjirappally, Tiruvalla, Kottayam and a small portion of the High Ranges. The rulers of Thekkenkur resided at Kottayam.[159] Most of the pepper produced in this region was brought to the markets of Iratuperha (Erattupetta), Erumelin (Erumely), Quanhara Pee (Kanjirappilly), Koon (Konni?), Irroonny (?) and from there to the port of Cochin. Also, good amount of it was taken to the Coromandel coast through the ghat route.[160] In a letter by Gaspar Luis da Veiga, we read that in the kingdom of Thekkenkur, the Portuguese had various interests besides procuring of the spices. The son of Gaspar Lopez, the *vereador* of the city of Cochin, was employed by the Thekkenkur king for making cannons for him.[161] The ruler of Thekkenkur also used to receive an annual amount of 72,000 *reais* as remuneration for regularly making pepper available in Cochin.[162]

The most important and principal hinterland of Cochin was the kingdom of Vadakkenkur which was often called *reyno da pimenta* (pepper kingdom).[163] It was bounded on the west by the Vembanadu lagoon, on the east by Poonjar, on the north by Kothamangalam and on the south by the kingdom of Thekkenkur.[164] The kingdom of Vadakkenkur included the areas of Ettumanoor, Vaikkom and the northern portion of Meenachil taluk. Its capital was the town of Kaduthuruthy, located between Vaikkom and Ettumanoor.[165] Kizhumalainad, which comprised Muvattupuzha and Thodupuzha taluks merged into Vadakkenkur by 1600, thereafter the pepper kings resided at Turubuli[166] (Thodupuzha) or more exactly at Caricotti[167] (Karikode near Thodupuzha). A road called *Kotta vazhi* starting from Poonjar and running along places such as Bharananganam, Lalam, Puliyannor, Kidangoor (till Kidangoor, along Meenachil river), Ettumanoor, Kottackapuram, Kanakkary, Manjoor, Kaipuzha reached Kayalkara via Kudavechur. This road is said to have separated the Vadakkenkur kingdom from the Thekkenkur kingdom.[168] Bardela (Vaduthala), Perimpalam (near Vaduthala), Chembe, Palliporão (Pallipuram), Bayquette (Vaikkom), Mannato (Mannar), Vechu (Vechur), Curru Vechur (Kudavechur) were important centres connected with pepper production and trade in the kingdom of Vadakkenkur.[169] During the period between 1548 and 1552, the pepper king with the help of the Zamorin waged war in Vaduthala against the king of Cochin as well as the Portuguese, consequently, the latter found it very difficult to send pepper to Portugal.[170] However, by 1553-4 the differences were patched up and this landspace continued to feed the port of Cochin for the remaining period. There were two customs houses in this kingdom to extract taxes from the merchandise taken to and from Cochin: One was by Rio Largo (the Vembanadu lake) and the other was by the river Urupule (Muvattupuzha).[171] For supplying regular pepper consignments to Cochin, the ruler of Vadakkenkur kingdom was paid 72,000 *reais.*[172]

The other important hinterlands of Cochin were Diamper[173] (Udayamperur), Aluva[174] (Alwaye), Anchekaimal[175] (Ernakulam), Muterte[176] (Muthedathu), Lerte[177] (Iledathu), etc. Of these, the ruler of Diamper used to get an annual amount of 72,000 *reais*[178] and the Karta of Aluva 42,000 *reais*[179], for ensuring a regular supply of pepper to the Portuguese factory in Cochin. Thus, the land which was located around the Vembanadu lake and extending to the eastern slopes, was used extensively for growing pepper on a large scale. This land space scattered in different petty kingdoms was attached as hinterland to the port of Cochin by the Portuguese, and ensured them a continuous supply of pepper and other commodities there, by means of distributing annual monetary rewards to their respective rulers. Table II-1 gives the details of the annuities paid by the Portuguese to the various native rulers for their co-operation in allowing their territory as hinterland to supply pepper cargo to Cochin.

Of these, the king of Thodupuzha (Turuguly) who became also the king of Vadakkenkur by 1600, began to receive annuities from 1603 onwards.[180] In 1607 Francisco da Costa writes that it was the king of Thodupuzha (Turuguly) and Vadakkenkur (Pimenta) who was supplying the greatest quantity of pepper to the Portuguese factory of Cochin. He was said to be the only ruler who regularly supplied pepper to the Portuguese. Other kings such as the ruler of Porcad often failed to send pepper to the Portuguese factory of Cochin.[181] In 1554, the major pepper supplying kings like those of Vadakkenkur, Alengad, Parur, Porcad and Diamper were paid 240 *pardaos* or 72,000 *reais* each per year.[182] However, in 1564 and

TABLE II-1: DETAILS OF ANNUITIES

Name of the Ruler	1554[183]	1564[184]	1574[185]	1605[186]
King of Cochin (*copa*)[187]	640 cr.	640 cr.	640 cr.	640 cr.
King of Vadakkenkur	240 par.	200 par.[188]	200 par.	
Mother of the king of Vadakkenkur [189]		100 par.	100 par.	220 xer.
King of Thodupuzha and Vadakkenkur[190]				240 xer.
King of Alengad	240 par.	200 par.	200 par.	240 xer.
King of Parur	240 par.	200 par.	200 par.	240 xer.
King of Porcad	240 par.	200 par.	200 par.	240 xer.
King of Diamper	240 par.	200 par.	200 par.	240 xer.
Karta of Alwaye	140 par.	140 par.	140 par.	140 xer.
The two kings of Thekkenkur kingdom		200 par. (100 each)	200 par. (100 each)	240 xer. (120 each)

1574, these kings and those of the Thekkenkur kingdom received only 200 *pardaos* and it may seem that some portion of the annuity was curtailed; in actuality it was not so. In terms of the *reais* they received, it was equivalent to that of previous annuities, i.e. each of these kings received 72,000 *reais*. The difference in the figures given in *pardaos* was because of the price fluctuations in the currency of *pardaos*.[191] These monetary rewards were usually given to the rulers of the hinterland sufficiently early every year, so that pepper supplies might reach the weighing place of Cochin before the advent of the ships from Portugal. These annuities were more or less fixed. However, the difference in the annuities given to the local rulers shows that the rulers of large centres of pepper production used to get higher amounts by way of annuity. It has to be specially mentioned that these overhead expenditures were added to the original price of pepper so as to get the actual price of the commodity. As the price of pepper was fixed, the fixed annuity scheme was devised to ensure a continuous supply of the commodity through the assistance of the recipients of annuities. In fact, what the cultivators should have received as price for their product was curtailed. This was because, an attempt was made to please the native rulers and purchase their co-operation by giving them a portion of the price which actually belonged to the cultivators. Paying a regular annuity to the local rulers (this annuity did not form a considerable amount, as the maximum paid per year was only 240 *pardaos*) seemed more profitable to the Portuguese than allowing the price of pepper to fluctuate.

II. THE CULTIVATORS

In the Portuguese documents, St. Thomas Christians were described as the major cultivators of pepper in Kerala. In the early information given to Portugal, we read that pepper was cultivated by the native Christians.[192] In a letter written in 1529 to the king of Portugal, it was said that all the pepper was in the hands of the St. Thomas Christians and that majority of the pepper that went to Portugal was sold by them.[193] The St. Thomas Christians, who trace back their origin to St. Thomas who preached Gospel in Kerala and Mylapore during the period between AD 52 and 72,[194] were distributed in the kingdoms of Calicut, Paru (Parur), Angamali, Managate, Cochin, Carturti (Kaduthuruthy), Cottette (Kottayam), Porcad, Marta, Callicoulam and Travancore.[195] The centres of Christian settlements became specialized regions of pepper cultivation. They dissociated themselves from the Muslim traders from whom they had had to suffer a lot of atrocities in the past, and the producers themselves began to take pepper to the Portuguese factory of Cochin.[196] This actively co-operating cultivator group was a great source of support to the Portuguese in obtaining pepper from hinterland almost till the middle of sixteenth century, when elements of tension began to strain their relationship. Besides St. Thomas Christians, there were others, such as the Hindus who were also involved in the production of pepper.

There were three categories of people, who were connected with pepper cultivation: Proprietors (*janmi* or *janmakaran*), tenants (*kanamkkaran*) and cultivators (*kutiyans* or *verumpattakkaran*).[197] The origin of this three-tier land system was the consequence of the Aryanization of the region[198] and was linked to the control over land established by the Nampoothiri Brahmins between the ninth and twelfth centuries, when they made profit out of their position in the *sabhas* which administered temple property.[199] The Brahmins from north India, had begun to enter Kerala in large numbers and as organized bodies in the seventh and eighth centuries, being whole-heartedly welcomed by the Perumals. Gradually a Brahmin-centred land system evolved with the frequent land grants made to them by the Perumal. When the latter was threatened by the western Chalukyas, and also later during the wars between the Chera and Chola powers, the Nampoothiri Brahmins acquired vast areas of land from other social groups and became wealthy and powerful *janmis*. The cultivators who had more or less customary proprietary rights to their lands, transferred their lands to Brahmin temples and through the temples to the Brahmins themselves. The Brahmins gained control over the entire affairs through the legitimizing myth spread by them.[200]

The end result of these land transfers was the emergence of Brahmins as *janmis* or *janmakarans* (holder of *janmam* tenure). As landlords, they enjoyed a fixed share of one-third of the total produce of the soil. Brahmins, meanwhile, transferred their lands on *kanam* tenure to the Nairs. *Kanam* included the right to supervise or protect all the inhabitants of the particular *nad* wherein the land lay. Usually *kanamkkaran* or the holder of *kanam* was the hereditary protector of his *nad* and not the hereditary protector of any particular piece of it. Though they were socially subordinate to the *janmi*, the *kanamkkarans* enjoyed for their service a fixed share equal in amount to that of the *janmi*, i.e. one-third of the total produce of the soil. Thus, *kanamkkarans* were, like the *janmi*, part-proprietors of the soil with the right to sell, subdivide and sublet their holdings. For all practical purposes, the *kanamkkarans* were permanently attached to their holdings, as the *janmi* would not dare to expel them, for they were not only the chief means of providing the *janmi's* income, but composed his retinue of armed followers, and the expulsion would only create problems for him.[201] However a system of renewal of the *kanam* agreement also existed. The *janmis* used to receive *kanappanam* from *kanamkkarans* in advance, either as advance of rent or as security for payment of rent. This advance was periodically revised, often at the time of succession to *janmam* or *kanam*, which was considered the occasion for *polichezhuthu* or renewal of the *kanam* deed.[202] The *janmi* could also turn to a third person or another *kanamkkaran* and accept an advance payment (*melcharth*) on condition that he would transfer the land to him after having terminated his contract with the earlier *kanamkkaran*. But in this case, the *janmis* were under a customary obligation to pay compensation to those whom he wanted to evict.[203] Since the Nairs or other *kanamkkarans* were placed in a higher strata of the society and since they spurned manual labour, their holdings passed on to people of the lower strata of society on inferior tenures.[204]

The actual cultivator under the *kanamkkaran* was called *verumpattakkaran*. He was also considered part-proprietor to the extent of the one-third of the produce, including the right to sell or sublet his holding and to payment for the improvements he made in his holdings. Usually the *janmis* were Nampoothiri Brahmins. Most of the *kanamkkarans* were Nairs and majority of the actual cultivators or *verumpattakkarans* who produced pepper in the hinterland of Cochin were from the St. Thomas Christians. There were also some Nair and Ezhava cultivators.

However this division was not a watertight one with regard to central Kerala.

Many St. Thomas Christians were also real landowners. Those members of this community, who had held land from days prior to the emergence of Brahmin-centred land system, enjoyed considerable proprietary rights over their cultivable land. Moreover, during the period of large land grants made to the Brahmin temples, many churches of St. Thomas Christians also received considerable land grants from the local Hindu rulers in remuneration for the favours they received from the churches.[205] This led to some sort of communal ownership of land among the St. Thomas Christians. The influential members of the *palliyogams* (administrative council of the churches) were the administrators and caretakers of such lands, who transferred this to ordinary farmers for cultivation. Many local rulers and Brahmin families also used to grant sizable portions of land to some families of the St. Thomas Christians and made them settle down in and around the settlement of high-caste Hindus with a view to touch and purify the vessels and other household utensils polluted by the use of low caste Hindus and untouchables. The belief behind this practice was that the members of these particular families of St. Thomas Christians, whose ancestors were said to have been Brahmins and were converted to Christianity by St. Thomas, could remove the pollution by a simple touch, so that these utensils could be later used by the Brahmins without fear of contamination.[206] One important advantage of this system was that many members of this community acquired personal property with ownership rights. Thus, it seems that a considerable number of St. Thomas Christians enjoyed proprietary rights over significant portions of the land which they cultivated. It was highly probable that some of them held land as *kanamkkarans*, as well. However, a good majority of them seems to have been *verumpattakkarans* cultivating the land for one-third of the produce. The *lavradores* or the cultivators from whom the Hindu, Muslim and Christian merchants purchased pepper in *serra* (that is, in the interior production centres) could be in either one or other of the categories mentioned above.[207] However, the big cultivators as well as the *janmis* and *kanamkkarans*, who had large amounts of pepper at their disposal and could organize transport of pepper to the ports, played a very significant role in the regular supply of cargo in Cochin.[208]

The Portuguese did not have any way of controlling the producers. Moreover, they had no particular reason to be interested in the actual volume of pepper grown. Their main concern was only with regard to the ways and means by which pepper could be purchased and supplied regularly for the Portuguese factory in Cochin.[209]

III. TRADE ROUTES

A. Land Routes

There was an intricate network of land routes (often connected with water routes) which conveyed commodities from the hinterland to the port of Cochin. Because of the geophysical position of Malabar, wheeled traffic was difficult and scanty.[210] Overland transport was based on caravans of oxen and donkeys as well as porters. Transport along straight routes was made difficult by the existence of steep inclines, tropical forests and rivers.[211]

People, who took to land routes, followed a method, as mentioned by Ibn

Batuta, for carrying merchandise. The merchants of Malabar hired men for carrying baggage and other movables on their backs. One merchant was accompanied by approximately one hundred men carrying his wares. Every one of them carried a stout stick fitted with an iron point at the lower end and a hook of the same metal at the top. When the porters wanted to take rest, he stuck his baton into the ground and suspended his burden from the hook. After resting, he took up his charge without anyone to assist him and resumed his journey.[212] It seems that this practice of the merchant caravans continued all through medieval Kerala. Visscher reports that the porters usually carried two packs: one on the shoulder and the other on the head. A *fanam* was to be paid in every kingdom through which they travelled, as tax for the packs which they carried on their backs, while no charge was imposed on those which were carried on the head.[213] These goods thus brought by land routes required the help of water routes to reach Cochin, because of its geophysical position. In many cases, the land routes reduced the distance of travel; however, the cost of land traffic was heavy, so the merchants preferred water routes whenever they reached the navigable part of a river. In fact, both land and riverine transport took the merchandise of the hinterland to the port of Cochin.

B. The Riverine Routes

Most of the commodities were taken from the hinterland to Cochin through several riverine routes. The seven rivers which flow into Vembanadu lake formed the principal waterways.

Periyar, which even today, holds a very important position among the wide and diverse networks of rivers, played a major role in linking the far-flung hinterlands lying in the north-eastern part with Cochin. It originates near Sabarimala on the southern side of the Peerumedu hills. But the waters of its tributaries like Mullayaru, Muthirapuzhayaru, Kuttampuzhayaru and Deviyaru, coming from distant hilly forests[214] make Periyar quite navigable by the time it reaches the low land. An important centre situated on the banks of Periyar in the land low, is Thrikkariyoor.[215] Kothamangalam, an important pepper-growing centre[216] is located some 5 kilometres to the east of Thrikkariyoor. Kothamangalam had a large bazaar, as it was an important halting centre for the traders from Tamil country who went on to Thrikkariyoor and other neighbourhood places.[217] The other spice-growing regions which this river integrated with Cochin were Perumpaulur (Perumbavoor), [218] Curupanpady (Kuruppumpady);[219] Maleatur (Malayattoor),[220] and Mekkattur.[221] Periyar, as a means of communication between the port of Cochin and its hinterland, had a very significant and decisive role when it reached Alwaye.[222] Alwaye was a major market place where there was a fair. At Alwaye, Periyar bifurcates and flows into the Arabian sea by two mouths: one into the opening at Cranganore and the other into the mouth of Cochin. The first branch passing through Alengad merges into the sea at Cranganore. The second branch or the southern branch that flows south, again bifurcates into two branches of which one joins Varapola (Varapuzha)[223] while the other passing Rapolim, [224] merges into the backwaters of Tripunithara.[225] These two branches of the Periyar, joining the backwaters of Vembanadu, flow into the Arabian sea along Cochin. Through Periyar, which has a length of

228.5 kilometres[226] were carried down to Cochin with the help of *tonis* and small boats, various spices and large quantities of teak, mast wood as well as *angelins* for shipbuilding.[227]

Besides these spice-pockets which were situated on the river side, there were other agrarian centres in the interior extending to the north. The most important among them was Angamali which, having a great market place and three big churches, was the seat of the bishop of the St. Thomas Christians. Antonio de Gouveia says that there were two rulers in Angamali: *rey branco* or *Velutha tavazhi* and *rey preto* or *Karutha tavazhi.*[228] In the same kingdom of Angamali or exactly in Velutha tavazhi, was located Agaparambim (Akaparambu)[229] which was peopled mostly by the St. Thomas Christians. Other important agrarian pockets were Mourikolam (Moozhikulam) and Manjappra,[230] situated in the kingdom of Parur as well as Cheguree (Chowara)[231] and Canhur (Kanjoor).[232] These parts of the *serra* were connected with Cochin, first by a network of land routes and then with the help of water routes.

The Chalakudy river, which has a length of 144.8 kilometres merges into the northern branch of Periyar at Elanthettikkara, six miles to the east of Cranganore.[233] It seems that a smaller amount of spices were carried down through Chalakudy river to Cochin via Cranganore, as most of the agrarian centres around this river like Koratty, Chalakudy, etc., were in the kingdom of the Zamorin. The ghat route trade from Chalakudy also diverted much of pepper to the Coromandel coast. However, through this water passage, a lot of teak wood, *angelins* and logs for masts were taken to Cochin for shipbuilding activities.

Muvattupuzha river, having a length of 120.7 kilometres connected the hinterland of the Vadakkenkur region with Cochin.[234] The three rivers of Thodupuzha, Kothamangalam and Kaliyar joined at Muvattupuzha to form this river, which was navigable except during the peak of summer. Turubuli (Thodupuzha—sometimes written as Turuguly) situated on the banks of this river was a centre of hectic trade and political activities. Caricotti (Karikode) near Turubuli was the seat of Vadakkenkur after 1600.[235] The ruler of Turubuli championed the cause of the St. Thomas Christians and their leader the Archdeacon. The very king himself intervened for them through a letter written to the queen of Kaduthuruthy when Dom Alexis Meneses tried to Latinize them and convert them into *vassalos e sogeytos a el Rey de Portugal,*[236] which was an indirect device to control the pepper-producers. Turubuli had intense trade relations with the Tamil country and commodities from Tamilnadu were brought through the Cumbam and Kumily passes via Udumpannoor and Marubuli (Muthalakodam).[237] The land route from Turubuli passed through Juncam (Chunkam) as well as Nediale (Nediasala)[238] and reached Prouto (Piravom)[239] from where they were again interlinked with the water routes provided by the Muvattupuzha river and through it commodities were taken to Cochin via Vembanadu lake. A major spice-growing centre near Turubuli and situated in the basin of this river was Melucompil (Mailakompu).[240] Other important spice-growing regions on the banks of this river were Aragosha (Arakuzha),[241] Muyattupula (Muvattupuzha),[242] and Palur (Pazhur).[243] Land routes from Ramrat (Ramapuram),[244] Baragore (Vadakara near Koothattukulam),[245] Ignapeli (Elenji)[246] and Molecalao (Mulakkulam)[247] intersected at Piravom from where commodities were taken down to Cochin through the waters of the Muvattupuzha river. This river that flows down into Baiqueta (Vaikkom)[248] bifurcates at Vettikkattumukku: one branch passing Ithipuzha falls at Vadakkemurry and the other branch passing Murinjapuzha reaches Chembu.[249] The other important centres around Baiqueta lake (Vaikkom lake is only an extension of Vembanadu lake) were Bechu (Vechur), Muttão (Muttam) situated in the kingdom of Muterte (Muttedathu),[250] as well as Palliporao (Pallippuram)[251] and Collegeira Mangalao (Kulasekhara-mangalam),[252] located in the pepper kingdom.

Meenachil river with a length of 67.6 kilometres was an integrating link with the northern part of Thekkenkur kingdom. The hilly regions from which this river originates were ruled by Punhati Perumal (king of Poonjar).[253] The royal family of Poonjar had its origins in Pandi (Tamilnadu). *Malleas* or the high-ranges, through which the trade routes from Poonjar, Thodupuzha and Kanjirappilly ran to Madurai, were under the king of Turubuli and Punhati Perumal.[254] It seems that the king of Poonjar controlled the land route that went from Meenachil basin via Periate (Periyar) to Tamilnadu.[255] Irattuperha (Erattupetta)[256] was an important bazaar located on the banks of the Meenachil river down below Poonjar. The presence of a large number of enterprising St. Thomas Christian farmers ensuring a regular supply of a sizeable volume of spices (their settlement was often called Aruvithara), and the presence of equally enterprising Muslim merchants in Erattupetta made this region a famous trade centre. It had flourishing trade relations with the Tamil country through the Kumily pass.[257] Anagalengal (Anakallunkal or the present-day Bharananganam),[258] Larat (Lalam in Pala), Palaya (Pala), Cherpungal, (Cherpunkal) and Punnathara[259] were other pepper pockets in the Thekkenkur kingdom located near the Meenachil river. It was navigable except during summer. The commodities from the interior were taken to Cotette (Kottayam)[260] and from there to Cochin through the Vembanadu lake. Important spice-growing centres of Puthuppalli as well as Manarcad (Manarkad)[261] in the kingdom of Thekkenkur, Coramallur (Kudamaloor)[262] in the kingdom of Porcad, and Athirampuzha in the kingdom of Vadakkenkur were located near Cotette (Kottayam). Carturte (Kadathuruthy),[263] the first capital of the pepper kingdom was integrated with Cochin (via Vembanadu lake) through Valiathodu. Pepper pockets like Kadaplamattam in the kingdom of Thekkenkur,[264] Corlengate (Kuravilangadu),[265] Ettumanur,[266] Kothanalloor,[267] Nagpili (Muttuchira),[268] etc., in the kingdom of Vadakkenkur were in the immediate vicinity of Carturte.

The land routes connecting Raakate (Rakkad), Kadamattam, Kolencherri[269] of the kingdom of Cochin intersected at Tripunithara part of Vembanadu lake. Kandanatt (Kandanad)[270] and Molendurte (Mulanthuruthy)[271] also part of the kingdom of Cochin, were so located that the land routes from these agrarian pockets had an immediate opening to the backwaters of Vembanadu.

Manimala river starting from Peerumedu hills, has a length of 91.7 kilometres. It integrated the important inland market of Quanhara Pee (Kanjirappally)[272] as well as the agrarian pockets of Changanachere (Changanacherry)[273] and Tiruvalla[274] in the kingdom of Thekkenkur with the lake of Vembanadu which was further linked with Cochin.

The river Pampa originates on the eastern part of Sabarimala hills and

Azhuthayaru, Kakkattaru as well as Kallaru are its main tributaries. With a length of 177 kilometres, it linked Changanor (Chengannoor),[275] Naranao (Niranam) and Maramon[276] in the kingdom of Thekkenkur and Poligunde (Pulinkunnu)[277] in the kingdom of Vadakkenkur, with the Vembanadu lake.

Achankovil river having a length of 128.7 kilometres joins Pampa river near Niranam and merges into Vembanadu lake as a part of Pampa. It formed a main water passage for the regions of Pathanamthitta, Karthikappally and Tiruvalla. The major agrarian pockets located around it were Podiagabo or Maelicare (Puthiakavu or Mavelikkara),[278] Calucate (Kalloorkad or Champakulam), Batimeni (Venmani),[279] Tuumpone (Thumpamon),[280] Calupare (Kallooppara),[281] Catiapely (Karthikappilly).[282] These seven rivers flow into a long stretch of back waters called Vembanadu lake which made the integration process of the spice hinterland with the port of Cochin smooth and constant. A considerable portion of these rivers, except Pampa and Periyar, were not navigable during the peak summer period. But land routes always intersected at the navigable parts of these rivers which provided easy and cheap accessibility[283] to the Vembanadu lake.

IV. THE BACK WATERS: A 'HIGHWAY' BETWEEN COCHIN AND ITS HINTERLAND

A system of backwaters which encircled Cochin, played a very significant role in integrating the various riverine routes with the port. The back waters in the vicinity of Cochin have two parts: 1. The northern part called Cranganore lake. 2. The southern part called Vembanadu lake.

Vembanadu lake is the long stretch of back waters or the land-locked water that extended from Cochin down to south. It is eighty-four kilometres in length, and an average of 32 kilometres of width.[284] On the border of this lake were situated the kingdoms of Karappuram, Karthikappally, Porcad, Thekkenkur, Vadakkenkur, Cochin, Rapolim, Anchekaimal, etc.

Some parts of this lake are very deep , though shallow places are not rare.[285] However, this lake was fully navigable and bigger boats and ships could be used for trade traffic.[286] Merchandise brought up to the banks of this lake from the hinterland either with the help of small country boats or *tonis* or with the assistance of pack-oxen, or carried by men, were taken by big boats and barges to the port of Cochin.

Cranganore lake is actually the northern extension of Vembanadu lake. This, being joined by the Periyar and Chalakudy rivers, extends 25 kilometres north of Cochin.[287] These two lagoons served as highways for the spice-carriers that moved constantly from the hinterland to the port of Cochin.

The Portuguese claimed that as the king of Portugal was the lord of the sea, and of the coast of India, all rivers and ports must be under his command.[288] So the backwaters and the lagoons into which the various riverine routes and land routes from the hinterland merged were patrolled very vigilantly by the Portuguese fleet.[289] Every loophole for diverting commodities from Cochin's hinterland to other ports was closed by well-thought out strategies. The Portuguese fleet patrolled the mouths of various rivers as well as the junctional points in the water routes. It seems that the patrolling of the junctions of rivers and lagoons was undertaken by Portuguese with the help of Indian auxiliaries. Those who were patrolling the lagoon used to get 369 *xerafins*, 4 *tangas* and 68 *reais* as salary.[290]

The cost of river patrolling and the annuities given to the native rulers had to be added to get the actual price paid for the pepper. If one totals the protection money, the 'fixed-price' dictated by the Portuguese would appear to be higher. At the same time, the money actually paid to the cultivator would appear to be less as compared to the 'protection cost'. The protection cost increased as the Portuguese paid a lower price to the cultivators,[291] so the producers increasingly resorted to the diversion of spices to the centres which paid rather better prices.

V. SATELLITE MARKETS

The exchange system in the hinterland led to the emergence of wide and intricate network of bazaars (*angadi*), markets, fairs and mega markets. Each of these acted as satellite economic units for the port of Cochin, in varying degrees. In almost all the pepper-growing centres, there were *angadis* or bazaars attached to the settlements. They were often located near the churches or temples. These places experienced a concentration of population.[292] Thus Antonio de Gouveia says that there were bazaars in Vaipicota (Vaipinkotta), Palla (Pala), Mangate (Alengad), Cranganore, Changanachere (Changanacherry), Cheguree (Chowara) Canhur (Kanjoor), Molendurte (Mulanthuruthy), Corlengate (Kuravilangad), Cotette (Kottayam), Coramallur (Kudamaloor), Baiquete (Vaikkom), Changanor (Chengannoor), Calucate (Kalloorkad), Podiagabo (Puthiyakavu), Poligunde (Pulinkunnu), etc.[293] In these bazaars all the necessities of life were sold.[294]

Besides these, markets or centres of greater economic activities also existed at some important nodal points. Diogo Gonçalves says that there were four centres that belonged to this category. They were Angamale (Angamali), Carturte (Kadathuruthy), Diamper (Udayamperur) and Paraur (Parur).[295] They were the capitals of the kingdoms of Angamali, Vadakkenkur, Udayamperur and Parur respectively. As centres of hectic political activities, they must have played a very significant role in the economic life, as well. Moreover these four towns were important as far the ecclesiastical life of the St. Thomas Christians was concerned. Angamali was the seat of their bishop and in three other places, the St. Thomas Christians formed almost the majority of the population. They also became important inland trade centres. The inhabitants of these market towns varied between one hundred and one thousand.[296]

There were *feiras* or fairs in connection with the important festivals of the churches and temples. Most of these fairs, which were conducted after the harvest of pepper and other spices gave the people a better exchange opportunity. The 'modernities of life' entered the hinterland through these fairs. Thus, there were fairs in Aragosha, Prouto, Rapolim, Maleatur, Athirampuzha, Palaya, Ettumanoor, Cranganore, etc., in connection with important festivals. But *Feira d'Alwa* (the fair of Alwaye probably in connection with Sivarathri festival) was the most important among them.[297]

On the eastern side of the hinterland six centres namely, Zaruquly (Chalakudy),[298] Codemangalao (Kothamangalam),[299] Turubuli (Thodupuzha),[300] Iratepely

(Erattupetta), Canharapely (Kanjirappally) and Erimamoly (Erumely)[301] developed the network of a mega-market because of their trade connections with the Tamil country.[302] These six centres from where began the ghat routes that ran to the Coromandel coast, are located almost 80 to 120 kilometres east of Cochin and were thus on the peripheral zone of Cochin's hinterland and were available for Tamil contacts. In reality the vitality of these inland markets depended on their relationship with Tamilnadu. The Tamil merchants took to these places metal utensils, opium, rice, oil seeds, groundnut and peas for exchange. But the most important items that came from 'Pande' (from Pandyanad—a general expression to denote Tamil country), to these market centres were various types of clothes,[303] rice and cereals. As the areas around these markets suffered scarcity in food supplies, it seems that the rulers not only allowed, but also encouraged the Tamil traders to come to these markets, which would ensure a regular rice-supply in their kingdoms. They often sold rice and cloth in exchange for pepper, which was in high demand along the Coromandel coast. Thus, a large amount of pepper from these markets was carried off to Tamilnadu with the help of pack oxen.[304] Their network ultimately extended to the Coromandel ports, as they collected enough cargo for their return journey, thus greatly reducing the transportation costs. As pepper and other spices were a return cargo, these merchants could cheaply transport these items to the ports of the Coromandel coast from where they were further taken to different destinations in Asia. Merchants from distant regions came to these markets of inland Kerala to sell spices, areca nut, etc., and to buy rice, clothes and some foreign items brought from the Tamil country. These bazaars with active processes of exchange and transactions occupied almost a one-mile length,[305] and eventually developed into mega-markets.

Erumely, Kanjirappally, Erattupetta, Thodupuzha, Kothamangalam and Chalakudy were interrelated by a network of roads. From Erumely, there was a road going to Kanjirappally via Koratty and crossing the Chittar river. It intersected at Chirakkadavu Areekkal near Kanjirappally and this was one of the ancient routes taken by the Ayyappa pilgrims going to Sabarimala.[306] The trade route from Kanjirappally to Erattupetta ran through Nellimalapetta.[307] However, the routes from these two places namely, Kanjirappally and Erattupetta ran in the direction to Tamil country via Pazhoomala.[308] This route, which was later joined by the trade route from Erumely, crossing Periate (Periyar)[309] entered the Tamil border through the Kumily pass. It was a very old and traditional route, through which the *Vellalas* and the *Ravuthar* Muslims from Madurai reached Kanjirappally and Erattupetta by the fourteenth century.[310] There was a land route running from Erattupetta to Thodupuzha via Edamaruku and Muttam. Thodupuzha, which was the capital of Kizhumalainad and later by 1600, that of Vadakkenkur, had strong trade relations with Tamilnadu. The usual trade-route from Thodupuzha to Tamilnadu ran through Muthalakodam,[311] Cheenikuzhy, and crossed the Kerala border either through the Cumbam pass or through the Kumily pass. The active Tamil contact with Thodupuzha is evident from the existence of the Annamalai temple of Karikode, Thodupuzha (the seat of the kingdom), which was dedicated to Siva and built in the Chola style of architecture. The presence of *Vellalas* and Tamil-speaking *Ravuthar* Muslims still living in and around Thodupuzha, who entered this region through this traditional trade route as early as the fourteenth century, attests to the connection of this portion of hinterland and its market, with Tamilnadu.[312] From Karikode-Thodupuzha, there was a *kottavazhi* or a land route running to Kothamangalam via Vazhakala (West Kodikulam), Kalloorkad (near Vazhakulam) and Ayavana (from where a branch ran to Muvattupuzha, which had been the former seat of the Kizhumalainad). Kothamangalam had strong trade relations with the regions of Thirunelveli and Dindigul in Tamilnadu.[313] The remnants of the *athanis* (stone structures) with which the Tamil traders used to stabilize their carriages are still seen in the vicinity of its markets. The Jacobite bishop Mar Basil who landed in the Coromandel coast in the seventeenth century, came via Pallivasal using this trade route to Kothamangalam, where he died and where his mortal remains are even now interred.[314] It also seems that there was a land route between Kothamangalam and Chalakudy running through Thrikkariyoor, which initially served as a land route to connect Kothamangalam with Muziris (Cranganore).[315] From Chalakudy commodities were taken to Tamilnadu through Peringalkuthu.

Thus, from Erumely to Chalakudy one can trace along the ghats some sort of continuous land route connecting the various markets. It seems that these routes which connected the different market centres were often used for distributive trade by the native peddlers but much less by the Tamil merchants who conducted the bulk trade. As the trade touching different markets involved a journey through different kingdoms and petty principalities, where the payment of taxes consumed all the possible profits, it seems to have been an usual practice for the Tamil traders to bring commodities only up to the mega-markets, and leave the local distribution to the native traders of the locality. But the trade of Erattupetta, Kanjirappally and Erumely seems to have been conducted as one unit and the same Tamil traders distributed commodities for these three mega-markets, since these places formed part of one and the same kingdom, namely, that of Thekkenkur. With regard to other places, the Tamil traders seem to have preferred to take the hilly ghat route to reach each of the other markets instead of going through the land routes which connected the markets, since the latter route would be tantamount to losing profit by paying taxes to the various kings and *naduvazhis*, who ruled the territories lying between these markets. Moreover, as we have already seen, the Tamil merchant groups, who were visiting these markets, were coming from different but specialized regions of Tamilnadu like Madurai, Thirunelveli or Dindigul. The traders from each of these regions seemed to have established some sort of monopolistic hold over one or more of these inland markets, linking its trade activities to the places of their origin and commercial operations. These commodities taken from the inland markets of Kerala to Madurai, Dindigul and Thirunelveli, were further distributed to interior India for domestic consumption, and to the Coromandel coast from where they were taken to different destinations in Asia. This distribution was often undertaken by the same merchant groups. But it was not unlikely that merchants with better resources and networks from other places actively participated in this trade to Coromandel coast.

However, these markets were not totally cut off from Cochin. Most of them were important political centres of the Vadakkenkur and Thekkenkur kings, to whom regular annuities were given by the Portuguese. (The king of Thekkenkur had a palace in Kanjirappally. It seems that of the two kings of Thekkenkur to whom the

Portuguese used to give annuities, one actually stayed in Kanjirappally.) The respective rulers had to see to it that pepper, ginger and other commodities reached Cochin regularly. At the same time, they did not dare to close the ghat routes which provided food-materials to their kingdoms and which ensured a regular source of income coming from market transactions, even though these routes were associated with the diversion of pepper to the Coromandel coast. It must be said that in times of tensions in the hinterland, these inland markets served as feeding centres for the ghat route that went to the Coromandel coast via Madurai or Dindigul.

Thus, with the emergence of Cochin as a port in the middle of the fourteenth century, the political and economic life of Kerala experienced a new turn of events. The establishment of the royal residence of the Perumpadappu kings in Cochin gave to the port security and safety, which were required for conducting trade and attracted traders from China, Persia and Arabia. Attempts were also made to convert considerable portions of the interior land into the hinterland of Cochin. This process of carving out of the hinterland for Cochin adversely affected Calicut, which naturally led to frequent clashes between the two. However, with the arrival of the Portuguese under Pedro Alvarez Cabral in 1500, and later with the establishment of the headquarters of the Portuguese *Estado* in Cochin in 1505, Cochin seems to have had a more advantageous position than Calicut, as the Portuguese tried to attach to Cochin more and more hinterlands by paying annuities and subsidies to the rulers of various inland territories. In the initial phase the fact that most of the pepper cultivators were St. Thomas Christians also helped them to integrate the spice-growing regions with Cochin. Different land and riverine routes which merged into the Vembanadu lake helped easy transportation of commodities from the hinterland to the port of Cochin. Moreover, the economic activities of the peripheral zone of the hinterland was often linked with six satellite markets, which, while maintaining relations with Cochin, had trade relations with Tamilnadu through the Tamil merchants as far as the Coromandel coast. These markets served as the entrance for the ghat route going to the eastern coast via Madurai and Dindigul; in addition, they supplied food materials and clothes for the entire hinterland lying in the eastern slope. In spite of their susceptibility to the Tamil contacts, these satellite markets as a part of the hinterland were linked with Cochin, as well. In short, though Cochin and its hinterlands, which were scattered over different kingdoms and principalities, were politically and administratively different, they still formed one economic unit.

NOTES

1. K.M. Panikkar, *A History of Kerala*, p. 8; C. Achyuta Menon, *The Cochin State Manual*, Ernakulam, 1911, p. 2; K.P. Padmanabha Menon, 'The Fort of Cochin', in *Fort Cochin Municipal Centenary Souvenir*, Cochin, 1966, p. 60.
2. K.P. Padmanabha Menon, *History of Kerala*, vol. I, p. 161; K. Rama Varma Raja, 'The Cochin Harbour and the Putu Vaipu Era', in *The Bulletin of the Rama Varma Research Institute*, no. 2, Cochin, 1933, pp. 49-51.
3. Ibid.; W.W. Hunter, *The Imperial Gazetteer of India*, vol. IV, London, 1885, p. 11.
4. Ibid.; According to Innes, this era commemorates either the establishment of the first church on the island or the date when the island first became cultivable. C.A. Innes,

Madras District Gazetteers: Malabar, Madras, 1951, p. 429. But these events are too insignificant to be commemorated by an era. As events with long-term significance are usually related to the commencement of an era, the geographical changes caused by the flood of 1341 must be the most probable event behind the Puthu Vaippu Era as well.

5. Nicolo Conti calls it Kocchi after the small river that flowed by that place. (Actually this is not a river, but a water passage between the lagoons and the sea.) R.H. Major (ed.), *India in the Fifteenth Century: A Collection of Narratives of Voyages to India in the Century Preceding the Portuguese Discovery of the Cape of Good Hope: From Latin, Persian, Russian and Italian Sources*, New Delhi, 1974, p. 19; K.P. Padmanabha Menon argues that this Kocchazhi appeared about AD 1000 by an earlier flood in Periyar and it became broadened and a deeper water passage appeared with the great flood of AD 1341. K.P. Padmanabha Menon, 'The Fort of Cochin', p. 60.
6. There are authors who say that the Permpadappu chief transferred his residence to Cochin to escape from the constant attacks of the Zamorin. See, A. Sreeddhara Menon, *A Survey of Kerala History*, p. 173. But it seems to me that besides these political motives, there was a preponderant desire in the chief to take part in the gains that accrued from the emerging trade activities of the port.
7. A. Sreedhara Menon, *A Survey of Kerala History*, pp. 173-4.
8. Ibid. *Perumpadappu Swarupam* was the name of the royal family of Cochin. It is so-called, after the village of the same name in Vanneri in Ponnani Taluk of Malabar, which is said to have been the original seat of the family. C. Achyuta Menon, op. cit., p. 2. It was also called *Madathumkal swarupam.*
9. Ibid. In Kerala, the kings preferred to have kingdoms with coastal outlets rather than mere land-locked kingdoms, as the former ensured regular revenue by way of trade. The situation was such that the kings, who had high political ambitions, centred their designs around a port.
10. K.V. Krishna Ayyar, op. cit., pp. 1-2.
11. Ibn Batuta, *Die Reise des Arabers Ibn Batuta durch Indien und China*, edited by Hanz von Mzik, Hamburg, 1911, p. 302.
12. Ibid., pp. 302-3, 305-8. The earliest account of Calicut is given by Ibn Batuta. Marco Polo who visited Malabar towards the end of the thirteenth century, though mentioning the kingdom of Eli, speaks nothing of Calicut or its ruler. It seems that Calicut became a considerable force only by the beginning of the fourteenth century.
13. Nycolão Gomçallvez, *Livro que trata das cousas da India e do Japão*, edited by Andelino de Almeida Calado, Coimbra, 1957, p. 45.
14. K.P. Padmanabha Menon, *History of Kerala*, vol. II, pp. 68-82.
15. C. Achyuta Menon, op. cit., p. 44; K.P. Padmanabha Menon, *History of Kerala*, vol. II, pp. 69-70. In spite of this link with the Brahmin ruler of Edappilly the king of Cochin was never considered a Brahmin. It shows that the caste of Kulasekhara rulers, to which the Perumpadappu kings originally belonged through the matrilineal system, continued even when the father was a Brahmin. But it also suggests that the Brahmin links, which this royal family had claimed, included claims over temples.
16. K.P. Padmanabha Menon, *History of Kerala*, vol. II, p. 71; K.M. Panikkar, *A History of Kerala*, p. 24.
17. K.P. Padmanabha Menon, *History of Kerala*, vol. II, p. 71.
18. The Ming ruler Yung Lo (1403-24) took a keen interest in maritime activities and despatched a big fleet under Grand Eunuch Cheng Ho (1405-33) to overseas countries in an ambassadorial role, as well as with a plan to induce foreign delegates and traders come to China to submit tribute and to conduct supplementary trade. Roderich Ptak, 'China and Portugal at Sea: The Early Ming Trading System and the Estado da India

Compared', in *The Asian Seas 1500-1800: Local Societies, European Expansion and the Portuguese, Revista de Cultura*, vol. I, Ano V, 1991, pp. 23-4; K.N. Chaudhuri, *Trade and Civilization in the Indian Ocean: An Economic History from the Rise of Islam to 1750*, New Delhi, 1985, p. 60.

19. Ma Huan, *Ying Yai Sheng lan* 12, 'Kochih', as translated by W.W. Rockhill, 'Notes on the Relations and Trade of China with the Eastern Archipelago and the Coast of the Indian Ocean during the Fourteenth Century', *T'oung Pao*, vol. XVI, 1915, pp. 450-1.
20. Ibid.
21. Duarte Barbosa, *The Book of Duarte Barbosa: An Account of the Countries Bordering on the Indian Ocean and their Inhabitants*, trans. Mansel Longsworth Dames, vol. II, Nendeln, 1967, p. 93.
22. W.W. Rockhill, op. cit., vol. XVI, p. 450 and footnotes.
23. K.P. Padmanabha Menon, *Kochi Rajya Charitram*, pp. 17-18; K.P. Padmanabha Menon, *History of Kerala*, vol. I, p. 167. There are authors who say that Saudi, a place at the southern end of the present day Fort Cochin, got its name from Saudi Arabia where from the Arabs came to trade K.L. Bernard, *History of Fort Cochin*, p. 2.
24. W.W. Rockhill, op. cit., p. 452.
25. Fei Hsin, *Hsing Ch'a Sheng lan* 30, 'Kochih', translated by W.W. Rockhill, 'Notes on the Relations and Trade of China . . .', in *T'oung Pao*, vol. XVI, p. 452.
26. For further details on the relationship between China and Malabar, see Haraprasad Ray, 'An Enquiry into the Presence of the Chinese in South and South East Asia after the Voyages of Zheng He in Early Fifteenth Century', A Paper presented in the *Second International Symposium on Maritime Studies*, Pondicherry, 16-20 December 1991.
27. Ma Huan, *Ying Yai Sheng lan* 12, 'Kochih', in Rockhill, op. cit., p. 451. *P'o-ho* is *bahar* or *bharam* which is equal to about 3 cwts, C. Achyuta Menon, op. cit., p. 45. The value of the *tael* has undergone much variation over time. In 1666, the value of 1 *tael* was 5 shillings. Richard Carnac Temple (ed.), *The Travels of Peter Mundy in Europe and Asia:1608-1667*, London, 1919, p. 309.
28. Fei Hsin, *Hsing Ch'a Sheng lan* 30, 'Kochih', translated by Rockhill, op. cit., p. 452.
29. Duarte Barbosa, op. cit., vol. II, p. 95.
30. Robert Bristow, *Cochin Saga*, p. 25.
31. Aubin Jean, 'l'apprentissage de L'Inde. Cochin 1503-1504', in *Moyen Orient et Ocean Indien*, 1988; Genevieve Bouchon, 'Calicut at the Turn of the Sixteenth Century', in *The Asian Seas 1500-1800: Local Societies, European Expansions and the Portuguese, Revista de Cultura*, vols. I and V, 1991, p. 44; see also 'Reisebericht des Franciscus Dalbuquerque vom 27. December 1503', in B. Greif (ed.), *Tagebuch des Lucas Rem aus den Jahren 1494-1541*, Augsburg, 1861, p. 146. *Korran* might have been a derivation from the Tamil word *Kurran* meaning association.
32. 'Letter from King Manuel to Ferdinand and Isabella', in William Brooks Greenlee (ed. and trans.), *The Voyage of Pedro Alvares Cabral to Brazil and India*, Nendeln, 1967, p. 49.
33. Fei Hsin, op. cit., p. 452.
34. Ma Huan, *Ying Yai Sheng lan* 12, 'Kochih', p. 451.
35. R.H. Major, op. cit., p. 19.
36. The idea of a major central port supported and reinforced by satellite ports and subordinate nodal centres of exchange is adapted from Ashin Das Gupta's observation of one principal port strengthened by the activity of subordinate ports on the Gujarat coast. Ashin Das Gupta, *Indian Merchants and the Decline of Surat*, Wiesbaden, 1979. Authors like Genevieve Bouchon and Denys Lombard find a similar situation on the Malabar coast. Genevieve Bouchon and Denys Lombard, 'The Indian Ocean in the Fifteenth Century', in *India and the Indian Ocean 1500-1800*, edited by Ashin Das

Gupta and M.N. Pearson, Delhi, 1987, p. 59; B.S. Boyle while studying East African sea ports, says that in the port complex, the individual ports are functionally interrelated and form a hierarchy. He also says that the character and functions of ports within this hierarchy are subject to change over time as a result of the differential impact of factors influencing port growth. B.S. Boyle, 'Indian Ocean Gateways: Some Maritime Perspectives on East African Sea Ports', A Paper presented in the *Second International Conference on Indian Studies* held in Perth, Western Australia, 5-12 December, 1984, p. 6. It seems that a similar port complex with functional interrelation and hierarchical structure and with the role of principal port changing over time, existed on the Malabar coast.

37. The fact that Cranganore, Quilon and Calicut were the major ports which occupied a pivotal position on the Malabar coast till the end of the fifteenth century in successive phases, is based on the early writings on this coast. For details see the unpublished M.Phil. dissertation of Pius Malekandathil, 'Urban Growth of Cochin in the Sixteenth and Seventeenth Centuries', submitted to Pondicherry Central University, 1992, pp. 24-37.
38. K.P. Padmanabha Menon, *Kochi Rajya Charitram*, pp. 15-16; Ramesan Thampuran, op. cit., p. 6.
39. Francis Day says that among the innumerable kings of Malabar, only the Perumpadappu ruler was considered a Kshatriya by birth. For details see Francis Day, op. cit., p. 45.
40. C. Achyuta Menon, op. cit., p. 39.
41. A. Sreedhara Menon, *A Survey of Kerala History*, p. 174.
42. The king of Cochin also had control over the Tiruvalla and Haripad Devasams in Travancore. C. Achyuta Menon, op. cit., p. 50.
43. Tomé Pires, *The Suma Oriental of Tomé Pires: An Account of the East from the Red Sea to Japan, written in Malacca and India in 1512-1515*, Nendeln, 1967, p. 80
44. K.P. Padmanabha Menon, *Kochi Rajya Charitram*, p. 17; C. Achyuta Menon, op. cit., pp. 46-7.
45. K.M. Panikkar, *A History of Kerala, 1498-1801*, p. 24; C. Achyuta Menon, op. cit., p. 47.
46. William Logan, *Manual of Malabar*, vol. I, New Delhi, 1989, p. 278.
47. A. Sreedhara Menon, *A Survey of Kerala History*, pp. 178-9.
48. Tomé Pires, op. cit., p. 80. It seems that this geographical unit mentioned by him was only the political territory ruled by the king in Cochin. The other branches of Cochin royal family used to control land territories other than the ones held in Cochin. These developments took place by the end of fifteenth century. C. Achyuta Menon, op. cit., p. 43.
49. Duarte Barbosa, op. cit., vol. II, p. 95.
50. K.V. Krishna Ayyar, *The Zamorins of Calicut*, p. 131. King Manuel in his letter to Ferdinand and Isabella mentions that the harbour (of Cochin) has much better and much more extensive trade, '*since of almost all the merchandise which goes to Calicut, most of it is to be found in that land (of Cochin)', and others go there first without going to Calicut*' from 'Letter from King Manuel to Ferdinand and Isabella' (29 July 1501) in William Brooks Greenlee (ed.), *The Voyage of Pedro Alvares Cabral to Brazil and India*, London, 1938, p. 49.
51. K.P. Padmanabha Menon, *History of Kerala*, vol. I, p. 167; O.K. Nambiar, op. cit., p. 40.
52. K.P. Padmanabha Menon, *History of Kerala*, vol. I, p. 167.
53. After the withdrawal of the Chinese, the power and influence of the Arab traders were on the increase. William Logan, op. cit., vol. I, p. 294; Genevieve Bouchon, 'Calicut at

the Turn of the Sixteenth Century', in *The Asian Seas 1550-1800*, p. 42. For details about the Arab traders who were a source of strength and financial support to the Zamorin, see Genevieve Bouchon, 'Les Musulmans du Kerala à L'Epoque de La Découverte Portugaise', in *Mare Luso-Indicum*, tom. II, Paris, 1973, p. 54; Henry E.J. Stanley (ed.), *The Three Voyages of Vasco da Gama and His Viceroyalty from Lendas da India of Gaspar Correia*, New York, 1869, pp. 154-6, 358-60.

54. Unlike other parts of India, Malayalis do not congregate in closely-built villages; but live in houses in their own premises and farmland. The urban phenomena or the cluster of closely built houses was the result of the influence and example of non-Malayali Hindus, native Christians or Mohammedans. C. Achyuta Menon, op. cit., pp. 3-4. These communities made their appearance in Kerala either through trade or activities connected with trade.
55. The most important obligation on the foreigners was that they should not kill cows. Later, during the Portuguese phase, tensions fomented because of the killing of cows. Paduronga S.S. Pisurlencar, *Assentos do Conselho do Estado*, vol. II, Bastora/Goa, 1953, p. 430. The existence of extra-territorial jurisdiction in Cochin was indirectly alluded by Philip Baldaeus, when he writes that 'all the different nations live (in Cochin) in perfect liberty as to religion, each having its own temple and that they all live in peace'. Philip Baldaeus, *A True and Exact Description of the Most Celebrated East Indies Coasts of Malabar and Coromandel, as also of the Isle of Ceylon, with all the Adjacent Kingdom, Principalities, Cities, Chief Harbours, Structure, Pagan Temples, Products and Living Creatures*, London, 1672, p. 632.
56. When the Portuguese came to India, the residence of the king of Cochin was in Calvethy. K.P. Padmanabha Menon, *Kochi Rajya Charitram*, p. 129; Gaspar Correia, *Lendas da India*, tom. I, Lisboa, 1858, p. 209.
57. It seems that the characteristic features usually seen in the settlement pattern of a pre-colonial port town, as mentioned by Arasaratnam, was also applicable to Cochin. For details see, Sinappah Arasaratnam, 'Pre-colonial and Early Colonial Port-towns', in Indu Banga (ed.), *Ports and their Hinterlands in India 1700-1950*, p. 373.
58. F.C. Danvers, *The Portuguese in India*, vol. I, New Delhi, 1988, p. 71.
59. W.W. Hunter, *The Imperial Gazetteer of India*, vol. IV, p. 13.
60. Ibid.
61. Philip Baldaeus, op. cit., p. 632.
62. For details about the settlement pattern of pre-colonial port towns of Malabar, see Bouchon's study of Calicut. The same pattern seems to have existed in Cochin. According to Bouchon's analysis, the Zamorin's palace was some distance from the port area, while in Cochin the royal residence was very close to the port. Genevieve Bouchon, 'Calicut at the Turn of the Sixteenth Century', in *The Asian Seas 1500-1800*, p. 42.
63. Fei Hsin, *Hsing Ch'a Sheng lan 30*, 'Kochih', p. 452.
64. Surendranath Sen (ed.), *Indian Travels of Thevenot and Careri*, New Delhi, 1949, p. 122.
65. This fact is testified to with the help of field study and interviews with the local people.
66. Sinappah Arasaratnam, 'Pre-colonial and Early Colonial Port-towns', p. 373.
67. Henry E.J. Stanley (ed.), op. cit., p. 35.
68. B. Greiff (ed.), *Tagebuch des Lucas Rem aus den Jahren 1494-1541*, p. 120. The writers vary in opinion with regard to the date of departure of Vasco da Gama. Roteiro says that on 8 July, Saturday, from Restello he started the journey. Gernot Giertz, *Vasco da Gama, dieEntdeckung des Seewegs nach Indien: Ein Augenzeugenbericht 1497-1499*, Tübingen, 1980, p. 35, Gaspar Correia gives March 25, Henry E.J. Stanley,

op. cit., p. 58. Barros gives July 8, João de Barros, *Decada*, parte I, p. 277. Duarte Pacheco gives 8 June, Duarte Pacheco, *Esmeraldo de Situ Orbis*, translated and edited by H.T. Kimble, Nendeln, 1967, p. 166. July 9 seems to be more probable.

69. Gernot Giertz, op. cit., p. 14.
70. In Calicut Vasco da Gama explained the purpose of his voyage in these words to the sceptic Arab trader from Tunis. Gernot Giertz, op. cit., p. 79.
71. Ibid., pp. 78-9. There is again a difference of opinion among the early writers regarding the date of his arrival. Barros gives May 20, João de Barros, *Decada* I, parte I, p. 328. Castanheda gives May 22. Fernão Lopes de Castanheda, *Historia do Descobrimento e Conquista da India pelos Portugueses*, liv. vi, Cap. 72, Coimbra, 1924, p. 72. It seems that May 20 is more probable.
72. Gernot Giertz, op. cit., pp. 92-8.
73. The ignorance of the native language (Malayalam) was a great handicap to the Portuguese. The Arab traders who read and translated Portuguese letters gave a wrong interpretation to them. This capacity as interpreters of Portuguese letters seems to have given the Arab traders an extra opportunity to turn the decision-making machinery in their favour. For further details see, Gernot Giertz, op. cit., pp. 95-6.
74. The various spices brought by Vasco da Gama are mentioned in 'King Manuel's letter to the King and Queen of Castile, July 1499'. They include cinnamon, cloves, ginger, nutmeg and pepper. For a full text of the letter see the appendix of E.G. Ravenstein (ed.), *A Journal of the First Voyage of Vasco da Gama 1497-1499*, 1898, p. 113.
75. King Manuel assumed this title for the first time in his 'Letter to the Cardinal Protector (Cardinal Alpedrinha), 28 August 1499'. For the full text see, E.G. Ravenstein, op. cit., pp. 114-15. Later this title was confirmed by the Pope in 1502. Marino Sanuto, *I Diarii de Marino Sanuto: 1496-1533*, edited by Rinaldo Fulin and Nicolo Barozzi, vol. III, Venice, 1880, cols. 1593-95.
76. William Brooks Greenlee, op. cit., p. xviii; Marino Sanuto, op. cit., vol. IV, cols. 66-7; Rinaldo Fulin, *Diarii e Diaristi Veneziani*, Venice, 1881, pp. 157-60.
77. 'The Anonymous Narrative' in William Brooks Greenlee, op. cit., p. 56. Though Cabral had the chief command of the fleet, commercial activities were in the charge of Ayres Correia and the latter was given the power to negotiate commercial treaties.
78. 'Fragment of Instructions to Pedro Alvares Cabral', in William Brooks Greenlee, op. cit., p. 169.
79. 'Anonymous Narrative', in William Brooks Greenlee, op. cit., pp. 83-4; Marino Sanuto, op. cit., vol. IV, cols. 66-7. It is estimated that out of the thirteen ships of Cabral, ten were of 200 to 300 tons and the smallest one was of 100 tons. William Brooks Greenlee, op. cit., pp. 191-2; H. Lopes de Mendoça, *Estudos Sôbre Navios Portuguêses nos Séculos XV e XVI*, Lisbon, 1892, pp. 12-25.
80. 'The Anonymous Narrative' in William Brooks Greenlee, op. cit., p. 83.
81. Ibid., p. 83.
82. Marino Sanuto, op. cit., vol. IV, cols. 66-7. Letters sent by Bartolomeo Marchioni to Florence dated 27 June 1501 in William Brooks Greenlee, op. cit., pp. 147-8. The factor who was killed in this uprising was Ayres Correia.
83. Ibid. F.C. Danvers, *The Portuguese in India*, vol. I, New Delhi, 1988, pp. 69-70; K.M. Panikkar, *Malabar and the Portuguese*, p. 40.
84. Marino Sanuto, op. cit., vol. IV, cols. 66-7; Gaspar da Gama was a Jew from India whom Vasco da Gama had taken to Portugal and he was later baptized, E.G. Ravenstein, op. cit., p. 179.
85. 'The Anonymous Narrative', in William Brooks Greenlee, op. cit., p. 86.
86. Marino Sanuto, op. cit., vol. IV, cols. 66-7.
87. Luis de Albuquerque (ed.), *Cronica do Descobrimento e conquista da India pelos*

Portugueses: codice anonimo Museu Britanico, Egerton 20901, Coimbra, 1974, p. 25; F.C. Danvers, *The Portuguese in India*, vol. I, p. 72. Ca' Masser, the Venetian, who was in Lisbon at this time says that the Portuguese made a fortress there on a point of the 'Chuchi river' as an habitation for the factor and security for his merchandise. 'The Report of Ca' Masser', in William Brooks Greenlee, op. cit., p. 143; C. Achyuta Menon identifies the then reigning king of Cochin as Goda Varma or Unni Goda Varma Koil Tirumulpad. C. Achyuta Menon, op. cit., p. 61.

88. The Letter of Giovanni Francesco de Affaitadi in Marino Sanuto, op. cit., vol. IV, col. 664; F.C. Danvers, *The Portuguese in India*, vol. I, pp. 75-6.
89. Luis de Albuquerque (ed.), *Cronica do Descobrimento . . .*, pp. 36-7.
90. Henry E.J. Stanley, op. cit., pp. 329-340; João de Barros, Decada I, liv. vi, cap. V; 'Calcoen' in Gernot Giertz, op. cit., p. 188.
91. Thomé Lopes, 'Navegação as Indias Orientaes', in *Collecção de Noticias para a Historia e Geografia das Nações Ultramarinas que vivem nos Dominios Portugueses ou Ilhes são Vizinhas*, tom. II, nos. 1 & 2, Lisboa, 1812, pp. 199-200; Walter de Gray Birch (ed.), *The Commentaries of the great Afonso Dalboquerque, Second Viceroy of India*, New York, 1875, p. 9; Gernot Giertz, op. cit., p. 173.
92. R.S. Whiteway, op. cit., p. 95; C. Achyuta Menon, op. cit., p. 65.
93. K.M.Panikkar, *A History of Kerala*, p. 54; A Sreedhara Menon, *A Survey of Kerala History*, p. 213; C. Achyuta Menon, op. cit., pp. 65-7.
94. C. Achyuta Menon, op. cit., p. 67.
95. Walter de Gray Birch, op. cit., pp. 1-2.
96. Ibid., pp. 3-5.
97. Ibid., pp. 6-7.
98. C. Achyuta Menon, op. cit., pp. 68-9; Bailey W. Diffie and George D. Winius, *Foundations of the Portuguese Empire 1415-1580: Europe and the World in the Age of Expansion*, Minneapolis, 1977, p. 226. The king of Cochin created Duarte Pacheco a Dom. Gundert, *Kerala Pazhama*, Trivandrum, 1961, pp. 65-8.
99. Barros, *Decada* I, parte I, pp. 351-3; Luis de Albuquerque, *Cronico do Descobrimento...*, pp. 48-51; C. Achyuta Menon, op. cit., p. 73.
100. Damião de Gois, *Cronica do Felicissimo Rei D. Manuel*, parte II, Coimbra, 1953, pp. 26-30. When Goda Varma died in 1510, Elaya Raja, the next candidate but with an anti-Portuguese and pro-Zamorin outlook was denied the throne. Unnirama Koil Tirumulpad was retained on the throne, instead of allowing him to become a religious recluse as dictated by custom. K.M. Panikkar, *A History of Kerala*, p. 24; A. Sreedhara Menon, *A Survey of Kerala History*, p. 175.
101. R.A. de Bulhão Pato (ed.), *Cartas de Afonso de Albuquerque, Seguidas de Documentos que as elucidam*, tom. III, Lisbon, 1903, pp. 72-80; C. Achyuta Menon, op. cit., p. 73; João de Barros, *Decada* I, parte II, pp. 355-6.
102. R.A. de Bulhão Pato, *Cartas*, tom. II, Lisboa, 1884, pp. 297, 323.
103. Ibid., tom. III, p. 396.
104. For details about the native spy network maintained by the Nampoothiri Brahmins, see C. Achyuta Menon, op. cit., p. 48; William Brooks Greenlee, op. cit., p. 86. The native spies, moreover, informed Duarte Pacheco of the designs of the Zamorin and the Muslim merchants to blockade supplies to Cochin. Gaspar Correia, *Lendas da India*, tom. I, pp. 430-1; Castanheda, *Historia do Descobrimento e Conquista da India*, liv. I, p. 74.
105. Tens and thousands of Nairs fought and died for the Portuguese. The services of these Nairs were utilized for the capture of Goa, Malacca, Ormuz and other coastal belts as well as for the wars against all anti-Portuguese forces. On 6 August 1547, the Vadakkenkur king promised to send 2000 soldiers from the St. Thomas Christian

community to fight for the Portuguese in Diu. ANTT, *Cartas de Dio a D. João de Castro*, Letter of Damião Vaz dated 6 August 1547, fol. 93. The St. Thomas Christian soldiers were used for the military operations of the Portuguese in the island of Ceylon by the end of sixteenth century and the beginning of seventeenth century. HAG, *Livro das Monções*, no. 8 (1601-2), Royal Letter sent to Aires de Saldanha, fol. 106.

106. The Mohammedan merchants were kept as collaborators of the Portuguese trade till the end of the viceroyalty of Afonso de Albuquerque. After 1515 they were estranged and thrown into the network of corsairs. The details are furnished in Chapters IV and VI.
107. C.G. Weigend, op. cit., pp. 192-3.
108. Atiya Habeeb Kidwai, op. cit., pp. 18-19.
109. Frank Broeze, 'The External Dynamics of Port-city Morphology', pp. 250-2.
110. Ibid., p. 248.
111. Jan Kieniewicz, 'Pepper Gardens and Market in Pre-colonial Malabar', in *Moyen Orient and Ocean Indien, XVIe- XIXe. S.*, 3, Paris: 1986, pp. 1-3.
112. Ibid., p. 2.
113. Ibid., p. 2; Paolino da San Bartolomeo, *Viaggio alle Indie Orientalie*, Roma, 1796, p. 116.
114. Diogo Gonçalves, *Historia do Malavar*, Josef Wicki (ed.), Münster, 1955, p. 7.
115. Luis de Albuquerque (ed.), *Cronico do Descobrimento*, p. 25.
116. ANTT, *Cartas dos Vice Reis*, doc. 71.
117. Antonio da Silva Rego (ed.), *Documentação Ultramarina Portuguesa*, vol. III, Lisboa, 1963, pp. 312-3
118. Cf. Supra n.91.
119. Diogo Gonçalves, op. cit., p. 88.
120. Tomé Pires, op. cit., p. 79.
121. Duarte Barbosa, op. cit., vol. II, p. 89.
122. A. Sreedhara Menon, *A Survey of Kerala History*, p. 197.
123. Tomé Pires, op. cit., p. 79. By 1540s the relationship between the kings of Cranganore and Cochin became worse. BNL, Fundo Geral, MSS 201, doc. 8. The Letter of Estavão da Gama sent to the king of Portugal narrating the differences betwen the two, dated 23 December 1541. By 1548 it became still worse. Elaine Sanceau, *Colecção de São Lourenço*, vol. III, Lisboa, 1975, pp. 488-9. However this tension was only a transient phenomenon.
124. Faria y Sousa, *Asia Portuguesa: The History of the Discovery and Conquest of India by the Portuguese*, translated by John Stevens, vol. III, London, 1695, p. 204.
125. Gaspar Correia, *Lendas da India*, tom. I, p. 906.
126. Paduronga S.S. Pissurlencar, *Regimentos das Fortalezas da India*, Bastora/Goa, 1951, p. 227 and see its footnote.
127. Biblioteca da Ajuda, *Documentos da India*, 51-VII-I. Rellacio de las Ciudades fortalezas de la India, y de los reys vezinos dellas, assi de pax como de guerra, 12 de Dezembro de 1596.
128. K.S. Mathew, 'Indian Merchants and the Portuguese Trade on the Malabar Coast during the Sixteenth Century', in *Indo-Portuguese History: Old Issues—New Questions*, New Delhi, 1985, p. 3.
129. Antonio da Silva Rego (ed.), *Documentação para a Historia das Missões do Padroado Portugues do Oriente*, vol. II, Lisboa, 1949, pp. 352-4.
130. Antonio Bocarro, *Fortalezas, Cidades Povoações do Estado da India Oriental*, vol. II, Transcrição de Isabel, Lisboa, 1992, p. 194.
131. Antonio da Silva Rego (ed.), *Documentação para as Historia...*, vol. I, p. 106._
132. BPE, *Nucleo de Manuscritos da Casa Forte CIX/2-3*, Maço 3, doc. 15, fol. 5v 'Carta

de Frei Vicente a El Rey dando-lhe conta do collegio que edificara em Cranganore, Estatutos dos Collegiaes delle e outras noticias daquella Estado', Cranganore: dated 1 January 1549.
133. Antonio Bocarro, op. cit., p. 197.
134. For details see Diogo Gonçalves, op. cit., pp. 7-8; Vitorino Magalhaes Godinho, *Les Finances de l'état Portugais des Indes Orientales (1517-1635)*: Matériaux pour une Étude Structuralle et Conjoncturelle, Paris, 1982, p. 307 and its footnote.
135. Ibid.
136. Antonio Bocarro, op. cit., p. 196.
137. Antonio de Gouveia, *Jornada do Arcebispo*, Lisboa, 1988, p. 107.
138. ANTT, *Cartas dos Vice-Reis da India*, doc. 124. Carta do Mangate Caimal para El Rey de Portugal. The date and year of this letter are not mentioned.
139. Elaine Sanceau, *Colecção de São Lourenço*, vol. III, p. 499.
140. Simão Botelho, 'O Tombo do Estado da India', in *Subsidios para a Historia da India Portuguesa*, Rodrigo José de Lima Felner (ed.), Lisboa, 1868, p. 25.
141. Antonio Bocarro, op. cit., p. 196.
142. Diogo Gonçalves, op. cit., p. 7.
143. Elaine Sanceau, *Colecção de São Lourenço*, vol. II, Lisboa, 1975, p. 317.
144. Ibid., vol. III, p. 499.
145. Antonio de Gouveia, op. cit., p. 103.
146. Antonio Bocarro, op. cit., p. 196.
147. Faria y Sousa, op. cit., vol. III, pp. 203-4.
148. Simão Botelho, op. cit., p. 25.
149. Diogo Gonçalves, op. cit., p. 6. In the Malayalam poem *Kokasandesam*, Edappally is described as a town and first ruler, as a recipient of tributes from other kings. But it seems that this was not tribute but money and land which he received from other kings in his capacity as the official priest (*santhikaran*) of the temple of Thrikkakara. Elamkulam P.N. Kunjan Pillai (ed.), *Kokasandesam*, Kottayam, 1952, pp. 88-9.
150. Barros, *Decada* IV, parte II, pp. 292-8.
151. Elaine Sanceau, *Colecção de São Lourenço*, vol. II, pp. 306, 317.
152. Ibid., p. 317.
153. Diogo Gonçalves, op. cit., p. 87.
154. Ibid., pp. 5-6.
155. Antonio de Gouveia, op. cit., pp. 210, 225, 274.
156. Simão Botelho, op. cit., p. 25.
157. Diogo Gonçalves, op. cit., p. 87.
158. Ibid., p. 4.
159. A. Sreedhara Menon, *A Survey of Kerala History*, p. 193.
160. K.P. Padmanabha Menon, *History of Kerala*, vol. II, p. 309; A Galletti, *The Dutch in Malabar*, New Delhi, 1984, p. 57.
161. Elaine Sanceau, *Colecção de São Lourenço*, vol. III, p. 85.
162. There were two kings in this kingdom residing at two different places, one probably at Kottayam and the other at Kanjirappally. Together they received 200 *pardaos* or 72,000 *reais*. For detailed figures, see below n.195.
163. Diogo do Couto, *Decada* XII, Lisboa, 1778, p. 286; Antonio da Silva Rego, *Documetação Ultramarina Portugues*, vol. III, p. 310; Vitorino Magalhães Godinho, *Les Finances de l'état Portugais des Indes Orientales* (*1517-1635*), p. 306.
164. K.P. Padmanabha Menon, *History of Kerala*, vol. II, pp. 122-6.
165. K.M. Panikkar, *A History of Kerala 1498-1801*, p. 25.
166. A. Sreedhara Menon, *A Survey of Kerala History*, p. 194.
167. A. Galletti, op. cit., p. 59.

168. Jacob Aerthail, *Kanjirappally Noottandukaliloode*, Kanjirappally, 1985, pp. 80-1.
169. Nycolão Gomçallves, op. cit, p. 45-7.
170. ANTT, *Cartas dos Vice-Reis da India*, doc.124, Carta do Mangate Caimal para El rey de Portugal. The pepper king quarrelled with the ruler of Cochin because of the claim he made on the temple in the island of Vaduthala. George Schurhammer, *Francis Xavier: His Life, His Times*, trans. by Joseph Costelloe, vol. III, Rome, 1980, p. 361; see also M.N. Pearson, *Coastal Western India: Studies from the Portuguese Records*, New Delhi, 1981, p. 29.
171. Diogo Gonçalves, op. cit., pp. 87-8.
172. Simão Botelho, op. cit., p. 25.
173. He used to receive 240 *pardaos* as annuity. Ibid., p. 25. For further details see below.
174. He used to receive 140 *xerafins* as annuity. Antonio da Silva Rego, *Documentação Ultramarina Portuguesa*, vol. III, p. 310.
175. Elaine Sanceau, *Colecção de São Lourenço*, vol. III, p. 312.
176. Diogo Gonçalves, op. cit., p. 7. Today it is called Arthunkal.
177. The kings of Muthedathu and Iledathu were cousins and they belonged to the *Kshatriya* caste. They had fourteen thousand Nairs. Ibid., p. 7.
178. Paduronga S.S. Pissurlencar, *Regimentos das Fortalezas da India*, p. 219; Vitorino Magalhães Godinho, *Les Finances de l'état Portugais*, p. 308.
179. Ibid. Paduronga S.S. Pissurlencar, *Regimentos das Fortalezas da India*, p. 219.
180. Account of Francisco da Costa, in Antonio da Silva Rego, *Documentação Ultramarina Portuguesa*, vol. III, pp. 310, 312.
181. Ibid., p. 312.
182. Simão Botelho, op. cit., p. 25.
183. Ibid.
184. Paduronga S.S. Pissurlencar, *Regimentos das Fortalezas da India*, pp. 217-19.
185. Vitorino Magalhães Godinho, *Les Finances de l'état Portugais*, pp. 306-8.
186. Account of Francisco da Costa, in Antonio da Silva Rego (ed.), *Documentação Ultramarina Portuguesa*, vol. III, p. 310.
187. Usually the *copa* also included the remuneration for the help which the king of Cochin used to render for the supply of pepper in Cochin. 640 *cruzados* was equivalent to 2,56,000 *reais*. Paduronga S.S. Pissurlencar, *Regimentos das Fortalezas da India*, p. 217; Vitorino Magalhães Godinho, *Les Finances de l'état Portugais*, p. 306.
188. The amount of 200 *pardaos* was equivalent to 72,000 *reais* which was given in 1554. Paduronga S.S. Pissurlencar, *Regimentos das Fortalezas da India*, p. 218; Simão Botelho, op. cit., p. 25.
189. The mother of Vadakkenkur referred to here was living at that time in Kaduthuruthy. Even when the seat of the Vadakkenkur kingdom was transferred to Thodupuzha, the queen continued to receive an annuity for the help she rendered for the supply of pepper in Cochin.
190. The kingdoms of Vadakkenkur and Thodupuzha were combined into the kingdom of Vadakkenkur and Thodupuzha by 1600, with its capital seat in Thodupuzha. From 1603 onwards, the ruler of this combined territory began to receive the annuity which the ruler of Vadakkenkur previously used to receive. Account of Francisco da Costa, in Antonio da Silva Rego, *Documentação Ultramarina Portuguesa*, vol. III, pp. 310, 312. But the mother of the king was in Kaduthuruthy and her support and co-operation was ensured by giving a regular annuity to her, as well.
191. For details, see Paduronga S.S. Pissurlencar, *Regimentos das Fortalezas da India*, pp. 217-19; Vitorino Maglhães Godinho, *Les Finances de l'état Portugais*, pp. 306-8.
192. ANTT, *Cartas dos Vice-Reis da India*, doc. 95; E.R. Hambye, 'Medieval Christianity

in India: The Eastern Church', in *Christianity in India*, E.R. Hambye and H.C. Perumalil (eds.), Alleppey, 1972, p. 34; Samuel Mateer, *The Land of Charity: A Descriptive Account of Travancore and its People*, New Delhi, 1991, pp. 237-8.

193. Antonio da Silva Rego (ed.), *Documentação para a Historia*, vol. II, pp. 175-6.
194. E. Tisserant, *Eastern Christianity in India*, trans. by E.R. Hambye, Calcutta, 1957, pp. 5-6.
195. BNL, *Reservados*, Cod. 464, Vida do Ilustrissimo D. Francisco Garcia Arcebispo de Cranganore por Francisco Teixeira, 1659, fol. 7.
196. Antonio da Silva Rego, *Documentação para a Historia*, vol. II, pp. 352-4.
197. This three-tier land system existed all over Kerala during pre-British times. For details, see D. Rothermund, *Government, Landlord, and Peasant in India: Agrarian Relations under British Rule, 1865-1935*, Wiesbaden, 1978, pp. 160-2; Jan Kieniewicz, 'Pepper Gardens and Market in Pre-colonial Malabar', in *Moyen Orient*, p. 13; K.N. Panikkar, *Against Lord and State: Religion and Peasant Uprisings in Malabar, 1836-1921*, Delhi, 1989, pp. 18-20; P. Radhakrishnan, *Peasant Struggles, Land Reforms and Social Change: Malabar, 1836-1982*, New Delhi, 1989, pp. 24-9.
198. P.N. Elamkulam Kunjan Pillai, *Janmi Sampradayam Keralathil*, Kottayam, 1966, pp. 8-10.
199. Kesavan Veluthat, *Brahman Settlements in Kerala*, Calicut: 1978, p. 3; K.N. Panikkar, 'Land Control, Ideology and Reform: A Study of the Changes in Family Organisation and Marriage System in Kerala' in *The Indian Historical Review*, vol. IV, no. I, July 1977, pp. 30-46.
200. P. Radhakrishnan, op. cit., pp. 24, 27; M.G.S. Narayanan, 'Political and Social Conditions of Kerala under the Kulasekhara Empire (800 A.D. to 1124 A.D.)', unpublished Ph.D. thesis, University of Kerala, 1972, pp. 330-5; Elamkulam Kunjan Pillai, *Studies in Kerala History*, Kottayam, 1970, pp. 332-8.
201. P. Radhakrishnan, op. cit., pp. 25, 28.
202 K.N. Panikkar, *Against Lord and State*, pp. 19-20.
203. D. Rothermund, *Government, Landlord and Peasant in India*, pp. 161-2.
204. T.C. Varghese, *Agrarian Change and Economic Consequences: Land Tenures in Kerala, 1850-1960*, Calcutta, 1970, pp. 12-16; P. Radhakrishnan, op. cit., p. 29.
205. One such case was that of Arakuzha, where the local ruler (Unniyathi) granted lot of cultivable land for the church of this community. Several grants which this community received from the local rulers were referred to by Father Bernard. Bernard, *The History of the St.Thomas Christians*, Palai, 1916, pp. 296-324.
206. BNL, *Reservados Cod.* No. 536. *Noticias do Reino do Malabar anteriores a chegada dos Portugueses e até ao sec. XVIII. Geografia, Clima, Etnais, Linguas, Costumes, Politica, Religões, confronte entre Carmelitas, e Jesuitas e a de Cristandade de São Tomé*, fol. 6.
207. Duarte Barbosa, op. cit, vol. II, p. 332; R.A. de Bulhão Pato, *Cartas.*, tom. I, p. 330; Diogo Gonçalves, op. cit., p. 9; Ashin Das Gupta, *Malabar in Asian Trade, 1740-1800*, Cambridge, 1967, pp. 23, 45.
208. For details, see Jan Kieniewicz, 'Pepper Gardens and Market in Pre-colonial Malabar', pp. 15-18.
209. Ibid., p. 3.
210. K.P. Padmanabha Menon, *History of Kerala*, vol. I, p. 77.
211. B. Ziegenbalg, *Ausfürliche Beschreibung der Malabarische Heidentums*, Leipzig, 1926, p. 211.
212. Ibn Batuta, op. cit., p. 292.
213. Visscher's Letters in K.P. Padmanabha Menon, *History of Kerala*, vol. II, p. 18.
214. K.A. Vasukuttan, *Bhoomisastram*, vol. III, Trivandrum, 1973, p. 260.

215. It is a very ancient place. Some say that Thrikkariyoor was the capital of the ancient Chera kingdom. Ruins and remnants of old buildings are still seen here. K.P. Padmanabha Menon, *Kochi Rajya Charitram*, p. 50; Velayudhan Panikkasserry, *Sancharikalum Charitrak karanmarun*, Kottayam, 1972, pp. 44-5.
216. It was called Codemangalão in Jornada do Arcebispo. Antonio de Gouveia, op. cit., p. 261.
217. K.P. Padmanabha Menon, *History of Kerala*, vol. II, p. 122; A. Galletti, op. cit., p. 58.
218. See the map of James Horsebury, Hydrographer to the East India Company who has published it according to an Act of the Parliament on 1 May 1829. A copy of this map is preserved in the Padroado Museum of Cochin.
219. See the map of Malabar in Paolino da San Bartolomeo, *Viaggio alle Indie Orientalie*, Roma, 1796.
220. Antonio de Gouveia, op. cit., p. 266.
221. The upper Cattur in opposition to Kizhcattur or lower Cattur. Nycolão Gomçallves, op. cit., p. 44.
222. Alwaye was the seat of Karta of Alwaye. See Antonio da Silva Rego, *Documentação Ultramarina Portugesa*, vol. III, p. 310.
223. For Varapuzha see the map of Paolino da San Bartolomeo.
224. In Kokasandesam we read that Edappally is situated on the banks of the river Periyar. Elamkulam P.N. Kunjanpillai (ed.), *Kokasandesam*, p. 89.
225. For Tripunithara, see the map of Paolino da San Bartolomeo.Varapuzha lake and Tripunithara lake are the extensions of the Vembanadu lake.
226. K.A. Vasukuttan, op. cit., p. 259.
227. *Angelins* or *Anjili* and teak were found in abundance in the *Serra*. Diogo Gonçalves, op. cit., p. 79. *Tonis* or small boats were used for both travel and carrying merchandise through water. Antonio de Gouveia, op. cit., pp. 99, 105, 111, 125.
228. Antonio de Gouveia, op. cit., pp. 215-16. See also the list of places given by Perron du Anquetil, in P.V. Mathew, *Sugandhanadu: Nazarani Charithram*, Ernakulam, 1984, p. 622.
229. Perron du Anquetil, in P.V. Mathew, *Sugandhanadu*, p. 622.
230. Ibid. See also the map of Paolino da San Bartolomeo.
231. Antonio de Gouveia, op. cit., pp. 108-11.
232. Ibid., p. 111.
233. K.A. Vasukuttan, op. cit., p. 259.
234. Diogo Gonçalves, op. cit., pp. 4, 87.
235. A Sreedhara Menon, *A Survey of Kerala History*, p. 194; Diogo do Couto, *Da Asia*, p. 77; A Galletti, op. cit., p. 59; Antonio de Gouveia, op. cit., p. 206.
236. Antonio de Gouveia, op. cit., p. 127.
237. Antonio de Gouveia, op. cit., p. 258; Perron du Anquetil calls it Modelakerte. Perron du Anquetil, in P.V. Mathew, *Sugandhanadu*, p. 623.
238. See the map of Paolino da San Bartolomeo. Jongam and Neriani were the names given by Perron du Anquetil. They were situated in the kingdom of Vadakkenkur. Perron du Anquetil, in P.V. Mathew, *Sugandhanadu*, p. 623.
239. Antonio de Gouveia, op. cit., p. 258.
240. Antonio de Gouveia, op. cit., p. 258. This agrarian settlement is very old. The inscriptions on the church bell say that it was made in AD 686 after the birth of Christ. For details see, Bernard, *The History of St. Thomas Christians*, pp. 296-7.
241. Paolino da san Bartolomeo, *Viaggio alle Indie Orientalie*, p. 116; see his map, as well. It is called Aracore in Jornada. Antonio de Gouveia, op. cit., p. 258.
242. The ruins of a fortress of the Vadakkenkur Raja are still seen here near the Siva

temple (in Sivankunnu). A. Sreedhara Menon, *Kerala District Gazetteers: Ernakulam*, Trivandrum, 1965, p. 859.

243. It is located near Piravom.Mathias Mundadan, *St. Thomas Christians, 1498-1552*. Bangalore, 1967, p. 5.
244. See the map of Paolino da San Bartolomeo. The list given by Perron du Anquetil, in P.V. Mathew, *Sugandhanadu*, p. 623.
245. Antonio de Gouveia, op. cit., p. 258.
246. It is near Mutholapuram and Vadakara. Antonio de Gouveia, op. cit., p. 261.
247. Ibid., p. 258. It is situated near Piravom.
248. Nycolão Gomçallvez, op. cit., p. 47; Antonio de Gouveia, op. cit., p. 223.
249. A. Sreedhara Menon, *Kerala District Gazetteers: Ernakulam*, pp. 9-10.
250. For Vechur see, Nycolão Gomçallves, op. cit., p. 47. For Muttam see, Antonio de Gouveia, op. cit., p. 223.
251. Antonio de Gouveia, op. cit., p. 223.
252. Ibid., p. 263.
253. For the king of Poonjar, see Antonio de Gouveia, op. cit., p. 206.
254. Ibid., pp. 203-9.
255. Periate is probably Vandiperiyar near Elappara and Kumily. It is located on the banks of the river Periyar and is also called Periyar, its place name. Antonio de Gouveia says that it is situated 26 leagues (26 x 4 = 104 kilometres) from Madure and that cloth from Tamilnadu pass through this place. The Portuguese ecclesiastical authorities asked permission from the king of Poonjar to erect a church here. Antonio de Gouveia, op. cit., p. 208. See also the map of Paolino da San Bartolomeo which gives dot-marks to show the trade route from Poonjar to Tamilnadu.
256. A Galletti, op. cit., p. 57; K.P. Padmanabha Menon, *History of Kerala*, vol. II, p. 85. It is so-called because in Erattupetta, the two main tributaries of the river Meenachil converge. Perron du Anquetil calls it Iratur. Perron du Anquetil, in P.V. Mathew, *Sugandhanadu*, p. 624; Antonio de Gouveia also calls it Iratur. Antonio de Gouveia, op. cit., p. 261. It is called Eratuzhe in the map of Paolino da San Bartolomeo. In the inscriptions of the church it is called Irattida.
257. The Muslim merchants mentioned here are the *Ravuthar* Muslims or the Tamil Muslims who came from Tamilnadu. Edamaruku, *Sthalapuranangal*, Kottayam, 1972, p. 191. It is said that the first Muslim to come and settle down in Erattupetta from Madurai was one Chandu Khan around 1375. For details, see Jacob Aerthail, op. cit., p. 95. In ancient days both the names of Aruvithara and Erattupetta were interchangeably used. But Aruvithara is often now referred to as the Christian settlement, while Erattupetta is used for the Muslim area of inhabitation. For further discussions on this, see Thomas Arayathinal, *A Short History of Irapuzhai or Aruvithurai Church*, Erattupetta, 1953, pp. 8-9.
258. Perron du Anquetil, in P.V. Mathew, *Sugandhanadu*, p. 624.
259. These places were in the kingdom of Thekkenkur. Ibid., p. 624. Pala was ruled by Gnamacata Caimal and was a unit of Tecancut (Thekkenkur) kingdom. Antonio de Gouveia, op. cit., p. 261.
260. In Kottayam there were two churches. Antonio de Gouveia, op. cit., pp. 193-4. See also BNL, *Reservados Cod*, no. 464, *Vida do Ilmº. D. Francisco Garcia*, fols. 41-2. Kottayam was the seat of the Thekkenkur kings. A. Sreedhara Menon, *A Survey of Kerala History*, p. 193. During this period, as we have already seen, two kings were ruling this kingdom: one was in Kottayam, while the other must have been in Kanjirappally.
261. These two places were located in the kingdom of Thekkenkur. Perron du Anquetil, in P.V. Mathew, *Sugandhanadu*, p. 624.

262. Antonio de Gouveia, op. cit., pp. 210-11. Athirampuzha was a famous trade and agrarian centre. See the map of Paolino da San Bartolomeo.
263. Nycolão Gomçallves, op. cit., p. 11; Antonio de Gouveia, op. cit., pp. 121, 258-61. See also BNL, *Reservados*, Cod. 464, Vida do Ilustrissimo D. Francisco Garcia, fol. 42. Kaduthuruthy was called *Sindhudeepam* in *Unnuneeli Sandesam* which was written before the arrival of the Portuguese. It mentions that a road for chariots starting from Muttuchira and reaching Kaduthuruthy was built by Bimbali (Vadakkenkur) kings. Elamkulam Kunjan Pillai, *Unnuneeli Sandesam*, Kottayam: 1989, pp. 123-5.
264. See the list of places in Thekkenkur kingdom given by Perron du Anquetil, in P.V. Mathew, *Sugandhanadu*, p. 624.
265. Antonio de Gouveia, op. cit., pp. 259-61.
266. A land route passing through Manikandapuram and Thiruvanchapuzhakadavu of the Thekkenkur kingdom reached Ettumanur (of the Vadakkenkur kingdom). *Unnuneeli Sandesam* gives a detailed description about this. Elamkulam Kunjan Pillai, *Unnuneeli Sandesam*, pp. 120-2.
267. The land-route from Ettumanur to Kaduthuruthy passed through Kothanalloor. Elamkulam Kunjan Pillai, *Unnuneeli Sandesam*, p. 123.
268. Antonio de Gouveia, op. cit., p. 138.
269. These places were in the kingdom of Cochin as testified by Perron du Anquetil, in P.V. Mathew, *Sugandhanadu*, pp. 619-20.
270. Ibid., p. 619.
271. Antonio de Gouveia, op. cit., pp. 139-43.
272. A. Galletti, op. cit., p. 57; Nycolão Gomçallves, op. cit., p. 47; K.P. Padmanabha Menon, *History of Kerala*, vol. II, p. 85. Antonio de Gouveia calls it Canharpily. Antonio de Gouveia, op. cit., p. 261. Kanjirappally had hectic trade relations with Tamilnadu. The Muslims of this area trace back their origin to Moosavannan Ravuthar, Kulasekhara Khan and Mollamiya Mahadul Labba who came to Kanjirappally from Madurai in AD 1373. They settled down near the Ganapathiyar Kovil. The *Kannanoor Chetties* of this locality came here in AD 1150 from Chettinadu near Dindigul. The same trade route from Madurai to Kanijrappally was taken by the *Daiva Vellalar* in 1399 and they setttled down near the Meenakshi temple. The presence of Tamil elements in the population of Kanjirappally opened new vistas of trade. Jacob Aerthail, op. cit., pp. 88-97; Mathew Madukkakuzhy, *Purathana Kraisthava Kendrangalilude*, Kanjirappally, 1995, pp. 99-104.
273. Antonio de Gouveia, op. cit., p. 254.
274. Thiruvalla is situated on the banks of the river Manimala. Elamkulam Kunjan Pillai doubts whether the ancient name of this river had been Valla. Elamkulam Kunjan Pillai, *Unnuneeli Sandesam*, p. 115.
275. Antonio de Gouveia, op. cit., pp. 251-2.
276. These two ancient centres of trade and agrarian activities were located in the Thekkenkur kingdom. Perron du Anquetil, in P.V. Mathew, *Sugandhanadu*, p. 624. Niranam was called as Naranão by Antonio de Gouveia, op. cit., p. 251.
277. Antonio de Gouveia, op. cit., p. 256.
278. Ibid., p. 250.
279. Ibid., pp. 225, 249-50. There is a tradition that people from Kalloorkad (near Muvattupuzha) came and settled down in Champakulam and that they began to call this place as Kalloorkad.
280. Antonio de Gouveia, op. cit., p. 254.
281. Ibid.
282. It was situated in the kingdom of Batimeni. Antonio de Gouveia, op. cit., pp. 248-9.

283. The water routes often reduced the cost of transportation, which helped the supply of commodities in Cochin at cheaper price.
284. K.A. Vasukuttan, op. cit., p. 265.
285. Ibid.
286. The remnants of big ships were excavated from some place bordering on Vembanadu lake. Recently, some remnants were unearthed from Kaduthuruthy.
287. K.A. Vasukuttan, op. cit., p. 265.
288. K.M. Mathew, *History of the Portuguese Navigation in India*, Delhi, 1988, p. 132.
289. Jan Kieniewicz 'The Portuguese Factory and Trade in Pepper in Malabar during the 16th Century', in *The Indian Economic and Social History Review*, vol. VI, no. 1, March 1969, pp. 64, 67.
290. Antonio Bocarro, op. cit., p. 200. See also Simão Botelho, op. cit., p. 19.
291. The protection cost of the Portuguese included the annuities given to the native rulers and the money spent for the patrolling of coastal Kerala as well as for the guarding of the junctional points of rivers and lagoons.
292. This fact is testified by Antonio Bocarro, op. cit., p. 196.
293. Antonio de Gouveia, op. cit., pp. 99-262.
294. Antonio Bocarro, op. cit., p. 196.
295. Diogo Gonçalves, op. cit., pp. 92-3.
296. Ibid., p. 93.
297. K.P. Padmanabha Menon, *History of Kerala*, vol. II, p. 122.
298. Francisco da Costa, 'Relatorio sobre o Trato da Pimenta', in Antonio da Silva Rego, *Documentação Ultramarina Portugesa*, vol. III, p. 315.
299. Cf. Supra notes 215 and 216.
300. A. Galletti, op. cit., p. 59.
301. Francisco da Costa, 'Relatório sobre o Trato da Pimenta', in Antonio da Silva Rego, *Documentação Ultramarina Portuguesa*, vol. III, p. 315.
302. These six places are connected with Tamilnadu by dot-marks in the map of Paolino da San Bartolomeo, suggesting the trade route through which this trade was carried out.
303. Antonio de Gouveia, op. cit., p. 208.
304. A. Galletti, op. cit., p. 208.
305. Jacob Aerthail, op. cit., p. 89.
306. Ibid., p. 290. This information on land routes connecting the various inland markets is corroborated with field study.
307. Ibid., p. 125.
308. Mathew Madukkakuzhy, op. cit., p. 121.
309. Vandiperiyar. Cf. supra n. 255.
310. Jacob Aerthail, op. cit., pp. 85-110: Mathew Madukkakuzhy, op. cit., pp. 99-104.
311. Muthalakodam was said to have been a halting centre for the traders going to Tamilnadu.
312. A. Sreedhara Menon, *Kerala District Gazetteers: Ernakulam*, p. 868; Edamaruku, *Sthalapuranangal*, pp. 57, 163, 165.
313. The remnants of this *kottavazhi* are still seen from Thodupuzha up to Kallorkad-Ayavana. For the contacts of Kothamangalam with Tamilnadu; see A. Sreedhara Menon, *Kerala District Gazetteers: Ernakulam*, p. 851.
314. The mortal remains of this bishop are kept and revered in *Cheriappally* of Kothamangalam. The inscriptions kept in Kothamangalam *Valiappally* (built *c.* AD 800) mention the agrarian nature of this area and its vicinity.
315. Some portion of this ancient land route is still traceable.

CHAPTER III

The Portuguese and the Changing Topography of Urban Cochin

With the advent of the Portuguese, the area in and around the port of Cochin experienced an unprecedented urbanizing process affecting both the native as well as the Portuguese segments of Cochin. This civic phenomenon was further accelerated by the intensification of private as well as European trade in this port. But, it was the the Portuguese part of Cochin which was quick to respond to this process. Though some elements of city life were noticeable in the Portuguese unit of Cochin as early as 1503, it became a fully organized urban unit with the establishment of the capital of *Estado da India* there in 1505. Setting up the capital was a turning point, making the administrative, ecclesiastical and naval-military institutions of the Portuguese Asia concentrate in this town. This coincided with a high demographic growth and in 1527, Cochin was officially and juridically raised to the status of a city. The establishment of the Diocese of Cochin, and the building of houses as well as educational institutions for the various religious orders such as the Franciscans, the Jesuits, the Dominicans and the Augustinians in this city, gave a new dimension to this urban growth. The culture, which sprang up within the city wall of Portuguese Cochin was linked more with the European world than with native Cochin. However, the elements of sophisticated urban life introduced by the Portuguese in Santa Cruz slowly permeated into the already existing city of native Cochin. This chapter deals with the urban development experienced in Cochin after the advent of the Portuguese.

1. THE URBAN MORPHOLOGY OF COCHIN

I. THE MANUEL FORT: THE INITIAL PHASE

The history of the Manuel Fort is linked with the specific portion of the port area and the land adjacent to it, which Pedro Alvarez Cabral received from the king of Cochin,[1] for the establishment of a Portuguese factory in 1500. The king did this to attract an ally to fight against Calicut and its political as well as economic suzerainty.[2] This geographical area extending from the mouth of Calvethy canal westward to the seashore formed the nucleus of the Portuguese settlement. The need for the fortification of this area arose after the war which Calicut fought against Cochin for the expulsion of the Portuguese.[3] In this war the Portuguese were routed and the king of Cochin was defeated, having to take refuge in the *Sanketam* of *Elankunnapuzha*. When he was reinstated by Francisco d'Albuquerque, the first thing the king did was to give permission for the building of a fort for the Portuguese in their settlement, to protect them permanently from all possible future attacks.

The native ruler not only granted the permission but also undertook the work at his own expense.[4] The site for the fortification was selected at the spot where Duarte Pacheco had previously built a bulwark. Many natives and the Portuguese, including Afonso Albuquerque and his cousin Francisco de Albuquerque participated in the construction work.[5] In Cochin, there existed no facilities for building with stone, so a stronghold was constructed of large palisades and palm-trees, filled in with earth in the shape of a square, with flanking bastions at the corners, each mounted with ordnance pointing towards the sea to protect the fleet.[6] The responsibility of this fort was entrusted to João Pegas.[7] It was inaugurated on 1 November 1503. After the religious functions officiated over by the Dominican priest, Domingos de Sousa, the king of Cochin who arrived on an elephant escorted by Nair soldiers, officially gave the fortress the name of Manuel Fort, in honour of king Manuel of Portugal.[8]

The first viceroy, Francisco Almeida who came to Cochin in 1505 with a view to making it the capital of the *Estado da India*, wanted to strengthen the fortress.[9] Seeing the obvious faults in the wooden fort, he tried to erect a stone fort. But as the king of Cochin was against such a move, the viceroy deliberately set the wooden frames on fire. Immediately, he was given the necessary permission from the king of Cochin to build a fireproof stone fort.[10] The king of Cochin conceded that this fort, which was strengthened with masonry walls as well as bastions and equipped with powerful cannons, be a property solely of the Portuguese.[11] D. Alvaro de Noronha was made the captain of this re-built fort.[12] This fortified part of Cochin was made the seat of the Portuguese Government in India, by Francisco Almeida.

Portuguese Cochin or the city of Santa Cruz of Cochin which evolved around the Manuel Fort continued to be the political capital of the *Estado da India* until it was transferred in 1530 from Cochin to Goa.[13] Even after the transfer of the political establishments, Cochin continued to be the commercial headquarters of Portuguese India. With the addition of many political and ecclesiastical institutions, it became an important urban centre in the east; eventually, a significant portion of the newly developed urban parts of Portuguese Cochin was also fortified.[14]

II. THE PORT OF COCHIN

The port of Cochin was outside the Portuguese city and was located in the territory of the king of Cochin by virtue of which he levied customs duties from the Portuguese traders.[15] The port, as a point where ocean and inland transport lines met and intervened, was situated in the area between the present Mattancherry and Calvethy. The mouth of Calvethy river was a busy trade centre, and it was quite navigable for ships and Patemares.[16] Though the land routes were confined to a very limited geographical area—the present Mattancherry area, Fort Cochin and the region south of it—there was a very extensive and diverse network of water routes, as we have already seen,which linked the port of Cochin with the socio-economic and human environment of the hinterland and with the exchange systems of other Malabar ports, as well as of the overseas ports.

The wide river, which carried a large volume of water of Periyar (actually it is not a river, but an outlet of the lagoons to the deep sea), divided Cochin and Vaipin and connected the deep sea and the inland back waters, served the purpose of a good harbour. This water passage, often known as the Cochin river gave good anchorage and safe shelter to the ships and vessels that came thither.[17]

There were docks and jetties on the water side off the Portuguese Cochin, but the *casado* traders of Cochin were not allowed to take any material from their vessels beyond the weighing place of pepper, into the free port area.[18] It seems that this restriction on the free movement of vessels was placed with a view to preventing illegal transactions in the port area. However there did exist a jetty in the city of Portuguese Cochin, constructed in 1590 for facilitating movements in the port which served also as a mini-port for the Portuguese.[19] Many parts of the water front which were not fortified were utilized by the *casados* to despatch their vessels. As these outlets were utilized by private traders to send ships without the permission and notice of Portuguese authorities, the *casados* were, as reported by Conde de Vidigueira in 1599, strongly against the fortification of waterfront of Portuguese Cochin.[20]

Thus it seems that the entire water passage that separated Cochin from Vaipin was used as a harbour and for the movement of vessels. But the nucleus of the port area was Calvethy where the principal transactions were conducted and customs duties were levied.

III. COCHIN DE CIMA

Cochin de Cima refers to native Cochin which was occupied by the king of Cochin as his seat together with the Pazhayannor temple, the settlement of the local people as well as the merchants with a market of their own.[21] In Cochin de Cima, a fort was constructed to commemorate the victories of Duarte Pacheco over the Zamorin, and it came to be known as *Castelo de Cima de Cochin.*[22] In 1507, D. Francisco Almeida appointed Luis Alvares with eight men to assist him, as the captain of *Castelo de Cima de Cochin.*[23] This fort was situated near the 'river' and even as early as 1550 it was well equipped with good artillery and munitions. Next to this fort was the church of *Reis Magos*, where the people who went in for military service were given opportunities for worship and general confession.[24] Many Jews and *Cristãos novos* or new Christians lived in Cochin de Cima.[25] As a unit reinforcing the city of Cochin, the fort of native Cochin was always under able leadership. Because of the strategic importance of the fort, located near the royal residence of the native kings, noble and able men like Tristão de Sousa,[26] Manuel Pereira Camelo,[27] and Antonio Rebelo[28] were appointed captains of the Castelo of the native Cochin. In spite of the Portuguese fort, Cochin de Cima was predominantly non-European. Various merchant groups controlled the economic activities of this city.

IV. THE LOCATION OF THE CITY OF SANTA CRUZ

The Portuguese city of Santa Cruz of Cochin lay on a triangular tongue of land, that extended from the mouth of the Calvethy canal westward up to the seashore, southwards along the coast for about a mile and a half in length and one mile in breadth.[29] (Its latitude was 9° 55' N and longitude 76° 15'E.) It corresponds to the present day Fort Cochin; *Livro das Cidades* written in 1582 mentions that this city with the fortress was situated along the banks of the river (outlet of the lagoon into the sea) and was called *Cochin de Baixo* in order to distinguish it from Cochin de Cima.[30] The plans and maps of the city of Cochin of the sixteenth and the seventeenth centuries show that a small narrow river called *rio de estreito* (which could be identified as Calvethy canal) flowed outside the city wall in a south-east direction to the outlet of the lagoons, separating Portuguese Cochin from native Cochin, 'the locus of the port'.[31] As these plans suggest, the space between the two cities was initially unused. But Francois Pyrard de Laval noticed in the seventeenth century continuous houses in the area as in the suburbs.[32]

The Cochin de Cima, which housed the very port as well as the Santa Cruz de Cochin developed simultaneously, even though the development of the latter was within the spatial boundaries of city wall. The structure and functions of the port of Cochin determined the urban layout in both these cities. The various mercantile groups like the *Chetties*, *Konkanis*, Jews, Muslims, and St. Thomas Christians occupied particular portions of native Cochin adjacent to the port.[33] Each of the streets on which they congregated was known after the faith or religion of the occupants. Even today this fact is evident in the Mattancherry area where Cochin de Cima was situated, though the numerical strength of these communities and castes has undergone great change, due to a variety of reasons. Moreover, the degree of the involvement in the exchange systems of the port also determined the proximity of their habitations to the port.

The urban layout in Portuguese Cochin was quite different. On the eastern tip of the city of Santa Cruz was located the weighing place of pepper, probably because of its proximity to the port. Adjacent to it, stood the monastery of St. Augustine.[34] From east to north-west, along the water side up to the seashore were located the important establishments in the city such as the church of St. Sebastian, the fortress, the cathedral, the bishop's House, the hospital, and the church of St. Bartholomew (used by the German mercenaries). *Misericordia* and the Municipal Council hall were just behind the cathedral.[35] The municipal jetty, constructed for facilitating the movement of vessels and goods in the port area was located on the side of the outlet of the lagoon into the sea, some hundred and sixty feet to the west of the weighing place of pepper.[36]

The plans of the city suggest that there was on the eastern side over the *rio de estreito* a bridge connecting the fortified city with the kingdom of Cochin. The bridge as a symbol (the city gates must have been at the entrance of this bridge) of land route interactions not only provided the way to Cochin de Cima, but also to the outward expansion of the city. Thus, many Portuguese settlers, establishments, including churches of Nossa Senhora de Graça, St. Thomas, and the leprosy centre St. Lazaros, grew up in the area outside the city walls.

Meanwhile, the urban process that started in Portuguese Cochin began to expand northward across the river to Vaipin.[37] The southern tip of Vaipin island which was soon incorporated into the intermediate zone of the urban Portuguese culture had a good number of Portuguese settlers, a church and Bishop's residence.[38] As a result, the fortified city of Santa Cruz of Cochin (the core area) together with the southern tip of Vaipin and the north-western tip of land across *rio de estreito* (intermediate zones) developed as a unit of urban environment which was entirely different and

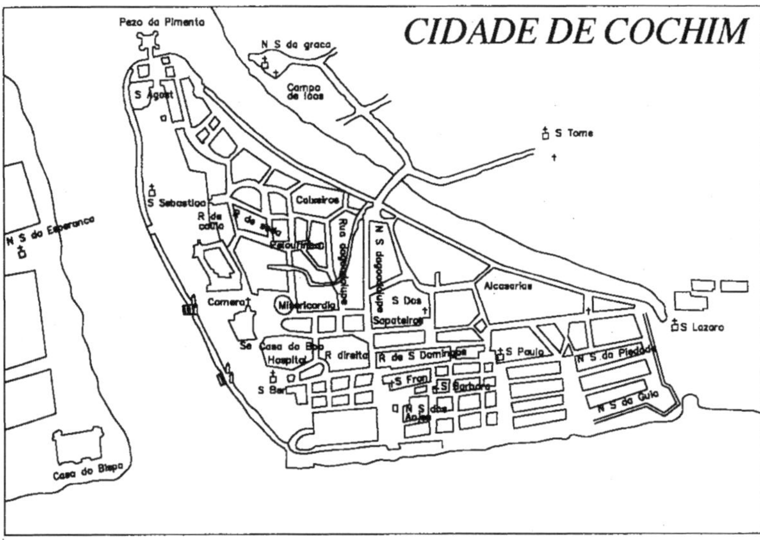

E.A.
Pezo da Pimenta – Bazar – S.Agosto – N.S. da graca – Campo de Iao's – N.S. da Esperaca – S. Sebastiao – R de coula – R.de seda – Caixeiros – Pelourinho – Rua dagoadolupe – N.S. dagoadolupe

E. B.
Caza do Bispo – Misericordia – Camera – Casa do Bpo –R. direita – Se – S. Ber. meu – Hospital

D. A.
CIDADE DE COCHIM – S. Thome – Hospital dos pobres –

D. B.
Alcasarias – S. D.os – Sapateiros – R. de S. Domingos – S. Paulo – N. S. da Piedade – S. Lazaro – S. Fran.co – S. Barbora – N. S. dos Anjos – N.S. da Guia.

Plan 1: The Plan of Cochin showing the Development of the City. The plan is based on the plan given in Luiz da Silveira, *Livro das plantas, Fortalezas, cidades e povoações do Estado da India Oriental, com as descrições do maritimo dos reinos e provinciais onde estão situados e outros portos principais daqueles partes, contribuição para a historia das fortalezas dos Portugueses no Ultramar.* Reproduction of the Codice no. 1471 existing in the Biblioteca do Paço Ducal de vila Viçósa, Lisboa, 1991, no. 72, p. 88.

distinct from the one that evolved in native Cochin. But this distinct pattern of urban development was in no way, it seems, completely watertight, but mutually supplementing and enriching because of the political umbrella of the king of Cochin and the interaction link provided by the bridge over the *rio de estreito* both of which greatly attempted to link the two Cochins.

V. THE ESTABLISHMENT OF THE CITY OF COCHIN

The town of Santa Cruz of Cochin, the Portuguese settlement in Cochin, was raised to the juridical status of a city by the King of Portugal John III, by a royal charter issued on 12 March 1527. It, being the abode of many of the Portuguese citizens and their families, was brought on par with the Portuguese city of Evora and was given all the privileges and rights attached to a city.[39] When it was raised to the status of a city, Portuguese Cochin was given a new and unique status in the structure of the *Estado da India* and was to be administered not only by a captain, but by a council of aldermen elected from among the citizens.[40] Seeing that the city of Cochin was an effective means of linking the exchange system of Lisbon with that of Cochin port, all the rights and privileges granted to it were confirmed and re-confirmed successively by the later kings and viceroys. Even though the political establishments of the *Estado da India* were shifted from Cochin to Goa in 1530, the original rights and privileges enjoyed by the city were retained and confirmed by Dom Sebastian, Dom Philip and by all the later viceroys as well.[41] The Portuguese authorities saw to it that the various privileges and rights of the city were sufficiently safeguarded and protected on the outbreak of any disturbance due to administrative deadlock. In 1551, the viceroy D. Afonso de Noronha asked the captains and other officials to respect the autonomy of the city of Cochin and not to encroach upon its privileges.[42]

VI. POPULATION

As urbanization refers to the process of an increasing concentration of people in cities, its demographic characteristics have to be analysed in order to understand the nature of the growth of the city of Cochin. Lazarus Nürnberger who visited Cochin in 1517 wrote that in this city there were about 300 Portuguese houses.[43] There were also many native Christians in the city. Thus, as mentioned by Padre Sebastião Pires, the vicar of the church at Cochin, there were about 10,000 to 12,000 Christians in Cochin (including probably the vicinity of Cochin) in 1518.[44] The presence of non-Christian elements was also considerable. As early as 1510, there were about 3,000 Nairs in the city, employed as daily wage workers in the service of the Portuguese. The movement of commodities and other works connected with the trade gave more employment opportunities to the local people, leading to this demographic increase.[45]

In 1525, there were 2,220 men in Cochin in the military service.[46] But it seems that the number of the soldiers always fluctuated. On 12 July 1527, Luis Martins from Portalegre wrote that there were only 1,000 men in Cochin and the number of married people was only 160.[47] Later, with the flow of people from the mother country, the number of married people living in Cochin increased considerably. By 1542, there were altogether 15,000 Christians in the Cochin (area) of whom more than 300 were *casados*, married and settled down in the city of Santa Cruz of Cochin.[48] By 1546, there were 570 Portuguese residents in Cochin, out of whom 343 were married settlers.[49] The number of the married Portuguese settlers rose to 500 by 1551.[50] The large increase in the number of orphans and church institutions in the city indirectly hints that Cochin experienced a very high demographic growth during the period under survey. Thus, we read that in 1584, the Christians in Cochin numbered 15,000, of whom 10,000 were natives and the remaining 5,000 Portuguese.[51] According to the report sent by the bishop of Cochin in 1598, there were besides children, 19,495 Christians who went to confession and communion in the city of Cochin.[52] This shows that Cochin was densely populated. But the population of the city began to decrease considerably after 1611, when a good number of the *casados* shifted their base of activities from Cochin to the Coromandel ports and elsewhere, because of the tensions in the hinterland which caused a decrease in the flow of commodities from the hinterland to the port of Cochin. The population of the city was reduced to one-third by the end of the second decade of the seventeenth century.[53] By the 1630s, the number of *casados* in Cochin was about five hundred: three hundred whites and the rest natives (the reference to native *casados* might include the *mestiços* or the married people of mixed race).[54] But the number of the *soldados* or the unmarried and the people of the other religious groups seems to have been much higher.[55] At the time of the Dutch conquest it was estimated that there were 900 old houses in the Portuguese quarter, though only 173 were actually inhabited.[56] After the ousting of the Portuguese from the city, the size of the population was 8,000 including 4,000 *topassen*.[57] This almost corresponds with the information given in Jesuit letters which say that after the Dutch conquest, there were five Franciscans and more than 10,000 Catholics in the city of Cochin.[58] Thus, there is every reason to believe that the urban population in its heyday, fluctuated, between 10,000 to 15,000 though the white element was considerably smaller. The city of Santa Cruz of Cochin was not an exclusively white settlement. The urban population included non-European elements like the Muslims, Hindus and native Christians, including the St. Thomas Christians. There were about 200 married native Christians inside the city.[59] Traders from Canara and Muslim merchants had shops in the city and formed component units of the urban population.[60] There were many other European traders and trade-agents in the city such as the Italians and the Germans. The German presence in Cochin, who came to this city as soldiers and traders, was great enough as to form a separate church for them.[61]

2. THE ADMINISTRATIVE STRUCTURE OF THE CITY

As M.N. Pearson observes, there were four areas of authority during the Portuguese period: in financial matters, the *vedor* (later *conselho da Fazenda*); in religious matters the clerics; in legal matters, the High Court; and in local government the Municipal Council. The Governor exercised appreciable control only over the first and assisted by the Council of State, also had control over military matters and external relations.[62] Above all, the city administration was entrusted to a popular body called *Senado da Camara* or Municipal Council.[63] From 1527 on, the administration of the city of Santa Cruz of Cochin was looked after by a Municipal Council which permeated into every sphere of urban activity.

I. THE ORGANIZATION AND STRUCTURE OF THE MUNICIPAL SYSTEM IN COCHIN

Municipal authority was invested in two kinds of office-holders: 1.Those having voting rights, 2.Those who had no voting rights. The first group comprised three or four *vereadores* (councillors or aldermen), two *juizes ordinarios* (justices of the peace or magistrates), the *procurador* (Municipal Attorney) and four *mestres* (the representatives of the working class guilds). These were collectively called the officials of the municipality and they had voting rights in council meetings. The *escrivão* (clerk or secretary) however, was not given voting rights, but was often included in the officials of the municipality. There were occasions when this term was loosely used to include subordinate municipal officials like *almotacels* (market-inspectors) and the *tesoureiro* (treasurer). To the category of municipal functionaries who did not have voting rights, belonged the *juiz dos orfãos* (judge in charge of orphans and widows), the *alferes* (standard bearer), the *porteiro* (the door-keeper), the *contador* (accountant) and the *veador das obras* (foreman of works).[64]

The municipal council was an elected body whose membership was exclusively restricted to married Portuguese male citizens. Not only *casados* but also resident *fidalgos* (noblemen) could vote for and sit in the Municipal Council.[65] The officials of the Municipal Council were elected through a system of annual balloting from voter's lists which were drawn up every three years in accordance with the procedure laid down in 1504.[66] The council represented only the Portuguese settlers of the city. There were occasions however, when strangers and people with little known backgrounds took part in the elections. So, in 1616, Dom Jeronimo d'Azevedo, the viceroy decreed that only virtuous people who were the inhabitants of Cochin and properly known in the city (to which people from the neighbourhood also could be added) should be included in the voters list.[67]

The municipal system in Cochin functioned in subordination to the king of Portugal, viceroy or governor, and permission was sought from them on serious and important issues. Thus, the appointments to posts such as *Meirinho dos Almotaseis*, supervisor for shipbuilding, officer in charge of the mint, inspector for the cleanliness of the city, and writer for the judges were made by the council with the approval of these higher administrative heads.[68] The king of Portugal Dom Sebastian, on account of his great concern for the city of Cochin, permitted in 1571 the construction of a municipal house for its meetings and for co-ordinating its administrative activities.[69]

The captain of Cochin, who was the most important officer in the fortress, was dissuaded by the viceroys in 1551 and 1585 from interfering in the activities of the municipality.[70] This was to safeguard the autonomy enjoyed by the municipal body. The viceroys and the kings of Portugal always made it a point that the institutional and administrative autonomy of the municipal council and the sanctity of its various privileges were well preserved and respected. Thus, in 1569 the viceroy Dom Luis de Ataide asked the captain-in-chief who arrived at Cochin not to upset the administrative set-up of Cochin by creating confusion for the soldiers and the residents.[71]

Most of the functions of the municipal council were related to public welfare activities. It laid out a road with necessary permission from the viceroy, Dom Duarte de Meneses to the *mandovi* (*mandapam* or square from where food materials were supplied) of food materials.[72] It even took up the responsibility of distributing rice through retail shops. Since rice was very scarce in this area, about 40,000 *candis* of rice was brought every year from outside into Cochin. But, very often this was hoarded in the houses and stores of captains and influential persons of the city so that they could sell it at a higher price elsewhere.[73] Hence the king of Portugal, Dom Philip decreed in 1593 that rice should be sold only under the supervision of the municipality of Cochin and for this purpose fifteen retail shops were instituted.[74]

The municipality had to look into the cleanliness and tidiness of the city of Cochin[75] and the problems of orphans.[76] Even shipbuilding came under the purview of the municipality. The municipal council elected a person to look after the construction of ships and another person for the collection of one per cent duty at the port of Cochin from every trader for the purpose of shipbuilding and keeping the city clean and tidy.[77]

The officials of the municipality enjoyed several privileges including judicial inmmunity and received regular salaries.[78] But if they did not perform well, or abstained from exercising their civic responsibilities, they were deprived of these privileges.[79]

The income of the municipality came mainly from the rents of the municipal property including houses which were leased as shops and from the taxes it levied on a variety of foodstuffs and from fines.[80] In order to tide over financial difficulties, one *pardao* each was collected from the Muslims and the people from Canara who put up shops in Cochin.[81] In 1572, the viceroy assigned a portion of the revenue coming from the Department of Justice (which it collected by way of fines and other pecuniary punishments) for the general expenditure of the city of Cochin.[82] There were occasions, when the municipality decided to dispose of land in the city in order to raise funds.[83] At times, the royal benevolence came to its rescue and in 1546 the king of Portugal sanctioned the necessary funds for the activities of this city.[84]

Thus, we find that the municipal system which developed in the city of Santa Cruz of Cochin was an autonomous, self-governing, and to a great extent, self-financing body.

II. THE CAPTAIN OF COCHIN

The function of the captain of Cochin, as the chief Portuguese official in the city, supplemented and complemented the activities of the Municipal Council. The captain as the official representative of the various interests of *Estado da India*, was in charge of trade, diplomacy, maintenance of law and order, defence, as well as war and peace.[85] He lived in the fortress which was located on the border of the river of Cochin or the outlet of the lagoon into the sea.[86]

The captains were assisted in the discharge of their duties by a number of functionaries such as the factor, beadle, scribes of the factory, storekeeper, treasurers, superintendent of provisions, supervisor of the weighing place, judge, peons, constables, officers for the deceased, master of the dockyard, master of caulkers, master of coins, interpreters, guards of the ships and the river. They were all paid directly from the Portuguese treasury.[87]

There was a clear-cut division between the administrative spheres of the captain of the city and the municipal council. The responsibility of the local government was given to the municipal council and the captains were asked to respect the autonomy and independent functioning of the *Senado da Camara*.[88]

3. THE ECONOMIC ACTIVITIES IN THE CITY

The most vibrant economic activities of the city were related to trade and urban life. The key productive activities in the secondary sector were shipbuilding, minting of coins and building of houses.

I. SHIPBUILDING

As the Portuguese did not have sufficient ships for the *carreira da India*, vessels both for battles and long voyages in the east were constructed in Cochin.[89] A large quantity of teak, *angelins* and other strong wood were floated down from the interior hinterland to Cochin for this purpose.[90] The base for the shipyard of Cochin was laid when Duarte Pacheco, who in course of the preparation of war against the Zamorin of Calicut, sent the *caravela* of João Serrão for repair and ordered the construction of small vessels for the naval encounter.[91] Later in 1506, for the construction of a ship in Cochin, the mast of São Gabriel (the ship that had accompanied Vasco da Gama on his first voyage), was made use of.[92] The shipyard of Cochin constructed the necessary vessels for the conquest of Goa and Diu.[93]

The ship called *Saint Catherine of the Mount Sinai*, which was constructed in Cochin during the period between 1511 and 1513 was said to have had a capacity of eight hundred tonnes.[94] Later, after having served its purpose in India it was sent to Portugal to Dona Beatriz, the daughter of King Manuel I.[95] Meanwhile private Portuguese citizens also began to build vessels for their personal use. Thus, in 1509, Jorge Barreto the captain of Cochin took timber to Cochin to build a ship for his personal use.[96]

Gaspar Correia makes mention of a ship that was built in Cochin and used in the maritime battle against the Sultan of Aden in 1516.[97] Some of the vessels built in this city were sold to indigenous merchants as well. Manuel Godinho refers to the ships that had been built in Cochin and sold to the merchants of Surat.[98] As Indian teak was preferable to European pine or oak, shipbuilding in the city received a boost. One particular advantage of Cochin was that the local ruler helped the Portuguese to get the necessary timber. One of the important ships built in Cochin was *Santa Cruz* completed in 1527 and fully equipped with pieces of artillery.[99] In 1545, João de Sepulveda took it to Lisbon as the principal vessel of the *Armada*.[100]

Meanwhile, with the increase of private trade, more individuals began building ships in Cochin for commercial use. As a result, from 1523 onwards, we hear that wood for shipbuilding had become scarce in Cochin.[101] The availability of timber for the construction of official vessels kept falling in Cochin, with the increasing number of concessions granted to private individuals in 1540s for shipbuilding and conducting voyages. During this phase of private trade a new situation arose: most of the timber that came to Cochin from the hinterland was reserved and used for manufacturing vessels for private individuals. Some of the timber was also taken to other ports for the same purpose. In 1558, when the scarcity of construction materials became a serious problem, the viceroy forbade the export of timber to any ports other than Cochin.[102]

In view of the order of the viceroy issued in 1572, the 'one per cent' duty levied from the port of Cochin was set apart for shipbuilding. The next year, the viceroy asked the municipality to elect two officials: one to supervise the construction of ships and the other to collect 'one per cent' duties from the port for the purpose of shipbuilding activities.[103] To realize this amount, the latter official was empowered in 1573 to raise a fleet and to go out at night to discover which vessels bypassed Cochin.[104] The municipality and the *Estado da India* placed great importance on shipbuilding activities, as they were intimately related to trade, the basic econmic activity of Cochin.

Mathias de Albuquerque, the viceroy, reported to the king of Portugal that Cochin was a very suitable centre for building ships for the kingdom. In 1596, King Philip ordered that at least two large vessels must be built in the city every year.[105] This royal command was again repeated in 1602 and Aires de Saldanha, the viceroy was asked to do the needful to encourage shipbuilding activities of Cochin.[106]

Meanwhile, with the decrease of the Portuguese population and with the diminishing manufacture of ships in the city of Santa Cruz of Cochin, a phenomenon which appeared after the second decade of the seventeenth century, the shipbuilding activities in native Cochin acquired greater importance. In 1630, we find the Portuguese authorities trying to enter into a contract with the king of Cochin for the construction of big vessels including galleons which could carry sixty pieces of artillery.[107] Though timber was scarce in Cochin, the rich hinterland with its abundant resources of teak and *angelins*, made available to the shipbuilding centres, timber at a reasonable price. Moreover, the Portuguese acquired a lot of expertise and technical co-operation from the local people. Indian co-operation was essential and decisive at all stages, because although the master shipwrights were Portuguese, the ordinary shipwrights, carpenters, and dockyard workers were nearly all Indians.[108]

II. MINTING OF COINS

With the development of trade and commerce in Cochin, there was a great demand for coins. The Portuguese therefore established a mint in this city in 1530 to issue coins.[109] In 1532, the official in charge of the mint in Cochin was Fernando de Silva.[110] Eventually, copper coins called *bazarcus*, were also issued from Cochin. It was in 1544 that the Governor Martim Afonso de Sousa ordered the re-minting of copper coins or *bazarcus* in the city of Santa Cruz.[111] The copper imported from Europe supplied the metal required for this minting. The process of minting could

TABLE III-1. THE COINS OF COCHIN IN 1554[112]

Year	Name of the coins	Value of the coins in *reais* in 1554
1554	*Pardau de Ouro*	360
	Xerafins	300
	Fanão (in the factory)	21 2/3
	Cruzado de Ouro	390
	Cruzado de Ouro (During the governorship of Martim Afonso de Sousa)	426

be carried out only by persons who had experience and knowledge of precious metals. Taking this fact into account, King John III sent to Cochin João Gomes as the master of the mint in 1552.[113]

In 1568, the viceroy, Luiz de Ataide, appointed Diogo Rodrigues Cavaco in charge of minting gold and silver coins (*xerafins*) in the city.[114] Often, the Municipal Council of Cochin elected competent persons to mint coins in the city. Thus, in 1577, the municipal council was permitted by the governor Antonio Munis Barreto to elect a competent person to issue coins called *bazarcus*.[115]

The coins made in Cochin in the early part of the sixteenth century rarely had any special mint mark, so it is difficult to differentiate the various existing species. But it is believed that they were marked with the cross of the order of Christ, a predominant motif on the contemporary coinage of Portugal.[116] During the time of the viceroy, Dom Luiz de Ataide, improvement was made with the help of Diogo Rodrigues Cavaco in the quality of the the coins, by minting gold and silver coins.[117] We have a few details of coins from Cochin as shown in Table III-1.

We do not know whether the other coins that were in circulation in Cochin were minted in the city. The wide circulation of coins and money accelerated trade and monetization of the economy.

III. HOUSE BUILDING

With the fast development of the city, house building thrived in Cochin.[118] Large quantities of timber were carried down to the city from the hinterlands for this purpose. In Cochin, a good number of carpenters were engaged in the various activities of house building. There was a master carpenter to inspect the work. The masonry work was carried out under the guidance of a master-mason.[119] Most of these houses were built with verandas on bungalow models.[120]

Many auxiliary activities connected with trade and shipbuilding received momentum in Cochin. The manufacture of sacks, ropes, etc, also flourished in the city.[121] Cochin had even a gun-manufacturing factory which employed expert cannon makers. The two Italian founders who deserted and joined Calicut in the first decade of the sixteenth century had been previously associated with this centre.[122] Thus, the important productive activities that developed in Cochin in the secondary sector were subservient to and oriented towards its military and commercial interests.

4. THE SOCIAL LIFE

With the growth of the city and its population, the social life in Cochin became complex. A new social milieu appeared in the city as a result of the mixed marriages and the mingling of Iberian and Indian elements, initiated by Afonso Albuquerque.

The policy of mixed marriage was encouraged by the Portuguese authority for two reasons: On the one hand, because of the hazards and long duration of the voyages only a very few women came to India.[123] On the other hand, as the supply of men from Portugal could not always be depended upon, it was decided by the Portuguese leadership headed by Albuquerque to bring into existence a body of Eurasians to whom could be entrusted the defence of the *Estado da India*.[124] Afonso Albuquerque made his Portuguese men marry Indian women. Horses, land and houses were allotted to them to encourage this mingling.[125] In the letter by Antonio Real written to the King of Portugal, reference is made to the marriage of Portuguese men with native captive women.[126] But Afonso Albuquerque wished the marriage of the Portuguese to be limited to women of Aryan origin. He stressed that he did not want his men to marry the dark-skinned women of Malabar.[127]In the city of Cochin, the majority of women whom the Portuguese married seem to have been converts from Islam. The Muslim links, thus acquired through marriage, helped some Portuguese citizens develop an easy network of private trade, as we shall see later.[128] The number of Christians in Cochin increased as a result of these inter-marriages, forming a class by themselves, called Topaz. The policy of inter-marriage brought out not only a new element called Eurasian community in the urban society of Cochin, but also helped the Portuguese to penetrate into the indigenous world because of their native wives.

The policy of conversion followed by the Portuguese effected an upward mobility in the social ladder and structure of urban society. The low-caste people by their conversion to Christianity, the religion of the ruling class, appeared to enjoy high social status. Even the higher officials of the native rulers embraced Christianity during the early period. The most notable among them was the Arel of Cochin (the Araya and the chief port officer of the king of Cochin) who converted to Christianity with 1,000 members of his clan and took on the name of Antony Real in 1510.[129] Most of the newly-converted were women and merchants. Some members of relatively higher castes like the Panikkars and Nairs also turned to Christianity.[130] Conversion was presented as a condition for the native women to get married to Portuguese men. In order to curb prostitution and promiscuous life, the Portuguese tried to restrict the relation of their men with only those women who were converts.[131] Many women, as a result, sought baptism with a view to marrying Portuguese soldiers. In 1514, in the city of Cochin, about one hundred women including those of Muslim, Nair, Canarese, Gujarati and Brahmin origin, were converted to Christianity.[132]

I. SOCIAL STRATIFICATION

Though the Portuguese society in Cochin was caste-free, differentiation on the basis of blood, profession and religion caused it to be stratified. In the hierarchy of

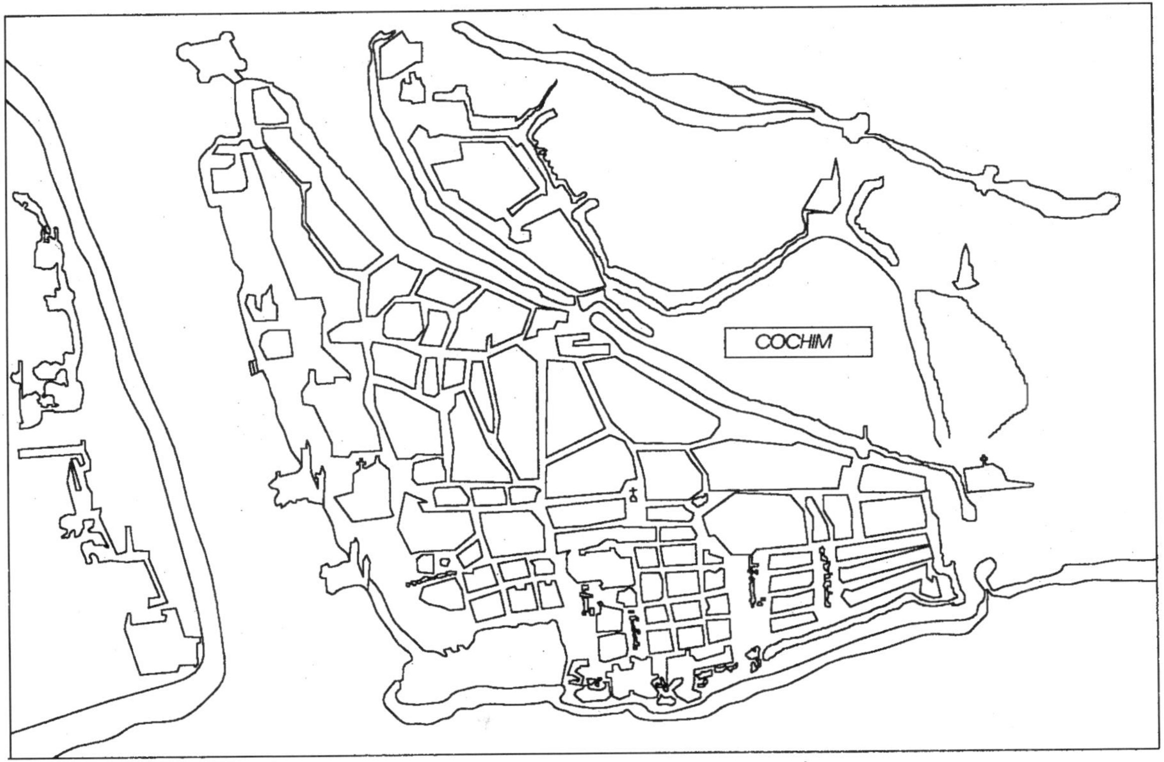

Plan 2: The Plan of Cochin shwing the Development of the City. The plan is based on the plan given in the Luiz da Silveira, *Ensaio de Iconografia das cidades Portugueses do Ultramar*, vol. III, Lisboa (n.d.), p. 414.

the urban society of Cochin, the clergy seems to have taken the top-most position. There was some kind of gradation even among them: 1.The higher clergy or the religious groups exclusively European. They denied admission to Indian as well as Eurasian candidates. 2. The lower clergy or the secular priests.[133] Down below them came the nobles. Among them as the Italian Jesuit Pe. Alexander Valignano testifies, the European-born Portuguese (*reinões*) were better placed than those born in India of Portuguese parents (*castiços* or *indiaticos*). Though those born of Portuguese and Indian parents (*mestiços*) could also be nobles, they held the lowest position.[134] The third estate or common people were again divided into *casados* and *soldados*.[135] The *casados* were those men who married after having reached india and who were allowed to leave the royal service and settle down as citizens or traders. The *soldados* were soldiers or the unmarried group who were liable for military service until they died, married, deserted or were incapacitated by wounds or diseases.[136] The ownership of wealth was again used as a criterion to stratify the position of the *casados*.

The rank of the common people in such a ladder differed also on the basis of religion and profession. The new converts to Christianity were ranked after the *mestiços*. The last stratum of the society was occupied by the non-Christians among whom the lower castes were put in the lowest position. It seems that this stratification of urban society was mapped out on to the settlement pattern and that the social status determined the intra-city location of different social groups. A careful and detailed study of the plan of Cochin attests and reinforces Gideon Sjoberg's view on the pre-industrial city, as an urban centre where the central area is occupied by the elite, while the disadvantaged members of the city had to make do with the periphery (the south-west tip of Vaipin island and the north-western track of land lying across the *rio de estreito*), while the poorest as well as the outcastes lived in the suburbs.[137]

II. EDUCATION

The first school in Cochin was started in 1510 by Afonso Albuquerque. He employed a teacher to instruct children in 1512. There were about 100 young men including the children of the Panikkars and nobles.[138] The first teachers were selected from the married Portuguese men residing in Cochin. In 1512, Afonso Alvarez was made the teacher for sixteen native students and arrangements were made for the provision of one *fardo* (sack) of rice every eighth day for them.[139] In 1514, the new teacher Ruy Pereira received 33 *cruzados* and 4 *fanões* for three months for imparting education to twenty-nine students.[140] Thus, there was an increase of thirteen students within two years.

The educational policy of Afonso Albuquerque suffered a setback during the time of his immediate successor Lopo Soares de Albergaria. In 1518, Friar Antonius de Loureiro wrote to the king of Portugal, 'in the city of Cochin, there used to be a school where the children were taught. At present there is none. May your Highness provide for one as it is a service to God.'[141] The request of the religious men was accepted and in 1521 the new governor Dom Duarte de Meneses re-established the old educational structure. In November 1521, for the education of the youngsters and orphans, about 200 primers (*cartilhas*), five biographies of saints and four prayer books were sent from Cochin to Goa.[142]

The Franciscans started a seminary or a centre of higher learning for candidates to the priesthood in Cochin. This seminary, though its actual date of foundation is unknown, was in existence in 1527 as evidenced from a letter by Friar Gonçalo de Lamego.[143] There were only five clerics in that year. The Mestiços or the sons of the Portuguese men from Indian women were admitted to the seminary for the first time in 1530. The Franciscan superiors of Portugal objected to their admission; but this practice continued.[144] As the number of the candidates increased, a new friary-cum-seminary which could accommodate fifty to sixty members was erected in 1580 with the money raised from sources other than *padroado*.[145] In the seminary of St. Antony of Cochin, the Portuguese professors gave lectures on arts and philosophy. In 1585, Frei Antonio do Rosario was the professor of Philosophy.[146] Later in the seventeenth century, much importance was given to the improvement of the seminary education with a view to having better priests.[147]

St. Francis Xavier came to Cochin in 1543, and again in 1544 and 1545, he visited the city. The citizens together with the vicar of Cochin, Pedro Gonçalves requested him to start a college in the city for the education of their children.[148] Balthasar Gago, a member of the Jesuit order, was sent as Superior for this purpose. In the beginning, the students were taught to read and write and were given lessons in the Latin language.[149] It seems that the higher levels of learning were incorporated into the Jesuit educational system of Cochin with the advent of Professor Francisco in 1548.[150] The *Madre de Deus* church of Cochin which originally belonged to the sodality was given to the Jesuits for setting up a college in 1550. Though the sodality members protested against this move and got back the church in 1552, it was finally given back to the Jesuits for the running of the college in 1557, thanks to the intervention of King John III. This college later came to be called *Madre de Deus* college and it had 300 students (it seems that either all or most of them were seminarians) in 1558.[151] As distinct from modern colleges, it was a residential institution. This college was a three-storeyed building and had twenty-three spacious apartments. It was situated on the south-west of the present Bishop's house, facing the seashore.[152] *Madre de Deus* eventually became the main seminary and chief of all the colleges and houses in the Malabar province of Jesuit order or south India. Arts, humanities and theology were taught to the aspirants for priesthood.[153]

As one of the new methods of teaching, in this college of *Madre de Deus* theatrical presentations were staged. Padre Amador Correia and Padre Francisco Lopes took the lead in presenting theatrical pieces in Cochin.[154] Short plays such as the '*Auto de Santo Aleixo*' (written by Padre Sebastian Pires) and '*Auto da Muita Dolorosa Morte e Paixão de Nosso Senhor Jesus Christo*' (written by Padre Francisco Vaz) were staged by the Jesuits under the auspices of *Madre de Deus*.[155]

III. *MISERICORDIA* (HOUSE OF MERCY)

The *Misericordia* founded in Portugal in 1498 was to assist the old, the disabled, the sick and the weaker sections among those involved in the overseas expansion.[156] The first *Misericordia* in India appeared in Cochin in 1527, two years before one was erected in Goa.[157] The *Misericordias* were established in centres where there were hospitals and they began to render help to hospital services and the poor.[158] In a letter written in 1527 from Cochin, a member of the House of Mercy refers to the various functions of *Misericordia*, such as absolution for the dying, help to orphans, the sick and the poor.[159] The members of the *Misericordia* made regular visits to the sick in hospital and the poor in prisons bestowing love and care on them. They used to give an honourable burial to the poor deceased, dowries to poor young ladies, alms to the poor, they supported the destitute and abandoned children.[160] In 1554 the *Misericordia* of Cochin received 30 *pardaus* per month for the marriage of orphans.[161] In 1574 according to the budget of the *Estado da India*, an amount of 9,000 *reais* per month was set apart for the *Misericordia* to help the poor.[162] This shows that after a period of twenty-nine years, the priority was shifted from the marriage of the orphans to financial help of the poor. By the end of the sixteenth century, this amount increased to 1,20,000 *reais*.[163]

The *Misericordia* in Cochin also undertook the responsibility for contacting the relatives of the deceased in Portugal if the dead person had originally come from there. Thus, the House of Mercy of Cochin contacted the *Misericordia* of Porto to find out the mother (living in Travassos) of one Antonio Jorge who died in Cochin and handed over 10,000 or 11,000 *reais* to her.[164] If it did not succeed in discovering the legitimate heir, the money reverted and was used for the maintenance of the orphans and the poor.[165]

In 1612, the *Misericordia* of Cochin obtained many privileges from Dom Philip II (of Portugal).[166] With the royal privileges and with the accumulation of the bequests and legacies of the individuals, it eventually became an institution with great economic significance. It seems that the *Misericordia* of Cochin received Government money for safe deposit and advanced loans to the *Estado da India* in times of necessity. Thus, the contribution of one per cent made by the municipality of Cochin for relieving the burden of the Portuguese Government was kept in the *Casa da Santa Misericordia* of the city in 1572.[167] In 1605, when Martin Afonso de Castro's *armada* was sent to defend Malacca, the *Casa da Misericordia* of Cochin was asked for a loan well in excess of the already given amount of 19,000 *xerafins*.[168] The bishop of Cochin pledged, in the *Misericordia* of this city, the silver vessels of the church in order to defend it from the European invader;[169] but these were later restored to the diocese, because of the firm stand taken by the citizens of Cochin.[170]

IV. HOSPITAL AND MEDICAL ASSISTANCE

In the early days of Portugese settlement, medical facilities were provided to them by the king of Cochin. The native physicians healed the wounded soldiers (injured in the war with Calicut), with hot coconut oil and lime juice.[171] The first hospital in Cochin was founded by Dom Francisco de Almeida on 21 January 1505.[172] As verified by *Ensaio de Iconografia das cidades do ultramar*, the hospital, erected in a rectangular shape, was parallel to the 'rio' (the outlet to the sea). In later years, there appeared another medical centre known as the 'hospital of the poor' and it was situated some distance from the fortress, but amidst the settlement of the ordinary folk.[173] From as early as 1512, various types of remedies and medicines were available in the pharmacy of Cochin.[174]

Right from the very beginning, the Cochin hospital was provided with a surgeon, a physician and a health worker.[175] The surgeons were, at least in some rare cases, appointed by the King of Portugal. Thus, the *Chancelaria* of Dom John III shows that Manuel Duarte who worked as a surgeon in Cochin for three years,[176] and Simão da Rosa who was sent to Cochin for a period of four years,[177] were both appointed by royal orders.

The administration of the hospital service was entrusted to *provedores*. The factors or the *almoxarifes* gave them the necessary equipment and medicines. In 1512, the *providor* (purveyor) of the Cochin hospital received from the *almoxarife* Alvaro Lopes, the wine required for the sick.[178] The hospital was provided with beds and other necessary items. It appears that the diet administered to the sick was nutritious and included bread, chicken, eggs, lentils, olive oil, wine, etc.[179]

For the maintenance of the hospital of Cochin, Afonso Albuquerque contributed twenty-two *cruzados*.[180] Later, 180 *paras* of wheat and one *fardo* of sugar were given by the *almoxarife* to the *provedores* of hospital.[181] There were cases when the penalties and the money paid to the *Justiça* in criminal and civil cases were offered for the running of the hospitals. In the letter sent to Pedro Vaz, the captain of Cochin, Dom John III asked him to hand over the money received by way of penalties and fines to be utilized for the hospital services.[182] Later, the hospital was entrusted to the *Misericordia* (1541-2) for better administration.[183] But the hospital was run badly and its transfer to the *Misericordia* did not improve the situation. In 1548, St. Francis Xavier writes about the dilapidated condition of the hospital.[184] But the crown felt deep concern for this medical institution. In 1554, the hospital of Cochin was given 3,00,000 *reais* for its administration.[185] This seems to have been utilized for the routine activities of the hospital. No concrete steps were taken to protect the building, and soon, in 1564, the hospital had to be closed down. However, this was only a transient phase in its history. The Jesuits, with the help of the wife of captain of Cochin, built a new edifice with a veranda for nursing the sick.[186] The House of *Misericordia* was located next to the hospital, and was able to give help to the sick and the infirm.[187]

According to Figueiredo Falcão, an amount of 6,00,000 *reais* was set apart for the hospital of Cochin, by the end of the sixteenth century.[188] But eventually the financial help given to this hospital began to decrease considerably. By 1630s it was reduced to 50 per cent. Antonio Bocarro mentions it to be only 3,00,000 *reais*.[189]

Leprosy had been a common sickness in Cochin, as was observed by Ralph Fitch.[190] The Portuguese built a leprosy asylum called *Lazaretto* which was outside the walls of the city.[191]

V. PRISON

Prison was another institution to which the helping hands of the *Misericordia* were extended. The prison of Cochin was situated on the side of the '*rio*'[192] (outlet of the lagoon into the sea) and was modelled on the prison in Lisbon.[193] There were persons who had been in this prison for five or six years. According to Pyrard de Laval, the Cochin prison had two divisions: the upper part was occupied by the sick and those who were put into irons. Usually the upper prison was set apart for those who would give money to the jailer. The lower level was occupied by ordinary Portuguese, Indians, Christians, Mohammedans and all other non-Christian groups.[194] The Cochin prison as seen by Pyrard de Laval in 1608, was a filthy and overcrowded place. The conveniences were minimal; the prisoners had to perform all their natural needs, in turn into vessels which were kept there till their removal in the evening, which made the atmosphere smelly and insanitary. Everybody had to lie sideways because of lack of space in the overcrowded prison. However, some slaves and paupers were employed to refresh the prisoners with a large fan. Every Portuguese was given a demy *tanga* while others were given, some cooked rice, fish and water once a day. There was an elderly person among the prisoners who commanded the obedience of the rest and acted as a kind of judge. This judge received a fee from everyone admitted to prison, half of it going to the jailer. It was his duty to maintain the lamp before the image of the blessed virgin Mary and to make arrangements for Sunday Masses.[195] Pyrard de Laval while describing the prison of Cochin observes: 'It (prison of Cochin) is built in the form of a large and lofty square tower, and high above, in the middle of the floor, is a square hole, like a very trap or the hatches of a ship, which is closed and locked; there they let down the prisoners in a scale or wooden table, which they lower with a rope and draw up again by a pully. It is six or seven fathoms in depth, like a well, and below there is no door, but only a large square window in the wall of an arm and a half's length in thickness to admit some light. This hole or window is trellised with thick, square cut bars of iron through which you can pass a two-pound loaf of bread and through which the gaoler does pass whatever he gives to the prisoners.This prison is verily the most frightful and cruel one that exists in the world.'[196]

Later in 1610, because of the overcrowding of the prison, Viceroy Dom Lourenço de Tavora permitted the municipality of Cochin to build another prison. Moreover, for its construction, the city of Cochin was asked to raise the necessary funds.[197]

VI. PROSTITUTION

The institution of prostitution had emerged as a necessary and consequent evil of the social structure of Portuguese India. As the Portuguese came to India unaccompanied by their women, illegitimate relations with native women became quite common.

A good number of women of Cochin exploited this situation to make money. Gradually prostitution became legalized. Viceroy Dom Francisco de Almeida by an order of 1506, decreed that the women whom the Portuguese kept as concubines should be set free and that those women who wanted to stay on with the Portuguese were to live in the house of a newly-converted lady by the name of Beatriz. The Portuguese were not allowed to keep mistresses at home, so they had to visit this house of prostitution for their sexual needs. The rate was fixed at three caixas (Kashu) each.[198]

Several mothers made a profitable business by selling their virgin daughters into prostitution. Dom Almeida, under threat of severe punishment forbade this, even ordering priests to convert attractive women to Christianity with a view to eradicating promiscuity. The result was that the women converts multiplied rapidly.

Afonso de Albuquerque made strict rules in selecting and maintaining prostitutes in consideration of the health of his men. Though the prostitutes were converted to Christianity, their relatives still lived as Hindus and Muslims. These non-Christian relatives visited and cohabited with these prostitutes frequently, consequently, many problems affecting the faith and health of the Portuguese cropped up.[199] Hence the viceroy ordered strict segregation of the Christian population from the non-Christian groups.[200] It has to be specially mentioned that the institution of prostitution with its diverse problems connected with the health and faith of the Portuguese played a rather important role, at least in the initial phase, in separating Portuguese Cochin as a separate urban entity from native Cochin.

Even in later days, prostitution thrived in Cochin mainly due to the presence of large number of unmarried men in the city. Even the married Portuguese were said to have drifted, sometimes, into immoral habits. The viceroy, Dom Afonso de Noronha ordered in 1551 that the unmarried women of native Cochin should be prevented from visiting the married men of Portuguese Cochin.[201] Similarly in 1556, the governor, Francisco Barreto issued an order to the officials of the municipality of Cochin to drive away all those, including married Portuguese settlers, who were leading an immoral life.[202]

5. THE ECCLESIASTICAL INSTITUTIONS

City life in Cochin was greatly influenced by the various church institutions. The Papal Bulls gave the Portuguese the sole right to sail the seas, conquer new lands that had been discovered or would be discovered on condition that in these places they would build churches, monasteries and other religious establishments and would send missionaries to these newly-discovered areas.[203]

The religious and ecclesiastical matters in these territories occupied by the Portuguese came to be administered by a new system of royal patronage called *Padroado*. The king of Portugal, being the permanent administrator of the Order of Christ, enjoyed patronage over the dioceses, religious orders and also held the right of presenting prelates and other persons to vacant monasteries of all the orders.[204] In the initial phase, this royal power was limited to sending chaplains for the *armadas*.[205]

The first ecclesiastical institution in the Portuguese settlement of Cochin was an oratory, the site of which was later in 1503 taken over by the church of St. Bartholomew (used by the German soldiers). It was located near the old wooden fortress.[206] Afonso Albuquerque, in 1509 collected money from the nobles for the construction works of the new church in the city.[207] It seems that this money was not properly utilized. So he complained in October 1514 to the king of Portugal that on coming to Cochin, after two years of absence from the city, he found that nothing had been done. 'There was neither stone nor money.'[208] But some months later, the construction work was resumed. In December 1514, Frei Domingos wrote to Dom Manuel that the new church would be the principal church in the city which, when completed, would have three naves with crosses, three *capelas* with arches and a bell-tower.[209]

I. THE ORDER OF ST. FRANCIS

The first Franciscan group came to Cochin in 1500 along with the fleet of Pedro Alvares Cabral. Four of them remained in Cochin while the superior of the group, Frei Henrique Alvares de Coimbra went back to Lisbon.[210] During the time of Afonso Albuquerque, the Franciscan activities did not get much encouragement; so there were fewer members of this order in Cochin. In 1517, the situation changed and thirteen Franciscans came to India to start houses in Cochin and Goa. The superior who accompanied this group came to be called *comissario*, a designation which was in use till 1542. The Franciscan monasteries in India formed a comissary under the province of Portugal.[211]

The Franciscans started the construction of St. Antony's Friary and St. Francis Assisi Church in 1518, both of which were completed in 1522. This new church was almost entirely made of wood. The monastery of the Friary was a two-storeyed building with dormitory below. There were fourteen cells with windows facing the sea.[212] The Friary had a school and a seminary attached to it. The king of Portugal used to send the necessary books for the library of the Franciscan seminary.[213] Among the Franciscans of Cochin, Frei Lourenço de Gois (who became superior in 1536) was significantly famous because of his association with the mint of Cochin and his efforts to convert the king of Tanur.[214] In 1583, Frei Andre de Santa Maria was elected as custodian. He came to Cochin and called the chapter in 1584, with a view to electing the superior and the councillors.[215] It was mainly because of the efforts of the Franciscans that the veneration of St. Antony assumed greater importance in Kerala. The fisherfolk of Cochin began to offer coconuts, candles and oil to the images of the saint.[216]

The maintenance for the Franciscan Friary was contributed by the crown, with assistance from the private contributions and gifts which it received from believers.[217] The restoration works of the monastery building of the Franciscans were carried out in 1580 with royal support. Moreover, the community used to receive wine and oil from Portugal for its sustenance.[218] By the 1630s there were twenty Friars in the monastery of St. Francis and they received an amount of 50 *xerafins* for their maintenance.[219]

The Friary-cum-seminary in Cochin gathered greater significance in the further development of the Franciscan mission. In 1633, this house became the head of a custody or vice-province to which the Franciscans in south India, including the Friaries of Cranganore, Quilon, and Ceylon belonged.[220]

II. THE DOMINICANS

In 1503, about five monks of the Dominican order came to Cochin with Afonso Albuquerque.[221] It was one of them, Frei Rodrigo Homem, who delivered the sermon on the occasion of the blessing of the church of St. Bartholomew in 1503.[222] From a letter of Padre Sebastian Pires, the vicar general of India, it becomes evident that a Dominican monk called *mestre* João was exercising spiritual functions in Cochin and that he was a great master of theology.[223]

The attempts of the Dominicans to move on to Cochin as an organized group were delayed due to the objection of the bishop of Goa and of the *Padroado*

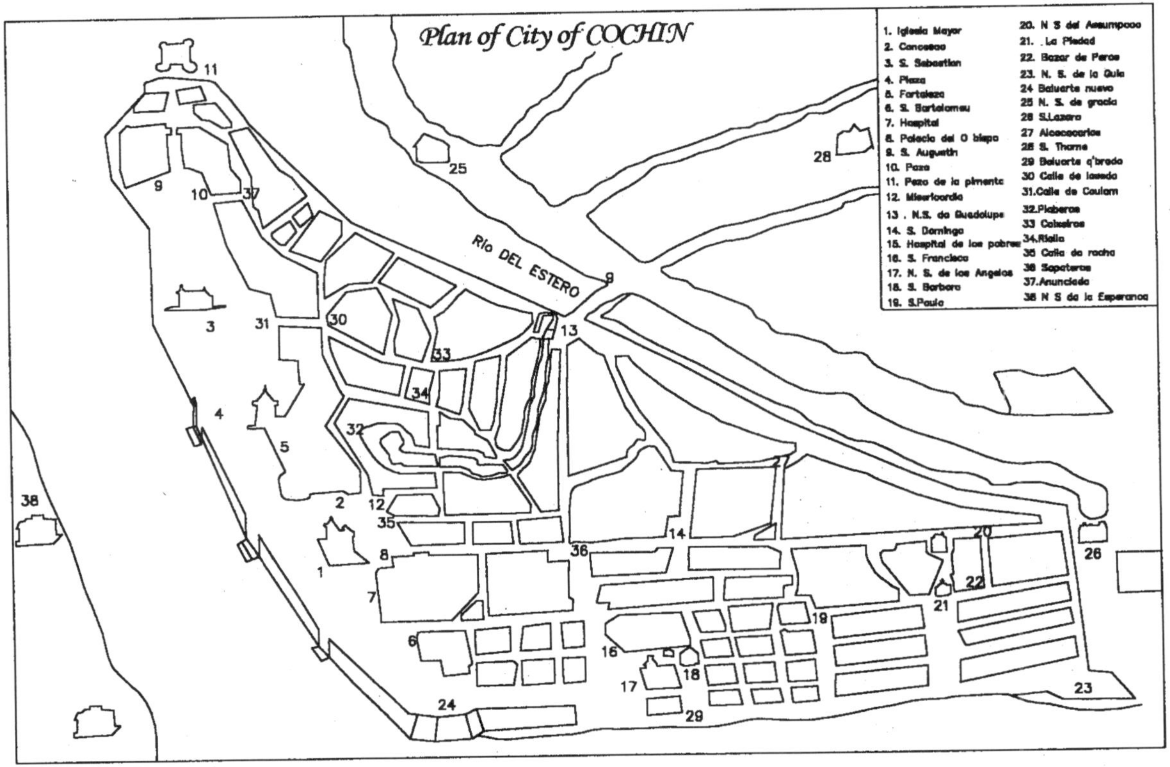

Plan 3: The Plan of Cochin showing the Development of the City. The plan is based on the plan given in Faria y Sousa, *Asia Portuguesa*, vol. I, 1661, p. 59.

authorities. It was only in 1551 that they managed to establish a house in Cochin.[224] The first superior of this monastery was Padre Frei Simão.[225] A monk of this house called Frei Andre de Santa Maria complains to his provincial in his letter of 25 February 1557, about the laxity seen among the members of this congregation. Reference was also made to the monks, who abandoning their spiritual duties, concentrated on visiting the Muslims, the native kings and the viceroys.[226] Despite its temporality and worldliness, one notices that the spirituality of this order was also considerably vibrant, as evident from the fact that the first bishop of Cochin, Dom Jorge Temudo was selected from this Dominican order.[227]

The Dominican monastery of Cochin, besides receiving a regular supply of wine and oil from Portugal also got from the governor Antonio Moniz Barreto in 1574 about 100 quintals of cinnamon coming from Ceylon.[228] In 1621, there were 18 priests and 13 brothers in this community of Cochin.[229] By the 1630s the number of the Friars in this religious house varied between 25 and 30 for whose sustenance 20 *candis* of wheat, 20 *candis* of rice, 2 barrels of wine and 6 *cantaras* of oil were supplied from Portugal.[230]

III. THE JESUIT ORDER

Diogo de Gouveia, the Rector of the college of Saint Barbara of Paris communicated in 1539 to King John III that this institute was training a group of youngsters who would be highly suitable persons to convert the gentiles. He also pointed out that this new order was quite different from other mendicant orders. Accordingly the Portuguese crown contacted Dom Pedro de Mascarenho, the ambassador in Rome to get some Jesuit missionaries to come to India.[231] The first and the foremost among them, St. Francis Xavier, came to Cochin in 1542. His subsequent visits to this city eventually made it the centre of Jesuit activities in the south.[232] On a request made by the city-dwellers of Cochin to Francis Xavier, a college was implanted on the site of the existing church of *Madre de Deus* for the education of their children, which came to be known as *Madre de Deus* college.[233]

In Cochin, between 1541 and 1560 there were sixty-five Jesuits,[234] most of whom later went to other parts of India. The office-bearers of the *Madre de Deus* for the period from 1557-9 were as follows: Pe.Belchior Nunes Barreto (rector), Pe. Francisco Lopes (priest), Pe. Francisco Peres (priest), Pe. Henrique Henrique (priest and compiler of Malayalam vocabulary), Br. Bernard Rodrigues (professor), Br. Gaspar Soeiro (procurator), Rui Mendes (in charge of the church), and Estevão de Ataide (in-charge of the house).[235] The priests had the responsibility of looking into the instruction of the seminarians.[236]

According to Antonio Bocarro, the church of St. Paul and the Jesuit college of *Madre de Deus* received 1,500 *pardaus* of gold and rent from the island of Divar of Goa for sustenance. The total amount, thus received was 1,800 *xerafins*. Besides this, the Jesuits rceived another 1,000 *xerafins*.[237] The various documents of the *Cartório dos Jesuitas* say that the Jesuits of Cochin had villages of Assolona, Velly and Ambelly of Goa as their property and that they were enjoying the rent from these villages for years.[238] In 1602, the Jesuit house of Cochin was raised to the status of vice-province while in 1605, it was made the independent Malabar province under which was brought the famous Madurai and other missions of the south.[239]

In 1600 there were about 48 Jesuits out of which 23 were in Cochin. In 1610 there were 133 Jesuits of whom 66 were in Cochin. As Bishop Roz S.J. complained, the Jesuits preferred to work in Cochin rather than elsewhere, since life in Cochin was more comfortable and no language other than Portuguese was needed.[240] In 1621, the number of the Jesuits in Cochin was as follows: Besides the provincial and rector, there were 20 priests, 15 seminarians and 13 brothers. For their maintenance the king of Portugal used to give 1,600 *xerafins* in the 1620s. In addition, the Jesuits of Cochin had other sources of income like the rents from the island of Divar in Goa, from the island of Vaipin and some other parts within the kingdom of Cochin.[241]

IV. THE AUGUSTINIANS

The Augustinians who came to India in 1572 were the fourth religious order to be established in Cochin.[242] The church and the monastery of St. Augustine was located near the weighing place of pepper.[243] In 1621, there were four Augustinian priests and two brothers for whose maintenance they received eighteen *xerafins* from thirty shops and rents from the coconut palms of 'castelo' (in native Cochin) and of some other parts of the kingdom of Cochin.[244] By the 1630s the number of Augustinian Friars varied between twelve and fifteen and they received five hundred *xerafins* from the king of Portugal for maintenance.[245]

All of these Friars, except those *mestiços* who were admitted by the Franciscans, were Europeans. In 1626, among the six religious who came to India as members of the Jesuit, Dominican, Augustinian and Franciscan orders, two were from Italy, one was from France and the remaining monks were from Portugal.[246] The natives were denied admission to these orders on the grounds that Indians were inclined to wrong-doing and were animated by base instincts.[247]

V. THE BISHOPRIC OF COCHIN AND THE CATHEDRAL OF SANTA CRUZ

The erection of the diocese of Cochin became inevitable as the bishop of Goa had difficulties in governing the distant region of Malabar.[248] Demands for a bishop and for monks of various religious orders were raised for 'teaching religion to the newly converted and for effective pastoral work'.[249] Cochin was taken as the centre of this bishopric because of the importance of this city, it being the seat of a king, as a harbour of great importance, as well as the centre of a large number of new Christians and finally, because of its great distance from Goa.[250] The new diocese of Cochin was created by Pope Paul IV by the bull *Pro Excellenti* on 4 February 1558.[251] The already existing diocese of Goa was made the Archdiocese and the diocese of Cochin along with Malacca was made suffragans or subordinate dioceses to it.[252] The bishopric of Cochin comprised the entire southern region of India that extended from Cannanore in the north-west, to Bengal in the north-east, and outside India it included Burma as well as Ceylon.[253] Though the bishopric was erected in 1558, the first Bishop Dom Jorge Temudo could assume the office only in 1559. Dom

Henrique de Tavora, his successor, was a participant in the Council of Trent (1545-63) and carried out the administration of the diocese according to the spirit of the council.[254]

Along with the erection of the bishopric, the church of Santa Cruz was elevated to the level of the Cathedral church. The king of Portugal had to provide for the bishop of Cochin, a dean, an archdeacon, cantors, schoolmaster, treasurer and twelve canons of the chapter with twelve prebendaries. The Pope ordered that the king of Portugal should pay 500 *ducates* to the bishop, 100 *ducates* to the dean, 75 to each of the cantors as well as prebendaries, and 50 *ducates* to each of the canons.[255]

Being the patron of ecclesiastical activities in India, the crown of Portugal extended monetary help to the cathedral and the bishopric of Cochin. Thus, in 1566, Dom Sebastian issued orders to give a 1,00,000 *reais* each year for six years, for the construction of the cathedral of Cochin.[256] By the end of the sixteenth century, the various office-bearers of the cathedral received 5,80,000 *reais*. An additional amount of 1,80,000 *reais* was allotted for the construction of the cathedral.[257] By the 1630s, the bishop of Cochin used to receive 9,00,000 *reais* which was equivalent to 3000 *xerafins*. Out of this 8,00,000 *reais* formed the annual salary for the bishop and the remaining 1,00,000 *reais* were paid to the *provizor* and the vicar-general. Besides this, the various prominent office-bearers of the cathedral received 3,600 *xerafins*. The others like the sub-treasurer, the choir, the assistant priest, master of the chapel, the gate-keeper, the organist as well as the sacristan got 776 *xerafins* 3 *tangas* and 26 *reais*.[258]

The cathedral, besides being a place of worship acted both as an integrating link for the city dwellers as well as a venue for incorporating the city of Cochin into the socio-political milieu of Portugal. Thus, it provided a venue to the citizens of Cochin to express their allegiance to Dom Philip II of Spain when he became the king of Portugal. The bishop of Cochin, the prelates of the various religious orders, the prince of Cochin and the several top officials of the King of Cochin who were present at this function to express allegiance to the new king of Portugal[259] were the chief factors in this integrating process.

Besides the Santa Cruz cathedral, there came up several churches in Cochin. Sieur de Rennefort says that there were twenty-three churches in Portuguese Cochin and its suburbs during the seventeenth century.[260] This fact is further testified to by the list of churches given in the *Descripsão de Cochin* and by the plans of Cochin given in the *Ensaio de Iconografia das Cidades do Ultramar*. The names of these churches were: St. Bartholomew's church (which was initially used by the German mercenaries in the Portuguese army), St. Sebastian's church, St. Augustine's church, the Church of our Lady of Guadelope, the Church of our Lady of Protection, St. Paul's Church, St. Dominic's Church, Church of our Lady of Pity, Church of our Lady of Guide, St. Francis Assisi's Church, St. Barbara's Church, Church of our Lady of Good Voyage and the Church of our Lady of Anunciation. These were within the walls of the city. Outside the city, but within the urban and ecclesiastical orbit of Cochin existed the Church of our Lady of Grace, St. Lazarus Church, Church of our Lady of Hope, Church of St. Luis, St. John's Church, St. Thomas Church, church of St. Lawrence de Castelo.[261] It seems that some of these were only *capelas*. However, the multiplicity of the churches as seen in the urban layout made the settlement distribution more church-centred and transformed the urban network of the city into a multi-church complex.

VI. INQUISITION

From 1533 onwards, many new Christians (Jews converted to Christianity) began to flee from Portugal as their life there had become precarious; they came to India in search of greater security and tolerance as well as to take advantage of the new opportunities for trade and commerce. A good many of them managed to reach Cochin, which had emerged as a major trading centre in the Portuguese empire. On reaching Cochin, these new Christians developed a commercial network in the Indian Ocean with the help of the Jews of native Cochin.[262] The association with the native Jews of Cochin helped them to revive their old faith and practices, as most of these new Christians changed their Jewish religion (in Portugal) out of compulsion. In 1540, Dinis de Azevedo wrote from this city to Dom John III about the vibrant mercantile activities of the newly converted Jews.[263] Immediately their judaizing activities came to the notice of Portuguese authorities who wanted to establish a branch of the Inquisition in Cochin to purge them of Semitic influence. St. Francis Xavier was one among the first to write to the king of Portugal to set up the inquisition in India. In 1546, he wrote to John III from Amboina '. . . in order to make the people who live in India into good Christians, [it is necessary] for your Majesty to send out the Holy Inquisition, for there are many here who live according to Mosaic law or who are of the Moorish sect. . . . And as they are many and spread out among all the fortresses, many preachers as well as Holy Inquisition are required. . . .'[264]

Luis de Panamo, the inquisitor of Sicily in 1598 alluded to the existence of an inquisitional tribunal working in Cochin from 1560 for the trial of the new Christians or the newly converted Jews of the city.[265] In fact, the process against the new Christians of Cochin began in 1557, when the Jesuit priest Dom Gonçalo da Silveira began an enquiry into the judaizing group of the new Christians. The pretext for the inquisitional proceedings against the new Christians was the appearance of blasphemous and provocative written words on the stand on which the Holy Sacrament was placed in the Church of Santa Cruz in Cochin on 30 April 1557, the feast day of *Corpus Christi* (Eucharist). This writing evidently condemned the basic Christian dogmas and was signed 'the tribes of Israel'.[266] It was followed by a similar statement found in the offertory box of the church of the Dominican monastery of Cochin.[267] The matter was taken very seriously and suspicion fell on the new Christians. Consequently most of the new Christians of Cochin were imprisoned by about 1557,[268] almost three years before the official establishment of the Inquisition in Goa (1560).[269] Immediately with their arrest an inquisitional court was set up in Cochin. It was presided over by Pero Gonçalves, the vicar of Cochin and he conducted the proceedings with the help of Jesuit priests such as Pe. D. Gonçalo da Silveira, Pe. Belchior Carneiro, the Franciscan monk, Friar Lopo, as well as the Dominican monk Friar Nicolau do Rosario. The notary was Francisco Fernandes.[270] After the arrival of Dom Jorge Temudo, the first bishop of Cochin, in 1559, the inquisitional proceedings were presided over by him, instead of the vicar of Cochin.[271]

Cochin as Depicted on the eve of 1663. The sketch of the city of Cochin was drawn by Ms. LisaThomas on the basis of sketches provided in NAAUWKEURIGE BESCHRYVINGE VAN MALABAR EN CHOROMANDEL, Der Zelver aangrenzende RYKEN, En het machtigé EYLAND CEYLON Door PHILIPPUS BALDAEUS, t'Amsterdam, by Johannes Janssonius van Waasberge, Johannes van Someren, Ano 1572.

Diogo do Couto[272] and several documents of the Inquisitional proceedings of Lisboa (housed in the archives of Torre do Tombo), make a reference to the various stages of enquiries and trials conducted for the new Christians of Cochin as well as the punishments meted out to them.[273] As a part of this inquiry, the tribunal questioned the persons concerned, their relatives and slaves and collected detailed reports about the accused.[274] Almost twenty new Christians were arrested and tried in this court of inquisition during this period before 1560. Among them figured Jácome de Olivares,[275] Leonor Caldeira, her son, Simão Nunes and daughter Clara Caldeira,[276] Manuel and Maria Rodrigues,[277] Luis Rodrigues,[278] etc., who were actively involved in the trade of Cochin. Many of these new Christians were arrested and punished for interacting with the Jews of native Cochin, taking part in their rituals and ceremonies, and for contributing to the construction of a new synagogue (Kadavumbhagam Synagogue built during the period between 1539 and 1549-50). Thus, Jácome de Olivares was accused of going to the house of Isaac do Cairo (a prominent Jew of native Cochin) and participating in the ceremonies of Purim. There they were said to have aided in the stoning of the crucifix in the manner in which it was done by the Jews. He was also accused of having given donations for the construction of a new synagogue in Cochin de Cima (Kadavumbhagam Synagogue).[279] He was said to have pronounced blasphemous words similar to those which had appeared on the stand of the Holy Sacrament in the Church of Santa Cruz in Cochin.[280] Diogo Soares was tried in the Inquisitional tribunal for not eating the flesh of the pig and observing Saturday celebrations, because of which he was accused of deviation from the faith.[281] Some were accused of blasphemy while others for disrespect to the faith and the articles of the faith.[282] All the new Christians, whose genuineness of faith and belief were questioned in one or another way were arrested and brought before the inquisitional tribunal of Cochin. After having tried them in Cochin, they were taken to Goa for further interrogations. Later they were taken to the Inquisition of Lisbon, where '*auto da-fe*' was carried out (in the Praça da Ribeira in Lisbon) and the accused were punished according to the gravity of their offences. Only one among them, Leonor Caldeira, the oldest of the group, was exempted from punishment.[283]

The economic result of this inquisitional process was that almost all the new Christian traders of Cochin, as in the case of Jácome de Olivares (a prominent trader of Cochin) who was sent to the prison of Lisbon in 1560 and was imprisoned for four long years, lost all their fortunes. The accused were stripped of all wealth at the very beginning.[284] Moreover, the prisoners had to pay for the costs of their own trials and support themselves, while these were going on, which again drained their resources.[285] The accused were to wear the penitentiary habit and were to be instructed in 'Things of the Faith' in prison. Jácome Olivares and his wife were to go in penitentiary habits in the mornings, to the monastery of Nossa Senhora da Graça, and in the evenings to the college of the Doctrine of the Faith (in Lisbon) in order to hear Masses and services.[286] Along with economic losses, these accused had to undergo public humiliation by wearing the penitentiary garb as well as by taking part in the '*auto-da-fe*'.

Thus, the existence of various ecclesiastical institutions (good and bad), in Cochin, shows that religion was a major force in the urban life of Cochin. The urban phenomena in Cochin, with a self-governing municipal system, a diverse but complex social pattern, a system of productive operations oriented towards port-life and shipbuilding, and a network of ecclesiastical institutions acting as cohesive and integrating forces in the city, was unique but vibrant. The economic role and functions of the Portuguese city of Cochin acquired an added momentum and diverse dimensions in its urban framework. The urban entity of Cochin did not constrain itself to the limits of the city wall, but went out to relate to the Indian Ocean economy with the exchange systems of the ports and nodal points in other parts of the world.

NOTES

1. Luis de Albuquerque (ed.), *Cronico do Descobrimento e Conquista da India*, p. 25.
2. O.K. Nambiar, op. cit., p. 34.
3. R.S. Whiteway, op. cit., p. 95.
4. Antonio Galvão, *Tratado dos Descobrimentos*, Porto, 1972, p. 98.
5. Ibid., pp. 97-9; Walter de Gray Birch, op. cit., pp. 6-7.
6. Gaspar Correia, *Lendas da India*, tom. I, cap. IV, pp. 393-5.
7. Fernão Lopes de Castanheda, op. cit., tom. I, liv. II, cap. XXVIII, pp. 273-4.
8. Gaspar Correia, *Lendas da India*, tom. I, cap. IV, pp. 393-5.
9. ANTT, *Gavetas*, 14, Maço 3, doc. 14.
10. Antonio Galvão, op. cit., pp. 99-100.
11. Gaspar Correia, *Lendas*, tom. I, cap. XV, pp. 625-33; cap. XVI, pp. 633-7.
12. Fernão Lopes de Castanheda, op. cit., tom. I, liv. II, cap. XXVIII, p. 274; Gaspar Correia, *Lendas*, tom. I, cap. XVII, p. 641.
13. Vitorino Magalhães Godinho, *Os Descobrimentos e a Economia Mundial*, vol. III (Editorial presença), Lisboa: 1982, p. 34.
14. The fortress of Cochin later came to constitute the walled structure that encircled the city. R.A. de Bulhão Pato, *Docummentos Remetidos da India ou Livro das Monções*, vol. V, Lisboa, 1935, doc. 1072, pp. 115-17; doc. 1169, pp. 308-9.
15. K.S. Mathew and Afzal Ahmad, *Emergence of Cochin*, doc. 53, pp. 73-82.
16. K.L. Bernard, *History of Fort Cochin*, pp. 5-9. This fact is testified and confirmed in the interview with the local people.
17. Francois Pyrard Laval, *The Voyages of Francois Pyrard of Laval to the East Indies, the Maldives, the Moluccas and Brazil*, trans. Albert Gray, London, 1887, p. 435.
18. K.S. Mathew and Afzal Ahmad, *Emergence of Cochin*, doc. 21, p. 34.
19. Ibid., doc. 56, p. 87.
20. BNL, *Fundo Geral*, Cod.1976, Letter of the Conde de Vidigueira sent to Philip II in 1599, fols. 158-9.
21. A.M. Mundadan, 'Town of Cochin and the Portuguese', in *II Seminario Internacional da Historia Indo Portuguesa, Actas*, Lisboa, 1985, p. 251
22. Antonio Bocarro, *Fortalezas, Cidades, povoações do Estado da India*, vol. II, p. 203.
23. Gaspar Correia, *Lendas*, tom. I, cap. X, p. 738.
24. Gaspar Correia, *Lendas*, tom. IV, cap. XVII, p. 705.
25. ANTT, *Inquisition de Lisboa*, Proc. no. 12292 de Luis Rodrigues de 1557, fols. 80-5 and Proc. no. 6369 de Maria Nunes de 1557, fols. 55-6 and 62-5.
26. ANTT, *Chancelaria de D. João III*, liv. 42, fol. 56, 'Capitania do Castelo de Cima de Cochin: Carta á Tristão de Sousa' Lisboa, 5 de Março de 1530.
27. ANTT, *Chancelaria de D. João III*, liv. 9, fol. 25 'Carta á Manuel Pereira Camelo', Palmela: 7 de Março de 1531.

28. ANTT, *Chancelaria de D. Sebastião e D. Henrique*, liv. 17, fol. 49 ' Capitania do Castelo de Cima de Cochin: Carta á Antonio Rebelo', Lisboa, 5 de Março de 1566.
29. K.P. Padmanabha Menon, *History of Kerala*, vol. I, p. 167.
30. 'Livro das Cidades e Fortalezas que a Coroa de Portugal tem nas partes da India e das Capitanias mais Cargos, que nelas há e da Importancia delles'. Pub. by Francisco Mendes da Luz, in *Boletim da Biblioteca da Universidade de Coimbra*, vol. XXI, Coimbra, 1953, pp. 70-1.
31. See Luis da Silveira (ed.), *Ensaio de Iconografia das Cidades do Ultramar*, vol. III, Lisboa: Images 720 and 724, pp. 414-15 Faria y Sousa, *Asia Portuguesa*, tom. I, p. 59.
32. Francois Pyrard de Laval, op. cit., p. 427. This area between the two Cochin roughly rcminds us of thc idca of 'opcn-space' mentioned by Jane Jacobs, which was deliberately kept empty as a space of separation. See Jane Jacobs, *Economy of Cities*, New York, 1969, p. 23; Harold Carter, *An Introduction to Urban Historical Geography*, London, 1983, p. 6.
33. Each of these communities used to live together in a cluster. This settlement pattern of native Cochin did not undergo much change, overtime.
34. See the plans of Cochin given in Luis da Silveira (ed.), *Ensaio de Iconografia das Cidades*, vol. III, pp. 413-16.
35. Ibid., pp. 414-16.
36. Ibid., Antonio Bocarro, op. cit., p. 198.
37. See the plans of Cochin given in Luis da Silveira (ed.), *Ensaio de Iconografia das Cidades,* vol. III, pp. 413-16.
38. Ibid., Francois Pyrard de Laval, op. cit., p. 427. This church in Vaipin was attached to a Franciscan Friary. Another important centre of devtion was the Miraculous Cross of Vaipin. Gervasis J. Mulakkara, op. cit., vol. I, p. 58.
39. K.S. Mathew and Afzal Ahmad, *Emergence of Cochin*, doc. 1, pp. 1-3.
40. Sanjay Subrahmanyam, *The Political Economy of Commerce*, p. 142.
41. K.S. Mathew and Afzal Ahmad, *Emergence of Cochin*, doc. 6, p. 18; doc. 24, p. 38; doc. 43, p. 60; doc. 70, p. 104; doc. 81, p. 120; doc. 82, p. 122.
42. Ibid., doc. 9, p. 22.
43. Miloslav Krasa, Joseph Polisensky and Peter Ratos (ed.), *European Expansion 1494-1519: The Voyages of Discovery in the Bratislava Manuscript*, Lyc. 515/8, Prague, 1986, p. 106.
44. Antonio da Silva Rego (ed.), *Documentação para a Historia*, vol. I, p. 340.
45. Ibid., p. 117.
46. 'Lembranças de Cousas da India' (Lembranças d'algumas cousas que sam passadas em Malaqua e assy outras partes da Imdea), in *Subsidios para a Historia da India Portuguesa*, edited by Rodrigo José de Lima Felner, pp. 10-11.
47. ANTT, *Gavetas*, 15, Maço 17, doc. 19.
48. Mathias Mundadan, *History of Christianity*, vol. I, Bangalore, 1984, p. 359.
49. Elaine Sanceau, *Colecçâo de São Lourenço*, vol. II, p. 321.
50. The Letter of the viceroy written to the king dated 16 January 1551, in ANTT, *Corpo Cronologico*, II, Maço 242, doc. 44.
51. M.N. Pearson, *Coastal Western India: Studies from the Portuguese Records*, New Delhi, 1981, p. 56.
52. Jesuit Archives of Rome, *Goa*, 32, fols. 653-5. See also Placid J. Podipara, *The Latin Rite Christian of Malabar*, Kottayam, 1986, pp. 40-1.
53. AHU, *Caixas da India,* Caixa 2, doc. 107. The letter of the city council of Cochin sent to Philip II of Portugal giving an account of the economic condition of Cochin dated

21 Dec. 1613, HAG, *Livro das Monções*, no. 12 (1613-17), fols. 254-80, dated March 1617.

54. Antonio Bocarro, op. cit., p. 199.
55. The size of population of the Portuguese soldiers in the fort depended on the season. It was at its largest during the period of the south-west monsoon from June to September, for during this time the strong offshore winds prevented patrolling along the western Indian coastline. M.N. Pearson, *Coastal Western India*, p. 42.
56. This was the estimation of 1670. See for details, H.K. Jacob (ed.), *De Nederlanders in Kerala, 1663-1701, De Memories en instructies betreffende het commandement Malabar van de Verenigde Ost Indische Compagnie*, The Hague, 1976, pp. lii-liii.
57. Sanjay Subrahmanyam, 'Cochin in Decline', p. 84.
58. D. Ferroli, *The Jesuits in Malabar*, vol. II, Bangalore, 1939, p. 290.
59. Livro das Cidades e Fortalezas, p. 71; Antonio Bocarro, op. cit., p. 199.
60. K.S. Mathew and Afzal Ahmad, *Emergence of Cochin*, doc. 14, p. 27.
61. Antonio da Silva Rego, *Documentação para a Historia* , doc. 105, p. 217.
62. M.N. Pearson, *Merchants and Rulers in Gujarat*, New Delhi, 1976, pp. 34-5.
63. M.N. Pearson, *Coastal Western India*, p. 52.
64. C.R. Boxer, *Portuguese Society in the Tropics: The Municipal Councils of Goa, Macao, Bahia and Luanda, 1510-1580*, Madison, 1965, p. 5.
65. M.N. Pearson, *Coastal Western India*, pp. 52-3.
66. The procedure is clearly specified in the *Regimento dos Officiais das Cidades, Villas e lugares destes Reynos Com Privilegio del Rey nosso Senhor,* Lisbon, 1504. For details see, C.R. Boxer, *The Portuguese Society in the Tropics*, pp. 5-8.
67. K.S. Mathew and Afzal Ahmad, *Emergence of Cochin*, doc. 80, pp. 119-20.
68. Ibid., doc. 10, pp. 23-4; doc. 25, p. 39; doc. 33, p. 47; doc. 44, pp. 61-2; doc. 52, pp. 71-2.
69. Ibid., doc. 38, pp. 53-4.
70. Ibid., doc. 9, p. 22; doc. 52, pp. 71-2.
71. Ibid., doc. 30, pp. 44-5.
72. Ibid., doc. 55, pp. 86.
73. Ibid., doc. 63, pp. 95-6.
74. Ibid., doc. 59, pp. 90-1; doc. 61, p. 93; doc. 63, pp. 95-6.
75. In 1551, the Municipal Council of Cochin employed the inspectors for maintaining tidiness in the city. Ibid., doc. 10, p. 23.
76. In 1575, the municipality appointed two judges to safeguard the interests of the orphans. Ibid., doc. 45, p. 62.
77. Ibid., doc. 33, pp. 47-8.
78. C.R. Boxer, *The Portuguese Society in the Tropics*, p. 10.
79. K.S. Mathew and Afzal Ahmad, *Emergence of Cochin*, doc. 67, pp. 101-2.
80. C.R. Boxer, *The Portuguese Society in the Tropics*, p. 10.
81. K.S. Mathew and Afzal Ahmad, *Emergence of Cochin,* doc. 14, p. 27.
82. Ibid., doc. 35, p. 49.
83. Ibid., doc. 18, p. 31.
84. Ibid., doc. 7, pp. 19-21.
85. Such powers were included in the appointment orders. See ANTT, *Chancelaria de D. João III*, liv. 9, fol. 21v, 'Capitania de cochin:Carta á Pedro Vaz', Palmela, 24 March 1531, ANTT, *Chancelaria de D. Sebastian*, liv. 15, fol. 24v, 'Capitania de Cochin: Carta á João da Foneseca', Lisboa, 2 March 1564.
86. Antonio Bocarro, op. cit., p. 199.
87. Simão Botelho, 'O Tombo do *Estado da India'*, pp. 18-21; *Livro das Cidades e Fortalezas*, p. 72; Antonio Bocarro, op. cit., pp. 199-201.

88. K.S. Mathew and Afzal Ahmad, *Emergence of Cochin*, doc. 9, p. 22.
89. Alfredo Botelho de Sousa, *Subsidios para a Historia Militar Maritima da India*, Lisboa, 1930, p. 38.
90. Antonio Bocarro, op. cit., p. 204.
91. Gaspar Correia, *Lendas*, tom. I, cap. VII, p. 410.
92. Antonio da Silva Rego, *Documentação para a Historia*, vol. I, doc. 10, pp. 40-2.
93. Gaspar Correia, *Lendas*, tom. II, cap. XVIII, p. 139.
94. Ibid., tom. II, cap. VII, p. 488.
95. Henrique Lopez de Mendonça, *Estudo sobre Navios Portugueses nos Séculos XV e XVI*, Lisboa, 1892, p. 10.
96. R.A. de Bulhão Pato, *Cartas . . .*, tom. II, pp. 430-41.
97. Gaspar Correia, *Lendas*, tom. II, p. 488.
98. John Correia Afonso (ed.), *Intrepid Itinerant: Manuel Godinho and his Journey from India to Portugal in 1663*, Bombay, 1990, p. 73.
99. *As Gavetas da Torre do Tombo*, vol. X, doc. 5575, p. 661.
100. Elaine Sanceau, *Colecção de São Lourenço*, vol. II, doc. 4, p. 4.
101. M.N. Pearson, *Merchants and Rulers in Gujarat*, pp. 37-9.
102. K.S. Mathew and Afzal Ahmad, *Emergence of Cochin*, doc. 20, p. 33.
103. Ibid., doc. 42, pp. 58-9; doc. 33, p. 47.
104. Ibid., doc. 34, p. 48.
105. K.S. Mathew, 'Cochin and the Portuguese Trade with India during the Sixteenth Century', in *Indica*, March 1989, p. 80.
106. HAG, *Livros das Monções*, no. 7 (1600-1603), fols. 113-15. Royal letter sent to Aires de Saldanha, dated 7 February 1602.
107. *Boletim da Filmoteca Ultramarina Portuguesa*, no. 6, p. 558.
108. C.R. Boxer, *Portuguese India in the Mid-seventeenth Century*, Delhi, 1980, p. 28.
109. K.S. Mathew, 'Money Economy in the Portuguese India, 1510-1640', in *The Journal of the Gujarat Research Society*, vols. 46/47, July, Bombay, 1984, p. 25.
110. ANTT, *Chancelaria de D. João III*, liv. 16, fol. 31v, 'Carta á Fernando De Silva mestre do moeda de Cochin', Setubal, 27 March 1532.
111. K.S. Mathew, 'Money Economy in the Portuguese India', p. 25.
112. Antonio Nunez, 'Livro dos Pesos da Ymdia, e assy Medidas e Moedas Escripto em 1554', in *Subsidios para a Historia da India Portuguesa*, edited by Rodrigo José de Lima Felner, p. 62.
113. ANTT, *Chancelaria de D. João III*, liv. 68, fol. 42v 'Carta á João Gomes mestre da moeda de Cochin', Lisboa, 4 March 1552.
114. K.S. Mathew, 'Indo-Portuguese Coinage in the Sixteenth and Early Seventeenth Centuries', in *The Journal of the Numismatic Society of India*, vol. XLVI, 1984, p. 122.
115. K.S. Mathew and Afzal Ahmad, *Emergence of Cochin*, doc. 44, p. 61.
116. Fenelon Rebello, 'Early Indo-Portuguese Coins', in *International Seminar on Indo-Portuguese History*, Bombay, 27 November 1978, pp. 39-40.
117. A.C. Teixeira de Aragão, *Desrição Geral em Nome dos Reis e Regentes e Governadores de Portugal*, vol. III, Porto, 1964, p. 102.
118. For detailed description of the living houses in the city, see Antonio Bocarro, op. cit., p. 199.
119. K.S. Mathew, *Portuguese Trade*, pp. 216-17.
120. Antonio Bocarro, op. cit., pp. 119-207; see the plans of the city in Luis da Silveira, *Ensaio de Iconografia das Cidades*, vol. III, pp. 413-16.
121. K.S. Mathew, 'Cochin and the Portuguese Trade', p. 80.
122. G.V. Scammell, 'Indigenous Assistance in the Establishment of Portuguese Power in

Asia in the Sixteenth Century', in *Modern Asian Studies*, 14, I, Cambridge, 1984, p. 3.

123. C.R. Boxer, *Mary and Misogyny: Women in Iberian Expansion Overseas, 1415-1815*, London, 1975, pp. 63-9. At the beginning women were not allowed to come to India. When some women surreptitiously made a voyage, Vasco da Gama punished them severely. R.S. Whiteway, op. cit., p. 20. It was only during the time of the Regent Catherine of Austria (1557-62) that women and that too some orphan girls were sent to India so that they could find husbands, Josef Wicki, 'The Portuguese Padroado in India in the Sixteenth Century and Francis Xavier', in E.R. Hambye and H.C. Perumalil (eds.), *Christianity in India*, Alleppey, 1972, p. 47.
124. K.M. Panikkar, *A History of Kerala*, p. 84.
125. Antonio da Silva Rego, *Documentação para a Historia*, vol. I, doc. 44, p. 118.
126. Ibid., doc. 76, p. 171.
127. Ibid., doc. 106, pp. 22-221.
128. This link with the Muslim relatives helped the *casados* later to collect commodities for their trade and develop the commerce which the Portuguese authorities often called 'illegal'. A detailed discussion on this, is given in Chapter IV.
129. Antonio da Silva Rego, *Documentação para a Historia*, vol. I, doc. 75, p. 170.
130. Ibid., vol. I, doc. 108, p. 225.
131. Ibid., vol. I, doc, 10, p. 44.
132. Ibid., vol. I, doc. 110, pp. 232-9.
133. This kind of division among the clergy was testified by Visscher's account. See Visscher's Letter sent from Malabar, in K.P. Padmanabha Menon, *History of Kerala*, vol. II, p. 38.
134. Antonio da Silva Rego, *Documentação para a Historia*, vol. XII, pp. 577-81; M.N. Pearson, *Coastal Western India*, pp. 41-2.
135. Ibid., p. 42.
136. C.R. Boxer, *Race Relation in the Portuguese Colonial Empire 1415-1825*, Oxford, 1963, p. 58. The *casado* population was not a clearly defined group: it often shaded off into the bulk of the native population. M.N. Pearson, *Coastal Western India*, p. 52.
137. Gideon Sjoberg, *The Pre-Industrial City*, New York, 1960, pp. 97-8.
138. R.A. de Bulhão Pato, *Cartas*, tom. I, pp. 44-5.
139. Antonio da Silva Rego, *Documentação para a Historia*, doc. 65, p. 159. On 16 July 1512 the provision was raised to one and a half *fardo* rice. Ibid., doc. 66, p. 160.
140. Ibid., doc. 107, pp. 222-3.
141. Antonio da Silva Rego, *Documentação para a Historia*, doc. 148, p. 355. Pe. Sebastian Pires, the vicar of Cochin, in his letter dated 8 January 1518, places almost the same request before the king of Portugal. Ibid., doc. 144, p. 341.
142. Ibid., doc. 194, pp. 419-21.The primer or the *cartilha* found in the Biblioteca Nacional de Lisboa has the following contents:
-The art for learning how to read.
-The prayer 'Our Father' in Latin and native language.
-The prayer 'Hail Mary' in Latin and native language.
-The 'Creed' in Latin and native language.
-The 'Confession' of Holy Mass.
-The prayers before and after the meals.
-The articles of faith made by the apostles and the commandments of the church.
-The sacrament of the Holy mother church, mortal sins and venial sins and the way of ablution.
-The seven mortal sins.

See, BNL, *Fundo Geral*, Cod. 3837, 'Cartilha para ensinar a ler'.

143. A. Meersman, *The Ancient Franciscan Province in India*, Bangalore, 1971, p. 314.
144. Georg Schurhammer, *Francis Xavier,* vol. II, p. 162.
145. A. Meersman, op. cit., p. 314; Georg Schurhammer, *Francis Xavier*, vol. II, p. 405 and its footnote 2.
146. Frei Paulo da Trindade, *Conquista Espiritual do Oriente*, vol. I, Lisboa, 1962, p. 264.
147. Antonio da Silva Rego, *Documentação para a Historia*, vol. V, doc. 75, pp. 401-9.
148. Gervasis J. Mulakara, op. cit., pp. 91-2. See also Josef Wicki, *Documenta Indica*, vol. I, Rome, 1948, pp. 417 and 521.
149. Antonio da Silva Rego, *Documentação para a Historia*, vol. IV, doc. 36, p. 183.
150. Ibid., p. 184.
151. Gervasis J. Mulakara, op. cit., pp. 92-3.
152. K.L. Bernard, 'Fort Cochin under the Portuguese', in the *Souvenir of Fifth International Seminar on Indo-Portuguese History*, Cochin, 1989, p. 9.
153. Fernão Guerreiro, *Relação Anual das Coisas que fizeram os Padres da Companhia de Jesus nas suas Missões(1604-1606)*, tom. II. cap. VIII, Coimbra, 1934, p. 334.
154. Antonio da Silva Rego, *Documentação para a Historia*, vol. IX, doc. 40, p. 288; doc. 60, p. 416.
155. These theatrical pieces having connections with the Jesuits of Coimbra were popularized in Kerala by Fr. Sebastião Pires and Fr. Francisco Vaz. See, Luis Francisco Rebelo, *Historia do Teatro Portugues,* Lisboa, 1968, p. 39.
156. K.S. Mathew, *Portuguese Trade*, p. 222.
157. Joaquim Verissimo Serrão, *Historia de Portugal*, vol. III, Lisboa, 1978, p. 158.
158. Later *Misericordias* appeared in Cannanore, Cranganore and Quilon. All of them, including the *Misericordia* of Cochin worked in correlation with the hospitals of the locality. Luis de Pina, *Expansão Hospitalar Portuguesa Ultramarina, Séculos XVI & XVII*, Lisboa, 1943, pp. 31-5.
159. Antonio da Silva Rego, *Documentação para a Historia*, vo. II, doc. 52, pp. 111-15.
160. A. Meersman, 'Notes on the Charitable Institutions the Portuguese Established in India', in *Indian Church History Review*, vol. II, no. 2, Bangalore, December 1971, pp. 96-7; Mathias Mundadan, *History of Christianity in India*, vol. I, pp. 370 and 516.
161. Simão Botelho, 'O Tombo do *Estado da India*', pp. 22-3.
162. Jean Aubin, 'Le Orçamento do *Estado da India* de Antonio Abreu (1574)', in *Studia*, vol. IV, Lisboa, 1959, p. 260.
163. Luiz de Figueiredo Falcão, *Livro em que se contem toda a Fazenda e Real Patrimonio dos Reinos de Portugal, India e Ilhas Adjacentes e outras Particularidades*, Lisboa, 1859, p. 109.
164. A. de Magalhães Basto, *Historia da Santa Casa da Misericordia do Porto*, vol. I, Porto, 1934, p. 457.
165. Antonio da Silva Rego, *Documentação para a Historia*, vol. III, doc. 94, pp. 442-7.
166. ANTT, *Chancelaria de Filipe* II, liv. 23, fol. 330, 'Misericordia de Cochim, Alvara para gozar os Privilegios', Lisboa, 23 February 1612.
167. K.S. Mathew and Afzal Ahmad, *Emergence of Cochin*, doc. 42, p. 58.
168. Sanjay Subrahmanyam, *The Political Economy of Commerce*, p. 225.
169. R.A. de Bulhão Pato, *Documentos Remetidos da India ou Livro das Monções*, tom. I, Lisboa, 1880, doc. 56, p. 157.
170. Ibid., tom. IV, doc. 844, p. 74 and tom. V, doc. 1192, pp. 344-5.
171. Gaspar Correia, *Lendas*, tom. I, cap. XII, p. 217.
172. Luis de Pina, *Expansão Hospitalar*, p. 33.

173. Luis da Silveira, *Ensaio de Iconografia das Cidades do Ultramar*, vol. III, plans. 720 and 724, pp. 414-15.
174. For details see, Antonio da Silva Rego, *Documentação para a Historia das Missões*, vol. I, doc. 63, pp. 154-6.
175. Ibid., vol. I, doc. 12, p. 51.
176. ANTT, *Chancelaria de D. João III*, liv. 44, fol. 150v, 'Cirurgião do Hospital de Cochim. Carta á Manuel Duarte', Lisboa, 15 January 1533.
177. ANTT, *Chancelaria de D. João III*, liv. 62, fol. 27v, 'Cirurgião do Hospital de Cochim. Carta á Simão da Rosa', Lisboa, 8 March 1540.
178. Antonio da Silva Rego, *Documentação para a Historia*, vol. I, doc. 67, p. 161.
179. Ibid., vol. I, doc. 12, p. 51.
180. Ibid., vol. I, doc. 68, p. 162.
181. Ibid., vol. I, doc. 99, p. 206 and doc. 129, p. 280.
182. ANTT, *Chancelaria de D. João III*, liv. 9, fol. 21v, 'Capitania de Cochim Carta á Pedro Vaz', Palmela, 24 March 1531.
183. A. Meersman, 'Notes on the Charitable Institutions', p. 96.
184. Antonio da Silva Rego, *Documentação para a Historia*, vol. IV, doc. 6, p. 27.
185. Simão Botelho, O Tombo do Estado, pp. 22-3.
186. Antonio da Silva Rego, *Documentação para a Historia*, vol. IX, doc. 40, p. 27l; doc. 60, p. 421.
187. Ibid., vol. II, doc. 103, p. 331; vol. III, doc. 94, p. 443.
188. Luis de Figueiredo Falcão, op. cit., p. 109.
189. Antonio Bocarro, op. cit., p. 202.
190. William Foster (ed.), *Early Travels in India, 1583-1613*, New Delhi, 1985, p. 44.
191. For the location of *Lazaretto*, see the plans of Cochin in Luis da Silveira, *Ensaio de Iconografia das Cidades do Ultramar*, vol. III, p. 415.
192. Antonio Bocarro, op. cit., p. 199.
193. Francois Pyrard de Laval, op. cit., p. 429.
194. Ibid., pp. 429-30.
195. Ibid., pp. 431-2. The French equivalent of this demy *tanga* was 5 *sols*. But the value of this coin was such that it was sufficient for one's daily sustenance, during this period. Tavernier writes: 'while the Portuguese held Cochin, one could live better with 5 *sols* than under the Dutch with 10 *sols*'. V. Ball (ed.), *Travels in India by Jean Baptista Tavernier*, vol. I, New Delhi, 1977, p. 194.
196. Francois Pyrard de Laval, op. cit., p. 429.
197. K.S. Mathew and Afzal Ahmad, *Emergence of Cochin*, doc. 75, pp. 113-14.
198. Antonio da Silva Rego, *Documentação para a Historia*, vol. I, doc. 10, p. 44.
199. Ibid., vol. I, doc. 61, p. 148.
200. Antonio da Silva Rego, *Documentação para a Historia*, vol. I, doc. 10, p. 44
201. K.S. Mathew and Afzal Ahmad, *Emergence of Cochin*, doc. 16, p. 29.
202. Ibid., doc. 19, p. 32.
203. Josef Wicki, 'The Portuguese Padroado in India', p. 49.
204. Thomas Pallippurathukkunnel, *A Double Regime in the Malabar Church*, Alwaye, 1982, pp. 3-4. Gervasis J. Mulakara, op. cit., pp. 25-6.
205. Casimiro Christovam da Nazareth, *Mitras Lusitanas no Oriente Catalogo Chronologico-Historico dos Prelados de Egreja Metropolitana de Goa e das Dioceses Suffraganeas com a Recopilação das Ordenanças por Elles Emittidas e Summario dos Factos Notaveis da Historia Ecllesiastica de Goa*, Nove Goa, 1887, pp. 1-2.
206. Fernão Lopes de Castanheda, op. cit., liv. IV, cap. XIII, p. 893; R.A. de Bulhão Pato, *Cartas...*, tom. II, p. 157. See also the plans of Cochin given in Luis da Silveira,

Ensaio de Ioconografia, vol. III, pp. 414-16. It seems that the German soldiers used this church only initially, when they formed a considerable portion of the Portuguese fighting force.

207. Antonio da Silva Rego, *Documentação para a Historia*, vol. I, doc. 20, pp. 72-3.
208. Ibid., vol. I, doc. 105, pp. 216-17.
209. Ibid., vol. I, doc. 112, pp. 251-2.
210. Gervasis J. Mulakara, op. cit., p. 49.
211. Frei Paulo da Trindade, *Conquista Espiritual do Orient*, vol. I, Lisboa, MCMLXII, pp. 102-3.
212. Gervasis J. Mulakara, op. cit., pp. 51-2.
213. The detailed list of the books is given by Antonio da Silva Rego, *Documentos para a Historia*, vol. I, doc. 143, pp. 336-9.
214. Frei Paulo da Trindade, *Conquista Espiritual*, vol. I, pp. 104-5.
215. R.A. de Bulhão Pato, *Documentos Remetidos da India ou Livro das Monções*, tom. III, doc. 571, pp. 284-5.
216. Antonio da Silva Rego, *Documentação para a Historia*, vol. II, doc. 105, pp. 347-8 and vol. III, doc. 39, p. 128.
217. F. Felix Lopes, 'Os Franciscanos no Orient Portugues de 1584 á 1590', in *Studia*, Lisboa, 1962, p. 44.
218. Joaquim Verissimo Serrão, *Historia de Portugal*, vol. III, p. 149.
219. Antonio Bocarro, op. cit., p. 202.
220. A Meersman, 'Development of the Church under the Padroado' in E.R. Hambye and H.C. Perumalil (eds.), *Christianity in India*, p. 69.
221. Gervasis J. Mulakara, op. cit., p. 98.
222. Fernão Lopez de Castanheda, op. cit., liv. I, cap. LXI, p. 130.
223. Antonio da Silva Rego, *Documentaç'ão para a Historia*, vol. I, doc. 200, p. 440.
224. Gervasis J. Mulakara, op. cit., p. 117.
225. Antonio da Silva Rego, *Documentação para a Historia*, vol. VI, doc. 38, pp. 291-2.
226. Ibid., vol. VI, doc. 38, pp. 297-9.
227. Diogo Barbosa Machado, *Biblioteca Lusitana*, tom. II, Lisboa, 1747, p. 818.
228. Antonio da Silva Rego, *Documentação para a Historia*, vol. V, doc. 49, pp. 379-80.
229. AHU, *Caixas da India*, Caixa 6, doc. 142, dated 2 July 1621, fol. 9.
230. Antonio Bocarro, op. cit., p. 202.
231. Fortunato de Almeida, *Historia da Igreja em Portugal*, vol. II, Porto, 1968, p. 169.
232. Gervasis J. Mulakara, op. cit., pp. 90-1; Josef Wicki, 'The Portuguese Padroado', pp. 62-3
233. Josef Wicki (ed.), *Documenta Indica*, vol. I, doc. 81, Rome, 1948, p. 521.
234. Gervasis J. Mulakara, op. cit., p. 65.
235. Josef Wicki, *Documenta Indica*, vol. III, doc. 118, p. 787.
236. Antonio da Silva Rego, *Documentação para a Historia*, vol. VIII, doc. 25, p. 98.
237. Antonio Bocarro, op. cit, p. 202.
238. ANTT, *Catório dos Jesuitas*, Maço 89, docs. 21 and 23.
239. Josef Wicki, *Documenta Indica*, vol. XVII, p. 13.
240. Placid J. Podipara, *The Latin Rite Christian of Malabar*, Kottayam, 1986, pp. 40-1; see also D. Ferroli, *The Jesuits in Malabar*, vol. II, Bangalore, 1951, p. 283.
241. AHU, *Caixas da India*, Caixa 6, doc. 142, dated 2 July 1621, fol. 8.
242. Josef Wicki, 'The Portuguese Padroado', p. 55.
243. See the plans of Cochin in Luis da Silveira, *Ensaio de Iconografia das Cidades*, vol. III, pp. 414-15.
244. AHU, *Caixas da India*, Caixa 6, doc. 142, dated 2 July 1621, fol. 10.

245. Antonio Bocarro, op. cit., p. 202.
246. AHU, *Caixas da India*, Caixa 9, doc. 17, dated 3 February 1626, fol. 1.
247. R. Wernham (ed.), *The New Cambridge Modern History: The Counter-Reformation and Price Revolution, 1559-1600*, vol. III, Cambridge, 1968, p. 549.
248. Joaquim Verissimo Serrão, *Historia de Portugal*, vol. III, p. 152.
249. ANTT, *Cartas dos Vice-Reis da India*, doc. 34 '*parecer dos letrados sobre negocio dos Christãos da India*'.
250. BNL, *Fundo Geral*, Cod. 737, *Erecção da villa em Cidade* (de Cochim), *Creação do bishpado á pedido de D. Sebastião 1557*, fols. 271-4.
251. Ibid., Fortunato de Almeida, *Historia da Igreja em Portugal*, vol. II, Porto, 1918, p. 25.
252. Antonio Castilho, *A Cronica de D. João III*, published by Joaquim Verissimo Serrão, Paris, 1970, p. 356.
253. Gervasis J. Mulakara, op. cit., p. 19.
254. Josef Wicki, 'The Portuguese Padroado', p. 54.
255. BNL, *Fundo Geral*, Cod. 737, *Erecção da Villa em Cidade* (de Cochim), *Creação do bishpado á pedido de D. Sebastião* 1557, fol. 273.
256. ANTT, *Chancelaria de D. Sebastião*, liv. 19, fol. 45, 'Alvara de Esmola para a fabrica da Sé', Lisboa, 28 February 1566.
257. Luiz de Figueiredo Falcão, *Livro em que se contem toda a Fazenda*..., pp. 108-9.
258. Antonio Bocarro, op. cit., p. 201.
259. K.S. Mathew and Afzal Ahmad, *Emergence of Cochin*, doc. 5, p. 11.
260. Sieur de Rennefort as quoted by K.P. Padmanabha Menon, *History of Kerala*, vol. I, p. 173.
261. See F. Figueiredo, 'Descripsão de Cochin' in the *Souvenir of the Fifth International Seminar on Indo-Portuguese History*, Cochin, 1989 (without page number); Luis da Silveira, *Ensaio de Iconografia das Cidades do Ultramar*, vol. III, p. 415; Antonio Bocarro, op. cit., p. 201; For details on the church used by the Germans, see Antonio da Silva Rego, *Documentação para a Historia das Missões*, vol. I, doc. 105, p. 217; Pius Malekandathil, *The Germans, the Portuguese and India*, Münster, 1999.
262. For details, see José Alberto Rodrigues da Silva Tavim, 'Outras Gentes em Outras Rotas: Judeus e Cristãos-Novos de Cochim-entre Santa Cruz de Cochim e Mattancherry, entre o Império Português e o Medio Oriente', a paper presented in *VIII Seminario Internacional de Historia Indo-Portuguesa-Angra de Heroismo*, 7-11 de Junho de 1996, pp. 4-9; Anant Kakba Priolkar, *The Goa Inquisition*, Bombay, 1961, p. 22; Ana Cannas da Cunha, *A Inquisição no Estado da Índia: Origens (1539-60)*, Lisboa, 1995, pp. 217-19; ANTT, *Inquisição de Lisboa*, proc. 7296, fols. 4-6; proc.12292, fols. 3-5; proc. 5808, fols. 3-5
263. ANTT, *Corpo Cronologico*, I, Maço 66, doc. 96. In 1547 Pero de Sequeira complained from Cochin to D. João de Castro about the active involvement of the new-Christians in the commercial activities of Cochin. Elaine Sanceau, *Colecção de São Lourenço*, vol. II, Lisboa, 1975, pp. 211-12.
264. Georg Schurhammer and Josef Wicki (ed.), *Epistolae S.Francisi Xaverii aliaque eius Scripta*, vol. I, Rome, 1945, pp. 346-7.
265. Luis de Panamo, *De Origine et Progressy Officii Sanctae Inqvisitionis eiusque dignitate et Vtilitate, De Romani Pontificis Potestate et Delegata Inqvisitorum: Edicto Fidei, et Ordine Iudiciario Sancti Officii, Quaestiones decem*, L.II, Matriti, Ex Typographia Regia, 1598, tit. 2, cap. XVIIII, p. 237.
266. See the Letter of Belchior Carneiro sent to Cardinal D. Henrique, Goa, dated 20 December 1559 in Josef Wicki, *Documenta Indica*, vol. IV, 1956, pp. 5-13.

267. See the Letter of D. Gonçalo da Silveira sent to Pe.Miguel de Torres, Goa, dated 19 December 1559, in Josef Wicki, *Documenta Indica*, vol. III, 1954, pp. 758-78.
268. The New Christians like Jácome de Olivares, Luis Rodrigues, etc., of Cochin were arrested in Malacca in 1557, on orders of Pero Gonçalves, the vicar of Cochin, as they were implicated in the inquiry conducted by D. Gonçalo da Silveira. See. ANTT, *Inquisição de Lisboa*, Proc. 5265 de Jácome de Olivares, fol. 123; Proc. 12292 de Luis Rodrigues, fol. 100; José Alberto Rodrigues da Silva Tavim, 'From Setubal to the Sublime Porte: The Wanderings of Jácome de Olivares, New Christian and Merchant of Cochin, 1540-1571', in Sanjay Subrahmanyam and Kenneth McPherson (eds.), *Santa Barbara Portuguese Studies*, vol. II, California, 1995, pp. 97-8.
269. It was in 1560 that the Inquisition of Goa took official shape. Antonio Baião, *A Inquisição de Goa*, vol. I, Lisboa, 1930, p. 35.
270. Josef Wicki, *Documenta Indica*, vol. III, pp. 758-75; ANTT, *Inquisição de Lisboa*, Proc. no. 7296 de Leonor Caldeira, fol. 11.
271. ANTT, *Inquisição de Lisboa*, Proc. no. 5808 de Grçea Lopes, fols. 23-30, 45 and 51.
272. Diogo do Couto refers to the steps taken against the new Christians of Cochin. Diogo do Couto, *Da Asia, Decada* VI, liv. VII, cap. V, pp. 92-3.
273. For the inquisitional proceedings connected with the New Christians of Cochin, see ANTT, *Inquisição de Lisboa*, Proc. nos. 5265; 12292; 4656; 7246; 7296; 10096. About 20 New Christians including 9 women and 11 men were accused of going back to Judaism.
274. For example, see the *proçesso* of Leonar Caldeira. ANTT, *Inquisição de Lisboa*, Proc. no. 7246 de Leonar Caldeira de 1557, fols. 11-12.
275. For details on Jácome de Olivares, see José Alberto Rodrigues da Silva Tavim, 'From Setubal to the Sublime Porte', pp. 97-119.
276. For details about the matriarchal family of Leonar Caldeira, see ANTT, *Inquisição de Lisboa*, Proc. no. 7296 de Leonar Caldeira, fols. 4; 29-33; 37-41. Ana Cannas da Cunha, op. cit., pp. 222-3.
277. ANTT, *Inquisição de Lisboa*, Proc. no. 3836, fols. 3-4 and Ana Cannas da Cunha, op. cit., p. 219.
278. ANTT, *Inquisição de Lisboa*, Proc. no. 12292, fol. 3-5; 17-22, 33-8; 77-9; Ana Cannas da Cunha, op. cit., p. 218.
279. ANTT, *Inquisição de Lisboa*, Proc. no. 7296, fol. 77v; ANTT, *Inquisição de Lisboa*, Proc. no. 12292 de Luis Rodrigues, fols. 50-85; Proc. no. 6369 de Maria Nunes, fols. 55-6 and 65-5. There were three chief synagogues in Cochin: The *Kadavumbhagam synagogue* (situated near the sea), the *Thekkumbhagam synagogue* (for the black Jews) and the *Kochangadi synagogue* built in the seventeenth century, especially after the arrival of the Castilhan Jews. K.P. Padmanabha Menon, *History of Kerala*, vol. II, pp. 527-8
280. ANTT, *Inquisição de Lisboa*, Proc. no. 5265, fol. 83.
281. ANTT, *Inquisição de Lisboa*, Proc. no. 185 de Diogo Soares, fols. 116-42.
282. See Josef Wicki, *Documenta Indica*, vol. IV, pp. 10-11; ANTT, *Inquisição de Lisboa*, Proc. no. 5808, fol. 53.
283. ANTT, *Inquisição de Lisboa*, Proc. no. 7246, fols. 12, 138-9.
284. ANTT, *Inquisição de Lisboa*, Proc. no. 5265, fol. 125.
285. José Alberto Rodrigues da Silva Tavim, 'From Setubal to the Sublime Porte', p. 116.
286. Ibid. ANTT, *Inquisição de Lisboa*, Proc. no. 5265, fols. 120-4.

CHAPTER IV

The Portuguese and the Intra-Asian Trade in Cochin: 1500-1570

With the arrival of the Portuguese, the trade in Cochin assumed new proportions and direction. Replacing its commercial rival, Calicut, Cochin had come to centre stage to play the dominant economic role in the Indian Ocean world. The transformation experienced in its trading activities can be studied under four categories: namely, 1. Local trade, 2. Inter-local trade, 3. Intra-Asian trade, and 4. Indo-European trade. The local trade catered more to urban needs, which increased with the widening of the city boundaries. The inter-local trade centred in Cochin aimed at accruing profit not only by supplying what the city and the *Estado da India*[1] required, but also by the exchange of commodities in the adjacent regions. The Portuguese participated in the intra-Asian trade both directly, by way of direct investment and indirectly, by way of controlling the movements of native ships and merchants. Though the crown also participated to a certain extent, in the country trade, most of the transactions were carried out by licenced traders and illicit profit-makers. However, the Portuguese crown gave the highest priority to the Indo-European trade. This chapter deals primarily with the various strands of intra-Asian trade conducted in Cochin during the period up to 1570 when King Sebastian of Portugal officially renounced the royal spice monopoly.[2]

1. LOCAL TRADE

With the expansion of the city of Cochin and the increase in the number of city dwellers, the needs and demands for more and more commodities increased simultaneously. Both in Portuguese Cochin and in its native counterpart, various merchants began to set up shops to exploit the opportunities offered by local trade. Right from the early days of Portuguese settlement, Afonso de Albuquerque encouraged the *casados*[3] to conduct the local trade and to set up as bakers, shoemakers, tavern-keepers, and tailors.[4] Rice and other food materials imported to the city formed the major commodity of transaction. Since rice was very scarce in this area, about 40,000 *candis* of rice were brought every year to Cochin. In order to avoid its hoarding and diversion to places where it could be sold at a higher price, the municipality took up the responsibility of conducting rice-trade in Cochin through retail shops.[5] The bazaar situated near the *pezo da pimenta*, the *Rua de Sa Domingos* and *Sapateiros* situated near the Dominican monastery, *Rua Direita* situated near the important institutions like the *Misericordia*, Bishop's House, Municipal Council and the Cathedral church, *Rua de Coul* situated near St. Sebastian's church, *Rua de Seda* situated near *Rua de Coulo*, *Rua dagoadolupe* situated near the Goadalupe became the important centres of local trade.[6] The most thriving among them was *Rua Direita* because of its proximity to the principal urban institutions. The wealthy merchants established their business houses in this area. The new Christians who came to Cochin from Portugal by the 1530s were attracted by this mercantile pocket. Jácome de Olivares, who came in 1540 from Setubal (in Portugal),[7] set up a commercial centre in *Rua Direita* and began to sell pitch, porcelain as well as *pau-da-China.*[8] Manuel Rodrigues, another new Christian of the city, established a business house close by to sell silk, clothes, carpets and other commodities.[9] He used to sell velvets and silk to the monks of the Dominican order of Cochin.[10] Leonor Caldeira also developed her commercial establishments on this principal street of Cochin. She was assisted by her daughter Clara and a black female slave in her business, which dealt with, 'all varieties of commodities'.[11] Simão Nunes, the son of Leonor Caldeira following the family tradition of trade established a commercial centre near the same *Rua Direita* for trading in corals, camphor and other items.[12] He stated before the inquisitorial court of Lisbon, that a Jew of native Cochin called Moisès Real, who was referred to as 'the greatest known merchant of India', had two business centres in Portuguese Cochin: one in *Rua Direita* and the other in the *Casa do Vigario.*[13] It shows that the Portuguese as well as non-Portuguese had begun, by this time, to invest considerably in the local trade. But it also seems that with the imprisonment of the new Christian traders of Cochin in 1557 and with the establishment of the Inquisition in Cochin, the Semitic merchants were deprived of opportunities to participate in the local trade of city.[14]

Eventually Muslim and Kanarese merchants began to invest in this flourishing local trade. They put up shops inside Portuguese Cochin. The authorities who observed the bulk of profit which these merchants were amassing began to extract from them one *pardao* by way of taxation.[15] Commodities ranging from the category of necessities of life up to most sophisticated and luxurious goods were transacted in the local trade. Slave trade was equally active and vibrant. Young people from Sri Lanka, Africa, Pegu (in Burma) and China were brought to Cochin and sold into slavery. Most of these slaves were used for domestic work.[16] Some of the natives were purchased in Cochin and were taken to foreign cities to be sold at high prices, as was the case with a certain Constança, a Malayali from Cochin, who was taken by Jácome de Olivares to Malacca for re-sale.[17] With the intensification of urban growth, the pattern of local trade began to be re-designed in such a way as to incorporate the diverse needs and interests of the consumers in Cochin.

2. INTER-LOCAL TRADE

Inter-local trade became a necessity as Cochin, for its existence, had to depend on other regions. A good many of the commodities which the city of Cochin required, had to be imported from outside. In the initial phase, the natives played an active role in the inter-local trade. The *Marakkars* from the Coromandel coast, who had established themselves in Cochin before the arrival of the Portuguese, were the greatest suppliers of rice and textiles to this city.[18] This powerful clan monopolized the import of Coromandel rice, which was cheaper than the Kanara rice,[19] to Malabar. The family network and partnership that was extended along the rice-belt of the Kaveri region enabled the *Marakkars* to take part in the inter-local trade and to make regular supply of food materials to their customers in Cochin and Cannanore.[20]

These *Marakkar* merchants had not only a common trade interest, but also group solidarity and partnership: they were all friends and relatives. One of the powerful trader in the Kaveri Delta was the brother of Nine Marakkar, a merchant of Cochin. With the help of these family networks, the *Marakkar* merchants used to bring in rice, textiles and other goods from the various ports of Coromandel like Kunimedu, Kilakarai and Kayalpatanam to Cochin.[21] Mame (Muhammed) Marakkar was the chief of all the merchants of Cochin. He built a big warehouse in the native Cochin to store grain (which he brought from the Coromandel coast) so as to have ready constant supplies for the city-dwellers.[22] In 1503-4, when the Zamorin tried to block the rice supply and thus create an artificial famine in Cochin as a part of war-tactics, Duarte Pacheco made friend with Mame (Muhammed) Marakkar to ensure a regular supply of provisions to the city.[23] The *Marakkar* clan continued to be very active in the inter-local trade supplying the Cochinites with the necessities of life until the end of the Albuquerque era, and until the emergence of the *casado* private traders of the Cochin, who were looking for every opportunity to replace the former.

Later the dominant role in the inter-local trade was taken up by the *casados* who supplied Cochin with rice from Coromandel, Kanara and Bengal.[24] Some of these food commodities seem to have been taken by the Jews back to native Cochin when they returned after selling pepper and sandalwood in the Portuguese city.[25] The advent of a considerable number of new Christians (Jews converted to Christianity) to the Portuguese city of Cochin from Spain and Portugal in the 1530s (especially from 1533 onwards), gave a new dimension to the inter-local trade closely connecting with the Judaic involvement. Isaac the Red and other Jews residing in the native city began to come to the Portuguese Cochin to take merchandise from the shop of Jácome de Olivares, which he had brought from Malacca.[26] At the same time, he possessed shops in native Cochin and in the Portuguese city, which enabled him to conduct inter-city trade effectively.[27] By the 1540s, Luis Rodrigues, another new Christian merchant made frequent visits to native Cochin, 'where lived the great merchants of the land and of transactions'. During these visits, he sold the commodities which he had taken from Bengal, Ceylon and Malacca and collected wares for his next expedition.[28] Isaac do Cairo, who was a big Jewish merchant of native Cochin and who had commercial links with west Asia, was associated with the new Christian traders of Portuguese city.[29] Leonor Caldeira, who started business establishments in Portuguese Cochin, had a warehouse in native Cochin for storing rice, where she would go in connection with her business as well as to collect the money for the goods she had sold.[30] In order to conduct the intra-local trade effectively, as we have already seen, some Jews like Moisès Real, who had a base in native Cochin, began to set up shops in the Portuguese city.[31] This intra-local trade was not restricted to the native and European portions of settlement. Luis Rodrigues used to take weapons and artillery to the Jewish traders of native Cochin, who in turn sold them to the native kings and chieftains of the adjacent areas.[32] Commodities from Portuguese Cochin were taken to the markets of the native city, which were further distributed to the neighbouring hinterlands through a network of local merchants. Almost for twenty-four years from 1533 to 1557 (during the period of flourishing private trade), the common economic interests and religious ties that existed between the Jews and the ex-Jews helped to create a vast network of intra-local trade.[33] A few Muslim merchants of Cochin, whose position, by this time, had been reduced to that of peddlers and the Ezhava merchants also took part in this trade that extended up to the hinterland.

3. INTRA-ASIAN TRADE

The trade of Cochin did not confine itself to the regional level; it extended to different parts of Asia. Cochin's link with intra-Asian trade became so important because of its junctional position, that the flow of different streams of commodities like textiles from Gujarat, Coromandel and Bengal, rice from Coromandel, Bengal and Kanara, spices from the Molucas, Sumatra, Sunda, Ceylon and Kanara, finished products such as silk and porcelain, etc., from China, European wares such as copper, silver and vermilion from Lisbon intersected at Cochin making it an entrepot.[34] In the processes of distribution, these commodities began to be brought to and exchanged from Cochin with great frequency.

Among the European commodities, copper was the greatest single item that was distributed over Indian Ocean regions by this trade network. Cherina *Marakkar* of Cochin and the Jews of Cochin used to purchase copper from the Portuguese at fourteen *cruzados* a quintal.[35] It was taken to different parts of Asia for re-sale. In Diu and Cambay copper was in great demand.[36]

In 1513, Lourenço Moreno took from Cochin 52459 kgs of copper to Cambay, where he saw a prospective market. He wrote to the king of Portugal for a further supply of this metal, which India, in general, lacked.[37] Copper was taken from Cochin also to Malacca for bringing back produce from south-east Asia.[38] In 1543, we find the demand for copper in Cochin going up and a large quantity of copper being transported from Quilon to Cochin.[39]

The various spices from the extensive hinterland of Cochin formed another group of commodities that were exchanged in intra-Asian trade. Some of these spices were taken either directly from the hinterland of Cochin or from the port of Cochin where different branches of private trade, fabricated by individual entrepreneurs, ran almost parallel to the *Estado* arrangement. The crown and the individuals participated in the intra-Asian commerce in varying and disproportionate degrees, while the commodities of exchange, very often, followed an intermingled pattern. Non-spice items formed the greatest cargo in this trade in Asia. But contraband items also entered the list of merchandise because of royal concessions, licences, voyage-systems and above all, because of the network of private entrepreneurs established in Cochin.

On the basis of the space through which the commercial transactions were conducted, intra-Asian trade could be divided into two: 1. Trade through ghat routes which started from the hinterland of Cochin. 2. Trade through sea which started from the port of Cochin.

I. INTRA-ASIAN TRADE OVER LAND ROUTE ACROSS THE GHATS

The land routes across the ghats were the traditional links for the exchange of commodities between the eastern and western coasts. Pack animals were used to carry rice, textiles and other goods from the Coromandel coast to the interior markets of the hinterland in Kerala, and to take pepper back to Tamilnadu.[40] The Kumily pass was the chief route taken by these Tamil merchants to carry merchandise to the interior markets of Turubuli (Thodupuzha), Irattuperha (Erattupetta in the kingdom of Vadakkenkur), Thekkenkur, Kizhumalainadu, and Poonjar.[41] The Munnar Pass was another outlet through which the Tamil traders reached Codemangalao (Kothamangalam), an interior market and north-eastern tip of Cochin's hinterland.[42] Many traders from the east coast came to Zalakuti (Chalakudi) through Peringalkuthu for the exchange of pepper with Coromandel rice and textiles.[43] As the Aryankavu and Palaghat passes, the only ghat routes mentioned by early Indo-Portuguese historians, are located very far away from the spice-hinterlands of Cochin, [44] the above-mentioned three routes appear to have been the major land-outlets for the exchange of eastern and western commodities and for the diversion of spices, as far as Cochin was concerned. The Portuguese documents use the phrase '*pela terra dentro*' in order to describe the trade through the ghat routes.[45]

In the second decade of the sixteenth century, the total production of the pepper of Malabar was about 16,000 *bhars*. Some 2,000-2,500 *bhars* were consumed domestically. Through the ghat route 3,000 *bhars* went to inland. Some 500-600 *bhars* went to Diu by sea. Out of the remaining portion (9,900 *bhars*), the Portuguese got some and the rest went to Diu, Ormuz, the Red Sea and Coromandel.[46] This document shows that a very large amount of spices crossed the ghats and that the inland trade was as significant as the sea trade, right from the very beginning of the Portuguese establishment. As the diagram below shows, out of the total pepper production in Malabar, 19 per cent went through the ghat routes; while 25 per cent was taken through maritime routes for Asian trade. From the remaining, about 40 per cent of the total pepper was supposed to be taken to Europe in the early sixteenth century and 17 per cent was used for domestic consumption.[47]

Three reasons may be responsible for the heavy traffic of spices across the ghats: 1. The relatively higher price given by these inland merchants; 2. It provided an easy and safe outlet for smugglers; 3. During times of conflict with the Portuguese in the hinterland, spices instead of being taken to Cochin, were diverted to the

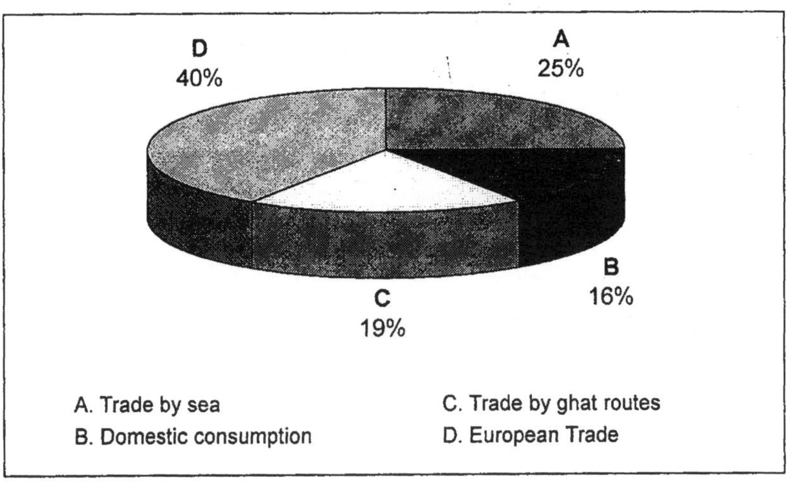

Figure 1: Distribution of Pepper for the period between 1500 and 1570.

profitable ghat routes. As the traders from the eastern coast gave higher prices for spices in comparison to what the Portuguese paid at Cochin, the producers as well as the merchants preferred the ghat-route traders. The king of Cochin remarked in 1516 that he found it difficult to arrange spices at the low rate paid by the Portuguese, because much of it was taken to places where it was better paid.[48] This reference to better pricing places must be to the ghat route. This was further testified to by a merchant who stopped the sale of spices to the Portuguese in Cochin. He explained the reason why he began to sell commodities to the traders of the ghat route by saying that these traders paid full and ready cash and purchased commodities at a higher price, while the Portuguese paid partly in copper and partly in cash and purchased the goods at a low rate fixed by Vasco da Gama.[49] Another document of 1545 says that the kings of Diamper (Udayamperur), Pimenta (Vadakkenkur), Cranganore, Cochin as well as the Christians of Diamper and *Serra* had several opportunities and ways of selling pepper to those who paid a higher price.[50] This gives the impression that the traders from the east coast and their agents were collecting spices from almost all the hinterlands of Cochin. Moreover, the Tamil merchants, who used to distribute rice and textiles in these hinterlands of Cochin, took back to Tamilnadu, pepper as their return cargo. This considerably reduced the transportation cost and enabled these traders to reap large profits.

As the streams of the ghat route were outside the Portuguese control systems, many found them safer channels for smuggling pepper for the intra-Asian trade. Spices were diverted and smuggled to the ghat from the very production centres themselves. In 1533, D. João da Cruz refers to the usual route taken by the smugglers. He says that a large amount of pepper was taken from the kingdom of Vadakkenkur (whose king was Chempenecoy) to the great kingdom (of Vijaynagar) touching the lands of Lerta Morte Trbery (Ilêdathu Mûthedathu Tiruvady), Teque Cute Nayre (Thekkenkur king), Cherabacoy (Chirvay Koyil), Yreme Trebery (Rama Tiruvady), Unyque Trebery (Unnikê Tiruvady), and Ylamana Lambratry (Lamgualur Nampiyathiri, the king of Edappilly).[51] It seems that the various routes from these places used to merge either into the ghat outlet of Kumily or into the interior land route that ran to Cape Comorin.

The flow of spices to Tamilnadu through the passes of Kumily and Munnar always used to be on the high side when there were conflicts with the Portuguese in the hinterland. Thus during the days of bitter war (1549-52) fought in Bardela (Vaduthala) between Cochin as well as the Portuguese on one side and Vadakkenkur, Calicut as well as Tanur on the other side, spices did not reach Cochin to be taken to Portugal; but were diverted instead to the inland routes.[52] The flow of spices from the hinterland to the ghat route was so well established during the days of conflict that even after the end of the war commodities did not appear in Cochin. So the king of Cochin went from king to king and trader to trader requesting them to make pepper available in Cochin for the *Carreiras*.[53] Finally the Portuguese decided to resort to military action to ensure a regular supply of spices from the hinterland to the port of Cochin.[54]

From the spices taken across the ghat to Tamilnadu, a significant portion was distributed all over India for domestic consumption. A considerable amount was taken to Bengal and China. But a great amount of this pepper was taken from the ports of Coromandel by the Gujaratis for re-distribution to the ports of Red Sea area.[55] Thus the ghat route was an alternative arrangement by land, for participation in Asian trade, and its networks were woven through the loopholes of the Portuguese control system.

II. INTRA-ASIAN TRADE BY SEA

The normal route for the intra-Asian trade originating from Cochin was by sea. The native merchant groups had been using it for centuries. But with the establishment of Portuguese rule in Cochin, the trade in Asian waters began to be shared by three different entrepreneurial groups, namely, the Crown, the private Portuguese entreprenuers and the native merchants. The entry of the Portuguese into Asian trade created a mixed reaction of co-operation, competition, and conflict among the natives. Some of the enterprising merchants like the Gujaratis, who were engaged in the intra-Asian trade resorted to co-operation and became collaborators of the Portuguese country trade.[56] But a group of Muslim merchants resorted to finding a parallel sea route touching all important Asian regions, but running outside the control systems of the Portuguese.[57] A good many of the Muslim merchants of Malabar, who were hit hard by the entry of the Portuguese in to the Indian Ocean region, were in conflict with the latter and resorted to piracy as a way of trading in Asian waters.[58] It appears that they had dealings on the side as well with the first group.

On the other hand, the Portuguese citizens of Cochin, who participated in the intra-Asian commerce represented a variety of persons including full-time traders, part-time traders conducting voyages, and officials who were trying to generate extra income by investing in clandestine commerce.

A third party that participated in the commerce of Asian waters was the Portuguese crown which looked at country trade as an additional source of income. The participation of these three groups in the trade of Asia was realized not with equal degrees of intensity and legitimacy. Moreover the commodities taken for the trade within Asia included a variety of items that encroached upon the royal monopoly. The movement of these wares in Asia was controlled by licences and passes, so that it might not adversely affect the Lisbon-bound *Carreira*. In general, based on its nature, intra-Asian trade could generally be divided into three: 1. Official Country Trade, 2. Licenced Country Trade, 3. Illicit Country Trade.

A. Official Country Trade

The crown participated in the intra-Asian trade by organizing voyages to the eastern space of Indian Ocean, especially to the ports of Bay of Bengal, Archipelago and the Far East. The captains and other officers of these vessels engaged in the country trade, were nominated by the Royal Chancellery, just as were the officers of the fortresses and factories.[59] Thus, for example, in March 1531, D. João III granted to one Tristão de Sousa, a *fidalgo* of the royal household, the captaincy of the trading carrack that went from Cochin to Malacca, for a period of three years.[60] The officers of the crown ships engaged in country trade, were entitled to some privileges. They enjoyed, besides the regular salaries for their service, a considerable amount of franchises which allowed them to participate in the profits of the enterprise.[61] These could also be seen as steps to ensure more private participation in the crown's official country trade. The opportunity to serve in the ships that took part in the official trade in Asian waters was also considered as an honour and a reward for the services. Along with such honour, these officers received a share of the profit. At times they could, with royal ascent, give up the nomination in favour of a relative, or even sell it.[62] Though the officers shared the profit, these commercial endeavours were primarily official as the crown did the investments and made the appointments.

The crown commercial voyages frequently left from Cochin. Thus, for example, Antonio Correia left from Cochin in April 1519, in a crown ship called Santiago Brandoa to the East. He carried along with him 21,500 pieces of Gujarati textiles and cumin from Cochin and took the following route: Cochin-Pasai-Malacca-Pasai-Martaban-Pasai-Malacca-Pasai-Cochin. The wares he carried from Cochin were exchanged for pepper in Pasai. This was again sold in Martaban from where he bought rice and sealing wax which he sold in Malacca. He went on buying and selling at each port and engaged himself in this chain of exchanges till January 1521, when he reached Cochin after almost twenty months.[63] Antonio Correia's ship was accompanied by two other ships, the names of which were Santiago and Santa Barbara, up to Malacca. These two vessels limited their routes to Cochin-Malacca-Cochin.[64] The royal ships going to Malacca for trade made a stop-over in Coromandel in 1547, probably for loading different varieties of clothes from there.[65]

The so-called *Carriera do Coromandel* with destinations to Pulicat and the *Carreira de Pegu* engaged in Pegu commerce[66] were carriers of the interests of the crown in the intra-Asian trade. On 5 February 1546, Luis Mendes de Vasconcelos was made captain of the *Carreira do Coromandel* that used to go to Malacca for trade.[67] Since he had gone to Diu to rescue it, he was given many additional privileges, but the privilege charter makes it clear that this should, in no way, hinder the official trade. The detailed instructions to Luis Vasconcelos are as follows: he could go to Pulicat to take on a cargo of textiles and clothes; no other ship should be allowed to load cargoes before having loaded the royal vessel; the captain of Malacca could screen the merchants who were travelling in the crown ship to Coromandel; he could nominate four merchants to this royal ship (to conduct trade to his advantage); but for the commodities they would carry, they had to pay freight charges; he could also use some space in the ship to carry rice, for which he was not to pay freight charges.[68] However, in some cases the grantees were clearly instructed to make use of the service of the merchants only after loading the official ships engaged in the intra-Asian trade. Thus, for instance, in 1547 João Nunes, who was permitted to take two merchants along with him from Coromandel in his voyage to Martaban, was particularly asked to take the merchants only after having loaded the 'ship of the king that was going to Pegu for trade'.[69] The crown and the grantees of the voyages found it profitable to trade with the ports bordering on the Bay of Bengal, such as Martaban, Mergui and the 'tin ports' of the Malay peninsula. Even in 1550, we find *Carreira de Pegu* returning to Cochin after completing the annual Pegu voyage.[70]

B. Licenced Country Trade

The Portuguese made the country trade a licenced commercial enterprise because spices and other items, which were reserved to the royal crown were included in the wares often taken for exchange within Asia. Despite Lisbon's statutory ban on the private movement of spices, the private enterpreneurs of Cochin prevailed upon the *Estado* officials to get licences to conduct trade on contraband items in Asian waters. The viceroys and governors had begun to show favour to some individuals and had started, as early as the beginning of the 1520s, to licence limited movement of pepper.[71] By the late 1540s, the Portuguese officials followed a liberal policy of issuing frequent licences to carry pepper within Asia to conduct commercial exchanges and often under the protection of these licences, large amounts of pepper were taken from Cochin to Bengal.[72] The licences usually stipulated the amount of pepper that could be carried by an individual. In 1545 opinions were sought from ex-officials of India as to whether this licenced trade should be permitted to continue in Bengal, as it was cheaper than the spices from Aceh and Sunda, sold by native merchants. They argued that the flow of pepper to Bengal would make it difficult to get sufficient pepper in Cochin to make up a cargo for the Lisbon-bound carracks.[73] Jorge Cabral (the future governor of Portuguese India) pointed out that it would also raise the prices of pepper in Cochin and would be detrimental to the European trade.[74] But nothing came of this polemic, and the licence system continued. The crown's tacit approval encouraged the private enterprises and spices continued to be taken in large amounts along with other commodities to different regions of Asia making the Portuguese authorities, as Braudel says, mere 'customs officials' or 'tax-gatherers'.[75] This system continued for almost fifty years till the 1570s, when vigorous legislation was again passed to ban it explicitly. The licenced trade could be divided into four: the trade of the *casados*, trade by Voyages, trade in ships with *cartazes* and trade through contracts.

a. The Trade of the Casados

The *casados* (family men, especially Portuguese citizens married to native women) of Cochin enjoyed special freedom to conduct commerce by virtue of their Portuguese origin and marital status. It was a social group continuously increasing in number and economic power and consequently extending their influence both politically and commercially for setting up an empire of their own interests.[76] They seemed to have exercised full freedom in conducting trade with all Asian regions and on all commodities except the items reserved for royal monopoly. But they were also engaged in the trade of pepper, cloves and other spices all over Asia, which they carried on in most cases, with due permission and viceregal licences. The maritime space between coastal India and South East Asia was the active area of their commerce. They even had trade with the Red Sea ports; but on a relatively minor scale, as the commerce from Malabar was dominated by shipping from Calicut and Cannanore.

As early as 1510, Affonso de Albuquerque, the protagonist of the policy of mixed marriage, encouraged the Portuguese who married native women to take up local trade as a means of livelihood.[77] The taste of profit generated by this trade induced in them a desire to participate in a wider commercial network. Eventually the Portuguese with private interests organized themselves into a lobbying group, known as 'the Cochin group', with a view to staging organized opposition to the state of intervention, which Albuquerque had implemented by an elaborate system of fortresses.[78] This move launched with the help of the king of Cochin was purely economic and was designed to evoke a liberal atmosphere, in which the trade within Asia would be made over to private parties.[79] The nomination of Lopo Soares de Albergaria, who was a representative of the Cochin group, as the successor to Affonso de Albuquerque in 1515 was a victory to the private enterprisers. This new governor demarcated for them a space east of Cape Comorin which was relatively free from state interference.[80]

The new situation favoured the private initiative of the *casados*. With the voyage of Fernão Peres de Andrade, who in 1515 was appointed the 'captain for discovering the Bay of Bengal and China',[81] Bengal and other eastern parts of Indian Ocean, along with Malacca, entered the commercial geography of the Portuguese. Pepper and other commodities were taken from Cochin to Bengal and other ports of the Gangetic delta in exchange for sugar, rice and textiles.[82] In 1518, D. João da Silveira sailed from Cochin to Bengal to explore further commercial prospects in the Gangetic delta.[83] In 1522-3, Diogo Pereira, who was greatly associated with the private trade of Cochin, was moving about in Bengal and Pegu trying to open the doors for the commerce of pepper from Cochin and procuring wares in exchange.[84] Along with the various usual wares of exchange the *casados* used to take pepper and other contraband items, but quite often they did so with permission. Diogo Pereira, on another occasion, took from Cochin pepper along with copper and silk to Cambay and Chaul and he was paid 16,000 *pardaos* in gold after sale.[85] In return, diverse types of cloth, indigo, sealing wax and gold were taken to Cochin.[86] The white cloth of Cambay was in high demand for exchange for pepper, timber, areca and other spices.[87] Some of this rice was again taken to the Maldives in exchange for coir and cowries. Thus in the letter of the town of Cochin to D. João de Castro, mention is made that the main source of living for the citizens of Cochin was navigation and that for years they were sending rice to the islands of Maldives, in exchange for coir and cowries.[88] These cowries were again taken to Bengal, Pegu and China, where they were used as monetary tender.[89]

The *casados* also began to import horses from Ormuz to Cochin. Though Goa was the main Indian port of import for the horses from Arabia (2,000 horses per year),[90] the *casados* of Cochin attempted to try their luck by importing horses to Cochin. In 1533, D. João da Cruz with due permission imported horses to Cochin to be taken to the fishery coast, Travancore and to the kingdoms of Chymbechenaque (Tumbhichi Nayak) and Beteperemal (Vettum Perumal).[91] In 1546, Henrique de Sousa Chichorro says that the horses taken to Cape Comorin from Ormuz via Cochin did not yield much profit. So he asked permission to take sugar, rice and lac from Satgão (*Porto Pequeno* of Bengal) to Cochin.[92] But in 1547, we find the *Ouvidor* of Cochin remarking that many *casados* of the city were taking horses to Cape Comorin from Cochin for trade, where they enjoyed themselves with girls, while their wives and children were dying of hunger at home.[93] During the period between 1546 and 1547 we find many *casados* taking horses imported to Cochin from Ormuz to Cape Comorin.[94] This trade appeared to be so lucrative that even the new Christian traders (also *casados*) like Luis Rodrigues, began to take horses to Cape Comorin for sale.[95] By 1568 the number of horses imported to Cochin from Ormuz for distribution in the kingdoms of south India created alarming situations in Goa, as it adversely affected the revenue of the latter.[96]

As early as 1520 the *casados* had begun to make use of a large amount of timber for the construction of their ships. As the private trade increased, the need for the timber to build more ships increased in proportion. This began to adversely affect the royal shipbuilding centre of Cochin. In 1523, it was reported that wood for shipbuilding was scarce in Cochin as it was being purchased by the Portuguese who had planned to settle in India, live by their own trade and die there.[97] By the 1540s, we find a lot of ships being built in Cochin in these centres. This was in response to the privileges they received for their participation in the rescue of Diu. It seems that most of those who were allowed voyages for their service in Diu were *fidalgos* while those who received the privilege to construct ships were only *casados*.[98] Simple logic would say that voyages were privileges for those who were not conducting trade regularly, while the means of livelihood for the *casados* was commerce. What the latter wanted was permission to build ships which was restricted because of the shortage of timber experienced in the royal shipbuilding centre.[99] About more than twenty different *casados* were allowed in 1546-7 to construct ships in Malabar as a reward for their services to defend Diu.[100] It seems that a good number of them were constructed in Cochin because of the advanced naval technology that was already utilized in Cochin for the construction of royal ships. With the possession of a large number of private ships at their disposal, the *casados* extended their commercial network to wider horizons.

How could the sudden rise of the *casados* in intra-Asian trade be accounted for? Most of the historians do not explain the reasons and factors that favoured the abrupt emergence of the *casados*, or their replacement of the traditional Muslim merchants of Cochin, from the pre-eminent position the latter had previously held in intra-Asian commerce. Three incidents seem to have played a major role in the transitional phase, whereby the *casados* came out as the principal merchant group. On the one hand, one could find the frequent attack and confiscation of Muslim ships in the name of *cartazes* by the Portuguese authorities, who favoured the private initiatives of the *casados* of Cochin. During the early days of Portuguese establishment the Muslim merchants of Cochin were their greatest allies and suppliers; this continued till the death of Affonso de Albuquerque.[101] By the 1520s, the Portuguese attitude towards them changed and the *Estado* officials began to frequently use *cartazes*, which authorized them to check and confiscate any vessel, as a convenient tool to weaken the commercial strength of these traditional Muslim traders (if not to destroy them) and to create out of their weakness a space for the emerging *casados*.[102] Many of them became a prey to torture tactics, which Zaynuddin describes as Portuguese high-handedness.[103] One among them was Kutti Ali who joined hands with Diogo Lopes, the Governor and another Portuguese in 1522 to send pepper to the Red Sea. When it was loaded the very same Diogo Lopes confiscated the whole as contraband and appropriated the vessel. This turned him against the Portuguese and he later became a corsair to fight against them.[104]

By 1524, being intolerably fed up with the confiscation of the ships and the Portuguese oppression, the leading Muslim merchants of Cochin such as Kunjali Marakkar, his brother Ahmad Marakkar, their uncle Mohammadali Marakkar and other dependants left Cochin and settled down in Calicut, with a staunch resolution to fight against the Portuguese.[105] This Kunjali Marakkar is the first reference to Kunjali ever made by Zaynuddin in his book. It is to be specially remembered that this offended Muslim merchant of Cochin, as some Kerala historians say, was the first Kunjali (Kunjali later became a title to designate the Admiral of Calicut) who organized guerilla warfare and corsair activities against the Portuguese.[106] Another important Muslim trader of Cochin to become a corsair when the Portuguese captured the two ships he sent to Cambay was Pate Marakkar.[107] He had been a great friend and collaborator of the Portuguese in the early days of their establishment[108] and had extensive commercial links on the Coromandel coast and in the gulf of Manar.[109] On the confiscation of his ships, he went to Calicut and joined his nephew, Kunjali Marakkar as a corsair.[110] It is to be specially noted that the *casados* of Cochin emerged as the principal traders of Asian waters only because of the estrangement of the traditional Muslim merchant magnates from Cochin, an estrangement which the Portuguese had created through an atmosphere of coercion and violence. With the transfer of residence to Calicut by prominent Muslim traders, the second-rate merchants of this group, who remained in Cochin were reduced to the role of peddling traders or petty shopkeepers. Those Muslim merchants, who had been alienated from Cochin as well as from the Portuguese system and moved to Calicut, had to resort to corsair activities as an alternative arrangement of trade.[111]

On the other hand, the royal monopoly over the spice trade in Malacca and the Moluccas ceased to exist in 1533 and 1537.[112] This allowed the *casados* bag huge profits by actively involving themselves in the Bengal-Malacca, Coromandel-Malacca and Cochin-Malacca routes.[113] In 1539, the trade in cloves and nutmeg was announced as free and every one was allowed to obtain these in the Moluccas; one-third of the transported amount however, had to be sold to the crown at the buying price.[114] This attracted the *casados* to the source of spices in South-East Asia. Diverse commodities like cloves from the Moluccas, nutmeg and mace from Banda, pepper from Sumatra and Sunda, sandalwood from Timor, camphor from Borneo, benzoin and aloes from Sumatra, and Cochin-China were brought to Malacca. Along with these plant products, the trade was also in Malacca musk, sealing wax and precious stones from Burma, and North Siam, exported through Pegu, tin from the Malay Peninsula and some gold from Sumatra. Though one part of these commodities went to China and Japan, from Malacca a strong stream moved through the *casados* to Cochin, from where some were taken to Portugal and the rest to Cambay and Ormuz for distribution in West Asia.[115] After the establishment of Macao in 1557, merchandise from China, especially finished goods such as porcelain, silk, lac, jewellery and minted brass began to be taken to Cochin and other Malabar ports with the help of the *casados*.[116]

Indian textiles were taken in large volume for exchange in the Malay Archipelago, as the spices from South-East Asia were to be paid in textiles rather than in money.[117] The three main weaving places in India were Gujarat, the Coromandel coast and the kingdom of Bengal. The *casados* took from Cochin pepper, ginger, coir, coconuts and other wares from China and Malacca to Diu, Surat and Chaul in exchange for raw cotton and textiles.[118] Meanwhile the *casados* who were exchanging pepper for the rice of Coromandel also began to extend their links to the Coromandel-Malacca trade carrying textiles from Nagapatanam and Mylapore to the entrepot of the Archipelago for the spices of South-East Asia.[119] The textiles from Bengal formed an important commodity in the distribution trade of Cochin. The *casados* who used to take pepper from Cochin to Bengal played a crucial role in this textile trade. Though some commodities were taken to Malacca, Cochin was the major outlet for the textiles of Bengal that came through the ports of Pipli, Chittagong, Satagon, and Dianga.[120] By the 1540s, Bengal turned out to be the chief destination of the *casados* who conducted licenced trade in the pepper of Cochin.[121]

The third factor which influenced the situation was the relatively low customs duty that the native king collected from the *casados* of Cochin. As early as 1520s, the king of Cochin had begun to demand port dues from the private traders because the port of Cochin was situated in his kingdom. But the Portuguese authorities were not prepared to give the native king the customs money which they had collected. In 1529, the king wrote to John III repeating his claim to the duties on all the ships that came from Malacca and Bengal and saying that these port dues levied on the private traders would lessen the burden of his expenditure.[122] The governor, Lopo Vaz de Sampayo, who was dead against the sharing of customs duties with the native ruler, reacted by interning the king of Cochin in his own palace.[123] Finally on 24 February 1530, John III explicitly renounced all rights to customs-duties collected at Cochin and yielded this right to the native ruler, after considering the fact that the latter was the owner of the port of Cochin.[124] This was later confirmed on 12 January 1543, by Martim Afonso de Sousa, on 24 January 1550 by Jorge Cabral, and on 17 November 1561, by Francisco Coutinho.[125] Initially the rate of customs duty at Cochin was six per cent and was equivalent to that of Goa and other Portuguese customs houses. To attract more trade to Cochin, the native ruler reduced the rate to three and a half per cent for the *casado* merchants, who could bring commodities directly to the port. All others who had wares destined for Cochin had to go first to Goa and pay six per cent duties there and only then were allowed to come to Cochin. But they evaded Goa by entering into side-deals with the *casados* of Cochin, who used to bring their goods through the customs-house, claiming ownership.[126] This led to a wider and deeper nexus: on the one hand, between the *casados* and the non-Muslim traditional merchants of Asian region and on the other hand between the *casados* and the king of Cochin who, emerging as a powerful lobby, had almost created a parallel commercial network sidelining the *Estado* set-up.

Along with the Portuguese, the new Christians who came to Cochin in the 1530s from Portugal and Spain, also began to exploit trade opportunities in the Asian waters, and by virtue of their status as family men, they also enjoyed the privilege of the *casado* traders.[127] Till 1557 they were virtually regarded as Portuguese citizens, with the privileges of *casados* and with the right to become members in the Municipal Council of Cochin.[128] Making use of the economic freedom given to the *casados* some of them like Jácome de Olivares and his brother-in-law Diogo Vaz used to conduct trade in South East Asian commodities in Malacca, in exchange for cloth taken from Cochin.[129] Luis Rodrigues, another merchant from this group, had Malacca, Bengal, Coromandel, and Ceylon as the major destinations of his commercial transactions.[130] But the participation of the *casados* from the new Christian group in the trade of Asia lasted only till 1557, when the feelings of anti-semitism choked this enterprising group.

The *casado* traders of Cochin, who are often viewed as an emerging bourgeois class in the Portuguese empire by scholars like Rothermund,[131] had achieved their economic stature and commercial growth in an atmosphere of vacuum, created by the ouster of Muslim merchants. They had always been a source of support and defence both economically and politically. Eventually, however, there arose a conflict between the *casados* and the mother-country born *fidalgos*, whom the crown preferred, while distributing concessions and public charges.[132] As Diogo de Couto in *Soldado Pratico* says, the kingdom 'could maintain only one more child'[133] and all members of the Portuguese noble class, except the first-born who alone inherited family property, looked at India as a country where they could set up for life and make a fortune if they could get the captaincy of some of its fortresses.[134] The *casados* and ecclesiastical dignitaries like Dom Jorge Temudo, the first bishop of Cochin, strongly opposed the mass reservation given to the *fidalgos*. The bishop wrote that India needed only two dozens of good *fidalgos* to be appointed as the governors and the captains. The rest, the *casados* could manage by themselves.[135] With the support of the ecclesiastical dignitaries, the *casados* opposed the hegemony of the *fidalgos*, which the latter exercised in politics as governors and captains as well as in commerce which they used to enjoy as the grantees of frequent voyages.[136] These *casados* had even developed a system almost parallel to and relatively independent of arrangements with the mother country. By 1559 a rumour had spread that the *Estado da India*, taking advantage of the presence of Dom Constantino de Bragança, a noble of royal blood, as viceroy, had severed ties with Lisbon.[137] The move against the *fidalgo*-dominated *Estado* by the *casados*, who had acquired sufficient financial basis and had established trade networks all over Indian Ocean regions independent of *Estado* control, had alarmed the Lisbon administration. The crown felt it necessary to appease this group, and made attempts to protect the *casado* trade from competition as well as to reserve some lines for their regional trade.[138]

b. Trade by Voyage Concessions

The second segment of licensed trade was the voyages farmed out to individuals on a monopolistic basis. The voyages were of two types, those rented to an individual for a fixed price, because the individual concessionaires could not use the state-owned ships; but had to use their own boats; and voyages conceded to individuals as honour and reward in recognition of their meritorious service. Here the individual concessionaires could build ships and send commodities to the destination permitted or could use the space of the crown ships to transport their wares. Voyages of the first category came into existence only after 1570.[139] So here we shall deal only with the voyages freely granted to the individuals on personal grounds such as reward for meritorious services and contributions.

Initially, as we have already seen, those who were to be rewarded and honoured were allowed by the crown to take part in the official country trade by making them officers in the ships, which had ensured them a considerable source of income and a share in the profits. Later, the grantees of these benefices or voyages were not appointed as officers of the ships but were given particular space in the crown ships for their cargo or were allowed to convey the stipulated commodity in their own ships.

We have evidence of this type of voyage granted to individuals for a variety of reasons. On 21 February 1547 Manuel Lourenço, the legal advocate for the Order of the Franciscans of Cochin was conferred a voyage to Bengal, in recognition of the services he had rendered to the monastery. He was allowed to send the ships in 1548.[140] Many Portuguese, who fought in the war of 1546 to protect Diu, were rewarded by D. João de Castro with the grant of voyages. Most of these voyages had Cochin as the boarding or terminal port. On 15 December 1546, one Diogo Lopes d'Aguiãr was allowed to send one big ship, two boats, one *catur* and two *galeotas* from Diu to Cochin, whenever he desired.[141] On 16 December 1546, Antonio Leme was given the permission to get a ship built in Malabar and to send commodities to any of the ports in Bengal.[142] From Cochin, its factor, Antonio Correia brought a *caravela* with a lot of soldiers (both native and Portuguese) to Diu. He provided these people engaged in war, with food supplies while he stayed on with the captain to defend the fortress. On 3 February 1547, Antonio Correia was given permission to conduct an annual voyage to Malacca. With the profit he got out of it, he was also instructed to look after an orphan girl who came from Portugal. On 19 February he was given another privilege to send a ship to Bengal every year. He was even given privileges, 'to which no other person in Cochin was ever entitled', to send ships and commodities outside and inside the limits of Cochin.[143] This privilege entitled him to conduct free trade more or less. On 21 February 1547, Manoel de Sousa de Sepulveda was permitted to send a ship to Bengal, for having served in Diu and for having spent a lot of money feeding the fighting forces.[144]

Fernão Peres de Andrade had come to Diu from Cochin in his own *catur* and he took along with him a lot of people to fight in the war. As a reward, he was permitted on 4 May 1547, to make or to buy a ship and to send commodities to Bengal in 1548.[145] On 6 May 1547, one Francisco Fernandes Moricalle was allowed to conduct a voyage to Bengal for having come to Diu from Cochin.[146] These voyages were intended to reward exceptional services, which were at times also rewarded by allotting space in the city of Cochin—a plot near the fortress of Cochin was granted to Christovão de Azevedo[147]—or by permitting the individuals, as in the case of Antonio Pereira to buy or to make ships in Cochin to serve the crown (by collecting spices for the *Carreira da India*).[148]

Some of the grantees such as Antonio Cardosa and Duarte Barbudo were permitted to conduct voyages by sending cloth in the special space of the royal ship which went via Coromandel to Malacca.[149] The voyage conceded to João Nunes on 19 March 1547, included the following privilege. He could go in his ship to Coromandel and from there he was allowed to take his wares to Martaban. He was also allowed to take two merchants from Coromandel to Martaban after they had loaded the royal ship going to Pegu (*Carreira de Pegu*).[150] Some others like Luis de Vasconcelos had a different privilege in this voyage system. He was given the right in 1547 to nominate four merchants to the royal ship going to Coromandel (*Carreira do Coromandel*).[151] On 11 July 1547, Francisco Fernandes was given the favour, along with the grant of a voyage, to take with him four *casados* from Cochin for his trade in Malacca.[152] Another voyage was granted on 17 February 1548, to Sebastião Luis, *alcaide-mor* of Cochin, who was entitled to take commodities from Cochin to exchange with textiles and other goods in Bengal.[153] The next day Alvares Teles, the factor of Cochin was also honoured and rewarded with two voyages to the Maldives.[154]

Though most of these voyages seem to have been granted to the *fidalgos* and to members of the higher social strata, some of the *casados* of Cochin were also conferred with the privileges of voyages. On 23 November 1547, Francisco da Silva, a *casado* of Cochin was given a grant of a voyage by which he could send every year, one ship each to Bengal, Arracão and Moluccas.[155] Two other *casados* of Cochin, one Gonçalves Caldeira and another Gomes de Carvalho obtained on 3 February 1548, grants for conducting commercial voyages to Malacca.[156]

Most of the voyages started from Cochin were conducted in the ships either built or bought in Cochin, as stipulated in the privilege charter. The well-known shipbuilding tradition and the advanced naval technology of Cochin must have been the reason for associating voyages with shipbuilding, when concessions and privileges had to be granted.

c. *Trade of the Natives in Ships with Cartazes*

Cartaz, which is a loan-word from the Arabic 'qirtas', meaning paper or document, was some sort of licence of movement or safe-conduct for navigation issued by the Portuguese to native ships, with the exclusive view of showing that these vessels did not belong to the enemy camp.[157] The Portuguese considered that the right over the sea and the land which was conquered and discovered by them, exclusively belonged to them by virtue of the series of papal bulls issued from 1441 onwards, and also that the Hindus, Muslims and all other natives who wanted to ply their vessels in the sea should purchase *cartazes*.[158] The ships that did not buy *cartazes* were confiscated along with their cargo, and the people on board were enslaved.[159] The first written *cartazes* were issued in 1502 by Vasco da Gama who took a belligerent approach to every seafarer, except those from Cannanore, Cochin and Quilon.[160] From then onwards, a permanent fleet stayed in the Indian Ocean to protect Portuguese interests and to blockade the entry of spices to the Red Sea. Usually the victims of the search conducted in the name of *cartazes*, were the Arabs and their allies such as native Muslim merchants, and the Zamorin's men. Though the *cartaz* was introduced as to implement political hegemony, it turned out equally to be an economic tool to control the movement of merchant ships.[161] All the native ships had to take *cartazes*, which contained the following particulars: the name of the vessel and of the captain, the nature of the cargo, its origin and destination (which factors attest the economic significance of these licences) and the name of the authority issuing the *cartaz*.[162] Initially these passes were issued from Cochin and then from Cannanore, Calicut (during the period of peace 1513-25) and Diu. Though the fee charged for the *cartaz* was only one *pardao* (13 *fanams*) per ship, by 1535, the annual revenue from the sale of this safe-conduct in Cannanore alone was 8,000 or 9,000 *cruzados*,[163] showing the degree and frequency with which the natives with licences were made to participate in the Asian trade.

The merchants of Cochin such as Cherina Marakkar used to take *cartazes* from the Portuguese factory at Cochin in order to send merchandise to Ormuz.[164] In the first decades of the sixteenth century, some of these passes were issued by local rulers like the king of Cochin who were friendly with the Portuguese; later they began to be given out by the Portuguese with the recommendation and the approval of the native rulers of the Malabar coast.[165] But when these native kings wanted to send ships, they also had to take *cartazes* from the Portuguese.[166] The system of *cartaz* required the ships to call at a Portuguese port, both coming and going, and pay duties at both places.[167] This diversion of merchant ships plying in the Indian Ocean to the Portuguese ports also provided enormous possibilities of commercial transactions and exchange in these ports, making them entrepots.

We have already seen how the principal Muslim traders of Cochin moved over to Calicut because of the atrocities they suffered in the name of *cartazes*. The second string of Muslim merchants of Cochin who continued to still co-operate with the Portuguese, used to take *cartazes* for the shipment of their commodities. Thus in 1526, we find a Muslim merchant of Cochin taking a *cartaz* from the Portuguese governor to go to Colombo to convey cinnamon in his ships.[168] Some of them had taken *cartazes* from Cochin to trade in the fishery coast, which eventually led to some sort of religious tension between the Christians and Muslims. So Padre Gaspar Barzeus asked King John III not to issue *cartazes* to the Muslims sailing from Cochin to Chilau as these Muslims were creating lot of trouble for the missionaries working in that area.[169]

One great merchant, who appears in the intra-Asian trade of the 1540s and 1550s as a favourite of the Portuguese, was Khwaja Shams-ud-din Giloni.[170] He was actually a Persian by birth and an employee of Asad Khan of Belgaum. Asad Khan planned to buy a piece of land in Cannanore and to transfer his enormous wealth to Malabar. Shams-ud-din was deputed to carry out this project. But with the death of Asad Khan his entire wealth, which was estimated to be about 10 million ducates, passed into the hands of Shams-ud-din and the latter used it as the capital for his future commercial endeavours.[171] In the process of converting black money into white and to ensure support and confirmation for his trade activities, he gave half of it in bars of gold to be sent to Portugal,[172] besides the frequent monetary help he used to render to the *Estado*.[173] In return he could establish a commercial empire with bases in Cannanore and Bassein which were linked with those in Mecca where his brother was running the business.[174] In 1547, the Portuguese (in particular, one Dom João da Cruz), as a token of gratitude for the service he received from Shams-ud-din, bought a plot in Cochin for 1605 *pardaus* for him and made arrangements to extend his commercial network to Cochin.[175] From Cochin and

Cannanore he used to take *cartazes* to send commodities to other trading centres. Manuel de Vasconcellos wrote from Cannanore to the governor that he could not prevent Shams-ud-din from sending pepper to Mecca, as all his ships, making voyages in that direction, had *cartazes* issued by the governor.[176]

Cartaz, in a nutshell, could thus symbolize a state-of-war in the navigation zone against those who did not comply with the Portuguese system. In actuality, it was the principal legitimate means by which the natives could conduct trade in the Asian waters.

d. Trade through Contracts

Another way by which the Portuguese allowed the natives to participate in the country trade was by entering into contract with the local merchants to supply, in prescribed quantity, the commodities which were in high demand in Cochin. Most of these contracts with indigenous merhcants were made to ensure regular supply of food materials as well as ancillary materials needed for shipbuilding like timber and coir. Thus, for instance, on 4 February 1560, Jorge de Sousa Pereira, the captain-in-chief of the *armada* went to the island of Maldives to conclude a contract with Mame (Muhammed) de Patydor and Habrao (Abraham) Patydor, the administrators of the islands, to obtain coir. In keeping with the conditions of this contract, these administrators undertook to send every year, 150 *bhares* of coir to Cochin at their own cost. Chaudela Marakkar, Ade Ramao, Ali Poera and Coje Ahmed, the Muslim merchants of native Cochin and the adjacent places like Palliport, took up this responsibility of supplying the stipulated quantity to Cochin.[177] Usually these contracts were concluded for commodities, which, by virtue of their high demand, had to be supplied constantly and regularly.

C. Illicit Country Trade

Despite the vast system of fortresses and patrolling set up by the Portuguese, unlawful trade thrived as intensely as licensed trade. A great part of the illicit trade, conducted by the Portuguese with the connivance or outside the cognizance of the *Estado*'s authorities, was in contraband items such as pepper and other spices. A network of illegal commercial transactions, with the active involvement of many Portuguese officials, *casados* and native merchants, spread from Cochin all over Indian Ocean regions, in a manner almost parallel to the official licenced system. Broadly speaking, the illicit country trade could be divided into three: smuggling, cheating and corsair activities. These are nothing other than different degrees and stages involved in the process of smuggling. Meanwhile there developed also an illegal system of ware and vessel exchanges between the *casados* and the native merchants to avoid the high customs duties and evade Portuguese control. Its main purpose was to cheat the *Estado* as well as the native customs arrangements in Cochin. The final aspect was the corsair activities spearheaded by the anti-Portuguese Muslims of the Malabar coast under the leadership of the Kunjalis.

a. Smuggling

Smuggling as an unlawful country trade included a variety of illegal activities: The licences usually stipulated the quantity of pepper that could be carried by private individuals. But very often these people used to take twice the amount stipulated by the licence. Just as frequently, these individuals also changed the destination mentioned in the licence, diverting the commodities to more profitable routes. In this atmosphere of great confusion, and difficulty in enforcing the law, many would not even bother to take viceregal licence for such shipment.[178] In contrast to the smuggling through the ghat route, smuggling by sea was often nourished by the *Estado* officials and *casados* who had begun to set up an empire of private entrepreneurs after the death of Afonso de Albuquerque. By the 1540s, the Cochin group widened the network of their private interests in co-operation with Martim Afonso de Sousa (the governor, 1542-5), Tomé Lopes (judge for the orphans and procurator of the king), and Pedro de Sequeira (treasurer). Later, a captain, Henrique de Sousa Chichorro, whom Dom João de Castro sent to Cochin to check the private trading lobby of Cochin, being unable to act against them, actually joined hands with them.[179] These officials raised funds for illicit trade by illegally selling artillery to the native rulers. Tomé Lopes had been lending the orphanage money to enterprising individuals to go to the native states to buy pepper and to take it to profitable destinations.[180] The captain of Cochin, Henrique de Sousa Chichorro allowed free movement for these illegal traders and he was dismissed from service in 1547 for not preventing, despite the orders of the viceroy, a part of the Portuguese population of Cochin from departing to participate in the trade of Bengal and Malacca, thus leaving the Malabar coast open to piracy and to the contraband trade with Aden and the Red Sea.[181] The captain and other officials used to get handsome pay-offs for the roles they played in helping 'smuggling' trade in pepper. The smuggling of spices from Cochin had grown to such an extent that the accusation, 'went to Bengal without licence', can be seen endlessly reiterated in Portuguese documents.[182] Goertz, commenting on this, says, 'pepper smuggling was a way of life in Cochin'.[183]

By 1545 the pepper smuggling to Bengal, Pegu and China became so frequent that the European trade began to dwindle.[184] These three regions were fed by the pepper not only of Cochin but also of Malacca and other South-East Asian production centres.[185] However, this large volume of spices was not entirely consumed in these places. Some of the documents even say that Bengal needed only a small quantity of pepper, probably because of the overflow of this commodity from Cochin and South-East Asia.[186] Though a lot of pepper was going to China every year, in 1543 pepper was even brought back from China because of the excess and disproportionate supply, caused by private trade and smuggling.[187] This excess flow obviously reduced the profits.[188] So, in many cases pepper was also distributed and diverted to other places, once they reached the safe pockets of the eastern Indian Ocean region. Thus, in 1545 we come across at least some instances when many Turkish traders from West Asia coming to Bengal, Pegu and Tenasserim to take pepper to Red Sea.[189] Such a hazardous and time-consuming venture of the Turks seems to have been an exceptional attempt to trade in 'smuggled pepper'.

As illegal transactions in pepper increased, the officers of Cochin were directed to examine every ship going from this port to Bengal and Coromandel to see whether the pepper was unlawfully loaded.[190] In 1546, we find that many ships engaged in pepper-smuggling in Cochin were captured and burnt.[191] But this did not stop the smuggling. On the contrary it flourished with the help of the natives. The Jews of Cochin were actively co-operating with the smugglers to obtain the necessary cargo. Thus we read that in 1546, the Jews of native Cochin were secretly selling pepper to be taken to Bengal.[192] The enterprising *casados* visited the neighbouring kingdoms of Rapolim (Edappilly), Vadakkenkur, and Parur to collect the necessary pepper for the consortium of smugglers.[193] Moreover, a large number of *casados* used to go to the eastern area of the Indian Ocean to carry on illegal commercial traffic. In certain cases, some of them seemed to have acted as agents of the big *casado* traders who had a wider network in this belt. These principal merchants among them used to hire the services of the small-scale *casado* entrepreneurs to collect and exchange commodities in South-East Asia. The principal merchants seem to have invested the money for all kinds of transactions, whereas, the small-scale traders carried out only the local exchange of goods. A strong bond of solidarity and partnership, involving mutual trust and mutual defence, grew up among them. Clandestine elements were of cource never absent in this system, as the extension of their commercial interests necessarily involved a certain amount of violation of the restrictions and regulations of the *Estado*. The most evident example of this type of transaction must be that of João Fernandes Correia who claimed that the entire eastern coast of India from Cape Comorin to Satgão and the whole of Bengal belonged to him. He used to take a very large number of *casados* with him for trade. In 1547 he took with him 70 *casados* and went to the Fishery coast and Nagapatanam from where he and his mercantile team moved 300 leagues along the coast to Bengal. The fact that he had taken such a large number of people with him, (instead of the normal number of 10-15 men) shows that he was one of the chief merchants among the *casados*. On 25 December 1547, Ruy Gonçalves de Caminha wrote to the governor that João Fernandes Correia was doing all this illegally and without permission.[194]

Much of the smuggled pepper went to the Red Sea and the Persian Gulf regions, as well.[195] A good amount of it from the Persian Gulf reached Venice through Syria.[196] By the 1540s, the spices and drugs that first arrived in Ormuz from Cochin and other ports were later taken by sea to Baçora (Basra). From Baçora, they were carried to Tripoly of Syria by two routes: Through the desert of Arabia which terminated at the city of Damascus, and the other by old Babylonia which is now called Bagdad. To Babylonia, the merchants travelled in caravans up to the city of Aleppo. From Aleppo the spices were taken to Tripoly of Syria.[197] It seems that the frustrated Muslim merchants who remained in Cochin as well as those who shifted allegiance to Calicut, played a major role in smuggling out pepper to the Red Sea ports. On 30 September 1541, Martim Correia wrote to the Portuguese Crown that two ships loaded with pepper from Cochin were going to Mecca.[198] The diversion of pepper to the Suez-Red Sea area appears to have become frequent by the mid-1540s. In 1546, Antonio de Sotomaior wrote that ships from Mecca were coming often to the Malabar coast to take pepper.[199] The anti-Portuguese feelings of the frustrated Muslim merchants seem to have been an important factor that kept the Red Sea route vibrant, a route which terminated finally at Venice. Moreover the Zamorin, the head and the authoritative symbol of this faction, also joined them, giving them protection, to send pepper to the various ports of West Asia.[200] The rising Ottoman empire (which intervened in the Indian Ocean in 1546-54) began to give the required protection to this route, as it ensured a considerable amount of protection rent.[201]

b. Illegal Commercial Partnerships

Another illicit device developed in Cochin with regard to intra-Asian trade was the commercial partnerships between the *casados* and the native merchants (especially Gujaratis), new Christian traders and the Jews of native Cochin with a view to avoiding high customs duty and other trade regulations stipulated by the Portuguese. We do not know the extent to which the *casados* and the native merchants arranged ware-vessel exchanges to ensure immunity and protection to the other commercial partners. However, the most evident fruit of this partnership, enjoyed by the indigenous merchants (other than the natives of Cochin), was the evasion of high customs duty of Goa. The Gujarati merchants who had goods from South-East Asia destined for Cochin were bound to go to Goa to pay 6 per cent customs duty there, and then only could they come to Cochin. However, the *casados* of Cochin (just like the natives of Cochin) could take commodities directly to Cochin after paying only three and a half per cent customs duty to the native ruler, which was a concession and a privilege granted to them by the latter.[202] The *casados* made use of this opportunity to help their commercial partners to avoid the extra journey to Goa and also from paying high duties there, by bringing the goods of the Gujaratis through the customs house of Cochin, claiming ownership.[203] This was cheating, and caused severe loss to the revenue of the *Estado*. But the king of Cochin, who profited out of it, encouraged this commercial partnership and maintained a lower rate of duty for the *casados* throughout this period.

Meanwhile, the new Christian group among the *casados*, began another partnership with the Jewish traders providing them vessels for their commerce in the 'paradises' of Portuguese private trade: Bengal, Tenasserim, Pegu and Malacca; and from this last port, via Martaban, they arrived in Ceylon with goods from the far east.[204] Luis Rodrigues, one of the new Christians in Cochin, confessed before the inquisitors of Lisbon that he had taken a white Jewish trader in his vessel from Malacca to Ceylon.[205] He also provided space in his ship for a Jewish trader whom he took with him from Malacca to Pegu.[206] Jácome de Olivares, another new Christian of Cochin, had as his trade partner in Malacca a Jew from the native Cochin called Abra.[207] He had established good commercial relations with the Jews.[208] This arrangement helped the new Christians to get commodities easily from the hinterland through their Jewish partners; the Jews equally profited, as they could move freely in the waters of Indian Ocean for trade, using the licence and vessel of their new Christian partners, a freedom which they enjoyed till 1557 as Portuguese *casados*.

c. Corsair Activities

Corsair activities, usually, do not fall under the category of trade. But most of the so-called corsairs who sailed along the west coast of India attacking the trade vessels of the Portuguese were ex-traders, namely, Kunjali and his men. They felt alienated and were converted to this life-style after their vessels had been confiscated and after they had been tortured by the Portuguese for want of *cartazes*.[209] Since the Portuguese had made legal trade a property only of the mighty and the powerful, and those associated with them, the Kunjali and his men with the support of the Zamorin resorted to force and violence constantly attacking the Portuguese vessels, not only as a means of making profit, but also as a struggle to establish the right to free and equal status in maritime trade. They resorted to those very same acts, such as confiscation of the commodities and all other cruelties, which they had experienced from the Portuguese. Their activity was more of a fight against the monopolistic policies of the Portuguese, leaving little outlet for legitimate trade. Some historians consider them patriots and nationalists;[210]some others like M.N. Pearson picture them as something between pirate and privateer. According to him, some of them were pirates, some were corsairs, some were guerilla warriors and many were inoffensive traders.[211]

One should distinguish between piracy and privateering: a pirate is a sea-robber acting on his own account, whereas a privateer is an armed vessel owned and manned by private persons holding commission from government authorizing them to use it against a hostile nation, especially in merchant shipping.[212] But in practice, it was not easy to distinguish one from another, as the concept of legality from the point of view of the plunderer does not necessarily coincide with how the plundered sees it; and therefore a seizure lawful in the eyes of the former can appear as a pure act of piracy to the latter.[213] Theoretically speaking, till the last decades of the sixteenth century, the estranged Muslim merchants had not developed into strict pirates.

The corsair activities organized by the Zamorin and his naval chieftain Kunjali seem to have had the co-operation of some Muslim merchants of Cochin, because of their close and continued association with Kunjali, their one-time collaborator in Cochin. Kunjali and others after having estranged themselves from Cochin, intensified their commercial activities largely in the gulf of Manar and Coromandel, as it relatively was a free zone, where they traded hand in hand with the Muslim merchants of native Cochin, who had *cartazes* from the Portuguese officials.[214] The *armada* which patrolled the Coromandel coast during this period[215] could do little to contain them. In 1527, Pate Marakkar, the ex-merchant of Cochin who joined Kunjali, captured near Pulicat, a ship coming from Malacca with a lot of merchandise.[216] Later these corsairs extended their pillage to Nagapatanam, causing great hindrance and alarm to the Portuguese merchants who had settled down in Nagapatanam, Mylapore and Pulicat.[217] These Muslim merchants of Cochin and the Kunjali's men had special interests in the pearl trade of the fishery coast and in the cinnamon trade of Kotte which further clashed with the commercial interests of the Portuguese. The situation became very tense by 1537 when direct confrontations began to take place. In 1538, Miguel Ferreira wrote to the governor to send three hundred men to expel these Muslim merchants from the kingdom of Kotte.[218]

Meanwhile, some *casados* of Cochin also joined hands with these corsairs and Muslim merchants. These Portuguese lived almost five or six leagues away from Cochin in places like Culimute (?) making armaments for the Kunjali's men, and trading with them in contraband commodities. The *casados* built ships for the Muslim corsairs and helped the latter to enlarge their fleet.[219] With the help of the corsairs these *casados* even attacked the fleet of the *Estado*, an act which arose out of common economic interests. The reason for the association of the *casados* with the corsairs was explained by one Diogo Fernandes as due to the Muslim origin of the wives of the *casados*. In 1537, he wrote to King John III that these Portuguese were married to native women whose parents were Muslims, [220] evidently referring to the fact that most of the *casados* were under the influence of Muslim merchants and corsairs.

In the military encounter of 1537-9, the Muslim merchants of Cochin were divided into two groups, one group supporting Pate Marakkar and Kunjali, their one-time collaborators while the other group stood by the Portuguese.[221] In 1538 the Muslim merchants were defeated in Vedalai by Martim Afonso de Sousa and in the next year they were again decisively defeated in Negombo by the forces of Martim Afonso de Sousa, and Miguel Ferreira.[222] Kunjali Marakkar and Pate Marakkar, the leaders of the corsair activities, who had left Cochin in the 1520s to fight against the Portuguese, were beheaded in 1539 in Ceylon.[223] After this event and especially after the termination of the peace which the Portuguese made with Calicut in 1540,[224] the so-called corsair activities began to take two different types of operation: 1. To patrol the west coast with the tacit or explicit consent of the Zamorin, blockading the enemy and plundering the vessels of the Portuguese. 2. To send spices regularly to the Red Sea–Venice route. The former provided them the wealth for continued resistance and space for the vessels destined for the Red Sea. Most of the anti-Portuguese factors seem to have co-operated with these corsair endeavours, which provided both political and economic outlets for the exercise of freedom. This corsair activity, as we have analysed above, did not develop as purely piratical, but as an alternative trade arrangement, where plundering and confiscation of the enemy vessels coincided with parallel shipment of commodities to destinations of their choice.

Thus the first seventy years of Portuguese establishment in Cochin witnessed intense and hectic commercial activities in Asian waters. It is very difficult to quote the exact volume of intra-Asian trade for this period, except the one for the second decade of sixteenth century as given by Afonso de Albuquerque.[225] Though the crown through the *Careirras* and the nobles through the voyages participated in the country trade, the great bulk of it was transacted by *casados* and the *mestiços* who, with the help of *Estado* officials and native merchants, had set up a vast commercial network all over the Indian Ocean. This merchant class emerged at the expense of the native Muslim traders, though on common ground they used to co-operate each other. Often their trade transactions were conducted with the permission of Portuguese authorities; but in many cases they resorted to ways and means which the Portuguese viewed as illegal to achieve their economic goals, and commercial transactions. Whether they conducted licenced trade or illicit trade as normally categorized by the Portuguese, their top priority was their personal economic interest and they were less bothered about the crown's commerce. Very often the dream of Albuquerque that the *casados* would be the strongest supporters of the *Estado* was seen to be collapsing at least in the economic sphere.[226] One wonders whether intra-Asian trade by sea, starting from the port of Cochin or the country trade by land, starting from the hinterland of Cochin, ever took place during this period, without the direct or indirect involvement of the *casados* in one or other stages of the transactions.

NOTES

1. Many Indian writers resent the usage *Estado da India* or Portuguese Empire in India as the Portuguese never did occupy any significant land area in the Indian subcontinent. What they possessed was some disjointed territory or tiny footholds on the coastal belts of India, which were established for the free flow of their trade and which actually appeared insignificant in size on the map of India. K.N. Menon, *Portuguese Pockets in India*, New Delhi, 1953, pp. 7-10. Luis Filipe Thomaz has, in his collection of essays, evolved the concept of the Portuguese 'network' and not an 'empire' to describe *'Estado da India'* and thus he tries to purge the pejorative connotations attached to it. Luis Filipe Thomaz, *De Ceuta a Timor*, Lisboa, 1994. In another place, he says that the *Estado da India* was a thalassocracy rather than a clearly defined territory. Luis Filipe Thomaz, 'The Portuguese in the Seas of the Archipelago during the 16th Century', in *Archipel* 18 (1979) SPAFA Consultation Workshop on Research in Maritime Shipping and Trade Networks in South East Asia (1-W7) Cisarua, West Java, 20-7 November 1984, p. 75.
2. João Lucio de Azevedo, *Epocas de Portugal Economico, Esboços de Historia*, Lisboa, 1929, pp. 136-7; Vicente M.M.C. Almeida d'Eça, *Normas Economicas na Colonização Portuguesa até 1808: Memoria*, Coimbra, 1931, pp. 62-6. He incorrectly gives the date as 1577. See also Bailey W. Diffie and George D. Winius, op. cit., pp. 424-5.
3. The word *casados* means married Portuguese men or family men. They were usually married to the native women and were allowed to leave the royal service and to settle down as citizens as well as traders.
4. R.S. Whiteway, op. cit., pp. 176-7.
5. K.S. Mathew and Afzal Ahmad, op. cit., doc. 61, pp. 93-4; doc. 63, pp. 95-7.
6. See the city plan of Cochin in Luis da Silveira, *Livro das Plantas das Fortalezas, Cidades e Povoações do Estado da India Oriental, com as Descrições do Maritimo dos Reinos e Provincias onde estão situados e outros Portos Principais daquelas partes: Contribuição para a Historia das Fortalezas dos Portugueses no Ultramar*, Lisboa, 1991, no.72, p. 88.
7. For details about Jácome de Olivares see, Jose Alberto Rodrigues da Silva Tavim, 'From Setubal to the Sublime Porte', pp. 94-134.
8. ANTT, *Inquisição de Lisboa*, Proc. 5265 fols. 45 and 55. *Pau-da-China* is a creeper seen in China, Japan and Western India and is classified under the name of *Smilax China*. It was often used to cure venereal diseases.
9. ANTT, *Inquisição de Lisboa*, Proc. 3836, fols. 3-4, 16-17 and 29; and Proc. 7543, fols. 28-9 and 39-40.
10. ANTT, *Inquisição de Lisboa*, Proc. 7543, fols. 27-8.
11. ANTT, *Inquisição de Lisboa*, Proc. 7296, fols. 4, 29-33, 37-41.
12. ANTT, *Inquisição de Lisboa*, Proc. 4516, fols. 3, 15; Proc. 15411, fols. 11, 34 and 36.
13. ANTT, *Inquisição de Lisboa*, Proc. 4516, fols. 15 and 20.

14. The details about the imprisonment and inquisition procedures were mentioned in Chapter III when the institution of the Inquisition of Cochin was dealt with.
15. K.S. Mathew and Afzal Ahmad, op. cit., doc. 14, p. 27.
16. Jácome de Olivares had a slave from Sri Lanka by name, Isabel. ANTT, *Inquisição de Lisboa*. Proc. 5265, fol. 71. He had another slave from Africa by name, Andre. Proc. 5265, fol. 70. Diogo Vaz had a slave from Pegu, Proc. 5265 fol. 76. He also had another slave from China by name, Joane. ANTT, *Inquisição de Lisboa*, Proc. 4656, fol. 74.
17. ANTT, *Inquisição de Lisboa*, Proc. 5265, fol. 77.
18. Etymologically the word 'marakkar' means captain or owner of a ship and is derived from the Tamil word 'Marakalam' meaning ship. For details see O.K. Nambiar, *The Kunjalis, Admirals of Calicut*, London, 1963, p. 76. Barros says that Mamale Marakkar and Cherina Marakkar were the leading merchants of Cochin. The ship with seven elephants which Cabral captured on the Zamorin's bid belonged to Cherina Marakkar, who sent them to Cambay. João de Barros, *Decadas* II, liv. V, Cap. VI, p. 140. For details about the trade of Marakkars with the Coromandel coast in rice and textiles see Genevieve Bouchon, 'Les Musulmans du Kerala', pp. 52-4; Jorge Manuel Flores, 'The Straits of Ceylon and the Maritime Trade in Early Sixteenth Century India: Commodities, Merchants and Trading Networks', in *Moyen Orient and Ocean Indien*, XVIe-XIXe. S., vol. VII, Paris, 1990, pp. 30-6.
19. Gaspar Correia, *Lendas da India*, tom. I, pp. 428-30.
20. During the failed expedition to Malacca in 1506, Francisco Pereira, Estevão de Vilhena, Nine Marakkar and one of Gaspar da Gama's sons arrived in the port of Coromandel where they were welcomed by a brother of Nine Marakkar, who was a great merchant of that port. R.A. de Bulhão Pato, *Cartas*..., tom. II, pp. 377-8. For more details about the family network of the *Marakkar* Muslim merchants see Genevieve Bouchon, 'Les Musulmans du Kerala', pp. 52-3. These Marakkars especially Cherina Marakkar of Cochin used to sell rice even to the Portuguese factory of Cannanore in 1516. ANTT, *Nucleo Antigo*, no. 804, fol. 37.
21. ANTT, *Nucleo Antigo*, no. 808; Duarte Barbosa, op. cit., vol. II, pp. 120-4; Gaspar Correia, *Lendas*, tom. II, p. 722. See also Jorge Manuel Flores, 'The Straits of Ceylon', p. 33.
22. Gaspar Correia, *Lendas*, tom. I, p. 430.
23. Fernão Lopes de Castanheda, *Historia do Descobrimento*, p. 74; Gaspar Correia, *Lendas*, tom. I, pp. 430-1; R.S. Whiteway, op. cit., p. 97.
24. Vitorino Magalhães Godinho, *Ensaios: Sobre Historia de Portugal*, vol. II, Lisboa, 1968, pp. 231-40.
25. ANTT, *Inquisição de Lisboa*, Proc. 5808, fol. 69.
26. ANTT, *Inquisição de Lisboa*, Proc. 5265, fols. 31 and 73.
27. ANTT, *Inquisição de Lisboa*, Proc. 5265, fols. 37; 45-7.
28. ANTT, *Inquisição de Lisboa*, Proc. 12292, fols. 17-22, 36-8, 42-3, 72, 77-9.
29. Diogo Vaz, a new Christian of Cochin, was one among them who was even said to be taken by Isaac to Cairo, the capital of Egypt. ANTT, *Inquisição de Lisboa*, Proc. 7296, fol. 77. For more details about the activities of Isaac do Cairo see José Alberto R. Silva Tavim, 'Os Judeus e a Expansão Portuguesa an India durante o Seculo XVI . O Exemplo de Isaac do Cairo: Espião, Lingua e Judeu de Cochim de Cima', in *Arquivos do Centro Cultural Calouste Gulbenkian*, vol. XXXIII, Lisboa, 1994, pp. 167-187.
30. ANTT, *Inquisição de Lisboa*, Proc. 7296, fols. 4, 29-33, 37-41.
31. Cf. Supra note 13.
32. ANTT, *Inquisição de Lisboa*, Proc. 5265, fol. 8.
33. For more details about the mercantile ties between the Jews and the new Christians

during this period, see Jose Alberto Rodrigues da Silva Tavim, 'Outras Gentes em Outras Routas: Judeus e Cristãos-novos de Cochim-Entre Santa Cruz de Cochim e Mattancherry, entre O Imperio Português e o Medio Oriente'. A Paper presented in *Seminario Interna cional de Historia Indo-Portuguesa-Angra do Heroismo*, Açores, 7-11 de Junho de 1996, pp. 4-17.

34. Adelino de Almeida Calado, *Livro que trata das Cousas da India e do Japão*, Coimbra, 1957, pp. 52-9;Vitorino Magalhães Godinho, *Ensaios*, vol. II, p. 235; Sanjay Subrahmanyam, *The Political Economy of Commerce*, p. 221.
35. ANTT, *Nucleo Antigo*, no. 804, fol. 10; K.S. Mathew, *Portuguese Trade*, p. 175.
36. R.A. de Bulhão Pato, *Cartas...*, tom. I, p. 240.
37. Ibid., tom. I, p. 265; tom. III, p. 396.
38. Ibid., tom. III, 52, 83, 269; tom. VII, pp. 41-2, 78.
39. See the letters of Alexis de Sousa sent from Cochin to Francisco Correia the captain of Quilon dated 19 December 1542, 2 January 1543 and 22 December 1543 which speak about the copper that was being sold to Cochin by the captain of Quilon. Bibliotheca do Palacio da Ajuda, *India Portuguesa*, 51-8-43, fols. 61-2. On 16 January 1544, we find Alexis de Souza sending money to Francisco Correia for the copper the former bought from him. Ibid., 51-8-43, fol. 63.
40. Fernão Lopes de Castanheda, op. cit., tom. V, p. 7; Gaspar Correia, *Lendas*, tom. II, pp. 558-9. By 1547, the land routes were said to have had two directions: one towards south to Cape Comorin while the other which was more frequent to Coromandel across the ghats. See the letter of Manuel Lobato to the governor written on 25 August 1547. Elaine Sanceau, *Colecção de São Luorenço*, vol. II, p. 390. From Cape Comorin these spices were again taken to Masulipatanam, Orissa, and Bengal by the lobby which was engaged in illegal trade transactions. See Elaine Sanceau, *Colecção de São Lourenço*, vol. III, p. 356.
41. For details about these hinterland routes see the second chapter on Native Cochin and the hinterlands.
42. Kothamangalam was an important pepper growing area of this period. Jan Kieniewicz, 'Pepper Gardens and Market', p. 2
43. Zaruquly (Chalakkudy) was referred to as the main centre of pepper deviation to Tamil Nadu. Luys da Costa, in *Documentação Ultramarina Portuguesa*, vol. III, Lisbon, 1963, p. 315.
44. F.C. Danvers, *The Portuguese in India*, p. 346; K.S. Mathew, *Portuguese Trade*, p. 209.
45. For more details see M.N. Pearson, *Coastal Western India*, pp. 27-32.
46. R.A.de Bulhão Pato, *Cartas*, tom. IV, pp. 174-6.
47. The main sources for this graph are R.A.de Bulhão Pato, *Cartas*, tom. IV, pp. 174-6; tom. III, p. 258; The details for European trade were furnished by Marino Sanuto which are further explained in this chapter. These details are carefully analysed against the study already done by Vitorino Magalhães Godinho, *Os Descobrimentos e a Economia Mundial*, vol. III, Editorial Presença, Lisboa, 1982, pp. 73-4; K.S. Mathew, *Portuguese Trade*, pp. 115-45.
48. Ibid., pp. 71-3.
49. This is based on a report sent to the crown in 1533 explaining the reasons why the latter got so little pepper. ANTT, *Corpo Cronologico*, I, Maço 50, doc. 65.
50. Bibliotheca do Palacio da Ajuda, *India Portuguesa*, 51-8-45, fol. 141; ANTT, *Corpo Cronologico*, II, Maço 240, doc. 56.
51. ANTT, *Corpo Cronologico*, I, Maço 52, doc. 25.
52. The tension between Cochin and Vadakkenkur fomented over Bardela (Vaduthala) and its temple from where the King of Cochin had taken away the money. Elaine

Sanceau, *Colecção de São Lourenço*, vol. III, p. 15. According to the obligations of the treaty concluded between the Portuguese and the Zamorin in 1540, the Zamorin undertook not to wage direct war with Cochin and the Portuguese. Faria y Sousa, op. cit., tom. II, p. 14; C. Achyuta Menon, op. cit., p. 82. But when the Vadakkenkur king started war he found a loophole in this treaty whereby he joined the enemy of Cochin, i.e. the Vadakkenkur king and began to wage an indirect war with the Portuguese. The association of Tanur king and Zamorin with the Vadakkenkur king made this fight fierce both on land and water. ANTT, *Chancellaria de D. João III, Privilegios*, I, fol. 10v; III, fol. 51v, 168v; ANTT, *Gavetas*, 15, Maço 20, doc. 8.

53. ANTT, *Corpo Cronologico*, I, Maço 87, doc. 50.
54. For see details Diogo Couto, *Decada VI*, part II. book X, Chaps.15 and 17; *Decada VII*, part I, book I, Chaps. 6 and 7; Francisco de Andrade, *Chronica do Muyto alto e Muyto Poderoso Rey destes Reynos de Portugal, D. João III*, part III, Coimbra, MDCCLXXXXVI, pp. 168; 470; part IV, p. 240.
55. ANTT, *Corpo Cronologico*, I, Maço 30, doc. 36; see also M.N. Pearson, *Coastal Western India*, p. 30. For the details of the routes through which this pepper was taken through the ghat route to Bengal and China see the map of Vitorino Magalhães Godinho, *L'Èconomie de L'Éempire Portugais aux Xve et XVIe Sicles*, Paris, 1969.
56. The partnership between the *casados* and the Gujarati merchants has been discussed later in this chapter.
57. This route free from the zone of Portuguese influence was created and encouraged by the Zamorin, Kunjali's men as well as Mamale of Cannanore who possessed Maldives. This was the usual route for the anti-Portuguese merchant groups. For details see Genevieve Bouchon, 'Les Musulmans du Kerala', p. 41; Genevieve Bouchon, 'Sixteenth Century Malabar and the Indian Ocean', in Ashin Das Gupta and M.N. Pearson (eds.), *India and the Indian Ocean 1500-1800*, Delhi, 1987, pp. 166-7, 174.
58. The so-called piratical activities to which they resorted were not mere plunder of the vessels, though it was a part of the strategy to block the ships of the enemy. It also had a trade dimension, which created safe space for the anti-Portuguese vessels to ply to destinations of their interests. For further details see the discussion on corsair activities.
59. Luis Filipe Thomaz, 'The Portuguese in the Seas of the Archipelago', p. 77.
60. See the royal letter from Palmela dated 15 March 1531, ANTT, *Chancelaria de D. João III*, liv. 9, fol. 18.
61. For details see Luis Filipe Thomaz, 'The Portuguese in the Seas of the Archipelago during the 16th Century', p. 77.
62. Ibid.
63. ANTT, *Nucleo Antigo*, No. 807. The details of this voyage are given in Luis Filipe Thomaz, *A Viagem de Antonio Correia a Pegu em 1519*, Lisbon, 1975. See also Genevieve Bouchon, 'Les Premiers Voyages Portugaises á Pasai et á Pegou', *Archipel*, 18 (1979), pp. 127-56.
64. Ibid.
65. For details see the grants given to various persons who took part in the defence of Diu. Duarte Barbudo was granted the privilege on 18 March 1547, to send 10 *bhares* of clothes in this royal ship that went to Malacca via Coromandel. In the same year the Ouvidor Geral and Antonio Cardoso were also granted privileges to send clothes to Malacca in the royal ship that was engaged in the country trade via Coromandel. Antonio Baião, *Historia Quinhentista do Segundo Cêrco de Dio*, Coimbra, 1927, pp. 314-15.
66. Sanjay Subrahmanyam, 'Cochin in Decline', p. 64.
67. Document of 5 February 1546, summarized in Luciano Ribeiro, *Registo da Casa da India*, vol. I, Lisboa, 1954, no. 373, p. 87.

68. See the favour granted to Luis de Vasconcelos. A. Baião, *Historia Quinhentista*, p. 308.
69. Ibid., p. 315.
70. See the letter of Jorge Cabral from Cochin to the king of Portugal dated 21 February 1550. ANTT, *Corpo Cronologico*, I, Maço 83, doc. 90. This particular voyage ended in failure.
71. Luis Filipe Thomaz, 'The Portuguese in the Seas of the Archipelago', p. 77; Sanjay Subrahmanyam, 'Decline in Cochin', p. 65.
72. Ibid., p. 66.
73. ANTT, *Corpo Cronologico*, I, Maço, 76, doc. 8.
74. ANTT, *Corpo Cronologico*, I, Maço, 77, doc. 26. See also Sanjay Subrahmanyam, *The Portuguese Empire in Asia 1500-1700: A Political and Economic History*, London, 1993, pp. 98-9.
75. Fernand Braudel, *The Mediterranean and the Mediterranean World in the Age of Philip II*, vol. 1. Translated from the French by Siân Reynolds, London, 1978, p. 546; see also Niels Steensgaard, *The Asian Trade Revolution of the Seventeenth Century: The East India Companies and the Decline of the Caravan Trade*, London, 1974, p. 83; K.N. Chaudhuri, *The Trading World of Asia and the English East India Company: 1660-1760*, London, 1978, p. 314.
76. For details see Sanjay Subrahmanyam, 'The Tail Wags the Dog or some Aspects of the External Relations of the Estado da India, 1570-1600', in *Moyen Orient & Ocean Indien*, XVIe-XIXe. S., no. 5, Paris, 1988.
77. Cf. Supra note 4.
78. For details see Vitor Luis Gaspar Rodrigues, 'O Grupo de Cochim e a Oposição à Afonso de Albuqueque', *Studia*, 51, Lisboa, 1992, pp. 119-44; Luis Filipe Thomaz, 'Diogo Pereira, O Malabar', *Mare Liberum*, 5, 1993, pp. 49-64. See also Genevieve Bouchon and Luis Filipe Thomaz, *Voyage dans Les Deltas du Gange et de l'Irraouaddy 1521*, Paris, 1988, pp. 58-68, 359-80; Genevieve Bouchon, *Albuquerque, le lion des mers d'Asie*, Paris, 1992.
79. The King of Cochin was interested more in the trade of Cochin than in the well-being of *Estado da India*. So he joined hands with the *casados* giving them tax-concessions. He turned against Albuquerque after the peace treaty which the latter concluded with the Zamorin. ANTT, *Chancelaria de D. Manuel*, I, liv. II, fol. 83. The king of Cochin strongly protested against this move and even wrote letters to Dom Manuel manifesting his displeasure over Albuquerque's alliance with Zamorin. ANTT, *Cartas dos Vice-Reis da India*, doc. 69. With the transfer of the capital of the *Estado* from Cochin to Goa in 1530, the King's alignment with the private traders became more evident, as the *casados* were his main source of income. He began to encourage them by taking a benevolent approach and by reducing the customs.
80. Sanjay Subrahmanyam, *The Portuguese Empire in Asia 1500-1700*, p. 97.
81. Document dated 26 March 1515 summarized in Luciano Ribeiro, *Registo da Casa da India*, vol. I, p. 3.
82. Sanjay Subrahmanyam, 'Notes on the Sixteenth Century Bengal Trade', in *IESHR*, 24/3, 1987, pp. 266-89.
83. Genevieve Bouchon and Luis Filipe Thomaz (eds.), *Voyage dans les Deltas du Gange et de l'Irraouaddy*, pp. 56-60.
84. Luis Filipe Thomaz, 'Diogo Pereira, O Malabar', pp. 50-64.
85. R.A. de Bulhão Pato, *Cartas...*, tom. I, p. 197. Luis Filipe Thomaz, *A Viagem de Antonio Correia*, p. 36.
86. Adelino de Almeida Calado, op. cit., p. 59.

87. Sanjay Subrahmanyam, 'Cochin in Decline', p. 63.
88. Gaspar Correia, *Lendas*, tom. II, pp. 129-30; Elaine Sanceau, *Colecção de São Lourenço*, vol. III, p. 482. The rice trade with Maldives, by the *casados* of Cochin, was very frequent. See also the letter of Manuel Barradas written to D. João de Castro on 16 April 1548. Ibid., p. 506.
89. See for details Roderich Ptak, 'China, Portugal und der Maldiven-Handel vom frühen 15. bis zum frühen 16. Jahrhundert: Einige Bemerkunen zur Wirtschaftsgeschichte Südasiens', in Roderich Ptak (ed.), *Portuguese Asia: Aspects in History and Economic History (Sixteenth and Seventeenth Centuries)*, pp. 123-8.
90. These 2,000 horses imported yearly from Arabia to Goa brought an annual income of 1,00,000 *Xerafins* by way of Customs duties. ANTT, *Corpo Cronologico*, I, Maço 87, doc. 2.
91. ANTT, *Corpo Cronologico*, I, Maço 52, doc. 25. Chymbechenaque and Beteperemal seem to to have been the rulers of southern territories of present day Tamil Nadu.
92. Elaine Sanceau, *Colecção de São Lourenço*, vol. II, p. 275.
93. Ibid., p. 391. See also Vitorino Magalhães Godinho, 'Os Portugueses e o Oriente' *Ensaios*, vol. II, p. 212.
94. Elaine Sanceau, *Colecção de São Lourenço*, vol. II, pp. 347, 380, 391.
95. Antonio Ferreira gave witness before the Inquisition court of Lisbon that Luis Rodrigues used to take horses beyond Cape Comorin to sell them in Bembar (Vembar in the Pearl Fishery coast). ANTT, *Inquisição de Lisboa*, Proc. 12292, fol. 82.
96. J.H.da Cunha Rivara, *Archivo Portuguez Oriental*, Fasciculo 3, New Delhi, 1992, p. 14.
97. M.N. Pearson, *Merchants and Rulers*, pp. 37-9.
98. For details about the favours and privileges granted to those who defended Diu, see Antonio Baião, *Historia Quinhentista*, pp. 296-333. These grants were basically of a dual nature: 1. The privilege to conduct specific voyages in crown ships or in personal vessels; 2. The privilege of mere ship-building without any specific mention of voyages.
99. M.N. Pearson, *Merchants and Rulers*, pp. 37-9.
100. Antonio Baião, *Historia Quinhentista*, pp. 296-333.
101. For details about the co-operation of the Muslim traders till the death of Afonso de Albuquerque see K.S. Mathew, *Portuguese Trade with India*, pp. 100-6; Genevieve Bouchon, *Les Musulmans du Kerala*, pp. 52-3.
102. Though *cartazes* were introduced right from 1502 on, the Muslim traders became the constant victims of raid and torture, conducted in the name of this safe-conduct, only after the death of Albuquerque. This was partly because of the change in the policy of king Manuel which explicitly demanded that the officers favour merchant-groups other than Muslims. R.A. de Bulhão Pato, *Cartas*, tom. I, p. 306. But the moves against the merchant-groups of the Muslim community became more evident and organized with the assumption of offices by those who supported the private entrepreneurial class among the Portuguese in Cochin.
103. Zaynuddin writes: 'Every vessel, however small, being provided with a distinct pass . . . and if this pass was not to be found, they would invariably make a seizure of the ship, its crew and its cargo.' Zaynuddin Shaykh, *Tuhfat-ul-Mujahidin*, trans. S. Muhammed Husain Nainar, Madras, 1942, pp. 89-91.
104. R.S. Whiteway, op. cit., p. 196.
105. Zaynuddin Shaykh, op. cit., p. 66; see also Faria y Sousa, op. cit., vol. I, p. 284.
106. A.P. Ibrahim Kunju, *Studies in Medieval Kerala*, Trivandrum, 1975, p. 60. These Muslim merchants from Cochin seem to have got prominence in Calicut, in the vacuum already created by the foreign Muslims (who traditionally controlled the chief affairs of Calicut), when they left Calicut for places like Ormuz, Gujarat, Vijayanagar and

the Red Sea ports in 1513, as a reaction against the peace treaty which the Portuguese made with the Zamorin. R.A. de Bulhão Pato, *Cartas*, tom. I, p. 126.

107. João de Barros, *Decada IV*, part 8, p. 12.
108. Genevieve Bouchon, 'Les Musulmans du Kerala', pp. 52-3.
109. Jorge Manuel Costa da Silva Flores, *Os Portugueses e o Mar de Ceilão, 1498-1543: Trato, Diplomacia e Guerra*, Dissertação de Mestrado em Historia dos Descobrimentos e da Expansão Portugesa apresentada á Faculdade de Ciências Sociais e Humanas da Universidade nova de Lisboa, Lisboa, 1991, p. 212.
110. Kunjali was said to be the cousin of Pate Marakkar; see the letter of Francisco de Sousa Tavares written to Dom John III dated 14 January 1535. *As Gavetas da Torre do Tombo*, vol. X, Lisboa, 1975, p. 577. But Diogo Couto says that Kunjali was the brother of Pate Marakkar. Diogo Couto, *Da Asia*, *Decada* V, part 2, p. 4.
111. After these incidents the Muslim merchants of Cochin appear only very occasionally in Portuguese documents, a factor which attests to the considerable amount of degradation, from the economic importance and the role which they once used to have. Some of them seem to have resorted to peddling trade. Some of them began to put up small shops for their livelihood. K.S. Mathew and Afzal Ahmad, *Emergence of Cochin*, doc. 14, pp. 27-8.
112. See the treatise on the drugs and spices of Malacca dated 23 September 1533, ANTT, *Cartas* dos Vice-Reis, no. 21; see also Luis Filipe Thomaz, *Os Portugueses em Malacca (1511-1580)*, vol. II, Mestrado thesis submitted at the Faculdade de Letras de Lisboa, 1964, doc. 98, pp. 278. Luis Filipe Thomaz, 'The Portuguese in the Seas of the Archipelago', p. 76. Even during the time of the royal monopoly some individuals used to receive licences to carry contraband goods from South-East Asia to Cochin. Thus, Rui Araujo, the first agent of Malacca, received licence to send to Cochin 29,000 kg. of cloves every year. The letter of king Dom Manuel to Rui Araujo, dated 2 March 1514, ANTT, *Corpo Cronologico*, II, Maço 42, doc. 260. See also the permission given to Martim Afonso de Melo dated 26 March 1521, ANTT, *Corpo Cronologico*, II, Maço 84, doc. 54.
113. Luis Filipe Thomaz, 'Malaka et ses communaut's marchandes au tournant du 16e siécle', in Denys Lombard et Jean Aubin (eds.), *Marchands et Hommes d'affaires asiatiques dans l'Océan Indien et la Mer de Chine 13e -20e siécles*, Paris, 1988, pp. 43-6; Luis Filipe Thomaz, 'The Portuguese in the Seas of the Archipelago', pp. 78-83. See also Sanjay Subrahmanyam, 'Cochin in Decline', p. 63.
114. Diogo de Couto, *Da Asia*, *Decada VI*, liv. viii, p. 19; Luis Filipe Thomaz, 'The Portuguese in the Seas of the Archipelago', p. 76.
115. Ibid., pp. 82-3; Adelino de Almeida Calado, op. cit., pp. 52-3.
116. Luis Filipe Thomaz, 'The Portuguese in the Seas of the Archipelago', p. 83. From 1522 onwards (till the temporary closing of China gate), the Portuguese had regular *carreira* from Cochin to China. There were usually three ships or *junks* in this annual Chinese expedition. Vitorino Magalhães Godinho, 'Os Portugueses e o Oriente', pp. 243-4.
117. See the details of the negotiations connected with the establishment of the Portuguese protectorate at the Javanese ports of Gresik and Panarukan ANTT, *Corpo Cronologico*, I, Maço 48, doc. 47. See also the letter of the captain of Ternate, Antonio de Brito, to the king dated 11 February 1523, published by Basilio de Sá, *Documentação para a Historia das Missões do Padroado Português do Oriente-Insulindia*, vol. I, Lisboa, 1954, doc. 20, p. 132.
118. Sanjay Subrahmanyam, 'Decline in Cochin', pp. 62-3. Almeida Calado, op. cit., pp. 54-9.
119. Vitorino Magalhães Godinho, 'Os Portugueses e o Oriente', pp. 240-1. Seeing the

prospects of trade between Malacca and Coromandel many *casados* of Cochin concentrated their activities in Nagapatanam and São Tomé.

120. Right from 1526, we have evidence of Bengali cloth being brought to Cochin for sale. For example, see the case of Manoel da Gama, who was the factor and captain of the coast of Coromandel and who brought textiles from Bengal to Cochin. ANTT, *Nucleo Antigo*, no. 808, fols. 5-6.
121. Bengal was the chief destination because of the high price that prevailed there. In 1545, a secret enquiry was made by the governor to know the price of Bengal. It led to the discovery of the fact that the net profit from each *Zentner* was 950 *reais*. ANTT, *Corpo Cronologico*, II, Maço 240, doc. 60. During the 1540s we find a lot of treatises on the navigation to Bengal, attesting to the frequency with which the ships used to visit the ports of Bengal. See for example, A. Fontoura da Costa (ed.), *Livro de Marinharia de Bernardo Fernandes (cerca de 1548)*, Lisboa, 1940, pp. 89-91.
122. ANTT, *Corpo Cronologico*, I, Maço 52, doc. 23.
123. K.M. Panikkar, *Malabar and the Portuguese*, pp. 111-13.
124. K.S. Mathew and Afzal Ahmad (eds.), *Emergence of Cochin*, doc. 53, pp. 73-6; Sanjay Subrahmanyam, 'Cochin in Decline', p. 67; K.M. Panikkar, *Malabar and the Portuguese*, pp. 112-13.
125. K.S. Mathew and Afzal Ahmad (eds.), *Emergence of Cochin*, doc. 53, pp. 73-84.
126. M.N. Pearson, *Coastal Western India*, p. 55; Sanjay Subrahmanyam, *The Political Economy of Commerce*, pp. 218-19.
127. This exodus of New Christians to Cochin began with the anti-Semitic religious policy taken by King John III. The *bull Cum ad nihil magis* issued by pope Clement VIII on 17 December 1531 (at the request of John III), and the law of 14 June 1532, prohibiting the exit of the New Christians from the kingdom were the first steps to purge the latter from semitic practices. On 23 May 1536, 'the Holy Office' for inquisitorial proceedings, was established in Portugal by Pope Paul III to deal with them on matters of faith. In this adverse situation many New Christians, expecting more religious freedom and commercial opportunities, migrated to Cochin and other centres in the Orient. For all practical purposes they were considered as Portuguese citizens. For details see J. Lucio de Azevedo, *Historia dos Cristãos Novos Portugueses*, Lisboa, 1975, pp. 72-3, 76 and 109; Israel Salvador Revah', 'Les Marranes Portugais et l'Inquisition au XVIe siécle' in Charles Amiel', *Ètudes Portugaises*, Paris, 1975, pp. 202-4, 213. See also Alexandre Herculano, *Historia da Origem e do Estabelecimento da Inquisição em Portugal*, vols. 1&2, Lisboa, 1987.
128. It was in 1557 that these New Christians were arrested and began to be accused of semitic practices. The inquiry in Cochin against them was spearheaded by the Jesuit Gonçalo da Silveira. For details see Ana Cannas da Cunha, *A inquisição no Estado da India: Origens* (1539-1560) part 2, Lisboa, 1995. These New Christians could until then come to any high post in *Estado da India* like any other Portuguese citizen. For example, Jácome Olivares was made a member of the Muncipal council of Cochin. But the very moment it was known that he was a New Christian, he was expelled from the council. ANTT, *Inquisição de Lisboa*, Proc. 5265, fol. 36.
129. ANTT, *Inquisição deLisboa*, Proc. 4516, fol. 110; Proc. 4656, fol. 110; Proc. 5265, fols. 45, 55, 77.
130. His route seems to have been Malacca -Pegu-Martaban-Ceylon-Cochin, Cochin-Mergui (on the coast of Tennaserim in Siam)-Pegu-Cochin, Cochin-Nagapatanam-Bengal. For details see, ANTT, *Inquisição de Lisboa*, Proc. 12292, fols. 4, 17-22, 33, 36-8, 42-3, 72, 77-9, 82.
131. Dietmar Rothermund, 'Introduction: The Fate of the Portuguese in Asia', in Roderich Ptak, *Portuguese Asia: Aspects in History and Economic History*, p. vii.

132. Luis Filipe Thomaz, 'A Crise de 1565-1575 na Historia do Estado da India', in *Mare Liberum*, no. 9, July 1995, pp. 503-8.
133. Diogo de Couto, *O Soldado Pratico*, cap. viii, edited by M. Rodrigues Lapa, Lisboa, 1937, pp. 38.
134. Luis Filipe Thomaz, 'A Crise de 1565-1575 na Historia do Estado da India', p. 506.
135. Joseph Wicki, 'Duas Relações sobre a situação da India Portuguesa nos anos de 1568 e 1569', in *Studia*, no. 8, Lisboa, 1961, pp. 200-1. This comment was made when he was in the office of Archbishop of Goa in 1569.
136. Luis Filipe Thomaz, 'A Crise de 1565-1575', pp. 507-8.
137. See the letter of Lourenço Pires de Tavora (the Portuguese ambassador in Rome) written to the king on 19 July 1561 in Luis Augusto Rebello da Silva, *Corpo Diplomatico Português*, vol. IX, Lisboa, 1910, p. 303. This news reached Rome via Alexandria and Venice and finally the ears of the Portuguese ambassador.
138. Luis Filipe Thomaz, 'Portuguese Control on the Arabian Sea and the Bay of Bengal—A Comparative Study'. A Paper presented in the Conference on Bay of Bengal, New Delhi, December 1994, p. 27.
139. Luis Filipe Thomaz, 'The Portuguese in the Seas of the Archipelago', p. 77. Voyages of the second category were, as we have already seen, rewards and recognitions and so the crown happily provided space in the royal vessels. Thus in 1548, D.Pedro da Silva was given permission to bring yearly 20 *bhares* of mace and 80 *bhares* of nutmeg in the royal ship, besides the privilege of sending a ship twice a year to Bengal, Pegu and Moluccas. Bibliotheca da Ajuda, *Livro das Mercés que fez D. João de Castro (1545-1548)*, 51-8-46, fol. 57.
140. Antonio Baião, *Historia Quinhentista*, p. 312. On 25 June 1547, he was again allowed to send one more ship to Porto Grande of Bengal, ibid., p. 327. See also Bibliotheca do Palacio da Ajuda, *Livro das Merces que fez D.João de Castro*, 51-8-46, fol. 129.
141. Antonio Baião, *Historia Quinhentista* , p. 298.
142. Ibid.
143. Ibid. , pp. 306 and 309-10.
144. Ibid., p. 312.
145. Ibid., p. 321.
146. Ibid. See also Bibliotheca do Palacio da Ajuda, *Livro das Merces que fez D. João de Castro*, 51-8-46, fol. 121.
147. Antonio Baião, *Historia Quinhentista do Segundo cêrco de Dio*, p. 328; See also Bibliotheca do Palacio da Ajuda, *Livro das Merces que fez D. João de Castro*, 51-8-46, fol. 129v.
148. Antonio Baião, *Historia Quinhentista do Segundo cêrco de Dio*, p. 321; some others like Francisco de Sequeira who wore the habit of the Order of Christ and who came to Diu from Cochin with four of his *caturs* was given 45,000 *reais* and the permission to build a ship in Malabar. Bibliotheca do Palacio da Ajuda, *Livro das Merces que fez D. João de Castro*, 51-8-46, fol. 122.
149. Ibid., p. 315.
150. Ibid., pp. 315-16.
151. Ibid., p. 308.
152. Bibliotheca do Palcio da Ajuda, *Livro das Merces que fez D. João de Castro*, 51-8-46, fol. 133v.
153. Ibid., fol. 182.
154. ANTT, *Chancellaria de D. João III, Doações*, 69 fol. 98v; On 22 November 1547, Alvares Teles had been granted the permission to send ships from Chittagong to Pegu and Malacca. Bibliotheca do Palacio da Ajuda, *Livro das Merces que fez D. João de Castro*, 51-8-46, fol. 170.

155. Ibid., fol. 193v.
156. Ibid., fol. 179.
157. In the technical sense of safe-conduct this appears from 1518 onwards.
158. C.R. Boxer, *The Portuguese Sea-borne Empire 1415-1825*, London, 1969, pp. 20-3: Through famous papal bulls like *Inter cetera* and *Exime Devotionis* of 13 May 1493, *Inter cetera* of 14 May 1493, and *Dudum siquidem* of 26 September 1493, Pope Alexander VI granted to the Catholic kings, the regions discovered by Columbus and divided the world between Portugal and Spain. Luis Adão da Fonseca and José Manuel Ruiz Asenzio (eds.), *Corpus Documental del Tratado de Tordesillas*, Valladolid, 1995, doc. 75, 76, 77 and 91, pp. 119-30 and 137-9. The Portuguese believed that they had full sovereignty over the maritime space occupied by them and granted to them by the Popes. Most of the Indo-Portuguese scholars hold the view that 'sovereignty of the seas' or *mare clausum* as propounded by João de Barros is the basis of the cartaz system. K.S. Mathew, 'Portuguese Trade with India and the Theory of Royal Monopoly in the Sixteenth Century', *Proceedings of the Indian History Congress*, Waltair, 1979, pp. 389-96; C.R. Boxer, *João do Barros: Portuguese Humanist and Historian of Asia*, New Delhi, 1981, p. 100. This view is recently questioned by Luis Filipe Thomaz by citing numerous examples from twelth century onwards, when safe conduct was often used for navigation . See Luis Filipe Thomaz, 'Portuguese Control on the Arabian Sea and the Bay of Bengal', pp. 1-22. It seems that though the practice of giving safe conduct was there from the early twelfth century, the papal bulls gave jurisdictional weight to the claims of these passes and that is why papal intervention, demarcating a particular space in the sea, was always sought after.
159. Zaynuddin Shaykh, op. cit., pp. 89-91. Luis Filipe Thomaz says that the practice of enslavement of crews and passengers of ships caught in the sea was unprecedented in the Indian Ocean, even though some sort of safe conduct for travel and considerable corsair activities existed in this region prior to the arrival of the Portuguese. The targets of the eastern marauders were ships and cargoes not human beings. The practice of enslavement was introduced by the Portuguese and also by the Turks who had intervened in the Indian Ocean since 1508. Luis Filipe Thomaz, 'Portuguese Control on the Arabian Sea and the Bay of Bengal', pp. 8-9.
160. Gaspar Correia, *Lendas*, tom. I, p. 298; Sanjay Subrahmanyam, *The Portuguese Empire in Asia 1500-1700*, p. 77.
161. According to Luis Filipe Thomaz, *cartaz* was a means to establish political hegemony and sovereignty over the seas, having little economic significance. For details see, Luis Filipe Thomaz, 'Portuguese Control on the Arabian Sea and the Bay of Bengal'. But the large network of fortresses and frequent patrolling in the west coast, careful scrutiny of the shipments to Red Sea ports, large and strict restrictions for issuing *cartazes* to west Asia (not even the intimate friends of the Portuguese did get *cartaz* to Red Sea ports) were introduced with economic purposes and with a view that contraband commodities did not enter Europe through the ports of West Asia. So one has to accept that though *cartaz* had often been a political symbol, it was equally an economic tool as well, to control the movements of ships from using the Red Sea–Venice Route. For all practical purposes *cartaz* was a licence which the native traders should, invariably, possess for their commercial movements.
162. Luis Filipe Thomaz, 'Portuguese Control on the Arabian Sea and the Bay of Bengal', p. 23.
163. Letter of Francisco de Sousa Tavares to the king, Cannanore dated 14 January 1535, in *As Gavetas da Torre do Tombo*, vol. X, Lisboa, 1974, pp. 606-9.
164. R.A. de Bulhão Pato, *Cartas*, tom. I, p. 41.

165. Gaspar Correia, *Lendas*, tom. I, p. 523. Letter of Afonso Albuqueque to the king, Cannanore 1 December 1513 in R.A. Bulhão Pato, *Cartas*, tom. I, p. 165; see also Luis Filipe Thomaz, 'Portuguese Control on the Arabian Sea and the Bay of Bengal', p. 8; K.S. Mathew, *Portuguese Trade with India*, pp. 60-2.
166. R.A. de Bulhão Pato, *Cartas*, tom. I, p. 347.
167. M.N. Pearson, *Merchants and Rulers in Gujarat*, pp. 41-4.
168. Letter of Afonso Mexia written to Dom John III, Cochin dated 20 January 1526, ANTT, *Corpo Cronologico*, I, Maço 33 doc. 65.
169. Letter of Fr. Gaspar Barzeus written to Dom John III, in Josef Wicki, *Documenta Indica*, vol. II (*1550-53*), Rome, 1949, doc. 119, p. 608.
170. For the details of the various entrepreneurial activities of Khwaja Shams-ud-din Giloni see K.S. Mathew, 'Khwaja Shams-ud-din Giloni: A Sixteenth Century Entrepreneur in Portuguese India', in Roderich Ptak and Dietmar Rothermund (eds.), *Emporia, Commodities and Entrepreneurs in Asian Maritime Trade, c.1400-1750*, Stuttgart, 1991, pp. 363-71.
171. Faria y Sousa, op. cit., tom. II, pp. 87-8; F.C. Danvers, op. cit., vol. II, p. 285. Asad Khan was the protector of the kingdom of Bijapur when Ismail Adil Shah died (1510-34); Mohamed Kasim Ferishta, *History of the Rise of the Mohamedan Power in India*, vol. III, New Delhi, 1981, p. 44.
172. Faria y Sousa, op. cit., tom. II, pp. 87-8. In 1545, he swore by touching the Koran that he had already given 7,50,000 gold *pardaos* to the Portuguese king and 30,000 gold *pardaos* to the Governor Martim Afonso de Sousa (20,000 for him and 10,000 by way of jewellery for his wife). ANTT, *Corpo Cronologico*, I, Maço 76, doc. 103.
173. In 1544, he was said to have given 70,000 gold *pardaos* for the Portuguese fleet. Luis de Sousa, *Annaes de El Rei Dom João Terceiro*, Lisboa, 1844, p. 413. In the previous year the Governor Martim Afonso de Sousa had come over to Cannanore to çollect an amount of 4,00, 000 *cruzados* from Shams-ud-din. Diogo do Couto, *Da Asia. Decada* V, part II, pp. 388-89.
174. Georg Schurhammer, *Die Zeitgenössischen Quellen zur Geschichte Portugiesisch-Asiens und seiner Nachbarländer*, Rome, 1962, n. 1636, p. 108; n. 2202, p. 145, n. 2632, p. 176, n. 3291, p. 216; ANTT, *Corpo Cronologico*, I, Maço 79, doc. 134; Gaspar Correia, *Lendas da India* , tom. IV, part I, Lisboa, 1864, p. 341; Armando Cortesão and Luis de Albuquerque (eds.), *Obras Completas de D. João de Castro*, vol. III, Coimbra, 1976, p. 174.
175. Elaine Sanceau, *Colecção de São Lourenço*, vol. III, fol. 178.
176. Ibid., fol. 134; his brother who had commercial establishments in Mecca facilitated Shams-ud-din in sending regular cargo to the ports of Red Sea. ANTT, *Corpo Cronologico*, I Maço 78, doc. 108.
177. J.H. da Cunha Rivara, *Archivo Portuguez Oriental*, Fasc. 5, pp. 425-6.
178 Sanjay Subrahmanyam, 'Cochin in Decline', pp. 66-7.
179. R.O.W. Goertz, 'The Portuguese in Cochin', in *Indica*, pp. 63-7; see also R.O.W. Goertz, 'The Portuguese in Cochin', in *Studia*, pp. 5-38.
180. R.O.W. Goertz, 'The Portuguese in Cochin', *Indica*, p. 66.
181. Ibid., pp. 66-7.
182. Elaine Sanceau, *Colecção de São Lourenço*, vol. II, p. 308; vol. III, p. 80, 501, 505.
183. R.O.W. Goertz, 'The Portuguese in Cochin', in *Indica*, p. 69.
184. ANTT, *Corpo Cronologico*, I, Maço 77, doc. 15 , doc. 25 and doc. 27. On 8 January 1547, Henrique de Sousa Chichorro wrote to the governor to hinder this large-scale pepper smuggle to Bengal. ANTT, *Colecção de São Lourenço*, vol. IV, fol. 520. The men of Martim Afonso de Sousa in Cochin were very active in this pepper

smuggle to Bengal. Elaine Sanceau, *Colecção de São Lourenço*, vol. II, p. 283.

185. About 12-15 Chinese junks were sent yearly to get pepper from these places. ANTT, *Corpo Cronologico*, I, Maço 77, doc. 18; ANTT, *Corpo Cronologico*, II, Maço 240, doc. 57.
186. On 26 November 1545, Bernaldim de Souza wrote that Bengal needed much less pepper than what was sent there. ANTT, *Corpo Cronologico*, I, Maço 77, doc. 30.
187. On 15 May 1546, Henrique de Souza Chichorro wrote to the Governor that Alexis de Souza permitted the Chinese junks to load pepper from Cochin. Bibliotheca do Palacio da Ajuda, *India Portuguesa*, 51-8-43. These transactions seem to have been conducted with the help of the promoters of private trade. In 1543 and 1544 the pepper that reached China seem to have caused excess supply. So in these two years the traders had to bring the pepper back from China. See the letter of Duarte de Miranda d'Azevedo, Goa, dated 27 November1545. ANTT, *Corpo Cronologico*, I, Maço 77, doc. 31.
188. See the remarks of Domingos Rabelo about pepper diversion to China written in 1545 in ANTT, *Cartas* dos *Vice-Reis da India*, no. 75. He says that the pepper that reached China was in such a great quantity that the profit from it was very little.
189. See the remarks of João Fernandes Galego about the flow of pepper to various destinations in the Indian Ocean in ANTT, *Cartas dos Vice-Reis da India*, no. 75.
190. Elaine Sanceau, *Colecção de São Lourenço*, vol. II, p. 240.
191. Ibid., vol. II, pp. 366, 368.
192. Ibid., vol. II, pp. 304-7. The native merchants from the Jewish and the Muslim communities had better networks and opportunities for penetrating into the hinterland. So they were often used by the smugglers for collecting cargo from the production centres.
193. For details see R.O.W. Goertz, 'The Portuguese in Cochin', in *Indica*, p. 66.
194. The letter of Ruy Gonçalves de Caminha to the Governor, Cochin, dated 25 December 1547, in Elaine Sanceau, *Colecção de São Lourenço*, vol. III, p. 408.
195. See the remarks of Cosme Anes about the diversion of pepper to various places like Ormuz, Bengal, Pegu, Dabul. ANTT, *Corpo Cronologico*, I, Maço 77, doc. 27. From the 1540s, the Red Sea-Venice route became again very active and a lot of documents speak of this fact. Thus, for example, on 16 October 1541, Estevão da Gama wrote to the king that pepper and other contraband items were continuously taken to Suez and Mecca. ANTT, *Corpo Cronologico*, I, Maço 70, doc. 109. In another letter of Estavão da Gama to the king dated 25 October 1541, a detailed report about the diversion of pepper to Suez and the Red Sea area was given. ANTT, *Gavetas*, 18, Maço 5, doc. 19. The Muslim merchants of Cochin seem to have engaged themselves in collecting spices for these illegal networks. Elaine Sanceau, *Colecção de São Lourenço*, vol. III, p. 449.
196. See the reports on pepper traffic given by Domingos Rodrigues d'Azevedo, Bibliotheca do Palacio da Ajuda, *India Portuguesa*, 51-8-45, fol. 151.
197. Adelino de Almeida Calado, op. cit, p. 74.
198. ANTT, *Corpo Cronologico*, I, Maço 70, doc. 102.
199. Elaine Sanceau, *Colecção de São Lourenço*, vol. II, p. 210.
200. Zamorin used to send pepper and other commodities regularly to Mecca as testified by the king of Tanur in his letter to the Portuguese crown. See the letter of king of Tanur dated 6-1-1549 in ANTT, *Corpo Cronologico*, III, Maço 17, doc. 11.
201. Dietmar Rothermund, *An Economic History of India: From Pre-Colonial Times to 1986*, New York, 1988, p. 11.
202. Cf. Supra note 129.

203. Sanjay Subrahmanyam, 'Cochin in Decline', p. 68.
204. Jose Alberto Rodrigues da Silva Tavim, 'From Setúbal to the Sublime Porte', p. 109. See also Jose Alberto Rodrigues da Silva Tavim 'Outras Gentes em Outras Rotas', p. 7.
205. ANTT, *Inquisição de Lisboa*, Proc. 12292, fol. 4.
206. ANTT, *Inquisição de Lisboa*, Proc. 12292, fols. 20-1.
207. ANTT, *Inquisição de Lisboa*, Proc. 5265, fol. 77. See also José Alberto Rodrigues Silva Tavim, 'Os Judeus e a Expansão Portuguesa na India', p. 206.
208. ANTT, *Inquisição de Lisboa*, Proc. 5265, fols. 98-9.
209. Cf. Supra notes 108, 109, 110.
210. See O.K. Nambiar, op. cit., pp. 14-16. K.M. Panikkar also gives a similar title to them: 'Admirals of the Zamorin'. K.M. Panikkar, *Malabar and the Portuguese*, p. 143.
211. M.N. Pearson, *Coastal Western India*, pp. 25-6.
212. Luis Filippe Thomaz, 'Portuguese Control on the Arabian Sea and the Bay of Bengal', pp. 2-3. Privateering is fostered by a state for political reasons, especially to blockade an enemy power.
213. Luis Filipe Thomaz, 'Portuguese Control on the Arabian Sea and the Bay of Bengal', p. 2.
214. See the letter of Afonso Mexia to Dom John III , Cochin, dated 20 Jan 1526, in ANTT, *Corpo Cronologico*, I, Maço 33, doc. 65. See also Jorge Manuel Costa da Silva Flores, *Os Portugueses e o Mar de Ceilão*, pp. 210-15.
215. This *armada* was meant to guard the coast of Ceylon and Coromandel against the diversion of pepper, cinnamon and other spices. In the early part of the sixteenth century, it was very vigilant, although in the later part the patrolling of the east coast seems to have ceased to exist, when the *armada* starting from Cochin began to stop at Cape Comorin as its terminal point. Initially this armada used to centre its activities in Ceylon and Coromandel. For details see Regimento de Pero Lopes de Sampaio, Evora, 11-2-1520, in ANTT, Livro do Registo de Leis e Regimentos de D. Manuel, fols. 134-6. In the time of Lopo de Azevedo, who was appointed as the captain of this *armada* in 1524, the *armada* began to take the pattern of Cochin-Pulicat-Cochin as the frequent route. ANTT, *Corpo Cronologico*, II, Maço 113, doc. 174; doc. 176. See also Jorge Manuel Costa da Silva Flores, *Os Portugueses e o Mar de Ceilão*, pp. 175-8.
216. Gaspar Correia, *Lendas da India*, tom. III, p. 235.
217. João de Barros, *Decada* IV, part 4, p. 25.
218. The letter of Miguel Ferreira written to King John III dated 26 November 1539, in Georg Schurhammer and E.A. Voretzsch, *Ceylon zur Zeit des Königs Bhuvaneka Bâhu und Franz Xavers, 1539-1552*, vol. I, Leipzig, 1928, doc. 1, p. 82.
219. Gaspar Correia, *Lendas*, tom. II, p. 830; tom. III, p. 712. The exact geographical location of Culimute could not be identified. It could be Calmutão which Georg Schurhammer identified as Muttamtura in Travancore. See Georg Schurhammer, *Die Zeitgenössischen Quellen*, n. 6147, pp. 461 and 540.
220. The letter of Diogo Fernandes to Dom John III dated 1 June 1537, in ANTT, *Corpo Cronologico*, II, Maço 211, doc. 65, fols. 5-6.
221. Jorge Manuel Costa da Silva Flores, *Os Portugueses e o Mar de Ceilão*, p. 214.
222. For details see Georg Schurhammer, 'Die Geschichte Ceylons, 1539-1552', in Georg Schurhammer and E.A. Veoretzsch, op. cit., pp. 1-78 Gaspar Correia, *Lendas*, tom. III, pp. 818-37; tom. IV, pp. 77-84.
223. João de Barros, *Decada* IV, liv. 8, chaps. 12-14; Diogo do Couto, *Da Asia*, *Decada* V,

chaps. 2, 4-6; and 8; Jorge Manuel Flores, *Os Portugueses e o Mar de Ceilão*, p. 221.

224. For the details of the treaty see Faria y Souza , op. cit., tom. II, p. 14. This atmosphere of alliance, as we have already seen, ended with the outbreak of the Cochin - Vadakkenkur war in which the Zamorin took an anti-Portuguese stand.

225. Cf. Supra note 46.

226. Actually Albuquerque, who encouraged mixed marriages by allowing the Portuguese to marry native women, had a dream that his policy would create a body of people to whom could be entrusted the defence and protection of the *Estado*. K.M. Panikkar, *A History of Kerala 1498-1801*, p. 84.

CHAPTER V

Cochin and the Indo-European Trade: 1500-1570

The urban segment of Portuguese Cochin was grafted on to its Indian counterpart to integrate the various spice-growing centres of the Indian Ocean region through the port of Cochin (which belonged not to the Portuguese; but to the native ruler) with Lisbon, and thus to make the surplus extracted from the production centres of Malabar accrue at the metropolis. Though spices including pepper continued to reach Europe in varying and diverse proportions and situations through the traditional gateway of Venice, Lisbon was the chief destination of the majority of the spices transhipped from the Indian Ocean region through the port of Cochin. Besides spices, precious stones, slaves, clothes and even living animals were exported to Lisbon from Cochin; while copper and other precious metals and bullion formed the bulk of commodities of import. The Indo-European trade, which was controlled by the Portuguese State till 1570 and carried out through the Cochin-Lisbon axis, was not static all through this period. A substantial and marked difference can be seen between the three early decades and the succeeding period on matters related to this trade through the *carreira* route. So this study is divided into two parts: 1. Phase of monopoly and state-controlled trade (1500-35); 2. Weakening of royal monopoly and intensification of private trade (1535-70). The export-import trade of these phases is analysed, taking into account the Indo-European background, which influenced greatly the pattern and organization of commerce.

1. THE PHASE OF ROYAL MONOPOLY AND STATE-CONTROLLED TRADE (1500-1535)

The years from 1500 to 1535 were marked by several common features and characteristics, which makes this period a convenient chronological unit for study and assessment. The trade index of this period shows the greatest amount of transactions ever carried on between Cochin and Lisbon. A contextual analysis of this phenomenon requires a brief reference to Indo-European situations without which 'the change over time' can not be properly understood.

Till 1530 Cochin was the commercial as well as the political headquarters of the *Estado da India*. It was in that year that the Governor Nuno da Cunha transferred the seat of Portuguese Asian government from Cochin to Goa.[1] Because of the strong political and military base, during these years, Cochin not only received much attention and consideration, but also created awe and fear among those native rulers and merchants who otherwise would have been reluctant to co-operate. The use of force and intimidation started by Cabral (1500)[2] and continued by Vasco da

Gama (1502), became the most important ingredient of the Portuguese policy of this period to seal off the traditional Red Sea–Venice routes. Moreover, with the establishment of Cochin as the commercial capital, a long chain of fortresses was set up at key strategic centres, as well as a vigilant patrolling system along the coast, to control the trade in the maritime space of the Indian Ocean and to make it converge it at Cochin.

This period also witnessed the greatest amount of indigenous co-operation and assistance. Along with this native involvement, the Portuguese could incorporate the participation of Italian and German merchants in to the commerce of Cochin, thus ensuring a regular supply of copper and silver required for the trade transactions in India. These various factors which influenced the export-import trade of Cochin are analysed in detail below.

I. NETWORK OF FORTRESSES

The nucleus of the Portuguese maritime trade activities in India was the network of fortresses erected on strategic and select places on the land along the coast. The long chain of fortresses along the strategic borders of the Indian Ocean was a symbol of vigilance and constant watch over trade traffic. This fort system, which extended from Ormuz to Malacca, was meant to safeguard the royal monopoly on spice-trade.

As we have already seen, the first Portuguese fort was built in Cochin in 1503.[3] Cochin as the 'source of all pepper' and the principal supporter of the Portuguese in the fights against the Zamorin[4] occupied the key position in this chain of fortresses. In 1505, Cochin was made the capital of the *Estado da India* by D. Francisco da Almeida. The next three forts, which were constructed by Almeida, were in and around Cochin: Kilwa, Anjediva and Cannanore. Though the forts of Anjediva and Kilwa (constructed in 1505) played a significant key role in the initial phase of Portuguese establishment, they were abandoned in 1507 and 1512 respectively.[5] The fortress of Cannanore was erected to control the movement of the spices in north Malabar. Its construction began in 1505 and was completed in 1508. The Viceroy D. Francisco da Almeida named it the fortress of St. Angelo.[6] Along with these forts in and around the production centres of spices, equal attention was given to the African coast where the first fort was built in Sofala, a place which supplied gold and ivory; its construction began in 1505 on the order of Dom Manuel.[7] The work was completed in 1507 by captain Vasco Gomes.[8] Meanwhile an initial step for a fortress was begun in Moçambique by erecting a tower there in 1507.[9] In the same year, another fort was constructed in Socotra; but its lifespan was only till 1511.[10]

Meanwhile a major incident took place in the Arabian sea which greatly influenced the further policies of fort establishment. It was the confrontation of the Portuguese in 1508/9 with the multi-continent forces near Diu. The four main parties namely, the Zamorin of Calicut, the ruler of Gujarat, the Arab merchants patronized by the Sultan of Egypt and the Venetian alliance joined together to fight against the Portuguese, and to revive the traditional route to eastern Mediterranean.[11] But the Portuguese under Almeida, who having purchased the support of Malik Ayaz (the governor of Diu), came out victorious in the engagement off Diu on 3 February

1509.[12] With this defeat, Venice and its supporters had to temporarily accept the Portuguese as the masters of the spice-route and the Indian Ocean. But the Portuguese though victorious, had already taken a decision to move to a safer place, a reasonable place distant from the troublesome Zamorin and at the same time, a place from where they could control the movements of spice ships to the Red Sea–Venice routes. This led to the conquest of Goa by Afonso de Albuquerque in 1510 and the consequent erection of a fortress in the island of Tissuary or Tisvady.[13] The next target was Malacca, the key port of South-East Asia. The potential of Malacca as a trading centre was first discovered by Diogo de Sequeira in 1509. Afonso de Albuquerque conquered it on 17 July 1511, and built a fortress there.[14] Afonso Albuquerque then, made a move to get into the very camp of the enemy. He succeeded in having the reigning Zamorin poisoned, and installed his own nominee on the throne. Albuquerque concluded a peace treaty with this Zamorin and managed to erect a fort in Calicut in 1513.[15] But this treaty and the fort lasted only up to 1525 when this oddly expedient relationship had to be given up. After this, the estranged Muslim merchants from Cochin became the trusted lieutenants of the Zamorin. Meanwhile, the move of the Portuguese to fortify the strategic centres continued. In the extreme west, in the island of Ormuz was located the key port of the entire Persian gulf region. Though the construction of a fort had already begun in Ormuz in 1507,[16] the Portuguese could not establish mastery over the land for some time. Afonso de Albuquerque recaptured the city from the Muslims and the work of the fortress was completed only in 1515.[17] This fort, which was named 'Our Lady of Victory', was described by Luis Figueiredo Falcão as the key to *Estado da India*.[18]

During the period of the next Governors, viz., Lopo Soares de Albergaria (1515-18, the leader of the anti-Albuquerque group in India),[19] and Diogo Lopes de Sequeira (1518-21, who himself was a corrupt official)[20] and Duarte de Menezes (1521-4), private trade and corruption became rampant and spices began to enter Europe through Venice.[21] Once more King João III realized the gravity of the situation and in order to purge the incompetency and corruption, he sent Vasco da Gama to India in 1524 for the third time. But he himself died on Christmas eve of that year.[22]

Even during these nine years of relative laxity, the Portuguese continued their policy of extending the chain of fortresses. A small fort was built in Colombo in Ceylon in 1518.[23] Another fort was also built in the same year in Manar on the western coast of Ceylon.[24] With the erection of these fortresses, as we have already seen, the Portuguese came into conflict with the *Marakkar* traders, who had already concentrated in this area.

The attention of the Portuguese now turned to Quilon, another pepper port in Malabar, where the Muslim attacks threatened the Portuguese presence. Though Afonso de Albuquerque had already established a factory in Quilon in 1503,[25] it was only in 1519 that a fortress was erected in its place.[26] This new fort was placed under the patronage of St. Thomas.[27] Another Portuguese settlement was established at Chaul, which had originally belonged to the Sultan of Ahmadnagar. In 1521, the Governor, Diogo Lopes de Sequeira, constructed a fortress in this place.[28] The extreme south end of East Asia, the land of cloves, nutmeg and mace, was brought under the vigilant watch with the erection of a fortress by Antonio Brito, who was sent by Governor Diogo Lopes de Sequeira, in 1521 for this very purpose.[29] He laid the foundation of the fortress on 22 June 1522, and named it after St. John the Baptist.[30]

The governors who succeeded da Gama namely, Henrique de Meneses (1524-6),[31] Lopo Vaz de Sampaio (1526-9)[32] and Nuno da Cunha (1529-38),[33] were rather honest officials who wanted to improve the situation. During the time of Nuno da Cunha, a fortress was erected in Diu on 25 October 1535, on the spot conceded to the Portuguese by Sultan Bahadur Shah of Cambay.[34]

This chain of fortresses had created some sort of militarized and centralized system, which, in spite of the thriving private trade through loopholes, controlled, to a great extent, the movements of both vessels and spices.

II. *ARMADA* AND THE PATROLLING OF THE COAST

There were two *armadas* which conducted the patrolling of the western coast: 1. The *armada* of the north patrolling the coast from north of Cochin up to Cambay, and 2. The *armada* of the south guarding the west from Cochin, down the entire southern coast to Cape Comorin. Initially there was only one *armada* for the entire west coast. We have an instance in 1507 when Viceroy Dom Almeida sent eight ships under Dom Lourenco to Chaul to guard the coast.[35] After 1510, a fleet was maintained to patrol the Kanara and Malabar coasts; there was regular patrolling of this coast except during the monsoon months (the period between May and September).[36] By the 1520s, the *armada* of the south seemed to have been introduced to control the movements of spices from Cochin. On 11 February 1520, Pero Lopes de Sampaio was appointed as the captain of the *armada* of the south, and began to patrol the coast between Cochin and Pulicat.[37] In 1522 this office was taken away from Lopes de Sampaio, and in 1524 we find Lope de Azevedo assuming charge of this *armada*. He introduced Cochin-Pulicat-Cochin as a regular pattern in this patrolling of the southern coast of India.[38] Eventually the extension of the *armada* to Coromandel coast was dropped and Cape Comorin was made the southern terminal point for the patrolling fleet, starting from Cochin. As far as Cochin was concerned, the *armada* of the south played a key role in checking diversion of the spices.

III. INDIGENOUS CO-OPERATION

This period was marked by the greatest amount of native co-operation which the Portuguese ever got from Malabar and which stands as the largest factor responsible for the transhipment of the huge volume of spices from Cochin to Lisbon. Most important was the royal assistance extended by the native king. Cochin had never been conquered by the Portuguese, but was a free gift given to them by the local ruler, when Cabral reached the port on 24 December 1500. Initially he protected them by accommodating them within his own palace when the Zamorin attacked Cochin in 1503. He demanded the expulsion of the Portuguese from the city, but even against the plea made by the members of his own council to comply with the Zamorin's demand, the native ruler stood by and for the Portuguese. The price that he had to pay for this commitment was that he lost the three ablest princes of the royal family in battle (the other losses being much beyond quantification).[39] When the Portuguese lacked sufficient funds to buy spices, the king of Cochin either gave them loans or supplied commodities on credit. Thus the amount due to the native ruler from the Portuguese in 1513, was 10,000 ducats.[40]

With the help of the king of Cochin, the Portuguese could recruit a great number of the natives for their military service (both Nairs and St. Thomas Christians), whose assistance was utilized not only for capturing Goa, Malacca and winning the Indian battles,[41] but also for carrying out the auxiliary services related to commerce. It was only with the help of these natives that the Portuguese could establish themselves in India and engage in commerce. The great significance of the native co-operation will be evident only when we look at the Portuguese situation. Portugal, at this time, had only 11,00,000 people.[42] The outbreak of famine and pestilence in Portugal in 1504 and 1506 adversely affected the economy of the mother country. Because of the pestilence of 1506, about 120 men died in Lisbon and Tristão da Cunha could not get enough men from Portugal for his *armada* to Cochin. Even in the fleet of Tristão da Cunha seven men died because of this contagious disease, before his departure from Lisbon.[43] In 1507, a plague which broke out in Alentejo took away the lives of 7,500 people; an average of 30 to 120 lives per day.[44] The situation in Portugal was so grave that not enough men were available to be sent to India. In 1510, the king offered a lot of benefices and privileges to those who would come forward to serve in India.[45] But, as Fortunato de Almeida says, despite this attractive offer, the Lisbon administration got only a very few people to go to the east.[46] So the Portuguese had to depend heavily on the natives for all their enterprises in the Indian Ocean.

At first the Lusitanians had no other choice but to depend on the various native merchant groups, since they themselves had no contact with the distant production centres of spices, and also for want of the enviably vast commercial networks which the native mercantile groups enjoyed. Though many of the Muslim traders were, initially, against the Portuguese, the latter succeeded in winning over the co-operation of the leading merchants of the *Marakkar* clan who had commercial links in the coasts of Malabar, Coromandel and Ceylon. By 1504, Cherina Marakkar and Mamale Marakkar, the great merchants of the land were befriended and were given 6,000 *cruzados* (2,000 in cash and 4,000 in rice, copper and other merchandise) for supplying 3,000 *bhares* of pepper for the ships that would be arriving in Cochin in the fleet of Lopo Soares.[47] They soon became the chief merchant agents for the Portuguese in Cochin. At a time when the Portuguese did not have a strong base in India, it was these two merchants who procured pepper at cheap prices from various parts of Malabar and supplied it to the Portuguese factory in Cochin.[48] Eventually a legion of Muslim traders was enlisted into the category of collaborators. Though Edappally was an enemy of Cochin, the Portuguese obtained the support of the prominent merchants of that place. Ali Apule,[49] Coje Mappila and Abraham Mapila were the important merchants of Edappally who used to regularly supply pepper to the Portuguese in Cochin.[50] Though the Portuguese reached Ceylon in 1505, till the second decade they could not penetrate too deeply into the cinnamon gardens. It was the *Marakkar* traders, especially Mitos Marakkar who were the chief suppliers of cinnamon to the Portuguese in Cochin to be taken to Lisbon.[51] However, there were traders like Nino Marakkar, who besides supplying commodities to the Portuguese, gave them ships and a fighting force; in fact, Nino once gave them

1,500 soldiers to fight against the Zamorin.[52] The commercial services of Cherina Marakkar, Mamale Marakkar and his brothers were so great and invaluable that the Governor requested Dom Manuel in 1513 to bestow some special privileges on them in recognition of their co-operation.[53] But after the death of Afonso de Albuquerque, this relationship did not last long. The idea of a crusade was very strong in the decision-making body of Portugal. D. Manuel asked the officials to prefer Christian (the emerging *casado* group as well as the native St. Thomas Christians) and Hindu traders and to keep the Muslim merchants away from trade activities.[54] The initial signs of distance and conflict between the Portuguese and the Muslim traders became evident in their transactions as well. Some Muslim merchants began to supply to the Portuguese factory only adulterated pepper and spices of inferior quality; while the best quality was often reserved to be sent to the Red Sea–Venice route.[55] Slowly, by the 1520s, the emerging *casado* traders who had started to establish extensive commercial networks, had begun to step into the shoes of the traditional Muslim merchants.The most prominent among the latter were slowly ousted from the rank of collaborators, and the frequent confiscation of the Muslim ships and cargoes in the name of *cartazes*, as we have already seen, threw them into the hostile camp. During this period of conflict, a good many of the principal merchants of Cochin moved to Calicut under the leadership of the Kunjali. However, a group of them, though probably second rate merchants, remained in Cochin and continued to co-operate with the Portuguese in their trade endeavours. Without this assistance the Portuguese would not have been able to make grass root contacts with the producers.

Another prominent group from whom the Portuguese enlisted co-operation was the native Christians or the St. Thomas Christians. They formed the great majority of the growers of pepper and ginger which were taken to Portugal.[56] Equally they played a major role in the mercantile activities of Cochin-based trade guild of *Korran* (might be Tamil *Kurran*) from whom Francisco de Albuquerque bought 4,000 *bhares* of well-dried pepper.[57] The leading merchants who used to supply pepper to the Portuguese in Cochin from Quilon, Kayamkulam and even Edappally were St. Thomas Christians. From Quilon (where the St. Thomas Christians had the privilege of keeping under their custody the seal and standard weight of the city)[58] and from Kayamkulam, pepper was brought to Cochin by two leading merchants called Mathias and Bragaida Taquatome.[59] In Cranganore, Bishop Jacome Abuna, the spiritual head of this community, himself came forward to lead the cultivators to take pepper to the Portuguese factory in Cochin.[60] During this period, the Portuguese were very keen on fostering the relationship with this community and ensuring their constant co-operation, as it was the easiest way of penetrating into the distant hinterland. The St. Thomas Christians, on the other hand, viewed the Portuguese as brothers in faith and the Portuguese King as a Christian ally, while the latter used to protect them from the frequent attacks which the Muslims made on their bazaars, churches and settlements in Cranganore.[61]

Though anti-Semitic feeling was very strong in the mother country during this period, it did not penetrate into Cochin with much intensity in the first half of this century.[62] The Portuguese made use of Jews and their commerical links in the early days of their establishment in Cochin. It was Gaspar da Gama, a Jew taken from Anjedive and converted to Christianity by Vasco da Gama, who showed the way to

Cabral to reach Cochin in 1500.[63] The Jews of Cochin used to bring cloth from Cambay and sell it for pepper in Malabar.[64] The pepper they collected was sold to the Portuguese factory in Cochin. The relatively free atmosphere in Cochin attracted the Jews of Spain to this city, especially when there was a massive expulsion of the Jews in 1512.[65] From 1533 on, the new Christians from Portugal also began to flow to Cochin.[66] These Jewish elements from the Iberian Peninsula forged links of co-operation between the native Jews and the Portuguese in economic activities.

The Hindu assistance to the Portuguese in Cochin was in various capacities: as traders, fighters, spy-workers, negotiators of trade and growers of spices. Hindus were also employed in the various categories of the service sector in the Portuguese city of Cochin. Though they did not have as much capital as the Muslims,[67] the contribution of the Hindu merchant community was not insignificant. Yte Couna (Ittikunju), a Nair merchant used to bring pepper from Cranganore to the Portuguese. Thus, for instance, in 1508, an Ezhava cultivator took pepper and other spices directly to Cochin in exchange for cash and copper.[68] Besides this, a number of Hindu merchant groups such as the *Chetties*, Konkanis, Gujaratis and the Kanarese, co-operating with the Portuguese system, conducted trade in Cochin.[69] The Nair militia of Cochin and the neighbouring principalities formed an important part of the fighting force that waged wars for the Portuguese. Thousands of Nairs fought and died for the Portuguese in the early days of their establishment.[70] Even the non-Nairs like the *Pulayas* (the low caste agricultural labourers) joined hands with the Portuguese to fight against the Zamorin, and Duarte Pacheco asked the king of Cochin to elevate them to the Nair caste.[71]

The Nairs were also employed for the collection of pepper from the hinterland. Two Nairs were permanently employed to go to the distant production centres to get spices for the *carreira da India*. For this job each of them was paid a monthly salary of 800 *reais* (19200 *reais* per year).[72] One Panikkar and four Nairs were employed to deal with pepper in the Portuguese factory and were given an annual remuneration of 5120 reis.[73] Besides this, there was another native hand called 'weigher' (*pesador*) of pepper, whose services were absolutely indispensable in the entire transactions, who was given an annual pay of 7200 *reais*.[74]

Native co-operation was also available to the Portuguese as the caretakers of the weighing houses where the river-craft brought pepper from hinterland, coolie-labourers who had to carry the sacks of pepper to and from boats, the store and weighing houses, guards who kept a watch on the commodities, makers of straw-mats, baskets and gunny bags (necessary for drying, packing and carrying pepper), suppliers of oil and candles for lighting.[75]

In general, this first phase was marked by remarkable co-operation from the various native factors which was responsible for, more than any other thing, for a greater volume of export trade from Cochin.

IV. PRICE-FIXATION AND UNDER-PRICING OF THE COMMODITIES

The price of the spices were lower in Cochin than in Calicut and other spice ports of Malabar. Thus in 1498 1 *faraçola* (8.31 kg.) of pepper in Cochin cost only 9 *panams* while the same quantity of pepper in Calicut cost 14 *panams*.[76] But the entry of the Portuguese into the spice market made the prices shoot up and the merchants were reluctant to sell their commodities at the old price offered by the Portuguese. The Manueline strategy found price-fixation to be the solution for the instability of the market. Accordingly, Vasco da Gama in consultation with the King of Cochin and the local merchants fixed the price of the spices on 3 January 1503.[77] According to this agreement, the price of a *bhar* (166.3 kg.) of pepper ws fixed at 152.5 *panams* (8.3 *cruzados*) and the king of Cochin was given half a *cruzado* per *bhar* as customs duty.[78] This price-fixation was, certainly, an under-pricing of the commodities, as the price for the same quantity of pepper in Calicut in 1500 was 360 *panams*[79] and the loss for the merchants was almost 207.5 *panams* per *bhar*. The native merchants and the cultivators, who suffered this great loss, had no other easy outlet and so had to co-operate with the Portuguese. With the low prices in Cochin, the price of even Calicut was forced to be brought down and in 1516, one *bhar* of pepper there cost only 10.17 *cruzados*.[80] It shows that the price of Calicut was reduced almost to half and was brought clos:: to that of Cochin. The price-fixation, thus, developed into a mechanism to under price the commodities of even other ports of Malabar and the templation to divert spices to non-Portuguese ports of Malabar to gain big profits, by selling at high prices, was thus drastically reduced. The possible alternative was to carry them across the ghat to Tamilnadu and to tranship them from the ports of the Coromandel coast to traditional destinations in Asia.[81] But this route, besides being risky, seems to have involved much expense reducing the percentage of profit. Though the price they would receive in Cairo and Venice was very high, the expenses incurred due to the risk factor, the long and secret journey and the taxes to the lords of the lands through which they had to pass, took away much of the possible profit. So even in this price situation many of the indigenous merchants and cultivators were compelled to co-operate and to make available spices for the ships to Lisbon.

Table V-1 shows that increase in the price of the commodities, effected with the entry of the Portuguese into Malabar was only a transient phenomenon. The price-fixation and the treaty with the Zamorin made the price come down to a rate lower than that of the pre-Portuguese times. This price-reduction strategy was also used as a weapon to seal off diversion to other ports and to strengthen the Cochin-Lisbon route.

Meanwhile there occurred a great fluctuation in the price of pepper in the three important re-export centres of spices namely, Cairo, Venice and Lisbon. In 1498, the price of pepper in Venice was 56 ducats per quintal. The news of Portuguese entry to Indian market made the price shoot up to about 100 ducats in February 1500. Whereas in Cairo, it was 78 ducats in 1498. However the Portuguese discovery of the Cape route affected the price of this traditional commercial city as well. The price of pepper rose up to 90-102 ducats in 1500-1.[82] Meanwhile in Lisbon, the price of pepper in 1498-9 was 80 ducats. But by 1500-2 it fell to 40 ducats.[83] By 1516, when the Portuguese had established almost total sovereignty over the trade routes in the Indian Ocean, the price indexes began to show a different trend. The price in Cairo shot up to 135 ducats in 1516, revealing the problem of obtaining this commodity in the Suez area. Venice also seems to have had some difficulty in getting spices during this period, as the price remained almost around 80 ducats in 1516.[84] The abundant flow of pepper to Lisbon is evident from the fact that the price fell by 1504 to 20 ducats and below. In the following year the price was fixed at 22 ducats and in 1516 it remained at this rate.[85] These fluctuations are indicated in Graph 1.

TABLE V-1: PRICE OF SPICES (Per Quintal in Ducats)

Commodity	Calicut		Cochin		Malabar after the entry of the Portuguese	Alexandria		Venice
	1498[86]	1500[87]	1516[88]	1498[89]	1502/3[90]	1500/2[91]	1498[92]	1498[93]
Pepper	4.64d	5.96d	3.02d	2.98d	2.5d	14d	25d	56d
Ginger		2.01d (dried)				10d	11d	16d
Cloves	9.88d				6.25d	26d	20d	
Cinnamon	6.41d				4.00d	22d	25d	
Cardamom		8.96d						
Nutmeg	7.40d	3.65d			2.35d	6d	16d	
Sealing Wax	4.25d					20d	25d	
Brazil Wood	2.64d					5d	10d	
Aloe Wood	132.82d				15.6d		25.6d	
Benzoin	2.01d	20.47d			7.9d	74d	12.8d	
Camphor	53.13d				1.56d			
Opium	132.82d	78.88d						
Sandal Wood–red	1.35d	1.92d						
Sandal Wood–white	11.45d	19.06d						

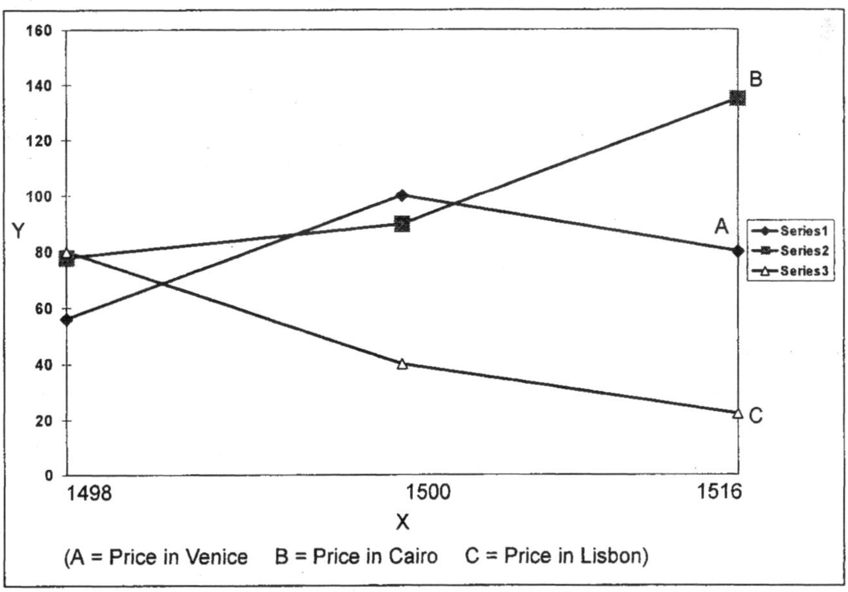

Graph 1: Price Fluctuations in Cairo, Venice and Lisbon in 1498, 1500 and 1516.

By keeping a fixed price both in Cochin and Malabar Coast (around 2.5 ducats) as well as in Lisbon (around 22 ducats during this period), the fluctuation in the market was controlled; but it under-priced the commodity. The higher prices in Cairo and Venice, though an attraction, were nothing but the prices offered for the risk in the diversion of pepper. The cultivators and the ordinary merchants, who received only pre-Portuguese price for their commodities were the victims of this under-pricing.

V. MONOPOLIZATION OF THE SPICE TRADE

The elements of force and violence introduced in the Indian Ocean region by the Portuguese with the systems of *cartaz-armada*-fortress were to bring the spice route under a perfect monopoly. After the initial experiments of allowing the participation of private merchants (in the early years of the first decade of sixteenth century), the crown began to reserve the trade on spices as a royal monopoly. Right from 1510 on, the king barred the people going to India from trading in spices, drugs, sealing wax, dyes, indigo and benzoin.[94] On 26 February 1518, the crown prohibited the Portuguese in India from buying and selling pepper, whether little or much.[95] Eventually, the ban on trading in spices was extended to all other sections of traders. The king ordered that no one should be allowed to deal with pepper, and all ships which took pepper should be confiscated along with the commodity.[96] *The Ordenaçoes da India* issued on 8 September 1520 (at Evora), ordered that pepper, cloves, ginger, cinnamon, maces, nutmeg, sealing wax, silk and borax should be commodities reserved for the crown.[97] The stringent measures to enforce the monopolistic trade in spices made the Cochin-Lisbon route relatively stronger.

Although, even during this period, the Portuguese could not have a perfect and monopolistic control over the spice trade in the Indian Ocean region, as we have already seen, and pepper as well as other spices continued to be taken to the Red Sea–Venice route as well as to other destinations in Asia,[98] commodities which entered Europe via the Cochin–Lisbon axis was so great and significant that the Portuguese, as the greatest and continuous suppliers of spices, exercised some sort of monopoly at least with regard to Europe.

VI. *CARREIRA* FACTOR

This period witnessed the greatest number of *Naos*[99] of the *Carreira* operating in the Indian Ocean. An India-bound *Nao* of the *Carreira* with a crew of 120 men and boys usually carried at least 400 to 500 soldiers sent out for service in the East.[100] The Portuguese despatched about 86 ships from Lisbon during the period from 1500 to 1505 and the sailors and soldiers aboard them must have numbered around 7,000.[101] For the first 35 years, about 365 ships departed from Portugal out of which 323 reached India. The average tonnage of these *Naos* ranged between 300 and 450.[102] Usually the ships to India left Lisbon every year in March or April, in view of the monsoon factor in the Indian Ocean. An early departure from Lisbon would compel the ships to take an unavoidable and long stay at Moçambique (sometimes Melinde or Socotora), as a further journey from there to India before the month of May, would be extremely risky and difficult because of the adverse monsoon wind.[103] The ships which left Lisbon in March/April reached Cochin in September.[104] These ships were loaded with spices in October and November, having to make the return voyage from Cochin to Lisbon in the second half of December, and in most cases, in the beginning of January.[105] Otherwise they would miss the favourable winds. But the pepper was harvested in Malabar in late December or January. The processes of threshing and drying in the sun took considerable time. Portuguese were not able to procure fresh supplies of pepper before late February or March.[106] So the ships of the *Carreira* had to be loaded with the supplies of the previous year which were stored in the various factories of south-west India and brought to Cochin. These ships on their way back often called on Moçambique for fresh water and provisions[107] and they reached Tejus between the middle of June and September.[108] Thus the round voyage between Lisbon and Cochin took about a year and a half in the most favourable circumstances.[109]

This period, though it was the initial phase, witnessed a smaller percentage of shipwrecks. Though different reasons could be assigned as explanations for this, *Caixas de Liberdade* or the liberty chests which the various officials and crew of the ships were allowed to take along with them to Portugal seem to have compelled the crew and officials to invest additional care, alertness and caution. This originated from the fact that the crown was either unable or unwilling to pay adequate and full wages and consequently strove to recompense its servants by allowing them to import limited quantities of spices wholly or partly, freight and duty free.[110] These chests were to a standard measurement of 6 *palmos de vara* (about 4 feet) in length by three in height, and two and a half in breadth.[111] The quantity of the commodities permitted to be taken to Portugal varied according to the status of the officials. Thus while a captain-major could carry fifteen *caixas*, a cabin boy could take only one *fardo* (bundle).[112] This practice, as a boost to private initiative and enterprise, though it tempted too many people to give more attention to the storage and safe-keeping of their own goods than to those of the crown, also prompted them to conduct the homeward journey of the *Carreira* more safely and securely as well, and thus to gain profit for their own entrepreneurial involvement.

The following statistics show that during this period (1500-30) the percentage of losses in the homeward ships (5.7 per cent) was less when compared to the losses incurred in the outward voyages (10 per cent). Table V-2 also points to the fact that the annual percentage of ships which safely reached India from Lisbon during this period (till 1529) was 9.3 out of which an annual average of 5.6 ships reached Portugal in 26 years during the period from 1501 to 1530.

The *Carreira* system with the *liberdade* practice incorporated a space for private initiative whose outcome was safety and the carefulness with which the homeward *Naos* of *Carreira* were tended.

VII. THE EUROPEAN CONTEXT

Any study of the Cochin–Lisbon axis and Indo-European trade relations requires a contextual analysis of various factors and developments in Europe which influenced the export-import indexes of Cochin.

TABLE V-2: MOVEMENT OF THE SHIPS OF THE *CARREIRA DA INDIA*

Outward Voyages[113]

Year	No. of ships departed from Portugal	Lost/destroyed sent back	Percentage of loss	No. of ships arrived in Cochin and Goa
1500-9	138	10	7.3%	128
1510-19	96	6	6.3%	90
1520-9	76	15	19.7%	61
1530-9	80	11	13.0%	69
1540-9	61	6	9.8%	55
1550-9	51	11	21.0%	40
1560-9	49	7	14.2%	42
Total	551	66	12.0%	485

Homeward Voyages[114]

Year	No. of ships departed from Cochin & Goa	Destroyed/ lost	Percentage of loss	No. of ships arrived in Lisbon
1501-10 (lacks 1507)	64	7	10.8%	57
1511-20 (lacks 1516 and 1520)	56	1	1.8%	55
1521-30 (lacks 1521)	37	1	2.7%	36
1531-40	Data not available			
1541-50 (lacks 1546)	46	5	10.9%	41
1551-60	45	14	31.1%	31
1561-70	37	5	13.6%	32
Total	285	33	11.6%	252

A. The Portuguese Situation

The strong maritime and explorative traditions initiated by Prince Henry the navigator and pursued by João II was followed by King Manuel, with the same intensity, when he ascended the Portuguese throne in 1495.[115] He became the king only because Afonso, the son of João II and heir to the throne, was killed when his horse fell in 1491, and because João II had executed his other relatives for treason.[116] It was chiefly because of the firm determination of this new king that the measures for Portuguese expansion and trade in the Indian Ocean were followed and given top priority. In a debate which took place at Monte-mor O Novo in the Alentejo during the month of December 1495, a faction of the councillors of the new king, Manuel, argued that Portugal should be content with the comparatively peaceful exploitation of what had already been discovered in Africa and that Portugal should give up the Indian expedition as it might arouse the hostility of every monarch then involved in the Indian trade[117] and the big expenses it would involve.[118] By voting with the councillors who wished to pursue the Indian enterprise, King Manuel took the risks in and initiatives for the Indian voyages and trade. The first generation of officials and captains sent to India like Da Gama, Cabral, Almeida and Albuquerque realized what he had dreamt of, although the last three appointees of King Manuel (Lopo Soares de Albergaria, Diogo Lopes de Sequeira and Duarte de Meneses—governors of India from 1515-24) proved to be bad lieutenants.

King Manuel, in order to announce Portuguese discoveries and to gain publicity for Portugal's conquests made in India, sent an embassy of obedience to Pope in 1505[119] and in 1514.[120] These embassies to the Pope were meant to suggest that Portugal was no longer small or constrained by geographical limits, as well as to establish a position in Europe equivalent to that of the recent achievements they had made in their trade with India. With the establishment of the Cochin-Lisbon axis, a great change was introduced in the organization of commerce in Portugal. The *Casa da Guine* which was established in the middle of the fifteenth century in Lagos in Algarve for the sake of the African trade,[121] and later transferred to Lisbon under the name of *Casa da Guine e Mina* (1480)[122] was re-organized for conducting trade with India. By 1500, with the beginning of spice-trade it was renamed *Casa da India*, this transformation being essential, as the Indian trade had already outstripped Portugal's other overseas trade, in importance and potential.[123] The *Regimento* of 1509, according to which the *Casa da India* was organized, makes it clear that all the three sections of India, Guinea and the slave trade, were subordinate to a single factor, generally known as the factor of the *Casa da India*.[124] It served as the warehouse for commodities purchased from Europe to be sent to India. At the same time it also functioned almost like a market where the oriental goods were sold to wholesale and retail merchants.[125] It was necessary that the entire cargo from each ship was to be deposited directly in *Casa da India* upon arriving at Lisbon. The factor of the *Casa* informed the king of the size as well as the composition of the cargo, and entered in an account book all receipts and disbursements of the spices. The factor was also charged with maintaining overseas correspondence, keeping lists of all the ships and their crew and checking on the factors in the overseas world. In effect he was the superintendent of practically all of Portugal's overseas trade.[126] Moreover, the dues to the king from those who participated in Indian trade were also collected in the *Casa da India*,[127] which had also the responsibility to pay in advance for the people who were sent to India in the annual fleets.[128]

The spices brought to Lisbon from Cochin were distributed all over the Mediterranean region through the *Casa da India*. In 1506, three Portuguese ships with brasil wood, pepper and other spices reached Valona.[129] Later in 1527, the Venetian senate even proposed to King John III that the sales contract for all pepper imported to Lisbon be farmed out to Venice, after allowing for Portuguese home consumption; but the project was never realized.[130] By 1532, the royal ships from Portugal began to re-export the spices brought from Cochin to the cities of Marseilles in France and Genova in Italy.[131] The trade with north Europe, especially the royal trade in Antwerp was also carried out through the *Casa da India*.

B. The Factory at Antwerp

The spices from Cochin that reached *Casa da India* were further taken to the Portuguese factory at Antwerp. With the establishment of the Cochin–Lisbon commercial axis, Antwerp in Flanders had pushed Bruges into the background and had emerged as a great centre of re-distribution for Asian goods in Europe.[132] The Portuguese collected copper and silver to be sent to Cochin and Goa from Antwerp where the merchants from the Aachen area and south Germany (especially the Fuggers and Welsers), were selling both these metals in increasing quantities.[133] The first ship from Lisbon carrying spices from Cochin arrived at Antwerp harbour, situated on the banks of the Scheldt river, in 1501.[134] From 1503, the re-exports of Indian spices from Lisbon to Antwerp were large and regular.[135] During this period, Nikolaus of Rechterghem, who was from Aachen and commercially associated with Jacob Fugger, began to buy pepper from the Portuguese in Antwerp and send it to upper Germany.[136] In 1508 the rights to the Portuguese crown monopoly of spices were leased to the Affaitadi and Gualterotti and they maintained this exclusive right till 1514. They took pepper to the fairs of Lyons and even to Italy.[137] The south German merchants like the Fuggers and the Welsers became a part of this monopoly at third hand.[138] In 1507 the *Magna Societas* of Ravensburg decided to henceforth buy pepper and spices at Antwerp. In 1512-13 the Viennese merchants complained that they were getting less pepper and spices from Venice, hence they requested the emperor to authorize foreign merchants to bring spices from Antwerp, Frankfurt or Nürnberg[139] (which were supplied by the Antwerp factory). Flanders and Antwerp had maintained land connections with Cologne, Frankfurt and Nürnberg, the former being a great centre of trade for the Hanseatic and English merchants who came by sea.[140] With the establishment of Cochin-Lisbon-Antwerp commercial axis, we see in the first three decades of the sixteenth century, a phenomenon appearing in Europe by which the commercial centre of gravity was shifted from the Mediterranean (Venice) to the north-west Atlantic (Antwerp fed by Lisbon).[141]

C. The Participation of Italians and Germans

The participation of the Italians and the Germans became inevitable because of three factors: 1. The mode of payment for the pepper of Malabar necessitated that a large quantity of copper be imported to India which inevitably required the participation of the German and Italian copper merchants who held monopolistic control over the production and distribution of copper in Europe. From 1503 onwards, the mode of payment was fixed at three-fourths of the price of pepper, being paid in cash and one-fourth in the form of copper.[142] This seemed to have been an advantageous arrangement both for the Portuguese as well as for the natives. The partial exchange in copper gave an added profit to the Portuguese commercial endeavour, as one quintal of copper purchased at Flanders for 4½ *cruzados* was exchanged at a value of 14 *cruzados* and the net profit after all expenses were paid, was around 5 *cruzados* per quintal.[143] Initially, the payment in copper was not greatly appreciated by some native merchants and cultivators, as it necessitated another exchange for cashing it. But very soon the demand for this metal in India, which lacked copper sources, became very high, as it began to be used on a very large scale for the making of household utensils. Eventually the household utensils made of copper and bronze became symbols of social status and aristocracy especially in Malabar, which further increased the demand for copper and continuous participation of the Italian and German copper dealers. Even in 1552, when the king of Cochin, prompted by the scarcity of pepper in Cochin because of the Vaduthala war, made a contract with the native merchants for pepper-supply, the condition stipulated by the latter was that they should get one-third of the price of pepper in copper.[144] Foreigners especially the Germans were instructed to get the required quantity of copper for every ship destined for India. 2. The difficulty felt in the initial phase, as we have already seen, of getting enough of a Portuguese fighting force necessitated the incorporation of many Germans and Italians as soldiers and *bombardeiros*. 3. The Portuguese crown had also felt it necessary to involve the wealthy entrepreneurs of Portugal, Italy and Germany in the Indian trade, at least in the initial years of establishment, for want of enough resources. The observations which Quirini made in 1506 throws some light on the general financial position of the Portuguese, and on the role played by the financiers and wealthy merchants. He remarks that out of the annual income of 3,50,000 ducats, Portugal had to spend 3,00,000 ducats domestically and that the King had only 50,000 ducats at his disposal for the Indian enterprise. For fitting out ships to India and for the purchase of spices and other commodities in Kerala, the Portuguese king had to find out an extra amount of 1,70,000 ducats. The crown invested only 25 per cent of the total amount required for the purchase of the commodities and the balance was supplied by the financiers and the merchants.[145]

a. The Italians

The Italian merchants who made their voyages to far-off Flanders in big merchant galleys and who stopped over at Lisbon on both the outward and return voyages began to play an active role in Portugal from the thirteenth century on.[146] Though among the Italians the Venetians were generally neglected, the Genoese and the Florentines were specially favoured. The Doria, the Lomellini, the Grimaldi, the Catanei and the Pessanha were the important Genoese families which played an active role in the commercial and maritime activities of Portugal.[147] Along with Cabral's fleet a Genoese, probably Antonio Salvago, in company with a Florentine named Girolamo Sernigi sent a ship to Cochin in 1500.[148] In 1516, Andrea Corsali came to Kerala for trade.[149] The Genoese continued to send ships along with the Portuguese fleet in the following years, as well. Thus, in 1518, we find Leonardo Nardi, from Genoa sending a ship to India in 1518.[150]

The Florentines were great merchants and bankers in Portugal. By 1338 the famous Bardi family of bankers from Florence was given the first charter containing commercial privileges by the Portuguese crown.[151] The elimination of their merchant fleet in 1494 by the Pisans forced the Florentines to look abroad for investment opportunities. The commercial and financial needs created in Portugal with the expulsion of the Jews and the discovery of the Cape route, gave the Florentines ample opportunities to involve themselves in the commercial enterprises of the Lusitanians.[152] The most prominent of the Florentine families was that of the Marchioni headed by Bartolomeo Marchioni. He was the richest man in Lisbon at the beginning of the sixteenth century.[153] It was from Bartolomeo Marchioni that John II secured for Pedro da Covilhão and Afonso de Paiva (for their travels to India and Ethiopia) in 1487, a letter of credit for 400 *cruzados*.[154] The *Anunciada*, a small ship which went to India along with Cabral in 1500 was financed by Bartolomeo and it brought back from Cochin 300 *chantara* of pepper, 160 *chantara* of cinnamon, 60 *chantara* of lac and 14 *chantara* of benzoin.[155] In 1501, a consortium was formed under the leadership of Bartolomeo and out of the four ships of João da Nova sent to India in 1501, two were despatched by the consortium. They were put under the captaincy of the Florentine, Messer Fernam Vineti.[156] Girolamo Sernigi, another Florentine financier in Lisbon,[157] had participated in sending a ship to India along with the fleet of Cabral in 1500.[158] In 1503, out of the nine ships which moved to Cochin in the fleet of Afonso de Albuquerque, four ships belonged to the merchants. Prominent among these merchant-groups were Girolamo Frescobaldi and Filippo Gualterotti, the heads of the great Florentine banking groups which had established factories in Flanders, and Girolamo Sernigi. Giovanni da Empoli was the factor of these Italian ships.[159] In 1505, joining hands with the German financiers, Bartolomeo and other Italians invested 29,400 *cruzados* for their trade with Cochin.[160] In 1506 once again, the Italian capitalistic groups, including the Genoese and Florentines with Bartolomeo Marchioni at the head, sent ships to India.[161] Among the four private ships sent by Portugal (the voyage was organized by *Estado*) to Malacca under the captaincy of Diogo Mendes de Vasconcelos, one ship was commanded by the Italian Sernigi, while the factor of another ship was said to have been the Italian Empoli.[162] In 1512, Girolamo Sernigi fitted out a ship directly for Malacca which returned to Lisbon the next year.[163] By 1515 the Factor Giovanni da Empoli had become a ship-owner, and we see him in that year accompanying Lopo Soares, the new governor, as captain of his own ship.[164]

The Affaitadi was another banking family from Italy that was actively involved in the economic life of Portugal. Actually Giovanni Francesco de Affaitadi was from Cremona (which during this period was under the control of Venice) and he engaged himself at first in the sugar trade with the Portuguese island of Madeira.[165] But with the arrival of Cabral's fleet from India, the Affaitadi became interested in the trade in spices. Because of his wealth, his banking and commercial links, he occupied an almost diplomatic position at Lisbon.[166] He participated in the trade with Cochin by sending Mateo do Begnino as his factor in the fleet of Vasco da Gama in 1502.[167] He travelled with Estavão da Gama and in his letter (dated 30 March 1503), he narrates the trade conditions of Cochin in detail to Giovanni Francesco de Affaitadi, his master.[168] As we have already seen, the Affaitadi obtained exclusive trade rights in spices with Flanders for some time. The Portuguese received copper and silver in exchange for spices and these precious metals were in great demand for the Portuguese trade with India. The Portuguese had, later, agents at Seville, Valencia and at Medina del Campo (where the largest fair in Spain was held), at London, at Lyons and in various cities in Italy and the Low country.[169] Giovanni continued to be in Lisbon till his death in 1528; later, his nephew João Carlos de Affaitadi began to take care of the enterprise.[170]

Many Italians came to India as soldiers, as well. Some of these Italian mercenaries on their arrival in India left the service of the Portuguese crown and entered the service of native rulers, e.g. the Milanese renegades who joined the Zamorin,[171] or Khwaja Safar, another Italian renegade who served as governor of

Diu later in 1538.[172] However, a good many of them did seem to have continued their service in the Portuguese regiment.

b. The Germans

The first German merchants who established themselves in Portugal were said to have been the timber merchants. Timber, iron (for shipbuilding purposes), and military goods such as war weapons from the ports of the Hanseatic League were brought in large quantities to Portugal. In 1433 Afonso Bernardes was the *procurador* for all German and Flemish merchants in Lisbon.[173] German ships known as *holks* (*urca* in Portuguese) were in high demand in Lisbon, and were used by John II (1481-95) in his African expeditions.[174] The German and Flemish soldiers had formed an important military group in Portugal during the time of John II and the German soldiers and *bombardeiros* had established the Brotherhood of St. Bartholomew in Lisbon.[175] The Brotherhood was intimately associated with the German mercantile community in Lisbon where the chapel of St. Bartholomew was the centre of German religious activities in Portugal.[176] The first Germans who came to India were soldiers from this Brotherhood of Bartholomew. They seem to have formed an important part of the artillery men who accompanied every Portuguese ship to Cochin.[177] The largest number of German soldiers seems to have reached Cochin in 1502, along with Vasco da Gama.[178] In 1503, these German soldiers built the chapel of St. Bartholomew near Calvethy in Cochin.[179] By 1525, the number of the German soldiers in Cochin rose to fifty.[180] In 1525, a request had been made to the Portuguese crown from Cochin to send 100 *bombardeiros* urgently to the East out of which half should be German mercenaries.[181] The German soldiers were generally used for all the Portuguese battles of expansion and defence fought in Asia. Later by 1546, in the defence of Diu, some of these German *bombardeiros* took active part. One among them was Antonio de Bos, who was given 10 *parados* of salary for his service, out of which 2 *pardaos* were given extra for the fact that he was a foreigner.[182]

Meanwhile the big German merchants, who had been trading at Venice for a long time, were forced in 1499-1500 to shift their business elsewhere because of the war which broke out between Sultan Bajesid II of Turkey and the Republic of Venice.[183] So in 1501, as the diarist Marino Sanuto says, four German trading houses under the leadership of the Fuggers tried to conduct direct trade on spices with Levant through Genoa, though it did not bring about any desired result.[184] The commercial developments in the Iberian peninsula attracted the German merchants to Lisbon. Anton Welser of Augsburg and Konrad Vöhlin of Memmingen and their company approached King Manuel through their representative, Simon Seitz.[185] On 12 December 1502 Simon in the company of Lukas Rem and Scipio Lowenstein went to Spain, then leaving Rem behind in Spain, the others continued on to Lisbon.[186]

There Simon was aided in his negotiations by Valentim Fernandes, a printer from Moravia who was influential at the Portuguese court.[187] Simon Seitz concluded a treaty with the Portuguese crown on 13 February 1503 by which, not only these companies but also all German merchants who had a capital of 10,000 ducats were given the privilege of conducting trade in Lisbon, and participating in the spice-trade of India.[188] The German merchants could buy in small or large amounts, spices or brazil-wood or any other wares from India or other places, or as yet undiscovered lands, without paying any duties, unless they had bought these wares from the fleet or from the ships coming from India.[189] It seems that shortly after this contract, the German merchants began to participate directly in Indian trade and began to come to India. Peter Holzschuher, the German merchant who died in Calicut in 1504, seems to have reached Cochin as a result of this contract. He came to India along with Afonso de Albuquerque in 1503.[190] Moreover, according to this contract, timber, tar, and pitch from north Germany, items which were in short supply in Lisbon and very essential for the construction of ships, were brought to Portugal at a duty of ten per cent or less.[191] King Manuel maintained good relations with the Germans as they ultimately controlled the production and distribution of most of the silver, copper and lead of Europe which in turn were essential for trade with India.[192] In 1504, two younger Welser merchants came to Lisbon for going out to India. Earlier the Welser agents had already come down to Lisbon through Antwerp with letters from Emperor Maximilian and Archduke Philip the Fair, for this purpose. These agents brought with them the metals and merchandise worth 20,000 ducats. The Portuguese king refused the offer of these young Welser merchants to invest in the fleet to India and to accompany Lopo Saores to India.[193] However, the German merchants from Augsburg and Nürnberg continued their efforts to participate directly in Indian trade. In August 1504, Lukas Rem signed a contract with King Manuel in the name of these merchants by which the German merchants obtained permission along with the Italian syndicates to send three ships of their own to Cochin.[194] They were also allowed to send their own agents to buy spices, but were put under the supervision of the Portuguese royal factor. The cargoes which these merchants brought to Lisbon from India were to be turned over to the crown.[195] The Portuguese king was said to have been forced to make concessions to the merchants because of his financial inability in 1504-5 to fit out from his own resources alone, a fleet of twenty-two ships under Francisco de Almeida.[196]

Along with Almeida's fleet (1505), the German-Italian syndicate sent three ships: *Leonarda*, *Rafael* and *Hieronymus*.[197] The German merchants who took part in this Indian expedition were the Welsers, the Fuggers, the Gossenbrots, the Höchstetters, the Imhofs and Hirschvogel. Anton Welser had already established a firm in Augsburg in 1496 in company with his brother-in-law Konrad Vöhlin of Memmingen and it was called Anton Welser, Konrad Vöhlin and Company. This company, which had based its activities on the silver mines of Tyrol, soon flourished.[198] As we have already seen, in 1503, a Welser factory was founded in Lisbon and from that year till 1508, Lukas Rem acted as the factor of this factory.[199] In the Indian expedition of 1505, the Welsers invested an amount of 20,000 *cruzados*.[200] The Fuggers of Augsburg, especially Ulrich Fugger (who died in 1510) and Jacob Fugger (often called Jacob the Rich, 1459-1522) had great economic influence all over Europe as great bankers and merchants.[201] They had started trade in copper in 1495.[202] Eventually they bought up the entire copper and silver of Tyrol especially of Schwarz. The loans which they used to advance to the Archduke Sigismund of Tyrol and Emperor Maxmilian I, enabled the Fuggers to have a monopoly hold over these mines.[203] The ownership of copper and silver mines made the participation of the Fuggers in the Indian trade inevitable. In the Indian expedition of 1505, the Fuggers invested an amount of 4,000 *cruzados*.[204] Another big business house in Augsburg was of the Höchstetters. Ambrosius Höchstetter, the head of this business house,[205] invested an amount of 4,000 *cruzados* in 1505 in sending ships to India.[206] The Imhofs were an important trading house in Nürnberg. By the end of the fifteenth century, Endres Imhof formed a consortium of which the Welsers of Augsburg were members.[207] They had a branch in Lisbon and in 1505, they invested 3,000 *cruzados* in the ships sent by the German-Italian syndicate to Cochin.[208] The Gossenbrots were members of the copper syndicate of the Fuggers along with Paumgartner and the Herwarts.[209] They invested an amount of 3,000 *cruzados* in the Indian expedition of 1505.[210] The Hirschvogels were yet another trading house of Nürnberg who had a factory in Lisbon.[211] In the Indian expedition of 1505, they invested 2,000 *cruzados*.[212] Balthasar Sprenger was sent to India as the agent of the German merchants in the ship *Leonarda*.[213] Hans Mayr, another German was also in the fleet as the authorized representative of the Portuguese Crown and as writer in the ship *Rafael*.[214] These German-Italian merchant syndicates which participated in the trade with Cochin and Cannanore in 1505 brought to Europe 12,000 quintals of pepper. After paying 30 per cent to the crown, these merchants had 8,400 quintals with them which was worth 1,68,000 *cruzados*, the profit being around 160 per cent.[215] As the price of the spices fell drastically in Lisbon with the arrival of the last ships, the crown decreed that private merchants like the Germans and the Italians should place their cargo in the warehouse of the *Casa da India* under lock and key. In order to stabilize the price and to ensure profits, the king further decreed that these merchants, should buy their pepper back again at a price dictated by the crown.[216] This disillusioned the German merchants and the Welser company instituted legal proceedings against the crown for the breach of contract.[217] The Welsers had every reason to do this, as they had invested the greatest share in the expedition of 1505, and moreover, they were also said to have invested a considerable amount in the next Indian expedition of 1506 through their representative Lukas Rem.[218] The legal move from the Welsers enraged the king who forbade the active participation of foreign merchants in the spice trade with India. But the king was very often compelled to allow exceptions to this law, as he did with the Italian and Portuguese private traders.[219]

Henceforth, the big German merchants such as the Welsers and the Fuggers, began to concentrate more on the re-export trade in Europe. The Welsers, who had factories in Nürnberg, Venice, Danzig, Milan, Rome, Genoa, Freiburg, Bern, Zurich, Lyons, Saragossa, Antwerp and Lisbon, [220] entered into contracts with the Portuguese crown to purchase a stipulated quantity of pepper at Lisbon to be taken to Antwerp and other places for re-sale. They continued to supply the copper and silver to the Portuguese factory at Antwerp to be taken to India.[221] The Portuguese king needed 5,000-6,000 quintals of copper every year to be taken to India. The Fuggers who had monopolistic control over the copper fields of Europe were invited to participate in copper-pepper contracts.[222] He was even ready to buy 15,000 quintals of pepper annually for six years. (But this project did not materialize.)[223] But the Fuggers' plan to purchase spices against copper faced strong competition from the

Höchstetters, and had also to face strong opposition and agitations from the Lutherans who were against the monopoly exercised by the upper Germans.[224] However, the main concern of the Fuggers' factory in Lisbon was spices.[225] From here, the spices appear to have been distributed to various places of Europe, like Narva, Reval, Riga and Kiev (in Russia), Danzig, Thorn, Warsaw, Krakau, Lemberg (in Poland), Klausenburg, Pest, Often and Banska Bystrica (in Hungary), Augsburg, Ulm, Nürnberg (in Germany) and so on, where the Fuggers had factories and agents.[226] Far beyond and besides the role of distribution of spices, the Fuggers supplied copper and silver (from the copper fields of Sweden, Denmark, Hungary and Tyrol), required for the purchase of spices in India to the Portuguese King either at the factory in Antwerp or the *Casa da India* in Lisbon.[227] In 1519 Rui Fernandes de Almada, the secretary of the factory in Flanders, went to Augsburg to meet Jacob Fugger where he entered into a contract with the Fugger for the supply of 12,000 quintals copper to be taken to India for the next two years.[228]

Meanwhile some other Germans were looking for opportunities to continue direct trade wtih India. Since the crown was not ready to share the spice trade with any other private trader, these German merchants began to concentrate on diamond, pearls and precious stones. The Hirschvogels of Nürnberg sent the sixteen year old Lazarus Nürnberger to India. On 2 April 1517, he left Lisbon for India. He reached Goa and spent some time in Cannanore and remained in Cochin for a considerable time.[229] The Herwarts of Augsburg, who specialized in jewels and pearls, sent Jörg Imhoff to India to procure precious stones. Imhoff travelled to Goa, Cannanore and spent some time in Cochin to collect commodities for his master.[230] The Hirschvogels employed Jörg Pock to collect precious stones from India. He left for India in 1520.[231] In search of pearls and jewels he travelled to Goa, Cannanore and to the kingdom of Vijayanagara. In 1522 he spent some time in Cochin in connection with his business.[232] Thus even when the royal monopoly was upheld, the economic participation of independent and foreign private traders was allowed, in varying degrees, in the Indian trade both in spice and non-spice items. The Portuguese would not have been able to collect and mobilize the copper and silver required for the Indian trade and to effect the timely distribution of spices in Europe without the involvement and co-operation of these private entrepreneurs.

VIII. VOLUME OF EXPORT TRADE DURING THE PERIOD BETWEEN 1500-1535

In 1506, the Venetian ambassador Vincenzo Quirini estimated that 25,000 to 30,000 quintals of spices, out of which two-thirds was pepper, were exported annually from Cochin, Cannanore and Quilon.[233] According to the estimate of Ca' Masser, another Venetian, the total quantity of annual export exceeded 35,000 quintals.[234] In 1509, an amount of 40,000 quintals of pepper was taken to Lisbon from Cochin.[235] By the end of 1512, Affonso de Albuquerque wrote to the king that he would be sending 38,000 quintals of spices to Lisbon.[236] The five ships which left Cochin in 1518 carried 50,000 quintals of pepper besides a large quantity of ginger and other spices.[237] In 1519, the volume of export trade increased to

TABLE V-3: EXPORT TO LISBON

Commodities	1501[238]	1502[239]	1503[240]	1504[241]	1505[242]	1506[243]	1513[244]	1514[245]
Pepper	1,04,920	52,459	9,44,262	5,24,590	11,54,120	9,07,534	10,50,249	10,70,865
Ginger	20,984	2,623		6,820	23,607	36,722	2,10,203	2,13,131
Cinnamon	31,476	23,607	3,14,754	26,230	18,361		66,518	42,650
Cloves				23,607	10,492	2,623	1,102	
Lac	3,148	1,312				2,098	708	
Brasil wood					3,148		2,361	3,804
Camphor				367	786	525		
Mace				131	367		1,90,898	26,2,348

56,000 quintals of pepper and 20,000 quintals of other spices.[246] A few details regarding the volume of export to Lisbon are given in Table V-3.

Thus we see that a relatively larger volume of spices was taken to Lisbon from Cochin and other ports of Malabar. A good number of them were not local products but were brought from other parts, as we have already seen, and re-exported from Cochin. During the period from 1515, we find Malabar spices entering Europe through the Red Sea–Venice route[247] (but the volume of this trade was very low). However this does not mean that the export trade to Lisbon dwindled. On the contrary, there was a remarkable increase in the volume of Indo-European trade, which was mainly because of the intensification of commercial activities in Cochin and because of the increase in production in its hinterlands.

The following table, in comparison with the one given earlier, shows an upward trend in the export trade of 1517 and 1519. Though the same record could not be maintained in the 1520s, the volume of spices that reached Lisbon from Cochin and other ports of Malabar was increasingly high.

The general trend of spice-export from Cochin is depicted in Graph 2. The sources mentioned above are used to draw the graph, whose main function is to depict the ups and downs of export of the principal three commodities, viz., pepper, ginger and cinnamon. As the graph clearly shows, the pepper curve stands up above

TABLE V-4

Commodities (in kg.)	1517[248]	1519[249]	1523[250]	1526[251]	1530[252]	1531[253]
Pepper	23,09,875	18,36,065	3,93,442	10,49,200	8,09,862	9,89,902
Ginger	1,29,574	15,738	1,20,658	17,836	46,636	17,889
Cinnamon	16,551	41,967	10,492	52,459	38,085	27,436
Cloves	9,755	34,623	62,951	31,476	37,403	31,318
Mace	971	2,098	3,148	10,492	4,879	4,249
Nutmeg		6,295	39,344		9,757	6,295
Camphor				13,115		105
Sandalwood	787				1,626	1,784
Rhubarb	4,669					105
Incense	2,256					210
Tamarind					735	

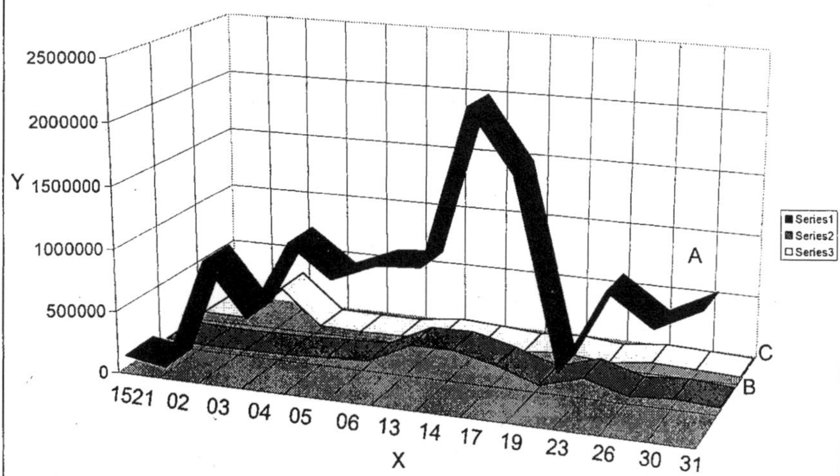

(A = Pepper, B = Ginger, C = Cinnamon)

Graph 2: Export of Spices from Cochin during the period from 1500-35.

the ginger and cinnamon curves. Right from the period immediately after the establishment of the Portuguese capital in Cochin in 1505, we find the pepper curve relatively going up, a phenomenon which continued upto 1519-20.

The early part of the 1520s, was marked by the emergence of private trade, the official laxity and the estrangement of the Muslim merchant magnates of Cochin, thereby witnessing lower pepper supply and causing the curve to fall steeply. But the vigilance and the strong measures taken with the arrival of Vasco da Gama in 1524 and the steps followed by his successors helped to improve the situation, which fact is evident from the once again upward-moving curve. Ginger seems to have been the second greatest commodity exported from Cochin. But, as the graph shows, sometimes the cinnamon brought from Ceylon occupied second position in the export trade.

During this period, though the greater part of the export consisted of pepper, ginger and cinnamon, other spices like cloves, nutmeg and mace were also exported to Lisbon in large quantities. Besides these spices, precious stones, cotton cloth (both painted and white), silk, pearls, and seed-pearls were also exported to Lisbon by private persons in the name of *liberdades*. In 1502 João de Nova brought from Cochin precious stones worth 4,000 *cruzados*.[254] All these pearls, silks and precious stones taken to Portugal were required to pay a tax of *quarto* and *vintena*.[255] After the declaration of the spices as royal monopoly, as we have already seen, the non-Portuguese Europeans especially the Germans, began to concentrate more on the trade in pearls and precious stones, which they took to Europe through their agents, Lazarus Nürnberger, Jörg Imhof and Jörg Pock.

IX. COMMODITIES

Vasco da Gama after his first encounter with the market of Calicut in 1498, came back to Portugal with a list of commodities that could be imported into Malabar. Gold, silver, coral and scarlet were the items which were in high demand in Calicut and the Zamorin suggested in his letter that they could be imported into Kerala.[256] Cabral returned to Lisbon collecting information about the price of copper (45 *panams* per *faraçola*), lead (18 *panams* per *faraçola*), silver (54 *panams* per *faraçola*), alum (20 *panams* per *faraçola*), white coral (1,000 *panams* per *faraçola*), branched coral (700 *panams* per *faraçola*) and bastard coral (300 *panams* per *faraçola*) in Calicut.[257] Because of the high demand for copper in Cochin, this metal had become an important means for trade transactions from 1502 onwards. The spices had to be partially paid for in copper. The 3,000 Faß pepper which Vasco da Gama bought from Cochin in 1502 was paid partly in copper while the balance price was paid in cash (bar money) and opium.[258] In the first decade of the sixteenth century, an annual amount of 4,000 quintals of copper, which rose to 6,000 quintals in the second decade, in addition to coral, vermilion, mercury, tin and lead were imported to Cochin.[259] Initially it was from Cochin that copper was distributed to Gujarat and other parts of India. In 1513, one bania merchant of Gujarat, estimated that an amount of 30,000 or 40,000 quintals of copper was required in India.[260] The participation of German and Italian merchants (who had monopolistic control over the production and distribution of copper in Europe) in the Portuguese trade with India, ensured a regular supply of copper to be imported to Cochin. It is estimated that the merchandise which each ship brought from Lisbon to Malabar was worth 50,000 *cruzados*.[261] During the period between 1510-18, copper worth 49,464 *cruzados*, silver equivalent to 16,107 *cruzados*, coral worth 13,750 *cruzados* and lead valued at 3,582 *cruzados* were imported into Cochin.[262] Table V-5 gives a picture of the volume of import into Cochin.[263]

With the increased demand for copper, the volume of this metal imported into Cochin increased in the later period. Even ivory from the African coasts was also brought to Cochin. The register of 22 January 1528, signed by Afonso Mexia, the *vedor da Fazenda* of Cochin, gives the details about the commodities imported into Cochin (Table V-6).[264]

TABLE V-5: VOLUME OF IMPORT

Commodities	1502-6	1506-7	1510-18
Gold		60 marcos, 2 onças, ½ oitava	5 marcos and 6 oitavas
Silver		405 marcos, 7 onças, 2 oitavas	2,478 marcos
Copper	745-1½	1,167-0-26½	4,122-3
Coral	3,999 onças	10,308 onças	
Vermilion	42-3	54-1-6	
Lead	360	598-1-13½	597-1
Tin		7	60

TABLE V-6: IMPORT OF COMMODITIES

Commodities	Quantity
Copper	5,700 quintals
Alum stone	360 quintals
Ivory	542 quintals
Lead	596 quintals
Tin	26 quintals
Worked coral	18,731 onças

Besides the gold from Europe (which came from Guine, Mina and Arguim),[265] the yellow metal from Sofala was also brought to Cochin. In 1507 the ship *Rinha Belem* took to the Malabar ports, an amount of 4,000 *miticais* of gold from Sofàla.[266] The value of gold taken annually to Cochin and Goa, during this period, varied from 12,000 to 29,000 *cruzados*.[267] Most of the silver that was imported into Cochin came from the German merchants.[268] The silver which the ships brought annually to Cochin and Goa was about 2,000 to 4,500 *marcos* and its value ranged between 12,000 and 27,000 *cruzados*.[269] Copper, which was in high demand for the purchase of pepper, formed the major part of the imports into Cochin. The Portuguese who bought pepper and other spices with gold and silver bullions induced some to say that it was India which discovered Portugal, implying that it was a phenomenon of adverse trade-balance in mercantilist terminology.[270] But these precious metals were often used to generate further profit in the system of multiple transactions and the flow of bullion was intended to maximize the profit. As these precious metals imported from Portugal to Cochin were meant to accumulate wealth in the home country through further transactions, the balance of the trade was never adverse for the Portuguese during this period.[271]

2. WEAKENING OF THE ROYAL MONOPOLY AND INTENSIFICATION OF PRIVATE TRADE (1535-1570)

The commercial activities of the Portuguese began to take a different turn after 1535. Though private trade was not unknown during the first three decades of the sixteenth century, it became rampant with the fourth decade. This period also witnessed some sort of relaxation and weakening in the royal arrangements made to maintain the monopoly. Spices began to enter Europe via Venice in continuous and increasing proportions. Scholars like Hildebrandt call the phenomenon, experienced during this period, as Oligopoly, in contrast to the monopolistic phase of early decades.[272] The commodities reserved for the crown became wares for regular Asian trade both for the Portuguese and non-Portuguese merchants. The export of spices from Cochin to Lisbon began to show a downward trend. A variety of reasons could be given as explanations for this development among which I would like to highlight three significant ones: 1. The exigency to incorporate the Portuguese individuals into trade, 2. Tensions in the hinterland, 3. The general economic crisis.

I. EXIGENCIES OF PERMITTING PRIVATE TRADE

In order to understand the reasons for allowing private trade on a mass basis, one should see the general situation of the Portuguese in India and in the mother country. When King Manuel died at the close of 1521, his nineteen-year-old son by Maria of Spain ascended the throne.[273] During his reign, from 1521 onwards, we find recurring famines and pestilence visiting Portugal, which compelled many to move to India. In 1521, a great famine broke out in Portugal and the poverty situation continued in 1522, its effects were felt even in the following years.[274] A great pestilence broke out in Lisbon and Coimbra in 1524 which took away 373 lives.[275] In 1530-1 the pestilence returned to Portugal, of which Lisbon was the most severely affected zone. There the people entered into clashes and fights with the Jews accusing the latter of being the cause of frequent pestilences.[276] As the disease was contagious, the inhabitants began to flee the capital. An eyewitness remarks that Lisbon was a completely deserted city.[277] The Braga area was affected by famine in 1539. In 1546 famine-related sufferings began to torture Beiras, Alentejo and Lisbon for many months and people of the capital even resorted to robbery for their living.[278] The famine of 1555-7 and the pestilence of 1563-6 lasted long and the people in Coimbra, conducted processions praying for God's mercy asking for relief.[279] The pestilence which came to Lisbon in 1569 was so great that in the months of July and August, there was no day without 600 or 700 deaths; about 50 to 60 people were buried in the same grave.[280] These famines and pestilences were followed by successive waves of migration to India which, they hoped, would be better than the miserable conditions of life at home.[281] Most of them came as soldiers; later they married and settled down in the prospective trade centres like Cochin and Goa. As a result the number of the Portuguese in Cochin began to increase. On 12 July 1527, Luis Martins from Portalegre wrote that there were 1,000 Portuguese men in Cochin; but the number of *casados* were only 160.[282] Later with the flow of people from the mother country as a result of the natural catastrophes, the number of *casados* increased, and simultaneously, private trade also thrived. According to the documents of 15 May 1546, there were 570 Portuguese in Cochin out of which 343 were *casados*.[283]

Within five years the number of the *casados* in Cochin rose up to 500, according to the data of 16 January 1551.[284] These newcomers began to take up trade as a means of their livelihood and to co-operate with the first generation of *casados*, who had already established a vast commercial network. The Portuguese authorities had to accommodate themselves to this situation and adopt a policy in which sufficient space was carved out for the commercial enterprise of this people. Chances for a decent livelihood and opportunities for private initiatives were offered to them through the system of licences, voyages and other trade concessions, details of which we have already seen. Even their participation in the diversion of pepper seems to have been tacitly allowed, to a certain extent. The Governor Jorge Cabral (1549-50) wrote that over half of the Portuguese in Asia refused to obey his mobilization orders for the Diu campaign, implying that they were not interested in royal service; but only in private trade.[285]

The crown seems to have encouraged these traders not only because commerce provided a livelihood to them; but also because they were slowly emerging as a substitute to the prominent and traditional Muslim merchants who left Cochin for Calicut. So the creation of a mercantile class from the Portuguese was a need of the time. Some sort of relaxation in the royal monopoly was allowed in such a way that their private initiatives could get better exposure. On the other hand, with regard to the *quintaladas*, the voyages, licences and other trade concessions, they had created a system in which the king was required only to pay less, while individuals had to earn the rest by their personal initiatives. When the crown itself faced a financial crisis at home, this arrangement saved the King from paying salaries due, and at the same time secured for him an extra income by way of customs duty.

During this period, the private participants began to overload the liberty chests and other spaces of the Lisbon-bound royal ships, with personal merchandise which led to frequent shipwrecks. Though in the first phase, as we have already seen, the liberty chest was a mechanism by which the crown ensured safe conduct of a homeward-bound *Carreira*, from the 1540s onwards, the practice of allotting space on royal vessels for the private entrepreneurs, turned out to be detrimental, affecting the lifespan of ships. A good many of the ships that departed from Cochin during this period to Lisbon were wrecked, as we read in *Historia Tragico Maritima*, because of overloading.[286] Besides merchandise, even human cargo was loaded to the maximum from Cochin without looking into the capacity of the vessels which the private traders took for sale in Lisbon. The most striking case was that of ship *São João* which left Cochin on 3 February 1552 but sank into the Ocean near the coast of Natal (Africa) on 24 June 1552. It had taken 4,500 quintals of pepper from Quilon and 7,500 quintals of pepper from Cochin. We do not know exactly how much the officials loaded in the liberty chests. Because of the war between Cochin and Vadakkenkur king in Vaduthala, the ship did not get as much pepper as they had expected from Cochin. But they filled the space with human cargo. A large number of slaves were taken from the Cochin slave market. The reporter of the shipwreck of 1552, says that there were about 500 men in this ship, most of whom were slaves from Cochin.[287] During the years between 1541 to 1550 five out of forty-six ships (10.9 per cent loss), engaged in homeward journeys were lost at sea. During the period between 1551 to 1560, the percentage of loss increased to 31.1 per cent, where fourteen out of forty-five Lisbon-bound ships were destroyed. The percentage of loss for the period between 1561 to 1570 was 13.6 per cent and five out of thirty-seven vessels that made the homeward journey were lost.[288] It is to be specially noted that the percentage of shipwrecks increased with the liberal phase of private trade. The voyages within Asia for which space in the crown ships was often parcelled out, the liberty chests granted to the officials of the vessels, the practice by which private traders overloaded the Lisbon-bound ships with human and non-human cargo, not only reduced the space for crown commodities, but also negatively affected the longevity of *Carreira* ships which often led to their destruction in the deep seas.

II. TENSIONS IN THE HINTERLAND

This period was marked by a diminishing trend in native co-operation and the beginning of tensions in the hinterland. There were two types of tensions: 1. Political tensions between Cranganore and Cochin and another between Cochin and the pepper (Vadakkenkur) kingdom which led to the Vaduthala war (1549-52). 2. Religious tensions, which led to the estrangement of Jewish traders and the merchant-cum-cultivator group of St. Thomas Christians, by the end of the 1550s.

The quarrels between Cochin and Cranganore started by 1540. On 23 December 1541, D. Estavão da Gama wrote to the Portuguese king about the tensions between these kingdoms which adversely affected the trade in Cochin.[289] The bone of contention between them was the claim to the principal temples of Cranganore. In those days temples played a great role in the State formation. Temples which were situated in the territories of other kings were used as tools for exercising hegemony. Moreover, the temple was also a source of royal revenue. The dispute was chiefly over the temples of Tribanchyaqualaa (Thiruvanchikulam) and Chiriguorumba, situated in Cranganore. The king of Cochin claimed complete rights over the Thiruvanchikulam temple (which was the principal temple of this royal family before it was transferred to Cochin), its money, and half of the share of the Chiriguorumba temple. Only one-fifth of the revenue from the latter went to the Cranganore king; three-fifth of the income was supposed to go to the king of Cochin and the remaining one-fifth went to Biliarty Coilo (Villiarvattam Kovil). The king of Cochin sent his men from Cochin to collect money from these temples and to guard them. In 1548, these temple guards sent by the Cochin king were killed by the ruler of Cranganore who appropriated the entire temple money.[290] The quarrel over the temple-revenue dragged Cochin into a tense phase of relationship with Cranganore, whose ruler had already antagonised Cochin by switching over allegiance to Calicut. The conflict went on till the 1560s.[291] Though this tension did not explode into battle, it affected the free flow of spices from the hinterlands in and around Cranganore.

Still worse was the tension that arose between Cochin and Vadakkenkur over Bardela (Vaduthala) which was ruled over by the Vadakkenkur chief. In the process of territorial expansion, the king of Cochin claimed lordship over Vaduthala and its temple from where the latter began to take money.[292] These tensions could not be patched up, finally leading in 1549, to the outbreak of a long and bitter war which continued up to 1552. The king of Vadakkenkur was supported by the Zamorin of Calicut and the newly-converted Christian king of Tanur, [293] who even went from king to king canvassing help for the Vadakkenkur and Calicut kings.[294] On the other hand, the king of Cochin was supported by the Portuguese. He met the combined forces of Vadakkenkur, the Zamorin and Tanur in Chembe and Vaduthala areas which were then under the Vadakkenkur kingdom.[295] Some 30,000 native soldiers and 600 Portuguese fought for Cochin.[296] In the course of the war, the king of Vadakkenkur was killed in the battlefield, which caused much uproar, leading the soldiers of Vadakkenkur to form a *Chaverpada* to avenge the death of their king. They ran amok, killing every one they saw and burning the city of native Cochin and *Castelo de Cima*.[297] The economic result of this continuous war which lasted up to 1552, was that spices stopped coming to Cochin for transhipment to Lisbon.[298] Most of the spices were diverted to different destinations through the ghat route. The king of Cochin felt duty-bound to reciprocate the help he received from the Portuguese: he went from king to king and traders for making pepper available in Cochin for transhipment to Lisbon. He made contracts with the native merchants for this, accepting all their terms and conditions. The most important condition of this contract was that the Portuguese should pay two-thirds of the price in cash and the remaining one-third in copper, the metal most in demand in Malabar for the manufacture of household utensils.[299] These two areas of political conflict intensified the ghat route traffic, providing only very little commodity at the port of Cochin.[300] Moreover the shadow of these tensions helped the private entrepreneurs to get these diversion routes linked with the commercial empire they had already established.

This period also witnessed the widening of the areas of conflict. The Portuguese, during this time, had robbed the temple treasure of Tevelakkara and had taken away two casks of pure gold and precious stones from it which antagonized the Hindus of Quilon and Kayamkulam.[301] They refused to supply further pepper to the Portuguese. In 1547, the Brahmins of the locality threatened that if 1,800 *pardaos* taken from this temple were not paid back, they would see to it that no pepper reached Quilon.[302] In the face of strong opposition and the cutting off of the pepper supply, King John III ordered the wealth to be returned to the temple.[303] After the temple robbery of Tevelakkara, the Portuguese plotted to take the treasure of Pallurithi temple, which was the family temple of the Pallurithi *tavazhi* of the Cochin royal family. Francisco da Silva, the captain of Cochin, took along with him 500 men and entered the temple when the Pallurithi chief was away. In the attempt to plunder the temple, three were killed and many were injured. The plunder of the family temple of Pallurithi *tavazhi* by the Portuguese greatly incensed the king of Cochin,[304] who was already in conflict with the Portuguese over the issue of converting his subjects to Christianity.[305] As the tension increased, the Portuguese tried to win the co-operation and goodwill of the native king by offering him a palace in 1555 (the present day Mattancherry palace), constructed at the expense of the former.[306] This was followed by the raising of customs duty paid by the Portuguese to the native king from 213 *reais* (1/2 *cruzados*) to 900 *reais* (2 *são tomes*) per *bhar* in 1569.[307] This temporarily succeeded in patching up the tensions that had arisen with the native king.

The religious tensions which adversely affected the Cochin trade began with the transplantation of European religious concepts to India. The anti-Semitic measures designed for Portugal and Spain as well as the Protestant reformation movements which occupied the centre-stage in Europe made the Portuguese look at everything strange in India with suspicion and doubt. The Manueline tolerance, if there was any, was set aside and the religious fanaticism of John III was transplanted to the East.[308] Instead of looking at common and basic points of co-operation, the attempt was to find out as many points of difference as possible and to categorize them as a part of heresy. This move antagonized the partners in Portuguese commerce such as the Jews and St. Thomas Christians.

The inquisition established in Lisbon for dealing with the new Christians who were said to be following Jewish practices, was eventually extended to Cochin. By 1557, the new Christian traders of Cochin began to be arrested and tried in the Inquisitorial Court of Cochin, one by one.[309] The result of the first round trial in Cochin was that they lost all their wealth and the fruit of all their commerce which they had conducted for years, as all of them were found to be guilty of the charges.[310] Later they were taken to Goa and finally to the Inquisition of Lisbon where all of them, except one were punished as offenders of faith.[311] The captain of Cochin strongly reacted against this large-scale arrest and transportation of new Christians to Lisbon, condemning it as a part of strategy to deprive Cochin of its eminent merchants.[312] This incident, on the other hand, spread panic and fear among the Jews of native Cochin in general, who began to look at the Portuguese with increased suspicion and viewed them as their greatest enemies. They feared that if the approach of the Portuguese towards the new Christians, who had collaborated with the latter in all their endeavours including the battle against Vadakkenkur king (1549-52), [313] was as cruel as this, then the fate of the Jews who were always hated by the Portuguese would be still worse. Their fear was based on the fact that all these new Christians were punished for their participation in Jewish ceremonies, and their contribution to the construction of Kadavumbhagam synagogue in native Cochin built between 1539 and 1550,[314] and from which, they inferred that the next target of Portuguese attack would be the Jews. Meanwhile, another development took place in Mattancherry. Many Jews from Cranganore migrated to native Cochin bacause of the religious persecutions thay faced in their traditional abode.[315] The last group of these successive waves of migration reached Mattancherry by 1564-5. The king of Cochin received them in the native part of the city and gave them space for their settlement adjacent to his palace.[316] According to the *paradesi* tradition, this part of land was given by the king to Samuel Castiel, David Belila, Efraim Sala and Joseph Levi, who constructed the *paradesi* synagogue (the only surviving synagogue in Mattancherry) and the Jews' town in 1568.[317] With the advent of this group, the strength of the Jews increased and the anti-Portuguese feelings cemented their ties of solidarity. Under the umbrella of royal protection from the king of Cochin, the Jews of Cochin began to develop a parallel commercial arrangement and from this time on, we find these ill-treated Jews emerging as the greatest agents of the pepper diversion in Cochin.

The steps for ensuring the co-operation of the St. Thomas Christians were taken also during the time of John III, who used to generously fund the study of the seminarians of this community, either in Portugal or in Cranganore,[318] though the purpose of this expenditure was to get them Latinized which would ensure them as regular collaborators for the Portuguese ecclesiastical and commercial systems. The cultivators and the merchants had grievances against the fraudulent practices of the Portuguese, who used to underweigh their commodities, using false weights. This must have prompted many to sell their commodities to the non-Portuguese. This was a matter of concern for the Portuguese officials and some of them including St. Francis Xavier, wrote accordingly to the crown. King John III wrote to the officials concerned repeatedly, to redress the grievances which the community of St. Thomas Christians had against the Portuguese traders who resorted to malpractices in the weighing of pepper.[319] But it seems that despite the crown's interference, fraudulent practices continued to exist in pepper dealings. Moreover, along with the phase of co-operation, some of the Portuguese clergy such as Pe. Alvaro Penteado and Pe. Michael Carneiro had begun to label St. Thomas Christians as heretics and acuse non-Latin practices of Nestorian heresy.[320] When Mar Joseph came to Malabar from the Persian Chaldean Church to take charge as the Bishop of this community, the Portuguese tried to arrest him, accusing him of heresy. It created much tension among the principal cultivator groups in the hinterland. In 1557, the St. Thomas Christians organized an *amocos* or suicide squad, comprising 2,000 soldiers to protect their bishop from being arrested.[321] Seeds of unrest were sown among the pepper producers, who deemed their liturgical and ecclesiatical traditions greater than the commercial links with the Portuguese. In spite of the strong resistance from the St. Thomas Christians, their bishop Mar Joseph was arrested and taken to Lisbon as a heretic. In the trial that was conducted there, he succeeded in convincing the crown of his innocence and came back to Malabar in 1565. But two years later he was again arrested with the same accusations, and in the trial that was conducted in the first council of Goa, the accusation that he was a heretic was confirmed. From Goa, he was sent to Lisbon from where he was again sent to Rome where he died in 1569.[322] The arrest of their bishop and the way in which the latter was treated, antagonized the majority of the pepper-growing St. Thomas Christains, who had been under the jurisdiction of this bishop. This tension which started by the end of the 1550s continued all through the next decade causing a downward flow of pepper to Cochin.

III. THE GENERAL ECONOMIC CRISIS

Portugal had been experiencing a terrible economic crisis in 1521, 1524, 1535 and 1545-52 which along with the above mentioned factors affected the Indian situation.[323] It was actually the balance sheet of the famines and pestilences which affected Portugal during these years. Added to this were the heavy expenses incurred in the royal marriages, and the settlement of the Moluccan issue, which drained the Portuguese exchequer. Thus, in 1526, King John III paid 9,00,000 *cruzados* to the Spanish Emperor Charles V, on the occasion of the marriage of his sister Isabella to the latter, the largest dowry in European history.[324] According to the matrimonial negotiations between the two crowns, the amount of dowry was to be paid in three instalments of 50,000 quintals of pepper at the Portuguese factory of Antwerp.[325] Three years later the Portuguese crown paid another amount of 3,50,000 *cruzados* to the Spanish emperor to settle the Spanish claims over Moluccas.[326] These and other related issues led to a flow of about 17,90,000 *cruzados* to Spain from Portugal, causing the debt of John III to rise up to 19,46,000 *cruzados*.[327] Meanwhile, the factory at Antwerp, which was the centre of the distribution of spices in northern Europe, and collection centre for wares to India from Germany and other northern countries, registered an enormous debt. By the end of 1548, a decision was taken by John III to close this royal factory and on 15 February 1549, this was done.[328] The strain on the finance of the mother country began to affect economic activities in India. The amount sent to the Portuguese factories in India both for the payment of Portuguese officers as well as for the purchase of spices began to dwindle. Very often a complaint is found registered, that the fleet from Portugal was coming in without sufficient money. Thus, in the letter of Martim Afonso de Souza, to the king dated 24 December 1537, we read that the ships which had recently arrived in Cochin were without money.[329] Later we find this economic crisis becoming acute as the number of ships coming to Cochin for taking on cargo was decreasing. On 28 December 1541, Miguel de Cunha wrote to the crown that in that year no ship came to Cochin from the kingdom.[330] Moreover, the Germans who used to participate in the Indian trade in the early decades of the sixteenth century were facing another problem. The waves of Protestant reformation in Germany triggered off a peasant uprising and revolt against the monopolists who used to supply to the Portuguese, copper and other merchandise for exchange in India. The Protestant move against the Catholic monopolists like the Fuggers and other merchant magnates affected, to a certain extent, commercial activities in Germany, which further tightened the Portuguese position to supply to Cochin the wares of exchange in sufficient quantities.

On the Indian side, the existing political order was undergoing a significant phase of change with some economic repercussions. The Turks had begun to enter the Indian seas quite frequently from 1538 on, when the Turkish fleet came under Sulaiman Pasha to capture Diu.[331] Though with the advent of Viceroy Garcia de Noronha (1538-40), they had to retreat, they changed their activities to the Persian Gulf region, where they thwarted Portuguese control. Meanwhile, the Turkish Sultan had made a suggestion to the Portuguese king through a letter dated 28 May 1544, that the Portuguese could supply 4,000 *zentner* (1 *zentner* = 50 kg.) pepper and other drugs to the Turkish governor in Aden, without causing damage to Portuguese commerce. He showed his readiness to buy these spices as the French and Venetians were purchasing from them.[332] But this dream was not realized and the Sultan's fleet continued tightening its control in the Persian Gulf. In 1546 it conquered Basra, the gate of the Tigris and Euphrates valleys and the eastern terminus of the desert route to Aleppo. In 1551 and 1553 too, he sent fleets to the Indian Ocean and captured the Portuguese-held Muscat (though they abandoned it later after destroying the city).[333] This hindered the Portuguese trade with the Persian Gulf ports, reducing the amount of income generated locally through Asian trade. Along with these maritime developments, significant changes could be seen in the mainland of India, as well. The combined forces of Muslim rulers under Adil Shah of Bijapore and Qutb-ul-Mulk of Golconda defeated the Vijayanagara king Rama Raya in the battle of Talicotta on 23 January 1565.[334] The great significance of the battle of Talicotta was that it sealed the fate of the Vijayanagara kingdom, which had been the major market for the horses imported by the Portuguese through Goa and Cochin and a major source of diamonds and other precious stones taken to Lisbon.[335] In this changed situation, the league of Muslim rulers of Bijapore, Ahmadnagar, and Achin, joined by the Zamorin of Calicut seemed to overwhelm the Portuguese settlements in the Indian Ocean regions. Many scholars like Luis Filipe Thomaz view the fall of Vijayanagara kingdom as followed by a period of acute crisis, both political and economic, for the *Estado da India* which lasted from 1565 to 1575.[336] Meanwhile, though the economic situation did not improve, the course of the political developments was moving towards a safer direction. The Moghuls who had already established a base[337] in north India in 1526, were tightening their grip over the rest of the country especially with the ascension of Akbar (1556-1605). The southward march of Akbar resulted in the destruction of the kingdom of Cambay and the conquest of half of Ahmadnagar. This move from a totally unexpected corner made Adil Shah and other traditional anti-Portuguese forces concentrate on the safety of their own land rather than fight against the Lusitanians.[338]

Out of this troubled situation, the Portuguese could make political profit, and strengthen their position by erecting further fortresses. The space for the erection of a fortress in Bacaim was given to the Portuguese by the Sultan Bahadur Shah of Cambay in virtue of a contract ratified on 23 December 1534. The Governor, Nuno da Cunha, laid the foundation stone for this fortress in March 1536.[339] The fortress of Daman was given to the Portuguese by the Sultan of Cambay and the Viceroy Dom Constantino Bragança occupied it on 2 February 1559. It was given the name of Our Lady of Purification.[340] After the downfall of the Vijayanagara empire, three fortresses were erected in Kanara: the fortress of St. Sebastian contructed in Mangalore in 1568 by the Viceroy Dom Antão de Noronha, [341] the fortress of Barcelor constructed by the viceroy Dom Luis de Ataide in 1568,[342] and the fortress of Onor (Honawar) erected by the same Viceroy in 1569.[343] The general picture we get for this period is that the political position of the Portuguese in India was more stable than ever. But the entire Portuguese structure, at the same time, was tormented by economic ills, which assumed chronic proportions in matters related to export trade.

The economic ills, which emerged out of the situations mentioned, led to the revival of the eastern Mediterranean trade.[344] Lourenco Pires de Tavora, the Portuguese ambassador to the papal court reported in 1560 to Lisbon that 40,000 hundred weight of pepper and other spices were entering Alexandria annually. He says that while very little came to Lisbon, a large amount went to the dominion of the Turks.[345] Ferdinand Braudel says that the quantities of spices arriving at Lisbon by 1560 were just about equal to those entering Alexandria.[346] The imports of spices to Venice, which controlled most of the trade with Syria and Egypt, was said to have reached the level of the pre-Portuguese period.[347] In this changed situation, even the prominent foreign merchants began to change their commercial establishments. Thus, for instance, in 1558, the Fuggers closed their business house in Lisbon, and in the years following they began to buy pepper directly at Alexandria from whence, via Ragusa and Fiume, they transported the commodities directly into central Europe.[348] Eventually Venice also began to face sharp competition in the Levant from the French, Genoese and Ragusans. The years after the death of Sulaiman the Magnificent in 1566 were characterized by the outbreak of disorders in the Ottoman empire and revolts in places like Arabia and Yemen. A peaceful relationship had existed between Venice and the Turks in 1570 over the control of Cyprus. By this time, the French cities like Marseilles were trying to exploit this situation of tension to establish hegemony over the spice trade in the Levant.[349] Because of the large flow of spices, the prices in Levantine and Egyptian marts began to come down to a lower level than those which existed in the market services through Lisbon; this attracted other Europeans, to also enter into commercial competition in the eastern Mediterranean.[350]

IV. VOLUME OF EXPORT

For want of continuous data, the volume of export trade to Europe via Lisbon can not be exactly presented. However, the available sources give us an impression that despite the factors mentioned above and the entry of a considerable amount of pepper into Europe via Venice, the *Carreira* used to take equally enormous quantity of spices to Lisbon. The increase in the production, growth of which was supposed to have been 1340 quintals per year,[351] must have been the reason for the relatively high volume of pepper export to Portugal, even when great volume was diverted to traditional routes and other commercial destinations within Asia. In 1545, the ship *St. Thomas* alone was loaded with 9860 quintals of pepper from Cochin and moved towards the kingdom.[352] In 1546, five ships and an amount of 41,266 *pardaos* were sent from Lisbon to buy spices.[353] These five ships were loaded with 40,000 quintals of spices out of which 36,412 quintals were pepper. On 26 January 1547, Francisco da Maya wrote to the governor that the profit that the crown would get out of this transaction would be 12,00,000 *cruzados*. In 1547, four ships were sent to Cochin with 30,000 *cruzados* for the pepper purchase. These ships carried back to Lisbon 23,827 quintals of pepper.[354] On 29 January 1552, João Anes wrote to the crown that five ships from Cochin were moving to Lisbon.[355] We do not know for certain, how much spice was taken in each of them, as this transhipment took place during the difficult days of the Vaduthala war when spices did not reach Cochin regularly. However, we have evidence that one of these ships, alone, the *São João* which wrecked near the African coast, had 12,000 quintals of pepper.[356] A few details regarding the volume of export from Cochin to Lisbon are given in Table V-7.

The available data should not lead one to the misunderstanding that there was regular and constant export trade to Lisbon during this period in the volume as stated above. The fact that the frequency with which the spices were taken to Lisbon was increasingly diminishing, can also be seen from the lack of documents for the European trade from Cochin for this period. The transhipments of 1547 and 1548 show an improvement of the situation, which was the result of the vigilant

TABLE V-7: VOLUME OF EXPORT FROM COCHIN 1545-52

Commodities (in kg.)	1545[357]	1547[358]	1548[359]	1552[360]
Pepper	5,17,246	19,10,138	12,49,941	6,29,508
Ginger		81,784	50,466	
Cinnamon	8,551	15,371	11,381	
Nutmeg	8,341	37,614	7,449	
Mace	1,836	14,479	4,197	
Incense			2,833	
Sealing Wax	5,141		14,636	
Medicinal drugs	2,518			
Benzoin			1,259	
Aloe			262	
Camphor			315	
Long pepper			525	

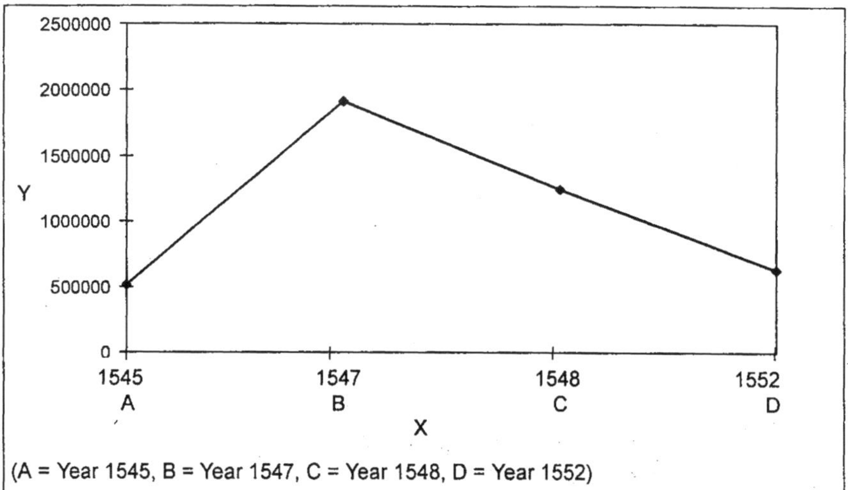

Graph 3: Pepper Export from Cochin to Lisbon (1545-52).

steps taken by *Estado* authorities which included even the transfer of officials involved in private trade.[361] But the volume of trade decreased considerably from the next year onwards, because of the outbreak of Vaduthala war and other related tensions. These facts are depicted in Graph 3 to show the general trend of this period.

Besides spices, a good variety of other commodities and animals were exported to Protugal from Cochin. Thus, for instance, we read in the letter of Ruy Goncalvez de Caminha dated 2 January 1548, elephants were sent to Lisbon from Cochin.[362] On 30 December 1548, Cosme Anes wrote to the king from Cochin that he was purchasing very precious diamonds for the crown which he found to be the most perfect and valuable things in the land.[363] Precious stones were brought from different places to Cochin to be taken to the kingdom. On 24 January 1551, Sebastian Ferreira wrote to the Portuguese Queen that the precious stones brought by Diogo Vaz from Ceylon and the gold necklace and bracelets offered by Bhuvaneka Bahu were already sent to Lisbon from Cochin.[364] Other items like coir, necessary for shipbuilding, were also exported from Cochin. The newly-converted King of the Maldives had, we read in the letter of Henrique de Souza Chichorro dated 8 January 1557, offered to deliver 500 *bhars* of coir every year to Cochin to be taken to Portugal.[365]

It is worth giving a diagram presenting the total volume of pepper export to Europe from Cochin during the period between 1500 and 1570, so as to enable one to understand the transactions conducted in Cochin. For want of continuous data, one cannot depict all the trends of trade in this diagram. Still, this graphic presentation shows that even in the 1540s, when private trade thrived in Cochin, some attempts were made by the Portuguese, at least occasionally, to despatch more cargo to Lisbon. The interrupted tendencies of the trade index to move upward is to be understood against this background.

Thus the commercial activities fostered by the Portuguese in Cochin included different strands. The groupings into local, intra-local, intra-Asian and Indo-

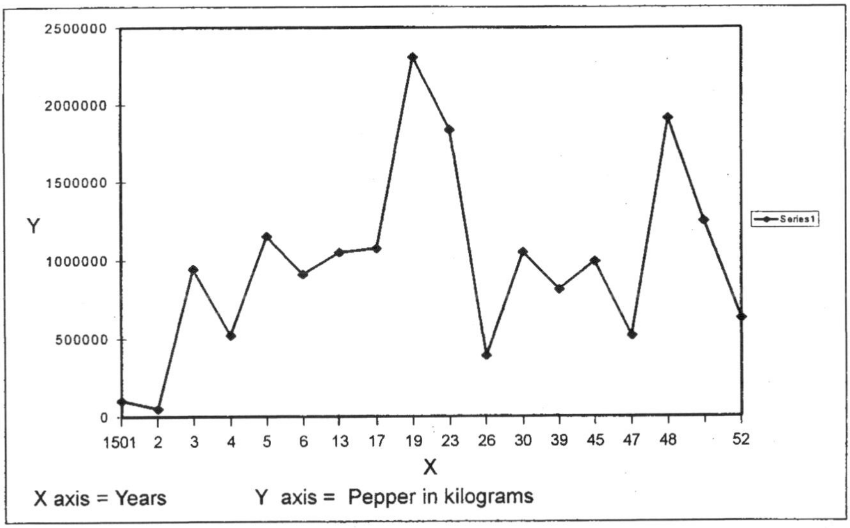

Graph 4: Total Volume of Trade in Pepper with Portugal (1500-70).

European trades have been done to understand properly the nature of this strand structure. The participation of German and Italian merchants in Indo-European trade, the under-pricing of the commodities by determining a fixed price, and the liberty chests provided for the officials of the ships, were all first steps of the initial phase in organizing Indian trade. But they proved very decisive as the German and Italian participation ensured a regular supply of copper for exchange in Cochin, the price-fixation ensured a constant supply of commodities at cheaper rates for about a century, the practice of encouraging private initiatives through liberty chests was extended to other fields where entrepreneurial commercial concessions were given as reward and recognition for the service. There was a marked difference between the first phase which ended in 1535, and the second phase which started in 1535 and ended in 1570. In the first phase we find a relatively great volume of spices going to Lisbon in which process the continuous co-operation and assistance of the natives played a key role. The different native mercantile communities, with vast resources and wide networks enabled the Portuguese to get commodities without much strain and difficulty. In the second phase we see these traditional merchants being slowly replaced by the *casado* traders. Since the latter did not have sufficient resources and networks as the traditional merchant groups did, the *casados* began to concentrate more on acquiring them rather than feeding the *Carreiras* of the crown. Private trade and even illegal commercial traffic, which dominated the commercial scenario of the period from 1535 to 1570, to a great extent, were exigencies of the time. With the increase of tensions in the hinterland and the gradual estrangement of pepper growing communities, the diversion of pepper became a frequent phenomena. The result was that from 1535 onwards, the indexes of Indo-European trade began to show diminishing trends, while the commerce in Asia and with Venice registered an upward growth.

NOTES

1. Vitorino Magalhães Godinho, *Os Descobrimentos e a Economia Mundial*, p. 34.
2. See J. Cortesão, *A Expedição de Pedro Alvares Cabral*, Lisbon, 1922; Brooks Greenlee, op. cit., pp. 83-5.
3. For details see Chapter III.
4. Gaspar Correia, *Lendas*, tom. I, part I, liv. I, pp. 384-7.
5. Sanjay Subrahmanyam, *The Portuguese Empire in Asia*, p. 72; see also Jaime Cortesão, *Os Descobrimentos Portugueses*, vol. VI, Lisboa, 1978, p. 1421.
6. Gaspar Correia, *Lendas* , tom. I, pp. 583 and 728; see also Castanheda, op. cit., liv. I, cap. XCI, pp. 226-8; liv. II, caps. XLV-LII, p. 142. The factory of Cannanore was already established in 1503, Diogo Couto, Da Asia, *Decada* VIII, liv. I, cap. XVIII, pp. 138-9.
7. Duarte Barbosa, op. cit., I, pp. 6-7.
8. Gaspar Correia, *Lendas* , I, p. 784; see also Simão Botelho, op. cit., p. 13.
9. Simão Botelho, op. cit., pp. 7-8.
10. Jaime Cortesão, *Os Descobrimentos Portugueses*, vol. VI, p. 1421.
11. Damião de Gois, *Cronica do Felicissimo Rei D. Emmanuel de Gloriosa Memoria*, part II, Coimbrà, 1953, pp. 128-32; Barros, *Da Asia Decada*, II, part I, pp. 231, 296; 300.
12. Antonio Brasio, *Uma Carta inedita de Valentim Fernandes*, Coimbra, 1959, p. 20; Luis de Albuquerque, *Cronica do Descobrimento...*, p. 187; see also R.B. Serjeant, *The Portuguese off the South Arabian Coast-Hadrami Chronicles*, Oxford, 1963, pp. 44-5.
13. Joaquim Verissimo Serrão, *Um Voyageur Portugais en Perse au debut du XVIIe siécle, Nicolau de Orta Rebelo*, Lisbon, 1972, p. 14; Diogo Couto, *Da Asia*, *Decda* IV, liv. X, cap. IV, p. 426. R.A. de Bulhão Pato, *Cartas*, tom. I, pp. 21ff.
14. Barros, *Decada* II, part II, pp. 40ff.
15. R.A. de Bulhão Pato, *Cartas*, tom. I, pp. 152-3, 188 and 249; see also Barros, *Decada* II, part II, p. 181; *Decada* III, part II, pp. 451-2.
16. Joaquim Verissimo Serrão (ed.), *Comentarios de Afonso de Albuquerque*, tom. I, Lisboa, 1973, p. 140; see also Antonio Brasio, *Uma Carta Inedita de Valentim Fernandes*, p. 18.
17. Duarte Barbosa, op. cit., I, p. 59.
18. Luis de Figueiredo Falcão, op. cit., p. 160.
19. Bailey W. Diffie and George D.Winius, op. cit., pp. 273-5.
20. It was Diogo Lopes who confiscated the commodities and vessels of Kutti Ali after having made arrangements with the latter to send them to the Red Sea. The pro-Portuguese Kutti Ali, as a consequence, became anti-Portuguese and began to engage in corsair activities. R.S. Whiteway, op. cit., p. 196.
21. A native official of the king of Cochin writes that mariners were deserting the royal service and were joining hands with private traders. The Portuguese officials bought pepper in Cochin for their own illegal private trade at prices higher than the fixed official price at which it was bought for the king. Now the local merchants wanted to sell all their pepper at this high price. He further says that private trade had eaten into the very vitals of Portuguese commercial administration. ANTT, *Corpo Cronologico*, I, Maço 27, doc. 69. In 1519, when the Governor was engaged in the duty of cruising the Red Sea, other officials in Malabar took this opportunity to send pepper to Cambay in the ships of the 'pirates' of Malabar. ANTT, *Corpo Cronologico*, I, Maço 25, doc. 108.
22. Henry E.J. Stanley, op. cit., pp. 405-6. Vasco da Gama was buried in the principal chapel (present day St. Francis church) of St. Antony in Cochin. In 1538 his body was

removed from there and taken to Lisbon. It now lies buried in the Church of St. Jeronymus in Belem, Lisbon, which was built mostly with the money from India.

23. Paduronga S.S. Pissurlencar, *Regimentos das Fortalezas*, p. 509. The Portuguese had already reached Ceylon in 1505.
24. Antonio Bocarro, op. cit., p. 362.
25. Gaspar Correia, *Lendas*, tom. I, p. 407.
26. Ibid., tom. II, p. 577.
27. Antonio da Silva Rego, *Historia das Missões*, vol. I, p. 403.
28. Gaspar Correia, *Lendas*, tom. II, pp. 659-61; J. Gerson da Cunha, *Notes on the History and Antiquities of Chaul and Basseim*, Bombay, 1876, pp. 3, 60-5.
29. Simão Botelho, op. cit. , p. 112; Gaspar Correia, *Lendas*, tom. II, pp. 624, 647, 711-15.
30. Ibid.
31. It was Henrique de Meneses who stormed Ponnani, the naval station of the Zamorin. Faria y Sousa, op. cit., vol. I, p. 284.
32. In 1526 Henrique de Meneses died. Then there arose a strong dispute over the governorship, as Pero Mascarenhas and Lopo Vaz de Sampaio had legitimate claims to the Office. According to the first order from the King of Portugal, Pero Mascarenhas should have been the governor. At that time he was away in Malacca. In the meantime, new orders were received from Lisbon appointing Lopo Vaz de Sampaio as governor. Lopo Vaz was supported by the *fidalgos* and by the officials of the Camara of Goa. Diogo de Couto, op. cit., IV, i, p. 3. The residents of Cochin and the municipality of Cochin also lobbied strongly for the selection of Lopo Vaz. All the residents of Cochin walked in a barefoot procession to the churches with their wives and children, with many tears and prayers, begging God to inspire the judges not to choose Pero Mascarenhas as Governor: Barros, op. cit., IV, ii, p. 6. The dispute finally ended Lopo Vaz being chosen.
33. Bailey W. Diffie and George D. Winius, op. cit., pp. 286-7; K.M. Panikkar, *Malabar and the Portuguese*, pp. 113-14.
34. Simão Botelho, op. cit., pp. 220-3; Gaspar Correia, *Lendas*, tom. II, pp. 622-4.
35. Barros, *Decada* I, part I, p. 181.
36. M.N. Pearson, *Merchants and Rulers in Gujarat*, pp. 44-5.
37. See for details Regimento de Pero Lopes de Sampaio dated 11 February 1520 (Evora) in ANTT, *Livro do Registo de Leis e Regimentos de D.Manuel*, fols.134-6.
38. ANTT, *Corpo Cronologico*, II, Maço 114, docs. 21, 41, 44, 45, 46, 47, 129. For details see Jorge Manuel Costa da Silva Flores, *Os Portugueses e o Mar de Ceilão*, pp. 177-8.
39. R.S. Whiteway, op. cit., p. 95; K.M. Panikkar, *A History of Kerala History*, p. 213.
40. R.A. de Bulhão Pato, *Cartas*, .tom. III, p. 396.
41. For the conquest of Goa about 100 Malayalee soldiers were utilized, out of which 80 seem to have been from Cochin. See the letter of Afonso de Albuquerque dated 1 April 1512, in Jose Ramos Coelho (ed.), *Alguns Documentos do Archivo Nacional da Torre do Tombo acerca das navegações e Conquistas Portuguezas*, Lisboa, 1892, p. 238. For further details see Fortunato de Almeida, *Historia de Portugal (1385-1580)*, tom. III, Coimbra, 1925, p. 572; A.J.R. Russell-Wood, *A World on the Move: The Portuguese in Africa, Asia and America, 1415-1808*, Manchester, 1992, p. 18.
42. It is the estimate of Costa Lobo, *Historia da Sociedade em Portugal no Seculo XV*, Lisbon: p. 32; C.R. Boxer says that later it increased slowly to about one and a half or one and three-fourth million. C.R. Boxer, 'War and Trade in the Indian Ocean and the South China Sea (1600-1650)', in *The Great Circle, Journal of the Australian Association for Maritime History*, 1/2, Nedlands, Western Australia, 1979, p. 6.
43. Fortunato de Almeida, *Historia de Portugal*, tom. III, pp. 571-2.

44. Cristovão Rodrigues Acenheiro, *Croniqua dos Reis de Portugal, Colecção de Ineditos de Historia Portugueza*, tom. V, Lisboa, 1926, pp. 334-5.
45. Jose Ramos Coelho (ed.), *Alguns Documentos*, p. 226.
46. Fortunato de Almeida, *Historia de Portugal*, tom. III, p. 572.
47. *As Gavetas da Torre do Tombo*, vol. IV, Lisboa, 1964, p. 132.
48. R.A. de Bulhão Pato, *Cartas*, tom. I, p. 320; tom. II, p. 361.
49. Ibid., tom. V, pp. 503-4.
50. K.S. Mathew, 'Indian Merchants and the Portuguese Trade on the Malabar Coast during the Sixteenth Century', in Teotonio R. de Souza (ed.), *Indo-Portugese History: Old Issues-New Questions*, New Delhi, 1985, pp. 6-7.
51. Ibid.
52. R.A. de Bulhão Pato, *Cartas*, tom. II, pp. 377-8. Chilay Marakkar was another native Muslim merchant who gave his ship for the use of the Portuguese. He provided ships for sending commodities to Goa. Ibid., tom. VI, p. 31.
53. Ibid., tom. III, p. 401.
54. Ibid., tom. I, p. 306.
55. Antonio da Silva Rego (ed.), *Documentação para a Historia*, vol. II, pp. 353-4; vol. IV, pp. 479-80; Ricahard Hakluyt (ed.), *The Principal Navigations, Voyages, Traffiques and Discoveries of the English Nation*, vol. I, New York, 1969, p. 392.
56. Antonio da Silva Rego (ed.), *Documentação para a Historia*, vol. II, pp. 175-6.
57. Reisebericht des Franciscus Dalberquerque vom 27, December 1503, in B. Greiff, *Tagebuch des Lucas Rem aus den Jahren 1494-1541*, p. 146; Genevieve Bouchon, 'Calicut at the Turn of the Sixteenth Century', p. 44.
58. Walter de Gray Birch, *The Commentaries*, p. 15. By 1504 this privilege was taken away from them by the king because of negligence of one of their members.
59. R.A. de Bulhão Pato (ed.), *Cartas*, tom. II, p. 268; tom. III, pp. 30, 258-9; tom. VI, pp. 114, 398-9; See also João de Barros, *Decada* I, part II, p. 350.
60. Antonio de Silva Rego (ed.), *Documentação para a Historia*, vol. II, pp. 352-4.
61. The Muslim forces of Calicut attacked the churches and the settlement of St. Thomas Christians in Cranganore in 1523-4. Vasco da Gama, to whom the members of this community complained against this, promised to re-build the church. For details see Atonio Silva Rego, *Historia das Missões do Padroado*, vol. I, p. 388; A.M.Mundadan, *A History of Christianity in India*, vol. I, Bangalore, 1984, pp. 302-3; João Paulo Oiveira e Costa, 'Os Portugueses e a Cristandade Siro-Malabar (1498-1530)', in *Studia*, no. 52, Lisboa, 1994, pp. 157-8.
62. The anti-Semitic moves began in Portugal from 1496 when all the Jews were asked to leave the kingdom. The crown took away all Jewish children below fourteen years for giving formation in Christian faith. For details see Damião Peres (ed.), *Historia de Portugal Edição Monumental*, vol. III, Barçelos, MCMXXXI, p. 221; Joaquim Verissimo Serrão, *Historia de Portugal*, pp. 16-17.
63. Franz Hümmerich, 'Estudo Critico sobre o Roteiro da Primeira Viagem de Vasco da Gama 1497-1499' Tradução do Comandanta Moura Bras, in *Diario da Viagem de Vasco da Gama*, vol. II, porto, 1945, pp. 242, 268; Marino Sanuto, op. cit., vol. IV, cols. 66-7. He accompanied Vasco da Gama in his second voyage. From 1505 to 1509 he rendered service to the viceroy Dom Francisco de Almeida in commercial matters as well as an interpretator. See S.S. Pissurlencar, *Agentes da Diplomatica Portuguesa na India*, Bastora, 1952, p. 552.
64. R.A. de Bulhão Pato, *Cartas*, tom. I, p. 330.
65. Mosses Pereyra de Paiva, *Notisias dos Judeos de Cochim*, p. 8;
66. For details see Ana Cannas da Cunha, op. cit., p. 218; José Alberto Rodrigues da Silva Tavim, 'Outras Gentes em Outras Rotas', p. 4.

67. See the discussions above.
68. R.A. de Bulhão Pato, *Cartas*, tom. VII, p. 174.
69. K.S.Mathew and Afzal Ahmad, *Emergence of Cochin*, doc. 53, pp. 73-83.
70. Around 10,000 to 15,000 native soldiers were supposed to have been involved in each battle waged for the Portuguese in the early years. By 1534, about 20,000 Nair soldiers joined hands with the Portuguese in the war against Calicut. Faria y Souza, op. cit., tom. I, pp. 398-400.
71. R.S. Whiteway, op. cit., p. 101. The descendants of these *Pulayas*, thus raised to the status of Nairs still retain the elevated position. T.H.P. Chentharasserry, *Kereala Charithrathile Avaganikkappetta Edukal*, Trivandrum, 1970, pp. 134-5.
72. S.S. Pissurlencar, *Regimentos das Fortalezas*, p. 216.
73. Ibid.
74. Ibid.
75. A.R. Disney, *Twilight of the Pepper Empire*, pp. 37-43.
76. Gernot Giertz, op. cit., p. 143.
77. Thome Lopes; 'Navegação as Indias Orientães' in *Collecçao de Noticias para a Historia e Geografia des Nações ultramarinas que vivem nos Dominios Portugueses ou lhes são visinhos*, tom. II, nos. I and 2, Lisboa, 1812, pp. 199-200; Barros, *Decada* I, part II, p. 61.
78. *Archivo General de Simancas secretarias Provinciales*, Cod. 1571; Luys da Costa, in Antonio da Silva Rego, *Documentação Ultramarina Portuguesa*, vol. III, Lisboa, 1963, p. 373.
79. 'The Anonymous Narrative', in William Brooks Greenlee, op. cit., p. 92.
80. For details see the price-list given by Duarte Barbosa, op. cit., vol. II, pp. 226ff.
81. As we have already seen, this route which ran across the ghat to the Coromandel ports from the pepper-growing hinterland which was situated on the periphery of Portuguese control systems was always active. Those who took the commodities to the markets situated in the outer periphery (we have already seen these markets in detail, when we discussed the Cochin-hinterland relationship), where the traders of ghat route flocked together, could make profits. And the geographical accessibility of the producers and native merchants to these markets, determined the amount of profit accrued from this trade. But, actually only those producers and native traders who were in and around these market centres could really reap profit. For others, because of the long and time-consuming transportation required and the customs duties to be paid in each kingdom, taking commodities to the inland market was the same as carrying them down to the port of Cochin, as far as profit was concerned.
82. Vitorino Magalhães Godinho, *L'Economie de L'empire Portugais aux XVe et XVIe Siécles*, Paris, 1969, pp. 720-5.
83. Donald F. Lach, *Asia in the Making of Europe*, vol. I (The Century of Discovery), book I, Chicago, 1965, p. 143.
84. Vitorino Magalhães Godinho, *L'Economie de L'empire Portugais*, pp. 720 and 725.
85. Donald F. Lach, *Asia in the Making of Europe*, vol. I, book I, pp. 143-4.
86. Gernot Giertz, op. cit., p. 143. This document says that the price of one *faraçola* of pepper in Calicut was 14 *panams*.
87. 'The Anonymous Narrative', in William Brooks Greenlee, op. cit., pp. 91-2.
88. Duarte Barbosa, op. cit., vol. II, pp. 227ff.
89. Gernot Giertz, op. cit., p. 143. This document says that during the time of the first voyage of da Gama, the price of one *faraçola* of pepper in Cochin was nine *panams*.
90. *Archivo General de Simancas, Secretarias Provinciales*, Cod. 1571; Luys da Costa, in Antonio Silva Rego, *Documentação Ultramarina Portuguesa*, vol. III, pp. 373-4; see Marino Sanuto, op. cit., tom. V, col. 318.

91. Sanuto, op. cit., tom. IV, col. 547.
92. Gernot Giertz, op. cit., p. 150.
93. Girolamo Priuli, *I Diarii di Girolamo Priuli 1494-1512*, vol. I, Citta di Castello, 1921, p. 75.
94. ANTT, *Corpo Cronologico*, I, Maco 8, doc. 68.
95. Cunha Rivara, *Archivo Portuguez Oriental*, Fasciculo 5, part I, p. 10.
96. Ibid., p. 46.
97. Historical Archives of Goa, *Regimentos, Provisões e Alvaras*, no. 52027, fol. 4ff; Cunha Rivara, op. cit., Fasciculo 5, part I, p. 48.
98. The merchants of Calicut like Mohammed Marakkar, used to send pepper to Cairo even during this period of royal monopoly. R.A. de Bulhão Pato, *Cartas*, tom. I, pp. 179-80. In 1513 about 13 ships with pepper left for Mecca and Aden from Malabar. Ibid., tom. III, p. 50. Usually these commodities were taken in small, light-oared craft called *parões*. Because of their small size these *parões* could easily escape the big Portuguese ships. In 1524, Vasco da Gama saw a lot of them making their way to the north. Barros, *Decada* III, ix, p. 2. In 1525 some 53 of these pepper ships of the Malabar traders were caught and burnt. Ibid., p. 5. Thus, even though the Red Sea route was risky, it was often active even in the early phase of Portuguese establishment which was characterized by strict patrolling.
99. The ships associated with the *Carreira da India* were first and foremost *Naos* which were big ships. There is a difference between a *Nao* and *Galeao*; but in practice this is blurred. A ship that started life as a Carrack (*Nao*) might end as a *galleon*, and vice versa. C.R. Boxer, *The Carreira da India* (Ships, Men, Cargoes, Voyages), O Centro de *Estudos Historicos Ultramarinos e as Comemorações Henriquinas*, Lisbon, 1961, p. 34.
100. Ibid., pp. 49-50.
101. Faria y Sousa, op. cit., vol. III, pp. 424-5; Bailey W. Diffie and George Winius, op. cit., p. 198.
102. C.R. Boxer, *The Carreira da India*, p. 3.
103. Vitorino Magalhães Godinho, *Os Descobrimentos e a Economia Mundial*, vol. III, pp. 43-4. All the ships to India started their voyages after the prayers and blessings in the 'capela do Restelo' and later in the church of Belem.
104. Ibid., p. 45.
105. Ibid.
106. A.R. Disney, op. cit., p. 37.
107. Moçambique was called on often, for fresh water and provisions, although through voyages between Lisbon and Goa without calling at any place en route were quite common C.R. Boxer, *The Carreira da India*, p. 56.
108. Vitorino Magalhães Godinho, *Os Descobrimentos e a Economia Mundial*, vol. III, p. 46.
109. C.R. Boxer, *From Lisbon to Goa 1500-1750: Studies in Portuguese Maritime Enterprise*, Variorum, Hampshire, 1990, p. 1.
110. C.R. Boxer, *The Carreira da India*, p. 53. The officials in the *Casa da India* deducted the duties and other shares due to the crown according to the authorization given to various officials. Damião Peres (ed.), *Regimento das Cazas das Indias e Mina (Manuscrito Inedito)*, Coimbra, 1947, p. 56. The officials were expected to pay to the King, the *vintena* (1/20) and *quarto* (1/4) of the quantities when they arrived at the *Casa da India* and it was almost 28.75 per cent of the total. ANTT, *Nucleo Antigo*, no.705, fols. 4-12. Genevieve Bouchon, 'Glimpses of the Beginnings of the Carreira da India (1500-1518)', in *Indo-Portuguese History: Old Issues and New Questions*, p. 51.

111. Damião Peres, *Regimento das Cazas*, pp. 147-8; C.R. Boxer, *The Carreira da India*, p. 53
112. C.R. Boxer, *The Carreira da India*, p. 53.
113. For details about the number of the India-bound ships see Luiz de Figueiredo Falcão *Livro em que se contem toda a Fazenda*, pp. 137-54; Faria y Sousa, op. cit., pp. 424-6; Vitorino Magalhães Godinho, *Os Descobrimentos e a Economia Mundial*, vol. III, p. 49; Fortunato de Almeida, *Historia de Portugal*, III, pp. 433-5.
114. Ibid., Vitorino Magalhães Godinho, *Os Descobrimentos*, vol. III, p. 49.
115. Fortunato de Almeida, *Historia de Portugal*, II, p. 162-70; Elaine Sanceau, *The Reign of the Fortunate King, 1495-1521*, Connecticut, 1969, pp. 1-25.
116. Elaine Sanceau, *The Reign of the Fortunate King*, pp. 3-22; Bailey W. Diffie and George D. Winius, op. cit., pp. 175 and 277.
117. Both Damião de Gois and Barros give two different reasons for the proposal to abandon the India project. It seems to me that the arguments given by both Gois and Barros must have been used by the councillors to substantiate their view-points. For the reasons given by Gois see Damião de Gois, *Cronica do Felicissimo Rey Manuel*, vol. I, Coimbra, 1949-55, p. 48.
118. Barros, *Da Asia*, *Decada* I, bk. 4, cap. 1.
119. Discussion in P. Mac Swiney de Mashanaglass, 'Une ambassade portugaise a Rome, sous Jules II', *Revue d'histoire diplomatique*, XVII, 1903, p. 51-63; Donald F. Lach, *Asia in the Making of Europe*, vol. I, book I, Chicago, 1965, p. 112.
120. Ibid., p. 167. King Manuel maintained good relationship with the Pope Leo X, who was the second son of Lorenzo Medici and the real ruler of the Republic of Florence. In 1516, King Manuel sent to this Medici Pope, 5,093 quintals of pepper, 1,093 quintals of cloves, 1,093 quintals of cinnamon, 1,593 quintals of ginger, 693 quintals of nutmeg, 1,093 quintals of Malagueta and 493 quintals of benzoin. But the ship carrying these commodities was lost near Genoa. Vitorino Magalhães Godinho, *Os Descobrimentos e a Economia Mundial*. vol. III, p. 178.
121. Donald F. Lach, op. cit., vol. I, book I, p. 93.
122. For details see Gustavo Couto, *Historia da Antiga Casa da India*, Lisbon, 1932.
123. Donald F. Lach, op. cit., vol. I, book I, pp. 93 and 120.
124. For details see Damião Peres (ed.), *Regimento das Cazas*, pp. 1-10.
125. Ibid., pp. 29-30; 65-6.
126. Francisco P. Mendes da Luz, *O Conselho da India*, Lisbon, 1952, pp. 42-7.
127. Damião Peres, *Regimento das Cazas*, p. 56.
128. Ibid., pp. 71-4.
129. M. Sanuto, *Diarii*, tom. VI, pp. 519-20; Vitorino Magalhães Godinho, *Os Descobrimentos e a Economia Mundial*, vol. III, p. 178.
130. Wilhelm Heyd, *Histoire du Levant au Moyen Age*, Leipzig, 1886, vol. II, p. 551; Angelo de Gubernatis, *Storia dei Viaggiatori Italiani nelle India Orientali*, Livorno, 1875, p. 380. Ferdinand Braudel, *The Mediterranean and the Mediterranean World in the Age of Philip II*, vol. I, translated by Sian Reynolds, London, 1978, p. 544.
131. M. Sanuto, *Diarii*, tom. LVII, p. 26; Vitorino Magalhães Godinho, *Os Descobrimentos e a Economia Mundial*, vol. III, p. 178.
132. Frederic Mauro, 'Merchant Communities: 1350-1750', in *The Rise of Merchant Empires, Long Distance Trade in the Early Modern World: 1350-1750*, James D. Tracy (ed.), New York, 1990, p. 261; see also J.A. Goris, *Etudes sur les Colonies Marchandes Meridionales ã Anvers: 1477-1567*, Louvain, 1925; Herman Van der Wee, *The Growth of the Antwerp Market and the European Economy*, 2 vols., Louvain, 1963. The foreign merchants began to abandon Bruges and settle down in Antwerp on the banks of the Scheldt river right from 1477. Hans Pohl, *Die Portugiesen in*

Antwerpen (1567-1648) zur Geschichte einer Minderheit, Wiesbaden, 1977, p. 25.

133. Herman van der Wee, 'Structural Changes in European Long-Distance Trade, and Particularly in the Re-export Trade from South to North 1350-1750', in *The Rise of Merchant Empires*, p. 28.
134. Ibid., Vitorino Magalhães Godinho, *Os Descobrimentos*, vol. III, p. 184.
135. Herman van der Wee, 'Structural Changes in European Long-Distance Trade', p. 28.
136. Hermann Kellenbenz, *Die Fugger in Spanien und Portugal bis 1560: Ein Großunternehmen des 16. Jahrhunderts*, Band I, München, 1990, p. 437.
137. Herman van der Wee, 'Structural Changes in European Long- Distance Trade', p. 28; See also Herman van der Wee, *The Growth of the Antwerp Market and the European Economy*, vol. II, p. 127; V. Vazques de Prada, *Letters Marchandes d'Anvers*, Paris, 1960, p. 89.
138. Donald F. Lach, op. cit., vol. I, book I, pp. 121-2.
139. Fernand Braudel, *The Mediterranean and the Mediterranean World*, vol. I, p. 544.
140. Ibid., see also Donald F. Lach, op. cit., vol. I, book I, p. 121.
141. During the first three decades of the sixteenth century, especially with the opening of the Cochin-Lisbon commercial axis and with the concentration of German and Italian merchants in Lisbon and Antwerp the supremacy of Mediterranean ports began to dwindle and the Atlantic became the focal area of commercial activities.
142. Thomé Lopes, op. cit., p. 200; see also Gernot Giertz, op. cit., p. 210.
143. K.S. Mathew, *Portuguese Trade with India*, pp. 197-8.
144. This document is dated 4 January 1552 (Cochin) in ANTT, *Corpo Cronologico*, I, Maço 87, doc. 50.
145. Vincenzo Quirini, 'Relazioni delle Indie Orientali di Vincenzo Quirini', in Eugenio Alberi, *Le Relazioini degli Ambasciatori Veneti al Senato*, vol. 15, Firenze, 1863, p. 16.
146. Bailey W. Diffie and George D. Winius, op. cit., p. 209. In 1278, a Genoese by name Don Vivaldo had become a citizen of Lisbon and was active in civic affairs. Bailey W. Diffie, *Prelude to Empire: Portugal Overseas before Henry the Navigator*, Lincoln, 1960, pp. 50-1.
147. Bailey W. Diffie, op. cit., p. 210; King Dinis banished the Venetian colony after 1309 as the Venetians were allied with his enemies. Bailey W. Diffie, *Prelude to Empire*, pp. 103-4.
148. Sanuto, op. cit., tom. IV, col. 66; William Brooks Greenlee, op. cit., p. 125.
149. Giovanni Battista Ramusio, *Delle Navigationi et Viaggi*, vol, I, Valencia: 1563, fols. 177-88.
150. Sanuto, op. cit., tom. XXVII, col. 641.
151. Bailey W. Diffie and George D. Winius, op. cit., pp. 210-11.
152. William Brooks Greenlee, op. cit., p. 145.
153. Barros, *Decada I*, part I, book V, cap. IV, p. 464.
154. Conde Ficalho, *Viagens de Pedro da Covilham*, Lisbon, 1898, p. 67.
155. The Letter sent by Bartolomeo Marchioni to Florence dated 27 June 1501 as translated in William Brooks Greenlee, op. cit., p. 148.
156. Vitorino Magalhães Godinho, *Os Descobrimentos e a Economia Mundial*, vol. III, pp. 53-4. The ship commanded by Buenagrazia and in which Giovanni de Empoli went to India in 1502 along with Vasco da Gama was also owned by Marchioni. William Brooks Greenlee, op. cit., p. 146.
157. E.C. Ravenstein, *A Journal of the First Voyage of Vasco da Gama*, London, 1898, pp. 119ff. King Manuel had conferred the citizenship of Lisbon on Serinigi. William Brooks Greenlee, op. cit., p. 125.

158. M. Sanuto, op. cit., tom. IV, col. 66.
159. Ramusio, op. cit., tom. I, pp. 145-7.
160. Wilhelm Heyd, *Histoire du Commerce du Levant*, pp. 530-1.
161. Ibid., p. 532.
162. Vitorino Magalhães Godinho, *Os Descobrimentos e a Economia Mundial*, vol. III, p. 54.
163. Wilhelm Heyd, op. cit., vol. II, p. 547.
164. Barros, *Decada* II, liv. X, cap. VIII.
165. William Brooks Greenlee, op. cit., p. 146.
166. Ibid., 118.
167. For more details see the Letter of Mateo de Begnino written on 30 March 1503, in Gernot Giertz, op. cit., pp. 30, 210-11.
168. Ibid., p. 210.
169. For details see A. Goris, *Les Colonies Marchandes meridionales a Anvers de 1488 á 1567*, Louvain, 1925; J. Denuce, *Inventaire des Affaitadi, banquiers italiens á Anves de l' annee* 1568, Antwerp, 1934.
170. K.S. Mathew, *Portuguese Trade with India*, p. 162.
171. These two Milanese, John Maria and Peter Antony, were said to have made 400 guns and cast a lot of cannon for the Zamorin. George Percy Badger (ed.), *The Travels of Ludovico di Varthema in Egypt, Syria, Arabia Deserta and Arabia Felix in Persia, India and Ethiopia AD 1503 to 1508*, New York, 1863, p. 260; O.K. Nambiar, op. cit., pp. 49-51.
172. Barros, *Decada* IV, liv. IV, caps.14-15; Correia, *Lendas*, tom. III, pp. 405-17; Bailey W. Diffie and Georg D. Winius, op. cit., p. 289.
173. Hermann Kellenbenz, *Fremde Kaufleute auf der iberischen Halbinsel*, Köln, 1970, p. 316.
174. Pieris-Fitzler, *Ceylon und Portugal*, vol. I, Leipzig, 1927, pp. 355-6.
175. Ibid., p. 296.
176. Horst G.W. Nusser, *Frühe Deutsche Entdecker: Asien in Berichten unbekannter deutscher Augenzeugen, 1502-1506*, München, 1980, p. 110.
177. Ibid., pp. 112-13; Damião de Gois, *Chronica do Felicissimo Rei Dom Manuel*, vol. IV, Lisbon, 1566, p. 623.
178. There were many German as well as Flemish soldiers with Vasco da Gama. It is believed that one (Flemish soldier) among them, who travelled with Vasco da Gama in 1502, wrote '*Calcoen*' (Calicut), the short travel report in German. For details Pius Malekandathil, *The Germans, the Portuguese and India*, Münster, 1999, pp. 31-3.
179. Antonio Silva Rego, *Documentação para a Historia das Missoes do Padroado*, vol. 1, doc. 105, p. 217. Pius Malekandathil, 'Mit den Portugiesen waren auch die Deutschen da: Erste deutsche Gemeinde in Cochin (Kerala)schon vor 485 Jahren', translated by Jose Punnamparambil, in *Meine Welt*, Heft 1/Jahrgang 15, Köln, Juni 1998, p. 11.
180. Horst G.W. Nusser, op. cit., p. 113.
181. ANTT, *Colecção de S. Vicente*, Caixa 11, 1-36.
182. Bibliotheca da Ajuda, *Livro das Merces que fez D. João de Castro*, 51-8-46, fol. 123v; see also Antonio Baião, *Historia quinhetista*..., p. 323.
183. Franz Hümmerich, *Die Erste Deutsche Handelsfahrt nach Indien 1505/06: Ein Unternemender Welser, Fugger und anderer Augsburger sowie Nürnberger Häuser*, München, 1922, p. 9.
184. Marino Sanuto, op. cit., vol. IV, p. 28; Konrad Haebler, *Die Überseeischen Unternehmungen der Welser und ihrer Gessellschafter*, Leipzig, 1903, p. 6.

185. Ibid., pp. 9-10.
186. B. Greiff (ed.), *Tagebuch des Lukas Rem*, pp. 7-8.
187. Franz Hümmerich, *Die Erste Deutsche Handelsfahrt nach Indien*, p. 11.
188. Johannes Philip Cassel, *Priviegia und Handelsfreiheiten, welche die Könige von Portugal ehedem den deutschen Kaufleuten zu Lissabon ertheilt haben*, Bremen, 1771, pp. 5ff.
189. Ibid., pp. 7ff.
190. Wolfgang von Stromer, 'Oberdeutsche Unternehmungen im Handel mit der Iberischen Halbinsel im 14. und 15. Jahrhundert', in Herman Kellenbenz, *Fremde Kaufleute auf der iberischen Halbinsel*, pp. 156-69. The travel report of Peter Holzschuher is preserved in 'Paumgartnerschen Usancenbuch' in the Fürstlich Waldburg-Zeilschen Archive in Leutkirch. The full text is given in Horst G.W. Nusser, op. cit., pp. 142-51.
191. Johannes Philip Cassel, op. cit., pp. 6ff.
192. Franz Hümmerich, *Die Erste Deutsche Handelsfahrt nach Indien*, pp. 12-16.
193. Konrad Haebler, *Die Überseeischen Unternehmungen der Welser*, pp. 15-16; B. Greiff, op. cit., pp. 163-6. It gives, in detail, the letter of Anton Welser. See also Marino Sanuto, op. cit., vol. I, p. 26. The crown refused their offer saying that he wanted in the future to make the Indian trade a royal monopoly.
194. Konrad Haebler, *Die Überseeischen Unternehmung der Welser*, pp. 16-17; B. Greiff, op. cit., pp. 8, 12-13.
195. Konrad Haebler, *Die Überseeischen Unternehmungen der Welser*, p. 17.
196. Donald F. Lach, op. cit., vol. I, book I, p. 110.
197. B. Greiff, op. cit., p. 8.
198. Richard Ehrenberg, *Capital and Finance in the Age of the Renaissance—A Study of the Fuggers and their Connections*, translated by H.M. Lucas, London, 1963, pp. 137-40.
199. B. Greiff, op. cit., pp. 8-9, 82-4.
200. Franz Hümmerich, *Quellen und Untersuchungen zur Fahrt der ersten Deutschen nach dem portugiesischen Indien 1505/6*, München, 1918, p. 67.
201. For details see Gots Freiherr von Pölnitz, *Jakob Fugger, Kaiser, Kirche und Kapital in der oberdeutschen Renaissance*, Tübingen, 1949; G.F. von Pölnitz, *Die Fugger*, Frankfurt, 1960.
202. The copper fields of Hungary were the most important source of the Fuggers' trade. Richard Ehrenberg, op. cit., p. 67.
203. Herman Kellenbenz, *Die Fugger in Spanien und Portugal bis 1560*, pp. 12-20.
204. Franz Hümmerich, *Quellen und Untersuchungen zur Fahrt*, p. 67.
205. Richard Ehrenberg, op. cit., pp.151-3.
206. Franz Hümmerich, *Quellen und Untersuchungen zur Fahrt*, p. 67.
207. Richard Ehrenberg, op. cit., pp. 168-70.
208. Franz Hümmerich, *Quellen und Untersuchungen zur Fahrt*, p. 67.
209. Herman Kellenbenz, 'Os Mercadores Alemães de Lisboa por volta de1530', in *separata de Revista Portuguesa de Historia*, vol. IX, Coimbra, 1961, pp. 9-12.
210. Franz Hümmerich, *Quellen und Untersuchungen zur Fahrt*, p. 67.
211. Joaquim de Vasconcellos, *Albrecht Dürer e a sua Influencia na Peninsula*, Coimbra, 1929, p. 25.
212. Franz Hümmerich, *Quellen und Untersuchungen zur Fahrt*, p. 67.
213. Franz Hümmerich, *Die Erste Deutsche Handelsfahrt nach Indien*, p. 22. His travel report was first published in 1509 as *Die Merfart vnn erfarung nüwer schiffung und wege zu viln onerkanten Inseln und Königreichen von dem grossmechtigen portugalischen Kunig Emanuel Erforschort/ funden/ bestritten vnnd ingenomen/ Auch*

wunderbarliche streyt/ordenung/ leben wesen handlung vnd wunderwercks/ des Volcks und Tyrer dar inn wonende/ findestu in diessein Buchlyn warhaftiglich beschryben vnn abkundterfeyt/ wie ich Balthasar Sprenger so sollichs selbs: in Kurtzverschynen zeiten: geschen vnn erfaren habe, 1509. The full text of this report is edited and published by Franz Hümmerich: *Quellen und Untersuchungen zur Fahrt*, pp. 104-26.

214. Franz Hümmerich, *Die Erse Deutsche Handelsfahrt nach Indien*, pp. 22-3. For the travel report of Hans Mayr (both in Portuguese and with German translation) see Franz Hümmerich, *Quellen und Untersuchungen zur Fahrt*, pp. 127-51.
215. Ibid., p. 67. Out of the 30 per cent 25 per cent went to the king and 5 per cent was to the support of Belem.
216. For details see Franz Hümmerich, *Die Erste Deutsche Handelsfahrt nach Indien*, pp. 135-9.Pius Malekandathil, *The Germans, the Portuguese and India*, pp. 52-4.
217. The merchants contended that the king was unilaterally setting aside the contract of 1504 and so instituted a suit against the crown in the hope of obtaining a judicial order to release their merchandise. Donald F. Lach, op. cit., vol. I, book I, p. 111.
218. Wilhelm Heyd, op. cit., vol. II, p. 532; Vitorino Magalhães Godinho, *Os Descobrimentos e a Economia Mundial*, vol. III, p. 54.
219. For details see Franz Hümmerich, *Die Erste Deutsche Handelsfahrt nach Indien*, pp. 137-42; Donald F. Lach, op. cit., vol. I, book I, p. 111.
220. For details see the list of factories and agents of Welsers mentioned in Herman Kellenbenz, 'Gewerbe und Handel 1500-1648', in *Handbuch der Deutschen Wirtschafts - und Sozialgeschichte*, vol. I, edited by Herman Aubin und Wolfgang Zorn, Stuttgart, 1971, p. 451.
221. Konrad Haebler, *Die Überseeischen Unternehmungen der Welser*, pp. 33-5.
222. ANTT, *Corpo Cronologico*, I, Maço 12, doc. 77; Herman Kellenbenz, *Die Fugger in Spanien und Portugal bis 1560*, vol. I, p. 53.
223. Ibid., p. 54; ANTT, *Corpo Cronologico*, I, Maço 17, doc. 126.
224. Herman Kellenbenz, *Die Fugger in Spanien und Portugal*, vol. I, p. 383.
225. Ibid., p. 53. The Fuggers were active in spice (distribution) trade till 1522.
226. For details on the factories, agents and distribution centres of the Fuggers see Herman Kellenbenz, 'Gewerbe und Handel 1500-1648', p. 451; see also Herman Kellenbenz, 'Wirtschaftsleben der Blütezeit', in *Geschichte der Stadt Augsburg von der Römerzeit bis zur Gegenwart*, Gunther Gottlieb and Wolfram Baer (eds.), Stuttgart, 1984, p. 273.
227. Herman Kellenbenz, *Die Fugger in Spanien und Portugal*, pp. 12-17, 52-61, 167-8.
228. Ibid., p. 373.
229. Miloslav Krasa, Josef Polisensky and Peter Ratkos, *European Expansion 1494-1519: The Voyages of Discovery in the Bratislava Manuscript Lyc. 515/8*, Prague, 1986, pp. 36ff, 66ff.
230. Herman Kellenbenz, 'The Portuguese Discoveries and the Italian and German Initiatives in the Indian Trade in the first two Decades of the 16th Century', *Congresso Internacional: Bartolomeu Dias sua Epoca: Actas*, vol. III, Porto, 1989, pp. 611-15; K.S. Mathew, 'Maritime Trade of India and the Germans in the Sixteenth Century', in *The Souvenir of the Second International Symposium on Maritime Studies*, Pondicherry: 16-20 December, 1991, pp. 39-40.
231. Stadtarchiv Augsburg, *The Letter of Georg Pock dated 14th March, 1520*, no. 24.11.
232. For details see Hedwig Kömmerling-Fitzler, *Der Nürnberger Kaufman Georg Pock (+1528/9) in Portugiesisch-Indien und im Edelsteinland Vijayanagar*, in Mitteilungen

des Vereins für Geschichte der Stadt Nürnberg (MVGN) vol. 55, Nürnberg, 1968.

233. Vincenzo Quirini, 'Relazione delle Indie Orientali di Vincenzo Quirini nel 1506', in E. Alberi, *Le Relazioni degli Ambasciatori Veneti al Senato*, vol. XV, Firenze, 1863, p. 12.
234. Ca' Masser, 'Relazione di Leonardo da Ca'Masser, alla Serinissima Republica di Venezia sopra il commercio dei Portoghese nell'India dopo la scoperta del capo di Bouna Speranza', in *Archivio Storioco Italiano*, Appendice tom. III, Firenze: 1845, p. 30.
235. R.A. de Bulhão Pato, *Cartas*, tom. III, p. 298.
236. Ibid., tom. I, p. 83.
237. A. Corsali in Giovanni Battista Ramusio, *Della Navigationi et Viaggi*, vol. I, Venetia, 1554, fol. 188v.
238. Rinaldo Fulin, *Diarii e diaristi Veneziani*, Venice, 1881, pp. 157-64; see also Girolamo Priuli, *I Diarii di Girolamo Priuli: 1494-1512*, vol. II, Bologna, 1933, p. 174; W. Heyd, op. cit., vol. II, p. 512; Castanheda, op. cit., liv. I, cap. XLI.
239. The Letter of Italian Factor Mateo di Begnino about his travel to India dated 30 Mar 1503, in Gernot Giertz, op. cit., pp. 210-11; Marino Sanuto, op. cit., vol. IV, p. 544; Castanheda, op. cit., liv. I, cap. XLIII.
240. The Travel Report of Francis Albuquerque in B. Greiff, op. cit., pp. 149-57; Girolamo Priuli, op. cit., tom. II, p. 305; W. Heyd, op. cit., vol. II, p. 526.
241. Ca' Masser, op. cit., p. 73; The German sources speak of 20,000 quintals of spices taken from Malabar ports to Lisbon. B. Greiff, op. cit., p. 158.
242. Ca' Masser, op. cit., p. 74.
243. Ibid., p. 77; M. Sanuto, op. cit., tom. VI, pp. 363, 373 and 383-4.
244. Only the merchandise brought by the three ships in August is accounted for here. M. Sanuto, op. cit., tom. XVII, p. 191.
245. Here the commodities brought by the remaining two ships of 1513 and the five ships of 1514 are combined together to give the statistics. See for details M. Sanuto, op. cit., tom. XVIII, p. 143 and ibid., tom. XXV, pp. 594-5.
246. Gaspar Correia, *Lendas*, tom. II, part II, p. 559.
247. But the amount of principal spices that entered Europe via Venice was relatively very meagre. Thus in 1515, the pepper that reached Venice through the traditional route was only 25 quintals; ginger 1540 quintals; cinnamon 45 quintals; cloves 85 quintals; mace 40 quintals. M. Sanuto, op. cit., tom. XIX, pp. 446-7. The volume of spices taken to Venice in 1518 was still less. 10 quintals of pepper, 457 quintals of ginger, 111 quintals of cinnamon, 23 quintals of cloves and 40 quintals of mace formed the principal merchandise that reached Venice. M. Sanuto, op. cit., tom. XXV, p. 621. In 1522 the quantity of spices which entered Venice was remarkably insignificant. Venice got only 88 quintals of pepper, 98 quintals of ginger, 51 quintals of cinnamon, 29 quintals of cloves, 6 quintals of nutmeg and 1quintal mace. M. Sanuto, op. cit., tom. XXXII, pp. 438-9.
248. Marino Sanuto, op. cit., tom. XXVII, p. 641.
249. Vitorino Magalhães Godinho, *Os Descobrimentos e a Economia Mundial*, vol. III, p. 73.
250. Ibid., p. 74.
251. Marino Sanuto, op. cit., tom. XLII, pp. 453-4.
252. Ibid., tom. LIV, p. 131.
253. Ibid., tom. LIV, p. 599 and LV, p. 63.
254. Artur Teodor de Matos, 'Some Aspects of the Portuguese Trade in the Malabar Coast: Cochin and the "Mercadorias Meudas" (1506-1508)', in *Indica*, March-September 1989, vol. 26, nos. 1 and 2 , pp. 93-7.

255. Maria Emilia Cordeiro Ferreira, 'Quintaladas' in *Dicionario de Historia de Portugal*, edited by Joel Serrao, vol. II, Lisbon, 1968, p. 528; Carta Regia of June 1510 giving instructions to Lourenço Moreno, the factor of Cochin, published by A.B. de Braganca Pereira, *Arquivo Portugues Oriental*, tom. IV, vol. I, part I, Bastora-Goa, 1937, pp. 349.
256. Henry E.J. Stanley, op. cit., p. 152. Fontoura da Costa, *Roteiro da Viagem de Vasco da Gama: 1497-99*, Lisbon, 1940, p. 63.
257. 'The Anonymous Narrative', in William Brooks Greenlee, op. cit., p. 92.
258. The Letter of the Italian factor Mateo di Begnino about his travel to India dated 30 March 1503 in Gernot Giertz, op. cit., p. 210.
259. Simão Botelho quoted by Vitorino Magalhães Godinho, *Os Descobrimentos e a Economia Mundial*, vol. III, p. 9.
260. Vitorino Magalhães Godinho, *Os Descobrimentos e a Economia Mundial*, vol. I, p. 37.
261. Ibid., vol. III, p. 10.
262. Ibid., p. 11.
263. Ibid., pp. 10-11.
264. ANTT, *Corpo Cronologico*, I, Maço 3, doc. 29.
265. Vitorino Magalhães Godinho, *Os Descobrimentos*, vol. I, pp. 139-218.
266. Ibid., vol. III, p. 9. Gold from Sofala, Quiloa, Mombaca and Melind frequently entered India. For details see ibid., vol. I, pp. 190-7.
267. Ibid., vol. II, p. 89.
268. Ibid., vol. I, pp. 95-138.
269. Ibid., vol. II, pp. 89.
270. The reference to the adverse trade balance is made by C.R. Boxer, who quotes an official dispatch written from Cannanore in 1534 and another anecdote, first recorded in a manuscript of the period 1550-70. The anecdote is as follows: when Vasco da Gama arrived in Portugal in 1499, he was enthusiastically received by King Manuel and his court. Meanwhile the Count of Vimioso asked Da Gama what merchandise could be got from India and what the Indians wanted in exchange. The explorer replied that what could be brought from India included pepper, cinnamon, ginger, amber and musk; what the Indians demanded in exchange was gold, silver, velvet and scarlet and cloth. To which the count retorted: 'In that case it seems to me that it is they who have discovered us'. Quoted by C.R. Boxer, *Portuguese Conquest and Commerce in Southern Asia: 1500-1750* (Variorum), Hampshire, 1985, p. ix.
271. Dietmar Rothermund, *Asian Trade and European Expansion in the Age of Mercantilism*, Delhi, 1981, pp. 49-51.
272. Reinhard Hildebrandt, *Die 'Georg Fuggerischen Erben': Kaufmännische Tätigkeit und sozialer Status 1555-1600*, Berlin, 1966, pp. 180-2.
273. Joaquim Verissimo Serrão, *Historia de Portugal*, vol. III, p. 31.
274. Cristovão Rodrigues Acenheiro, *Croniqua dos Reis de Portugal*, *Colecção Ineditos de Historia Portugueza*, tom. V, Lisboa, 1926, pp. 341-3; A. Braamcamp Freire, *Vida e Obras de Gil Vicente, Trovador e Mestre da Balança*, Lisboa, 1944, p. 149.
275. Antonio de Oliveira, *A Vida Economica e Social de Coimbra de 1537 a 1640*, part I, vol. I, Lisboa, 1971, pp. 250-1.
276. The people believed that pestilence and other calamities were divine punishment for the tolerance which the church was showing towards the Jews and the heretics. Alexandre Herculano, *Historia da Origem e Estabelecimento da Inquisição em Portugal*, tom. I, edited by Jorge Borges de Macedo, p. 171; Joaquim Verissimo Serrão, *Historia de Portugal*, vol. III, pp. 51 and 292. Antonio Sergio, *Obras Completas de Antonio Sergio: Introdução Geografico-Sociologica á Historia de*

Portugal, critical edition guided by Castelo Branco Chaves, Vitorino Magalhães Godinho, Rui Gracio and Joel Serrão, Lisboa, 1976, pp. 191-2.

277. The German eye-witness says that the King and family fled to Palmeda; while the inhabitants left the city. See for details Albert Haemmerle (ed.), *Stetten-Jahrbuch*, MCML, vol. II, Deren von Steten Geschlechterbuch MDXXXXVIII, pp. 52ff.; Hermann Kellenbenz, 'Os Mercadores Alemães de Lisboa por volta de 1530', *Separata da Revista Portuguesa de Historia*, vol. IX, Coimbra, 1961, pp. 12-13.
278. Joaquim Verissimo Serrão, *Historia de Portugal*, vol. III, p. 292.
279. Ibid., p. 293.
280. Manuel Lopes de Almeida, *Memorial de Pêro Roiz Soares*, tom. I, Coimbra, 1953, pp. 19-21.
281. Antonio Sergio, *Obras Completas de Antonio Sergio*, p. 191.
282. ANTT, *Gavetas*, 15-17-19.
283. The letter of Henrique de Souza written to the Governor dated 15 May 1546 in Elaine Sanceau, *Colecção de Sao Lourenço*, vol. II, p. 321.
284. The letter of the Viceroy written to the King dated 16 January 1551, in ANTT, *Corpo Cronologico*, II, Maço 242, doc. 44.
285. ANTT, *Corpo Cronologico*, I, Maço 76, doc. 8.
286. For details see Bernardo Gomes de Britto, *Historia Tragico Maritima: Berichte aus der grossen Zeit der portugiesischen Seefahrt 1552-1602*, Stuttgart, 1983.
287. Ibid., pp. 31-60.
288. See the table given above in the text.
289. ANTT, *Gavetas* 20-1-45.
290. The letter by the King of Cochin written to the Governor dated 31 January 1548, in Elaine Sanceau, *Colecção de São Lourenço*, vol. III, p. 9. The letter was written for the king by one Marcos Roiz Dalemanha, who probably must have been a German who entered the service of the native ruler. See also the letter of the king of Cranganore. Ibid., vol. III, p. 17.
291. Diogo do Couto, *Da Asia, Decada*, VII, parte II, liv. 8, cap. 14 and liv. 9, cap. 10.
292. Elaine Sanceau, *Colecção de São Lourenço*, vol. III, p. 15.
293. John Soarez, the vicar of the fort of Chale (Chalium) baptized the king of Tanur. *The Jesuit Archive of Goa*, 10 Letter of D. João the king of Tanur to the Bishop of Goa, fol.136; Faria y Souza, op. cit., tom. II, p. 133. For further details regarding this conversion see D. Ferroli, *The Jesuits in Malabar*, vol. I. Bangalore, 1939, pp. 130-7. Later he returned to his old ways.
294. The Tanur king asked the nobles and the small kings to support the Zamorin and to send pepper to Calicut, instead of sending it to Cochin. ANTT, *Corpo Cronologico*, I, Maço 87, doc. 50. Later the Tanur king justified his action saying that he was a Christian in the true spirit and that he would die as a believer in Christ. The support to the Zamorin was necessary as he was a vassal of Calicut and he would have lost the kingdom, had he not stood by the Zamorin. The letter of D. João, the king of Tanur written to the Portuguese crown in 1552. ANTT, *Gavetas*, 15-21-6.
295. The Viceroy gives a detailed account of this struggle in his letter to the Portuguese king dated 16 January 1551 in ANTT, *Corpo Cronologico*, II, Maço 242, doc. 44; See also ANTT, *Gavetas* 15-20-8.
296. ANTT, *Corpo Cronologico*, II, Maço 242, doc. 44; ANTT, *Gavetas*, 15-20-8.
297. Ibid. *Chaverpada* means the retainers of the dead king who run amok in order to avenge the death of the king and they usually die in this attempt. This practice of a suicidal squad was prevalent in south India, especially in Kerala. This prevailed among even non-Nair martial groups such as the St. Thomas Christians, as well.
298. The continuous fighting hindered the transport of pepper. Even after 1552, the pepper

king obstructed the movement of spice ships. Faria y Souza, op. cit., tom. II, p. 159.

299. ANTT, *Corpo Cronologico*, I, Maço 87, doc. 50.
300. On 26 January 1549, Cosme Anes wrote from Cochin to the Portuguese Crown that the trade had been going down in Cochin for the last three years (even before the outbreak of Vaduthala war and the reason for this must have been the tensions that grew between Cranganore and Cochin) and that small boats and other carriers of pepper were lying unused in Cochin de Cima. ANTT, *Corpo Cronologico*, I, Maço 82, doc. 36.
301. During this period the Portuguese resorted to temple wealth as a source of income. On the order of John III, they tried to rob Tremele (Thirumala or Thiruvannamala), which they could not because of bad weather. Then they came to Tebelicare (Tevelakkara) and took two casks of pure gold and precious stones under the leadership of Martim Afonso de Souza. Diogo do Couto, *Decadas*, liv. IX, cap. VII, pp. 93-9; Faria y Souza, op. cit., tom. II, pp. 72-83; Elaine Sanceau, *Colecção de São Lourenço*, vol. II, p. 390.
302. Elaine Sanceau, *Colecção de São Lourenço*, vol. II, pp. 390-4.
303. Faria y Souza, op. cit., tom. II, pp. 72-83.
304. Francisco d'Andrade, *Chronica do muyto alto e poderoso Rey destes Reynos de Portugal, Dom João*, vol. III, part III, Coimbra, MDCCLXXXXVI, pp. 233-4.
305. The king even threatened to confiscate the property of the converts and to deprive them of jobs. For details see Georg Schurhammer, *Francis Xavier*, p. 306.
306. Gervasis Mulakara, op. cit., pp. 17 and 38.
307. Vitorino Magalhães Godinho, *Os Descobrimentos*, vol. III, pp. 22-3.
308. For a study on the change in the religious approach with the accession of John III, see Joaquim Verissimo Serrão, *Historia de Portugal*, vol. III, pp. 50-8; 260-2.
309. The Inquisition proceedings of Cochin began in 1547 under the Jesuit priest D. Gonçalo da Siveira. For details see Jose Alberto Rodrigues da Silva Tavim, 'From Setubal to the Sublime Porte', pp. 96-8
310. As all of the new Christian traders were arrested almost simultaneously, they could in no way protect their hard-earned wealth, which they had to leave behind when they were transported to Goa and Lisbon.
311. These new Christians were sent from Cochin to Goa in 1558 or 1559. See Ana Cannas da Cunha, op. cit., p. 136. They were further taken to Lisbon in August, 1560. Ibid., p. 168. The documents relating to Maria Nunes (ANTT, *Inquisição de Lisboa*: proc. 6369), wife of Jácome Olivares and to Simão Nunes (his brother-in-law: proc. 4516) and his wife Elvira Rodrigues (proc. 4656) testify to this date. Only Leonor Caldeira, the oldest among them, was set free. ANTT, *Inquisição de Lisboa*, proc. 7296 de Leonor Caldeira, fols.12 and 138-9.
312. The captain of Cochin, Diogo Alvares Teles accused the inquisitors of emptying the city of inhabitants under the pretext of inquiry against the new Christians. Over this dispute between Belchior Carneiro and Diogo Alvares Teles see the testimony of Fr. Francisco Fernandes dated 5 May 1557 in Josef Wicki and John Gomes (eds.), *Documenta Indica*, vol. III, Rome, 1948, pp. 638-42.
313. The one-time *juiz dos orfãos* in Cochin, Estêvão Rebelo, gave testimony before the Inquisition that Jácome Olivares had served with arms and horses in the war with the pepper king. ANTT, *Inquisição de Lisboa*, proc. 5265, fol. 42.
314. ANTT, *Inquisição de Lisboa*, proc. 7296, fol. 77; Jose Alberto Rodrigues da Silva Tavim, 'From Setubal to the Sublime Porte', p. 113.
315. Jose Alberto Rodrigues da Silva Tavim, 'Uma Comunidade na Sombra', pp. 16-17.
316. L.K. Anantha Krishna Iyer, *The Cochin Tribes and Castes*, vol. II, London, 1912, pp. 404-5. K.P. Padmanabha Menon, *History of Kerala*, vol. II, p. 519.

317. David Mandelbaum, 'The Jewish Way of Life in Cochin', in *Jewish Social Studies*, vol. I, no. IV, 1939, pp. 440-2 and 448-50; see also David Mandelbaum, 'Social Stratification among the Jews of Cochin in India and Israel', in *Jews in India*, edited by Thomas A. Timberg, New Delhi, 1986, pp. 90-1.
318. In Cranganore, Fr. Vicente de Lagos OFM founded a Seminary for the St. Thomas Christians. BPE, *Nucleo de Manuscritos da Casa Forte* C IX/2-3, Maço 3, doc. 15, fol. 5v. In 1548, there were 70 Seminarians, 10 Deacons and 3 priests, all belonging to the St. Thomas Christian community. The crown used to give 1,00,000 *reais* for their sustenance. ANTT, *Corpo Cronologico*, I, Maço 80, doc. 7. Moreover, many were sent to Portugal for higher studies. Thus in 1539, there were 4 students in Lisbon. Georg Schurhammer, 'Three Letters of Mar Jacob Bishop of Malabar, 1503-1550', pp. 81-2; In 1549, there were 2 Seminarians in Coimbra. ANTT, *Corpo Cronologico*, I, Maço 82, doc. 1; in 1550, there were altogether 4 Seminarians in Portugal from this community. ANTT. *Corpo Cronologico*, I, Maço 83, doc. 71.
319. G.M. Moraes, 'St. Francis Xavier, Apostolic Nuncio, 1542-1552', *Journal of the Bombay Branch of the Royal Asiatic Society*, New Series, XXVII, 1950, p. 288.
320. Pe. Alvaro Penteado accused the St. Thomas Christians of being heretics. Antonio Silva Rego, (ed.), *Documentação para a Historia das Missões*, vol. II, p. 359. The accusations made by Fr. Michael Carneiro against Bishop Mar Joseph are given in D. Ferroli, *The Jesuits in Malabar*, vol. I, pp. 154-8.
321. Josef Wicki (ed.), *Documenta Indica*, vol. III, Rome, 1960, p. 801.
322. See Eugene Tisserant, *Eastern Christianity in India*, trans, by E.R. Hambye, Calcutta, 1957, pp. 35-8; D. Ferroli, op. cit., vol. I, p. 156.
323. Vitorino Magalhães Godinho, 'Crises et Changements Geographiques et Structuraux au XVIeme Siécle', in *Revista de Economica*, vol. XI, fasc. I, Lisboa, 1959. See also Vitorino Magalhães Godinho, *Ensaios*, vol. II, Lisboa, 1968, pp. 139-74.
324. Damião Peres (ed.), *Historia de Portugal*, vol. III, p. 261; A. Braamcamp Freire, *Vida e Obras de Gil Vicente*, p. 104; Joaquim Verissimo Serrão, *Historia de Portugal*, vol. III, pp. 36 and 42.
325. Damião Peres (ed.), *Historia de Portugal*, vol. III, pp. 261-2.
326. Ibid., p. 262. See also Joaquim Verissimo Serrão, *Historia de Portugal*, vol. III, pp. 37-8.
327. For more details see Frei Luis de Sousa, *Anais de Dom João III*, edited by Rodrigues Lapa, vol. I, Lisboa, 1938, pp. 194-200; vol. II, pp. 272-75.
328. Freire Luis de Sousa, *Anais de Dom João* III, pp. 421-4; Fortunato de Almeida, *Historia de Portugal*, vol. III, p. 564. With the closing of the Portuguese factory of Antwerp, many merchants left the place. The first who left Antwerp were the *maranos*, followed by the German, Baltic and English Protestants. Most of the catholic traders of France, Italy and Germany who were doing business in Flanders transferred their activities to Hamburg, the Rhenish cities, Zurich, Rouen and Lyons. By 1560, some of the chief spice-contractors like Affaitadi were forced into bankruptcy. For details see Jervis Wegg, *The Decline of Antwerp under Philip of Spain*, London, 1924; Donald F. Lach, op. cit., vol. I, book I, p. 127.
329. Elaine Sanceau, *Colecção de São Lourenço*, vol. I, p. 442.
330. ANTT, *Corpo Cronologico*, I, Maço 71, doc. 42.
331. Diogo do Couto, *Da Asia. Decada* V, book III, cap. 1; Lopo de Sousa Coutinho, *Livro Primeiro do cerco de Diu, que os Turcos poseram a Forteleza de Diu*, Coimbra, 1556.
332. The letter of the Sultan to the Portuguese crown in ANTT, *Corpo Cronologico*, I, Maço 74, doc. 108.
333. For more details see David Lopes, *Extractos da Historia da Conquista do Yemen*

pelos Othomanos-Contribuições para a Historia do Estabelecimento dos Portugueses na India Memoria destinada á X sessão do Congresso Internacional dos Orientalistas por..., Lisboa, 1892. See also R.B. Serjeant, *The Portuguese off the South Arabian Coast—Hadrami Chronicles*, Oxford, 1963; Salih Özbaran, 'The Ottoman Turks and the Portuguese in the Persian Gulf, 1534-1581', *Journal of Asian History*, vol. 6, no. 1: 45-87, 1972, pp. 45-87.

334. Diogo do Couto, *Da Asia, Decada* VIII, liv. II, cap. 10. See also Nilakanta Sastri, *A History of South India from Pre-historic Times to the Fall of Vijayanagar*, Madras, 1976; Burton Stein, *Vijayanagara*, Cambridge, 1989.
335. The trade in horses by the Portuguese, and in precious metals by the Portuguese and the Germans has already been treated above.
336. See for details Luis Filipe Thomaz, 'A Crise de 1565-1575 na Historia do Estado da India', in *Mare Liberum*, no. 9, Julho 1995, pp. 481-508.
337. John Briggs, *History of the Rise of the Mahommedan power in India till the year AD 1612*, trans. from the original Persian of Mahomed Kasim Ferishta, vol. II, New Delhi, 1989, pp. 5ff.
338. Diogo do Couto, in his 'Dialogo do Soldado Práctico', has the soldier say that only their fear of Akbar's attacking them kept the other Muslim rulers from continuing their fights against the Portuguese. Diogo do Couto, *O Soldado Práctico*, edited by Rodrigues Lapa, Lisboa, 1954, pp. 113-14.
339. Gaspar Correia, *Lendas da India*, tom. II, p. 689, S.S. Pissurlencar, *Regimento das Fortalezas*, p. 302.
340. Diogo do Couto, *Da Asia*, Decada VII, liv. III, Cap. I, II, III; Antonio Francisco Moniz, *Noticias e Documentos para a Historia de Damão-Antiga Provincia do Norte*, I, Bastora, 1900, pp. 27 and 65-71.
341. S.S. Pissurlencar, *Regimento das Fortalezas*, p. 494. This fortress was at the junctional point of two rivers which separated the land into the kingdom of Banguel (Bangher) and the kingdom of the queen of Olala (Ullal). The latter which was to the south of Mangalore used to pay tribute of vassalage to the Portuguese Crown. Henry Heras, *The Aravidu Dynasty of Vijayanagara*, vol. I , Madras, 1927, p. 188.
342. Antonio Bocarro, op. cit., p. 313; *Livro das Cidades e Fortalezas, que a Coroa de Portugal tem nas Partes da India; E das Capitanias, E Mais Cargos, Que Nelle ha, E da Importancia Delles*, Preface by Francisco P. Mendes da Luz, in *Boletim da Bibliotheca da Universidade de Coimbra*, vol. XXI, Coimbra, 1953, p. 63.
343. Diogo do Couto, *Da Asia*, Decada VIII, cap. XXXII, pp. 275-81.
344. This revival of the Levantine trade via Persia and Egypt was made possible also because of the stability re-established by Suleiman the Magnificent. Donald F. Lach, op. cit., vol. I, book I, p. 128. See also F.C. Lane 'The Mediterranean Spice-Trade. Further Evidence of its Revival in the Sixteenth Century', AHR, XLV, 1940 reprinted in B. Pullan (ed.), *Crisis and Change in the Venetian Economy*, London, 1968, pp. 47-58.
345. Lourenço Pires de Tavora quoted in F.C. Lane 'The Mediterranean Spice-Trade', in *American Historical Review*, XLV, 1939-40, p. 585.
346. Ferdinand Braudel, *The Mediterranean and the Mediterranean World*, vol. II, p. 492.
347. Gino Luzzato, 'La decadenza di Venezia dopo le scoperte geografiche nella tradizione e nella realtà', *Archivo Veneto*, Series 5, LIV-LV, 1945, pp. 168-70.
348. F.C. Lane, 'The Mediterranean Spice-Trade' in *American Historical Review*, XLV, 1939-40, p. 588.
349. For further details see Aldo Stella, 'La crisi economica veneziana della seconda metà delsecolo XVI', in *Archivo Veneto*, Series 5, LVIII, 1962, pp. 42-4; The emergence of Marseilles as an important distributing centre of spices is discussed by R. Gascon,

'Un siécle du commerce des épices à Lyon. Fin Xve-fin XVIe siécles', *Annales. Economies, sociétés, civilisations*, XV, no. 4, pp. 648-50.

350. Aldo Stella, 'La crisi economica veneziana della seconda metà del secolo XVI', p. 42; Donald F. Lach, op. cit., vol. I, book I, pp. 129-30.
351. K.S. Mathew, *Portuguese Trade with India* , p. 213.
352. See the letter of Braz d'Araujo written to the King dated 15 December 1545, in ANTT, *Corpo Cronologico*, III, Maço16, doc. 22.
353. See the letter of Braz d'Araujo written to the Governor dated 12 December 1546, in ANTT, *Colecção de São Lourenço*, vol. IV, fol. 288. See also Bibliotheca da Ajuda, *Livro das Merces que fez D. João de Castro*, 51-8-46, fol. 59.
354. See the letter of Francisco da Maya written to the governor dated 25 January 1547 in ANTT, *Colecção de São Lourenço*, vol. IV, fol. 326.
355. Bibliotheca da Ajuda, *Livro das Merces que fez D. João de Castro*, 51-8-46, fol. 62.
356. Letter of João Anes written to the king dated 29 January 1552 in ANTT, *Corpo Cronologico*, I, Maço 87, doc. 74.
357. Bernardo Gomes de Britto, *Historia Tragico Maritima*, p. 32.
358. ANTT, *Corpo Cronologico*, III, Maço 16, doc. 22.
359. Bibliotheca da Ajuda, *Livro das Merces que fez D. João de Castro*, fols. 59-60.
360. Bibliotheca da Ajuda, *Livro das Merces que fez D. João de Castro*, fols. 62-4.
361. Bernardo Gomes de Britto, *Historia Tragico Maritima*, p. 32.
362. Elaine Sanceau, *Colecção de São Lourenço*, vol. III, p. 422.
363. ANTT, *Corpo Cronologico*, I, Maço 83, doc. 60.
364. ANTT, *Corpo Cronologico*, I, Maço 86, doc. 11.
365. See the letter of Henrique de Chichorro Souza written to the king dated 8 January 1557, in ANTT, *Corpo Cronologico*, I, Maço 100, doc. 65.

CHAPTER VI

Intra-Asian Trade: A Drain on the Portuguese Commercial Establishment: 1570-1663

The official renouncement of royal monopoly over spices in 1570 coincided with a new phase in Cochin's commercial history. During the period between 1570 and 1663, the organization of local, inter-local, intra-Asian as well as Indo-European trade underwent very significant changes. The private trade in Cochin, during the period between 1570 and 1598 saw the highest watermark in its history. However, the general pattern in the intra-Asian trade of Cochin was not uniform all through these ninety-three years. The private traders of Cochin were extending the boundaries of their commercial empire within Asia, when there was chaos in the organization of Indo-European commerce. A large number of voyage concessions accorded to the Portuguese individuals and institutions which in most cases were conducted by private entrepreneurs who had large commercial networks, gave an added impetus to intra-Asian trade. However the diversion of pepper on a large-scale from the hinterland of Cochin to the Coromandel coast through the ghat route, coinciding with the diminishing supply of pepper in Cochin, made the enterprising *casados* shift their trading activities more to the eastern coast by the second decade of the seventeenth century, creating a crisis in Cochin's trade. With increasing tensions in the hinterland, which accelerated this diversion, and with increasing pressure on the Portuguese navigational lines from the Dutch and the English, the different strands of intra-Asian commerce emanating from Cochin became feeble and slender by the end of the 1630s. However, navigational lines to Moçambique and European commerce via the Goa–Cape route were still operating from Cochin even in the troubled days of 1650s. This chapter deals primarily with the different layers of intra-Asian trade conducted in Cochin during the period between 1570 and 1663.

1. THE ORGANIZATION OF LOCAL AND INTER-LOCAL TRADE

Cochin, being the most opulent and populous city in Portuguese India, second only to Goa,[1] had a great demand for a variety of commodities for local consumption and to maintain its sophisticated life-style. Almost all the articles transacted in local trade were imported from outside. Food materials, especially rice, were a very rare commodity, demand for which was always on the increase. In 1585, a road with a width of 25 palms, which started from the seaside and went through the *Casa da Moeda* and *Casa da Feitoria*, was constructed to connect the populous pockets with the square where the food materials were distributed.[2] Every year, more than 40,000 *candis* of rice were brought to the city, which the captains and other officials of Cochin joined hands to hoard in their houses and godowns, with a view to selling it later at a higher price. This created an artificial shortage of food materials in the city making the residents pay very high prices for them, especially during the rainy season. A good volume of this hoarded rice was also taken from these private godowns to the interior parts of Malabar where it was sold at a very large profit.[3] So the municipality of Cochin took a decision to open fifteen retail shops for the sale of food materials. On 18 April 1592 Matias de Albuquerque, the Viceroy, ratified this decision.[4] According to the royal order of 22 January 1593, Dom Philip decreed that rice should be sold only through these retail shops opened and operated under the jurisdiction of the municipality of Cochin. Those who violated this order would be punished with a fine of fifty *cruzados* and two years of exile to Daman.[5] The state intervention in the local trade was inevitable as far as trade transactions on food materials were concerned. In the city of Portuguese Cochin, there were two big godowns owned by the state for the storing of rice and other food materials. When they fell into a dilapidated condition, the Viceroy Francisco da Gama on 7 April 1598, ordered the repair of these godowns with the money taken from the 'one per cent collected from the merchants for maintaining the cleanliness of the city'.[6]

This period, especially after the 1590s also witnessed the entry of many new Christians into the commerce of Cochin and their dominance in the local trade as well as in intra-Asian trade. Most of them seem to have reached Cochin after 1592 as factors and collection agents of the contractors of Indian trade whose main partners in Portugal were new Christians. Duarte Gomes Solis (1561-1630), a new Christian who came to Cochin in 1586 was one among them.[7] This period of contract trade (1592-8) offered a good pretext for many new Christians of Portugal to come over to Cochin and to take up the commercial opportunities offered by this city.[8] Thus, in 1596, when Chryztoph Pawlowski from Poland visited Cochin, he noticed only new Christian merchants trading in the city of Santa Cruz.[9] Linschotten also testifies to the Semitic dominance in Cochin in the local as well as intra-Asian trade of this period.[10] The memories of the immediate past, when the new Christians of Cochin reviving their jewish practices were subjugated to inquisitional procedures in the 1560s with which we have already dealt with in the third chapter, must have prompted the new Christians engaged in local trade to make some compromise with Catholic teachings, initially at least, to protect their commercial interests.

Caesar Frederick who visited Cochin during the period between 1563 and 1581 remarked that the great quantity of silk that came from China and the great volume of sugar that came from Bengal (for which the married citizens were not required to pay any customs) formed the two principal commodities that were traded in Cochin's market.[11] Simultaneously, there arose a great demand for coins for carrying on trade in the city as well as with neighbouring regions. On 28 March 1577, the Governor Monis Barreto permitted the Municipality of Cochin to issue copper coins called *bazaruccos*.[12] This was in addition to the various copper and silver coins that were minted and circulated in Cochin, as we have already seen, right from the beginning of the Portuguese period.

Rice, silk, sugar, textiles and copper were the important commodities that were transacted in the inter-local trade. These wares were taken from the market of Santa Cruz of Cochin to native Cochin and to the interior as well as to distant parts of

Malabar, very often in exchange for pepper and other spices. Large quantities of areca nut and coir were also brought to Cochin for trade.[13] Moreover, as a part of the inter-local trade, pieces of artillery were taken from Cochin to different parts of Malabar for sale. Thus, in 1598, we find a Jew from Cochin selling artillery to the king of Travancore.[14]

However, it seems that after 1612, there was a setback to the local trade and even to the inter-local trade, as many *casados* had quitted Cochin. In January 1615, Dom Diogo Coutinho, who was the captain of Cochin for the period between 1614 and 1627, wrote to the Portuguese king that Cochin was then lacking in nobility and that this city was greatly depopulated.[15] A similar hint to the general condition of local and inter-local trade was given by King Philip in his letter addressed to the viceroy, on 11 February 1616, that the city of Cochin was, as he was informed, in a very difficult state and had been abandoned by its citizens.[16] This migration of people from Cochin took place mainly because of the shortage of spices and other commodities felt in Cochin as a result of the tensions which the Portuguese had with the pepper-growers in the hinterland and also because of the Dutch blockade in South-East Asia.[17] The depopulation of the city seemed to have continued throughout the remaining years of Portuguese rule reducing considerably the ratio of the consumer class, adversely affecting the volume of local trade and indirectly the intra-local trade.

2. THE GHAT ROUTE AND THE INTRA-ASIAN TRADE BY LAND

This period witnessed a proportionately high volume of trade transactions through the ghat route. The contemporary evidence suggests that the spices taken from the hinterland of Cochin through the ghat and other land routes for intra-Asian distribution were superior in quality and larger in volume, when compared to those taken from the port of Cochin to Europe. Thus, Caesar Frederick writes: '. . . the Pepper that goeth for Portugale is not so good as that which goeth for Mecca, because that in times past the officers of the king of Portugale made a contract with the king of Cochin, in the name of the king of Portugale, for prizes of Pepper, and by reason of that agreement betweene them at that time made, the price can neither rise or fall, which is a very lowe and base price, and for this cause the villaines bring it to the Portugales, greene and full of filthe. The Moores of Mecca that give a better price, have it cleane and drie and better conditioned. All the Spices and drugs that are brought to Mecca are stolen from thence (Cochin) as contrabanda. . . .'[18] It seems that most of these traders bought the commodities directly from the farmers through their agents and peddling-traders operating in the hinterland. The higher price offered by these traders was an attraction to the growers. Though the diversion of the spices through the ghat route and the despatch of pepper from Coromandel ports to Mecca may seem to have been an expensive affair, it appears that in reality it was not so. The Tamil merchants who used to distribute rice and textiles in the pepper-growing hinterland of central Kerala, brought back pepper to the Coromandel ports as return cargo, which considerably reduced the transportation costs.

The volume of spices taken across the ghat to Tamilnadu for intra-Asian trade increased considerably during the contract period (1570-98). As the burden of procuring necessary cargo for Europe ultimately fell upon the German and Italian agents of the contractors in Cochin and other parts of Malabar, a good many of the Portuguese citizens also seemed to have linked themselves with the ghat route trade.[19] On 26 December 1587, Ferdinand Cron, the agent of the Fuggers and the Welsers in Cochin, writes that although about 3,00,000 quintals of pepper were produced yearly in India, only a very little came into the hands of the contractors to be taken to Europe. The main reason for this phenomenon was the high price that prevailed in the hinterland, a price which was offered by the traders who took spices to the regions across the ghats. These powerful merchants with the help of a large caravan of 800 to 1,000 oxen used to carry the pepper to the Coromandel coast from where they were sent to Tartaria, Mogor (Moghul territory), Arabia, Persia, Pegu and China.[20] Francisco da Costa, the writer of the factory of Cochin during the period between 1586 and 1607, also says that much of the pepper was diverted through the ghat routes to destinations such as Bengal, Masulipatanam and other places. He further gives the information that the volume of the spices that went from the hinterland through these routes was relatively high, about 19,000 *bhars* of pepper: from Canharapely (Kanjirappilly) and Tecanqutes (the kingdom of Thekkenkur) 4,000 *bhars*, from Iratepely (Erattupetta) 1,000 *bhars*, from Erimamoly (Erumely) 3,000 *bhars*, from Zaruquly (Chalakkudi) 5,000 *bhars*, from Corgeira (Kodakara) 3,000 *bhars*, from Paleacate Cheri (it must be Palakkad Churam or pass) 3,000 *bhars*.[21]

This shows that the volume taken through the ghat route was relatively large when compared to the annual average of pepper exported from India to Europe during the period between 1590 and 1598. It was only 6,28,653 kilograms,[22] while

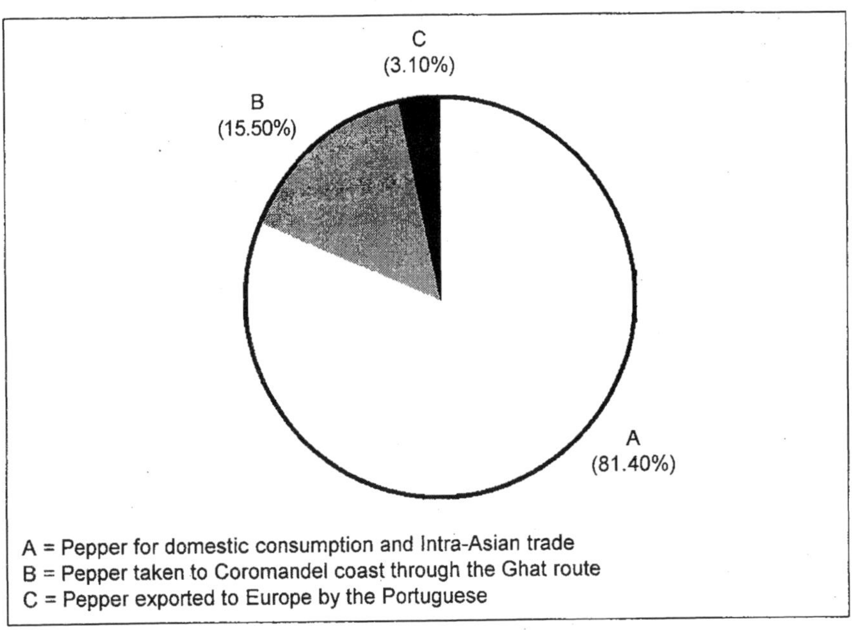

Figure 2: Distribution of Pepper for the period between 1570 and 1663.

the total production of pepper from Onor to Travancore, at the beginning of seventeenth century was 1,00,000 *bhars* or 2,58,000 quintals (1,66,30,000 kilograms).[23] On the basis of such data, we can get an idea of the volume of the ghat route trade. Only 3.1 per cent of the total pepper was exported to Europe. The ghat route commerce was almost five times greater than that of European trade and 15.5 per cent of the total production was taken through the ghat route for Asian commerce. The remaining 81.4 per cent included the share of domestic consumption and the volume of pepper taken for intra-Asian trade. It shows also that the European trade on pepper conducted by the Portuguese during this period was very insignificant, when compared to the other strands of commerce confined to Asia.

Kumily pass was the common outlet for the commodities conveyed from places like Erattupetta, Kanjirappilly and Erumely to Tamilnadu for further distribution. The spices from Chalakkudi reached Tamilnadu through Peringalkuthu and those from Kodakara through Kormala. Among these, the Kumily pass, into which the land routes from the Vadakkenkur and Thekkenkur kingdoms merged, seems to have been the most frequented and heavily-used mountain-route. When the Archbishop, Dom Alexis de Meneses visited the St. Thomas Christians of the hinterland, he happened to meet many traders coming through this route to take pepper in exchange for the textiles of Tamilnadu.[24]

One of the royal documents dated 6 February 1580, mentions that the crown was informed about the paucity of the pepper in the weighing place of Cochin, the main reason for which was that the merchants who got money from the king of Cochin for bringing spices, bought them at higher prices and with the help of the people of the native Cochin sold them to the traders who came with the oxen through the ghat route.[25] On 6 February 1587, the Viceroy was asked by the crown to take all the necessary steps to prevent the diversion of spices through these ghat routes.[26] But nothing could stop this well-established trade traffic. This phenomenon continued uninterruptedly all through the remaining period of Portuguese occupation. However some effort was taken to counter this flow of spices by increasing the price of pepper in 1632.[27]

Though the various native kings, who held sway over the hinterland, were given subsidies and monetary rewards to prevent the diversion of commodities through the ghat routes,[28] they were totally unable to control the situation. On the one hand, the traders associated with the land route used to quote a relatively high price. On the other hand, many of the St. Thomas Christians, the principal pepper cultivators, who had already estranged themselves from the Portuguese because of the latter's policies of grafting a colonial-Latin-structure on the former, had begun to co-operate with the traders of the ghat route. For them, this route provided an opening to ventilate their opposition and resistance to the Portuguese designs of Latinizing their liturgy and practices.[29] The seeds of this tension between the St. Thomas Christians and the Portuguese were already sown, when the latter labelled the native Christian group as Nestorian heretics and began to condemn their social practices, religious rites and ceremonies as heresy. Though Pope Pius IV (1559-65) had ordered that the administration of this native Christian community should be divided between the two Chaldean bishops, Mar Joseph and Mar Elias sent by the Patriarch Mar Abdiso,[30] and though the Diocese of Angamali, to which the

Malabar Christians belonged, was never put under the *padroado* jurisdiction, the council of Goa (1575) proclaimed that the St. Thomas Christians should be governed by the King of Portugal.[31] Moreover, another bishop, Mar Abraham, who arrived in Malabar in 1566 from Persia as the Bishop of the St. Thomas Christians, evading the Portuguese blockade, was also accused of Nestorian heresy at the third council of Goa (1585).[32] By usurping ecclesiastical jurisdiction over the native Christians, the Portuguese under the leadership of Archbishop Dom Alexis Meneses launched an organized programme to turn the former away from non-Latin rites, ceremonies and practices, as well as to make them conform to Latin tradition. With little command over native (and Syriac) languages and with little knowledge of native cultural practices, it seems, hasty steps were taken to label everything which was found to be non-European and which did not correspond to the western Latin tradition as heresy.[33] This move evoked much opposition from the St. Thomas Christian community and especially from the Archdeacon, who became the symbol of resistance against the Portuguese after the death of Mar Abraham in 1597. He convened a Synod in Angamali where the priests of this community pledged to uphold the traditions of the church without any change and, not to allow the priests trained in the Latin tradition at the Vaippinkotta Seminary to enter the church of the St. Thomas Christians. They also resolved not to accept any Latin bishop, but only the one sent by the Patriarch (of the Chaldean church).[34] A rebellion had already broken out in the hinterland: the leading pepper cultivators rose up against the Portuguese who were trying to impose on the former Latin ecclesiastical traditions. Reasons other than religious ones also seem to have been in operation behind this move. The Portuguese insistence on the uniformity of not only faith but also rituals, customs and practices seems to have been motivated by economic as well as political targets: to ensure easy penetration into the distant spice-hinterland. It appears to have been an indirect way of controlling the producers of the spices. As a continuation of this project, the Archbishop of Goa, Dom Alexis Meneses, convened a synod in Diamper (Udayamperur) in 1599, according to the canons of which a good many of the St. Thomas Christians were converted to the Latin traditions.[35]

However a great majority, which was the most powerful and wealthy group among them, led by their Archdeacon, continued their resistance against the Portuguese and the *Padroado* in order to preserve their age-old traditions and practices. The religious tensions in the hinterland were eventually transferred to the economic activities of Cochin and the supply of the spices from the hinterland in the port of Cochin to be exported to Europe began to show drastic downward trends. The agitated cultivators and merchants of the St. Thomas Christians were reluctant to co-operate with the Portuguese trade in Cochin.[36] They, in turn, found the lucrative ghat route an easy way of taking part in the resistance against the Portuguese whom they had begun to view as their enemies. Here, it is to be specially noted that the ghat route witnessed an unprecedented flow of spices during this period of tension in the hinterland.

The Portuguese authorities in Lisbon had already taken note of the estrangement of this community and the damage they had caused to the trade in Cochin by their participation in the ghat route trade network. In January 1601, two royal letters were sent to the Viceroy, Aires de Saldanha, asking him to specially favour the St. Thomas Christians and to win their goodwill.[37] The diplomatic visit of the archbishop Dom Alexis Meneses to the churches of this community to enforce the Synod decisions and to win back their co-operation did not yield good results.[38] During the years between 1603 and 1605, the pepper supply to the Portuguese factory in Cochin became scanty. So the Portuguese made strenuous efforts to placate and persuade the merchants of the St. Thomas Christians as well as their Archdeacon to make available spices in Cochin.[39] Nevertheless, the outcome of this move was not positive. On the other hand, with the diminishing supply of pepper in Cochin and with the increasing flow of pepper from the hinterland of Cochin to the Coromandel coast through the ghat route, there commenced a mass exodus of *casados* from 1612 onwards, from Cochin to Nagapatanam, Mylapore and other parts of the eastern coast, to take advantage of the changed situation. Some of them even moved to Bengal, Pegu and Ceylon.[40] These *casados*, with their new base in Coromandel, made more profit by distributing the pepper coming through the ghat route to Bengal, Pegu and China. Even the Dutch in Masulipatanam and Pulicat began to buy pepper increasingly from the traders of ghat route.[41]

However this tension between the pepper-growers of the native Christian community and the Portuguese was not a temporary phenomenon: on the contrary it continued throughout the remaining years of the Portuguese phase until it finally exploded into an open rebellion in 1652-3. The sparks were kindled in the hinterland, when the St. Thomas Christians heard that Ahatullah, a Syrian bishop sent to Malabar from the Chaldean church was drowned by the Portuguese in the sea. On 3 January 1653, members of this community led by Archdeacon and their clergy assembled at Mattancherry (native Cochin), in the vicinity of the Portuguese city of Cochin and touching the cross they pledged (which later came to be known in history as *Coonan* Cross Oath) not to allow themselves to be subjugated further by the Portuguese and the Jesuits.[42] Then they assembled at Alengad where twelve priests laid hands on the Archdeacon to 'consecrate' him a Bishop. With the making of this schismatic Bishop, the revolt of the influential section of the St. Thomas Christians against the Portuguese turned out to be complete and decisive.[43] The religious tensions were not constrained to the limits of rites and celebrations; but were always transferred into the economic sphere. Anti-Portuguese feelings influenced, throughout this period, the economic transactions of the St. Thomas Christians. Incidentally, the ghat route trade offered to the Malabar Christians a suitable outlet to show their spirit of rebellion and resistance against the Portuguese.

Moreover, the coastal wars that were fought between Cochin and Calicut as well as Cochin and Parur obstructed the trade in Cochin, which in turn favoured the ghat route commerce. The king of Cochin had already begun to feel uneasiness, when the Portuguese joined hands with the Zamorin to attack Kunjali in 1599.[44] The former feared that this new relationship would be harmful to the trade interests of Cochin. So, in order to disrupt it, the ruler of Cochin invaded the territory of Koratty Caimal, who was a feudatory of the Zamorin. The ruler of Calicut, who had by this time defeated Kunjali and captured Kottakkal with the help of the Portuguese,[45] was therefore, compelled to launch attacks against Cochin. By 1614, the Zamorin occupied the northern part of Cranganore and continued the war against the Perumpadappu king for which he got also the support of the king of Parur.[46]

Though the Portuguese were able to compel the king of Parur to sign a peace treaty, the state of war prevailing in and around Cochin, adversely affected the supply of spices to the Portuguese factory. The coastal war, with interrupted intensity, continued up to 1626 when peace was finally established between Cochin and Calicut through the mediation of Pe. Francisco Doliveira, the rector of the Jesuit college of Cochin.[47] However, the belligerent atmosphere that had prevailed in Cochin, for almost twenty-seven years, also favoured the ghat route trade.

The only period when the ghat route registered a smaller flow of pepper was between 1621 and 1629, when a war broke out in the interior land obstructing the ghat route commerce. Though the exact names of the kingdoms that were engaged in the war are not mentioned in a Portuguese document,[48] they seem to have been located on the eastern border of the hinterland of Cochin through which the ghat route passed. The passage of pepper to Tamilnadu was so greatly disturbed by this war that the merchants had no other option but to take the commodity to Cochin. This contributed to a fresh flow of pepper to Cochin where this phenomenon even effected a fall in the price.

Thus, we find that, during this period the hinterland of Cochin was often only loosely integrated with the economic orbit of Cochin. On the other hand, it appeared more as a source for inland and ghat route commerce, than as a hinterland for Cochin. The majority of the local rulers in the hinterland, who were given better monetary rewards by the traders of the interior, were permitting the spices to be diverted through the ghat route. Among them, only the pepper king and the king of Turuguli (Thodupuzha), as observed by Francisco da Costa at the beginning of seventeenth century, were making genuine efforts to ensure regular deliveries of pepper to the Portuguese factory in Cochin.[49] It should be specially mentioned that the intensity of the ghat route commerce, whose frequency was augmented unprecedentedly by the tension between the Portuguese and the pepper-grower-cum-trader group of the St. Thomas Christians, had sapped the vitality of the economic life of Cochin during the period between 1600 and 1663.

3. THE MARITIME TRADE WITHIN ASIA

Three distinct chronological phases can be observed in the intra-Asian trade by sea, which emanated from Cochin: 1. The period from 1570 to 1600 when the intra-Asian trade reached its highest level. 2. The period from 1600 to 1622 when much of the hinterland and trade space linked with Cochin's commercial empire was curtailed and cut off because of the tensions with the St. Thomas Christians and because of the Dutch occupation of South-East Asia. 3. The period from 1622 to 1663 when trade in Asian waters was stifled because of the overwhelming tensions, both domestic and external.

During this period, the crown abstained from participating in the country trade emanating from Cochin. Still, much of the intra-Asian trade by sea was left in the hands of Portuguese citizens and the native traders who supported Portuguese interests. However, this does not mean that the trade conducted in Cochin was always subservient to Portuguese commercial designs. On the contrary, there flourished as well, the notorious 'illegal commerce' by the natives as well as the

Lusitanians, which violated the trade restrictions imposed by the Portuguese authorities. The trade of Cochin conducted within Asia could be divided generally into two: 1. Licenced Country Trade, and 2. Illicit Country Trade.

I. LICENSED COUNTRY TRADE

With the reorganization of trade in 1570, the nature of licensed trade underwent considerable alteration. On the one hand, laws were made to ban the practice of issuing licences for pepper trade within Asia.[50] Though these royal orders issued from Lisbon and Valladolid were not seriously implemented in Cochin and even when pepper, as Boccarro testifies, continued to be taken from Cochin to Bengal in the early seventeenth century,[51] the frequency of the ships that moved under a strict licence system seems to have diminished considerably. Instead, the voyages conceded and farmed out to individuals and institutions, which were—in most cases—further sold out to real traders, became an oft-resorted alternative to licensed trade.

Moreover, the *cartazes* were continued to be used increasingly as an 'economic pass' rather than a 'political-allegiance-certificate'. For all practical purposes, the natives began to view the *cartazes* as a trade licence which conferred on them considerable economic freedom. Thus, the licensed country trade of this period could be divided into three: 1. The trade of the *Casados*, 2. Trade by Voyages, and 3. Trade in ships with *cartazes*.

A. The Trade of the Casados within Asia

By 1570 the *casados* of Cochin had already become a powerful mercantile group with considerable capital resources and vast commercial network. The crisis which the *Estado* experienced during the years between 1565 and 1570 as well as the liberal policy which the crown followed during the contract-trade-period (1570-97) had prepared a favourable commercial atmosphere for the *casados*. During the period between 1570 and 1600, the *casados* virtually turned Cochin into one of the biggest entrepots of Asia. The important commodities taken from Cochin to the trade centres, situated on the eastern spaces of the Indian Ocean, were pepper, textiles, wild-cinnamon, flour, wine, olive oil, gun powder, almonds and dried grapes.[52] From Bengal the *casados* of Cochin brought to this port large quantities of sugar, rice, laciron, textiles, long pepper, wheat, saltpetre, etc.[53] Rice and other food materials, during this period, were in high demand not only in Cochin but also all through Kerala. So the rice ports of Bengal and Pegu were often frequented by the *casados* of Cochin to take maximum advantage of the trade in food materials. On 17 May 1590, they brought to the city of Santa Cruz 900 candis of rice from Bengal and 500 candis from Pegu.[54] This transaction in rice was conducted in exchange for the pepper taken from Cochin. This barter proved to be more profitable and rice was frequently brought to Cochin from these distant ports of Bengal and Pegu, as testified by the trade records of 1592 and 1597.[55] Bengal was also a great production centre for textiles and was ranked along with the other large centres of Gujarat and Coromandel, even in the seventeenth century.[56] Textiles were also bought from Bengal in exchange for the pepper taken by the *casados* from Cochin. In the 1580s and 1590s, the *khasas*, *malmals* and silks of Bengal formed a great share in the entire cargo of textiles brought to Cochin, both for Asian and European trade.[57]

However, the frequency of the cargo ships that plied between Cochin and Bengal seems to have diminished considerably in the seventeenth century, due to the paucity of pepper that arrived in Cochin because of the tensions between the Portuguese and the St. Thomas Christians in the hinterland, and also due to the Dutch menace that often obstructed the routine trade. Even then, in 1615, we do find mention of Bengal ships coming to Cochin for trade and the customs revenue from Bengal commerce was relatively significant.[58] Moreover, textile items from Bengal such as the *khasas* and *malmals* used to figure in the list of the commodities taken from Cochin to Portugal, as we see, for example, in the case of goods carried by the ship *Nossa Senhora da Luz* in 1615.[59] Antonio Bocarro writing his *Livro das Plantas* by 1630 says that the *casado* traders of Cochin continued to send pepper to the Bengal port of Pipli and that the Bengal-Cochin trade of this period was worth 40,000 *xerafins* a year.[60] But this trade with Bengal does not seem to have continued for a long time. After 1632, with the capture of Hooghli from the Portuguese by the Mughal general Qasim Khan, one of the most profitable commercial links, which the *casados* of Cochin had enviously maintained for such a long period, was almost cut off.

It was with the same frequency almost, that the ports of Coromandel coast were visited by the *casado* traders of Cochin, in the last three decades of the sixteenth century, to collect textiles and food materials. Thus, for example, on 17 May 1590, the *casados* brought to Cochin from Nagapatanam 400 *candis* of rice of which 4 *candis* were given to Thome Roiz, the collector of 'the one per cent', as the share for the city of Cochin.[61] The settlers of Cochin continued to bring rice frequently from Nagapatanam in the subsequent years, as well, as we see from the trade records of 1592 and 1597.[62] Besides food materials, textiles formed a great portion of the commodities taken from the ports of Coromandel (among which Mylapore and Nagapatanam were the prominent ones) to Cochin. In 1605, the crown asked the Viceroy to see to it that the textiles brought from Coromandel ports were sold only in exchange for spices and drugs.[63] This royal direction was supposed to have been given to attract more spices from the hinterland to Cochin. However, as we have already seen, with the arrival of a great volume of spices in the Coromandel ports directly from the hinterland of Cochin through the ghat route, as early as 1612 many *casados* of Cochin shifted their sphere of activities to Mylapore and Nagapatanam. It gave them a secure and a better position to maintain their commercial links with Bengal, Pegu and Malacca and to bag greater profits out of the barter trade. With the intensification of the tensions between the Portuguese and the St. Thomas Christians, the major pepper-growing group, the flow of spices from the hinterland to Coromandel through the ghat route increased unprecedentedly, which attracted more and more settlers of Cochin to Coromandel. The large scale diversion of spices to the eastern coast and the subsequent exodus of the *casados* to Coromandel ports had a disastrous impact on the commercial activities and the urban life of Cochin, causing it to fall off drastically. By 1616, most of the enterprising *casados* had left Cochin. And by 1640, as Agostinho de Almeida Gato (the *ouvidor* of the city of Cochin) says, that about half of the inhabitants of Cochin had left the city and most of its residential areas were depopulated. Those who remained in the city were suffering because of acute poverty (caused by the lack of trading activities). Many who had been brought up in luxury, were seen to be begging from door to door; a good number of women even resorting to prostitution to support themselves and their families.[64] However, it seems that the *casados* continued to maintain with less frequency, even during this period, the lucrative commercial traffic between Cochin and the Coromandel ports. Thus, we see, for example, in 1644 the *casados* taking large quantity of cotton cloth, both white and coloured, to the various parts of the *Estado* including Cochin.[65]

With the liberalization of the spice trade in 1570, Malacca was proclaimed a free port and it was decreed that the spices bought there should not pay duties or fees on being taken to Goa and Cochin.[66] The *casados* of Cochin took a better advantage of this trade concession than had their counterparts in Goa, as they were required to pay less tax to the native ruler upon their arrival.[67] During the last decades of sixteenth century, many *casado* traders from Cochin used to conduct frequent commercial trips to Malacca, whereas in 1588 for example, through their trade tactics, they controlled the price of the market to their advantage.[68] Some of them also used to take commodities from Malacca and South-East Asia to Coromandel ports in exchange for textiles and bagged considerable profit. However, the crown often desired that this trade be conducted directly with Cochin or Goa so that the *Estado* also might profit out of it by extracting customs duty. In 1591 a royal order was issued notifying that no commercial embarkation from Malacca should be made to San Thome (Mylapore), Nagapatanam or any other ports except to Cochin or Goa under the penalty of losing their merchandise. This notice was affixed in the various public places of the city of Malacca.[69]

The role played by Malacca in the commercial life of the *casados* of Cochin was so significant, that the city of Santa Cruz sent every possible help to defend the former, which was under threat. In 1589, the food supplies sent to Malacca by the city of Cochin with a view to defending its fortress was worth 16,700 *pardaos*. The *casados* paid this amount, entirely, though not directly from their own pockets, but from the one per cent which the city levied on the commodities that reached Cochin.[70] Malacca was so dear to the commerce of the settlers of Cochin that besides food supplies, a lot of money was collected from its traders to be sent to the rescue of the former. About 1356 *xerafins* were collected in cash from the *casado* traders of Cochin, by way of one per cent taxation, to help Malacca during the period between 1587 and 1598.[71] A substantial contribution became necessary in 1605, when Martim Afonso de Castro's *armada* was sent to Malacca for its defence. Even the *Casa de Misericordia* of Cochin, on official request, paid a loan of 19,000 *xerafins* towards its expenditure.[72] However, with the mounting pressure from the anti-Portuguese powers on Malacca in the seventeenth century, the commercial links established by the *casados* of Cochin with this exchange centre of South-East Asia began to feel the increased strain. Even so, some *casados* of Cochin took the initiative to bring pepper from Malacca to Cochin. In 1615, some *casados* of Cochin went to Malacca and fetched 2,000 quintals of pepper. In some rare cases, they even enjoyed the freedom and permission to sell it to the traders of their own choice.[73] This seems to have continued for sometime. In 1616, Manoel de Fonsequa, a citizen of Cochin from whom the *Estado* often borrowed money for pepper purchase, was also found to be engaged in the pepper trade of Malacca. He used to buy pepper from Malacca with his own personal money and bring it to Cochin.[74] In the second and third decades of the seventeenth century, the Malacca trade began to dwindle. However, later with the capture of Malacca in 1641 by the Dutch, Cochin's commercial link with this traditional port of South-East Asia was totally cut off.

China, into which penetration was made possible after 1560, via Macao and Malacca,[75] was always a prospective market for the *casados*. A large volume of silk and porcelain was brought to Cochin from Chinese production centres by the *casados*.[76] As the import of copper from Europe stopped by the end of the sixteenth century, the settlers of Cochin went to China for collecting this metal, which had great demand all over India. There were instances when the individual traders were given licences to bring twelve quintals of copper per year.[77] Further, there were many cases, as for example in 1597, when ships from China were stopped at Cochin to unload the copper there.[78] The involvement of the *casado* traders in this deal became more evident, as the frequency with which the Chinese ships destined to Goa were stopped at Cochin to unload the merchandise under the pretext of a bad monsoon, increased.[79] Demand for copper in India increased against the backdrop of copper crisis in Europe and trade in this metal from China (Japan) appeared very lucrative to the *casados*. Copper, thus brought to India, was used not only for the minting of coins and the manufacturing of weaponries, but also for the manufacturing of household utensils for the aristocratic families in south India, particularly in Kerala.

With the Dutch blockade, the navigational lines between Cochin and China as well as other South-East Asian countries were frequently interrupted. The expulsion of the Portuguese from Ternate in 1570 and their loss of Amboina and Tidore to the Dutch in 1605 made it difficult for the *casados* to trade in cloves, nutmegs and mace. After 1605, these Indonesian spices reached Cochin only very seldom.[80] However, the *casados* of Cochin continued to send ships occasionally to other parts of South-East Asia. There are examples of maritime movements even between Cochin and Manila during this period. In a document dated 11 October 1632, mention is made of a ship going from Cochin to Manila with eight hundred slaves.[81] Again, in the middle of the 1630s, the traders of Cochin were said to have taken their ships to Macão, as well,[82] which suggests that they must have also played some part in the Macão-Nagasaki exchange-trade. Even in 1650s, the *casado* trade with China continued, even though the frequency was lower. In 1655, we hear of a ship engaged in the Cochin-Macão trade being captured by the Dutch.[83]

One of the important and interesting features of this period (1570-1663) was that the *armada* of the south, instituted initially to prevent the diversion of the spices, began to be used increasingly for protecting the private trade of the *casados* whose commercial empire stretched into the eastern space of Indian Ocean. It was because of the constant threat from the corsairs that the ships of the *casados* were given fleet protection from Cape Comorin to Cochin. The duty of conducting the coastal patrolling up to Comorin fell upon the shoulders of the city of Cochin and to maintain this *armada*, the city extracted 'one per cent' duty from every trader of

TABLE VII-1: PROTECTION EXPENSES ON *CASADO* TRADERS

Years	Captains of the Armada	Expense: *Pardaos*	*Tangas*	*Reais*
1587	Costa Manoel Botelho	5,288	4	20
1588	-not known-	300	0	50
1589	D. Jeronimo da Azevedo	593	0	51
1590	João Correa	2,434	1	10
1591	-not known-	1,408	3	48
1592	-not known-	1,507	0	0
1593	Alvaro da Branches de Pendeo	4,497	3	20
1594	-not known-	120	0	0
1595	Fernando Lobo	3,080	4	47
1596	Fernando Lobo	2,874	2	06
1597	Rui Dias de San Paio	2,444	0	41
1598	Diogo Couto	515	4	03

this port.[84] Even the ships from China destined for Goa were asked to enter the port of Cochin[85] so that the city might get a 'one per cent share' towards the expense of the *armada*. With the conversion of the southern *armada* into a military arrangement to protect the private trade of the *casados* of Cochin, the municipality of this city was given the right to appoint the captain-in-chief of these *armadas*, as in 1589, for example, when the Viceroy Dom Duarte de Menezes issued orders to the same effect.[86] During the period between 1587 and 1598, the amount which the city of Santa Cruz paid for conducting the patrolling up to Cape Comorin was 25,078 *pardaos* and it was collected as 'one per cent' from the traders.[87] The fleet that was used for patrol duty consisted of many ships, as in the case of the fleet of Fernando Lobo whose patrolling vessels were thirteen in number.[88]

Table VII-1 gives the amount spent by the city of Cochin, during the period from 1587 to 1598, to render protection to the *casado* traders coming from eastern part of Indian Ocean:[89]

The table shows the keen interest which the city of Cochin took in promoting and protecting the commerce of the *casados*, even though it also betrays the elements of negligence shown in some years. The transformation of the southern *armada* from a mechanism to safeguard the royal trade, into one to protect the private trade of the *casados* was a typical example of how the various *Estado* institutions were, during this period, made to serve and safeguard the private interests as well as initiatives of the Portuguese citizens, rather than those of the crown. During this period, especially towards the end of the sixteenth century, the merchant ships were asked to travel in caravans or small groups which were guarded by a fleet, and the *cafila* system, as this caravan arrangement was often called, was made a common practice in the seventeenth century to withstand the threat from the Dutch and the corsairs.[90] Antonio Bocarro refers to the fleet which used to take the caravans of merchant ships coming from Fishery coast, Coromandel ports and Bengal to Cochin from Cape Comorin, till the end of summer.[91] In the second and third decades of seventeenth century, as in 1621, for example, the *casado* traders of Cochin coming from China and Malacca moved in *cafilas* or caravans up to Cape Comorin from where they were taken to Cochin under the guard of an *armada* consisting normally of a galley and fifteen ships.[92] By 1640s, the Dutch tightened their control over the Indian Ocean and had begun obstructing the *casados* from maintaining commercial links with China and Malacca.[93]

Corresponding to the maritime movements linking Cochin with the ports in the eastern space of Indian Ocean, the *casados* developed trade relations with the Maldives as a supplementary commercial activity. The *casados* brought to Cochin, coir which was in high demand for the various purposes of the private ships as well as those of the *carreira*, and cowries, which were again taken from Cochin as a monetary medium for buying slaves from western African ports, indigo and textiles from Gujarat, food materials and clothes from Bengal, Pegu and Coromandel.[94] The king of the Maldives, who had fled to Cochin in 1552 and had become a Christian, was residing in the city of Santa Cruz, during this period, under the name of Dom Manuel. The Portuguese forces conquered the Maldive islands in 1554, and defeating the new King Hassan, they built a fortress in Male and compelled the islands to pay annual tribute to their old sovereign, now a resident of Cochin.[95] Dom Manuel in Cochin used to farm out annual voyages (a concession which he obtained from the Portuguese as the former ruler of Maldives) to Maldives, which made available coir and cowries for the *casados* of Cochin, to be taken to Bengal and Gujarat.[96] However, because of the native resistance, which became strong with the support of the Muslim merchants of Malabar, the Portuguese entered into an agreement in 1567 accepting the sovereignty of the native Muslim king.

Meanwhile, it was agreed that the external commerce of the islands be given to the Portuguese, while Dom Manuel, the exiled king in Cochin was to get, besides cowries, 500 quintals of coir as annual tribute and was given the right to have a warehouse with his own factor in charge, in Male. From the commodities that arrived in Cochin for the exiled king, the Portuguese collected one third as a tribute to them.[97] However, as a result of this arrangement, a large quantity of coir and cowries began to reach Cochin from the Maldives, by way of trade rights enjoyed by and the tribute given to the members of the royal family in exile in Cochin (like Dom Manuel, later his sons Dom João and Dom Paulo and finally on the death of Dom João, his son Dom Filipe) and by way of direct participation of the Portuguese in the trade of the islands. Besides this, the members of this royal family like Dom Filipe used to collect some taxes from every ship coming from Maldives to Cochin and other Portuguese ports, by virtue of being their old sovereign.[98]

Francisco Pyrard de Laval observed during the years 1606-7 that annually four ships with the capacity of 140 *toneladas* were taking coir and cowries from these islands to Cochin.[99] The *casado* traders of Cochin seem to have taken greater advantage of this Maldive commerce by carrying cowries and coir to Bengal and Gujarat for exchange trade. In Gujarat, one *candil* of coir was sold at 13 *xerafins* and one *tanga*.[100] The Portuguese often forced the ships coming from the islands to sell the commodities to them without paying taxes to the royal family in exile.[101] Even though Dom Jeronimo de Azevedo in 1615 decreed that a due share should be given to Dom Filipe, the heir of the royal family in exile in the city of Santa Cruz, for the coir and the cowries brought to Cochin, the situation continued to be the same and almost the entire commodity coming to Cochin from the islands went into the hands of the Portuguese, being further distributed all over Asia through the *casado* networks.[102] In the procurement and distribution of these commodities, the *casados* were frequently in competition with the king of Cannanore, who exercised great control over the politics and the commerce of Maldives, and his merchants.[103] By the 1620s, the Portuguese made a compromise with the king of Cannanore being reluctant to enter his political and commercial dominion with a view to avoiding the Dutch occupation of the islands and also to ensure the regular arrival of ships from the Maldives into Cochin.[104] In fact, with the diminishing supply of pepper in Cochin, the coir and cowries from Maldives began to occupy prime position in the wares used by the *casados* for exchange in the ports of Bengal and Gujarat.

The trade of the *casados* with the island of Ceylon continued even during this period. Cinnamon and precious stones, both for European trade as well as for intra-Asian commerce used to be brought to Cochin by the settlers of Cochin.[105] In 1598 as well as in 1601, when Vimala Dharma Suriya declared himself the king of Ceylon, and the Portuguese found their position threatened in the island, an army of the St. Thomas Christians (obviously from the pro-Portuguese group) was raised by Dom Alexis Meneses and by the Prince of Cochin respectively, for the defence of the Portuguese interests in Ceylon.[106] The special interest of the settlers of Cochin in the affairs of Ceylon was very evident from the fact that some 130 Portuguese citizens of Cochin came forward in 1630 under Dom Filipe Mascarenhas along with many native soldiers to defend this island. Besides this, the city of Santa Cruz, even in the midst of the economic pressure it was undergoing, offered 800 *candis* of rice towards the same purpose.[107] This service of the city did not go unrewarded. In 1635, we find the merchants of Cochin going to Ceylon to procure cinnamon.[108] It was evidently a reward for Cochin's participation in the defence of Ceylon. It was to be seen against the background of many pre-1630 requests, such as the one continuously made by the municipal council of Cochin from 1622 to 1629 for importing 50 *bhars* of cinnamon without paying customs duties, with a view to installing artillery,[109] most of which were often rejected. It seems that, though a portion of the cinnamon brought to Cochin was taken for intra-Asian commerce, a great bulk of it was reserved for European export.

Coastal Malabar used to depend greatly on the rice-ports of Kanara as well, for obtaining necessary food-stuffs. During the great drought and famine of 1587, to which Ferdinand Cron refers,[110] the demand for food materials unprecedentedly increased. The *casados* used to import a great volume of rice to Cochin during the period immediately after 1587 (especially till 1598) from the ports of Kanara, Bengal and Coromandel.[111] Mangalore was one of the important ports of Kanara from which the settlers of Cochin used to bring rice to the city of Santa Cruz.[112]

The *casados* played a considerable role in re-distributing the production of Kanara and rice was used to be taken from Cochin occasionally to feed Malacca as well as Ceylon and to Maldives for the exchange of commodities.[113] Rice trade with Kanara was often hindered by the Dutch and English blockade. Some of the rice-ships of the *casados* of Cochin coming from Kanara were captured by the English, as in the case of the vessel captured by the British ship *Dragon* off the Kanara coast on 24 January 1613.[114] Despite this fact, it seems that the *casados* had to depend more on Kanara rice, with the diminishing availability of food materials from Coromandel and Bengal, caused by the tightening of the Dutch blockade and also the loss of Bengal in 1632. Meanwhile, the war of succession, which began in Ikkeri (Kanara) in 1629 between Virappa and Virabadra, had already begun to obstruct the flow of food materials to Goa and Cochin. In 1630, the price of the food materials spiralled considerably and both Cochin as well as Goa were short of food supplies.[115] Though the new Viceroy, Pero da Silva, entered into a contract with Virabadra in 1635 to obtain the necessary food-stuff,[116] Cochin's situation did not seem to have made any significant improvement. There is every reason to believe that the misery and famine which had visited the city of Santa Cruz by the end of the 1630s, though linked with the absence of trade and consequent economic crisis, was aggravated by the shortage of adequate food supply, which became still worse when many *casados* who were trading in food materials had already transferred their residence and spheres of activities, due to the changed circumstances for more prospective locations.

The private trade of the *casados* with Goa was very small when compared with other commercial routes. The Cochin–Goa route was associated more with European trade than with intra-Asian commerce. However in 1615, Dom Diogo Coutinho observed that the commodities which the settlers of the city of Santa Cruz were taking from Cochin to Goa, were valued at 30,000 to 40,000 *xerafins*.[117]

The ports of Gujarat, from where commodities were taken to Persia, Arabia, East Africa and Europe via West Asia, were the leading and long-standing commercial targets of the *casados* of Cochin. Though the old Sultanate of Gujarat was incorporated into the Mughal territory in 1573, the settlers of Cochin procured the wares through Portuguese bases in Chaul, Baçaim, Daman and Diu. The *casados* took Gujarat spices from Cochin, wares from China and Malacca, coir and cowries from the Maldives, in exchange for textiles, indigo as well as opium. Coconuts also turned out to be a major commodity sent to the ports of Cambay from Cochin and other Malabar ports, as observed by Thomas Best in 1613.[118] Some of these commodities were taken on from here to the ports of West Asia, as well, using *cartazes*.

The *casado* trade between Cochin and the ports of Gujarat was always a controversial one, as on the one hand, the partners of the *casados*, the bania traders, used to send textiles and other commodities to the port of Cochin in the name of the settlers of the city of Santa Cruz, with a view to avoiding the Portuguese customs of Goa (where the customs rate was 6 per cent). The benefit of this illegal partnership was that the bania merchants were required to pay only 3.5 per cent to the king of Cochin and the one per cent tax to the city, as the wares were claimed by the residents of the city. However, this illegal partnership prevailed not only in the Gujarat trade. Even from China and Malacca, the native partners of the *casados* were bringing commodities into Cochin and paying only a concessional rate to the native king under the label of the settlers of the city of Santa Cruz, thus evading the excessive Portuguese customs rate.[119] But what was special with the Gujarat-Cochin trade was that because of the illegal partnership established between the *casados* as well as the bania merchants with a view to evading the customs house of Goa, as estimated in 1612, the *Estado* was losing an annual amount of 20,000 *pardaos* per year,[120] a heavy loss when compared to the possible profit that could be gathered from the declining navigational lines of the east. To solve this problem, as early as 1583, the Portuguese authorities had made secret negotiations with the king of Cochin to equalize the customs rate of Cochin with that of Goa, by raising the rate of *casado* settlers to six per cent which was to be paid to the native king and by imposing on all, the compulsory exit tax to the Portuguese Treasury.[121] This must have also been a part of the strategy to centralize trade in Goa and to minimize the commercial attraction which Cochin possessed. However, this deal provoked great protest and some 15,000 armed men (10,000 local Christians and 5,000 Portuguese) marched into the church of St. John in Cochin to defend their privileges. The crowd even attacked the captain in his fort, who took refuge in the palace of the King.[122] The authorities were compelled to reconsider this legislation. According to the agreement, made by the newly arrived Viceroy Dom Duarte de Menezes on 12 December 1584, (a) the *casados* were required to pay only 3.5 per cent to the king of Cochin and no export duties, (b) the unmarried Portuguese citizens of the city had to pay 6 per cent to the Portuguese Treasury at Cochin, (c) all non-Portuguese including the Muslims, Jews, Venetians, Armenians, local Christians and those Christians residing south of Cochin, were to pay the usual 6 per cent duties to the king, and (d) all *casados* not resident in Cochin had to pay 6 per cent on entry and exit to the Portuguese customs officials.[123] This again provided a loophole to the bania merchants to take cloth and commodities to Cochin, bypassing Goa and attributing ownership to the *casados*. As another solution to this problem, an order was issued, on 23 November 1607, asking the bania merchants of Chaul who were taking commodities to Cochin to pay customs duties at Goa.[124] However, the king of Cochin, who had always favoured the alliance between the *casados* of Cochin and the native traders to attract more trade to his port, complained in 1613, and 1615, that this decision was an encroachment on his privilege and was a violation of the contract made in 1584.[125] It has to be admitted that the partnership between the settlers of Cochin and the native merchants of Gujarat made the re-distribution trade of the *casados* centred around Cochin easier and smoother. On the other hand, the *casado* traders of Cochin, who were bringing commodities from the eastern spaces of the Indian Ocean and had paid customs duties to the king of Cochin, were permitted, in 1607, to carry merchandise to the ports of Gujarat without paying customs duties at Goa; they were required to take with them only the certificate of having paid tax at Cochin.[126] But, for all other commodities taken from Cochin, they were to pay duties at Goa. The high customs rate prevalent in Goa took away a great share of the profit earned in the *casado's* commerce with Gujarat.

Meanwhile, by the 1630s the *casados* had to face stiff competition from the English and the Dutch in the western littoral of India. However, even when the trade with the eastern spaces of the Indian Ocean had to be abandoned because of the Dutch threat, and later, with the loss of Bengal, the commerce with Gujarat remained hopeful, perhaps the last resort for the *casados* of Cochin. But, the hope did not seem to have lasted long. The obligation that all the *casados* of Cochin trading with the ports of Gujarat had to pay customs at Goa ruined even this branch of commerce. The advantage of the commerce with the eastern spaces of the Indian Ocean was, that there was no customs house for them other than the one in Cochin, where they enjoyed a concessional rate. But the ruinous regulations imposed on

Gujarat commerce was that the embarkations from Cochin had to pay almost double the rate of Cochin to the customs house of Goa. This was because the officials there always maintained antipathetic feelings towards the *casados* of Santa Cruz, who were said to have been affluent and who even often appeared to be a menace to the *Estado* because of their parallel commercial and strategic network. This attempt to tax the *casados* of Cochin at Goa played a crucial role in the decadence of Cochin's trade, as explained by the document of 7 October 1644. This letter of the city says that the decline of the commerce of Santa Cruz was because of the compulsory customs duties, which the *casados* of Cochin were obliged to pay at Goa, each time they moved to the north (evidently Gujarat ports). The city narrated the state of its poverty and suffering, and it hopefully requested the crown for the permission to conduct trade with the ports of Gujarat without paying customs at Goa, a concession which the early kings of Portugal had granted to the *casados* earlier.[127]

Ormuz in the Persian gulf provided an attractive exchange centre for the *casados*. Very often the commercial links of the residents of Cochin with Ormuz seemed to have been maintained through the ports of Gujarat and occasionally through Goa. The *casados* also made frequent and direct trips to this port of the Persian Gulf to bring horses to Cochin, whose distribution in south India continued to offer them attractive trade prospects, even after the disintegration of the Vijayanagara kingdom.[128] These horses, though a sum of 40 *ducats* as customs to the Portuguese in Ormuz had to be paid, were sold in south India for a value varying from 300 to 1,000 *ducats*.[129] Though some of the ships carried 80 horses[130] and some even 124 horses[131] to Goa, as observed by Caesar Frederick and Ralph Fitch respectively in their voyages from Ormuz to Goa, we do not know the approximate tonnage of the vessels or the number of the horses taken to Cochin. It is believed that they amounted to considerable proportions. That must have been the reason why the crown made a special intervention on 3 March 1594, saying that the import of horses from Ormuz to Cochin and Kanara was prejudicial to the royal service and that instead, they should be taken to Goa, where the *Estado* might extract customs duty.[132] As the taxes that were levied on the horses in Cochin went to the native king, there was strong pressure to centralize the trade on horses in Goa, this being a great source of revenue to the Portuguese Treasury. But even so, the *casado* trade in the horses continued for some time longer in Cochin, as we see in the letter of King Philip I dated 2 January 1596, for instance.[133] It is highly probable that the settlers of Cochin took with them a large volume of various spices including pepper to Ormuz in exchange for horses. This assumption is further reinforced by the testimony of Leonhard Rauwolf, who happened to see on 2 December 1574, as many as tweny-five ships loaded with the spices and drugs of India reaching Baghdad via Ormuz and Basra.[134] He adds that in return, besides horses, corals, emeralds, saffron, chermes-berries, raisins, dates, figs, almonds, and Turkish handkerchiefs were also taken to India.[135] Even in the early decades of seventeenth century, when the Dutch and English vessels made appearances in the Arabian sea, the shipping between Cochin and Ormuz continued, although it was with less frequency.[136] But by the end of the second decade of the seventeenth century the pressure of these European powers on this navigational line increased. Nevertheless, with the fall of Ormuz in 1622 (into the hands of the English and the Shah of Persia), the links of Cochin's *casados* with the caravan route trade were cut off, greatly affecting the economic life of Cochin.[137] As the *casado* network in the western space of Indian Ocean was intimately linked with commerce of Ormuz, its loss caused a general slackening of trade, which consequently further worsened the commercial position of the city of Santa Cruz.

The socio-economic position of all the *casados* were not always the same. The period between 1570 and 1600, which witnessed heavy traffic of private trade, seems to have introduced some sort of stratification among the settlers of the city of Cochin, on the basis of capital accumulated through commerce. 1. On the top rung of this ladder stood the rich, who were few in number and who had amassed huge wealth through private trade. To this group could also be added the upper-middle class, some of whom were also associated with administrative responsibilities. 2. They were followed by the middle class, who were the ordinary traders; but who had by this time already acquired sufficient capital resources and a wide commercial network. They seemed to have formed the bulk of the population of Cochin. 3. The next group comprised the lower-middle class who assisted the traders of the above classes as collection agents and peddling traders. It seems that the number of the *casados* who belonged to this category was not very small. The number of very poor people seems to have been negligible in the period up to 1600, although there did exist some who were visited by misfortunes, such as orphans, widows, and those infected with incurable diseases. But the entire picture changes by 1610, from which date the number of the poor people increased. The first category, especially the rich ones among the *casados* like Manuel da Fonseca, Isabel Ferreira, and Francisco Barbosa used to provide huge loans to the *Estado* for conducting pepper-trade.[138] In the second decade of seventeenth century, the loans given by them amounted to 60,000 *cruzados*,[139] which the *casados* were never paid back. Again, it was some of these rich settlers, as we shall see later, who began to undertake the contract to tranship spices to Portugal. When the rich *casados* continued their commercial activities with their base in Cochin, a good many of the adventurous middle-class and lower-middle-class trading settlers of the city shifted their commercial bases in the second decade of the seventeenth century to the eastern spaces of Indian Ocean, especially Nagapatanam, Mylapore, Bengal, Pegu and even Ceylon in the south, which offered better trade prospects. Some seem to have even preferred Portuguese bases in Gujarat such as Diu, Daman and Chaul. As we have already seen, the mass exodus of the *casados* began by 1612.[140] Dom Diogo Coutinho mentions the depopulation of the city and the decline of trade as early as January 1615.[141] On 6 February 1616, King Philip refers to the same problem of depopulation experienced in Cochin and the slackening of trade.[142] The Viceroy Dom Jeronimo de Azevedo refers in his letter addressed to the Portuguese king, dated March 1617, to the great losses and damage which 'the rebels' (*rebeldes*) had caused to the city of Cochin, to the point of reducing its population to one-third (*a ponto de só uma terça parte estar habitada*).[143] The reduction of the city's population to one-third was caused by the mass exodus of citizens from Cochin to other destinations in the eastern spaces of the Indian Ocean and to the Gujarat area. This migration seems to have been mainly because of (1) the shortage of pepper supply in Cochin caused by the tensions with the St. Thomas Christians (which the operators in the eastern part of Indian Ocean got in plenty for their trade from Coromandel ports as supplied by the ghat route) and (2) the frequent blockade which the Dutch, the English and the Danes were creating on the navigational lines to Cochin, which destroyed a great many of the *casado* ships conducting trade with the eastern spaces of Indian Ocean, as observed by Antonio Bocarro in 1635.[144] Operations from the Coromandel and Gujarat bases seem to have placed them in an advantageous position to adjust their commercial routes according to the movements of the enemies. With the arrival of the *casados* from Cochin the population of the Portuguese bases on the Coromandel coast swelled and their economic condition began to improve. Thus, in 1644, there were 800 Portuguese citizens with more than 20 *fidalgos* in Nagapatanam. Besides this, the number of people who used to come to confession was about 30,000 souls. (It must have been the approximate number of confessions heard in a year.) By this time, the Portuguese settlement in Nagapatanam had become richer and greater than the city of Cochin.[145] Even after arriving at the new bases of operations, these *casados* continued to enjoy almost the same commercial privilieges which they used to in Cochin. From Nagapatanam and other Coromandel bases, they continued to send commodities to China, Malacca and Bengal even during these troubled days. However, they were required to pay to the Portuguese Treasury of Naga-patanam, the entry-tax at the same rate as paid by the settlers of Cochin.[146]

The attempt to transplant the commercial ambience of Cochin into Nagapatanam was evident from the various efforts taken by these traders of this Coromandel port for securing the same rights and commercial privileges enjoyed by the residents of the city of Santa Cruz, as is demonstrated by the document of 29 November 1645.[147]

When Nagapatanam and other bases, to which a great number of enterprising settlers of Cochin had moved, grew in prosperity and richness, Cochin, which had been an opulent city sank into poverty and misery. The flight of the middle-class traders from Cochin, who had chiefly been responsible for the opulence of the city, had worsened the economic position of Santa Cruz as well as of those who stayed over in the city and made the number of the poor people increase unprecedentedly. The miserable situation, which arose as a result of the lack of trade, struck hard at the members of the upper middle-class and, as Agostinho de Almeida observed in 1640s, 'those who were brought up luxuriously in the midst of prosperity'. Many resorted to begging and prostitution. Deciding that this misery was caused by the wrath of God, the settlers of Cochin even began to practise self-torture, penance and fasting to seek the mercy of the Almighty and to get opulence back into the city.[148] Though the general public was suffering, it seems that some of the *casados* still continued their commercial activities and used to send very occasionally, ships to Macão in China, as they did in 1643,[149] as well as in 1655[150] (this vessel along with the one sent from Goa was captured by the Dutch) and to the ports of gulf of Cambay in 1644.[151]

B. Trade by Voyage Concessions

With the re-organization of trade in 1570, the voyages to the Spice Islands and other prospective centres turned into a regular means of licensed trade. As the eastern part of the Indian Ocean did not have any effective means of control, there was a lot of abuse, waste, as well as theft, and the profit that went to the royal treasury from the trade conducted with these centres was both small and irregular. So the crown began to resort to indirect exploitation by renting out voyages to these places at a fixed rate. The *Livro das Cidades e Fortalezas que a Coroa de Portugal tem nas partes da India* written around 1580, gives details of the selling price of these voyages to the ports in the Bay of Bengal, South-East Asia, China as well as Japan and the net average profit bagged from each voyage.[152] Though Cochin was not mentioned in it as the port of embarkation or the destination, it seems that some of the settlers of Cochin used to buy these voyages either directly from the crown or from the concessionaires. But the usual form of voyages that departed from Cochin, were those freely granted by the crown to individuals and institutions, as reward and recognition for their meritorious services. These voyages were also conceded by the crown as a way of showing its benevolence and providing some source of income to the recipients. Thus, the king of Cochin was granted two voyages to China, by Dom Sebastian in return for the help he might render for the fortification of the city of Santa Cruz.[153] Another voyage to China was also said to have been conceded to the king of Cochin by 1587, probably to win the goodwill and permission for the same fortification works.[154] On 8 March 1589, the city of Cochin was granted two voyages to China for raising funds for its fortification.[155] However, this construction work moved very slowly, and the delay was deliberately caused, not only to get more voyages, but also to stop the very work of the fortress, as the fortification would hinder the smooth trade on contraband items that thrived in Cochin.[156]

On 15 February 1594, we find mention of another voyage from Cochin to China granted for the same purpose.[157] Eventually, the fortification of this city seems to have been a pretext for undertaking profitable voyages to China. One is compelled to think so, as the work of the city wall remained unattended to, while the city acquired more and more voyages to China. Thus, on 8 February 1602, the city of Santa Cruz obtained another voyage to China.[158] Again, on 15 February 1603, this city was granted two more voyages to the same destination and for the same purpose.[159] It seems that most of the voyages conceded to institutions such as the city of Cochin, as in the above case, and in some cases to certain individuals were not conducted by the concessionaires themselves; but were sold by them further to a professional class of traders, who had wider networks . In one of the letters dated 23 January 1604, the captain of Cochin gives interesting information about the entire business associated with some of the voyages conceded to the city. King Philip II had granted a voyage to China to the city of Cochin for its fortification. But the Viceroy Aires de Saldanha sold this voyage for 27,000 *pardaos*, out of which he gave only 2,000 to the city. With this money, instead of attending to the fortification, the city built six ships which sailed to Cape Comorin to load food materials.[160] The most interesting thing with the voyages conceded for the fortification of the city, was that by 1615 only a bastion was built in the city and the remaining money went into the pockets of the individuals concerned, as in the case of most trade transactions.[161]

Sometimes these voyages were granted with a view to finding funds for the social and charitable activities of the city. Thus, in 1591, the city of Cochin was accorded two voyages from Coromandel to Malacca and the profit accruing from them had to be spent on the marriage-expenses of the orphans of the city.[162] With the tightening of the Dutch blockade, the practice of granting voyages from Coromandel to Malacca gained special significance, as this route, besides bringing huge profits in the exchange trade of Indian and South-East Asian commodities, did not have the risk of being attacked by the Dutch while circumnavigating Cape Comorin. This route seems to have been used with frequency even in the 1630s. Thus, on 28 February 1635, we hear about a certain Antonio Fogasse de Britto who was granted a voyage from Coromandel to Malacca for raising money for the marriage of one of his daughters[163] and on 31 March 1635, one Luis da Mota Leyte who was conceded two voyages from Coromandel to Malacca.[164]

By the 1640s, Moçambique became one of the principal targets of the voyages made from Cochin, mainly because of the fact that the eastern spaces of the Indian Ocean were often threatened by the Dutch presence. During this period, we see the city of Cochin making requests for two voyages to Moçambique. In the reply which the city received, mention was also made of the large number of applicants waiting for the voyage to Moçambique.[165] By the 1650s, even the religious orders of Cochin resorted to Moçambique voyages as a source of income for their multifarious activities. For instance, on 22 December 1653, the rector of the Jesuit College of Cochin asked the crown for a voyage to Moçambique to overcome the great poverty that the college was experiencing.[166] The next month, on 31 January 1654, the crown conceded this request. The crown also recalled specially the great service rendered by this college, while according the voyage to Moçambique.[167]

In most cases, these voyages conceded to individuals and institutions were again sold to real traders, who had better commercial experience and network. Thus the two Japan voyage concessions conferred to Dona Margarida, the queen of Spain, to make money for the Augustinian monastery of Encarnação in Madrid,[168] were handed over to Ferdinand Cron to conduct the trade and send the money to Europe.[169] Cron acted as a middleman who once again sold it to real traders, who then conducted the voyage. He secured a share of 13,000 *xerafins* as profit after having transacted one of these voyages.[170] The *casados*, who used to buy many of these voyages from the concessionaires, seem to have reaped the lion's share of the profits by converting them into actual trade, while the original recipients of the voyages seem to have got only a very meagre amount.

C. Trade of the Natives in Ships with Cartazes

During this period, the *cartazes* were increasingly used by the natives almost like a licence for the transhipping of contraband items to the ports of the Red Sea and the Persian gulf. Still the Portuguese authorities used to issue *cartazes* almost regularly to their friends and allies such as the kings of Cochin, Calicut and Cannanore.[171] Rama Varma, the king of Cochin (1601-15) used to send ships to Mecca using the *cartazes* issued by the Viceroy Aires de Saldanha from 1603 onwards.[172] In 1604, he sent 4,000 quintals of pepper, besides a large quantity of iron, timber and other contraband items, to Mecca using the label of *cartazes*. The king procured pepper and other commodities from the hinterland with the help of the Jewish and Muslim merchants of native Cochin.[173] It seems that the estranged group of the St. Thomas

Christians also co-operated in this project. Moreover, Rodrigo Rebelo, the Portuguese secretary of the native king was also said to have been involved in these attempts of the native entrepreneurs to annually send two ships with 4,000 quintals of pepper to the Red Sea, under cover of *cartazes*.[174] With the native king's participation in pepper trade using *cartazes*, the Jewish and Muslim merchants began to collect pepper from the hinterland and to hide the spices for the king's ships. This led to an increase in the price and created shortage of the commodity for Portuguese commerce.[175] Moreover, the sending of iron and timber by the ruler of Cochin to the ports of the Red Sea, which the Turks were using for the building of ships,[176] created great alarm and commotion among the Portuguese authorities.Dom Philip II repeatedly wrote letters in 1605 and 1606 to the officials concerned in India asking them not to allow the king to send contraband items to Mecca.[177] In 1607, we find Dom Philip II writing a letter to the king of Cochin in gratitude for the measures taken by the latter to make spices available for transhipment to Lisbon. However, he refused to allow further *cartazes* to the native ruler of Cochin.[178]

The native merchants of Cochin were also despatching commodities under the cover of *cartazes*. Thus, we see, in January 1613, three native ships carrying wares from Cochin to Cambay with *cartaz* issued by the Portuguese authorities.[179] Besides this, ordinary merchants of Cannanore and Cochin were also conducting trade with places like the Maldives under the cover of *cartazes*. In the seventeenth century, *cartazes* were said to have been frequently issued to the ships going to the Maldives for trade in cowries and coir. On 23 January 1615, we find the Viceroy Dom Jeronimo de Azevedo writing to Philip II asking him to prohibit the issuing of *cartazes* destined to Maldives.[180] In 1626, the captain of Tanur and Chale (Chalium) was issuing *cartaz* at a high rate of 30 to 40 *pardaos*. When the king of Tanur complained against this excessive rate, the place for issuing the *cartaz* was changed to Goa.[181]

Very often the ship carrying *cartaz* symbolised a system where voyage of the natives was conducted under the political hegemony of the Portuguese; but for all practical purposes, it had greater economic significance and was considered a way by which the natives could conduct trade within the system of licences.

II. NETWORKS OF THE ILLICIT COUNTRY TRADE: THE UPTURN

This period witnessed the network of illicit country trade emanating from Cochin and spreading all along the Indian Ocean rim, almost parallel to, and sometimes even hand in hand with the licensed trade. A long queue of entrepreneurs, both Indian as well as Europeans, were operating behind the so-called 'illegal trade-transactions'. It is to be specially remembered that the term 'illegal' and 'illicit' were used from the Portuguese point of view, for the sake of better understanding, even though the natives carried on this trade as a legitimate economic activity.

The trade in contraband items without proper permission, often termed smuggling, the 'illegal' partnership between the *casados* and the native merchants by which they exchanged wares and vessels, as we have already seen, to avoid higher customs duties and the corsair activities linked with commerce, can be treated as part of the 'illicit' trade. This illicit commerce had thrived since the second half of the sixteenth century, not only because the entrepreneurs circumvented the

Portuguese blockade, but also because the Portuguese had abandoned the attempt to hinder navigation to the ports of the Red Sea and the Persian Gulf by means of force.[182]

A. Smuggling and 'Illegal' Trade Transactions

The smuggling trade from Cochin with the West Asian ports assumed significant proportions during this period. Coincidentally it was also marked by various phases of tensions and conflicts between the Portuguese and the pepper cultivators from the St. Thomas Christian community of the hinterland, as well as native rulers of Cochin. The already estranged Muslim and Jewish merchants seem to have acquired the support of these antagonized native Christians and rulers of Cochin in smuggling out commodities, including spices, to the ports of the Red Sea and the Persian Gulf. Nevertheless, the Portuguese officials and the *casados* of Cochin were also frequently associated with this network, incorporating this stream into the licensed trade.

The merchants, as observed by Cåesar Frederick, who had side-deals with the smuggling trade, bought spices at a higher price and so they used to get clean and better conditioned pepper. He adds further 'all the spices and drugs that are brought to Mecca, are stolen from thence (Cochin) as contrabanda'.[183] When he speaks about the Ormuz trade, he says 'They lade ships in Cochin for Portugale and for Ormus, but they that goe for Ormus carrie no Pepper but by Contrabanda, as for Sinamome they easilie get leave to carrie that away, for all other Spices and drugs they may liberally carie them to Ormus or Cambaia, and so all other merchandize which come from other places.'[184] It seems that very often vessels carrying different wares were used to smuggle out the pepper and other prohibited commodities.

Sometimes, the smuggling of prohibited commodities including pepper, cinnamon, cloves, timber and iron to different destinations in Asia, were carried out under the pretext of taking them to Portuguese fortresses.[185] The Portuguese authorities in Lisbon were always worried about the diversion of spices, though they did not seem to have taken effective measures to prevent it. By 1599, the viceroy was asked to furnish details about the practice of conducting 'illegal' trade in prohibited items with the Red Sea and other parts of Asia.[186] Later, in the letter of the secretary of the state written around 1597 to Dom Francisco da Gama, special directions were given not to allow any ship to carry pepper to Ormuz and Muscat.[187]

But the routes of the 'illegal' traders were often linked with different navigational lines and could not, in any way, be checked by the ineffective control system of the Portuguese. The most prominent among them ran through the islands of Maldives. This was the route often taken by the king of Cannanore, Calicut and the Muslim merchants to send commodities to Mecca.[188] This navigational line was mostly in the hands of the Muslim merchants and their allies. Even the captains of Cochin who used to send ships to the Maldives, under the pretext of acquiring cowries and coir, were said to have been associated with this traditional network, running into the ports of the Red Sea and the Persian Gulf.[189] The natives of Malabar, including their kings, found the Maldives a good base for their West Asian contacts (both for licensed as well as illicit trade); as, in the case of the king of Cochin, who took pepper, timber, iron and food materials there with a view to sending them to Mecca, as we have already seen, under cover of *cartaz*.[190]

Another channel for diverting spices to these destinations was offered by the ports of Gujarat. The pepper taken from Cochin to the ports of Cambay were taken further on to Ormuz and to the ports of Arabia. Thus, for instance, in 1611, eight vessels and in 1612, twelve ships loaded with pepper were taken from Diu, Daman and Chaul to these destinations. The Muslim and the Hindu merchants were said to have played a major role in this illicit trade transactions.[191] This does not mean that the direct smuggling from Cochin decreased. On 18 February 1619, the Bishop of Cochin wrote that a lot of pepper and cinnamon (Malabar cinnamon) were taken from Cochin and other ports of Malabar to Ormuz and other parts of Asia, evidently without licence.[192] Even after the fall of Ormuz, pepper continued to be smuggled out to Muscat. On 24 January 1629, the Viceroy Conde de Linhares was asked by a royal letter, to take rigorous steps to prevent the flow of spices to Muscat.[193]

Meanwhile, smuggling and illegal trade transactions with links in Cochin thrived under the very nose of *Estado* establishments in Goa. The head of this project was one Rama Queny who had the charge and responsibility for collecting pepper for the Portuguese India Company. He was permitted to collect in his warehouse, 60 *candis* of pepper every year. But under this pretext, he collected a large quantity of pepper coming from Cochin. By 1633, he was said to have become very rich and the principal merchant of Goa, through this trade in smuggled pepper. On 10 February 1633, the king in his letter to the viceroy refers to the fact that Rama Queny used to buy almost all the pepper that was brought from Cochin and sell it through his shop. He transacted in pepper and other spice items outside the Portuguese system and often the company itself had to buy pepper from this rich merchant.[194]

Even in the eastern part of Indian Ocean, the smuggling trade thrived as intensely as the licensed one. Though there were frequent orders, as in 1589, to prevent the trade with Bengal, Borneo, Solor, Java, Sunda, Japan and Siam which were conducted without proper licences and permission,[195] they seem to have remained dead letters. A document of 1592 suggests that the *casados* were also engaged in illegal traffic in human cargo, which they carried from China as well as Malacca, and sold in the profitable markets of Malabar coast on their way to Cochin. The document says that many Portuguese merchants and a great number of people who were brought from China and Malacca, used to get down before the ships reached the port of Cochin, leaving only a very few people on board to protect the cargo. These people, assumed to be slaves, were brought without permission from the authorities.[196] In the third decade of the seventeenth century, we hear that the smuggling to Bengal was on the increase, as the punishment given to the smugglers was not corporal, but merely pecuniary.[197] Even the captains of Malabar such as the captain of Tanur and Chale, were great merchants of Cochin and using their official status, they used to trade in contraband items. These merchant-officials were a threat and a problem not only to the ordinary traders but also to the native kings, whose customs revenue they never bothered to pay. In 1627, it is said that the captain of Tanur and Chale was a great merchant of Cochin; but he never paid the customs duties of Cochin either to the native ruler or to the Portuguese treasury.[198]

B. Clandestine Commercial Partnerships

This, as a trade system developed by the *casados* and the native traders, consisted of ware-vessel-exchanges to avoid exorbitant customs duty, or other commercial regulations imposed by the *Estado* authorities. As we have already seen, the native merchants who were to pay six per cent customs duties, were helped by their partners, the *casados* of Cochin, by claiming the ownership of their wares and thus enabling them to pay only the concessional rate of 3.5 per cent to the king of Cochin. This partnership business saved the natives from paying excessive customs, even though the revenue loss incurred thereby on the *Estado* was considerable.[199] Another side of this illegal partnership was the use of the vessels of the native merchants for the transhipping of goods of the *casados*. This seems to have had two advantages for the partners: on the one hand, the native traders could evade the excessive customs duties for their commodities, by attributing ownership of the entire cargo to the *casados*. On the other hand, the *casados* used the native connections to despatch commodities to non-Portuguese ports and destinations. This matter came before the crown. On 9 October 1596, the Portuguese king issued an order asking the *casados* not to use the ships of the *chatins* (the native private traders) to carry out the trade of Cochin with northern ports, under the penalty of losing both the ship and the merchandise. This order was made known to the public by affixing a notice on the fortress walls in Cochin.[200] But even in the early seventeenth century, many *casados* used to send commodities in the vessels of the natives especially *banias*; but it seems that it was an arrangement mainly to avoid the blockade imposed by the Dutch and the English.[201]

The concessional customs rate charged from the *casados* by the native king of Cochin, forced many native merchants of Cochin to join hands with the married settlers of the city to despatch wares. On 6 April 1601, the crown asked the *casados* not to send commodities that actually did not belong to them.[202] On 6 January 1602, the crown again asked Aires de Saldanha not to allow the *moradores* (meaning residents, including both the natives and the non-married Portuguese) of Cochin to send merchandise to Goa in the name of the *casados*, paying only a concessional customs duty to the king of Cochin and thus causing great financial loss to the Portuguese treasury of Goa, into which they should have actually paid the full duty.[203]

C. Corsairs and Trade

The so-called corsair activities, with bases all along Malabar coast, consisted mainly of two streams of operations: on the one hand, there was the stream of piratical activities targeted at plundering Portuguese vessels, while on the other hand, this was supplemented by another strong stream interwoven with the native trade network targeted more at diverting commodities to Mecca. Both were inseparably interlinked.[204] The *armada* of Malabar had the double responsibility of curbing the corsair activities spearheaded by the Muslims of Malabar and obstructing their links with the Mecca trade, as we see in the royal letter of 13 March 1587, addressed to Dom Duarte Meneses.[205] A German document of this period sent from India and received in Augsburg on 15 December 1588, says that the entire western coast right from Diu up to Cape Comorin was infested with the activities of the Malabar corsairs.[206] Meanwhile, the Muslim merchants of the native Cochin also seem to have continued their links with these corsairs, who, besides being of the same faith, were interrelated by both family ties and commercial partnerships.

To counter the threat from the corsairs, as we have already seen, the Portuguese passed legislation by the end of the sixteenth century that the merchant ships were to move in caravans or *cafilas*.[207] These caravan arrangements only reduced the frequency of the movements of the Portuguese vessels, while the trade and corsair activities of the Malabar Muslims, on the other hand, thrived uninterruptedly under the leadership of Kunjali Marakkar. Gradually, with the weakening of the Portuguese position, the group linked to corsair activities began to wield more and more economic and political power, encroaching even upon the sovereignty of their very patron, the Zamorin. Kunjali Marakkar's assumption of titles such as 'Lord of the Arabian Sea', 'prince of Navigation' were viewed as a great threat to the suzerainty of the Zamorin. He consequently joined hands with the Lusitanians to lay siege to the fort of Kunjali in Pudupatanam and to capture the usurper.[208] Meanwhile, the king of Cochin began negotiations with Kunjali promising to help him in his fight against the Zamorin and the Portuguese.[209] This intervention of the king of Cochin in favour of the Kunjali was probably to show his displeasure towards the peace treaty recently established between the Zamorin and the Portuguese. Yet another reason, far stronger than this, seems to have played the key role. Nothing less than the fact that the Muslim merchants of native Cochin had links with Kunjali's corsair empire, must have prevailed upon the king of Cochin to come to the rescue of their leader. However, Kunjali was finally arrested in March 1600 and was taken to Goa to be beheaded.[210] But the Portuguese could not put an end to the corsair activities, which continued with almost the same intensity.

Royal letters were again sent to the Portuguese officials of India, for example, the one written to Aires de Saldanha on 12 February 1603, asking the latter to hunt down the 'pirates' of Malabar.[211] Meanwhile, there appears to have been some understanding reached between the Muslim merchants operating from the corsair network and the non-Portuguese Europeans in the early phase of their establishments. Thus, for example, Nicholas Downton who came to India to establish contacts for English trade in 1614-15, was on friendly terms with the Malabar Muslims. In February 1615, one Mousa Attale from Malabar came to visit Nicholas Downton and made agreements with the English to conduct 'mutuall trade and traffique one with another'. Downton even gave him some letters which were written personally by him and which could be utilized as a certificate for conducting this reciprocal trade.[212] The friendship between the corsairs of Malabar and the English (probably also with the Dutch) must have been a part of the tactics to create a commercial partnership between the forces which opposed the Portuguese trade system. This arrangement helped the Malabar Muslims to send commodities to the Red Sea ports and other destinations even when the English and the Dutch blockaded Portuguese navigational lines. Thus, we see in 1621, vessels from India, including one from Cochin—probably all operating from this network—reaching Mocha for trade.[213]

Even though the Zamorin played a major role in annihilating Kunjali who presented a threat to his sovereign position, the former continued to patronize ordinary corsair activities as ever before, since it was also a part of his trade strategy. Calicut was the main rallying point for the corsairs, who often used to publicly sell the goods robbed from the Portuguese, in its market, as observed by Pietro Della Valle in 1624.[214] The same Zamorin-corsair link was operating in the transhipment of pepper from Panane (Ponnani) to Mecca on 29 October 1624.[215] By the 1630s, when the movements of the mercantile ships diminished, it was often the Portuguese vessels moving to Cochin after having evaded or defeated the Dutch that were preyed upon by them. Thus, in 1637, as observed by Peter Mundy, a Portuguese ship which was coming to Cochin from Malacca and which the Malabar corsairs captured on the Malabar coast, had some Dutch prisoners whom the Portuguese had taken from the straits of Malacca. The corsairs sold the commodities, which were looted from the Portuguese vessel in the coastal markets through their local network.[216] In the years following, we find the corsair activities growing to menacing proportions, offering to the Portuguese at times even more of a serious threat than did the Dutch and the English, who were also frequently attacked by the corsair gang. The Patriarch of Ethiopia in his letter dated 21 December 1642, says that the Malabar corsairs were increasingly concentrating their activities along the ports of Gujarat and along other parts of the west coast to prey upon merchant ships coming from Sind, Muscat, Basra and Mombasa.[217] They eventually widened their resources and network recruiting more personnel for maritime operations. Jean Baptiste Tavernier while mentioning the Muslim corsairs who operated under the patronage of the Zamorin says that they used to go in squadrons consisting of 10 to 15 vessels (sometimes 25 to 30 vessels as when the English Captain Mr. Clerc was attacked), with 200 to 250 men to each vessel, to attack the European ships.[218] By the middle of the seventeenth century, all the Europeans including the Portuguese, the Dutch and the English became the target of their frequent attacks.[219] The whole operation had evolved into an anti-European maritime campaign with bases all over Malabar including Cochin. This gives the impression that had there been only the Portuguese as their enemy, the corsairs would have, with their vast personal and material resources, easily erased them from the scene and become the supreme masters of the Indian Ocean by this time. However, the Portuguese inability to contain the corsair activities reduced the maritime position of the Lusitanians into a mere bi-annual exercise of coastal patrolling by the *armada*. Except for the two periodical coastal patrols made by the *armada*, the vast seashore of India was, predominantly, under the suzerainty of corsairs for the rest of the year.

4. VOLUME OF ASIAN TRADE AND IMPORTS IN COCHIN

The volume of the various streams of intra-Asian trade that converged at Cochin can not be quantified commodity-wise, for want of continuous records. But from the one per cent tax which the city of Cochin levied on the various commodities brought to the port, one could draw a rough picture of the volume of intra-Asian commerce and in particular of the volume of imports made from other Asian ports to Cochin. During the period from 1587 to 1598, the total amount of money received

TABLE VI-2: IMPORTS INTO COCHIN: 1587-98[220]

Year	Amount in *pardaos*	Commodities Rice in kg.
1587	8,49,200	1,54,423
1588	5,29,300	12,35,876
1589	8,46,000	39,65,760
1590	9,48,100	27,76,532
1591	6,34,200	20,26,944
1592	6,32,500	27,77,232
1593	7,69,500	4,63,972
1594	6,99,100	36,57,712
1595	8,38,300	22,03,500
1596	8,66,600	46,70,804
1597	5,12,200	35,69,234
1598	6,94,700	36,13,268

as one per cent duty from the various commodities imported by the city of Cochin, was 88,195 *pardaos*, 4 *tangas* and 32 *reais*.[221]

The one per cent share that went to the city from the rice trade of this period was 1515 *candis* and 11.5 *paras*. An addition of 264.25 *fardos* of rice was also collected during this period from the rice ships. The one per cent share from the wheat trade was 10 *paras*.[222]

Table VI-2 shows that there was an average import of 7,34,900 *pardaos* per year during the period between 1587 and 1598. The annual average of rice import during this period was about 3,86,830 kilograms. Though we do not have any document to assess the volume of export made in the intra-Asian trade, there is every reason to believe that the exports almost equalled the imports. But one has to be very cautious here, as this figure shows a high volume of intra-Asian trade which can be attributed only to the period between 1570 to 1600 and not to the later period when trade in Asian waters suffered drastically. Even in the seventeenth century, one is compelled to assume on the basis of the sources available, that the trade indexes for the period between 1620 and 1663 were at a lower ebb, when compared to the commerce of the first two decades of the century.

A graphic presentation of the above table would give a glimpse into the ups and downs of the import trade. It is interesting to note that the relative fall in import trade corresponds with the years in which less money was spent on coastal patrolling by the city of Cochin as, in 1588 (300 *pardaos*), in 1594 (120 *pardaos*), and in 1598 (515 *pardaos*). However, the *armada* factor should not be held responsible as the sole reason for the fluctuations in the trade indexes, as in of 1589, when only 593 *pardaos* were spent by the city of Cochin for coastal patrolling, while the import was actually 8,45,900 *pardaos*.[223]

This picture of import trade also shows that Cochin's trade on food commodities and non-food items went on hand-in-hand, with almost equal velocity, although some fluctuations are also noticeable. Graph 5 throws light on the rice import to Cochin which had increased considerably from 1588 onwards, probably because of the great increase in the demand for foodstuffs in Malabar, the

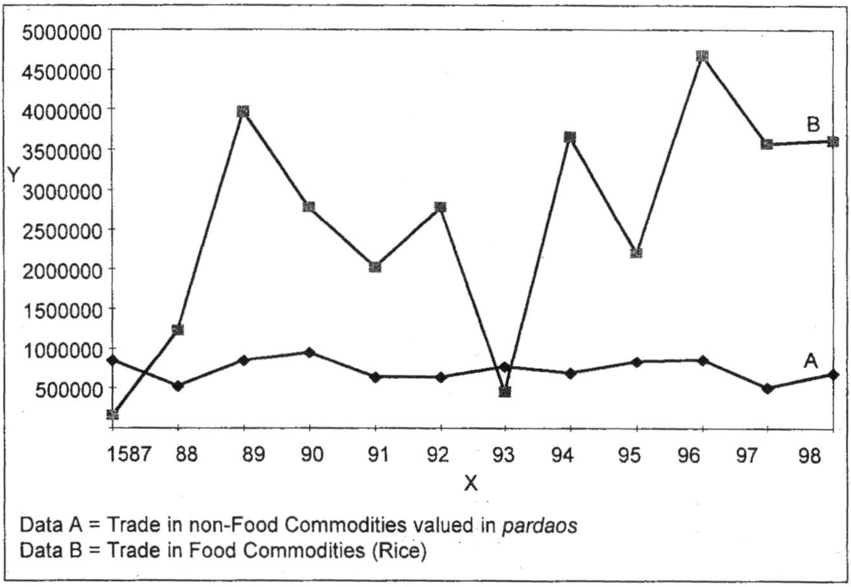

Graph 5: Intra-Asian Trade and the Volume of Import in Cochin.

result of the severe drought about which mention was made by Ferdinand Cron in December 1587.[224]

As the natives as well as the *casados* were charged the one per cent tax to the city and, moreover, as all vessels including those which were used to smuggle out pepper and other contraband items imported commodities to the port of Cochin through the proper channel paying the required duties, the figure presented above seems to incorporate almost all the different streams of intra-Asian commerce that were conducted in Cochin.

Thus we find that the various strands of intra-Asian trade emanating from Cochin had developed almost into an incubus draining the blood of the official Portuguese commercial establishment. Though the usual form of intra-Asian trade fostered by the Portuguese authorities was the one carried out by licenses as well as *cartazes* and through the grant of voyages, there also continued the highly organized 'system of mixed economy', in which the officials of the *Estado* joined hands with the private traders to send commodities to Asian destinations. Along with this, there flourished 'illegal partnerships' between the *casados* and the native merchants, which comprised ware and vessel exchange programmes.This exchange was not one-sided, but reciprocal, depending on the exigencies of time. It was so chalked out that the native merchants might escape the heavy rate prevalent in Portuguese customs houses and the *casados* might escape the threats from other European powers. From 1612 onwards, with the mass exodus of *casado* traders to more prospective trade centres as a result of the diminishing supply of pepper in Cochin, we find a declining trend in the intra-Asian commerce, which had entered a critical phase by the third decade of the seventeenth century.

NOTES

1. Richard Hakluyt, *The Principal Navigations, Voyages, Traffiques and Discoveries of the English Nation* (Caesar Frederick), vol. V, New York, 1969, p. 392; F.P. Mendes da Luz, 'Livro das Cidades e Fortalezas que a Coroa de Portugal tem nas partes da India, e das capitanias e mais cargo que nelas ha e da importância deles', in *Boletim da Biblioteca da Universidade de Coimbra*, vol. XXI, 1953, pp. 70-1; *Relação das Plantas & Dezcripsões de Todas as Fortalezas, Cidades e Povoações que os Portuguezes tem no Estado da India*, Lisbon, CMXXXVI, pp. 38-9.
2. K.S. Mathew and Afzal Ahmad, *Emergence of Cochin*, doc. 55, p. 86.
3. Ibid., doc. 63, p. 95. There was a high demand for the food materials in Malabar especially after the great drought and famine of 1587, to which Ferdinand Cron makes reference. For details see below n. 110. The food shortage must have been increasingly felt in Cochin as many took rice to the interior parts of Malabar, where it was better priced.
4. Ibid., doc. 61, p. 93.
5. Ibid., doc. 59, pp. 90-1.
6. Ibid., doc. 66, p. 100. The 'one per cent money' was often used for the welfare activities of the city.
7. Duarte Gomes Solis was adminitrator general of pepper employed by the new Christian merchant magnate, Heitor Mendes de Brito, who was also his future father-in-law. For more details about Duarte Gomes Solis, see José Calvet de Magalhães, 'Duarte Gomes Solis', *Studia* 19 (1966), pp. 119-71.
8. For details see below nn. 272 and 273.
9. Chryztoph Pawlowski visited Cochin in November 1596. For more details see, 'Relação de Chryztoph Pawlowski', in Stephan Stasiak', 'Les Indes Portugaises à la fin du XVI siecle d'aprés la Relation du voyage fait à Goa en 1596 par Christophe Pawlowski, gentil homme polonais', in *Rocznik Orjentalistyczny*, vol. III, 1926, p. 45.
10. Huyghen van Linschotten, *Histoire de la Navigation de Jean Hvgves de Linscot Hollandais et de son voyage es Indes Orientales*, translated by Bernard Palvdanvs, Amsterdam, 1610, p. 119.
11. Richard Hakluyt, *The Principal Navigations, Voyages, Traffiques*, vol. V, p. 393.
12. K.S. Mathew and Afzal Ahmad, *Emergence of Cochin*, doc. 46, p. 63.
13. *Relação das Plantas & Dezcripsões de Todas as Fortalezas, Cidades*, p. 39.
14. ANTT, *Miscelâneas Manuscritas do Convento da Graça*, Caixa 2, doc. 3. The letter of the king of Cochin to the Viceroy Conde da Vidigueira dated 26 Oct 1598.
15. AHU, *Caixa da India*, Caixa 3, doc. 29, dated 25 Jan 1615.
16. Letter of Philip III (Philip II of Portugal) to the Viceroy dated 6 Feb 1616, in R.A. de Bulhão Pato, *Documentos Remettidos da India*, vol. III, Lisbon, 1935, pp. 373, 388.
17. For details see infra nn. 40, 41.
18. Richard Hakluyt, *The Principal Navigations, Voyages, Traffiques*, vol. V, p. 392.
19. The Portuguese citizens appear to have acted as main distributors of spices coming to the Coromandel coast through the ghat route.
20. *Fürstlich und Gräflich Fuggersches Familien und Stiftungs Archiv*, Dillingen /Donau, MSS Codex no. 46.1. fols. 50-51v.
21. Francisco da Costa, 'Relatório sobre o Trato da Pimenta', p. 315.
22. For elaborate and separate list of the export trade of pepper for this period see Chap. VII.
23. Francisco da Costa, 'Relatório sobre o Trato da Pimenta', p. 351. This figure corresponds

almost to the estimate of Ferdinand Cron in 1587, who calculated it to be around 300,000 quintals. See *Fürstlich und Gräflich Fuggersches Familien und Stiftungs Archiv*, Dillingen /Donau, MSS Codex no. 46.1. fols. 50-51v.

24. Antonio de Gouveia, *Jornada*, p. 208.
25. J.H. da Cunha Rivara, *Archivo Portuguez Oriental*, Fasciculo 3, p. 91.
26. HAG, *Livro das Monçoes*, no. 3-A (1585-9), fols. 174-7; The crown continued to issue orders even in 1591 to the effect of obstructing the flow of pepper through the ghat route. But they remained dead letters. J.H. da Cunha Rivara, *Archivo Portuguez oriental*, Fasciculo 3, p. 301.
27. *Boletim da Filmoteca Ultramarina Portuguesa*, no. 8, Lisboa, 1958, p. 100.
28. For detailed account of the monetary rewards given to the native rulers see Chap. II.
29. Dom Alexis Meneses claimed that he was visiting the churches of St. Thomas Christians to bring them back to the Roman Catholic Church. AHU, *Caixas da India*, Caixa 1, doc. 20, fols. 4-5. But as Eugene Tisserant says this community had always believed in and acknowledged the supremacy of the Pope. E.Tisserant, op. cit., pp. 18-19. It was a time, when, against the background of Protestant Reformation in Europe, every non-Latin liturgical tradition, religious practices and celebrations other than Western Latin tradition was looked upon with suspicion and often termed as heresy. With little command over native and Syriac languages (in which the liturgical celebrations of this community were conducted), and with little knowledge of the cultural and social life of this community, hasty steps were taken to call everything, which were found to be non-European and which did not conform to Latin tradition as heretical practices. The label of Nestorianism, an easy and general epithet often mistakenly used to categorize all the Christians, who were using Syriac as liturgical language, was attributed to the St. Thomas Christians. The moves of the Portuguese which culminated in the Diamper Synod (1599), was motivated with the belief that they could make St. Thomas Christians Catholics only by making their rites and practices conformed to the Latin tradition. So, many prefer to call this phenomenon undertaken by the Portuguese as a process of Latinisation. For further details see Joseph C. Panjikaran, 'Christianity in Malabar with Special Reference to the St. Thomas Christians of the syro-Malabar Rite', in *Orientalia Christiana*, vol. VI, 1926, pp. 103-5.
30. Leslie W. Brown, *The Indian Christians of St. Thomas*, Cambridge, 1956, pp. 20, 39; Placid J. Podipara, 'Portuguese Religious Conquests in Malabar under the Diocese of Cochin during the Sixteenth Century', *NZM*, XII, 1957, pp. 287-306.
31. Ibid. Angamali was a diocese that was existing prior to the advent of the Portuguese and all the St. Thomas Christians were ecclesiastically under this diocese till the second council of Goa.
32. For further details see D'sa, *History of the Catholic Church in India*, vol. I, Bombay, 1910, p. 167. The details about the Jesuit charges of Nestorianism, of which Mar Abraham was accused, could be found in Ferroli, op. cit., vol. I, pp. 172-6.
33. It has to be mentioned here that most of the pre-Diamper liturgy and practices, which were condemned as heresy by the Portuguese, have been slowly re-introduced in the present day Syro-Malabar Catholic rites of the St. Thomas Christians, as a part of the attempt to preserve its age-old traditions.
34. K.M. Panikkar, *Malabar and the Portuguese*, p. 190.
35. For a critical study of the Diamper Synod from the point of view of the St. Thomas Christians, see Jonas Thaliath, *The Synod of Diamper*, Rome, 1958.
36. During this tension period and especially after the Synod of Diamper, the supply of pepper from Cochin to Portugal became small in comparison with the early

figures. For details, see the discussions on the Indo-European trade in Chap. VII.

37. HAG, *Livro das Monções*, no. 7 (1601-3), Royal letter sent to viceroy Aires de Saldanha dated 2 Jan 1601, fols. 21-4; another letter dated 22 Jan. 1601, fols. 27-30.
38. After the synod of Diamper, Archbishop D. Alexis Meneses visited the churches of the St. Thomas Christians to make them accept the synodal decisions. For details see Antonio de Gouveia, op. cit, pp. 198ff.
39. Antonio da Silva Rego, *Documentação Ultramarina Portuguesa*, vol. III, 320-1, 379.
40. AHU, *Caixas da India*, Caixa 2, doc. 107. The letter of the city council of Cochin sent to Philip II (Philip III of Spain) giving an account of the economic condition of Cochin dated 21 Dec. 1613.
41. BNL, *Fundo Geral* 1815. The letter of Philip II sent to Conde de Vidigueira, dated 26 March 1625, fols. 78-78v; Antonio Boccaro, *Livro das Plantas*, pp. 353-4, 360-2; AHU, *Caixas da India*, Caixa 8, doc. 38, dated 29 Dec. 1624.
42. AHU, *Caixas da India*, Caixa 22, doc. 23, dated 4 March 1653. It speaks about the Syrian Bishop (the document mentions that this dignitary was a Syrian patriarch) who was detained by the Portuguese in Goa. AHU, *Caixas da India*, Caixa 23, doc. 20, dated 5 Feb. 1655. Report on the causes of the rebellion which was spearheaded by the archdeacon and the priests of the hinterland. For more details on the rebellion of St. Thomas Christians see Jacob Kollaparambil, *The St. Thomas Christians' Revolution in 1653*, Kottayam, 1981; Jacob Kollaparambil, *The Archdeacon of all India*, Kottayam, 1972.
43. Ibid. During this tension period the Queen of Cochin was said to have supported the cause of the St. Thomas Christians. See S.S. Pissurlencar, *Assentos do Conselho do Estado*, vol. III (1644-58), doc. 149, pp. 274-8.
44. Though the Kunjalis were the traditional admirals of the Zamorin, tensions between them broke out with the accession of Muhammad Kunjali Marakkar (popularly known as Kunjali IV) as the chief of Kottakkal in 1595. He began to assert himself and assumed the title of 'the king of the Malabar Moors' and 'Lord of the Indian seas'. This antagonized the Zamorin, who joining hands with the Portuguese, launched attacks on the fort at Kottakkal. AHU, *Caixas da India*, Caixa 1, doc. 20, fol. 11; Faria y Sousa, op. cit, vol. III, pp. 99-100; F.C. Danvers, *The Portuguese in India*, vol. II, p. 112; A.P. Ibrahim Kunju, op. cit., pp. 81-2.
45. F.C. Danvers, *The Portuguese in India*, vol. II, pp. 113-18; K.M. Panikkar, *Malabar and the Portuguese*, p. 141; Faria y Sousa, op. cit, vol. III, p. 116.
46. Faria y Sousa says that the Zamorin had an added reason in attacking Cranganore as he wanted to occupy the temple of the city where the ancient rulers of Malabar used to be crowned. Faria y Sousa, op. cit., vol. III, p. 204.
47. S.S. Pissurlencar, *Assentos do Conselho do Estado*, Supplementary series, vol. I, part 2, Panaji-Goa, 1972, pp. 109-10.
48. AHU, *Caixas da India*, Caixa 8, doc. 38, dated 29 Oct. 1624.
49. Antonio da Silva Rego, *Documentação Ultramarina Portuguesa*, vol. III, p. 312; Francisco da Costa also says that during his service period he had never found vessels from Porcad bringing pepper to Cochin. Similarly, the pepper supply from Mangatti (Alengad), Parur, from the land of Quarto d'Alva (Karta of Alwaye) to Cochin also dwindled. Ibid.
50. Sanjay Subrahmanyam, 'Cochin in Decline, 1600-1650: Myth and Manipulation in the Estado da India', in *Portuguese Asia*, p. 67.
51. Antonio Bocarro, *Livro das Plantas de todas as Fortalezas, Cidades*, pp. 353-4.
52. *Relação das Plantas & Dezcripsões de todas as Fortalezas, Cidades*, p. 39. It seems that the gunpowder exported from Cochin to the eastern spaces was very little, as most

of the saltpetre that reached Cochin came from Bengal. There is the possibility that the gunpowder mentioned here could be of the refined category.

53. Ibid., pp. 38-9.
54. BNL, *Fundo Geral*, 1980, 'Livro das Despezas de hum Porcento', fol. 25.
55. Ibid., fols. 12; 40.
56. For details on the Portuguese trade in textiles, see Afzal Ahmad, 'Indian Textiles and the Portuguese Trade in the Seventeenth Century (1600-1663)', *Studia* 48, 1989, pp. 213-36.
57. See for details, the table of export given for the period between 1587 and 1609 by Niels Steensgaard, *Carracks, Caravans and Companies: The Structural Crisis in the European-Asian Trade in the early Seventeenth Century*, Kopenhaven, 1973, p. 166; Om Prakash, *The Dutch East India Company and the Economy of Bengal 1630-1720*, Princeton:1985, pp. 183-6; Sanjay Subṛahmanyam, 'Cochin in Decline', p. 65.
58. AHU, *Caixas da India*, Caixa 3A, doc. 162, dated 23 Dec. 1615.
59. Ibid., Caixa 3, doc. 152.
60. Antonio Bocarro, *Livro das Plantas*, p. 353.
61. BNL, *Fundo Geral*, 1980, Livro das Despezas de hum Porcento, fol. 25.
62. Ibid., fols. 16, 40.
63. HAG, *Livro das Monções*, no. 6-B (1605), fols. 39-40.
64. Biblioteca Publica de Evora, MSS. Codice, no. CXVI/1-23, fols. 2-4.
65. AHU, *Caixas da India*, Caixa 16, doc. 34, fol. 21, dated 12-2-1644.
66. Francisco P. Mendes da Luz, *O Conselho da India, Lisboa*, 1952, pp. 73-4; Vicente Almeida d'Eça, *Normas Economicas na Colonização Portuguesa até 1808*, Coimbra, 1921, Chap. II; Marie Antoinette Petronella Meilink-Roelofsz, *Asian Trade and European Influence in the Indonesian Archipelago between 1500 and about 1630*, Nijhoff, 1962, pp. 166; 171.
67. The customs rate in Goa was six per cent, while the *casados* had a concessional rate in Cochin where they were to pay only 3.5 per cent. For details see the discussion on customs duties of Cochin given below.
68. J.H. da Cunha Rivara, *Archivo Portuguez Oriental*, Fasciculo III, p. 123; HAG, *Livro das Monções*, no. 3-A (1585-9), fols. 308-11.
69. J.H. da Cunha Rivara, *Archivo Portuguez Oriental*, Fasciculo 3, pp. 328-9.
70. Ibid., pp. 220, 250.
71. BNL, *Fundo Geral*, Cod. no. 1980, Livro das Despezas (Taboada), fol. 17.
72. ANTT, *Documentos Remetidos da India*, liv. 28, fol. 158; letter of the king sent to the viceroy dated 31 March 1631; Sanjay Subrahmanyam, 'Cochin in Decline', pp. 73-4.
73. AHU, *Caixas da India*, Caixa 3, doc. 36.
74. Ibid., Caixa 4 doc. 107.
75. According to Vitorino Magalhães Godinho, about 75,000 quintals of pepper worth 1.5 million *cruzados* of gold were consumed in China. Almost three quarters of the production of South-East Asia and one-fourth of Malabar pepper were taken to Chinese markets. Vitorino Magalhães Godinho, *Ensaios*, vol. II, Sobre Historia Universal, Lisboa, 1968, p. 233. After the opening up of Chinese ports to Portuguese traders, *casados* stepped into this lucrative trade.
76. *Relaçãodas Plantas & Dezcripsões de todas as Fortalezas*, p. 39; Richard Hakluyt, *The Principal Navigations*, vol. V, p. 393.
77. J.H. da Cunha Rivara, *Archivo Portugez Oriental*, Fasciculo 3, p. 211.
78. Ibid., pp. 750, 761.
79. Ibid., Fasciculo I, part 2, p. 229. During this period we find Chinese junks

carrying the cargo of the *casados* of Cochin, coming frequently to India and the king of Cochin demanding that these Chinese vessels should touch Cochin and pay the customs duties to him as usual. In 1583 and 1598, these junks were said to have called at Nagapatanam. Moreland, *India at the Death of Akbar*, p. 169. For further details about the chinese junk that touched Nagapatanam in 1598 see Chap. VII.

80. R. Disney, *Twilight of the Pepper Empire*, p. 120.
81. *Boletim da Filmoteca Ultramarina Portuguesa*, no. 8, pp. 71-2.
82. AHU, *Caixas da India*, Caixa 10, doc. 105, dated 30 Dec. 1633; In 1643, we hear about another ship which departed from Cochin to China. AHU, *Caixas da India*, Caixa 15, doc. 116, dated 30 Dec. 1643.
83. AHU, *Caixas da India*, Caixa 23, doc. 20, dated 5 Feb. 1655. Though two ships, one from Cochin and another from Goa, moved to China in this year, both of them were captured by the Dutch.
84. For details, see BNL, *Fundo Geral*, Codice no. 1980, 'Livro das Despezas', fols. 19-26.
85. HAG, *Livro das Monções*, no. 3-B (1589-93), the royal letter sent to the viceroy Matias de Albuquerque, January, 1591, fols. 430-7; another letter dated 27 February 1595, fols. 605-8.
86. K.S. Mathew and Afzal Ahmad, *Emergence of Cochin*, doc. 51, p. 70.
87. BNL, *Fundo Geral*, Cod. 1980, 'Livro das Despezas', fol. 3.
88. Ibid., fols. 24; 26. Later with the appearance of the Dutch, the Portuguese intensified and strengthened the patrolling system using more vessels.
89. BNL, *Fundo Geral*, Cod. 1980, 'Livro das Despezas de hum porcento', fols. 4-11.
90. M.N. Pearson, *Merchants and Rulers in Gujarat*, p. 46.
91. Antonio Bocarro, *Decada XIII da Historia da India*, edited by Rodrigo José de Lima Felner, Lisboa, 1876, p. 39.
92. AHU, *Caixas da India*, Caixa 6, doc. 146, dated 17 Dec 1621, fols. 2-3, 10.
93. After the capture of Malacca by the Dutch in 1641, the vessels coming from the eastern spaces of the Indian Ocean, almost stopped touching Cochin. From the 1640s onwards, we hear that the vessels even from Nagapatanam and Mylapore were not coming regularly to Cochin. AHU, *Caixas da India*, Caixa 15, doc. 108, 28 Dec. 1643.
94. Vitorino Magalhães Godinho, *Os Descobrimentos e a Economia Mundial*, vol. II, pp. 7; 24-8; Antonio Bocarro, *Livro das Plantas*, pp. 325-6, 350-1; João Manuel de Almeida Teles e Cunha, *Economia de um Imperio: Economia politica do Estado da India em Torno do Mar Arabico e Golfo Persico Elementos Conjunturais: 1595-1635*, Mestrado Dissertation submitted to the Universidade of Nova de Lisboa, 1995, pp. 397-400.
95. João Manuel de Almeida Teles e Cunha, op. cit., p. 398.
96. J.H. da Cunha Rivara, *Archivo Portuguez Oriental*, Fasciculo 5, parte 1, pp. 455-7.
97. Ibid.; João Manuel de Almeida Teles e Cunha, op. cit., pp. 399-400.
98. Ibid., pp. 400-2; R.A. Bulhão Pato (ed.), *Documentos Remetidos da India ou Livro das Monções*, vol. I, Lisboa: 1884, pp. 262-3. Even in 1645, the members of the royal family of Maldives, who were living in Cochin, used to enjoy this privilege. Dom Pedro Inffant and later, on his death, his son Dom Manuel were entitled to have 500 *xerafins* of pension. AHU, *Caixas da India*, Caixa 17 A, doc. 167, dated 5 July 1645.
99. Francisco Pyrard de Laval, op. cit, vol. I, pp. 180-2.
100. ANTT, MSS, *S.Vicente*, doc. 26, fols. 93-4, dated 5 March 1626; ANTT, *ML* 816, fol. 258.

101. João Manuel de Almeida Teles e Cunha, op. cit., p. 400.
102. *Boletim da Filmoteca Ultramarina Portuguesa*, no. 4, p. 759. Letter of Dom Jeronimo de Azevedo sent to Philip II (of Portugal), dated 23 Jan. 1615.
103. João Manuel de Almeida Teles e Cunha, op. cit., pp. 400-4.
104. R.A. de Bulhão Pato (ed.), *Documentos Remetidos da India*, vol. IV, doc. 954, pp. 295-6; João Manuel de Almeida Teles e Cunha, op. cit., pp. 403-4. From 1619 on, coir and cowries began to come increasingly from the Maldives to Cochin.
105. AHU, *Caixas da India*, Caixa 3 A, doc. 179 fols. 1, 7, dated 30 Dec. 1615.
106. HAG, *Livro das Monções*, no. 7 (1600-3), Letter of the Principe Real to the bishop of Cochin, dated 15 Jan 1598; HAG, *Livro das Monções*, no. 8 (1601-2), royal letter to the Viceroy Aires de Saldanha, 22 Feb. 1601. In 1591, the anti-Portuguese Puviraja Pandaram, the ruler of Jaffna, was attacked and killed. Thereafter, in the meeting of chief men of Jaffna, often called the Convention of Nallur (1591), the king of Portugal was proclaimed the king of Jaffna, and a local ruler Hendaramana Sinha was appointed for routine governance. Meanwhile, with the death of childless Dharmapala in 1597, the kingdom of Kotte also passed into the hands of the Portuguese according to his will, and the king of Portugal became its official ruler. But Vimala Dharma Suriya, who seized the throne of Kandy under the name Don Juan of Austria (later he abandoned this foreign name and took a Sinhalese name), declared himself the ruler of Ceylon and raised a serious challenge to the entire scheme of the Portuguese to master the island. From 1602 onwards, he won the support of the Dutch in the battles against the Portuguese. The wars mentioned here were those waged to regain the Kandyan throne from Vimala Dharma Suriya (and from Senarat, who succeeded Dharma Suriya in 1604), which had previously been ruled by Catholic kings. For details, see L.H. Horace Perera, *Ceylon under Western Rule*, London, 1959, pp. 20-48.
107. HAG, *Livro das Monções*, no. 14 (1630-1), fol. 336, dated 23 Oct. 1630. The intervention of the citizens of Cochin became necessary in Ceylon when the king of Kandy attacked Kotte, the Portuguese stronghold, in 1627. The war continued and in 1630, 4 Mudaliyars and 2,000 soldiers who were fighting for the Portuguese deserted and joined Kandy. Moreover, Constantine de Sa, the captain-general was killed and the Portuguese could not conquer Kandy. For details, see L.H. Horace Perera, op. cit., p. 47.
108. AHU, *Caixas da India*, Caixa 11A, doc. 205, dated 6 Dec. 1635. As we shall see below, most of the cinnamon, brought by the *casados* from Ceylon was taken to Portugal in navetas.
109. BNL, *Fundo Geral*, Codice no. 1816, fol. 211, dated 17 Feb. 1624; ANTT, *L.M.*, doc. 26, fol. 121, dated 25 March 1629; ANTT, *L.M.*, doc. 28, fol. 276, dated 10 April 1631.
110. *Fürstlich und Gräflich Fuggers'ches Familien und Stiftungs Archiv*, Dillingen/Donau, Codex no. 46, 1, fol. 50. The Letter of Ferdinand Cron sent from Cochin, dated 26 Dec. 1587.
111. For more details, BNL, *Fundo Geral*, Codice no. 1980, 'Livro das Despezas', fols. 5-16.
112. Ibid., fols. 11-26.
113. Ibid., 11-16; BNL, *Fundo Geral*, Codice no. 1975, fol. 310, letter of Rui Lourenço de Tavora sent to Conde da Vidigueira (1609-10); Antonio Bocarro, *Livro das Plantas*, pp. 350-1.
114. William Foster (ed.), *The Voyage of Thomas Best to the East Indies: 1612-1614*, London, 1934, pp. 149-50.

115. BNL, *Fundo Geral*, Codice 11410, Relação do Estado da India (1630-31), fols. 169-72; João Manuel de Almeida Teles e Cunha, op. cit., pp. 553-4.
116. S.S. Pissurlencar, *Assentos do Conselho do Estado*, vol. I, Appendix no. 38, contract of peace with Virabadra Naique dated 5 April 1633, pp. 569-71; João Manuel de Almeida Teles e cunha, op. cit., pp. 556-7.
117. AHU, *Caixas da India*, Caixa 3, doc. 29, dated 25 Jan. 1615.
118. William Foster, *The Voyage of Thomas Best*, pp. 148-9, 188.
119. Antonio Bocarro, *Decada XIII*, p. 227; AHU, *Caixas da India*, Caixa 2, doc. 73, dated 23 Dec. 1612; BNL, *Fundo Geral*, Codice no. 1976, fols. 104-8, dated 13 Dec. 1599.
120. AHU, *Caixas da India*, Caixa 2, doc. 4, dated 12 Jan 1612; Caixa 2, doc. 73, dated 23 Dec. 1612.
121. Diogo do Couto, *Da Asia, Decada X*, part 1, liv. IV, cap. XIII, pp. 472-80.
122. Ibid.
123. K.S. Mathew and Afzal Ahmad, *Emergence of Cochin*, doc. 53, pp. 77-83.
124. J.H. da Cunha Rivara, *Archivo Portuguez Oriental*, Fasciculo 6, p. 745.
125. AHU, *Caixas da India*, Caixa 3 A, doc. 179, dated 30 Dec. 1615.
126. K.S. Mathew and Afzal Ahmad, *Emergence of Cochin*, doc. 74, pp. 11-112.
127. AHU, *Caixas da India*, Caixa 17, doc. 13, dated 7 Oct. 1644.
128. Most of these horses imported to Cochin were sold by the *casados* in the kingdoms of Tamilnadu and some in Kerala.
129. Karl H. Dannenfeldt, *Leonhard Rauwolf: Sixteenth Century Physician, Botanist & Traveller*, Massachusetts, 1968, p. 121.
130. Ibid., p. 122; Richard Hakluyt, *The Principal Navigations*, vol. V, p. 285.
131. Karl H. Dannenfeldt, op. cit., p. 122; Richard Hakluyt, *The Principal Navigations*, vol. V, pp. 333-4.
132. J.H. da Cunha Rivara, *Archivo Portuguez Oriental*, Fasciculo 3, p. 301.
133. HAG, *Livro das Monções*, no. 4 (1595-8), fols. 672-8, the royal instructions given to the Viceroy Conde de Vidigueira, dated 2 Jan. 1596.
134. Karl H. Dannenfeldt, op. cit., p. 121.
135. Ibid.
136. Sanjay Subrahmanyam, 'Cochin in Decline', pp. 78-9.
137. This theme is highlighted by Maria Manuela Sobral Blanco, op. cit., *O Estado Portugues da India da Rendição de Ormuz á Perda de Cochim: 1622-1663*, vol. I, unpublished Doctoral Dissertation submitted to the Faculdade de Letras da Universidade de Lisboa, Lisboa, 1992.
138. For a detailed list of the *casados* of Cochin with considerable capital, who used to lend money to the Portuguese Treasury, see AHU, *Caixas da India*, Caixa 2, doc. 89, fols. 1-4, 11, 15 dated 27 Jan. 1613.
139. AHU, *Caixas da India*, Caixa 3, doc. 174, dated 2 Jan. 1616. Another document of 1616 speaks about the money which the Royal Treasury owed to Manuel da Fonseca, the *casado* of Cochin AHU, *Caixas da India*, Caixa 4, doc. 133.
140. Cf. Supra n. 40.
141. AHU, *Caixas da India*, Caixa 3, doc. 29, dated 25 Jan. 1615; see also Caixa 3, doc. 31, dated 25 Jan. 1615.
142. R.A. de Bulhão Pato, *Documentos Remettidos da India*, vol. III, pp. 373, 388.
143. HAG, *Livro das Monções*, no. 12 (1613-17), fols. 254-80, dated March 1617.
144. Antonio Bocarro, *Livro das Plantas*, pp. 352-3.
145. AHU, *Caixas da India*, Caixa 16, doc. 34, dated 12 Feb. 1644.
146. Ibid., Caixa 17, doc. 42, dated 3 Dec. 1644.

147. Ibid., Caixa 18, doc. 57, dated 29 Nov. 1645.
148. Biblioteca Publica de Evora, MSS Codice no. CXVI/1-23, fols. 2-4.
149. AHU, *Caixas da India*, Caixa 15, doc. 116, dated 30 Dec. 1643.
150. Ibid., Caixa 23, doc. 20, dated 5 Feb.1655.
151. Ibid., Caixa 17, doc. 13, dated 7 Oct. 1644.
152. '*Livro das Cidades e Fortalezas que a Coroa de Portugal tem nas partes da India*', published by Francisco Mendes da Luz in *Boletim da Biblioteca da Universidade de Coimbra*, vol. XXI, Coimbra, 1953. For detailed table of voyages, see Luis Filipe Thomaz, 'The Portuguese in the Seas of the Archipelago during the 16th Century', p. 87.
153. HAG, *Livro das Monções*, no. 3A (1585-9), fols. 325-8.
154. J.H. da Cunha Rivara, *Archivo Portuguez Oriental*, Fasciculo 3, p. 81.
155. HAG, *Livro das Monçes*, no. 3 A (1585-9), fols. 346-7, dated 8 Mar. 1589; see also J.H. da Cunha Rivara, *Archivo Portuguez Oriental*, Fasciculo 3, p. 185.
156. For details see, BNL, Codice no. 1976, fols. 158-9. Letter of Conde de Vidigueira sent to Philip in 1599.
157. HAG, *Livro das Monções*, no. 2 A (1583-95), fols. 128-37. Royal letter sent to the Viceroy Matias de Albuquerque dated 15 Feb. 1594.
158. HAG, *Livro das Monções*, no. 7 (1600-3), fol. 100.
159. Ibid., fols. 193-5.
160. ANTT, *Corpo Cronologico*, I, Maço 114, doc. 97, Cochin, dated 23 Jan. 1604.
161. HAG, *Livro das Monções*, no. 12 (1613-17), fol. 88, letter of the Viceroy Dom Jeronimo de Azevedo, dated January, 1615.
162. HAG, *Livro das Monções*, no. 3-A (1589-93), fols. 419-25, dated 12 Jan. 1591.
163. AHU, *Caixas da India*, Caixa 11, doc. 54, dated 28 Feb. 1635.
164. Ibid., doc. 134, dated 31 March 1635.
165. ANTT, *Documentos Remetidos*, liv. 61, fols. 113-14.
166. AHU, *Caixas da India*, Caixa 22, doc. 71, dated 22 Dec. 1653.
167. Ibid., doc. 89, dated 31 Jan. 1654.
168. AHU, *Caixas da India*, Caixa 1, doc, 110, dated 26 Jan. 1611.
169. See for details C.R. Boxer, 'Uma Raridade Bibliografia sobre Fernão Cron', in *Boletim Internacional de Bibliografica Luso-Brasileira* 12.2, 1971, pp. 331; R.A. de Bulhão Pato, *Documentos Remetidos da India*, vol. II, pp. 106-10.
170. Sanjay Subrahmanyam, 'An Augsburger in Asia Portuguesa: Further Light on the Commercial World of Ferdinand Cron: 1587-1624', in Roderich Ptak and Dietmar Rothermund (ed.), *Emporia, Commodities and trade Entrepreneurs in Asian Maritime Trade, C.1400-1750*, Stuttgart, 1991, p. 408.
171. Niels Steensgaard, *Carracks, Caravans and Companies*, p. 90; R.A. de Bulhão Pato, *Documentos Remettidos*, vol. III, p. 35.
172. HAG, *Livro das Monções*, no. 7 (1600-3), fols. 192-5, royal letter sent to Aires de Saldanha, dated 15 Feb. 1603.
173. Ibid., no. 6 A (1604-5), fols. 71, 77, 79; all these three letters were dated 15 March 1605; ANTT, MSS, *S. Vicente*. 14, fol. 161, letter of Philip II (of Portugal) sent to D. Alexis de Meneses, dated 15 May 1605.
174. ANTT, MSS, S. Vicente, 14, fols. 163-1163v Letter of Philip II (of Portugal) to the bishop of Cochin, dated 15 May 1605; doc. 17, fols. 26v-27, Letter of Philip II (of Portugal) to D. Martinho Afonso de Castro, dated 15 March 1605; R.A. de Bulhão Pato, *Documentos Remettidos da India*, vol. I, doc. 8, p. 36, letter of Philip II to D. Martim Afonso de Castro, dated 6 March 1605.
175. HAG, *Livro das Monções*, no. 6 A (1604-5), fol. 79, royal letter sent to the bishop of Cochin, dated 15 March 1605.

176. Ibid., fol. 77.
177. Ibid., fols. 75, 77, 118.
178. Ibid., fol. 117.
179. William Foster (ed.), *The Voyage of Thomas Best*, p. 188.
180. *Boletim da Filmoteca Ultramarina Portuguesa*, no. 4, p. 759, the letter of Dom Jeronimo de Azevedo sent to Philip II dated 23 Jan. 1615. At least from 1612 onwards, we come to know that the *cartazes* were issued to the Maldives on a regular basis. R.A. de Bulhão Pato, *Documentos Remettidos da India*, vol. II, p. 259.
181. BNL, *Fundo Geral*, Codice 1975, fols. 172-172v, dated 6 Feb. 1627. *Cartazes* were also issued to the rulers of the Coromandel coast in exchange for food-supply. Thus from 1591on, the Portuguese began to issue *cartazes* to the king of Masulipatanam in exchange for an annual supply of 300 *candis* of rice. HAG, *Livro das Monções*, no. 3-B (1589-91), fols. 4224-5, dated 12 Jan. 1591.
182. Niels Steensgaard, *Carracks, Caravans and Companies*, p. 89.
183. Richard Hakluyt, *The Principal Navigations*, vol. V, p. 392.
184. Ibid., pp. 394-5.
185. *Boletim da Filmoteca Ultramarina Portuguesa*, no. 2, pp. 177-8. This diversion of commodities seems to have taken place through the distributive network, and often with the knowledge and approval of some bureaucrats of the *Estado da India*.
186. AHU, *Caixas da India*, Caixa 1, doc. 12, dated *c.* 1590.
187. HAG, *Livro das Monções*, no. 2-B (1595-1601), fol. 425.
188. R.A. de Bulhão Pato, *Documentos Remettidos da India*, vol. I, doc. 55, pp. 147-9, letter of Philip II sent to D. Martim Afonso de Castro, dated 10 Dec. 1607; HAG, *Livro das Monções*, no. 2-A (1583-95), fol. 417, dated 30 March 1598; AHU, *Caixas da India*, doc. 38, dated 29 Oct. 1624; João Manuel Almeida Teles e Cunha, op. cit., pp. 399-402.
189. João Manuel Almeida Teles e Cunha, op. cit., pp. 399-400.
190. Cf. supra nn.173 and 188.
191. AHU, *Caixas da India*, Caixa 2, doc. 119.
192. Ibid., Caixa 6, doc. 41, dated 18 Feb. 1619.
193. *Boletim da Filmoteca Ultramarina*, no. 5, p. 106. After the fall of Ormuz, Muscat turned out to be the commercial destination of many private traders.
194. HAG, *Livro das Monções*, no. 17 (1632-3), fol. 216, the letter of the king to the viceroy, dated 10 Feb. 1633; HAG, *Livro das Monções*, no. 18 (1633), fol. 81, letter of the king to the viceroy dated 10 Feb. 1633.
195. *Boletim da Filmoteca Ultramarina*, no. 2, p. 457.
196. J.H. da Cunha Rivara, *Archivo Portuguez Oriental*, Fasciculo 3, p. 353.
197. BNL, *Fundo Geral*, Codice 1816, fol. 151, report on the illegal pepper trade of Cochin with Bengal, dated 25 Jan. 1624.
198. Ibid., Codice 1975, fol. 172, letter of the viceroy sent to the king, dated 6 Feb. 1627.
199. Cf. supra nn.120 and 123.
200. J.H. da Cunha Rivara, *Archivo Portuguez Oriental*, fasciculo 3, pp. 660-1.
201. This was the usual way resorted to by the *casados* to escape the English blockade. The natives would either escape the enemy for being a native or would be made the scape-goat. Thomas Best gives a striking example, where the English captain Hermon capturing a vessel, tortured some bania merchants mistaking them to be Portuguese *casados*. Hermon did not believe that they were natives and he caused them hung upon a tree by "their hands, fingers and heads" to make them confess that they were Portuguese. William Foster, *Thomas Best*, pp. 129-30. However, the transhipment of wares in the vessels of banias usually provided some sort of immunity to the *casados* from the blockade of the enemies.

202. HAG, *Livro das Monções*, no. 7 (1600-3), fols. 35-44, letter of the king to viceroy, Aires de Saldanha, dated 6 Jan. 1601.
203. Ibid., no. 8 (1601-2), fols. 44-5, royal letter sent to Aires de Saldanha, dated 6 Jan 1602.
204. As we have already seen in the last chapter, corsair activities could not be considered as mere piracy; on the other hand it was an alternative trade arrangement developed on the Malabar coast.
205. HAG, *Livro das Monções*, no. 3-a (1585-9), fols.180-1, royal letter sent to Duarte Meneses, dated 13 March 1587.
206. National Bibliothek wien, Cod. 8961, fols. 891-2, dated 15 Dec. 1588.
207. Cf. supra n. 90.
208. Cf. supra n. 44.
209. BNL, *Fundo Geral*, Codice no. 1976, fols. 158-9, letter of Conde de Vidigueira to Philip, written in 1599.
210. For details see, C.R. Boxer and Frazão de Vasconcelos, *André Furtado de Mendonça (1558-1610)*, Lisboa, 1956, pp. 21-35.
211. HAG, *Livros das Monções*, no. 7 (1600-3), fols. 161-4, royal letter sent to Aires de Saldanha, dated 12 Feb 1603.
212. William Foster (ed.), *The Voyage of Nicholas Downton to the East Indies: 1614-1615*, London, 1939, p. 25.
213. Marie Antoinette Petronella Meilink-Roelofsz, *Asian Trade and European Influence in the Indonesian Archipelago*, p. 387.
214. James Talboys Wheller and Michael Macmillan, op. cit., p. 34.
215. AHU, *Caixas da India*, Caixa 8, doc. 38, dated 29 Oct. 1624.
216. Richard Carnac Temple (ed.), *The Travels of Peter Mundy, in Europe and Asia: 1608-1667*, vol. III, part I, London, MCMXIX, p. 110.
217. AHU, *Caixas da India*, Caixa 14 A, doc. 136, dated 21 Dec. 1642.
218. V. Ball (ed.), *Travels in India by Jean Baptiste Tavernier*, vol. I, London, 1889, pp. 177-8.
219. With the establishment of several trade-centres by these powers, the commercial opportunities left for the corsairs in the Indian Ocean were curtailed considerably. Therefore, they considered every European vessel plying in Asian waters as an encroachment upon their birth-right.
220. BNL, *Fundo Geral*, Codice no. 1980, 'Livro das Despezas', *Taboada* section, fols. 5-16.
221. Ibid., fol. 1.
222. Ibid.
223. Cf. supra n. 89.
224. Cf. supra n. 110.

CHAPTER VII

The Vicissitudes of Indo-European Trade: 1570-1663

The European trade of Cochin underwent different phases of organizational and managerial innovations during this period. While the *casados* and the ordinary Portuguese were increasingly engaging themselves, either independently or in association with the natives, in Asian trade, European commerce turned out to be a tough task for the *Estado*. The crown realized the gravity of the pro-Asian trends of *casado* traders, especially of the 'illicit' trade transactions, as well as the mounting pressure on Indo- European trade. The royal attempt to overcome this situation, led to several phases of innovations in the organization of Indo-European commerce: 1. The Phase of Contract trade (1570-98), 2. Re-introduction of the direct trade by the crown (1598-1629; 1634-63), 3. Trade through Portuguese India Company (1629-34), 4. The participation of the *casados* of Cochin in the European commerce (1628-38)

1. INDO-EUROPEAN TRADE DURING THE CONTRACT PHASE (1570-1598)

With the death of Dom John III on 11 June 1557, the Portuguese Government passed into the hands of regents for some time as the next candidate Dom Sebastian was a minor. The regency period, marked by a great amount of confusion, ended by 1568 when Dom Sebastian took up the reins of the government.[1] By this time, most of the spice trade in the East as well as in the home country had fallen into the hands of private individuals, who had amassed huge fortunes mostly through illicit trade. The crown, on the other hand, not being able to contain the illegal activities, had to bear all the burden of maintaining and protecting the vast trade empire, whose benefits, in most cases, were enjoyed by the private profiteers. In this situation, in order to reduce the crown's obligations, king Sebastian promulgated a new *regimento* liberalizing the Indo-European commerce. According to the new rules, all the subjects of the king of Portugal could trade privately in the products of India, on condition that all colonial goods, including spices, would be brought to Lisbon for payment of duties. Private trade was legally permitted in some ports of Malabar coast, as well.[2] By 1575, Dom Sebastian, who had stepped down from the role of merchant monarch and who was confronted with heavy expenses, began to give the spice monopoly to private contractors. In this new system of pepper trade, there were two contracts: the European contract which included the rights of distribution and sale in Europe as well as the Indian contract which included the right of purchase in the marts of India.[3] Though in 1575, the south German merchants were prepared to enter into the European contract of pepper distribution, the Portuguese court, which viewed this as an effort of Spain and her Fugger associates to extend their commercial designs to Portugal, thwarted the move.[4] Finally in the last months of the same year, the pepper contract was awarded for five years to Konrad Rott, an Augsburg merchant who, though he had been doing business in the Iberian Peninsula for a long time, was not one of the really important merchants. He pledged himself to buy 12,000 quintals of pepper in the first year and 20,000 thereafter, at 34 *ducats* per quintal. Rott, who soon found it difficult to carry out the project alone, sold three-eighths of his contract to Giacomo dei Bardi and the Company of Florence.[5]

In 1578, Rott entered into the India Contract, sending Gabriel Holzschuher of Nürnberg to Cochin on 4 April 1579, as his trade agent to procure pepper for his ships.[6] Rott's entry into the Indian trade coincided with the great tragedy of Alcaçer Quibir, where King Sebastian of Portugal himself, along with a great many important nobles were killed in the crusade against Morocco. Much of the wealth of Portugal, including the portable wealth of leading families, was to be paid out as ransom for the *fidalgos* who were taken as prisoners in Morocco.[7] During this critical period, though Cardinal Henry, who was then seventy-seven years old, ascended the throne,[8] the Indo-European trade and especially the pepper trade with Cochin was in the hands of the intrepid Konrad Rott.

With the acquisition of the India Contract, Rott tried to establish a world pepper monopoly. He divided the value of his contracts into thirty shares out of which he sold ten to Portuguese firms and seven-and-a-half to Italian firms while the remaining twelve-and-a-half he kept for himself. Once the pepper from Cochin and other Malabar ports came into the hands of Rott and his enterprise was properly organized in southern Europe, he entered into negotiations with the Elector Augustus of Saxony in 1579 to establish a base in Leipzig from where pepper could be distributed to Germany, the Netherlands, the Baltic states and Poland. In this connection, the Elector organized the Thuringian Company with a view to exchanging copper and tin for the pepper from Rott. However, by 1580, this ambitious scheme of the Elector to control the spice trade of northern Europe had to be abandoned and Rott went bankrupt.[9]

From 1580 on, Giovanni Rovellasca, an Italian merchant from Milan took up the Indian part of the contract that had already and originally been concluded by Rott, and began to control Cochin's pepper trade with Europe.[10] The entry of Rovellasca into Indian trade, with its base in Cochin, coincided with the union of the crowns of Spain and Portugal under Philip II. Upon the death of the childless Cardinal Henry in 1580, Philip's army entered Portugal and in 1581, he was proclaimed the king of Portugal by the Cortes as Philip I.[11] The terms of the Agreement of Union made at Tomar in 1581 provided that the Spanish and Portuguese overseas empires would be kept separate, each being administered by its own officials. During the reign of this Hapsburg king, the Secretary of State for India continued to operate as a separate administrative department in Lisbon and *Casa da India* had the responsibility of the sale and distribution of the commodities from Cochin and other parts of Asia.[12] The *Casa da India*, during this period, was buying pepper from the holders of the India Contract at the lowest possible price and selling to the holders of European contract at the highest possible price. This arrangement through the *Casa da India* helped to extract as much profit as possible from the contracting system, with minimum investment and risk on the Portuguese side.[13]

Filippo Sassetti (1540-88) the great Florentine humanist and a one-time commercial agent of the Cappioni in Spain and Portugal was sent out to Cochin as the factor for Rovellasca's commercial enterprise in India. He arrived in Cochin in November 1583 and worked as the supervisor for Rovellasca not only till the expiry of the first contract but right up to his death in 1588 at Goa.[14] Max Wolfmüller, who was associated with Konrad Rott in Augsburg came to India in 1583/4, to help Filippo Sassetti in this enterprise.[15] Meanwhile, Gabriel Holzschuher, who had served Rott in Cochin till his bankruptcy, was then in Malabar and his services were also employed for the enterprise of Giovanni Battista Rovellasca.[16] Rovellasca's Indian contract which continued up to 1585, was also supported in Europe by some Italians and by a Spanish branch of the Fuggers.[17] Meanwhile, as we have already seen, the private traders who had bases in Cochin and other Malabar ports were increasingly supplying the Levant with pepper, which flowed into the Italian cities. At this time, Philip who was in dire need of money because of his wars with the Netherlands and later with the English, began to negotiate with Venice as early as 1581 to make them part-takers in the pepper distribution of Europe. With the expiry of Rovellasca's European contract in 1585, he was even ready to sell 30,000 quintals annually to the Venetians at the rate of 30 *ducats* per quintal, which was much lower than the price to the European contractors, which varied between 36 to 38.[18] Neither Venice nor any other Italian city was ready to buy this pepper distribution contract in Europe from Portugal.

Unfortunately, we do not have enough details for the volume of trade carried out during the contract under Rott and Rovellasca. But there is evidence to say that the agents of these contractors did not confine themselves to the pepper trade alone, even though the agreement was only for it. We are told that besides pepper, a lot of nutmeg and ginger, which was not included in the contract, was also brought to Lisbon during the years from 1579 till 1581.[19]

In 1586, through the negotiations conducted in Spain by Giraldo Paris, who was a noble of Limburg and a copper trader, a new Asian contract was concluded between Philip I and Giovanni Rovellasca. According to the terms of the agreement signed at Valencia on 15 February 1586, the 'contractors' were to equip five ships annually for a period of six years (1586-91) to India and Malacca (however in certain years, five vessels were sent to India and one to Malacca). The holders of the Asian contract had to annually send 1,70,000 *cruzados* for the purchase of 30,000 quintals of pepper and had to deliver it to the *Casa da India*. Again, they had to pay 24,000 *cruzados* each year to the king for the vessels that would be used for the contract trade. The contractors could also send their own agents to India to conduct the trade. For their maintenance, the holders of contract were given a special privilege to import free of duty 450 quintals of 'drugs' including cloves and cinnamon which the contractors themselves could sell in Europe. The purchase price of the pepper was fixed at five and two-thirds *cruzados* per quintal. The pepper taken to *Casa da India* was to be sold at 12 *cruzados* per quintal and they might receive an additional amount of 4 *cruzados* for the freight and transhipping cost. Rovellasca and Giraldo Paris were also allowed to bring associates into their contract.[20] Eventually, Markus Mathäus Welser and Company bought 41.67 per cent (five-twelfths of a share) of the Asian contract. Out of this Octavian and Philip Edward Fugger bought 25 per cent (three-twelfths of a share) of the contract for 'Georg Fuggerischen Erben', in 1587. Giovanni Battista Rovellasca kept 58 one-third per cent (seven-twelfths of a share) of the contract with him.[21]

Ferdinand Cron (*c*.1559-1637) the son of Heinrich Cron, the Mayor of Augsburg, represented the Fuggers and the Welsers in Cochin. He reached Goa in 1587, as the chief factor of these south German firms (with an annual salary of 1,000 fl.). He concentrated his activities in Cochin to mobilize native co-operation and to ensure regular transhipment of pepper to Europe.[22] He was assisted by Christian Schneeberger, who was another agent of the Fuggers, and who had reached Goa along with Cron, in his efforts to procure pepper. His bases of operation were the ports of Cochin and Quilon.[23] When he became sick in 1588, Gabriel Holzschuher, who was previously acting as the trade agent for Konrad Rott and later for Rovellasca in Cochin took charge of Quilon.[24] Max Wolfmüller, who had previously served Sassetti for the Rovellasca, entered the service of Ferdinand Cron in 1586/7 and he was the chief collection agent for the Welsers and the Fuggers in Cannanore.[25] Sebastian Zangmeister was another link in Malabar in this collection network of the German contractors.[26]

Meanwhile, the interests of the Rovellasca were represented in India by some Italian agents, who had been operating right from the beginning of the first contract. Filippo Sassetti in Cochin continued to be the principal factor of the Rovellasca firm even during this contract.[27] He was assisted by another Italian (probably from Florence) called Oratio Nereti.[28] In connection with the processes of procuring pepper, he also seems to have concentrated his activities in Cochin. Along with these two, Filippo Margera, another Italian was also in Cochin in the service of Rovellasca.[29] These agents of the contractors procured pepper from Cochin, Cannanore and Quilon with the help of native merchants, very often paying higher prices.[30]

However, in no single year could the Italian-German syndicates deliver the stipulated 30,000 quintals of pepper to Lisbon. Because of the private traders, who, as we have already seen, were diverting pepper from Cochin and other Malabar ports to other parts of Asia as well as to the eastern Mediterranean routes, the agents of the contractors found it difficult to achieve their targets in India. Meanwhile, Malacca was under siege from the Achineses of Sumatra in 1586. Though a fleet sent from India could relieve the siege, the situation was no better for the contractors in the following years.[31] The international situation also contributed no less to the non-achieving of the target of contract. The English, who had been looking for a northern route to Cathay and India since 1553,[32] had emerged as a prospective commercial nation with the circumnavigation of the world by Francis Drake in 1580.

Meanwhile, the Dutch, who were struggling to throw off the yoke of Spanish hegemony, continued their fighting against Spain and Portugal.[33] The outbreak of war between Spain and England in 1585 united the interests of Protestant England

and the Dutch against the Catholic Iberian states. Mutual trade was forbidden by both the warring factions. Against this hostile background ships returning to Portugal from India were increasingly captured and looted by the English and Dutch corsairs.[34] This coincided with the transfer of the European spice market to Amsterdam, which was necessitated by the fall of Antwerp into the hands of the Spaniards in 1585.[35] The menace from the English and the Dutch, the greatest maritime powers of northern Europe, increased with the defeat of the Spanish Armada in 1588.[36]

Though six ships left Lisbon in March 1586, the first ship *Santa Maria* shortly after its departure was attacked by the English near Azores and had to return greatly damaged. One of the biggest vessels among them, *S. Felipe* did not reach India. Instead, it took from Moçambique the wares that belonged to the previous contract, and on its way back to Portugal it fell into the hands of the English corsairs.[37] The third vessel *S. Salvador* turned out to be a distressed ship on the east African coast. With a tattered mast, it was taken to Ormuz.[38] Only three ships reached India to take on board the pepper collected by Ferdinand Cron and other agents of the contractors. However, among them, the *Reliquias*, which was loaded with 1638 quintals of pepper sank into the sea at the mouth of Goa.[39] Finally what was brought to Europe in 1587 by the two remaining ships, the *S. Thomé* and the *Nostra Señora de Concepción*, was 10,368 quintals of pepper, being only one-third of the amount called for in the contract.[40] In the first year, this enterprise which invested a capital of 1,94,000 *cruzados* brought in only 1,64,979 *cruzados* and 80 *reales* in return.[41]

The five ships of 1588, loaded with pepper reached Lisbon safe. The agents of the contractors could send 22,963 quintals from Cochin, Quilon, Cannanore and Kanara.[42] On sale of this cargo, the contractors obtained about 3,65,262 *cruzados*.[43]

The trade of 1589 also fared relatively well. Out of a total cargo of 30,042 quintals of pepper loaded in India, 24,163 quintals reached Portugal, on 16 September 1589. The vessel *S. Salvador*, which set out in 1586 and was then taken to Ormuz, was used for the first time to take pepper to Europe in this year. However *S. Thomé*, which carried 5,877 quintals of pepper was wrecked near the coast of South Africa on its home-bound voyage. Still, about 80 per cent of the cargo reached the metropolis safely. The value of this cargo was about 3,82,400 *cruzados*.[44]

In the next year, the vessels left Lisbon very late, only on 20 May 1590. However the ship *Santa Cruz* broke before leaving the Lisbon harbour. Three ships, the *Nostra Señora de Concepción*, the *S. Cristobal* and the *S. Juan Battista*, were about to fall into the hands of the English corsairs and had to return home because of adverse winds. Only the fifth ship, *S. Antonio*, which carried the Viceroy Mathias de Albuquerque sailing to Brasil, reached India one year after its departure from Lisbon. As this ship arrived too late, there was no transhipment of spices from India that year. So the contractors got back a great portion of their payment made for 1590.[45] On 4 April 1591, in the last year of the contract, six vessels were fitted out for India and Malacca from Lisbon. Of these, only *S. Cristobal* reached Portugal in 1592 with a cargo of 8,438 quintal pepper. The *Santa Cruz* burnt down while trying to flee from the English corsairs. Three vessels, the *Buen Jesu*, the *S. Bernardo* and the *S. Luiz* seem to have been wrecked on their way back home. The sixth ship,

Madre de Dios with a cargo of 7,101quintal of pepper, fell into the hands of the English in Atlantic on its way back, and was taken to England in 1592.[46] The efforts of the contractors and the special intervention of the German Kaiser, who wrote letters to Queen Elizabeth on 25 January 1595 and 4 August 1597 to return the *Madre de Dios* did not achieve any result.[47] It is estimated that what was delivered to the *Casa da India*, over the entire contract period, did not reach half of the stipulated amount of pepper.[48]

Meanwhile King Philip I (of Portugal), whose fortunes were increasing with the large quantity of silver flowing into Castile from America, wanted to have proportionate control over the pepper trade by reorganizing its administration and introducing a centralizing programme in Portugal. He passed a decree on 20 November 1591, abolishing the old financial offices and the system of *vedores*. In its place, he created a Council of Finance composed of men of his own choice. The spice trade and the *Casa da India* were put under this council. Eventually, almost all the agencies of Portugal's home government and overseas management were brought under its umbrella making the centralization complete.[49] This reorganization hid an actual desire to take back the pepper trade for the Iberians, once the Indian contract of the Italian-German Syndicates terminated in 1591.[50]

However the termination of this Indian contract was not followed by the crown's direct trade. On the other hand, a new contract was negotiated in 1592 for a period of five years with Tomas Ximenes for bringing pepper from India.[51] The Indian contract was taken up by a Portuguese syndicate consisting of Pero Rodrigues of Lisbon, Fernão Ximenes, João Monteiro, Henrique Dias, André Ximenes, Heitor Mendes de Brito, Luis Gomes Furtado and Jorge Rodrigues Solis, all belonging to the group of new Christians.[52] According to the conditions of this contract, the signatories were required to deposit 1,70,000 *cruzados de dez reales* (silver) which they should use for the purchase of 30,000 quintals of pepper.[53] Meanwhile, the shipping service to India was handed over to another group of contractors to whom André Ximenes and his associates had to pay 4,800 *cruzados* for each vessel, towards the cost of repair and maintenance.[54] These contractors could send to Cochin and Goa their own trade agents, which gave the new Christians a fresh opportunity to despatch members of their community for trade, to Cochin and Goa. It seems that many of the new Christian traders whom Polanswski and Linschotten saw in Cochin must have originally come as agents of these contractors.[55] The clause of the contract for making use of their own agents to buy pepper in advance from Onor, Barcelor, Mangalore, Cochin and Quilon was used as a loophole for sending further men from this community to Cochin. Some of them seems to have later shifted to the profitable private trade abandoning their jobs as agents. As a result, this period of contract trade did not succeed in collecting what the Italian-German syndicates had in the previous contract.

Meanwhile a European contract was signed on 8 April 1591, between Philip I (of Portugal) and a group of his creditors, to ensure a regular distribution of pepper in Europe. These merchants who saw in this contract an opportunity to recover their money already been borrowed by Philip I (of Portugal), formed a syndicate to enter into this contract. The European contract was divided into thirty-two shares out of which André Ximenes, a Portuguese banker and a merchant doing business in Lisbon and Antwerp, bought twelve shares. The Fuggers had seven shares, while the Welsers took five. G.B. Rovellasca and Giraldo Paris, together kept four shares and the Spanish merchants Francisco & Pedro Malvenda of Bourgos had the remaining four shares. Later, Ximenes bought two more shares from Malvenda.[56] The Portuguese crown, which bought the pepper from the holders of Asian contract at 16 *cruzados* per quintal, sold it to the syndicate at 38 *cruzados* 218 *reales*.[57]

Meanwhile the signatories of the European contract agreed among themselves to sell the pepper in Europe at forty to forty-two *cruzados* per quintal. The merchant magnates sold their stocks at a reduced price to smaller contractors of Lisbon and elsewhere. Pepper was in great demand in the markets of northern Europe and the holders of the European contract began to send large shipments of pepper to the Hanseatic cities such as Danzig, Lübeck and Hamburg, as well as to Middleburg and Amsterdam from where it was distributed all over Northern Europe.[58] Hamburg which was least affected by the the Anglo-Dutch-Spanish war turned out to be the safest distribution centre in the northern Europe. Out of the pepper that was sent in 1591, Hamburg received the greatest share with 48.3 per cent, Amsterdam stood second with 28.3 per cent, and Lübeck at 23.4 per cent. Meanwhile, the Fuggers sold their seven shares in early 1592 to Ruy Lopez d'Evora, who was associated with André Ximenes.[59]

Thus, during the period between 1570 and 1598, the contract trade provided a wider distribution network in Europe for the pepper taken from Cochin. But there was a diminishing trend in the movement of vessels between India and Lisbon. Though the vessels of the *Carreira da India* of this period were bigger in size and in tonnage, solving the problem raised by the paucity of ships, the hectic overloading of the cargo led to frequent shipwrecks. Even if some vessels could safely return to the Atlantic many did not reach Lisbon, where they were captured either by the British or Dutch corsairs.[60] Thus during the period between 1570 and 1579, fifty-four ships left Lisbon out of which only fifty-one reached India. On the return journey to Lisbon (1571-80), forty-four vessels left India out of which one ship was lost. During the next decade (1580-9), though the vessels despatched to India increased to fifty-six, only forty-seven actually reached India. The number of losses on the return trip (1581-90), rose to five, and only forty-one ships arrived in Lisbon. The last decade of the sixteenth century witnessed the lowest number of ships sent from Portugal in that century. Out of forty-four vessels, only thirty-seven touched the ports of India. This decade also registers the record of the greatest number (sixteen ships) of vessels lost on the return journey (especially between the years 1500 and 1663). During the period between 1591 and 1600, thirty-nine vessels moved to the metropolis; but only twenty-three reached Lisbon,[61] because of the heavy losses incurred by the vessels of the *carreira* by way of wrecks and capture by the British and Dutch corsairs. What was extracted and exported from Cochin did not enter the metropolis in the same measure or volume.

However, while dealing with the export trade of pepper from Cochin (which, for want of separate details, cannot be dissociated from the general account of pepper-export from the ports of the west coast of India), I would like to present the volume of pepper sent from India, instead of that which reached Lisbon. A detailed table (Table VII-1) of the pepper trade during the contract period is given below:

TABLE VII-1: EXPORT TRADE OF PEPPER DURING THE CONTRACT PERIOD: 1582-98[62]

Year	Quantity (in kg.)
1582	11,27,675
1587	6,29,715
1588	12,04,409
1589	15,75,703
1590	12,42,121
1592	8,15,021
1593	2,62,336
1594	3,41,792
1595	9,23,697
1596	1,42,349
1597	8,87,821
1598	4,14,093

Thus, the period of contract trade witnessed the recuperation of the export trade of pepper with Europe. The annual average of the export, during this period, was 7,97,228 kgs. Because of the earnest efforts of the Italians under Filippo Sassetti and the Germans under Ferdinand Cron and Christian Schneeberger, the quantity of pepper that was sent from Cochin and other ports of Malabar remained significantly high till 1592. During the next six years, when export trade from India was again carried out by a syndicate, whose leading figure was Ximenes, the volume of export to Europe began to show diminishing trends and in 1598, the year in which Philip I died,[63] only 4,14,093 kgs. of pepper were sent from Malabar. Though the contractors from Portugal sent their own agents to Cochin and tried to collect the necessary cargo for the vessels to Lisbon, the tensions in the hinterland and the alienation of the pepper-growing community of the St. Thomas Christians from the Portuguese, which had by this time, assumed alarming dimensions, obstructed them from realizing their target. The tensions were renewed when Mar Abraham refused to ordain the priests trained in the Latin tradition at the Vaipinkotta Seminary. Moreover, he abstained from attending the fourth Provincial Council of Goa in 1592. In the succeeding years, tensions mounted and it became open and acute with the death of Mar Abraham and the convocation of the Diamper Synod in 1599.[64] While the non-Portuguese Europeans like the Italians and the Germans managed to collect a large quantity of pepper for European trade till 1592, with an annual average of 10,99,108 kgs., the Portuguese contractors could not procure even half of it during the period between 1593 and 1598, when the annual average was only 4,95,348 kgs. This obviously points to the fact that the anti-Portuguese feelings of the St. Thomas Christians had already begun to work negatively on the European commerce of Cochin of this period. Its repercussions were so great that no contractor dared to come forward in the years following, to take up the Indian trade. The various commercial trends exhibited during this contract period are illustrated with the help of a graph.The ups and downs of the indexes of this diagram indicating European export trade should be analysed against the general background of the hinterland and the ever-active intra Asian trade that thrived in Cochin under the leadership of the *casados*.

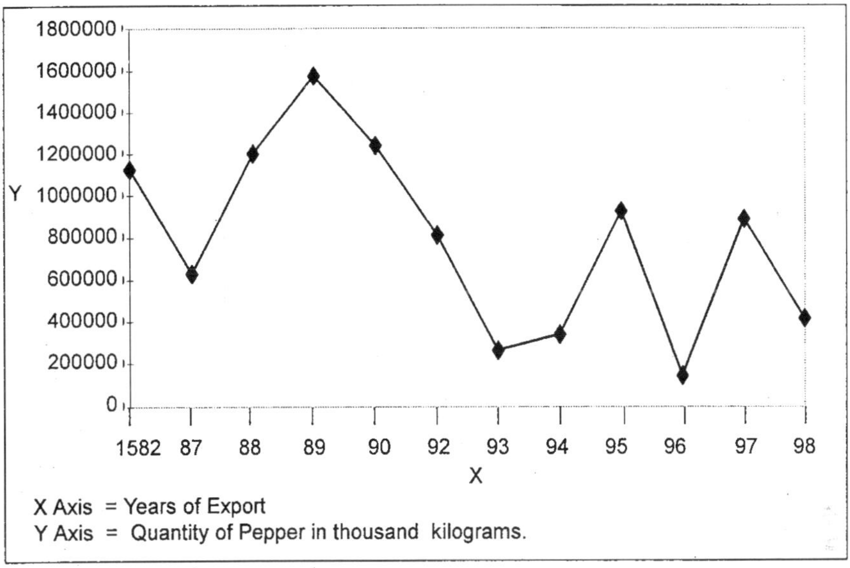

Graph 6: Pepper Export from Cochin to Europe (1582-98).

In general, the contract phase rendered Cochin's commerce with Europe as hectic as its Asian trade. Despite tensions in the hinterland relatively a better performance was seen in 1595 and 1597.

Besides pepper, other spices also entered Europe via Cochin. For want of continuous documents, we cannot assess this volume of trade. In 1588, different commodities such as 91,027 kgs. of cinnamon, 85,336 kgs. of indigo, 11,120 kgs. of nutmeg, 71,463 kgs. of ginger, 24,232 kgs of cowry shells as well as 1271 boxes of silk and textiles were sent to Lisbon.[65] It seems that the export of non-pepper commodities almost approached this figure, during this period. After the expulsion of the Portuguese from Ternate in 1570, there seems to have been a diminishing trend in the export of cloves, nutmeg and mace from Cochin, during this period,[66] even though some *casado* traders of Cochin appear to have continued supplying these sophisticated spices to their home city.

2. RE-INTRODUCTION OF DIRECT TRADE BY THE CROWN (1598-1629; 1634-1663)

The accession of Philip II (Philip III of Spain) to the throne of Portugal in 1598, coincided with the termination of both the Indian as well as European contracts. The export trade from India fell again into the hands of the crown in 1599 with the termination of the contract of the Portuguese syndicates. Meanwhile, because of the heavy losses incurred by the contractors and especially with the bankruptcy of Konrad Rott and Rovellasca, the merchant syndicates were not interested in taking up further commerce with India. In this situation, the Portuguese crown was again required to conduct the trade directly. In general, the direct trade by the crown seems to have continued up to 1663, even though we have clear evidence of an interval of some years (from 1628-38), when Indo-European trade from Cochin was conducted both by the *casados* of Cochin as well as by the Portuguese India Company for some time. Besides this, there were stray cases of enterprising native factors being invited to send ships to Lisbon. One most striking example was that of the King of Cochin who was invited in 1626 to take part in Indo-European commerce and to send vessels to Portugal.[67]

The situation in Cochin and Malabar had changed a lot by 1598. The most important among them was that the local king of Cochin, who had amassed great wealth by way of customs duty from private trade, emerged as a powerful factor often asserting his claims and placing his own interests in the forefront. King Kesava Rama Varma who had been ruling Cochin since 1565 was not at all happy with the Portuguese, right from their customs reform in 1583, which as we have already seen, antagonized the native as well as *casado* traders of Cochin. The popular revolt which followed, was said to have had the support of king Kesava Rama Varma, who feared a mass diversion of trade from his port.[68] Though the conditions of the final agreement made on 8 January 1585 were so prepared as to satisfy the demands of the native king and his commercial associates, the *casado* traders of Cochin,[69] customs duty continued to be the bone of contention between the Portuguese and Kesava Rama Varma, all through the lifespan of the latter. Thus on 5 January 1598, he sent two ambassadors to the Viceroy Conde de Vidigueira, when a Chinese junk carrying the merchandise of the *casados* of Cochin and resting in Nagapatanam was asked by the Viceroy not to call the port of Cochin to pay customs duty for the commodities of the *casados*. Finally, even when the vessel did call at Cochin, nothing was unloaded there in spite of constant insistence from the chief officer (*Regedor mor*) of the king of Cochin.[70] It was a part of the Portuguese strategy to sidetrack the ruler of Cochin who was amassing huge wealth by way of customs duty, and to make the customs money accrue in Goa where the *Estado* establishments were suffering a severe financial crisis.[71] Still worse was the financial condition of the home government which was greatly preoccupied with the severe famine and the terrific pestilence that broke out in Portugal from November 1598 to August 1599.[72] The increasing strain on Portuguese finances necessitated the bypassing of the customs-house of the king of Cochin. This irritated the king who in his letter to the viceroy dated 19 September 1599, insisted that the merchandise which the *casados* of Cochin brought from the south (the commercial space east of Cape Comorin) must be unloaded in Cochin for the payment of regular customs duties. He also showed his displeasure when the the viceroy further attempted to prevent the Chinese ships carrying the merchandise of the *casados* from touching Cochin.[73]

This coincided, as mentioned by Conde de Vidigueira in his letter of 1599 to Philip I, with the mounting tensions between the Portuguese and the natives of Cochin who had rallied under Pandaro Paramo, the chief officer of the king of Cochin. Though it began as a dispute between a Brahmin, an officer (*Recebedor*) of the king of Cochin, and a citizen of Santa Cruz, it spread and turned into a revolt against the Portuguese. Actually it was the extension and popular expression of the anti-Portuguese feelings nurtured by the local ruler. The king Kesava Rama Varma who maintained deep ill-feeling against the Portuguese seems to have tacitly approved and kindled this popular revolt against the Lusitanians. This is further verified by the fact that the prince of Cochin, who intervening to save the situation and prevent the rebellion from spreading into the entire city, was deprived of all his charges and responsibilities by his father. In addition, the Lusitanian alliance with Calicut, the eternal enemy of Cochin, forged in order to capture Kunjali, increased the hostile feelings of the ruler of Cochin, against the Portuguese and the Zamorin. The latter immediately began a correspondence with Kunjali offering him every possible help. Another area of tension between the king of Cochin and the Portuguese consisted in the fortification of the city of Santa Cruz. The reasons for it were both political and commercial. The commercial reasons seem to have played a major role by this time. Both the local ruler and the *casados* of Cochin feared that the attempt to build a wall around the entire Portuguese settlement, especially one on the water-front, would hinder and close down the places which the private traders of the city were using for the trade in contraband items. This heightened the resistance to the attempts to fortify the city.[74]

It was against this background of tension that King Kesava Rama Varma died in September 1600 in Bengal (80 leagues away from the Ganges), where he had gone to immerse the mortal remains of his mother.[75] Prince Goda Varma, who ruled Cochin during his absence, and later for some time after the death of Kesava Varma, began to take strong anti-Portuguese steps. He sent men to kill Sidra Mena (Chandra Menon), the pro-Portuguese *regedor mor*. He, also demanded 12,080 *pardaos*, which the *Estado* owed the king of Cochin as *copa*-dues, as a condition for permitting the fortification of the city.[76] As the debts of the Portuguese to the king of Cochin increased with the mounting financial crisis, strain in the relationship between the two seems to have proportionately increased . On the death of Goda Varma in March 1601, Virakerala, who was then twenty-eight years old ascended the throne on 13 October 1602.[77] His reign coincided with the diminishing flow of spices from Cochin to Europe, whose root causes could be attributed to the tension in the hinterland that broke out between the pepper-growing group of the St. Thomas Christians and the Portuguese and to the consequent diversion of spices to the Coromandel coast directly from the production centres through the ghat route. There was no loading of ships in Cochin in 1604.[78] During the period between 1606 and 1609 (both years inclusive), no ship departed from Cochin to Portugal. The spices which were collected during these four years were sent to Lisbon only in 1610, but the volume thus sent was very meagre, i.e. only 4,170 quintals.[79] In the first decade of the seventeenth century only thirteen ships left India with pepper cargoes. Out of this, six ships departed in 1600 with 32,415 quintals of pepper, and four ships in 1603 with 21,349 quintals. In 1602, two ships departed from India with only 7,598 quintals.[80] Though there is no means of finding out the exact figure of pepper export from Cochin to Lisbon from this description which covers the volume of export trade from the whole of India (and this includes a lot of pepper from Karnataka) to Europe, it still throws light on the prevailing phenomenon, i.e. the transhipment of spices to Europe was irregular and very meagre, as compared to the total production in India which was estimated to be 2,58,000 quintals per year.[81] The only exception was in 1600 and 1603. Corresponding to this phenomenon of dwindling European trade, private trade, which was sponsored by the native king, thrived in the first decade of seventeenth century. As we have already seen, around 1605, the king of Cochin bagged about 60,000 *pardaos* annually from the customs,[82] which indicates that the private trade had risen up to double the volume, in comparison with the period from 1587 to 1598. By 1612 the customs revenue which the native ruler used to get from private trade went up to 70,000 to 80,000 *pardaos* [83] indicating a further increase . It also shows that the king of Cochin was following an increasingly pro-Asian trade policy, as Asian commerce brought him more revenue than the *copa* and the annual subsidies of the Portuguese, which in most cases, were not paid in time.[84]

This period, as indicated by the Viceroy Rui Lourenço de Tavara in his report on the purchase of pepper for the period between 1606 and 1610, also witnessed very poor organization as far as the procurement of the pepper was concerned. It was usually bought in winter, immediately before the arrival of the ships from Europe. This meant that the Portuguese could buy only that portion of pepper which remained after being taken to ghat route and other Asian destinations, or, unripe pepper. As the Portuguese, for want of sufficient money to pay the prices in advance, had not made much of an effort to buy and collect pepper during the harvest season which fell between late December and January, or during the period thereafter, especially in the months between February and May when it would be available in the market after proper seasoning, a great portion of it was taken to the ghat route.[85] Along with this organizational failure, was the corruption of the officials which made things worse in Cochin. There was much falsification of weights in the factory; two types of weights namely, the light quintal (45.9 kgs.) and heavy quintal (52.46 kgs.) were used for cheating.[86] Garcia de Melo, who came to Cochin in 1605 as the *Vedor da Fazenda*, was accused of serious corruption and was arrested and sent back to Lisbon in 1610.[87]

Meanwhile, with the decreasing flow of spices to Cochin, preference was given to the pepper ports of Kanara, the chief among them being Onor, Barcelor and Mangalore. The pepper ports of Kanara were safer and more secure compared to the port of Cochin which was open to Dutch threats of varying degrees, from 1602 onwards. Though the prospects for a high volume of pepper trade were found in Kanara by the Viceroy Dom Antonio de Noronha as early as 1565,[88] it seems that the Kanara pepper began to overtake Cochin's export index only by the beginning of the seventeenth century. In 1602, two ships from Portugal brought in 66,000 *cruzados* as pepper money. The Governor Archbishop Dom Alexis Meneses did not allow Garcia de Melo, the *Vedor da Fazenda* of Cochin to take this money for purchasing pepper from Cochin, on the ground that the Dutch were moving about Cochin. The pepper money was, then, taken to Kanara to procure sufficient cargo for the ships of *carreira*.[89]

With mounting financial strain on the Portuguese treasury, the *casados* of Cochin were invited to lend money to procure cargo for the Europe-bound vessels. As one Portuguese document testifies, though sufficient money used to reach Cochin and other pepper trading centres for the purchase of commodities during the period of contract trade, the situation changed with the re-introduction of crown trade. The money that came to India from Portugal was so meagre that very often cash was borrowed from the *casados* at an interest of ten per cent.[90] In 1606, an amount of

93,744 *xerafins* was borrowed by Garcia de Melo, the *Vedor da Fazenda* of Cochin, from the *casados* of Cochin at the rate of 10 for the purchase of 8,918 quintals of pepper from Cochin, Quilon, Cannanore and Malacca.[91] Besides this, some silver vessels used in the churches of Cochin and some belonging to the *casados*, as well, were pawned at the *casa da Misericordia* of Cochin under the initiative of the Bishop to raise sufficient money for the purchase of pepper in 1606.[92] The general financial condition of the Portuguese treasury in Cochin during these years was so bad that the soldiers and even the ecclesiastical office-holders including the priests, who were used to being paid punctually, did not receive their salaries for months.[93]

Meanwhile the Portuguese authorities made a contract with Jorge Rodrigues Solis, a ship-owner, to send vessels of not less than 500 tons, to India for the period between 1602 and 1608 (both inclusive). He was required to annually send seven ships to the East, out of which five were to be destined for India and the remaining two for Malacca. The Indiamen should take 1,000 soldiers, while the vessels to Malacca should take 400.[94] However, in this case shipping was not co-ordinated with trade. This contract for the equipment of ships to India coincided with an abortive attempt to farm out the distribution of the spices in Europe to contractors. The main aim behind this negotiation was to oust the Dutch from the markets of Germany, where the former had begun to supply spices to the East in great bulk by the end of the last decade of the sixteenth century. The contract was negotiated with João Conserbeque, the consul of the Germans and the contractors were expected to supply the Hanseatic cities of Hamburg, Lübeck and Danzig with Portuguese spices. The crown promised to sell pepper to the contractors at a reduced rate of 30 *cruzados*. Though this subsidized rate would cause an annual loss of 50,000 to 60,000 *cruzados* to the crown, it wanted to re-capture the European market, especially the German ones and thus to eliminate the Dutch from the pepper trade.[95] Though this project did not materialize, the Portuguese expelled the Dutch merchants from Lisbon in 1605 when Dom Pedro de Castilho was the Viceroy of Portugal.[96]

The Dutch who had made their successful voyage to the East as early as 1595 bypassing the Portuguese control system raised a severe threat to Portuguese commerce. The *Compagnie van Veere* formed in 1594, despatched five ships in 1595 from Texel under the command of Cornelius van Houtman. These vessels avoided all Portuguese stations by skipping India and sailing to Bantam in western Java through the Sundra straits.[97] During the period between 2 April 1595, and 21 December 1599, thirty-seven Dutch vessels moved to the East [98] out of which the first vessel departed for the Netherlands in 1597.[99] In 1602, the various Dutch companies were amalgamated into the *Vereenigde Oost Indische Compagnie* (VOC– The United East India Company) in order to reduce the rivalry of different companies.[100] Meanwhile, another trade rival had entered the waters of Indian Ocean, with the formation of East India Company (EIC) in 1600, which by Royal Charter was given the 'exclusive right to trade beyond the Cape of Good Hope'.[101] Though the first English embarkation in 1601 took place at a time when England was still at war with Spain and Portugal, the second British voyage was in 1604 when peace prevailed between the two nations.[102] Actually, it was the Dutch Company, which raised challenges to the Portuguese in Malabar, where the Dutch made their first appearance in Cochin in 1602,[103] and later in 1604, to make a treaty with the Zamorin.

The Dutch under Van der Hagen obtained permission to trade at Calicut and to build a fort for their protection.[104] Later, the Zamorin was visited by Paulus Van Caerden in 1607 and by Admiral Verhoff in 1608, when the ruler of Calicut asked the Admiral for six ships to occupy Goa and Cochin.[105] These developments occurred at a time, when Calicut was waging war with Cochin, as we have already seen. In the first decade of the seventeenth century, though the vessels from Netherlands were continuously operating against the Portuguese especially from 1603 on,[106] the Dutch threat did not assume critical dimensions initially as far as the trade of Cochin was concerned. This, as we have already seen, is further testified to by the high volume of intra-Asian trade of Cochin. Besides the casual attacks directed against Goa or Moçambique and the capture of Portuguese vessels, the main concentration of the Dutch was in Indonesia where they had conquered Jakarta in western Java. Converting its name into Batavia, they made it the chief Dutch naval and military base and centre of their administration in the East. The Twelve Years Truce (also known as the Truce of Antwerp 1609-21), which was secretly arranged in 1609 by Philip III's (Philip II of Portugal) Spanish minister, the Duke of Lerma, relatively decreased the danger from the Dutch to the Portuguese establishments in Malabar, for some time in the next decade. Though the Dutch expansion activities continued in the East even during this period and the Dutch envoys continued to visit Calicut in 1610 (Cornelis Jacobs Van Breekvelt and Hans Bullard from Coromandel), as well as in 1616 (Van den Broecke as instructed by Dutch Governor-General of Batavia), and there were cases when they even blockaded and captured Portuguese vessels,[107] the Dutch military operations in Malabar assumed alarming dimensions only by the end of the 1610, especially with the termination of the Antwerp Truce in 1621. However, the great number of Dutch vessels with high tonnage, which used to enter the Indian Ocean during this period, offered the greatest and very real challenge to the Portuguese, who were lagging far behind as far as shipping was concerned. Many of the Dutch ships had an average tonnage varying between 300 to 800 in the first decade of the seventeenth century, even though there existed some vessels which were of low tonnage. In the later years, this varied from 500 to 1100.[108] The following table indicating the movements of the Dutch and Portuguese vessels for the period between 1600 and 1663 shows how poor was the Portuguese performance.

TABLE VII-2: OUTWARD-BOUND VOYAGES TO ASIA

Year	Portugal		Netherlands[109]	
	Departure	Arrival in India	Departure	Arrival
1600-9[110]	68	49	96	91
1610-19	56	44	112	109
1620-29	67	43	145	135
1630-35	16	16	72	70
1636-40[111]	14	11 or 12	103	99
1641-50	44	32 or 33	160	158
1651-60	32	29 or 30	207	195
1661-65	9	8	112	107

TABLE VII-3: MOVEMENT OF SHIPS FROM THE EAST TO EUROPE

Year	Portugal[112]		Netherlands[113]	
	Departure	Arrival in Lisbon	Departure	Arrival in Netherlands
1601-10	31	25	76	69
1611-20	30	24	48	44
1621-30	22	16	69	66
1631-35	12	9	34	34
1636-40			47	46
1641-50			94	93
1651-60			103	102
1661-5			49	41

The homebound voyages of the Portuguese vessels had several problems in contrast with those of the Dutch. Besides the number of vessels in which the Portuguese stood far behind the Dutch, some of these ships were old and dilapidated. Overloading of such vessels with personal merchandise and liberty chests led to frequent wrecks. Though the continuous shipwrecks prompted the Portuguese authorities to intervene in 1625 with the 'Carrack's Bill of Lading',[114] the situation did not improve. There were also cases when some of the returning ships were captured either by the Dutch or by the English. Though the above table shows that the figure of loss was not extraordinarily high in comparison with the previous period, it also indicates that the Portuguese had been reduced to the size of pygmies before the Dutch as far as the movement of ships was concerned. For want of data, we are able to furnish only the details of the homebound voyages of the Portuguese vessels for the period up to 1635.

In the second decade of seventeenth century significant changes were noticeable in Cochin. A detailed picture of these changes connected with the pepper trade in Cochin and the fund raised for this trade during the period is given in papers dealing with the enquiry procedures against Diogo Coutinho, the *Vedor da Fazenda* of Cochin.[115] In 1610, only 1,24,000 *cruzados* reached Cochin as pepper money. In order to raise further funds for the purchase of pepper, Dom Diogo Coutinho borrowed 69,145 *xerafins* from the *casados* of Cochin at the rate of 10 per cent. In the month of December of the same year another loan of 52,831 *xerafins* was raised from the *casados* at the rate of nine per cent for a period of two years for the same purpose. In 1611, the amount borrowed from the *casados* increased to 71,200 *xerafins* and that too, at ten per cent. Out of this 1,93,176 *xerafins*, a portion, i.e. 36,192 *xerafins* was used to clear the debt of money which was borrowed earlier by Garcia de Melo from the *casados*.[116] The remaining portion was mostly used for buying pepper from Cochin, Panane (Ponnani), Pallur (Palayur), Chetua, Tanur, Cannanore and Parur.[117] This document also suggests that strenuous attempts were made to placate the merchants of the St. Thomas Christians and to win their co-operation for the purchase of pepper from the hinterland. The merchants of this community were given one *xerafin* extra for each *bhar* of pepper that they brought to Cochin as a special remuneration for not diverting the commodity to the ghat route or other destinations. Thus the merchants of the St. Thomas Christians earned 440 *xerafins* extra for 440 *bhars* of pepper. The Tarega (Tharaka) merchants, also belonging to this group, were given special prizes and gifts such as sandal wood and knives.[118] The Tarega (Tharaka) of Canhur (Kanjoor) and the Cassanar Alexander (a priest of this community), who received 1,000 and 1,250 *xerafins* respectively from Diogo Coutinho, were prominent merchants who co-operated with the Portuguese trade even during tense times. The Archbishop of Cranganore was given a special gift of 534 *xerafins* so that the St. Thomas Christians, who were subject to him, might loyally supply the spices only to the Portuguese.[119] These were all part of the design to bring the estranged communities back to co-operative ways.

Thus, raising funds from local sources and ensuring the co-operation of the estranged community of St. Thomas Christians, Diogo Coutinho succeeded in 1611, in loading 4,895 quintals of pepper in the ship of *Nossa Senhora dos Remedios*, and 3,511 quintals in the ship of *Santa Elena*, which happened to be the last vessels of the *carreira* to leave Cochin.[120] Out of the total volume of 4,40,991 kgs. of pepper collected in Cochin, 1,29,084 came from Quilon and Kayamkulam and 4,72,83 from Ponnani. With the help of a contract made with the Aderajão (Ali Raja) of Cannanore 52,498 kgs. were fetched from north Malabar. The share from Malacca was only 4,818 kgs. The rest of the 2,07,308 kgs. were collected from the hinterland of Cochin alone, and that too, because of the efforts made by Diogo Coutinho to purchase the co-operation of the estranged groups.[121] However, another aspect of this entire project was that the debt of the crown to the *casados* of Cochin increased to 76,972 *xerafins*.[122] Though this was a sum of money raised by Diogo Coutinho for the purchase of pepper, the crown could not repay it and this fact made the possibilities of taking loans from *casados* in the future somewhat difficult.[123]

After the departure of the ships *Nossa Senhora dos Remedios*, and *Santa Elena* (1611), the vessels of *Carreira da India* stopped going to Cochin to take pepper and other commodities directly from this port. It seems that the dwindling of pepper supply in Cochin because of the tensions in the hinterland, the extra expenses incurred in purchasing co-operation, and the fear of the Dutch must have prompted the Portuguese authorities to take such a decision. As the ships of the *carreira* began to depart only from Goa from 1612 onwards, pepper was taken first from Cochin to Goa in smaller vessels, often operated and manned by the *casados* of Cochin.[124]

However, this change in the route of the *carreira* adversely affected the private trade from Cochin to Lisbon, which was conducted, almost on a regular basis, in the ships of the *carreira* under the cover of liberty chests.[125] There was a general protest from the king of Cochin and the *casados* against this decision not to send the ships of the *carreira* to load directly from Cochin. The officials of the municipality of Cochin made continuous requests as late as 1624 to the Portuguese authorities to reconsider this decision and to despatch at least one vessel from Portugal to the port of Cochin, as it had been in the past.[126] But the Goan lobby, which wanted to centralize commerce there (it knew quite well that the centralization of Indo-European commerce in Goa would eventually help it to centralize the distributive trade there, as well as the intra-Asian commerce, upon which much of Cochin's prosperity depended) had gained the upper hand in decision-making. However, the petitions were rejected, saying that Cochin was unsafe because of the Dutch presence along the coast of Malabar and that the pepper of Kanara which was dearer to the Europeans was available in Goa in great quantity.[127] The availability of a relatively large volume of pepper in Goa from Kanara was a major reason to abandon the request of Cochin, where supply was fluctuating with the tensions in the hinterland. However, the pro-Cochin group argued that the pepper from Kanara, that was available in Goa in great volume, was very costly, consequently, the preference shown to the Kanara pepper over that of Cochin would mean heavy losses to the *Estado*. Actually, the price of one *bhar* pepper in Kanara was 73 *xerafins* while it was only 48 *xerafins* in Cochin. There was a price difference of 25 *xerafins* in each *bhar* of pepper. Nuno Vaz de Castelo Branco, the *vedor da Fazenda* of Cochin argues in 1618, that in that year itself 300 *bhars* of pepper bought from Mangalore caused a loss of 7,500 *xerafins* to the Portuguese treasury (as compared to the price in Cochin).[128] Even the Bishop of Cochin came out openly against the Goan lobby in 1619 saying that the decision to load all the vessels of *carreira* in Goa would mean an extra expense of 24,000 *pardaos* for each ship (extra expense incurred in the collection, transportation, weighing, loading and re-loading, etc., of the commodities in various places of shipment). Moreover the pepper that was bought from different ports reached Goa, very late which often delayed and put at risk the homebound vessels of the *carreira*. Since the pepper of Cochin was somewhat better (this statement contradicts the argument of the Goan lobby which says that Kanara pepper was the best) and cheaper of that which was available in India, the crown could save more than 30,000 *pardaos* in each ship, if the pepper were to be loaded in Cochin (instead of the costly pepper of Kanara).[129] Subsequent to this phenomenon, the distributive trade of Cochin which consisted mostly in exchanging the wares of Europe with Asian commodities declined drastically, once the vessels of *carreira* stopped touching this port.

During the period between 1612 and 1620 the pepper from Kanara formed two-thirds of the total export from India. The annual average of pepper transhipped from Karnataka increased to 6,480 heavy quintals.[130] The years following 1611, which were marked by a period when the *carreira* ships stopped taking pepper directly from Cochin and when the tension between the Portuguese and their native collaborators mounted, the pepper export from Cochin fell to its lowest ebb. During the period between 1612 and 1620, the annual average export of pepper from the whole of India to Lisbon was 9,219 heavy quintals out of which the annual average share from Cochin alone was less than 1500 heavy quintals.[131] The volume of pepper exported from Cochin in 1615 was 2,475 quintals[132] and in 1616 it was 4,000 quintals.[133] In the following years, it fell drastically. In 1618, it was only 491 quintals. In the next year, the pepper export from Cochin was 814 quintals, which again fell sharply in 1620 when only 83 heavy quintals of pepper were exported from Cochin.[134] The crisis in supply and finance was so acute that the efforts of the Viceroy Jeronimo de Azevedo, to pawn his gold and silver in 1617 to raise money for the annual pepper fleet to Cochin,[135] did not improve the figures of the export trade.

From 1612 onwards, began the mass exodus of *casado* traders from Cochin to the Coromandel coast, to trade in the pepper reaching there in great volume from the one-time hinterland of Cochin through the ghat route. Some of the *casados* even went to Ceylon, Bengal and Pegu as they found the trade atmosphere of Cochin worsening, with the diminishing pepper supply in Cochin. On 26 January 1615, Diogo Coutinho wrote that for the past three years (i.e. from 1612 on) the *casados*, leaving their wives and children in Cochin, were trading outside Cochin and did not touch the city of Santa Cruz. They used to take their commodities to Goa paying the customs there, which they should have done at Cochin.[136] The king of Cochin who came to know of it demanded this customs money which he calculated to be around 13,000-14,000 *pardaos* for himself.[137] By 1616, most of the enterprising *casado* merchants of Cochin left the city, pulling it into a critical phase as far as its commerce was concerned. This mass exodus of enterprising *casado* traders from the city and the bypassing of Cochin by some *casado* traders reduced the income of the king of Cochin. The heavy fall in the customs revenue of the native ruler made things still worse, which resulted in the straining of his relationship with the Portuguese. He lost no time in contacting the Dutch. In 1618, the king of Cochin invited the Dutch to visit his land assuring them that they would always be welcome there and requested the Dutch, then or later on, to expel the Portuguese who were treating him harshly.[138]

However, the threat from the Dutch, who were bound by the Antwerp Truce, did not take on any serious and critical dimension in this decade. In its place, the English, who were keeping a low profile in the first decade of the seventeenth century, began to raise serious challenges to the Portuguese. Open conflicts between the two nations broke out, off Surat in 1612. The English, who were led by Captain Thomas Best defeated the Portuguese force and established their first base in Surat in December of the same year.[139] The Portuguese were again defeated off Swally near Surat in 1614-15 by the naval force under Thomas Best.[140] This was followed by the entry of the English into Malabar coast. In March 1615-16, Captain Keelinge arrived at Cranganore (which was then conquered and occupied by the Zamorin) and obtained liberty of trade and permission from the Zamorin to open a factory. Both the English and the ruler of Calicut had entered into an agreement to join forces and to expel the Portuguese from Cochin.[141]

The third decade of the seventeenth century put the European trade of Cochin into a very awkward position. On 31 March 1621, King Philip III (Philip II of Portugal) died in Madrid and Philip IV ascended the throne.[142] This coincided with the termination of the Antwerp Truce and the renewal of open conflict with the Dutch. The Dutch plans to attack Cochin and other Portuguese possessions on the Malabar coast had already begun as early as 1919, when the Anglo-Dutch treaty was concluded for concerted military operations against the Portuguese. According to this treaty, a joint fleet consisting of nine ships and two pinnaces, with 754 men on the Dutch side and 385 men on the English vessels, was despatched in the autumn of 1621 under Admiral Dedell and Vice-Admiral Fitzherbert. They were advised to blockade and attack the Portuguese by sailing along the coast from Cape Comorin to Cochin and thence to Goa. The joint operation was also meant to make use of trade opportunities availed by the native kings besides making a surprise attack on the Portuguese.[143] Though the result of this enterprise was not known in detail, it seems to have marked the beginning of open conflict between the Dutch and the Portuguese off Cochin and in the succeeding years it assumed alarming dimensions. Against the background of frequent blockade of Portuguese vessels, and further troubled by a scarcity of funds and very little military-defence materials, Cochin with its ruined fortress could be saved, wrote the Viceroy Francisco da Gama in 1623, only by making peace with the Dutch on any terms, even to allowing them to trade in Portuguese ports.[144] But in the European atmosphere of the Thirty-Years War, waged between the Catholics and the Protestants, nobody in the home government thought about the advantage of such peace efforts with the protestant Dutch traders. The general tendency was to settle things through the power of the sword.

Meanwhile, with the fall of Ormuz on 22 April 1622, into the hands of the English and the Shah of Persia,[145] Cochin's link with the traditional caravan route was almost cut off. The Dutch and British blockade of the gates of the Persian Gulf and the Red Sea, not only made the private trade with the eastern Mediterranean difficult,[146] but also drained the profit of the king of Cochin, which he gathered either directly by sending ships to these destinations or indirectly, by collecting taxes from those who participated in the commerce of this traditional route. The continuous strain on the income of the native king irritated him further, which led to frequent clashes with the Portuguese. Because of financial difficulties, the Portuguese could not pay him *copa* from 1622 on, and we hear that he was not paid the annual *copa* money for the next ten years, which further worsened the relationship between the two.[147] Meanwhile, Calicut, which had been continuously waging wars with Cochin for more than quarter of a century, began to be frequently visited by the Dutch in the hope of fishing in these troubled waters. In 1625, Van Speult made a treaty with the Zamorin by which the latter was obliged to supply 3,000 *candis* of pepper to the VOC.[148]

During the years after 1621, a long war broke out in the interior, which hindered the flow of spices through the ghat route. With the temporary closure of the ghat route, more pepper began to reach Cochin, which even reduced the price of the commodity there.[149] This, in spite of the strained relationship between the native ruler and the Portuguese and the mounting threats from the Dutch, was followed by an increase in the volume of export from Cochin during the period from 1621 till 1630, which even superseded the export from Kanara. The annual average of pepper export from Cochin increased to 5,106 quintals while that of Kanara was only 4,888 quintals.[150] Against this background, attempts were made to fulfil the oft-repeated orders from the Lisbon authorities that two-thirds of the pepper be bought from Cochin.[151] But that target was beyond reach. With the termination of the Calicut-Cochin war in 1626, which was brought about by the mediation of the Rector of the Jesuit college of Cochin,[152] Calicut abstained, temporarily, from providing a base for Dutch operations. The end of coastal wars had positive results on the export trade of Cochin. A relatively higher volume of pepper was collected in Cochin for transhipment to Lisbon in the atmosphere of peace that followed. An agreement was even reached between the king of Cochin and the Viceroy in this changed atmosphere of 1626, to send one ship of pepper to Portugal. But as Diogo Coutinho, the *Vedor da Fazenda* was not included in the negotiations, the entire project had to be cancelled.[153] However, the period immediately after the peace with Calicut, namely, from 1626 to 1629, witnessed an increase in the annual export of pepper from Cochin. It rose to 4947 heavy quintals.[154]

Though the peace with Calicut contributed to the relative improvement of the European trade from Cochin, the relationship of the king of Cochin, Vira Kerala Varma with the Portuguese continued to be strained. The native ruler was distancing himself more and more from the Portuguese as the years passed by. In his policy decisions, he was greatly influenced by Jewish councillors, which always gave an anti-Portuguese tone to his activities.[155] It is believed that Samuel Castiel, who had, by this time, begun to serve the king of Cochin as a translator and interpreter (a capacity which gave a lot of opportunities for manipulation) was the most important one among them.[156] Vira Kerala Varma was looking for new allies. Eventually he began diplomatic contacts with Iskandar Muda, the Sultan of Aceh. The initial steps of this relationship started with the arrival of Acehnese ambassadors in Malabar in 1627, where they were warmly received and protected by the king of Cochin in his kingdom.[157] Meantime, the estranged king was trying to re-take the land and properties granted by his predecessors to the Portuguese under various pretexts. The most striking among these, was the attempt in 1629 to capture the island of Bendure (Venduruthi), which had been granted to Dom Gaspar de Azevedo by an early king of Cochin and which he enjoyed as his personal property.[158] The king re-took it, amidst a lot of protests and tensions, under the pretext of arresting a murderer.[159]

The general atmosphere of mutual mistrust and ill-feeling was exhibited by yet another incident in 1630, when one *Desembargador* from Goa came to Cochin with orders from the viceroy to enter in to a contract with the king of Cochin to make one *galleão* (which could accommodate sixty pieces of artilleries), one *braça* and two *gales*. The *Desembargador* asked for security for the money which he was entrusting to the king for the construction of the ships. The ruler of Cochin, who was deeply irritated by this, replied: 'the kings are not required to give security'. With this reply, the project was wound up.[160] Still worse was its effect, as these incidents intensified tension between the native ruler and the Portuguese at a time, when, as the same document states, the Company office of Goa was 'waiting each moment eagerly' for the arrival of the fleet from Cochin with pepper.[161] Thus, though the peace with Calicut offered a favourable atmosphere for European trade, the estrangement of the king of Cochin hindered the Portuguese from achieving any remarkable progress in this export trade, making the indexes of export trade fall far below the volume of the sixteenth century.

This coincided with two different organizational arrangements which the Portuguese made in Cochin, besides the crown's commerce, to conduct pepper trade with Europe. As we shall see later, the financially prosperous *casados* of Cochin were made to participate in European commerce by allowing them to send pepper directly to Lisbon from 1628 onwards, and almost simultaneously, i.e. from 1629 onwards, the Portuguese India company also began to enter into the export trade of Cochin. Thus, though there were two different channels for European commerce, besides the crown's trade, the quantum of pepper that was carried through the ghat route increased considerably by the 1630s with the termination of wars in the interior. The resumption of the ghat route commerce made it difficult to get pepper in Cochin at the old prices. So an attempt was made to attract more pepper to Cochin by increasing the price in 1632.[162]

However this did not seem to have helped to improve the European trade which was almost on the verge of extinction. The period from 1635 to 1645 which was ruled by Goda Varma witnessed the tension between the Portuguese and the native ruler reaching its highest boiling point. In 1635, the Muringur *tavazhi*, which was about to become extinct, was merged into the Elaya *tavazhi*, and the heir apparent of the latter branch of the royal family, Goda Varma, was crowned the king of Cochin.[163] He was often described as a great enemy of the Portuguese,[164] which also suggests that in a situation of declining fortunes, he was trying to distance himself from the Portuguese. By 1640, the Elaya *tavazhi* was reduced to two members: himself and a princess. So he adopted some princes from all the surviving collateral branches namely, Palluruthi, Chazhur and even from the anti-Portuguese branch of the Mutta *tavazhi*.[165] Adoption of a prince from the Mutta *tavazhi*, whom the Portuguese had disliked all through the period, and whose members they always had prevented from coming to power, was suggestive of the anti-Lusitanian feelings that Goda Varma nurtured. Though this happened at a time when Portugal regained its independence from Spain (1640), and Dom João IV from the house of Bragança became the king of Portugal, which was followed by a ten-year truce signed between the Lusitanians and Holland,[166] Goda Varma was fully aware of the declining position of the Portuguese in the East. They were on the verge of being replaced by the Dutch. The latter had already made a treaty with the king of Kandy as early as 1638, and captured Trincomalee in 1639 and Negombo as well as Galle in 1640.[167] This was followed by the fall of Malacca in 1641,[168] which marked the severing of the navigational lines of the Portuguese with South-East Asia permanently. Meanwhile, the Dutch increasingly began to use Ceylon as a base for their operations in Malabar.[169] On 20 May 1642, the ruler of Porcad, a former ally of the Portuguese and of the king of Cochin, entered into a treaty with the Dutch for the pepper trade.[170] In 1643, about 2,36,584 lbs of pepper and 3,043 lbs of dry ginger were bought by VOC, from Malabar.[171] On 1 March 1643, the king of Kayamkulam entered into a treaty with P. S. Groes, a senior merchant of VOC, by which the former agreed to deliver all the pepper produced in his territory to the Dutch.[172] With the deepening of Dutch commercial operations along the Malabar coast strengthened by the political treaties, the general political scene in Cochin changed considerably.

Unprecedented in the history of both the Cochins, tension fomented acutely between the natives of *Cochin de Cima* and the citizens of the city of Santa Cruz by the 1640s. On 17 August 1642, the *patare regedor mor* (the chief officer) of the king of Cochin and his people were said to have destroyed the statues of St. Mary and St. Antony. It was also pointed out that they broke a big cross and made a ladder out of it.[173] The tempo of the conflict increased with the destruction of a church in Bendurte (Venduruthi), of crosses in Palaurte (Palluruthi), occupation of palm-trees of the *casados* in the region of Sam Tomé.[174] These excesses were said to have been part of the reactions to the murder of a *regedor* (officer) of the king of Cochin by the Portuguese in 1630. Besides this, cow slaughter in the city (in 1643 there were one hundred and fifty cases of cow slaughter in the city of Santa Cruz), frightening and disturbing the people by shooting of cannon, were said to have been the chief atrocities that provoked the inhabitants of native Cochin.[175] Underneath these religious tensions and mutual accusations, one can observe a wide gap of estrangement in the relationship between the Portuguese and the natives, which could also be explained as the exteriorization of the tensions that existed between the native ruler and the Portuguese. The tense situation adversely affected the meagre trade which the Portuguese were conducting in low profile. In 1643, it was said that the king of Cochin did not allow anything to come to the Portuguese city and the general atmosphere was almost like being under economic sanctions.[176]

In order to establish a good relationship with the native ruler, the city of Santa Cruz sent Antonio de Pinho da Costa, João Correia da Silveira and Miguel Freire Dalmeida, all persons with experience and good contacts with Goda Varma.[177] The representation yielded fruits and an agreement was made between the king of Cochin and the Portuguese in the church of Mattancherry on 22 July 1643, mutually pledging to remedy the excesses on both sides.[178] But this peace seems to have only short-lived, as from August of the same year, we hear about further tension between the two parties.[179] These tensions culminated in 1643, with the murder by some *casados* of Samuel Castiel, who was an influential Jewish trader of Cochin and very close to Goda Varma. His role as the interpreter and translator of the king of Cochin was believed to have been used to infuse anti-Portuguese feelings in the latter, this perhaps being the reason why Samuel Castiel was selected as the target of attack.[180]

By the middle of the 1640s, with the termination of the Thirty-Years war, the position of the Dutch in the east was greatly improved by the treaty of Westphalia. Meanwhile, with the death of Goda Varma in 1645, a feud broke out in the royal family of Cochin between the Palluruthi *tavazhi* and the member adopted from the Mutta *tavazhi*.[181] In course of time, in the internal conflicts and royal intrigues, which had shaken the very structure of the Perumpadappu Swarupam, the old queen gained the upper hand. She expelled the member of the Mutta *tavazhi*, who was then ruling the kingdom of Cochin, and instead placed one of her nephews on the throne in 1653. This, being contrary to the tradition of the land, created a lot of opposition from the kings of the neighbourhood, especially from Carturte (Kadathuruthy, the seat of Vadakkenkur kingdom), from the kingdoms of Paru (Parur), Mangate (Alengad), Rapolim (Edappilly) and of course from the Zamorin, as well.[182] Paying little attention to this opposition, the queen approached the Portuguese authorities to get approval for her nephew as the official ruler and get him crowned with a crown of gold, which Dom Manuel had sent to India through Francisco da Almeida in 1505 to crown the then king of Cochin.[183] At the beginning, i.e. till 1655, the Portuguese tried to maintain neutrality in this family feud, neither supporting the steps of the queen nor opposing the prince of the Mutta *tavazhi*.[184]

But later, the Portuguese seem to have changed their approach to favour the queen's choice. The change in the stand of the Portuguese must have been caused by the Dutch conquest of Colombo in 1656,[185] which gave out the message that the danger to the Portuguese strongholds in Malabar was imminent. Even in this changed situation, the old queen went further with her own schemes and plans. In 1658, ignoring the claims of the Mutta *tavazhi*, five princes from the Tanur (Vettathu) royal family were adopted and given the right to succeed.[186] This further heightened the tension. The prince of the Mutta *tavazhi* appealed to the Zamorin, who immediately came forward to champion the former's cause. The Portuguese supported the Tanur adoptees.[187] In 1661, the Zamorin, the prince of the Mutta *tavazhi* and Paliathachan (the hereditary prime minister of Cochin and the chief of the island of Vaipin) made an agreement with the Dutch to capture Cochin, and offered every help for the expedition.[188] In the ensuing battle, which was fought mainly to capture Cochin, the ruling king of Cochin and his two nephews (adoptees from the Tanur royal family) were killed, and the old queen arrested and taken as a captive.[189] Though all the resources of the kingdom of Cochin and the neighbouring places like Angamali were mobilized to defend the city of Cochin,[190] it fell before the combined forces of the Dutch-Zamorin-Mutta *tavazhi* axis on 5 January 1663.[191] Goda Varma, a Tanur adoptee and the heir apparent to the throne of Cochin was expelled from the kingdom by the Dutch. Even after losing everything, this intrepid warrior with a handful of soldiers continued fighting for the Portuguese till 1680, with all the loyalty of a friend and a collaborator.[192]

During the years between 1631 to 1634 the annual average of crown trade from India was 7,089 quintals.[193] In 1635, the total pepper supplied from Cochin and Quilon for two ships named *Capitania* and *Nossa Senhora de Belem* (under crown trade) was only 4,910 quintals.[194] But in the subsequent years, amidst the mounting tensions, the European trade from Cochin seems to have reached its lowest level.

Though there are no continuous documents available for quantifying the volume of trade for this period, a narrow and feeble strand of European commerce is visible at random intervals. It suggests that besides the *casado* trade with Lisbon, which continued to exist almost up to 1640, crown trade also continued simultaneously. But the increase of the pepper price in Malabar made the transactions less frequent. The frequent Dutch blockade made things still worse in Malabar and Kanara, as well. Thus, in 1637, though pepper money was brought to Cochin, Quilon and Kanara for the purchase of the commodity, and a contract with Sancara da Gama was signed to obtain 2,000 quintals of pepper from Kanara, the Portuguese did not get sufficient pepper to load the ship *S. João de Cruz*. So it was decided to fill the space with 1,200 quintals of cinnamon brought from Ceylon.[195] In March 1641, the Viceroy sent twelve ships of the fleet to bring pepper from Cochin to Goa from where the cargo was despatched to Lisbon.[196] Very often, the lack of appropriate exchange money created problems, even during this period. On 29 November 1643, a request was made to the crown to send pepper money to Cochin, Quilon and to Kanara only in the gold coin called *São Tomé* (usually the pepper money that was despatched during this period was in uncoined gold and silver in the form of Spanish reals-of-eight. But in all the pepper transactions in Malabar and Kanara, the gold *São Tomé*, which was struck at the mint in Goa since 1548, was used). For want of this coin, the factors were finding it difficult to get the necessary pepper for the ships of the kingdom.[197] But even then the European commerce managed to operate. In 1648, besides pepper, cinnamon from Ceylon and bastard cinnamon from Cochin and Quilon were sent to Lisbon through the liberty chests.[198]

Even during the troubled years of the 1650s pepper was collected from Cochin for European commerce. Thus, on 23 September 1654, we hear that 1,23,537 kgs. of pepper were taken from Cochin and Quilon. The share from Cochin was

TABLE VII-4: THE CROWN'S PEPPER TRADE WITH COCHIN[199]

Year	Pepper in kgs.	Years	Pepper in kgs.
1600	17,04,163	1621	2,26,627
1602	3,98,591	1622	18,046
1603	11,19,969	1623	3,24,098
1610	2,18,758	1624-5	1,99,138
1611	4,40,991	1626	3,69,843
1613	57,863	1627	5,07,413
1615	4,05,093	1628	1,90,245
1616	2,15,086	1629	1,94,889
1617	68,408	1630	4,20,047
1618	25,758	1634	1,51,767
1619	42,702	1635	2,57,579
1620	4,354	1654	1,23,537

73,548 kgs. while that of Quilon was 49,989 kgs.[200] The Europe-bound vessels were loaded with Cochin pepper even in 1656,[201] showing that the trade did not die out completely in Cochin even though the various internal and external tensions that had already begun to suck the vitality of its economic activities, reached their highest level.

However the crown trade formed only one of the three strands of European commerce. The Portuguese India Company and the *casados* of Cochin also undertook the European commerce from Cochin as a different organizational arrangement. So both these alternative commercial arrangements are dealt with here, in order to better understand the Indo-European commerce organized in Cochin.

3. INDO-EUROPEAN TRADE FROM COCHIN THROUGH THE PORTUGUESE INDIA COMPANY (1629-1634)

Inspired by the Dutch and the English East India Companies, a company named Portuguese India Company (PIC) was founded to conduct trade with India.[202] The idea of the company, whose initial discussions can be traced back to as early as 1619, got the special attention of the Portuguese authorities by 1624, with the work of Dom Jorge Mascarenhas. On 27 August 1628, the Portuguese India Company was founded by royal decree. It received a sixty-eight clause charter.[203] The liberal contributions from the crown, which amounted to 15,00,000 *cruzados* and formed almost two-thirds of the total investment and from various municipalities of Portugal whose contribution was about 3,18,867 *cruzados*[204] provided the financial assets for the company. Unlike other European companies, which had powers to found factories, organize settlements, make war and peace, sign treaties, and govern the Asians and Europeans in their trading posts, the Portuguese India Company did not exercise political and military powers. Actually it was grafted on to an existing administrative system and was required to perform only commercial functions.[205] In Lisbon, the company had a board of directors consisting of a president and six directors. All the directors, except Garcia de Melo and Luis de Figueiredo Falcão, and the president, Jorge Mascarenhas (who were all officers in the royal service), were members of the Lisbon business community. Some of these directors such as Garcia de Melo (the former *vedor da Fazenda* of Cochin (1605-10), who was suspended in 1610 for malpractices, and Francisco Dias Mendes de Britto (whose father had been a member of the syndicate which contracted for the pepper trade with India for the five-year period 1592-7) were associated with Cochin in one way or another.[206] Under this board set up by Lisbon, a subordinate board of administration was organized in Goa after the arrival of the Viceroy Dom Miguel de Noronha, the fourth Count of Linhares, in October 1629.[207] In Cochin, the Company's affairs were handled by an administrator whose name was Antonio de Pinho da Costa.[208] Pepper collected from Cochin was sent in small vessels to Goa for further transhipment to Lisbon.

In order to conduct trade, the company despatched during the period between 1629 and 1634, nine large carracks. The company's first ships, which brought with them the new Viceroy, the Count of Linhares, reached Goa in 1629 and the second lot of outward-bound ships reached in 1630. In 1631, the company vessels had to cancel the voyage and return, because of bad weather, while the attempt to send three ships in May 1632, also failed. The delays and losses which it suffered in these two years worsened the financial position of the company. It became increasingly difficult to meet the expenses of PIC. Coinciding with this financial crisis, there was strong criticism that the company had only decreased the trade of Portugal with India and that, besides spending all the capital given, it had incurred a net loss. A lot of money was wasted on the duplicated arrangements made for the company.[209] Liquidation of the company and resumption of the Indian trade by the Treasury Council was the only solution that appeared acceptable to the Lisbon authorities. On 12 April 1632, the crown declaring that the company was in too poor a financial condition for further operations, and that it had failed to attract private capital for Indian trade for which it was formed, officially announced the liquidation of the Portuguese India Company.[210] Though the company was liquidated in 1633, the last company ships left Goa for Portugal in 1634. The trade conducted through the company during the period between 1629 and 1634 is dealt with here.

Besides pepper, which accounted for 81 per cent of India's total export to Portugal in 1630, 96 per cent in 1631 and 98 per cent in 1633, other commodities such as indigo, saltpetre, cowries, rice, and ebony were also exported to Lisbon. In 1630, about 1,500 bales of rice, 1,638 *paras* of cowries, 7,682 kgs. of saltpetre, and 14,973 kgs. of indigo were taken to Europe. Saltpetre exported in 1631 was of 4,370 kgs., but in 1633 it accounted to only 2,622.[211] During this period between 1629 and 1634, when the Indian trade was left to the PIC, pepper from Cochin and other spice ports entered Lisbon through channels other than that of company.[212]

TABLE VII-5: VOLUME OF PEPPER EXPORT UNDER COMPANY TRADE [213]

Year	Pepper in kgs.
1630	5,72,194
1631	4,76,376
1633	5,09,174
1634	4,75,410

This gives the impression that the crown trade was not fully suppressed during this phase. In the meantime, the *casados* of Cochin were also furnishing the metropolis with pepper in relatively significant quantity.

4. THE PEPPER TRADE OF THE *CASADOS* OF COCHIN WITH PORTUGAL (1628-1638)

This was another arrangement made in Cochin to revive the trade and to ensure greater supply of pepper in Lisbon, on the basis of a royal letter dated 17 April 1626. It was on 9 January 1627, that the Portuguese authorities in Goa made the contract with André Simões, a *casado* of Cochin, to send one *naveta* (ship) every year to Portugal. With this, the *casados* were given an opportunity to take part in Indo-European commerce. This *naveta* was supposed to carry at least 2,000 quintals of pepper. According to the conditions of the contract, if the pepper-money were provided by the crown, the ship-owning citizens of Cochin would be paid 4½ *cruzados* for every quintal of pepper taken to Portugal. If the pepper-money was not given by the crown, the *casados* could collect the pepper from Cochin and Quilon according to the order of the *Vedor da Fazenda* of Cochin and send it to the kingdom. There they would get nineteen *cruzados* for each quintal upon the delivery of cargo. But the ship-owner had to bear all the expenses and the risk factors. The money would be paid to the *casados* within thirty days after the delivery of pepper. The pepper of the *casados* unloaded and sold to the *Casa da India*, would be free of the usual duties and levies which were charged on pepper brought in by others.[214] The commodity that was entrusted by the *casados* in the *Casa da India* would not be mixed up with other consignments of pepper and the factor of the *naveta* would be given a key to the warehouse where it was stored. It was the *Vedor da Fazenda* of Cochin who had to examine and decide on the quality of pepper, and give a certificate as to whether the pepper was to be allowed to be taken to the kingdom or prohibited, depending on the quality.[215]

There was a desire, when this agreement was contracted, to make the king of Cochin participate in this trade of the *casados*. So a clause was inserted requesting the native ruler to enter into this contract with 2,000 to 3,000 *xerafins* or with an amount as he desired. It was also stipulated that the shipowners should pay the customs duties due to the king of Cochin. This contract was to be made known to the officers of the municipal council of Cochin, so that other citizens of the city might also join this enterprise.[216]

The ship-owners could send up to 800 *paras* of cowries in their vessels to Portugal, on condition that they might sell the commodity only to the king or that they could sell it to others, but with royal permission. They could also take with them 150 *bhars* of cinnamon coming from Ceylon, on the order of the Viceroy. The Viceroy would provide the ship-owners, technical experts such as the pilot, assistant pilot, sailors and 4 *bombardeiros*.[217] The captain and other officials of the *naveta* were entitled to the privileges of liberty chests and other provisions enjoyed by the officers of the vessels of *Carreira da India*. The Portuguese authorities would provide them with ten to twelve pieces of artillery and the necessary gun-powder.[218] The duration of this first contract was three years[219] which could be renewed, or re-made in the next decade, as well.

The first *naveta* under this contract left Cochin to Lisbon in 1628 with a cargo of more than 2,000 quintals of pepper.[220] The second *naveta*, whose captain was Francisco Freire de Andrade and which left Cochin on 22 December 1629, carried more than 3,500 quintals of pepper. It reached Lisbon in 1630.[221]

Unfortunately, we do not have details for the *naveta* which departed from Cochin in 1630. Meanwhile, there arose a dispute in Lisbon between the officials of the *Casa da India* and the agent of the *casados* over the payment of duties on the pepper of 1629. The agent of the *casados* also argued that the price must be raised above nineteen *cruzados*. The captain of the *naveta*, Francisco Freire de Andrade submitted a petition to the court at Valladolid and thus succeeded in delivering the cargo without paying any duties. But the purchase price remained the same.[222]

We do not have enough evidence for the *naveta* trade of the *casados* in the years immediately after the termination of the first contract. But it is highly probable that against the background of the declaration, which the crown made in the early 1630s that settlers from any part of the *Estado* could send vessels on the Cape route with due permission from the council of the state of Goa,[223] the *naveta* trade continued, at least sporadically.

The next known contract for the *naveta* trade from Cochin was made in 1635. However, it seems that this contract was made not with the individual *casados* but with the municipal council of the city of Cochin. It was in 1635 that the city of Cochin made a request for permission to send one *naveta* each year to conduct trade with the kingdom.[224] In 1636, a *naveta* of the *casados* was loaded in Cochin under the supervision of Antonio de Pinho da Costa, who had been earlier nominated to the post of administrator of the Portuguese India Company in Cochin. For want of enough pepper, he persuaded the viceroy to get the permission to take on cinnamon instead.[225] This and the *naveta* of the following year (1637), as well, reached the kingdom, and their captains received the payment upon the delivery of the cargo in the *Casa da India*.[226] The last *naveta* of this series, called *Santa Maria Madre de Deus*, left Cochin for Portugal under the captaincy of Luis de Freitas de Maçedo on 11 February 1638. Five months after departing from Cochin, it was forced to put in at Moçambique. Finally, the *naveta* reached Lisbon in May 1639, almost fifteen months after its departure from Cochin.[227] Cinnamon brought from Ceylon was one of the chief commodities laden from Cochin, even in this *naveta*, *Santa Maria Madre de Deus*. Upon reaching Lisbon, Luis de Freitas de Maçedo, the captain of the *naveta* asked for new and fresh valuation for this commodity which he had entrusted to the *Casa da India*.[228] Besides spices, the *casados* used to despatch diamonds and other precious stones to Portugal in their *navetas*. In the *naveta*, which departed from Cochin in 1638, Gaspar Ribeiro had sent diamonds and some other precious stones through a sailor to Lisbon, which were later seized by the captain of the fortress of Cascaes.[229]

Though details of the volume of pepper exported in the *navetas* is not available for all the years of this period, the terms of the contract, which was made with the *casados*, allows us conclude that almost 2,000 quintals of pepper or a mixed cargo of pepper and cinnamon of the the same weight, departed from Cochin to Lisbon in each year.

5. TOTAL VOLUME OF EXPORTS FROM INDIA TO EUROPE: 1570-1663

Pepper and other commodities taken from India during this period at different phases through different channels and arrangements are given below, so that we may get an overall view of Indian trade with Europe. This table includes the cargo taken from the whole of India including Kanara, Cochin and the other ports in Malabar. The commodities taken through contract traders, crown ships, Portuguese India Company and *casado navetas* are combined together, wherever applicable, to present in Table VII-6.[230]

For the period between 1636 and 1663, very little data is available for quantifying the trade. However, the figure of 1654 gives a rough picture of the trade that was carried on during these troubled days. A graphic presentation of these trade activities would show how the mounting tensions from within, i.e. from their one-time collaborators as well as from outside, i.e. from the European rival powers, had slowed down, at different phases and stages, the flow of pepper to Portugal after 1592. It also shows that, in spite of the various trade arrangements made at different times, the index of pepper trade of the seventeenth century often remained far below than that of the contract trade of 1586-91.

Pepper formed almost 70 to 96 per cent of India's total trade with Portugal, even though the pepper export fell to probably 50 per cent of the average level of the sixteenth century commerce. Indigo, which was in great demand in Europe as a blue dye and grown in north India especially in Sarkhej in Gujarat, and Biana near Agra, often took second place. In 1587 and 1588, a total of 4,457 quintals and in

TABLE VII-6: PEPPER EXPORT TO EUROPE

Year	Pepper in kgs.	Years	Pepper in kgs.
1582	11,27,675	1616	8,31,019
1587	6,29,715	1617	2,30,142
1588	12,04,409	1618	6,08,064
1589	15,75,703	1619	5,71,394
1590	12,42,121	1620	3,14,708
1592	8,15,021	1621	3,97,962
1593	2,62,336	1622	3,08,360
1594	3,41,792	1623	4,80,429
1595	9,23,697	1624-5	11,11,228
1596	1,42,349	1626	5,23,026
1597	8,87,821	1627	7,77,981
1598	4,14,093	1628	4,10,289
1600	17,04,163	1629	4,72,402
1602	3,98,591	1630	5,72,194
1603	11,19,969	1631	4,76,376
1610	2,18,758	1632	29,640
1611	4,40,991	1633	5,09,174
1612	4,98,842	1634	4,75,410
1613	4,19,785	1635	2,57,579
1614	3,35,849	1654	1,23,537
1615	5,43,223		

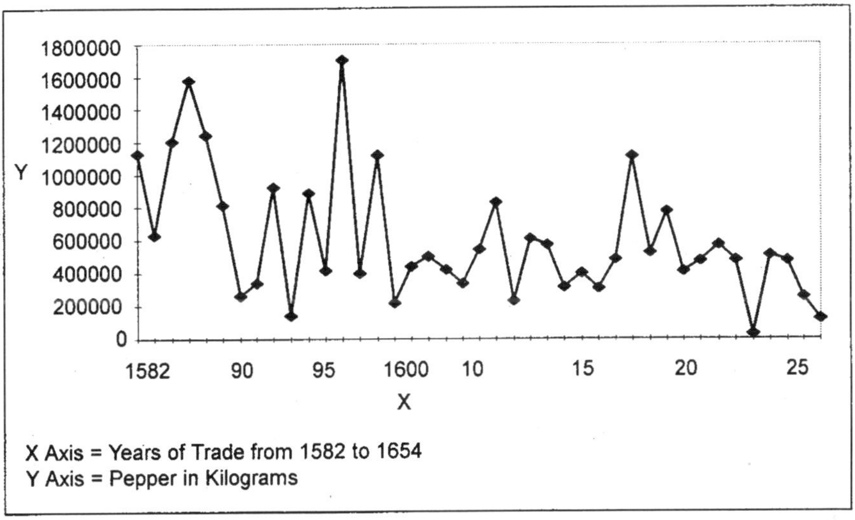

Graph 7: Cochin's Trade of Pepper with Europe during the period between 1570-1654.[231]

1600, about 1918 bales of indigo were exported to Europe. But during the period between 1601 and 1610, the annual average of indigo was only 215 quintals.[232] The export of this commodity in 1616 was 1,227 quintals 2 *arrobas*, in 1617, it was 1,500 quintals. But in the following two years it fell sharply: 825 quintals in 1618 and 794 quintals and 2 *arrobas* in 1619.[233] In 1630, indigo was 11 per cent of the total value of the Portuguese India Company's exports.[234] The export of cinnamon, another spice which all through this period was brought from Ceylon, was 1,598 quintals for 1587 and 1735 quintals for 1588. In 1600, it rose to 3,934 quintals. However in the first decade of the seventeenth century, the average annual export of cinnamon fell to 962 quintals.[235] As we have already seen, after 1635, with the diminishing availability of pepper, cinnamon began to occupy a substantial portion of the cargo space of the Europe-bound vessels. Both the crown vessels and the *casado navetas* began to increasingly carry cinnamon to Portugal, as they failed to procure the required quantity of pepper.[236] The export of ginger, another spice grown in Malabar, fluctuated all through this period. The volume in 1587 was 499 quintals, in 1588, it was 1750; but in 1600 it decreased to 899 quintals. The annual average of ginger exported to Lisbon for the period between 1601 and 1610 was only 316 quintals.[237] As we have already seen, after the fall of Ternate in 1570, cloves, nutmeg, mace and other South-East Asian spices were exported less frequently from India to Portugal. Only 388 quintals of nutmeg, 382 quintals of cloves and 99 quintals of mace were exported during the two-year period of 1587 and 1588. Of these three spices, only cloves occupied a somewhat significant place in the cargo list of the succeeding years. In 1600, a volume of 3,114 quintals of cloves was sent to Lisbon and during the period between 1601 and 1610, the annual average of this commodity exported from India was only 249 quintals.[238] Silk and textiles, coming from Bengal, Cambay and the Coromandel coast, formed an important cargo of the Portugal-bound vessels. In 1587, about 372 chests and 411 bales of textiles and silk were exported; however, in 1588 the export of cloth increased to 2,004 chests. In 1600, the five ships that departed from India took with them 414 chests, 151 big bales and 442 small bales of cloth. There was an average of 296 chests, 289 big bales and 1091 small bales of textiles and silk in the commodity list for the export trade of the period between 1601 and 1610.[239]

Saltpetre, which was in short supply in Europe, was another important commodity that was earnestly procured for the Portugal-bound carracks. Cochin acted as an intermediary port for the saltpetre coming from the Coromandel coast, Bengal and Madura. Sind, Cambay, Barçelor, Bijapur were other centres of supply. In 1625, Jorge de Sousa Pegado had supplied 200 quintals of saltpetre in Goa.[240] In 1630, the export of saltpetre to Portugal was 168 quintals, which decreased to 95 quintals in 1631. The export of this commodity again increased to 200 quintals in 1632. But in the following year, the figure fell to 57.[241] Often the saltpetre was sent to Portugal after having it refined in the new gun-powder plant constructed at Panelim in Goa by the Viceroy Linhares in the early 1630s, although there were cases when high quality saltpetre was directly sent to Lisbon.[242]

In 1616, the crown prohibited the private trade on coir and other naval materials. The aim behind this move was to get coir for the shipbuilding activities of Portugal.[243] Both coir and cowries, commodities coming from the Maldives, were exported to Lisbon on a monopolistic basis. In 1624-5, Bartolomeu Sanches Correia was authorized to export 1,000 quintals of cowries. In 1625, we find Francisco Tinoco de Carvalho sending cowries for the construction work of the monastery of Encarnação of Madrid.[244] However, during the company trade, the volume of cowrie export was so low that the Lisbon board gave instructions to stop further shipments of this commodity.[245]

Another item that was frequently exported to the kingdom was diamonds among other precious stones. Most of these precious stones came from Ceylon, Bijapur, Golconda and Madura.[246] Cochin was the southern base where the precious stones from Madura and Ceylon were collected for export to Europe. On the eastern coast, Mylapore was often used for penetrating into the mines of Golconda.[247] In 1609, we hear about the despatching of the precious diamond *rocha velha* to the kingdom.[248] In 1624, Dom Francisco da Gama sent in the liberty chest of Manuel dos Anjos about 157 diamonds to Portugal. Two years later, in 1626, the same Manuel dos Anjos was said to have received diamonds from Antonio Costa to be given to the Countess of Vidigueira.[249] Jacques de Coutre, the Augsburger, Ferdinand Cron who had previously been the agent of the Fuggers and the Welsers in Cochin and Goa, the new Christian traders namely, Fernão Jorge and his brother Francisco da Silveira were prominent traders in diamonds and precious stones which they exported to Europe almost on a routine basis.[250] Dom Miguel de Noronha, the viceroy and fourth count of Noronha, was another entrepreneur, who collected diamonds from Bijapur through agents and brokers such as the new Christian Vicente Ribeiro, whom the viceroy appointed as his chief gem broker.[251] Some of the diamonds exported to Europe by him were valued at 70,000 to 1,00,000 *ducats*.[252] Thus a variety of commodities were also exported to Europe, though the per centage of their composition in the export list was very small as compared with pepper.

6. VOLUME OF IMPORTS: 1570-1663

Precious metals including gold, silver and copper formed important commodities of import; though some copper was said to have been imported from Europe to India during the contract trade conducted by the Italians and Germans (1586-91),[253] this phenomenon did not last long. The copper crisis in Europe caused by the shortage of this metal experienced towards the end of the sixteenth century, compelled the Portuguese to look more to Chinese copper. From 1590 onwards, we find Chinese copper taking precedence over European copper.[254] During this period, silver and gold were the important metals that were sent to India as pepper money. However, as Linschotten said, silver in the form of 'Spanish reals of eight' was the greatest ware imported from Europe.[255] Silver from Spain, of course supplied by South America, formed almost 60 to 68 per cent of total imports and the profit on the sale of this metal was about 25 to 40 per cent at the end of the sixteenth and beginning of the seventeenth centuries. The merchants and money dealers of the native states of India were the most common buyers of this metal. In 1629, silver worth 29,481 *mil réis* (which was 62 per cent of the total import to India) was imported to India and the profit accrued from the sale of this specie was 70 per cent. In 1630, silver worth 22,695 *mil réis* were imported to India. It registered 68 per cent of total cargo imported. With increasing supply, this consignment was sold at a price 30 per cent lower than that of 1629 and despite this, the sale of silver in 1630 produced a profit of 53 per cent.[256]

If little gold was imported to India in the sixteenth century, as this metal was worth more in Europe, it was just the contrary in the seventeenth century. Gold became a common commodity of import. In 1627, about 80 per cent of the pepper money (32,847 out of 40,000 *cruzados*) was sent to India in gold and uncoined gold had higher demand in the market than silver.[257] In 1629, uncoined gold, gold bullion, worth 15,184 *mil réis* (i.e. 32 per cent of the total imports) was imported to India. Besides this, a small fraction in four-*cruzado* gold pieces worth 2,884 *mil réis* also was despatched to India. Both these consignments formed one-third of the total pepper money for 1629 and their sale fetched almost 62 per cent profit. In 1630, gold worth 6,349 *mil réis* (i.e. almost 19 per cent of total imports) was brought to India and its sale made a profit of 56 per cent.[258] Besides the import of gold bars on carracks from Europe, a lot of gold came to India from Moçambique. A good volume of this precious metal was sold in the open market in Goa and was taken all over India by the merchants and money dealers.[259] But a considerable portion of this gold was also used for minting SãoTomé, the gold coin which was used for buying pepper in Cochin and Quilon.[260] Gold other than in the coin-form of São Tomé was priced less in Cochin and Quilon: a mark of gold in 1629, was worth only 185 *xerafins* 2 *tangas* in Cochin and 176 *xerafins* 2 *tangas* 30 *reais* in Quilon, whereas it was 196 *xerafins* 4 *tangas* in Goa.[261]

Besides these precious metals, coral (which was collected from Italy and composed thirteen per cent of the total imports in 1630),[262] mercury, European cloth, jewellery, small arms, German toys, etc., were the other commodities that were imported to India at different phases.[263]

Thus we see the Indo-European trade emanating from Cochin for the period between 1570 and 1663 undergoing several changes. The Cochin's commerce with Europe, conducted by different contractors till 1597, registered a lower supply of commodities in the last decade of the sixteenth century. Though the crown took up the trade in 1598 and continued doing so till 1663, the situation did not improve. The arrangements made in 1628 to tranship pepper to Portugal through the *navetas* of the *casados* of Cochin (1628-38) and by means of the Portuguese India Company (1629-34), however, could be considered as extra streams of European commerce, and were suggestive of the crown's desire to revive the Cape route trade. However the European trade was beyond recuperation from the 1590s and from the early 1600s onwards. Both the intra-Asian as well as Indo-European commerce were hit hard by the diminishing flow of pepper to Cochin, caused by the tension between the St. Thomas Christians and the Portuguese and the subsequent diversion of the commodity to the ghat route. With tensions in the hinterland, the Portuguese had to confront less co-operative and more assertive kings in Cochin, who had more reason to become alienated as their revenue began to fall with the decreasing trade. Along with these two internal problems, which had already sucked the vitality of Cochin's trade, there came the external enemy: the rival European powers namely, the Dutch and the English who obstructed the Portuguese navigational lines. The mounting problems and tensions in the hinterland and from the one-time collaborators of the Portuguese had eaten up the flesh of Cochin; but the remaining bones, which continued as a vague symbol of trade till 1663, were finally devoured by the superior force of the Dutch.

NOTES

1. Joaquim Verissimo Serrão, *Historia de Portugal*, vol. III, pp. 60-4; see also Barbosa Machado, *Memorias para Historia de Portugal, que comprehendem o Governo delrey D. Sebastião*, part 1, Lisboa, 1736, pp. 330-78.
2. Mendes da Luz, op. cit., pp. 73-4; Vicente Almeida d'Eça, op. cit, Chap. II.
3. Sanjay Subrahmanyam, 'An Augsburger in Asia Portuguesa', pp. 402-3; T.A. de Caravalho, *As Companhias Portuguesas de colonização*, Lisboa, 1902, Chap. IV. Here he speaks about the trade monopoly of Cochin—China being given to Sebastião Pero da Cunha.
4. In 1578, the Fuggers alone held an amount of 40,000 *ducats* of Portuguese notes. For further details, see Konrad Häbler, 'Die Fugger und der spanische Gewürzhandel', in *Zeitschrift des historischen Vereins für Schwaben und Neuburg*, XIX, 1892, p. 40.
5. K. Häbler, 'Konrad Rott und die Thüringische Gessellschaft', in *Neues Archiv für sächsische Geschichte und Alterthumskunde*, XV, 1895, pp. 178-81; see also Reinhard Hildebrandt, 'Wirtschaftsentwicklung und Konzentration im 16. Jahrhundert: Konrad Rott und die Finanzierungsprobleme seines interkontinentalen Handels', in *Scripta Mercaturae*, I, 1970, pp. 28-49.
6. For further details, see the letter sent by Gabriel Holzschuher on 10 January 1580, from Cochin to Konrad Rott. Nationalbibliothek Wien: Cod. 8953, fols. 23-8.
7. Joaquim Verissimo Serrão, *Historia de Portugal*, vol. III, pp. 76-9.
8. Ibid., pp. 80-1. Cardinal Henry wanted to marry the queen mother of France. But he was blocked by Philip II of Spain in his efforts to get dispensation from the vow of celibacy and to get married.

9. K. Häbler, 'Konrad Rott', pp. 179-81; R. Hildebrandt, 'Wirtschaftsentwicklung und Konzentration', pp. 30-40.
10. See J.H. da Cunha Rivara, *Archivo Portuguez Oriental*, Fasciculo III, pp. 52-3.
11. Joaquim Verissimo Serrão, *Historia de Portugal*, vol. III, pp. 85-90. Though D. Antonio, Prior do Crato, raised resistance to Philip II's design to occupy Portugal, the army of the latter moved into Portugal and the court of Tomar accepted him as the ruler. For details, see Joaquim Verissimo Serrão, *Historia de Portugal*, vol. IV, pp. 14-15; Joaquim Verissimo Serrão, *O Reinado de D.Antonio, Prior do Crato*, vol. I (1580-2), Coimbra, 1956, pp. 330-45.
12. Mendes da Luz, op. cit., pp. 75-6.
13. Cf. infra n. 20.
14. Donald F. Lach, *Asia in the Making of Europe*, vol. I, book I, pp. 475-7; The details on Sassetti's own employment under Rovellasca are furnished in his letter to Francesco Valori, dated April, 1582, in Ettore Marucci (ed.), *Lettere edite e inedite di Filippo Sassetti*, Florence, 1855, pp. 204-10. He travelled to the cities of Onor, Mangalore, and in 1586 he accompanied Portuguese embassy to Zamorin.
15. Later Max Wolfmüller served Ferdinand Cron when the latter reached Cochin in 1587 as the agent of the Welsers and the Fuggers. See below n. 249.
16. Gabriel Holzschuher also shifted his service to the German firms after 1587.
17. F. Döbel, 'Über einen Pfefferhandel der Fugger und Welser, 1586-1591', *Zeitschrift des historischen vereins für Schwaben und Neuburg*, XIII, 1886, p. 125.
18. Ferdinand Braudel, *Mediterranean and the Mediterranean World*, vol. II, pp. 437-8. For details on price per quintal of pepper in Europe, see Reinhard Hildebrandt, *Die 'Georg Fuggerischen Erben': Kaufmännische Tätigkeit und sozialer Status, 1555-1600*, Berlin, 1966, p. 166.
19. AHU, *Caixas da India*, Caixa 1, doc, 7A, dated 16 July 1598.
20. For details about the terms and conditions of this contract, see Reinhard Hildebrandt, *Die 'Georg Fuggerischen Erben'*, appendix, pp. 191-6; F.A. MSS Cod. no. 46.1, fols. 33-8; M.A.H. Fitzler 'Der Anteil der deutschen an der Kolonial politik Philipps II von Spanien in Asien', in *Vierteljahrschrift für Social und Wirtschaftsgeschichte*, vol. 28, 1935, pp. 243-81.
21. Reinhard Hildebrandt, *Die 'Georg Fuggerischen Erben'*, pp. 148; Hermann Kellenbenz, 'Autor de 1600: le commerce du poivre des Fugger et le marché international du poivre', in *Annales, Economiés, Sociétés, Civilisations*, XI, 1956, pp. 1-26; Dietmar Rothermund, *Asian Trade and European Expansion in the Age of Mercantilism*, Delhi, 1981, pp. 20-2. The names of the contractors are also given by *Gavetas da Torre do Tombo*, vol. XI, pp. 331-2.
22. Hermann Kellenbenz, 'Cron, Ferdinand, 1559-1637', in Joel Serrão (ed.), *Dicionario de Historia de Portugal*, vol. I, Lisbon, 1963, pp. 752-3; C.R. Boxer, 'Uma raridade bibliografica', p. 236.
23. F.A. MSS Cod. no. 46.1, fols. 47v; 78v, letter of Ferdinand Cron sent from Cochin, dated 26 Dec. 1587.
24. Ibid., fol. 56.
25. Ibid., fol. 56v.
26. Ibid., fols. 78-9.
27. Ibid., fols. 54v, 55v, 64v, 66; Cf. supra n. 238.
28. Ibid., fol. 44v
29. Ibid., fols. 44v, 47v.
30. For details, see ibid., fols. 48, 51-3.
31. F.C. Danvers, *The Portuguese in India*, vol. II, pp. 68-80.

32. Donald F. Lach, *Asia in the Making of Europe*, vol. I, book I, p. 135.
33. The Union of Seven Provinces took place in January 1579 at Utrecht and was ratified by the States in July 1581. With this event, the Dutch intensified the struggle for independence.
34. In 1585, D. Antonio, the Prior do Crato got the support of England and Queen Elizabeth's attack of Portugal was organized also with a view to installing Prior do Crato on the throne of Portugal. For more details, see Joaquim Verissimo Serrão, *Historia de Portugal*, vol. IV, pp. 37-8. During this period, the English corsair activities in the Atlantic were often spearheaded by Francis Drake and with Queen Elizabeth's consent. After the circumnavigation of Drake, Philip called upon Elizabeth to punish him for having entered into the area of the so-called Portuguese monopoly. But the queen refused the Spanish demand and went on further to knight Drake. Francis Drake was considered by the English as a pioneer in the British maritime enterprise. For details, see J.A. Williamson, *The Age of Drake*, Oxford, 1938; Julian Corbett, *Drake and the Tudor Navy, with an History of the Rise of England as a Maritime Power*, vols. I-II, London, 1898.
35. Immanuel Wallerstein, 'Dutch Hegemony in the Seventeenth Century World Economy', in *Dutch Capitalism and World Capitalism*, edited by Maurice Aymard, London, 1982, p. 102.
36. For details, see Cesareo Fernandez Duro, *La' Armada Invencible*, vols. I-II, Madrid, 1884-5; Josen Knox Laughten (ed.), *State Papers relating to the Defeat of Spanish Armada Anno 1588*, London, 1894. After having concluded a treaty with the Dutch in 1585, the English joined hands with the Netherlands in their operations against Spain and Portugal. See also John Bruce, *The Annals of the Honorable East-India Company from their Establishment by the Charter of Queen Elizabeth, 1600 to the Union of the London and English East India Companies, 1707-8*, London, 1810, pp. 56-7.
37. F.A. 2.1.30d, fol. 3, letter sent to Ferdinand Cron/Schneeberger, dated 4 Jan. 1588; R. Hildebrandt, *Die 'Georg Fuggerischen Erben'*, pp. 158-9.
38. Ibid., p. 158; F.A. 46.1, fol. 48, letter of Ferdinand Cron sent from Cochin, dated 26 Dec. 1587.
39. F.A. 46.1, fols. 47v-48, letter of Ferdinand Cron sent from Cochin, dated 2 Dec. 1587; R. Hildebrandt, *Die 'Georg Fuggerischen Erben'*, p. 158.
40. Ibid., F.A. 46.1, fols. 48-9; Archivo General de Simancas, *Secretarias Provinciales*, libro. 1551, fols. 213-15. The cargo-list of the three ships which departed from Goa is furnished here.
41. R. Hildebrandt, *Die 'Georg Fuggerischen Erben'*, p. 159.
42. F.A. 46.1, the cargo-list given by Filippo Sassetti, dated 23 Jan. 1588; K.S. Mathew, 'Maritime Trade of India and the Germans in the Sixteenth Century', Paper presented in the *Second International Symposium on Maritime Studies*, Pondicherry, 16-20 December 1991.
43. R. Hildebrandt, *Die 'Georg Fuggerischen Erben'*, p. 159.
44. Ibid.
45. F.A. 2.1.31e, fol. 3, letter sent to Ferdinand Cron and Schneeberger, dated 5 Jan. 1591; R. Hildebrandt, *Die 'Georg Fuggerischen Erben'*, p. 161.
46. *Nationalbibliothek Wien*, Cod. no. 8964, fols. 635-6, report from Lyon, dated 16 May 1591; R. Hildebrandt, *Die 'Georg Fuggerischen Erben'*, p. 162.
47. For details, see G. Pölnitz, *Fugger und Hanse*, Tübingen, 1953, pp. 222-6.
48. Hermann Kellenbenz, 'Autor de 1600', p. 3.
49. Mendes da Luz, op. cit., pp. 81-3.
50. Hermann Kellenbenz, 'Autor de 1600', p. 19.
51. Antonio da Silva Rego, *Documentação Ultramarina Portuguesa*, vol. III, p. 340.

52. Ibid., p. 314; James C. Boyajian, *Portuguese Bankers at the Court of Spain 1626-1650*, New Jersey, (without date), pp. 6-8.
53. Antonio da Silva Rego, *Documentação Ultramarina Portuguesa*, vol. III, pp. 340-1.
54. BNL, *Fundo Geral*, Codice 1977, fol. 213, dated 4 April 1597.
55. Chryztoph Pawlowski, 'Relação de Chrystoph Pawlowski', p. 45; Huyghen van Linschotten, op. cit., p. 119.
56. Hermann Kellenbenz, 'Autor de 1600', p. 5; M.A. Hedwig Fitzler, 'Der Anteil der Deutschen an der Kolonialpolitik Philipps II', p. 267.
57. R. Hildebrandt, *Die 'Georg Fuggerischen Erben'*, p. 166, n.177.
58. Hermann Kellenbenz, 'Autor de 1600', pp. 9-11.
59. R. Hildebrandt, *Die 'Georg Fuggerischen Erben'*, pp. 167-8.
60. These so-called corsairs used to plunder in the Atlantic Portuguese vessels coming from India. Many documents speak about the robbing of Portuguese vessels by the English pirates. For example, see *Nationalbibliothek, Wien*, Cod. 8955, fol. 23. During the period between 1580 and 1594, about 28 ships coming from India were captured or destroyed by the English. See for deatails, Luis Figueiredo Falcão, *Livro em que se contem toda a Fazenda e Real Patrimonio dos Reinos de Portugal, India e Ilhas adjacentes e outras Particularidades*, Lisboa, 1859, pp. 137-86; Manuel Lopes de Almeida, *Memorial de Pêro Roiz Soares*, tom. I, Coimbra, 1953, p. 302. Because of the constant capturing by the English corsairs, Portugal did not have enough vessels to be fitted out to India. Joaquim Verissimo Serrão, *Historia de Portugal*, vol. IV, pp. 44, 154.
61. Vitorino Magalhães Godinho, *Os Descobrimentos e a Economia Mundial*, vol. III, p. 49.
62. Archivo General de Simancas, *Secretarias Provinciales*, libro 1551, fols. 213-15; F.A. MSS Cod. no. 46.1, cargo list furnished by Filippo Sassetti, dated 23 Jan. 1588; Luiz de Figueiredo Falcão, *Livro em que se contem toda a Fazenda*, pp. 59-69; Vitorino Magalhães Godinho, *Os Descobrimentos e a Economia Mundial*, vol. III, p. 75; R. Hildebrandt, *Die 'Georg Fuggerischen Erben'*, pp. 158-63.
63. Philip I (Philip II of Spain) died on 13 September 1598. See for details, Joaquim Verissimo Serrão, *Historia de Portugal*, vol. IV, p. 48; Manuel Lopes de Almeida, *Memorial de Pêro Roiz Soares*, tom. I, Coimbra, 1953, p. 352.
64. Donald F. Lach, *Asia in the Making of Europe*, vol. I, book I, pp. 267-8.
65. F.A. MSS Cod. no. 46.1, cargo list furnished by Filippo Sassetti, dated 23 Jan. 1588; Friederich Dobel, 'Über einen Pfefferhandel der Fugger und Welser, 1586-91', *Zeitschrift des Historischen Vereins für Schwaben und Neuburg*, 13, 1886, p. 133.
66. A.R. Disney, *Twilight of the Pepper Empire*, p. 120
67. BNL, Cod. 1975, fols. 125-125v, letter of Conde de Vidigueira sent to Philip III (of Portugal) dated 21 Dec.1626.
68. Diogo do Couto, *Da Asia*, Decada X, part I, liv. IV, Cap. XIII, pp. 472-80.
69. K.S. Mathew and Afzal Ahmad, *Emergence of Cochin*, doc. 53, pp. 77-83.
70. ANTT, *Miscelâneas Manuscritas do Convento da Graça*, Caixa 2, doc. 3, fols. 235-6 letter of the king of Cochin sent to Conde de Vidigueira dated 5 Jan. 1598; fol. 271, letter of the king of Cochin sent to Conde de Vidigueira dated 19 September 1599.
71. For details on the financial crisis of the *Estado* especially during the period between 1595 and 1610, see Joâo Manuel de Teles e Cunha, op. cit., pp. 319-31; A.R. Disney, *Twilight of the Pepper Empire*, pp. 50-70.
72. Joaquim Verissimo Serrão, *Historia de Portugal*, vol. IV, p. 50; Eduardo Freire de Oliveira, *Elementos para a Historia do Municipio de Lisboa*, tom. II, Lisboa, 1887, p. 120.
73. ANTT, *Miscelâneas Manuscritas do Convento da Graça*, Caixa 2, doc. 3, fol. 271,

letter of the king of Cochin sent to Conde de Vidigueira, dated 19 September 1599.

74. BNL, Cod. 1976, fols. 158-9, letter of the Conde de Vidigueira sent to Philip II in 1599.
75. Antonio da Silva Rego, *Documentação Ultramarina Portuguesa*, vol. III, pp. 355-6.
76. Ibid., p. 357.
77. Ibid., pp. 359-60.
78. J.H. da Cunha Rivara, *Archivo Portuguez Oriental, Fasciculo I*, part 2, pp. 128, 140; ANTT, MSS *S. Vicente*, doc. 14, fols. 163-163v, letter of Philip II (of Portugal) to the bishop of Cochin, dated 15 May 1605.
79. Niels Steensgaard, *Carracks, Caravans and Companies*, p. 166; Fernand Braudel and R. Romano, *Navires et marchandises á l'entreé du port de Livourne, 1547-1611*, Paris, 1911, p. 68; AHU, *Caixas da India*, Caixa 1, doc. 101, dated 25 Feb. 1611. But this document says that in 1606, a cargo 8,918 quintals of pepper was bought from Cochin, Quilon and Cannanore. However, it was transhipped from Cochin to Portugal only in 1610. See doc. 101, fol. 1.
80. Niels Steensgaard, *Carracks, Caravans and Companies*, p. 166.
81. Francisco da Costa, 'Relatorio sobre o Trato da Pimenta', p. 351
82. Antonio da Silva Rego, *Documentação Ultramarina Portuguesa*, vol. III, p. 315.
83. BNL, Cod. 11410, fol. 116v , *Orçamento de* 1612 (Cochin).
84. For details on the non-payment of *copas* in time, see Francisco da Costa, 'Relatorio sobre o Trato da Pimenta', p. 357.
85. AHU, *Caixas da India*, Caixa 1, doc. 101, *Devassa feito ao vedor da Fazenda Garcio de Melo* (*Compra da pimenta* 1606-1610), dated 25 Feb. 1611.
86. The heavy quintal was lacking half *arroba* (almost 6.6 kgs.) for a quintal and the light quintal was lacking 2 arráteis (almost 1 kg.) for a quintal. Ibid., AHU, *Caixas da India*, Caixa 2, doc. 86, letter of Francisco Rebelo Rodovalho sent to Philip II, dated 13 Jan. 1613; R.A.de Bulhao Pato, *Documentos Remettidos da India*, vol. II, pp. 6-8.
87. J. Gentil da Silva (ed.), *Alguns Elementos para a Historia do Commercio da india de Portugal existentes na Bibliotheca Nacional de Madrid*, Lisboa, 1950, pp. 41, 64-6.
88. BNL, Cod. 11410, fols. 129v-130, *Orçamento de* 1612, about the pepper that goes to Portugal.
89. AHU, *Caixas da India*, Caixa 1, doc. 101, *Devassa feito ao vedor da Fazenda*, dated 25 Feb. 1611.
90. Ibid., Caixa 4, doc. 133, year 1616. It became all the more necessary against the background of the strong financial crisis, which the *Estado* was experiencing.
91. Ibid., Caixa 1, doc. 101, *Devassa feito ao vedor da Fazenda*, dated 25 Feb. 1611.
92. Ibid., Caixa 2, doc. 107, dated 1 Dec. 1613.
93. Ibid.
94. BNL, Cod. 11410, fols. 29-29v, summary of the contract concluded with Jorge Rodrigues Solis, in 1602.
95. For details about this European contract, see ANTT, MSS. S. *Vicente*, 26, fols. 294-5.
96. J.J. Andrade Silva, *Collecção Chronologica de Legislação Portuguesa, 1603-1612*, Lisboa, 1854, p. 104; Joaquim Verrissimo Serrão, *Historia de Portugal*, vol. IV, p. 64.
97. J.R. Bruijn, F.S. Gaastra and others, *Dutch-Asiatic Shipping in the 17th and 18th Centuries*, vol. I, *Introductory Volume*, The Hague, 1987, pp. 2-3; Immanuel Wallerstein 'Dutch Hegemony in the seventeenth Century World Economy', p. 102; K.M. Panikkar, *Malabar and the Dutch (Being the History of the Fall of the Nayar Power in Malabar)*, Bombay, 1931, pp. 1-2.
98. J.R. Bruijn, F.S. Gaastra, and others, *Dutch-Asiatic Shipping in the 17th and 18th Centuries*, vol. II, *Outward-bound Voyages from the Netherlands to Asia and the Cape (1595-1794)*, The Hague, 1979, pp. 2-9.

99. J.R. Bruijn, F.S. Gaastra and others, *Dutch-Asiatic Shipping in the 17th and 18th Centuries*, vol. III, *Home-bound Voyages from Asia and the Cape to the Netherlands (1597-1795)*, The Hague, 1979, p. 2.
100. S. van Brakel, *De Hollandsche Handelscompagnieën der Zeventiende eeuw*. 'S'Gravenhage, 1908, pp. 15-20; J.R. Bruijn, F.S. Gaastra and others, op. cit, vol. I, pp. 3-7.
101. For details, see John Bruce, op. cit., pp. 136-47.
102. Niels Steensgaard, *Carracks, Caravans and Companies*, pp. 121-2.
103. AHU, *Caixas da India*, Caixa 1, doc. 101, *Devassa feito ao vedor da Fazenda.*
104. M. Antoinette P. Roelofsz, *De Vestiging der Nederlanders ter Kuste Malabar*, 'S' Gravenhage, 1943, pp. 29-35; T.I. Poonen, *A Survey of the Rise of the Dutch Power in Malabar (1603-1678)*, Trichinapoly, 1949, pp. 45-7.
105. M. Antoinette P. Roelofsz, *De Vestiging der Nederlanders*, pp. 36-45; T.I. Poonen, op. cit., pp. 48-50.
106. It seems that only from this period onwards, did the Dutch turn openly against the Portuguese possessions in the Indian Ocean.
107. M. Antoinette P. Roelofsz, *De Vestiging der Nederlanders*, pp. 47-9; T.I. Poonen, op. cit., pp. 51-2.
108. For details, see J.R. Bruijn, F.S. Gaastra and others, op. cit., vol. II, pp. 2-150.
109. J.R. Bruijn, F.S. Gaastra and others, op. cit., vol. II, pp. 10-150.
110. Vitorino Magalhães Godinho, *Os Descobrimentos e a Economia Mundial*, vol. III, p. 49.
111. C.R. Boxer, *From Lisbon to Goa, 1500-1750: Studies in Portuguese Maritime Enterprise*, Variorum, Hampshire, 1990, p. 64.
112. Vitorino Magalhães Godinho, *Os Descobrimentos e a Economia Mundial*, vol. III, p. 49.
113. J.R. Bruijn, F.S. Gaastra and others, op. cit., vol. III, pp. 4-80.
114. For details, see C.R. Boxer, 'On a Portuguese Carrack's Bill of Lading in 1625', in *Petrus Nonius*, Orgão do Grupo Portugués de Historia das Ciências, II, Lisbon, 1939, pp. 176ff.
115. For details, see AHU, *Caixas da India*, Caixa 2, doc. 89, dated 27 Jan. 1613.
116. Ibid., fols. 1-4, details about the pepper-money and the money borrowed from the *casados*.
117. Ibid., fols. 1-11.
118. Ibid., fol. 5.
119. Ibid., fol. 12.
120. Ibid., fols. 16-17.
121. Ibid., fols. 10, 16-17.
122. Ibid., fols. 14-15.
123. For details on the financial indebtedness of the crown to the *casados* of Cochin, see AHU, *Caixas da India*, Caixa 4, doc. 133, year 1616. The transfer of the commercial activities of the enterprising *casados* from Cochin to the Coromandel coast and elsewhere followed by a dull phase in the trade of Cochin, made it all the more difficult for the Portuguese to raise funds locally from the dwellers of the city.
124. For a detailed list of *casados*, who were engaged in the transport of pepper from Quilon to Cochin and from Cochin to Goa, see AHU, *Caixas da India*, Caixa 8, doc. 129; Caixa 8-A, doc. 231, dated 16 Feb. 1626; Caixa 9, doc. 26, dated 6 Dec. 1625. Manuel Carvalho, Antonio José, Pero Ribeiro, João Lopes, Paulo Moreno were some among them.
125. Sanjay Subrahmanyam, 'Cochin in Decline', p. 72.
126. See for details, AHU, *Caixas da India*, Caixa 3, doc. 29, dated 25 Jan. 1615;

Caixa 3, doc. 34, dated 29 Jan 1615; Caixa 8, doc. 66, dated 25 Jan 1624.

127. AHU, *Caixas da India*, Caixa 5, doc. 62, the letter of Nuno Vaz de Castelo Branco sent to Philip II (of Portugal) dated 1 Feb. 1618. See the opinion especially of Garcia de Melo in the same document; Lisbon, 28 Nov. 1618.
128. Ibid. See the letter of Nuno Vaz de Castelo. For further details on the difference of pepper price in Cochin and Kanara, see AHU, *Caixas da India*, Caixa, doc. 68, dated 12 Dec. 1612.
129. AHU, *Caixas da India*, Caixa 6, doc. 33, letter of the bishop of Cochin, dated 14 Feb. 1619.
130. A.R. Disney, *Twilight of Pepper Empire*, see appendix, p. 162.
131. Cf. infra n. 199.
132. AHU, *Caixas da India*, Caixa 3, doc. 1, dated 4 Jan. 1615.
133. A.R. Disney, *Twilight of Pepper Empire*, p. 162.
134. Ibid.
135. Ibid, p. 60.
136. AHU, *Caixas da India*, Caixa 3, doc. 31, dated 25 Jan. 1615.
137. Ibid., doc. 34, dated 29 Jan. 1615.
138. T.I. Poonen, op. cit., p. 52.
139. John Bruce, op. cit., pp. 163-4.
140. Ibid., 171.
141. Ibid., 178; M. Antoinette P. Roelofsz, *De Vestiging der Nederlanders*, pp. 49-50.
142. Joaquim Verissimo Serrão, *Historia de Portugal*, vol. IV, p. 91.
143. M.Antoinette P.Roelofsz, *De Vestiging der Nederlanders*, pp. 51-2. See also William Foster, *The English Factories in India, 1618-1621: A Calendar of Documents in the India Office, British Museum and Public Record Office*, Oxford, 1906, pp. 276-7.
144. F.C. Danvers, *Report to the Secretary of State for India in Council on the Portuguese Records Relating to the East Indies Contained in the Archivo da Torre do Tombo and the Public Libraries at Lisbon and Evora*, London, 1892; T.I. Poonen, op. cit., p. 54.
145. For details on the fall of Ormuz and the structural crisis see, Niels Steensgaard, *Carracks, Caravans and Companies*, pp. 193-342. However, after the fall of Ormuz, the Portuguese tried to concentrate more on Muscat.
146. The flow of commodities through the traditional caravan route, which the Portuguese could not completely blockade, almost stopped with the entry of the Dutch and the English into Persian gulf and the Red Sea area. For details, see Niels Steensgaard, *Carracks, Caravans and Companies*, pp. 345-411.
147. *Boletim da Filmoteca Ultramarina Portuguesa*, no. 8, Lisboa, 1958, p. 99.
148. T.I. Poonen, op. cit., pp. 54-5.
149. AHU, *Caixas da India*, Caixa 8, doc. 38, dated 29 Oct. 1624.
150. Cf. infra n. 199.
151. AHU, *Caixas da India*, Caixa 9-A, doc. 185, in 1626.
152. S.S. Pissurlencar and V.T. Gune, *Assentos do Conselho do Estado (Proceedings of the State Council at Goa), Supplementary Series*, vol. I, part 2, Goa, 1972, pp. 108-11.
153. BNL, Cod. 1975, fols. 125-125v, letter of Conde de Vidigueira sent to Philip III (of Portugal), dated 21 Dec 1626.
154. Cf. infra n. 199.
155. *Boletim da Filmoteca Ultramarina Portuguesa*, no. 8, p. 99. As early as 1619, we find David Levi, a Jew of native Cochin, being made Mudaliar and ambassador of the

king of Cochin. See HAG, *Livro das Pazes*, no. 1, fol. 34; J.H. da Cunha Rivara (ed.), *O Chronista de Tissuary*, vol. IV, no. 39, 1869, p. 47.

156. When Antonio Bocarro visited Cochin, Samuel Castiel was an interpreter and translator to the king of Cochin. See for details, ANTT, *Inquisição de Lisboa*, Cadernos do Promotor, liv. 20 (Caderno 9), fols. 437v-8; Pedro d'Azevedo, 'O Bocarro Francês e os Judeus de Cochim e de Hamburgo', *Archivo Histórico Portugués*, vol. VII, 1910, pp. 186-91; José Alberto Rodrigues da Silva Tavim, 'From Setubal to the Sublime Porte', p. 120. The Castiel family had been exercising the charge of the Mudaliar since 1570. For details about Samuel Castiel, who was exercising the charge of Mudaliar and had great influence over the native king, see ANTT, *Livros das Monções*, no. 40, fol. 132; no. 42, fol. 21, the letter of the Viceroy Pero da Silva sent to the king, dated 25 Nov 1637.
157. ANTT, *Livros das Monções*, no. 24, fols. 69v-70, letter of the Conde-Almirante sent to the king, dated 24 Feb. 1627; ANTT, *Livros das Monções*, no. 27, fol. 156, letter of the king of Portugal sent to the Viceroy of India, dated 6 March 1630; ANTT, *Documentos Remettidos da India*, liv. 24, fols. 69v-70; Sanjay Subrahmanyam, 'Cochin in Decline', p. 83.
158. *Boletim da Filmoteca Ultramarina Portuguesa*, no. 8, pp. 99-100; HAG, *Livros das Monções*, no. 14 (1630-1), fols. 184-5, dated 5 Dec. 1630.
159. HAG, *Livros das Monções*, no. 13-A (1629-30), fol. 10, dated 3 Jan. 1630.
160. HAG, *Livros das Monções*, no. 14 (1630-1), fols. 184-5, dated 5 Dec. 1630. This document also suggests that the shipbuilding industry thrived in native Cochin, as well.
161. Ibid.
162. *Boletim da Filmoteca Ultramarina Portuguesa*, no. 8, p. 100. With the termination of war in the interior regions, the ghat route commerce got revived and the price of pepper in Cochin marked an increase from 1628 onwards. In that year it rose to 11 *xerafins*, 4 *tangas* and 48 *reais* per quintal, which was the price that prevailed in Cochin before the outbreak of war in the interior regions. João Manuel Teles e Cunha, op. cit., p. 456.
163. C. Achyuta Menon, op. cit., p. 79.
164. This distance maintained by the local ruler widened all the more, with the decreasing flow of income from the customs. From the 1630s onwards, we hear that the King of Cochin was getting very little customs revenue from the port, because of the decline of trade. HAG, *Livros das Monções*, no. 14 (1630-1), fol. 29, dated 12 Nov. 1630.
165. C. Achyuta Menon, op. cit., p. 79.
166. Joaquim Verissimo Serrão, *Historia de Portugal*, vol. V, pp. 11-14; D. Antonio Caetano de Sousa, *Historia Genealogica da Casa Real Portuguesa*, vol. VII, Coimbra, 1949, pp. 1-149.
167. L.H. Horace Perera, *Ceylon under Western Rule*, pp. 79-80.
168. S. Arasaratnam, 'Merchants of Coromandel in Trade and Entrepreneurship circa 1650-1700', in Roderich Ptak and Dietmar Rothermund (ed.), *Emporia, Commodities and Entrepreneurs in Asian Maritime Trade, c.1400-1750*, p. 45.
169. K.M. Panikkar, *Malabar and the Dutch*, p. 3.
170. M. Antoinette P. Roelofsz, *De Vestiging der Nederlanders*, p. 106; T.I. Poonen, op. cit., p. 56.
171. T.I. Poonen, op. cit., pp. 56-7.
172. M. Antoinette P. Roelofsz, *De Vestiging der Nederlanders*, pp. 108-9.

173. S.S. Pissurlencar, *Assentos do Conselho do Estado*, vol. II, p. 379.
174. Ibid., pp. 435-6.
175. Ibid., pp. 431-2.
176. *El Rey nao deixava vir nada á ella* (Cochin city). Ibid., p. 431.
177. Ibid., 432.
178. For details of the agreement, see ibid., pp. 435-9.
179. Ibid., vol. II, pp. 447-8.
180. ANTT, *Documentos Remetidos*, liv. 50, fol. 110, liv. 56, fols. 27, 212; Sanjay Subrahmanyam, 'Cochin in Decline', p. 82. The assassination of the *Regedor mor*, the chief officer (which post Samuel Castiel seems to have borne, as well, at the time of his death) of the king of Cochin, created great damage to the relationship between the Portuguese and the native ruler. For details, see AHU, *Caixas da India*, Caixa 15, doc. 27, dated 28 Nov. 1643; Caixa 15, doc. 52, dated 4 Dec. 1643; Caixa 23, doc. 10, 26 Jan. 1655.
181. K.M. Panikkar, *Malabar and the Portuguese*, p. 155.
182. For details about the expulsion of the ruling king from the Mutta *tavazhi*, see AHU, *Caixas da India*, Caixa 23, doc. 20, dated 5 Feb. 1655, carta no.15; S.S. Pissurlencar, *Assentos do Conselho do Estado*, vol. III, pp. 148-9, 560-1. Some authors say that the Palluruthi prince, who was installed as king with the help of the Portuguese, died about the year 1650 and was succeeded by Rama Varma, the prince adopted from the Chazhur branch. C. Achyuta Menon, op. cit., p. 87. There is the possibility that the nephew of the queen, as mentioned in the Portuguese documents, must have been this prince adopted from the Chazhur branch. For the response of other native rulers on this issue see, S.S. Pissurlencar, *Assentos do Conselho do Estado*, vol. III, pp. 149, 272.
183. Ibid., pp. 560-1.
184. Ibid., pp. 149, 198, 367, 577.
185. L.H. Horace Perera, *Ceylon under Western Rule*, p. 80.
186. K.M. Panikkar, *Malabar and the Portuguese*, p. 156; C. Achyuta Menon, op. cit., p. 88.
187. Ulloor Parameswara Aiyyar (ed.), *Padapattu*, Trivandrum, 1924, p. 14.
188. The prince of the Mutta *tavazhi* contacted the Dutch authorities at Colombo in order to get back the kingdom and to expel the Portuguese from Cochin. It was against these circumstances that the Council of Ceylon decided to send van der Meyden to Malabar. On 12 March 1661, Paliathachan, the traditional Chief Ministers of Cochin, signed a treaty with the Dutch to fight against the Portuguese. The Zamorin concluded a treaty with the Dutch by which he agreed that if the Dutch should succeed in setting on the throne of Cochin the Mutta *tavazhi* prince, then the Zamorin and the king of Cochin would bear the whole cost. *A Translation of a Record Grandhavari*, pp. v-vi; T.I.Poonen, op. cit, pp. 72, 75; A. Galletti, *The Dutch in Malabar*, New Delhi, 1984, p. 121.
189. S.S. Pissurlencar, *Assentos do Conselho do Estado*, vol. IV, pp. 525; 566.
190. Ibid., p. 567.
191. Ibid.; AHU, *Caixas da India*, Caixa 25-A, doc. 205, dated 14 April 63; doc. 220, dated 11 May 1663.
192. Goda Varma calling himself '*irmão da Coroa de Portugal*' continued the offensive. For details see, S.S. Pissurlencar, *Assentos do Conselho do Estado*, vol. IV, pp. 525-9, 532-3, 566-8.
193. Cf. infra n. 199.
194. AHU, *Caixas da India*, Caixa 11, doc. 11, dated 23 Feb. 1635.

195. Ibid., Caixa 13, doc. 10, dated 8 Jan. 1638.
196. Ibid., Caixa 20-A, doc. 145, fol. 21, dated 1 Feb. 1650.
197. Ibid., Caixa 15, doc. 30, dated 29 Nov. 1643.
198. Ibid., Caixa 20, doc. 60, dated 9 Nov. 1648.
199. Niels Steensgaard, *Carracks, Caravans and Companies*, p. 166; AHU, *Caixas da India*, Caixa 2, doc. 89, fols. 16-17 dated 27 Jan. 1613; AHU, *Caixas da India*, Caixa 1, doc. 112; AHU, *Caixas da India*, Caixa 2, doc. 83 (1613); AHU, *Caixas da India*, Caixa 3, doc. 1, dated 4 Jan. 1615; Caixa 3-A, doc. 174 (1516); AHU, *Caixas da India*, Caixa 5, doc. 90, dated 16 Feb. 1618; AHU, *Caixas da India*, Caixa 8, doc. 38, dated 13 Oct. 1623; Caixa 8, doc. 129 (1624); Caixa 11, doc. 11, dated 23 Feb. 1635; Caixa 22-A, doc. 126, dated 23 Sept. 1654; A.R. Disney, *Twilight of Pepper Empire*, p. 162.
200. AHU, *Caixas da India*, Caixa 22-A, doc. 126, dated 23 Sept. 1654.
201. Ibid., Caixa 23, doc. 87, dated 12 Feb. 1656.
202. For details, see Tito Augusto de Carvalho, *As Companhias Portugueses de Colonização*, Lisbon, 1902; Joaquim Verissimo Serrão, *Historia de Portugal*, vol. IV, p. 190.
203. J.J. Andrade e Silva, *Collecção Chronologico de Legislação Portugueza (1620-1627)*, pp. 129, 137, 410; A.R. Disney, *Twilight of the Pepper Empire*, pp. 72-9, 87; C.R. de Silva, 'The Portuguese East India Company 1628-1633', in *Luso-Brazilian Review*, II, 1974, pp. 154-6; D. Jorge Mascarenhas was the president of Lisbon Municipal council.
204. A.R. Disney, *The Twilight of the Pepper Empire*, pp. 84-5;159-60.
205. Ibid., 87.
206. Ibid., 88-93.
207. Eduardo Freire de Oliveira (ed.), *Elementos para a Historia do Municipio de Lisboa*, vol. III, Lisbon, 1889, pp. 313-15.
208. AHU, *Caixas da India*, Caixa 10, doc. 90, dated 11 Nov. 1633; HAG, *Livros da Monções*, no. 17 (1632-3), fol. 208, dated 16 March 1632; Antonio de Pinho da Costa had served earlier as the captain-General-elect of Mylapore and *vedor da Fazenda* of Ceylon. Later he was associated with the sending of *navetas* from Cochin to Lisbon. Sanjay Subrahmanyam, 'Cochin in Decline', p. 76.
209. A.R. Disney, *The Twilight of the Pepper Empire*, pp. 124-9, 137-48, 166-7.
210. Ibid., p. 148.
211. AHU, *Caixas da India*, Caixa 12, doc. 3, fol. 15, dated 2 Dec. 1633; A.R. Disney, *Twilight of the Pepper Empire*, pp. 164-5, 168.
212. Even during the period of Company trade, crown vessels used to bring pepper to Portugal. A.R. Disney says that the pepper that reached Lisbon in 1632 was shipped on behalf of the crown. Ibid., p. 162.
213. AHU, *Caixas da India*, Caixa 12, doc. 3, fol. 15, dated 2 Dec. 1633; A.R. Disney, *Twilight of the Pepper Empire*, pp. 166-9.
214. BNL, Cod. 11410, fols. 173-8, contract to send *navetas* to Lisbon from Cochin.
215. Ibid., fol. 174v.
216. Ibid., fols. 175v-6.
217. Ibid., fol. 174-5.
218. Ibid., fol. 173v.
219. Ibid., fol. 176.
220. Andre Simois was the captain of this *naveta*, called *Madre de Deus*, which departed from Cochin on 9 January 1628. For details, see AHU, *Caixas da India*, Caixa 22-A, doc. 122, fol. 15, dated 13 Aug. 1653; see also BNL, Cod. 11410, fols. 91-2,

letter of the captain of the *naveta* (of 1629) sent to Philip III, dated 1 June 1630; ANTT, *Documentos Remetidos*, livro 26, fols. 123, 349, 581.

221. BNL, Cod. 11410, fols. 91-2v, letter of the captain (Francisco Freire de Andrade) of the *naveta* sent to Philip III, dated 1 June 1630.
222. Biblioteca da Ajuda, Cod. 51-X-1, fols. 120-2, dated 9 Dec. 1631.
223. Sanjay Subrahmanyam, 'Cochin in Decline', p. 76; ANTT, *Documentos Remetidos*, liv. 37, fol. 247. The Portuguese authorities in India feared that this arrangement would only increase the loss of competent seamen to the Dutch.
224. AHU, *Caixas da India*, Caixa 11-A, doc. 220, letter no. 6, written in 1635.
225. Sanjay Subrahmanyam, 'Cochin in Decline', pp. 76-7; ANTT, *Documentos Remetidos da India*, liv. 37, fol. 247; liv. 40, fol. 225.
226. AHU, *Caixas da India*, Caixa 13-A, doc. 162, fols. 1-1v, dated 8 June 1639.
227. Ibid., doc. 156, dated 4 May 1639; Caixa 13-A, doc. 162, dated 8 June 1639; Caixa 13-A, doc. 170, dated 9 Sept. 1639.
228. AHU, *Caixas da India*, Caixa 13-A, doc. 170, dated 9 Sep. 1639.
229. Ibid., doc. 156, dated 4 May 1639.
230. Cf. supra nn. 283, 422, 432. Besides, the details for the total export of pepper from India to Portugal during the period between 1612 and 1634 were taken from A.R. Disney, *Twilight of the Pepper Empire*, p. 162.
231. The above-mentioned source is used for this graph.
232. Archivo General de Simancas, *Secretarias Provinciales*, libro 1551, fols. 213-15; Niels Steensgaard, *Carracks, Caravans and Companies*, p. 166.
233. ANTT, *Miscelâneas Manuscritas do Convento da Graça*, Caixa 3, doc. 6, fol. 321.
234. A.R. Disney, *Twilight of the Pepper Empire*, p. 113.
235. Archivo General de Simancas, *Secretarias Provinciales*, libro 1551, fols. 213-15; Niels Steensgaard, *Carracks, Caravans and Companies*, p. 166.
236. AHU, *Caixas da India*, Caixa 13, doc. 10, dated 8 Jan. 1638; Caixa 13-A, doc. 170, dated 9 Sept. 1639; Cf. supra n. 446.
237. Archivo General de Simancas, *Secretarias Provinciales*, libro 1551, fols. 213-15; Niels Steensgaard, *Carracks, Caravans and Companies*, p. 166.
238. Ibid.
239. For details, see the cargo list of 1588 given in F.A. Cod. 46.1; Archivo General de Simancas, *Secretarias Provinciales*, libro 1551, fols. 213-15; Niels Steensgaard, *Carracks, Caravans and Companies*, p. 166.
240. AHU, *Caixas da India*, Caixa 10, doc. 81, dated 19 Oct. 1633; A.R. Disney, *Twilight of the Pepper Empire*, pp. 116-17. In 1632, the Portuguese in Cochin made contract with the Naique of Madura to get saltpetre in exchange for elephants. For details, see HAG, *Livros das Monções*, no. 15 (1631-2), fol. 26, dated 26 Nov. 1632.
241. Ibid., p. 168;
242. Ibid., p. 117.
243. R.A. de Bulhão Pato, *Documentos Remettidos da India*, vol. III; letter of Philip II sent to D. Jeronimo de Azevedo, dated 21 April 1615, p. 348; letter of Philip II, dated 5 March 1616, pp. 432-3.
244. BNL, *Fundo Geral*, Cod. no. 1983, fols. 55-6, dated 12 Dec. 1624, fols. 83-83v, dated 30 Dec. 1625; Antonio da Silva Rego, *Documentos Remettidos da India*, vol. IX, pp. 136-7.
245. A.R. Disney, *Twilight of the Pepper Empire*, pp. 114-15.
246. For details on the mines, see Jacques de Coutre, *Andanzas Asiaticas*, Madrid, 1991, pp. 258-60.
247. João Manuel Teles e Cunha, op. cit., pp. 519-20; Jacques de Coutre, op. cit., p. 268.

248. BNL, *Fundo Geral,* Cod. 1975, fols. 305-305v, letter of Rui de Tavora sent to Conde da Vidigueira, dated 10 Jan. 1609.
249. Ibid., Cod. 1981, fols. 74-5; 91-4; João Manuel Teles e Cunha, op. cit., pp. 526-7.
250. Jacques de Coutre, op. cit., p. .253; James C. Boyajian, *Portuguese Bankers at the Court of Spain, 1626-1650,* New Jersey (without year), p. 8.
251. A.R. Disney, 'The Viceroy as Entrepreneur: The Count of Linhares at Goa in the 1630s', in Roderich Ptak and Dietmar Rothermund (eds.), *Emporia, Commodities and Entrepreneurs in Asian Maritime Trade, c.*1400-1750, p. 440.
252. Ibid., p. 441.
253. K.S. Mathew, 'Maritime Trade of India and the Germans in the Sixteenth Century', p. 43.
254. By the end of 1580 the annual import of copper to Goa and Cochin from China was 2,000-3,000 quintals. The Jesuits were actively involved in this copper trade. BNL, *Fundo Geral,* Cod. 11410, fols. 123-4; *Boletim da Ultramarina Portuguesa,* no. 2, p. 298; João Manuel Teles e Cunha, op. cit., pp. 374-6.
255. A.R. Disney, *Twilight of the Pepper Empire,* p. 103.
256. Ibid., pp. 103-4, 178.
257. Ibid., p. 104.
258. Ibid., pp. 104-5.
259. AHU, *Caixas da India,* Caixa 10, doc. 10, 6 Aug. 1631.
260. A.R. Disney, *Twilight of the Pepper Empire,* pp. 104-5.
261. Ibid., p. 105.
262. Ibid.
263. Ibid., p. 106.

CHAPTER VIII

Conclusion

In the introduction to this work, a question was raised as to how far the urban unit of Cochin influenced the maritime trade of India by re-orienting and concentrating the international commerce in Cochin and what role did it, as the first Portuguese settlement in Asia, play in the colonial designs of the Portuguese. An attempt was made to examine the role which Portuguese Cochin played in the maritime trade of India as well as in its economic activities by highlighting several innovative features, and Portuguese superiority in relation to other phases. The extent to which this urban unit was utilized by the Lusitanians as a surplus extracting institutional arrangement for setting up a universal empire was analysed by reviewing the various strategies and actions of the Portuguese in Cochin.

1. Cochin which emerged as a major centre trade in the Indian Ocean region played a very significant role in the maritime commerce of India. The Portuguese who made it their political headquarters till 1530, and later their commercial capital almost till 1611, were chiefly responsible for the convergence of Asian as well as European commerce upon Cochin. Cochin with the help of the Portuguese began to control the trade of the Indian Ocean. Commodities that would have been taken by the native merchants to the traditional ports of the Red Sea and the Persian Gulf were controlled and diverted to a great extent to Cochin. The other traditional navigational lines were also largely modified to make the commodities of the Indian Ocean region to converge on this port. Commodities that were distributed through the East-West axis, i.e. via Malacca, Calicut, Cambay, Aden, Cairo, Alexandria and Venice began to reach Asian as well as European destinations through a new network which developed in the Indian Ocean region with Cochin as its core or centre. It eventually became what Calicut used to be, and changed the entire commercial balance through the Cochin–Lisbon commercial axis. The development of Cochin initiated by the Portuguese in the sixteenth century speaks for the present state of affairs in which Calicut is relegated to the background and Cochin is day-by-day coming to the fore as a major centre of trade and export.

All the control systems of *cartaz*, *armada* and fortresses were instituted to divert trade to Lisbon through the Cape route. However, it has to be said that only one stream of its commerce extended to Lisbon. Even so, the centralization of trade in Cochin realized through this control system, made this port a great distribution centre for Asian commodities. As a result, Cochin began to exercise a great measure of control even in intra-Asian trade. The relatively low rate of customs duties charged by the local ruler from the *casados* of Cochin gave it an added impetus. These *casado* traders, who entered into partnership with the native merchants and began to divert their own commodities as well as those of their own partners on a large scale to Cochin under their names, taking advantage of the concessionary rate granted to them by the king of Cochin, made Asian trade concentrate in this port unprecedented. The import of a large amount of precious metals such as gold as well as copper, and less frequently silver as well, from Europe to Cochin made traders from different parts of India visit Cochin frequently, to purchase these metals. These three metals were in high demand all over India for minting coins, silver and copper for making household utensils for the aristocratic families. Gold and silver were also largely used for making ornaments. These metals were brought to Cochin often in exchange for commodities from distant and far-flung areas of India.

Moreover, the rich pepper hinterland which Cochin enjoyed enabled the private traders (both native as well as *casados*) of Cochin to procure through their native links, the necessary merchandise for exchange with the rice and textiles of the Coromandel coast and the Bengal ports, or with the textiles and indigo of the Gujarat ports. Besides this, the rice from the Kanara ports was taken to Cochin for trading with the Maldives, Ceylon and Malacca. Horses were taken from Ormuz to Cochin to send them on to southern Kerala and Tamilnadu. Cowries were brought from the Maldives to Cochin to be taken to Gujarat and Pegu. Cloves, nutmeg and mace were brought from South-East Asia, as well as cinnamon from Ceylon, by the *casados* to Cochin and for further distribution all over India.

Cochin's contact was not limited to the ports and littoral centres of maritime India. Precious stones, diamonds and saltpetre from Madurai were brought to Cochin through the ghat route and taken to different Asian as well as European destinations. Thus the various commercial streams of India intersected at Cochin, where there existed a strong network of distributive trade. In short, the period from 1500 to 1663, when Cochin was ruled by the Portuguese, was quite unique in the history of Cochin.

Never before and never afterwards, under the other European powers such as the Dutch or the English, could this city re-gain the commercial importance which it acquired under the Portuguese. Though Cochin was later ruled by the Dutch (1663-95) and the English (1795-1947), this port did not regain its importance, which it had under the Portuguese. On the contrary it had to keep a low profile in these later periods, because the commercial capital of the Dutch was Batavia, and also they had other prominent trading centres even in India. Cochin was only one of the several feeding ports for the Dutch. Even during the English period, Cochin was reduced to a rather insignificant satellite port, as the prime English interest rested in Madras, Bombay and Calcutta. However, during the Portuguese period, though Goa was very important politically, the commercial activities were often dictated by Cochin. Cochin and its vast hinterland often formed one economic unit, which concentrated the economic and the commercial activities of Indian Ocean centre on this port. It is true that during this period Cochin emerged as the commercial capital of maritime India.

2. Cochin was the first port in the history of Asia to establish a direct trade relationship with the Atlantic ports. With the arrival of Cabral, Cochin began to establish a direct trade relationship with Lisbon, and the commodities of India and

other parts of Asia began to enter Antwerp and northern Europe. As discussed in the previous chapters, commodities from Quilon, Kayankulam and some of the hinterland areas were brought to this port. Spices such as cloves, nutmeg and mace from South-East Asia, textiles from Bengal, Coromandel and Gujarat were taken to this sea port for European export. It was chiefly from Cochin that all these commodities were loaded on to the ships and sent to Lisbon.

3. The ghat routes, which had already been used for a low-profile trade in the pre-Portuguese period, revived and flourished with the price fixation and the establishment of control systems in Cochin by the Portuguese. Actually the price fixation by the Portuguese underpriced the commodities and the producers as well, as the merchants began to look to the ghat route as a profitable outlet. Added to this, the *cartaz* system and frequent confiscation of the commodities in the absence of this Portuguese pass, made the natives co-operate with the traditional ghat routes, which were linked with the hinterland of Cochin. The tensions in the hinterland, especially between the St. Thomas Christians and the Portuguese, accelerated the flow of spices through this route to the ports of Coromandel, after the middle of the sixteenth century. Kumily, Munnar, Peringalkuthu were the important mountain outlets through which spices were diverted from the hinterland of Cochin to Dindigal and Madura, from where they were taken to the ports of Coromandel. It must be specially remembered that these ghat routes were more active than Aryankavu and Palghat passes, as far as the diversion of the spices from the hinterland of Cochin to the Tamil ports were concerned, as the latter passes were situated very far away from the production centres of Cochin. With the tightening of Portuguese control systems, trade through these ghat routes increased unprecedented. Consequently, as we have already seen in Chapters IV and V, the European export trade of pepper from Cochin, which formed 40 per cent of the total production in the second decade of the sixteenth century, fell to 3.1 per cent of total production by the first decade of the seventeenth century. Even though, there was a great increase in the production of pepper, almost 15.5 per cent of the total produce went through the ghat routes by the beginning of the seventeenth century, which was five times greater than the European export trade .

4. The amount of extraction, which Cochin as pre-colonial city did, was rather very little, as one single commodity, i.e. pepper, formed the seventy to ninety five per cent of the total cargo taken to Portugal. By the end of the sixteenth century, pepper became the greatest single commodity that was exported to Europe. Though at the beginning of the sixteenth century about 40 per cent of the total production was taken to Lisbon, it fell to 3.5 to 10 per cent by the beginning of the seventeenth century. The remaining ninety per cent was either distributed within Asia for consumption or taken to the ports of the Red Sea and the Persian Gulf for further distribution to Europe, via the Levant and Venice. This small figure in the pepper trade, which is significantly small in relation to the total production, gives us the impression that this trade did not seem to have risen to the dimensions of extracting commerce. The majority of the other commodities which filled the space of Lisbon-

bound vessels was also composed of spices and agricultural products. The products of the secondary sector like textiles from Bengal, the Coromandel coast and Gujarat entered the cargo list and often formed five to ten per cent of the total cargo. But they were not coming under the commodities reserved for the crown, so the profit from the trade in these items often went to private individuals settled in India. In general, taking the commodities together, one cannot actually perceive the element of extraction. But the tendency to grab more surplus was exhibited in the attempts at price fixation for pepper and other commodities, at a rate which was lower than that of pre-Portuguese times. It was actually an underpricing of the commodities and the elements of extraction of the surplus became increasingly evident from the fact that the Lusitanians did not allow a change in the price of pepper for more than 130 years, in spite of the value fluctuations of the currency and the increase in the cost of living or inflation. However, this impeded Portuguese commerce as well, for which they had to pay the price. The cultivators and merchants, over whom the Portuguese had no control, were in no way bound to sell the commodities at this low price to the Lusitanians, and naturally preferred to sell the commodities to the traders associated with the ghat route, who paid higher prices.

5. A look at the value of export trade from Cochin will shed further light on this issue. The pepper money imported to India could not be taken as the barometer to assess the value of export trade, as this money was often diverted to several purposes other than the purchase of spices. Though the crown officially used to ban the diversion of this fund, the practice continued throughout the period. The worth of the export trade from Cochin could easily be assessed by multiplying the quantity of cargo taken to Europe, with the price that prevailed in Cochin (where the fixed rate was 2.66 *cruzados* per quintal), as well as in Lisbon (where the minimum rate was 22 *cruzados* per quintal). The annual average export of pepper was estimated to be around 12,400 quintals. This shows that the value of pepper (which formed the major commodity of European export) taken to Lisbon was around 32,984 *cruzados*. However, besides the fixed price, the Portuguese used to pay quite a lot by way of 'protection cost' for the pepper trade. Thus we have to add to this figure the amount paid as annuities to the rulers of the hinterland, the cost of patrolling in the lagoons, at the junctional points of the rivers as well as along the western sea coast. The Portuguese practice of buying spices at a fixed price, which was lower than the pre-Portuguese period made an increase in the 'protection cost' inevitable, as the spices were often diverted to places where they were better priced. Besides this, the shipping cost would have to be added to the total expenditure. These various expenses added the price of pepper when it reached Lisbon. In Lisbon a quintal of pepper was sold at the minimum rate of 22 *cruzados*. Thus the value of the 12,400 quintals (which was estimated to be the annual average export from Malabar to Europe) was 2,72,800 *cruzados* in Lisbon, revealing a difference of 2,39,816 *cruzados* every year, which the Portuguese took as profit and as money to meet the expenses incurred in the trade between Cochin and Lisbon. Though we do not have details to assess the exact profit, it seems that the balance sheet was greatly favourable to the Portuguese. Besides pepper several other

commodities like ginger, cinnamon, cloves, nutmeg, diamonds and precious stones, which were greatly valued in Europe, were taken from Cochin to Lisbon. But pepper which formed the bulk commodity, has been taken as an example to assess the value of the export trade.

6. Since the hinterland was outside the control of the Portuguese, the possibilities for extraction were even lower. The economic decisions taken by the cultivators could, in no way, be influenced simply by the commercial policies of the Portuguese. The hinterland was integrated with the city of Cochin only insofar as the former enjoyed some advantages, and had their interests protected. When there was some clash of interests between the Portuguese and the various factors of the hinterland, as in the case of the war of Vadakkenkur king or the rebellion of the St. Thomas Christians, the hinterland put its interests in the forefront and was ready even to turn against the Portuguese. The same was true of the king of Cochin. He supported the Portuguese only as far as the latter helped him to protect his interests. When the Portuguese were against their plans and moves, the local kings used to assert themselves, and clashes ensued frequently. As Cochin was never a territory conquered by the Portuguese, but a free gift given by the local ruler of Cochin, there was a permanent dependency of the Lusitanians on the king of Cochin. This also made the Portuguese confer several concessions and favours on the local ruler. The king of Cochin too had a great sense of indebtedness to the Portuguese. They liberated him from the clutches of vassalage to the Zamorin and made him an independent king by officially performing his coronation ceremony in 1505. However, it must be said that the hinterland and the local ruler of Cochin often acted as a spontaneous machinery of check and control to the extracting tendencies of the Portuguese.

7. Though in all other Portuguese settlements, customs duty was used as a means for taking the surplus from the traders, Cochin had a different practice. As the port belonged to the local ruler, the Portuguese had to concede to him the right to collect customs duties. The king developed a strategy of collecting more money by reducing the rate for *casados*, which made commodities flow to Cochin from different directions under the name of *casados*, often belonging to them; at times belonging to native merchants but cleared the customs as merchandise belonging to *casado*. This practice reduced the Portuguese revenue from customs. All through the period of our study, as mentioned in previous chapters, the income of the local ruler from the customs of Cochin stood far higher than that of the Portuguese. It shows that customs was also a weak instrument in the hands of the Portuguese of Cochin, and that the possibilities of extraction were relatively little.

8. However, there was an indirect way of extraction in which the native vessels were allowed less frequently to conduct commerce. Actually this had emerged as a part of the Portuguese strategy to exercise control over the movements of ships, especially over merchant vessels. All the native vessels had to travel either with a pass or with the risk of being captured. It did greater harm to the trade of the local people than the direct way of extraction. The native traders who were less organized

(except the so-called corsairs), before the military-based arrangements of the Portuguese, had minimum options. The traditional native merchant groups were hit hard by this and they became relatively insignificant in the field of commerce by the second half of the sixteenth century. Most of the prominent Muslim merchants of Cochin were either pushed in to corsair activities or to donning the low-profile trade of peddlers. This gap was filled with the private Portuguese traders and the position of the traditional merchants was taken by the *casado* traders of Cochin.

9. However, the *casados* had more of a pro-Asian policy as far as their commerce was concerned. They took pepper from Cochin to Bengal or Coromandel and exchanged it with textiles which they further exchanged in South-East Asia for nutmeg, cloves and mace, etc., or pepper to China in exchange for porcelain and silk, and this exchange trade generated much more profit than the export trade to Europe. The various voyages and licences conceded to individuals increased the volume of this exchange trade. During the Portuguese period, often the profit from this exchange trade went into the hands of either *casados* who were settled in Cochin or of their native partners and this was further utilized as capital for further commercial enterprises. In contrast to the exchange trade, conducted under the Dutch or the British, where the profit of such trade was taken by the company and taken to Europe, there developed almost unknowingly an Asia-centred or India-centred trade policy among the *casados*, which made the drainage of wealth relatively negligible.

10. Precious metals like gold, silver and copper which were very rare in India, were imported to India from Europe in large volumes as pepper money. Though they were imported by the Portuguese to generate further profit either by sale in the open market or by investment in pepper, India had an abundant supply of these metals, which were in great demand for the minting of coins in the various native kingdoms. Most of the gold and silver was used for minting coins. A large volume of copper and some silver was also used for making ornaments, household utensils of aristocratic families. The flow of bullion to India, even if it was to generate further profit for the Portuguese, increased the wealth of the native kingdoms and chieftains and served to monetize the economy.

11. The features of pre-colonial cities began to appear, some in evident form and others in embryonic shape in Cochin, by this period. The city of Portuguese Cochin began to be dominated chiefly by the Europeans and later by mixed races but the predominant religion was Christianity. The presence of European women was very small, leading to the practice of the Portuguese marrying native women. The Portuguese city of Cochin maintained its identity by deliberately keeping it as a separate urban unit, comprising chiefly Europeans, and people of mixed races. Several characteristic features of a pre-colonial city can be traced in this part of Cochin. Several elements of European culture penetrated into Kerala through this urban unit.

12. There developed in and around Cochin new centres of economic importance

and commercial significance. It began with the Portuguese policy of transplanting the European concept of the balance of power in Malabar instead of the traditional norms existing in the region. They often supported the weak rulers and made alliances with them to compete or to fight against the powerful kings. Cochin was thus befriended to fight against Calicut. Later the kings of Vadakkenkur, Thekkenkur, Tanur and Porcad were supported with a view to serving their political designs. The end result of such political manoeuvring was that these places became not only places of political importance but also of economic significance. They became commercially important as well.

13. The export of pepper from Cochin to Europe, was only a stream of commerce parallel to the private trade from Cochin as well as the ghat route trade from the hinterland of Cochin. These three streams of commerce increased the demand for pepper which, in turn, intensified the pepper cultivation. More areas were brought under cultivation, making the agricultural tendencies of Kerala oriented towards commercial crops.

14. These three streams of commerce operating in parallel, and simultaneously, meant better economic conditions for the merchants and large scale cultivators, who could dictate the price of the commodities. This improved their life style. The bungalow model of architecture introduced by the Portuguese was imitated and taken to interior regions by the wealthy and the well-off. The sophisticated European way of life entered Cochin and the regions nearby.

15. The trade in nutmeg, cloves and mace with South-East Asia as well as in cinnamon with Ceylon led to the introduction of these plants in Kerala, especially in regions near Cochin which led to an agrarian as well as economic revolution in the later phase of its history. Different crops and plants like tapioca, which was the common man's bread in Kerala till the 1980s, pineapple, which is the main commercial crop of the present day Muvattupuzha, Vazhakulam and Kottayam regions, and cashew nut, which turned out to be the chief commercial crop of the Malabar regions, Quilon, central Kerala entered through Portuguese contact with Cochin. Though these items did not play an important role in the sixteenth and seventeenth centuries, they do play a major role in the present day economy of Kerala.

In general, Cochin, as far as its economic and commercial activities were concerned, went far beyond its city wall, to control the trade of Europe and Asia for more than a century. The conditions of Europe and India influenced, to a great extent, the ups and downs of Cochin's commercial activities, in various phases. However, Cochin, where the Portuguese, the first of the various European groups to come to Asia and India, established their first trade-oriented colony and urban centre, offers a rare, if not unique, development in history where the Asian trade was concentrated to promote European trade of exports and imports.

Bibliography

ARCHIVAL SOURCES

1. LISBON: ARQUIVO NACIONAL DA TORRE DO TOMBO

Cartas Missivas.
Cartas dos Vice-Reis da India.
Cartório dos Jesuitas.
Chancelarias Reais: D. Manuel I, D. João III, Privilegios (D. João III), D. Sebastião e D. Henrique, D. Filipe II.
Colecção de São Lourenço, vol. IV.
Colecção de São Vicente: Cod. no. 11, 12, 14, 17, 19, 22, 26.
Convento da Graça: Miscelâneas. Caixa e Cod. no. Caixa 2-1C, Caixa 2-3, Caixa 3-6D, Caixa 3-6L, Caixa 5-2, Caixa 5-3, Caixa 6-2E, Caixa 16-6F.
Corpo Cronologico: Parts I-III.
Documentos Remettidos: Cod. nos. 23-38.
Fragmentos: Caixas 4 and 5.
Gavetas.
Inquisição de Lisboa, Processo nos. 3836, 4516, 4656, 5265, 5808, 7296, 7543, 10096, 12292.
Leis: Livro do Registo de Leis e Regimentos de D.Manuel.
Miscelâneas Manuscritas, Cod. no. 1104, 1109, 1113, 1116.
Núcleo Antigo: nos. 705, 804, 807, 808.

2. LISBON: BIBLIOTECA DA AJUDA

46-XI-5; 51-VII-14; 51-VII-8; 51-VII-27, 51-VIII-43, 51-VIII-45, 51-VIII-46.

3. LISBON: BIBLIOTECA NACIONAL DE LISBOA

Fundo Geral. Cod. nos. 737, 1540, 1783, 1784, 1814, 1815, 1816, 1817, 1975, 1976, 1977, 1978, 1980, 1981, 1983, 1986, 2298, 2702, 3837, 4180, 7160, 7640, 11410.

4. ARCHIVO HISTORICO ULTRAMARINO, LISBOA

Caixas da India: Caixas 1-24.

5. EVORA: BIBLIOTECA PÚBLICA E ARQUIVO DISTRITAL

Nucleo de Manuscritos da Casa Forte CIX/2-3,
CXVI / 1-23, CIII/2-17, CXV/2-3.

6. ARQUIVO HISTORICO GENERAL DE SIMANCAS, SPAIN

Secretarias Provinciales, libros 1551, 1571.

7. ROMA: ARCHIVUM ROMANUM SOCIETAS IESU

Goa, 32 and 38; D. Duarte d'Eça, Relação dos Governadores da India (1571).

8. FÜRSTLICH UND GRÄFLICH FUGGERSCHES FAMILIEN UND STIFTUNGS ARCHIV, DILLINGEN/DONAU

MSS. Cod. no. 46.1.

9. STADTARCHIV AUGSBURG

MSS. no. 24.11, The letter of Georg Pock (1520).

10. NATIONAL BIBLIOTHEK, WIEN

Cod. 8955, 8961, 8964.

11. HISTORICAL ARCHIVES OF GOA

Livro das Monções

PRINTED DOCUMENTS (PRIMARY SOURCES)

Acenheiro, Cristovão Rodrigues, *Croniqua dos Reis de Portugal, Colecção de Ineditos de Historia Portugueza*, tom. V, Lisboa, 1926.

Aiyyar, Ulloor Parameswara (ed.), *Padapattu*, Trivandrum, 1924.

Alberi, Eugenio, *Le Relazioni degli Ambasciatori Veneti al Senato*, vol. 15, Firenze, 1863.

Albuquerque, Luis de (ed.), *Cronica do Descobrimento e Conquista da India pelos Portugueses: Codice anonimo Museu Britanico, Egerton 20901*, Coimbra, 1974.

Andrade, Francisco de, *Crónica do muyto alto e muyto poderoso rey destes Reynos de Portugal Dom João III*, 4 vols., Lisboa, 1613.

Andrade e Silva, Jacinta Freire de, *Vida de Dom João de Castro, quarto Vice-rei da Índia*, Lisboa, 1759.

Andrade e Silva, José Justino , *Collecção cronologica da legislação Portuguêsa*, 10 vols. and 5 supplementary volumes, Lisboa, 1954-9.

As Gavetas da Torre do Tombo, Lisbon, 1960-75, 11 vols.

Assemanus, J.S., *Bibliotheca Orientalis Clementino-Vaticana*, 4 vols., Rome, 1719-28.

A Translation of a Record Grandhavari in the State Archives, Trivandrum, 1973.

Baião, António (ed.), *Afonso de Albuquerque, Cartas para el Rei D. Manuel I*, Lisboa, 1942.

Baião, António, *Historia Quinhentista (inedita) do segundo cerco de Dio*, Coimbra, 1927.

Baldaeus, Philip, *A True and Exact Description of the Most Celebrated East Indies, Coasts of Malabar and Coromandel, as also of the Isle of Ceylon, with all the Adjacent Kingdom, Principalities, Cities, Chief Harbours, Structure, Pagan Temples, Products and Living Creatures*, London, 1672.

Barbosa, Duarte, *The Book of Duarte Barbosa: An Account of the Countries Bordering on the Indian Ocean and their Inhabitants*, tran. by Mansel Longworth Dames, 2 vols., Nendeln, 1967.

Barros, João de, *Asia. Dos feitos que os Portuguezes fizeram no Descobrimento e conquista dos Mares do Oriente*, ed. Livraria Sam Carlos, (facsimile of the edition of 1777-8), Lisboa, 1973, Decadas I-IV.

Bartolomeo, San, *Viaggio alle Indie Orientalie*, Roma, 1796.

Batuta, Ibn, *Die Reise des Arabers Ibn Batuta durch Indien und China*, edited by Hanz von Mzik, Hamburg, 1911.

Berjeau, J.B., *Calcoen: A Dutch Narrative of the Second Voyage of Vasco da Gama to Calicut*, printed at Antwerp *c.* 1504, London, 1874.

Biker, Julio Firmino Judice (ed.), *Collecção de Tratados e Concertos de Pazes que o Estado da India portuguesa fez com os Reis e Senhores com quem teve Relações nas Partes da Asia e Africa Oriental desde o Principio da Conquista até ao fim do seculo XVII*, Lisboa, 1881-7, 14 vols.

Birch, Gray (ed.), *The Commentaries of the Great Afonso Dalboquerque. Second Viceroy of India*, New York, 1975.

Bocarro, António, *Decada 13 da Historia da India*, edited by Rodrigo José da Lima Felner, 2 vols., Lisboa, 1876.

———, *Livro das Plantas de todas as fortalezas, cidades e Povoações do Estado da India Oriental*, vol. II, Transcricão de Isabel, Lisboa: 1992.

Botelho, Simão, 'Tombo do Estado da India (1554)', in *Subsídios para a Historia da India Portugueza*, edited by R.J.de Lima Felner, Lisboa, 1868, pp. 22ff.

Bouchon, Genevieve, *Navires et Cargaisons Retour de l'Inde en 1518, Caderno dos Officiaes da India da Carreguaçam das Náos que vieram o anno da b^c xviij* (ANTT, Nucléo Antigo, 705), Paris, 1977.

Bouchon, Genevieve et Thomaz, Luis Filipe (eds.), *Voyage dans Les Deltas du Gange et de l'Irraouaddy 1521*, Paris, 1988.

Boxer, C.R. (ed.), 'Uma raridade Bibliografica sobre Fernão Cron', in *Bibliofilia: De Bibliografia Luso-Brasileira*, vol. XII, no. I, Janeiro-Marco, 1871, pp. 323-44.

Boxer, C.R. and Vasconcelos (eds.), *Frazão de, André Furtado de Mendonça (1558-1610)*, Lisboa, 1956.

Brás, Alfonso de Albuquerque, *Comentarios de Afonso de Albuquerque*, Lisboa, 1973.

Brasio, Antonio (ed.), *Uma Carta Inedita de Valentim Fernandes*, Coimbra, 1959.

Brito, Bernardo Gomes de, *Historia Tragico-Maritima, 1552-96*, 2 vols., Lisboa, 1971.

Bullarium Patronatus Portugaliae Regum in Ecclesiis Africae, Asiae atque Oceaniae (ed.) Maria Levy Jordão, tom. I, Olisipone, 1868.

Bullarum collectio quibus Serenissimis Lusitaniae Algarbiorumque Regibus Terrarum omnium atque Insularum ultra Mare Transcurrentium sive jam acqisitae sint, sive in posterum acquirentur jus patronatus a summis Pontificibus liberaliter conceditur, Lisboa: 1707.

Caminha, Lourenço A. (ed.), *Ordenações da India do senhor Rei, D.Manuel de Eterna Memoria*, Lisbon, 1807.

Camões, Luis de, *Os Luciadas*, Lisboa, 1972.

Cassel, Johannes P., *Privilegia und handelsfreiheiten Welche die Könige von Portugal ehedem den deutschen Kaufleuten zu Lissabon erheilt haben*, Bremen: 1771.

Castanheda, Fernão Lopes de, *Historia do Descobrimento & Conquista da Índia pelos Portugueses*, 4 vols., 1924-33.

Castilho, Antonio, *A Cronica de D. João III*, published by Joaquim Verissimo Serrão, Paris, 1970.

Castro, Dom João de, *Roteiro em que se contem a viagem que fizeram os portuguêses no anno de 1541 partindo da nobre cidade de Goa atraves Suez que he no fim do Mar Roxo*, Lisboa, 1940.

Cha' Masser, *Relazione di Lunardo de Cha Masser, Apéndice à carta de El-Rey D. Manuel ao rei cathólico*, edited by Prospero Peragallo, in Memoria da Commissão no Centenário da Descoberta da America, Lisboa, 1892.

Coelho, Ramos (ed.), *Alguns Documentos da Torre do Tombo acerca das navegações e conquistas Portuguezas*, Lisboa, 1892.

Colecção da Legislação antiga do Reino de Portugal. Parte II da Legislação moderna. Ordenações e leis do Reino de Portugal, recopilado per mandado del Rei D. Filipe I., 3 vols., Coimbra, 1847.

Collecção de Notícias para a Historia e geografia das nações Ultramarinas que vivem nos domínios Portuguzes ou lhe são visinhas, 6 vols., Lisboa, 1812-56.

Coote, C.H. (ed.), *The Voyage from Lisbon to India, 1505-1506, being an Account and Journal by Albericus Vespuccius*, London, 1894.

Cordeiro, Luciano, *Batalhas da India.Como se perdeu Ormuz. Processo Inédito do século XVII*, Lisboa, 1896.

Correia, Gaspar, *Lendas da Índia*, 4 volumes in 8 parts, Lisboa, 1921-25.

Cortesão, Armando and Albuquerque, Luis de (eds.), *Obras Completas de D.João de Castro*, vols. I-III, Coimbra, 1976.

Costa, A. Fontura da (ed.), *Livro de Marinharia de Bernardo Fernandes (cerca de 1548)*, Lisboa, 1940.

Costa, Francisco da , 'Relatorio sobre o trato da pimenta feito por (....), escrivao da feitoria de Cochin', in Antonio da Silva Rego (ed.), *Documentação Ultramarina Portuguesa*, vol. III, Lisboa, 1963, pp. 310ff.

Couto, Diogo do, *Da Ásia dos feitos que os Portuguezes fizeram na Conquista e Descobrimento das Terras e Mares do Oriente*, 15 vols., Lisboa, 1973-5, Décadas IV-XII.

———, *O Soldado Práctico*, edited by Manuel Rodrigues Lapa, Lisboa, 1937.

Coutinho, Lopo de Sousa, *Livro primeiro do cerco de Diu, que os Turcos poseram a fortaleza de Diu*, Coimbra, 1556.

Coutre, Jacques de, *Andanzas Asiaticas*, edited by Eddy Stols, B.Teensma and J. Werberckmoes, Madrid, 1991.

Dannenfeldt, Karl H., *Leonhard Rauwolf: Sixteenth Century Physician, Botanist & Traveller*, Massachusetts, 1968.

Danvers, F.C., *Report to the Secretary of State for India in Council on the Portuguese Records Relating to the East Indies Contained in the Archivo da Torre do Tombo and the Public Libraries at Lisbon and Evora*, London, 1892.

Denuce, J., *Inventaire des Affaitadi Banqueirs Italiens á Anvers de L'Annee 1568*, Antwerp, 1934.

——— 'Privileges Commerciaux accordes par les Rois de Portugal aux Flammands et aux Allemands, XVe et XVIIe Siécles', in *Arquivo Historico Portuguez*, vol. VII, Lisboa, 1909.

Dinis, António Joaquim Dias, *Monumenta Henricina*, 15 vols., Coimbra, 1960-74.

Documentos inéditos para a história de D.Sebastião, edited by Joaquim Verissimo Serrão, Coimbra, 1958.

Documentos sôbre os portuguêses em Moçambique e na África Central, 1497-1840, 7 vols., Lisboa, 1962.

Falcão, Luis de Figueiredo, *Livro em que se contém toda a fazenda e real patrimonio dos reis de Portugal, Índia, e Ilhas adjacentes, e outras particularidades, escripta no anno de MDCVII*, Lisboa, 1859.

Felner, Rodrigo José de Lima (ed.), *Subsidios para a Historia da India Portugueza*, Lisboa, 1868.

Fernandes, Valentim, *O Manuscrito de Valentim Fernandes*, edited by Antonio Baião, Lisboa, 1940.

Ferreira, Godofredo, *Relação da viagem de um correio do vice-rei das Indias Orientais a sua magestade expedido de Goa no primeiro de Janeiro 1608*, Lisboa, 1953.

Ferreira, J.A.Pinto, 'Privilegios concedidos pelos reis de Portugal aos alemães nos seculos XV e XVI', in *Boletim Cultural da Camara Municipal do Porto*, vol. XXXII, fasciculos I, part 2, Porto, 1969, pp. 339-96.

Ferroli, D., *The Jesuits in Malabar*, 2 vols., Bangalore, 1939-51.

Filippo P.Amati di S., *Biografia dei Viaggiatori Italiani*, Roma, 1882.

Fonseca, Henrique Quirénio da (ed.), *Diários de navegação da Carreira da Índia nos anos de 1595, 1596, 1597, 1600 e 1613*, Lisboa, 1938.

Fonseca, Luis Adão da and Asenzio, Jose Manuel Ruiz (eds.), *Corpus Documental del Tratado de Tordesillas*, Valladolid, 1995.

Foster, William (ed.), *Early Travels in India 1583-1619*, Oxford, 1921.

———, *The English Factories in India, 1618-1621; A Calendar of Documents in the India Office, British Museum and Public Record Office*, Oxford, vol. II, 1622-3, vol. III, 1624-9, Oxford, 1906-9.

———, *Letters Received by the East India Company from its Servants in the East. Transcribed from the Original Correspondence of the India Office*, vol. II, 1613-15; vol. III, 1615; vol. IV, 1616; vol. V, 1616; vol. VI, 1617; London, 1897-1902.

———, *The Voyage of Nicholas Downton to the East Indies: 1614-1615*, London, 1939.

———, *The Voyage of Thomas Best to the East Indies, 1612-1614*, London, 1934.

Foster, William (ed.), *The Red Sea and Adjacent Countries at the close of the Seventeenth Century: as Described by Joseph Pitts, William Daniel, and Charles Jacques Poncet*, London: The Hakluyt Society, 2nd series, vol. 100, 1949.

Fulin, Rinaldo, *Diarii e Diaristi Veneziani*, Venice, 1881.

Galletti, A., *The Dutch in Malabar*, Madras, 1912.

Gama, Vasco da, *Diário da viagem de Vasco da Gama, Attributed to Alvaro Velho*, 2 vols. edited by A. de Magalhães Basto, Oporto, 1945.

Garcia, José Inácio de Abranches, *Archivo da Relação de Goa, contendo documentos dos séculos XVII, XVIII e XIX até á organização da nova Relação pelo decreto de 7 de Dezembro de 1836*, 2 vols., part I, 1607-40, Nova Goa, 1871.

Giertz, Gernot, *Vasco da Gama, die Entdeckung des Seewegs nach Indien: ein Augenzeugenbericht 1497-1499*, Tübingen, 1980.

Godinho, Vitorino Magalhães, *Les Finances de L'état Portugais des Indes Orientales (1517-1635): Matériaux pour une Étude Structuralle et Conjoncturelle*, Paris, 1982.

Góis, Damião de, *Crónica do seréssimo senhor Rei D.Emmanuel*, .ed.by Joaquim Martins Teixeira de Carvalho and David Lopes, 4 vols., Coimbra, 1926.

Gomçallvez, Nycolão, *Livro que trata das Cousas da India e do Japão*, edited by Adelino da Almeida Calado, Coimbra, 1957.

Goncalves, Diogo, *Historia do Malavar*, edited by Josef Wicki, Münster, 1955.

Gouveia, Antonio de, *Jornada do Arcebispo*, Lisboa, 1988.

Greenlee, W.B. (ed.), *The Voyage of Pedro Alvares Cabral to Brazil and India from Contemporary Documents and Narratives*, London, 1938.

Greiff, B. (ed.), *Tagebuch des Lucas Rem aus den Jahren 1494-1541: Ein Beitrag zur Handelsgeschichte der Stadt Augsburg*, Augsburg, 1861.

Grey, Edward (ed.), *The Travels of Pietro della Valle in India*, Hakluyt Society, 1st series, vols. 84-5, London, 1892.

Grotius, Hugo, *The Freedom of the Seas or the Right which belongs to the Dutch to take part in the East Indian Trade*, tran. by Ralph van Deman Magoffin, London, 1916.

Gubernatis, Angelo de, *Storia die Viaggiatori Italiani nelle India Orientali*, Livorno, 1875.

Guerreiro, Fernão, *Relação Anual das Coisas que fizeram os Padres da Companhia de Jesus nas suas Missões (1604-1606)*, tom. II, Coimbra, 1934.

Gune, V.T. (ed.), *Assentos do Conselho da Fazenda (1613-1621)*, vol. I, parte I (1613-17), Panaji/Goa, 1979.

Haemmerle, Albert (ed.), *Stetten-Jahrbuch*, MCML, vol. II, *Deren von Steten Geschlechterbuch*, MDXXXXVIII.

Hakluyt, Richard, *The Principal Navigations, Voyages, Traffiques and Discoveries of the English Nation*, 12 vols., Hakluyt Society; Glasgow, 1905-7.

Hümmerich, Franz, *Vasco da Gama und die Entdeckung des Seewegs nach Ostindien*, München, 1898.

Jordanus, Friar, *Mirabilia Descripta*, trans., by Colonel Henry Yule, London, 1863.

Klarwill, Victor von (ed.), *The Fugger News-Letters. Being a Selection of Unpublished Letters from the Correspondents of the House of Fugger during the Years 1568-1605*, 1st series translated by H.Gordon Selfridge, London, 1924. 2nd series translated by L.S.R. Byrne, London, 1926.

Krasa, Miloslav, Polisensky, Joseph and Ratos, Peter (ed.), *European Expansion 1494-1519: The Voyages of Discovery in the Bratislava Manuscript, Lyc.515/8*, Prague, 1986.

Laughten, Josen Knox (ed.), *State Papers Relating to the Defeat of Spanish Armada Anno 1588*, London, 1894.

Laval, Pyrard de, *The Voyage of Fraçois Pyrard of Laval to the East Indies, the Maldives, the Moluccas and Brazil*, translated by Albert Gray, London, 1887.

Linhares, Conde de (D.Miguel de Noronha), *Diário do Terceiro conde de Linhares, vice-rei da India*, 2 vols., Lisboa, 1937-43.

Linschoten, Jan Huyghen van, *The Voyage of Jan Huyghen van Linschoten to the East Indies*, 2 vols., London: The Hakluyt Society, vols. 70-1, 1885.

Lopes, David (ed.), *Historia dos Portugueses no Malabar: Manuscrito Arabe do século XVI*, Lisboa, 1898.

Lopes, Thomé, 'Navegação as Indias Orientales escrita em Português por Thomé Lopes', in *Collecção de Noticias para a Historia e Geografia das Nações ultramarinas que vivem nos dominios Portugueses ou lhes são vizinhas*, tom. II, nos.1 and 2, Lisboa, 1812, pp. 182-203.

Luz, Francisco Paulo Mendes da, 'Livro das Cidades e Fortalezas que a Coroa de Portugal tem nas Partes da India, e das Capitanias e mais cargo que nelas ha e da importancia deles', in *Boletim da Biblioteca da Universidade de Coimbra*, vol. XXI, 1953, pp. 63ff

———, *Regimento da Casa da India. Manuscrito do século XVII existente no Arquivo Geral de Simancas*, Lisboa, 1992.

Major, R.H., *India in the Fifteenth Century—Being a Collection of Narratives of Voyages to India in the Century preceding the Portuguese Discovery of the Cape of Good Hope from Latin, Persian, Russian and Italian Sources*, New Delhi, 1975.

Marucci, Ettore (ed.), *Lettere edite e inedite di Filippo Sassetti*, Firenze, 1855.

Mathew, K.S. and Afzal Ahmad, *Emergence of Cochin in the Pre-Industrial Era: A Study of Portuguese Cochin*, Pondicherry, 1990.

Montalboddo, Fracanzano, *Paesi nouvamente retrovati et novo mondo da Alberico Vesputio florentino intitulato*, Vicenza, 1507.

Mosseh Pereyra de Paiva, *Notisias dos Judeus de Cochim, mandadas por Mosseh Pereyra de Paiva, introduction by Moses Bensabat Amzalak*, Lisboa, 1923.

Nazareth, Casimiro Christovam da, *Mitras Lusitanas no Oriente: Catalogo Chronologico-Historico dos Prelados de Egreja Metropolitana de Goa e das Dioceses Suffraganas com a Recompilação das Ordenanças por Elles Emittidas e Summario dos Factos Notaveis da História Ecllesiastica de Goa*, Nova Goa, 1887.

Newton, A.P. (ed.), *Travel and Travellers of the Middle Ages*, New York, 1968.

Nunes, António, 'O Livro dos Pesos, Medidas e Moedas', in *Subsidios para a Historia da India Portuguesa*, Lisboa, 1868, pp. 61ff.

Nußer, Horst G.W., *Frühe Deutsche Entdecker: Asien in Berichten Unbekannter deutscher Augenzeugen 1502-1506*, München, 1980.

Oliveira, Eduardo Freiere de, *Elementos para a História do Município de Lisboa*, 19 vols., Lisboa, 1882-1911, 1942-3.

Orta, Garcia da, *Colóquios dos simples e Drogas da India*, edition of Conde de Ficalho, 2 vols., Lisboa, 1977.

Pacheco, Duarte, *Esmeraldo de Situ Orbis*, translated and edited by H.T. Kimble, Nendeln, 1967.

Pacifici, Sérjio J. (ed.), *Copy of a Letter of the King of Portugal sent to the King of Castile Concerning the Voyage and the Success of India*, Minneapolis, 1955.

Panamo, Luis de, *De Origine et Progressy Officii Sanctae Inqvisitionis eiusque dignitate et Vtilitate, De Romani Pontificis Potestate et Delegata Inqvisitorum: Edicto Fidei, et Ordine Iudiciario Sancti Officii, Quaestiones decem*, Liv. II, Matriti, 1598.

Pato, Raymundo Antonio de Bulhão (ed.), *Documentos Remettidos da India ou Livro das Monções*, vols. I-IV, Lisboa, 1884-1935.

Pato, Raymundo António de Bulhão and Mendonça, Henrique Lopes de, *Cartas de Affonso de Albuquerque seguidas de documentos que as elucidam*, 7 vols., Lisboa, 1884-1935.

Pereira, A.B. de Bragança, *Arquivo Português Oriental*, 10 vols., Bastora: 1937- 40.

Peres, Damião (ed.), *Regimentos das Cazas das Indias e Mina*, Coimbra, 1947.

Pirés, Tomé, *The Suma Oriental of Tomé Pires: An Account of the East from the Red Sea to Japan, written in Malacca and India in 1512-1515*, Nendeln, 1967.

Pissurlencar, Paduronga S.S. (ed.), *Assentos do Conselho do Estado*, vol. I *(1618-1633)*, vol. II *(1633-1643)*, Bastora/Goa, 1953-4.

Pissurlencar, Paduronga S.S., *Regimento das Fortalezas da Índia*, Bastora/Goa, 1951.

Pissurlencar, Panduronga S.S. and V.T. Gune (eds.), *Assentos do Conselho do Estado. Supplementary Series*, vol. I, parte 2 (1624-7), Panaji/Goa, 1972.

Polo, Marco, *The Book of Ser Marco Polo the Venetian Concerning the Kingdom and the Marvels of the East*, 2 vols., edited by Sir Henry Yule, London, 1903.

Priuli, Girolamo, *I Diarii di Girolamo Priuli, 1494-1512*, vol. I, Citta di Castelo, 1921; vols. II and IV, Bologna, 1933-46.

Quirini, Vincenzo, 'Relazioni delle Indie Orientali di Vincenzo Quirini', in Eugenio Alberi, *Le Relazioni degli Ambasciatori Veneti al Senato*, vol. XV, Firenze, 1863, pp. 15ff

Ramusio, Giovanni Battista, *Delle Navigationi et Viaggi*, 3 vols., Venice, 1550-6.

Ravenstein, E.G. (ed.), *A Journal of the first Voyage of Vasco da Gama 1497-1499*, Haklyut Society, vol. 99, London, 1898.

Rebello, Jacinto Ignacio de Brito, *Livro de Marinharia: Tratado da Agulha de Marear de João de Lisboa. Roteiros, Sondas e Outros Conhecimentos relativos a Navegação*, Codice do Seculo XVI, Lisboa, 1903.

Regimento dos Officiais das Cidades, Villas e Lugares destes Reynos com Privilegio del Rey Nosso Senhor, Lisboa, 1504.

Rego, António da Silva (ed.), *Boletim da Filmoteca Ultramarina Portuguesa*, nos. 1-10, Lisboa, 1954-8.

———, *Documentação para a Historia das Missões do Padroado Português do Oriente-India*, 12 vols., Lisboa, 1948-58.

———, *Documentos Remetidos da Índia ou Livros das Monções*, vols.VI-X, Lisboa, 1974-82.

———, *Documentação Ultramarina Portuguesa*, vols. I-III, Lisboa, 1960-3.

———, *Gavetas da Torre do Tombo*, vols.VI and IX, Lisboa, 1967-71.

Relação das Plantas & Dezcripsões de Todas as Fortalezas, Cidades e Povoações que os Portuguezes tem no Estado da India, Lisboa, MCMXXXVI.

Ribeiro, Luciano (ed.), *Registo da Casa da India*, 2 vols., Lisboa, 1954-5.

Rivara, Joaquim Heliodoro da Cunha (ed.), *Archivo Portuguez Oriental*, 6 fasciculos in 10 parts, New Delhi, 1992.

Sá, Artur Basélio de, *Documentação para a Historia das Missões do Padroado Português do Oriente - Insulindia*, 6 vols., Lisboa, 1954-88.

Sanceau, Elaine, *Colecção de São Lourenço*, 3 vols., Lisboa, 1975-8.

Sanderson, John, *The Travels of John Sanderson in the Levant, 1584-1602 with his Autobiography and selections from his correspondence*, edited by William Foster, London, 1931.

Sanuto, Marino, *I Diarii di Marino Sanuto: 1496-1533*, edited by G. Berchet, R. Fulin, N. Barrozi, F. Steffani and M. Allegri, 58 vols. Venice, 1879-1903.

Schulze, Franz, *Balthasar Springers Indienfahrt 1505-06*, Strassburg, 1902.

Schurhammer, George and Wicki, Josef (ed.), *Epistolae S. Francisi Xaverii aliaque eius Scripta*, vol. I, Rome, 1945.

Sen, Surendranath (ed.), *Indian Travels of Thevenot and Careri*, New Delhi, 1949.

Serrão, Joaquim Verissimo, *Comentarios de Afonso de Albuquerque*, Lisboa, 1973.

Serrão, Joaquim Verissimo (ed.), *Um Voyageur Portugais en Perse au debut du XVIIe siécle*, Nicolau de Orta Rebelo, Lisboa, 1972.

Serjeant, R.B., *The Portuguese off the South Arabian Coast; Hadrami Chronicles with Nemini and European Accounts of Dutch Pirates off Mocha in the Seventeenth Century*, Oxford, 1963.

Shaykh, Zaynuddin, *Tuhfat-ul-Mujahidin*, translated by S. Muhammed Husain Nainar, Madras, 1942.

Silva, J. Gentil da, *Alguns elementos para a Historia do comercio da India de Portugal existentes na Biblioteca Nacional de Madrid*, Lisboa, 1951.

———, *Marchandises et finances, Lettres de Lisbonne 1563-1578*, 2 vols., Paris, 1959-61.

Silva, J.J. Andrade, *Collecção Chronologica de Legislação Portuguesa, 1603-1612*, Lisboa, 1854.

Silva, Luiz Augusto Rebello da, *Corpo Diplomatico Português, contendo os actos e relações politicas de Portugal com as diversas potências do mundo desde o século XVI até aos nossos dias*, vols. 1-9, edited by José da Silva Mendes Leal, vols. 10-14 edited by Jayme Constantino de Freitas Moniz, Lisboa, 1862-1910.

Silveira, Francisco Rodrigues, *Memorias de um soldado da India*, edited by A. de S.S. Costa Lobo, Lisboa, 1987.

Silveira, Luis da, *Livro das Plantas das Fortalezas, Cidades e Povoações do Estado da India Oriental, com as Descrições do Maritimo dos Reinos e Provincias onde estão situados e outros Portos Principais daqueles partes: Contribuição para a História das Fortalezas dos Portugueses no Ultramar, Reproduction of the codice 1471*, existing in the Biblioteca do Paço Ducal de Vila Viçosa, Lisboa, 1991.

Sinclair W.F. and Ferguson D. (eds.), *The Travels of Pedro Texeira*, Hakluyt Society, vol. 9, London, 1902.

Solis, Duarte Gomes, *Alegacion en favor de la Companhia de la India Oriental Comercios Ultramarinos, que de nuevo se instituyó en le Reyno de Portugal*, edited by Moses Bensabat Amzalak, Lisboa, 1955.

———, *Discursos sobre los comercios de la dos Indias*, edited by Moses Bensabat Amzalak, Lisboa, 1943.

Sousa, Faria Y., *Asia Portuguesa: The History of the Discovery and Conquest of India by the Portuguese*, translated by John Stevens, 4 vols., London, 1695.

Sousa, Frei Francisco de, *Oriente conquistado a Jesu Christo pelos Padres da Companhia de Jesus da Provincia de Goa*, 2 vols., Lisboa, 1710.

Sousa, Frei Luis de, *Anais de Dom João III*, edited by M. Rodrigues Lapa, 2 vols., Lisboa, 1938.

Sprenger, Balthasar, *Die Merfart vnn erfarung nüwer schiffung und wege zu viln onerkanten Inseln und Künigreichen von dem grossmechtigen portugalischen Kunig Emanuel Erforschort/funden/bestritten vnnd ingenomen/Auch wunderbarliche streyt/ ordenung/leben wesen handlung vnd wunderwercks/des Volcks und Tyrer dar inn wonende/findestu in diessein Buchlyn warhaftiglich beschryben vnn abkundterfeyt/ wie ich Balthasar Sprenger so sollichs selbs: in Kurtzverschynen zeiten: geschen vnn erfaren habe*, 1509.

Stanley, E.J. Henry (ed.), *The Three Voyages of Vasco da Gama and His Viceroyalty from Lendas da India of Gaspar Correia*, New York, 1869.

Stasiak, Stephen, 'Les Indes Portugaises a la fin du XVI siecle d'apres la Relation du Voyage fait a Goa en 1596 par Christophe Pawlowski, Gentilhomme polonais', in *Rocznik Orjentalistyczny*, vol. III, 1926.

Tavernier, Jean Baptiste de, *Travels in India*, translated by V. Ball, 2 vols., London, 1889.

Temple, Richard Carnac (ed.), *The Travels of Peter Mundy in Europe and Asia, 1608-1667*, London, 1919.

Torre, Antonio de la, *Documentos sobre Relaciones internacionales de los Reyes Católicos, 1479-1504*, 4 vols., Barcelona, 1949-66.

Trindade, Frei Paulo de, *Conquista espiritual do Oriente: em que da relação de algumas coisas mais notaveis que fizeram os Frades Menores da Santa Provincia de S.Tomé da Índia Oriental em a pregação da fé e conversão dos infiéis em mais de trinta reinos, do Cabo da Boa Esperança até as remotéssimas ilhas do Japão*, edited by Felix Lopes, O.F.M., 3 vols., Lisboa, 1962-7.

Vallavanthara, Antony, *India in 1500 A.D.: The Narratives of Joseph the Indian*, Mannanam, 1984.

Varthema, Ludovico di, *The Travels of Ludovico di Varthema in Egypt, Syria, Arabia Deserta and Arabia Felix, in Persia, India and Ethiopia, A.D.1503-1508*, edited by George Percy Badger, New York, 1863.

Wiegas, Artur (ed.), *Relação anual das coisas que fizeram os padres da Companhia de Jesus nas suas missões*. vol. I, 1600-3; vol. II, 1604-6; vol. III. 1607-9.

Wicki, Josef (ed.), *Documenta Indica*, 8 vols., Roma, 1948-63.

Yule, Colonel Henry (ed.), *Cathay and the Way thither, Being a Collection of Medieval Notices of China*, vols. I-II, London, 1866.

SECONDARY SOURCES

Abraham, Meera, *Two Medieval Merchant Guilds of South India*, New Delhi, 1988.

Achyuta Menon, C., *The Cochin State Manual*, Ernakulam, 1911.

Aerthail, Jacob, *Kanjirappally Noottandukaliloode*, Kanjirappally, 1985.

Afonso, John Correa (ed.), *Intrepid Itinerant: Manuel Godinho and his Journey from India to Portugal in 1663*, Bombay, 1990.

Aghassian, M. and K. Kevonian, 'Le Commerce armenien dans l'Ocean Indien, aux 17e et 18e siecles', in Denys Lombard and Jean Aubin (eds.), *Marchands, et hommes d'affaires asiatiques dans l'Ocean Indien e la Mer de Chine 13e -20e siecles*, Paris, 1988, pp. 155-81.

Ahmad, Afzal, 'Indian Textiles and the Portuguese Trade in the Seventeenth Century (1600-1663)', in *Studia*, 48, 1989, pp. 213-36.

———, *Indo-Portuguese Trade in Seventeenth Century, 1600-1663*, New Delhi, 1991.

Aiya, V. Nagam, *The Travancore State Manual*, 3 vols., Trivandrum, 1906.

Albuquerque, Luis de (ed.), *Dicionario de Historia dos Descobrimentos Portugueses*, 2 vols., Lisboa, 1994.

Allen, W.E.D., *Problems of Turkish Power in the Sixteenth Century*, London, 1963.

Almeida, Fortunato de, *Historia da Igreja em Portugal*, 4 vols., Coimbra, 1910-22.

———, *História de Portugal*, 6 vols., Coimbra, 1922-9.

Almeida, Manuel Lopes de, *Memorial de Pero Roiz Soares*, vol. I, Coimbra, 1953.

Amaral, Maria Valentine Cotta do, *Privilegios de Mercadores Estrangeiros no Reinado de D.João III*, Lisboa, 1965.

Aragão, A.C. Teixeira de, *Descriçao Geral em Nome dos Reis e Regentes e Governadores de Portugal*, vol. III, Porto, 1964.

———, *Descrição Geral e Historica das Moedas cunhadas em nome dos reis, Regentes e Governadores de Portugal*, vol. III, Porto, 1966.

———, *Vasco da Gama e a Vidigueira - Estudo Historico*, Lisboa, 1898.

Arasaratnam, Sinnappah, 'Merchants of Coromandel in Trade and Entrepreneurship circa 1650-1700', in Roderich Ptak and Dietmar Rothermund (eds.), *Emporia, Commodities and Entrepreneurs in Asian Maritime Trade, c.1400-1750*, Stuttgart, 1990.

Arasaratnam, Sinnappah and Ray, Aniruddha (eds.), *Masulipatanam and Cambay. A History of Two Port-Towns*, New Delhi, 1994, pp. 44ff.

Arayathinal, Thomas, *A Short History of Irapuzhai or Aruvithurai*, Erattupetta, 1953.

Ashtor, Eliyahu, 'The Karimi Merchants', in *Journal of the Royal Asiatic Society of Great Britain and Ireland*, London, 1956.

———, 'The Venetian Supremacy in Levatine Trade: Monopoly or Pre-colonialism?', in the *Journal of the European Economic History*, vol. III, no. 1, Rome, 1974.

Atiya, Aziz S., *History of Eastern Christianity*, South Bend, 1968.

Aubin, Jean, 'L'apprentissage de L'Inde: Cochin 1503-1504', in *Moyen Orient & Océan Indien, XVIe -XIXe. S.*, IV, Paris, 1987, pp. 1-20

———, 'Le Orçamento do Estado da India de Antonio Abreu (1574)', *Separata de Studia*, Lisboa, 1959.

Ayyar, K.V. Krishna, *The Zamorins of Calicut*, Calicut, 1938.

Azevedo, João Lúcio de, *Epocas de Portugal Economico-Esboços de Historia*, Lisboa, 1973.

———, *História dos Cristãos Novos portuguêses*, Lisboa, 1975.

Azevedo, Pedro de and Antonio Baião, *O Arquivo da Torre do Tombo, Sua Historia, Corpos que o compõem e organização*, Lisboa, 1989.

Balandier, G., 'The Colonial Situation: A Theoretical Approach', in *Social Changes: The Colonial Situation* (ed.) Immanuel Wallerstein, New York, 1966.

Basto, A.de Magalhaes, *Historia da Santa Casa da Misericordia do Porto*, vol. I, Porto, 1934.

Beazley, Charles Raymond, *The Dawn of Modern Geography*, 3 vols., London, 1897-1906.

Beckingham, C.F. 'The Travels of Pero de Covilhão and their Significance', *Congresso Internacional de História dos Descobrimentos*, Lisbon, 1960 Actas, 2, 1961, pp. 1-14.

Bernard, Father, *The History of the St.Thomas Christians*, Palai, 1916.

Bernard, K.L., 'Fort Cochin under the Portuguese', in the *Souvenir of Fifth International Seminar on Indo-Portuguese History*, Cochin, 1989, pp. 5ff.

———, *History of Fort Cochin*, Cochin, 1991.

Blanco, Maria Manuela Sobral, O Estado Portugues da India da Rendição de Ormuz á Perda de Cochim: 1622-1663', 2 vols., Unpublished Doctoral Dissertation submitted to the Faculdade de Letras da Universidade de Lisboa, Lisboa, 1992.

Blitz, Rudolph C., 'Mercantilist Policies and their Pattern of World Trade, 1500-70', in *Journal of Economic History*, 27 March 1967, pp. 39-55.

Blusse, Leonard and George Winius , 'The Origin and Rhythm of Dutch Agression against the Estado da India 1601-1661', in Teotonio R. de Souza (ed.), *Indo-Portuguese History: Old Issues, New Questions*, New Delhi, 1985, pp. 73-83.

Bouchon, Genevieve, 'Calicut at the Turn of the Sixteenth Century', in *The Asian Seas 1500-1800: Local Societies, European Expansions and the Portuguese, Revista de Cultura*, vol. I, ano V, 1991, pp. 41ff.

———, 'Glimpses of the Beginnings of the Carreira da India (1500-1518)', in Teotonio R.de Souza, *Indo-Portuguese History: Old Issues, New Questions*, New Delhi, 1985, pp. 40ff.

Bouchon, Genevieve, *Albuquerque, le Lion des Mers d'Asie*, Paris, 1992.

———, *Mamale de Cananor-Un Adversaire de l'Inde Portugaise (1507-28)*, Paris, 1975.

———, 'Les Musulmans du Kerala a L'Epoque de la Découverte Portugaise', in *Mare Luso-Indicum*, II, Paris, 1973, pp. 1-54.

———, *Navires et cargaisons retour de l'Inde en 1518*, Paris, 1977.

———, 'Les Premiers Voyages Portugaises a Pasai et a Pegu', *Archipel*, 18, 1979.

———, 'Sixteenth Century Malabar and the Indian Ocean', in Ashin Das Gupta and M.N. Pearson (eds.), *India and the Indian Ocean 1500-1800*, Calcutta, 1987, pp. 162-84.

Bouchon, Genevieve and Lombard, Denys, 'The Indian Ocean in the Fifteenth Century', in *India and the Indian Ocean 1500-1800*, edited by Ashin Das Gupta and M.N. Pearson, Delhi, 1987.

Boxer, C.R., 'Anglo-Portuguese Rivalry in the Persian Gulf 1615-1635', in Edgar Prestage (ed.), *Chapters in Anglo-Portuguese Relations*, Watford, 1935, pp. 46-129.

———, 'The Carreira da India (Ships, Men, Cargoes, Voyages)', in *O Centro de Estudo Historico Ultramarinos e as comemorações e Henriquinas*, Lisboa, 1961, pp. 33-82.

———, *The Dutch Seaborne Empire, 1600-1800*, London, 1965.

———, *Four Centuries of Portuguese Expansion, 1415-1825*, Johannesburg, 1961.

———, *From Lisbon to Goa, 1500-1750: Studies in Portuguese Maritime Enterprise*, Variorum, Hampshire, 1990.

———, *João de Barros: Portuguese Humanist and Historian of Asia*, New Delhi, 1981.

———, *Mary and Misogamy: Women in Iberian Expansion Overseas, 1415-1815*, London, 1975.

———, 'On a Portuguese Carrack's Bill of Lading in 1625', in *Petrus Nonius, Orgão do Grupo Portugues de Historia das Ciensas, II*, Lisboa, 1939, pp. 176ff.

———, *Portuguese Conquest and Commerce in Southern Asia: 1500-1750*, Variorum, Hampshire, 1985.

———, *Portuguese in India in the Mid-seventeenth Century*, Delhi, 1980.

———, 'Portuguese Military Expeditions in Aid of the Mings against the Manchus, 1627-1647', in Charles Ralph Boxer, *Estudos para a Historia deMacau, seculos XVI e XVII*, vol. I, Lisboa, 1991, pp. 105-17.

———, 'Portuguese Roteiros 1500-1700', in *the Mariners Mirror*, XX, London, 1934.

———, *The Portuguese Seaborne Empire, 1415-1825*, London, 1969.

———, *Portuguese Society in the Tropics: The Municipal Councils of Goa, Macao, Bahia and Luanda, 1510-1580*, Madison, 1965.

———, 'The Principal Ports of Call in the Carreira da India (16th-17th Centuries)', in *Recueils de la Societe Jean Bodin XXXIII Les Grandes Escalas Zeme Partie: Les Temps Modernes*, Brussels, 1972, pp. 29-65.

———, *Race Relation in the Portuguese Colonial Empire 1415-1825*, Oxford, 1963.

———, 'Three Historians of Portuguese Asia' - *Barros, Couto and Bocarro in Boletim do Instituto Portugues de Hong Kong*, no. 1, July 1948, pp. 15-44.

———, 'War and Trade in the Indian Ocean and the South China Sea (1600-1650)', in *The Great Circle, Journal of the Australian Association for Maritime History 1/2*, Nedlands, Australia, 1979.

Boyajian, James C., *Portuguese Bankers at the Court of Spain 1626-1650*, New Jersey: (without date of publication).

Brakel, S. van, *De Hollandsche handelscompagnieën der Zeventiende eeuw*, 'S' Gravenhage, 1908.

Braudel, Fernand, *Civilization and capitalism 15th-18th Century*; vol. I: *The Structures of Everyday Life*; vol. II: *The Wheels of Commerce*; vol. III: *The Perspective of the World*, New York, 1981-4.

———, *The Mediterranean and the Mediterranean World in the Age of Philip II*, 2 vols., translated by Sian Reynolds, London, 1978.

Braudel, Fernand and Romano, R., *Navires et marchandises á l' entré du port de Livourne, 1547-1611*, Paris, 1951.

Bricker, Charles, *A History of Cartography: 2500 Years of Maps and Mapmakers*; Maps chosen by R. Vtooley, London, 1969.

Briggs, John, *History of the Rise of the Mahommedan Power in India till the Year A.D.1612*, translated from the original Persian of Mahomed Kasim Ferishta, vol. II, New Delhi, 1989.

Bristow, Robert, *Cochin Saga*, Cochin, 1967.

Brocahdo, José Idalino Ferreira da Costa, *O Piloto Árabe de Vasco da Gama*, Lisbon: Comemoração Centenário do Morte do Infante D.Henrique, 1959.

Broeze, Frank (ed.), *Brides of the Sea: Port Cities of Asia from 16th-20th Centuries*, Australia, 1989.

Broeze, Frank, 'The External Dynamics of Port-city Morphology: Bombay 1815-1914', in Indu Banga (ed.), *Ports and their Hinterlands in India 1700-1950*, New Delhi, 1992.

Broeze, Frank, Reeves, Peter and McPherson Kenneth, 'Port Cities in the Indian Ocean Region 1815-1939: Functional and Methodological Issues', A Paper presented at the *Second International Conference on Indian Ocean Studies*, held in Perth, 5-12 December 1984.

———, 'Studying the Asian Port City', in *Brides of the Sea: Port-Cities of Asia from 16th-20th Centuries*, Australia, 1989.

Brown, Leslie W., *The Indian Christians of St. Thomas Christians*, Cambridge, 1956.

Bruce, John, *The Annals of the Honorable East India Company from their Establishment by the Charter of Queen Elizabeth, 1600 to the Union of the London and English East India Companies, 1707-1708*, London, 1810.

Bruijn, J.R, Gaastra, F.S. and Schoffer, I. with assistance from A.C.J. Vermeulen, *Dutch-Asiatic Shipping in the 17th Centuries and 18th Centuries*, vol. I: *Introductory Volume*, The Hague, 1987; vol. II: *Outward-bound Voyages from the Netherlands to Asia and the Cape (1595-1794) with the assistance of E.S.van Eyck van Heslinga*, The Hague, 1979; vol. III: *Home-bound Voyages from Asia and the Cape to the Netherlands (1597-1795)*, with the assistance of E.S.van Eyck van Heslinga, The Hague, 1979.

Brustyn, Harold L., 'Theories of Winds and Ocean Currents from the Discoveries to the End of the Seventeenth Century', *Terrae Incognitae*, 3, 1971, pp. 7-32.

Carter, Harold, *An Introduction to Urban Historical Geography*, London, 1983.

Carvalho, Tito Augusto de, *As Companhias Portuguesas de Colonização*, Lisboa, 1902.

Chandra, Motti, *Trade and Trade Routes in Ancient India*, New Delhi, 1977.

Chang, Tien'Tse, *Sino-Portuguese Trade from 1514-1644*, London, 1933.

Chaudhuri, K.N., *Asia Before Europe, Economy and Civilization of the Indian Ocean from the rise of Islam to 1750*, Cambridge, 1990.

———, *Trade and Civilization in the Indian Ocean: An Economic History from the Rise of Islam to 1750*, New Delhi, 1985.

———, *The Trading World of Asia and the English East India Company: 1600-1760*, London, 1978.

Chauhan, R.R.S., 'Kunjali's Naval Challenge to the Portuguese', in Teotonio R. de Souza (ed.), *Essays in Goan History*, New Delhi, 1989, pp. 29-38.

Chentharasserry, T.H.P., *Kerala Charithrathile Avaganikkappetta Edukal*, Trivandrum, 1970.

Cherian, A., 'The Genesis of Islam in Malabar', in *Indica*, 1, March 1969, pp. 1-13.

Cipolla, Carlo M., *Before the Industrial Revolution: European Society and Economy, 1000-1700*, London, 1981.

———, *Guns, Sails and Empires*, New York, 1965.

———, 'The Economic Decline of Italy', in Brian Pullan (ed.), *Crisis and Change in the Venetian Economy*, London, 1968.

Coelho, Antonio Borges, 'O mercantilista Portugues Duarte Gomes de Solis (1561/2-c.1630)', *in Portugaliae Historica*, 2nd Series, 1991, pp. 183-257.

Coimbra, Álbaro da Veiga, 'Ordens militares de Cavalaria de Portugal', *Revista de Historia*, no. 53, São Paulo: 26, 1963, pp. 21-34.

Colenbrander H.T. and Coolhaas W.Ph. (eds.), *Jan Pietersz Coen, Bescheiden omtrent zijn bedrijf in India*, 8 vols., Haag, 1919-53.

Coles, Paul, *The Ottoman Impact on Europe*, New York, 1968.

Collier Raymond and Billoud Joseph, *Histoire de commerce de Marseille, 1480-1599*, Paris, 1951.

Corbett, Julian, *Drake and the Thudor Navy, with an History of the Rise of England as a Maritime Power*, 2 vols., London, 1898.

Correia, Afonso John, *Jesuit Letters and Indian History, 1542-1773*, Bombay, 1969.

Cortesão, Armando, *The Mystery of Vasco da Gama*, Coimbra, 1973.

Cortesão, Jaime, *A Expedição de Pedro Alvares Cabral e o Descobrimento do Brasil*, Lisboa, 1967.

———, *Os Descobrimentos Portuguêses*, vols.I-VII, Lisboa, 1960-78.

Costa, Abel Fontoura da, *A Marinharia dos Descobrimentos*, Lisbon, 1939.

Costa, Cristovão da, *Tratado das Drogas e Medicinais das Indias Orientais por Cristovão da Costa . No qual se verifica muito do que escreveu o Doutor Garcia da Orta*, introduction and notes by Jaime Walter, Lisboa, 1964.

Costa, João Paulo Oliveira e , 'Os Portugueses e a Cristandade Siro-Malabar (1498-1530)', in *Studia*, 52, Lisboa, 1994.

Costa, José Pereira da, 'Gaspar Correia e a lenda do Apostolo São Tome', in II *Seminario Internacional de historia Indo-portuguesa, Actas*, pp. 851-68.

Couto, Monsenhor Gustavo, *Historia da Antiga Casa da India*, Lisboa, 1932.

Couvreur, Raul da Costa, *Numismatica Indo-Portuguesa: Bazarucos*, Lisboa, 1943.

Cunha, Ana Cannas da, *A Inquisição no Estado da India: Origens (1539-1560)*, 2 vols., Lisboa, 1995.

Cunha, J. Gerson da, *Contribuições para o Estudo da Numismatica Indo-Portuguesa*, Lisboa, 1955.

———, *Notes on the History and Antiquities of Chaul and Basseim*, Bombay, 1876.

Cunha, João Manuel de Almeida Teles e, *Economia de um Imperio: Economia politica do Estado da India em Torno do Mar Arabico e Golfo Persico Elementos Conjunturais: 1595-1635*, Mestrado Dissertation submitted to the Universidade Nova de Lisboa, 1995.

Cunha Rivara, Joaquim Heliodoro da, *Catalogo dos Manuscriptos da Bibliotheca Publica Eborenese*, Lisboa, 1850-71.

Dalgado, Monsenhor Sebastião Rodolfo, *Glossario Luso-Asiatico*, 2 vols., Coimbra, 1919-21.

Dames, M. Longworth, 'The Portuguese and Turks in the Indian Ocean in the Sixteenth Century', in *Journal of the Royal Asiatic Society of Great Britain and Ireland*, part.I, London, 1921, pp. 1-28.

Danvers, F.C., *The Portuguese in India—Being a History of the Rise and Decline of their Eastern Empire*, 2 vols., New Delhi, 1988.

Das Gupta, Ashin, 'Changing Faces in the Maritime Merchant', in Roderich Ptak and Dietmar Rothermund (eds.), *Emporia, Commodities and Entrepreneurs in Asian Maritime Trade, c. 1400-1750*, Stuttgart, 1991, pp. 353-62.

———, *Malabar in Asian Trade, 1740-1800*, Cambridge, 1967.

Das Gupta, Ashin and M.N. Pearson (eds.), *India and the Indian Ocean 1500-1800*, Delhi, 1987.

Davies, F.S., *Cochin: British and Indian*, London, 1923.

Day, Francis, *The Land of the Perumals or Cochin: Its Past and its Present*, New Delhi, 1990.

D'Azevedo, Pedro, 'O Bocarro Frances e os Judeus de Cochim e de Hamburgo', *in Archivo Historico Portugues*, vol. VII, 1910.

D'Eca, Almeida, *Normas Economicas na Colonização Portuguesa até1808: Memoria*, Coimbra, 1921.

Deyon, Pierre, *O Mercantilismo*, Lisboa, 1989.

Dias, Manuel Nunes, *O Capitalismo Monarquico português (1415-1549)*, 2 vols., São Paulo, 1957 and Coimbra, 1963-4.

Diffie, W. Bailey, *Prelude to Empire: Portugal Overseas before Henry the Navigator*, Lincoln, 1960.

Diffie, W. Bailey and Winius, D. George, *Foundations of the Portuguese Empire 1415-1580: Europe and the World in the Age of Expansion*, Minneapolis, 1977.

Disney, Anthony R., 'Famine and Famine Relieves in Portuguese India in the Sixteenth and Seventeenth Centuries', in *Studia*, 49, 1989, pp. 255-82.

———, 'The Portuguese Empire in India *c.*1550-1650. Some Suggestions for a Less Seaborne, More Landbound Approach to its Socio-Economic History', in John

Correia-Afonso (ed.), *Indo-Portuguese History: Sources and Problems*, Bombay, 1981, pp. 148-62.

———, 'The Portuguese and Foreign European Overland Merchants Trading Between the Eastern Mediterranean and South and South-West Asia, c.1515-1645', in *Venice-Almirante A.Teixeira da Mota in Memorian*, vol. II, Lisboa, 1989, pp. 169-81.

———, 'Smugglers and Smuggling in the Western Half of the *Estado da India* in the Late Sixteenth and Early Seventeenth Centuries', in *Indica*, vol. 26, nos.1&2, March-September, 1989, pp. 57-75.

———, *Twilight of the Pepper Empire: Portuguese Trade in Southwest India in the Early Seventeenth Century*, London, 1978.

———, 'The Vice-Roy Count of Linhares at Goa, 1629-1635', in Luis de Albuquerque and Inacio Guerreiro (eds.), *II Seminario de Historia Indo-Portuguesa-Actas*, Lisboa, 1985, pp. 303-15.

———, 'The Viceroy as Entrepreneur. The Count of Linhares at Goa in the 1630s', in Roderich Ptak and Dietmar Rothermund (eds.), *Emporia, Commodities and Entrepreneurs in Asian Maritime Trade, c. 1400-1750*, Stuttgart, 1991, pp. 353-62.

Dobel, Friedrich, 'Über einen Pfefferhandel der Fugger und Welser, 1586-91', in *Zeitschrift des Historischen Vereins für Schwaben und Neuburg*, 13, 1886, pp. 125-38.

D'Sa, *History of the Catholic Church in India*, vol. I, Bombay, 1910.

Duro, Cesareo Fernandez, *La' Armada Invencible*, vols. I-II, Madrid, 1884-5.

Ehrenberg, Richard, *Capital and Finance in the Age of the Renaissance—A Study of the Fuggers and their Connections*, trans. H.M. Lucas, London, 1963.

Ehrhardt, Marion, *A Alemanha e os Descobrimentos Portugueses*, Lisboa, 1989.

Ehrhardt, Marion, 'Ein Gutachten Conrad Peutingers in Sachen der Handelsgesellschaften, Ende 1522', in *Zeitschrift des Historischen Vereins fur Schwaben und Neuburg*, 2, zweites Heft, Augsburg, 1875, pp. 189-215.

Elliot, J.E., *España y suo Mundo 1500-1700*, Madrid, 1990.

Faroqhi, S., 'The Venetian Presence in the Ottoman Empire (1600-1630)', in *The Journal of European Economic History*, 15-2, Summer 1986, pp. 345-84.

Ferrão, Antonio, *Os Arquivos e as Bibliotecas em Portugal*, Coimbra, 1920.

Ferrão, Jose E. Mendes, *A Aventura das Plantas e os Descobrimentos Portugueses*, Lisboa, 1992.

———, *Especiarias, Cultura, Tecnologia Comercio*, Lisboa, 1993.

Ferreira, Maria Emilia Cordeiro, 'Quintaladas', in *Dicionario de Historia de Portugal*, edited by Joel Serrão, vol. II, Lisboa, 1968.

Ficalhão, Conde, *Viagens de Pedro da Covilham*, Lisbon, 1898.

Figueiredo, F., 'Descrição de Cochin', in *The Souvenir of the Fifth International Seminar on Indo-Portuguese History*, Cochin, 1989.

Fischel, Walter J., 'The Spice-Trade in Mamluk Egypt—A Contribution to the Economic History of Medieval Islam', in *Journal of the Economic and Social History of the Orient*, vol. I, Leiden, 1958, pp. 67-82.

Fitzler, M.A. Hedwig, 'Der Anteil der Deutschen an der Kolonialpolitik Philipps II von Spanien in Asien', *Vierteljahrschrift für Sozial-und Wirtschaftsgeschichte*, 28, 1935, pp. 243-81.

———, *A Secção Ultramarina da Biblioteca Nacional. Inventarios I: Codices do Vindos de Moçambique. Inventarios III: Codices do Arquivo da Marinha*, Lisboa, 1928.

———, 'Überblick über die Portugiesischen Überseehandels gessellschaften den 15-

18 Jahrhunderts', in *Vierteljahrschrift für Sozial und Wirtschaftsgeschichte*, vol. XXIV, 1931, pp. 283-98.

Fitzler, Hedwig Kömmerling, Der Nürnberger Kaufman Georg Pock (+1528/9) in Portugiesisch-Indien und im Edelsteinland Vijayanagara, in *Mitteilungen des Vereins für Geschichte der Stadt Nürnberg* (MVGN), vol. 55, Nürnberg, 1968, pp. 137-84.

Fitzler, Pieris, *Ceylon und Portugal*, vol. I, Leipzig, 1927.

Flores, Jorge Manuel Costa da Silva, *Os Portugueses e o Mar de Ceilão, 1498-1543: Trato, Diplomacia e Guerra*, Dissertação de Mestrado em Historia dos Descobrimentos e da Expansão Portuguesa presented to the Faculdade de Ciencias Sociais e Humanas da Universidade Nova de Lisboa, 1991.

———, 'The Straits of Ceylon and the Maritime Trade in Early Sixteenth Century India: Commodities, Merchants and Trading Networks', in *Moyen Orient and Ocean Indien, XVIe-XIXe. S.*, vol. VII, Paris, 1990, pp. 30ff.

Freire, A. Braamcamp, *Vida e Obras de Gil Vicente, Trovador e Mestre da Balança*, Lisboa, 1944.

Furber, Holden, 'The History of East India Companies: General Problems', in Michel Mollat (ed.), *Sociétes et Compagnies de Commerce en Orient et dans l'Ocean Indien*, Paris, 1970, pp. 415-18.

Galvão, Antonio, *Tratado dos Descobrimentos*, Porto, 1944.

Glamann, Kristof, *Dutch Asiatic Trade*, 1628-1740, The Hague, 1958.

Godinho, Vitorino Magalhães, 'Crises et Changements Geographiques et Structuraux aux XVIeme Siecle', *Revista de Economica*, vol. XI, fasc. I, Lisboa, 1959.

———, *Os Descobrimentos e a Economia Mundial*, 4 vols., Editorial Presença, Lisboa, 1981-4.

Godinho, Vitorino Magalhães, *L'Economie de l'Empire Portugais aux XVe et XVIe siecles*, Paris, 1969.

———, *Ensaios: Sobre Historia de Portugal*, vol. II, Lisboa, 1968.

———, 'Le repli venetien et egyptien et la route du Cap, 1496-1533', *Eventail de l'histoire vivante: hommage à Lucien Febvre*, 2, Paris, 1953, pp. 283-300.

Goertz, R.O.W., 'The Portuguese in Cochin in the Mid-sixteenth Century', in *Indica*, vol. 23, nos. 1&2, March-September 1986, pp. 63-78.

———, 'The Portuguese in Cochin in the Mid-sixteenth Century', in *Studia*, 49, 1989, pp. 5-38.

Goris, A., *Les Colonies Marchandes Meridionales (Portugais, Espagnols, Italiens) á Anvers de 1488 a 1567*, Louvain, 1925.

Gracias, J.B. Amâncio, *Alemães na Índia nos séculos XV à XVIII*, Lisboa, 1941.

Grogan, H.T., *Numismatica Indo-Portuguesa*, Lisboa, 1955.

Guimarães, Vieira, *A Ordem de Cristo*, Lisboa, 1936.

Gulbenkian, Roberto, *L'Ambassade en Perse de Luis Pereira de Lacerda et des Peres Portugais de l'Ordre de Saint-Augustin, Belchior dos Anjos et Guilherme de Santo Agostinho 1604-1605*, Lisboa, 1972.

———, 'Jacome Abuna, an Armenian Bishop', in *Arquivos do centro Cultural Portugues*, vol. IV, Paris, 1972, pp. 149-76.

Guna, V.T., *Guide to the Goa Archives*, Goa, 1973.

Gundert, Herman, *Kerala Pazhama* (1498-1531), Trivandrum, 1961.

Habib, Irfan, 'Merchant Communities in Pre-colonial India', in James D.Tracy (ed.), *The Rise of Merchant Empires. Long-Distance Trade in the Early Modern World 1350-1750*, Cambridge, 1990, pp. 371-99.

Hall, Kenneth R., *Maritime Trade and State Development in Early Southeast Asia*, Honolulu, 1985.

Haebler, Konrad, 'Die Fugger und der Spanische Gewurzhandel', in *Zeitschrift des Historischen Vereins für Scwaben und Neuburg*, Zweiter Jahrgang, Erstes Heft, Augsburg, 1875, pp. 25-44.

———, 'Die Geschichte der Fugger'schen Handlung in Spanien', *Zeitschrift für Sozial- und Wirtschaftsgeschichte, Ergänzungsheft*, Sozialgeschichtliche Forschungen I, Weimar, 1897, pp. 25-44.

———, 'Konrad Rott und die Thüringische Gessellschaft', *Neues Archiv für sächsische Geschichte und Altertumskunde*, Bd.16, 1895, pp. 177-218.

———, *Die Überseeischen Unternehmungen der Welser und Ihrer Gessellschafter*, Leipzig, 1903.

Hambye, E.R., 'Medieval Christianity in India: The Eastern Church', *Christianity in India*, edited by E.R.Hambye and H.C.Perumalil, Alleppey, 1972.

Hamilton, Earl J., 'The Role of Monopoly in the Overseas Expansion and Colonial Trade of Europe before 1800', in *The American Economic Review*, Papers and Proceedings, 38, 1948.

Heckscher, Eli F., *Merkantilismen*, 2 vols., Stockholm, 1953.

Heras, Henry, *The Aravidu Dynasty of Vijayanagara*, vol. I, Madras, 1927.

Herculano, Alexandre, *Historia da Origem e do Estabelecimento da Inquisição em Portugal*, vols. I-II, Lisboa, 1987.

Hess, Andrew C., 'The Evolution of the Ottoman Seaborne Empire in the Age of Oceanic Discoveries, 1453-1525' *American Historical Review*, 75, December, pp. 1892-1919.

Heyd, Wilhem von, *Histoire du commerce du Levant au Moyen Âge*, 2 vols., Leipzig, 1885-6.

Hicks, John, *Une Theorie de l'Histoire Economique*, Paris, 1973.

Hildebrandt, Reinhard, *Die 'Georg Fugger ischen Erben': Kaufmännische Tätigkeit und sozialer Status 1555-1600*, Berlin, 1966.

Hildebrandt, Reinhard, 'Wirtschaftsentwicklung und Konzentration im 16. Jahrhundert: Konrad Rott und die Finanzierungsprobleme seines interkontinentalen Handels', in *Scripta Mercaturae*, I, 1970.

Hoffman , Paul E., 'The Portuguese Crown's Cost and Profits in the Indian Trade, 1580. A Report with a Proposal for Increasing the Profits', *Journal of the American Portuguese Cultural Society*, V, nos. 1 and 2, Winter-Spring, 1971, pp. 22-32.

Hornell, James, 'The Origins and Ethnological Significance of the Indian Boat Designs', in *Memoirs of the Asiatic Society of Bengal*, VII/3, 1920, pp. 139-256.

Hourani, George F., *Arab Seafaring in the Indian Ocean in Ancient and Early Medieval Times*, Princeton, 1951.

Hümmerich, Franz, *Die Erste Deutsche Handelsfahrt nach Indien 1505/6: Ein Unternehmender Welser, Fugger und anderer Augsburger sowie Nürnberger Häuser*, München, 1922.

———, 'Estudo Critico sobre o Roteiro da Primeira Viagem de Vasco da Gama 1497-1499', Tradução do comandanta Moura Bras, in *Diario da Viagem de Vasco da Gama*, vol. II, Porto, 1945.

———, *Quellen und Untersuchungen zur Fahrt der ersten deutschen nach dem Portugiesischen Indien*, München, 1918.

Hunter, W.W., *The Imperial Gazetteer of India*, vol. IV, London, 1885.

Innes, C.A., *Madras District Gazetteers: Malabar*, Madras, 1951.

Inalcik, Halil, 'Capital Formation in the Ottoman Empire', in *The Journal of Economic History*, vol. XXIX, no. I, 1969, pp. 97-140.

Iria, Alberto, 'A Organização dos Servicos do Archivo Historico', in *Boletim do Archivo Historico Colonial*, I, Lisboa, 1950.

Israel, Jonathan I., *Dutch Primacy in World Trade 1585-1740*, Oxford, 1991.

Iyyer, L.K. Ananthakrishna, *Castes and Tribes of Cochin*, Cochin, 1909.

Jacobs, Jane, *Economy of Cities*, New York, 1969.

Kaufmann, S.B., A Christian Caste in Hindu Society: Religious Leadership and Social Conflict among the Paravas of Southern Tamilnadu', in *MAS*, 15/2, 1981, pp. 203-34.

Kayserling, Meyer, *Historia dos Judeus em Portugal*, Lisboa, 1971.

Keay, John, *The Honourable Company. A History of the English East India Company*, New York, 1994.

Kellenbenz, Hermann, 'Autor de 1600: Le Commerce du Poivre des Fugger et le marché international du Poivre', in *Annales: Economies-Sociétes-Civilisations*, 11, 1956, pp. 1-28.

———, 'Cron, Ferdinand, 1559-1637', in Joel Serrão (ed.), *Dicionario de Historia de Portugal*, vol. I, Lisbon, 1963, pp. 752-53.

———, *Fremde Kaufleute auf der iberischen Halbinsel*, Köln, 1970.

———, 'From Melchior Manlich to Ferdinand Cron: German Levantine and Oriental Trade Relations (Second Half of XVIth and Beginning of XVIIth Centuries', in *The Journal of European Economic History*, vol. 19, no. 3, Winter, 1990, pp. 611-22.

———, 'Le front hispano-Portugais contre l'Inde et le rôle d'une agence de renseignements au service de marchands allemands et flamands', *Océan Indien et Méditerraniée* (travaux du Sixieme Colloque International d'Histoire Maritime et du Deuxieme Congres de l'Association Historique Internationale de l'Océan Indien-Section de Lourenço Marques: 13-18 Aout, 1962), Paris, 1964, pp. 263-90.

———, *Die Fugger in Spanien und Portugal bis 1560: Ein Grossunternehmen des 16. Jahrhunderts*, 3 vols., München, 1990.

———, 'Gewerbe und Handel 1500-1648', in *Handbuch der Deutschen Wirtschafts-und Sozialgeschichte*, vol. I, edited by Herman Aubin und Wolfgang Zorn, Stuttgart, 1971, pp. 424-84.

———, 'Os Mercadores Alemães de Lisboa por volta de 1530', *Separata de Revista Portuguesa da Historia*, vol. IX, Coimbra, 1961, pp. 5-20.

———, 'The Portuguese Discoveries and the Italian and German Initiatives in the Indian Trade in the first Two Decades of the Sixteenth Century', *Congresso Internacional Bartolomeu Dias sua Epoca: Actas*, vol. III, Porto, 1989.

———, 'Wirtschaftsleben der Blütezeit', in *Geshichte der Stadt Augsburg von der Römerzeit bis zur Gegenwart*, edited by Gunther Gottlieb, Wolfram Baer, Joseph Becker, Joseph Bellot, Karl Filser, Pankraz Fried, Stuttgart, 1984, pp. 258ff.

Kidwai, Atiya Habeeb, 'Conceptual and Metodological Issues: Ports, Port-cities and Port-hinterlands', in *Ports and their Hinterlands in India 1700-1950*, edited by Indu Banga, New Delhi, 1992.

Kieniewicz, Jan, 'Pepper Gardens and Market in Pre-colonial Malabar', in *Moyen Orient and Ocean Indien XVIe-XIXe. S.*, no. 3, 1986, pp. 1-36.

———, 'The Portuguese Factory and Trade in Pepper in Malabar during the 16th Century', in the *Indian Economic and Social History Review*, vol. VI, no. I, 1969, pp. 61-84.

———, 'The Stationary System in Kerala', in *Hemispheres*, I, 1985, pp. 7-40.

King, Anthony D., 'Colonial Cities: Global Pivots of Change', in *Colonial Cities: Essays on Urbanism in a Colonial Context*, edited by Robert Ross and Gerard J. Telkamp, Leiden, 1985.

Knabe, Wolfgang, *Auf den Spuren der ersten deutschen Kaufleute in Indien*, Anhausen, 1993.

Koder, S.S., 'Glimpses of Old Cochin, in *Fort Cochin Municipal Centenary Souvenir*', Cochin, 1966.

Kollaparambil, Jacob, *The Archdeacon of all India*, Kottayam, 1972.

———, *The St.Thomas Christians' Revolution in 1653*, Kottayam, 1981.

Kooiman, Dick, 'Bombay: From Fishing Village to Colonial Port-City 1662-1947', in *Colonial Cities: Essays on Urbanism in a Colonial Context*, edited by Robert Ross and Gerard J.Telkamp, Leiden, 1985.

Kunju, A.P. Ibrahim, *Studies in Medieval Kerala History*, Trivandrum, 1975.

Kunstmann, *Die Fahrt der ersten deutschen nach dem portugiesischen Indien*, München, 1861.

Kurup, K.K.N., *William Logan: A Study in the Agrarian Relations of Malabar*; Calicut, 1981.

Lach, Donald F., *Asia in the Making of Europe*, vols. I-II, Chicago, 1965.

Lach, Donald F. and Carol Flaumenhaft, *Asia on the Eve of Europe's Expansion*, New Jersey, 1965.

Lafittau, P.F., Joseph Françoise, *Histoire des Déscouvertes et Conquestes des Portugais dans le nouveau Monde*, Paris, MDCCXXXIII.

Lane, Federic C., 'The Mediterranean Spice Trade: Further Evidence of its Revival in the Sixteenth Century' *American Historical Review*, 45, 1939-40, pp. 581-90.

———, 'Pepper Prices before Da Gama', *Journal of Economic History*, 28, December 1968, pp. 590-7.

———, 'Venetian Shipping during the Commercial Revolution', in Brian Pullen (ed.), *Crisis and Change in the Venetian Economy in the Sixteenth and Seventeenth Centuries*, London, 1968.

———, *Venice: A Maritime Republic*, Baltimore, 1973.

———, *Venice and History*, Baltimore, 1966.

Leite, Duarte, *Descobrimentos português*, 2 vols., Lisbon, 1958-60.

Leod, N. Mac, *De Oost-indische Compagnie als Zeemogendheid in Azië*, 2 vols., Rijswijk, 1927.

Lewandowski, Susan, 'Urban Growth and Municipal Development in the Colonial City of Madras, 1800-1900', in *Journal of Asian Studies*, 1975, pp. 342-60.

Logan, William, *Malabar Manual*, 3 vols.; vol. I, reprinted in Trivandrum, 1981; vols. II and III reprinted in Madras, 1951.

Lopes, David, *Extractos da Historia da Conquista do Yemen pelos Othomanos-Contribuições para a Historia do Estabelecimento dos Portugueses na India: Memoria Destinada á X Sessão do Congresso Internacional dos Orientalistas por . . .*, Lisboa, 1892.

Lopes, F. Felix, 'Os Franciscanos no Orient Portugues de 1584 a 1590', in *Studia*, Lisboa, 1962.

Ludden, David, *Peasant History in South India*, New Delhi, 1989.

Luz, Francisco Paulo Mendes da, *O Conselho da India.Contributo ao Estudo da Historia da Administração e do Comercio do Ultramar Portugues nos Principios do Seculo XVII*, Lisboa, 1952.

Luzzatto, Gino, 'La Decadenza di Venezia dopo le scoperte geografiiche nella tradizioni e nella realta', *Archivo Veneto*, Ser. 5, LIV-LV, 1945.

———, *Storia Economica di Venezia dal XI al XVI secolo*, Venice, 1961.

Lybyer, A.H., *The Influence of the Rise of the Ottoman Turks upon the Routes of the Oriental Trade*, 2 vols., Washington, 1914.

———, 'The Ottoman Turks and the Routes of Oriental Trade', *The Economic History Review*, 30, no.120, October 1915.

Macedo, Jorge Borges de, *Historia Diplomatica Potuguesa. Constantes e Linhas de Forca. Estudo de Geopolitica*, Lisboa, 1987.

Machado, Diogo Barbosa, *Biblioteca Lusitana*, tom. II, Lisboa, 1747.

Machado, Jose Pedro (ed.), *Grande Dicionário da Lingua Portuguesa*, 11 vols., Lisboa, 1981-6.

Government of Madras, Malabar Special Commission, 1881-1882, Malabar Land Tenures, 2 vols., Madras, 1882.

Madukkakuzhy, Mathew, *Purathana Kraisthava Kendrangalilude*, Kanjirappally, 1995.

Malekandathil, Pius, 'Mit den Portugiesen waren auch die Deutschen da: Erste deutsche Gemeinde in Cochin Schon vor 485 Jahren', in *Meine Welt: Zeitschrift des deutschen-indischen Dialogs*, trans. by Jose Punnaparambil, Heft 1/Jahrgang 15, Köln (Germany), June 1998.

———, *The Germans, the Portuguese and India*, Münster, 1999.

———, *Urban Growth of Cochin in the Sixteenth and Seventeenth Centuries*, M.Phil. Dissertation submitted to the Pondicherry Central University, 1992.

Mandelbaum, David, 'The Jewish Way of Life in Cochin', in *Jewish Social Studies*, vol. I, 4, 1939, pp. 423-60.

———, 'Social Stratification among the Jews of Cochin in India and Israel', in *Jewish India*, edited by Thomas A. Timberg, New Delhi, 1986.

Mantram, Robert (ed.), *Histoire de l'Empire Ottoman*, Paris, 1989.

Martins, José Frederico Ferreira, *Historia da Misericordia de Goa*, Goa, 1910-14.

Mashanaglass, P. Mac Swiney de, 'Une Ambassade Portugaise a Rome, sous Jules II', *Revue d'Histoire Diplomatique*, XVII, 1903.

Masters, Bruce, *The Origin of Western Economic Dominance in the Middle East.Mercantilism and the Islamic Economy in Alleppo, 1600-1750*, New York, 1989.

Mateer, Samuel, *The Land of Charity: A Descriptive Account of Travancore and its People*, New Delhi, 1991.

Mathew, K.M., *History of the Portuguese Navgation in India*, Delhi, 1988.

Mathew, K.S., 'Cochin and the Portuguese Trade with India during the Sixteenth Century', *Indica*, 1989, pp. 80ff.

———, 'German Merchant Financiers in Goa during the 16th and 17th Centuries', in P.P. Shirodkar (ed.), *Goa's External Relations*, Goa, 1992, pp. 32-56.

———, 'India Contract of the Indo-Portuguese Trade in the Last Quarter of the Sixteenth Century', in V.K. Chavada (ed.), *Studies in Trade and Urbanisation in Western India*, Baroda, 1985, pp. 165-71.

———, 'Indian Merchants and the Portuguese Trade on the Malabar Coast during the Sixteenth Century', in *Indo-Portuguese History: Old Issues—New Questions*, New Delhi, 1985.

———, 'Indo-Portuguese Coinage in the Sixteenth and Early Seventeenth Centuries', in *Journal of the Numismatic Society of India*, vol. XLVI, 1984, pp. 120ff.

———, *Indo-Portuguese Trade and the Fuggers of Germany*, Delhi, 1997.

———, 'Khwaja Shams-ud-din Giloni: A Sixteenth Century Entrepreneur in Portuguese India', in Roderich Ptak and Dietmar Rothermund (eds.), *Emporia, Commodities and Entrepreneurs in Asian Maritime Trade, c.* 1400-1750, Stuttgart, 1991.

———, 'Maritime Trade of India and the Germans in the Sixteenth Century', A Paper presented in the Second International Symposium on Maritime Studies, Pondicherry, 16-20 December 1991.

———, 'Money Economy in the Portuguese India, 1510-1640', in *Journal of the Gujarat Research Society*, vols. 46/47, Bombay, July 1984, pp. 25ff.

———, 'Portuguese Trade with India and the Theory of Royal Monopoly in the Sixteenth Century', *Proceedings of the Indian History Congress*, Waltair, 1979.

———, *Portuguese Trade with India in the Sixteenth Century*, Delhi, 1983.

Mathew, P.V., *Sugandhanadu: Nazarani Charitram*, Ernakulam, 1984.

Matos, Artur Teodoro de, *O Estado da India nos anos de 1581-1588. Estrutura administrativa e economica. Alguns Elementos para o seu Estudo*, Ponta Delgada, Universidade dos Açores, 1982.

———, 'The Financial Situation of the State of India during the Philippine Period', in Teotonio R. De Souza (ed.), *Indo-Portuguese History: Old Issues*, New Questions, New Delhi, 1985, pp. 90-101.

———, 'Some Aspects of the Portuguese Trade in the Malabar Coast: Cochin and the "mercadorias meudas" (1506-1508)', in *Indica*, vol. 26, nos. 1 & 2, 1989, pp. 93-102.

Matos, Artur Teodoro de and Thomaz, Luis Filipe (eds.), *Vinte anos de Historiagrafia Ultramarina Portuguesa*, Lisboa, 1972-92.

Mauro, Frederic, 'Merchant Communities: 1350-1750', in *The Rise of Merchant Empires, Long Distance Trade in the Early Modern World: 1350-1750*, edited by James D. Tracy, New York, 1990.

Meilink-Roelofsz, M.A.P., *Asian Trade and European Influence in the Indonesian Archipelago between 1500 and 1630*, The Hague, 1962.

———, *De Vestiging der Nederlanders ter Kuste Malabar*, 'S. Gravenhage, 1943.

Meersman, A., 'Development of the Church under the Padroado', in E.R, Hambye and H.C. Perumalil (eds.), *Christianity in India*, Alleppey, 1972.

———, 'Notes on the Charitable Institutions the Portuguese Established in India', in *Indian Church History Review*, vol. II, no. 2, Bangalore, December 1971, pp. 90ff.

Mendes dos Remédios, *Os Judeus em Portugal*, 2 vols., Coimbra, 1895-1928.

Mendonça, Henrique Lopes de, *Estudos Sôbre Navios Portuguêses nos Séculos XV e XVI*, Lisbon, 1892.

Menon, A. Sreedhara, *A Survey of Kerala History*, Kottayam, 1970.

———, *Kerala District Gazetteers : Ernakulam*, Trivandrum, 1965.

Menon, K.N., *Portuguese Pockets in India*, New Delhi, 1953.

Menon, K.P. Padmanabha, 'The Fort of Cochin', in *Fort Cochin Municipal Centenary Souvenir*, Cochin, 1966.

———, *History of Kerala*, 4 vols., Ernakulam, 1929-37.

———, *Kochi Rajya Charitram*, Kozhikode, 1989.

Moniz, Antonio Francisco, *Noticias e Documentos para a Historia de Damão-Antiga Provincia do Norte*, vol. I, Bastora, 1900.

Moniz, Jose Antonio, *Biblioteca Nacional de Lisboa Inventarios*, Secção XIII, Manuscriptos, Lisboa, 1896.

———, *Collecção Pombalina*, Lisboa, 1889.

Monteiro, Armanto da Silva Saturnino, *Batalhas e Combates da marinha Portuguesa*, vols. I-VI *(till 1668)*, Lisboa, 1993-5.

Moraes, G.M., 'St. Francis Xavier, Apostolic Nuncio, 1542-1552', *Journal of the Bombay Branch of the Royal Asiatic Society*, New Series XXVII, 1950.

Moreland, W.H., *From Akbar to Aurangzeb: A Study in Indian Economic History*, Delhi, 1988.

———, *India at the Death of Akbar: An Economic Study*, Delhi, 1962.

Mulakara, Gervasis J., *History of the Diocese of Cochin: European Missionaries in Cochin 1292-1558*, vol. I, Rome, 1986.

Mundadan, Mathias, *A History of Christianity in India, vol. I (from the beginning up to the middle of the Sixteenth Century)*, Bangalore, 1984.

———, *St.Thomas Christians, 1498-1552*, Bangalore, 1967.

———, 'The Town of Cochin and the Portuguese', in *II Seminario Internacional de Historia*

Indo-Portuguesa-Actas, edited by Luis Albuquerque and Inacio Guerreiro, Lisboa, 1985, pp. 251-63.

Nambiar, O.K., *The Kunjalis, Admirals of Calicut*, Delhi, 1963.

Narayanan, M.G.S., 'Political and Social Condition of Kerala in the Kulasekhara Empire (800 A.D. to 1124 A.D.)', unpublished Ph.D. thesis, University of Kerala, 1972.

Neale, Walter C., 'Le marche des points de une thoeorique e historique', in Karl Polanyi and Conrad Arensberg (eds.), *Les Systemes Economiques dans l'Histoire et dans la Theorie*, Paris, 1975, pp. 331-43.

Oliveira, Antonio de, *Poder e oposição politica em Portugal no Periodo filipino (1580-1640)*, Lisboa, 1990.

———, *A Vida Economica e Social de Coimbra de 1537 a 1640*, vol. I, Lisboa, 1971.

Oliveira Marques, A.H. de, *Hansa e Portugal na Idade Média*, Lisbon, 1959.

———, 'Navegação prussiana para Portugal nos princípios do século XV', *Revista da Universidade de Coimbra*, 10, March, 1960, pp. 1-24.

———, 'Notas para a história da feitoria portuguêsa na Flanders no século XV', in *Studi in onore di Amintore Fanfani*, 3 vols., Milan, 1962, II, pp. 217-67.

Özbaran, Salih, 'The Ottoman Turks and the Portuguese in the Persian Gulf, 1534-1581', in *the Journal of Asian History*, 6, no. I, 1972, pp. 45-87.

Pallippurathukkunnel, Thomas, *A Double Regime in the Malabar Church*, Alwaye, 1982.

Panikkar, K.M., *Malabar and the Dutch (Being the History of the Fall of the Nayar Power in Malabar)*, Bombay, 1931.

———, *Malabar and the Portuguese, 1500-1663*, Bombay, 1929.

———, *A History of Kerala (1498-1801)*, Annamalainagar, 1960.

Panikkar, K.N., *Against Lord and State: Religion and Peasant Uprisings in Malabar, 1836-1921*, Delhi, 1989.

———, 'Land Control, Ideology and Marriage Reform: A Study of the Change in Family Organisation and Marriage System in Kerala', in *The Indian Historical Review*, IV, I, July 1977, pp. 30-46

Panikkasserry, Velayudhan, *Sancharikalum Charitrakkaranmarum*, Kottayam, 1972.

Panjikaran, Joseph C., 'Christianity in Malabar with Special Reference to the St. Thomas Christians of the Syro-Malabar Rite', in *Orientalia Christiana*, vol. VI, 1926, pp. 100ff.

Parry, J.H., *The Age of Renaissance*, New York, 1963.

Pearson, M.N., *Coastal Western India: Studies from the Portuguese Records*, New Delhi, 1981.

———, *Merchants and Rulers in Gujarat, the Response to the Portuguese in the Sixteenth Century*, London, 1976.

Peragallo, Próspero, *Cenni intorno alla colonia italiana in Portogallo*, Genoa, 1904.

Peres, Damião, *Historia dos descobrimentos portuguêses*, Oporto, 1943.

Peres, Damião (ed.), *Historia de Portugal: Edição Monumental*, 8 vols., Barcelos, 1928-38.

———, *Viagens e naufragios celebres dos séculos*, XVI, XVII, XVIII, 4 vols., Porto, 1937-8.

Perera, L.H.Horace, *Ceylon under Western Rule*, London, 1959.

Perlin, Frank, 'Changes in Production and Circulation of Money in Seventeenth and Eighteenth Century India: An essay on Monetization before Colonial Occupation'; in Sanjay Subrahmanyam (ed.), *Money and the Market in India 1100-1700*, Delhi, 1994, pp. 256-75.

Philips, Carla Rahan, 'The Growth and Composition of Trade in the Iberian Empire 1450-1750', in James D. Tracy (ed.), *The Rise of Merchant Empires. Long-*

Distance Trade in the Early Modern World: 1350-1750, Cambridge, 1990, pp. 351-70.

Philips, George, 'The Seaports of India and Ceylon, described by Chinese Voyagers of the Fifteenth Century together with an Account of Chinese Navigation', in *Journal of the China Branch of the Royal Asiatic Society for the Year 1884*, new series, vol. XIX, part I, Shanghai, 1885, pp. 209-26; vol. XXI, Shanghai, 1887, pp. 30-42.

Pillai, Elamkulam Kunjan P.N., *Koka Sandesam*, Kottayam, 1952.

———, *Janmi Sampradayam Keralathil*, Kottayam, 1966.

———, *Studies in Kerala History*, Kottayam, 1970.

———, *Unnuneeli Sandesam*, Kottayam, 1989.

Pina, Luis de, *Expansão Hospitalar Portuguesa Ultramarina*, Séculos XVI&XVII, Lisboa, 1943.

Pissurlencar, S.S., *Agentes da Diplomatica Portuguesa na India*, Bastora, 1952.

———, *Roteiro dos Arquivos da India Portuguesa*, Goa, 1955.

Podipara, J. Placid, 'Portuguese Religious Conquests in Malabar under the Diocese of Cochin during the Sixteenth Century', *NZM*, XII, 1957.

———, *The Latin Rite Christians of Malabar*, Kottayam, 1986.

Pohl, Hans, *Die Portugiesen in Antwerpen (1567-1648) zur Geschichte einer Minderheit*, Wiesbaden, 1977.

Polanyi, Karl, Conrad M. Arensberg, and Harry W. Pearson, (eds.), *Trade and Market in the Early Empires*, Illinois, 1957.

Pölnitz, Gotz Freiherr von, *Anton Fugger, 1548-1560*, 3 parts in 4 books, Tübingen, 1958-71.

———, *Die Fugger*, Frankfurt am Main, 1960.

———, *Fugger und Hanse: Ein Hundertjahriges Ringen um Ostsee und Nordsee*, Tübingen, 1953.

———, *Jakob Fugger, Kaiser, Kirche und Kapital in der Oberdeutschen Renaissance*, Tübingen, 1949.

———, *Jakob Fugger, Quellen und Erläuterungen*, Tübingen, 1951.

Poonen, T.I., *A Survey of the Rise of the Dutch Power in Malabar (1603-1678)*, Trichinapoly, 1949.

Prada, Vazques de, *Letters Marchandes d'Anvers*, Paris, 1960.

Prakash, Om, *The Dutch East India Company and the Economy of Bengal 1630-1720*, Princeton, 1985.

Priolkar, Anant Kakba, *The Goa Inquisition*, Bombay, 1961.

Ptak, Roderich, 'China and Portugal at Sea: The Early Ming Trading System and the Estado da India Compared', in *The Asian Seas 1500-1800: Local Societies, European Expansion and the Portuguese, Revista de Cultura*, vol. I, ano V, 1991, pp. 23ff.

———, 'China, Portugal und der Maldiven-Handel vom fruhen 15.bis zum fruhen 16. Jahrhundert: Einige Bemerkungen zur Wirtschaftsgeschichte Südasiens', in Roderich Ptak (ed.), *Portuguese Asia: Aspects in History and Economic History (Sixteenth and Seventeenth Centuries)*, Stuttgart, 1987, pp. 123ff.

———, 'The Maldive and Laccadive Islands (Liu-Shan) in Ming Records', in *Journal of the American Oriental Society*, 107/4, October-December, 1987, pp. 675-94.

Pullan, Brian (ed.), *Crisis and Change in the Venetian Economy*, London, 1968.

Queiroz Velloso, José Maria de, *D. Sebastião, 1554-1578*, Lisbon, 1945.

Radhakrishnan, P., *Peasant Struggles, Land Reforms and Social Change: Malabar, 1836-1982*, New Delhi, 1989.

Raja, K.Rama Varma, 'The Cochin Harbour and the Putu Vaipu Era', in *The Bulletin of the Rama Varma Research Institute*, no. 2, Cochin, 1933.

Raja, P.K.S., *Medieval Kerala*, Calicut, 1966.

Ramaswamy, Vijaya, *Textiles and Weavers in Medieval South India*, Delhi, 1985.

Rau, Virginia, 'Um Grande Mercador-Banqueiro Italiano em Portugal: Lucas Giraldi', *Separata de Estudos Italianos em Portugal*, no. 24, Lisboa, 1965.

———, 'Les Portugais et la route terrestre des Indes a la Mediterranée aux XVIe et XVIIe siécles' in *Mediterraneo e Oceano Indiano*, Firenze, 1970, pp. 91-8.

Raychaudhuri, Tapan, 'European Commercial Activity and the Organization of India's Commerce and Industrial Production', in B.N. Ganguli (ed.), *Reading in Indian Economic History*, London, 1964, pp. 64-77.

Ray, Haraprasad, 'An Enquiry into the presence of the Chinese in South and South East Asia after the Voyages of Zheng He in Early Fifteenth Century', A Paper presented in the Second International Symposium on Maritime Studies, Pondicherry, 16-20 December 1991.

Rebelo, Luis Francisco, *Historia do Teatro Portugues*, Lisboa, 1968.

Rebello, Fenelon, 'Early Indo-Portuguese Coins', in *International Seminar on Indo-Portuguese History*, Bombay, 27 November 1978.

Reeves, P., Mc Pherson, Kenneth and Broeze, Frank, 'Port-Cities: The Conceptual Problems', A Paper presented in the Australian Historical Association, Sydney, 1982.

Renouard, Yves, *l'hommes d'affaires italiens du Moyen Âge*, Paris, 1968.

Revah, Israel Salvador, 'Les Marranes Portugais et l'Inquisition au XVIe siecle', in *Charles Amiel, Estudes Portugaises*, Paris, 1975.

Ribeiro, Vitor, *A Santa Casa da Misericordia de Lisboa*, Lisboa, 1902.

Rich, E.E. and C.H.Wilson, *The Economy of Expanding Europe in the Sixteenth and Seventeenth Centuries*, 4 vols., Cambridge, 1941-67.

Rockhill, W.W., 'Notes on the Relations and Trade of China with the Eastern Archipelago and the Coast of the Indian Ocean during the Fourteenth Century', in *T'oung Pao*, vol. XV, Leiden, 1914, pp. 419-47; vol. XVI (1915), pp. 61-159, 236-71, 374-92, 435-67, 604-26.

Rodrigues, Vitor Luis Gaspar, 'O Grupo de Cochim e a Oposição a Afonso de Albuquerque', *Studia*, 51, Lisboa, 1992.

Rogers, Francis M., *The Quest for Eastern Christians: Travels and Rumor in the Age of Discovery*, Minneapolis, 1962.

———, *The Travels of the Infante Dom Pedro of Portugal*, Cambridge, 1961.

———, 'Union between Latin and Eastern Christians and the Overseas Expansion of the Portuguese, a Thematic Study of the Libro del Infante Don Pedro de Portugal', in *III Colóquio Internacional de Estudos Luso-Braileiros*, Lisbon, 1957, Actas, 2, 1960, pp. 148-63.

Romano, Rggiero, Tenenti, Alberto and Tucci, Ugo, 'Venise et la Route du Cap: 1499-1517', in *Mediterraneo e Oceano Indiano, Firenze*, 1970, pp. 109-39.

Roover, Florence Edler de, 'The Market for Spices in Antwerp 1538-1544', in *Revue Belge de Philogie et d'Histoire Recueil Trimestriel*, tom. XVII, Bruxelles, 1938, pp. 212-21.

Ross, Robert and Telkamp, Gerard J. (eds.), *Colonial Cities: Essays on Urbanism in a Colonial Context*, Leiden, 1985.

Rossabi, Morris, 'The "Decline" of the Central Asian Caravan Trade', in James D. Tracy (ed.), *The Rise of Merchant Empires. Long-Distance Trade in the Early Modern World 1350-1750*, Cambridge, 1990, pp. 351-70.

Rothermund, Dietmar, 'Asian Emporia and European Bridgeheads', in Roderich Ptak and

Dietmar Rothermund (eds.), *Emporia, Commodities and Entrepreneurs in Asian Maritime trade, c. 1400-1750*, Stuttgart, 1991, pp. 1-3.

———, *Asian Trade and European Expansion in the Age of Mercantilism*, Delhi, 1981.

———, *An Economic History of India: From Pre-Colonial Times to 1986*, New York, 1988.

———, *Government, Landlord, and Peasant in India, Agrarian Relations under British Rule, 1865-1935*, Wiesbaden, 1978.

———, 'Government, Landlord, and Tenant in India, 1875-1900', in *Indian Economic and Social History Review*, vol. 6, no. 4, 1969.

———, 'Introduction: The Fate of the Portuguese in Asia', in Roderich Ptak (ed.), *Portuguese Asia: Aspects in History and Economic History (Sixteenth and Seventeenth Centuries)*, Stuttgart, 1987.

Ruddock, Alwyn A., *Italian Trading Fleets in Medieval England in History*, 106, September 1944, pp. 192-202.

Sanceau, Elaine, *Portugal in Quest for Prester John*, London, 1943.

———, *Henry the Navigator*, New York, 1947.

———, *The Reign of the Fortunate King, 1495-1521*, Connecticut, 1969.

Sapori, A, *Le marchand italien au Moyen Âge*, Paris, 1952.

Saraiva, António José, *Para a historia da cultura em Portugal*, 3 vols., Lisbon, 1969.

Saraiva, Cardeal D. Francisco de S. Luiz, *Obras Completas*, 10 vols., Lisbon, 1872-83

Sastri, Nilakanta, *A Hitory of South India from Pre-historic Times to the Fall of Vijayanagar*, Madras, 1976.

Scammel, G.V., 'Indigenous Assistance in the Establishment of Portuguese Power in the Indian Ocean', in John Correia Afonso (ed.), *Indo-Portuguese History: Sources and Problems*, Bombay, 1981, pp. 163-73.

Schick, Leon, *Un Grand Homme d'Affaires au debut u XVIe siécle: Jacob Fugger*, Paris, 1957.

Schmeller, J.A., *Über Valenti Fernandez Alemã und seine Sammlung von Nachrichten über die Entdeckungen und Besitzungen der Portugiesen in Afrika und Asien bis zum Jahre 1508 enthalten in einer Portugiesischen Handschrift der königl. Rof-und Staates Bibliothek zu München*, München, 1845.

Scholberg, Henry, *Bibliography of Goa and the Portuguese in India*, New Delhi, 1982.

Schurhammer, Georg S.J., 'Armenian Bishop in Malabar', in *Arquivos do centro Cultural Portugues*, vol. IV, Paris, 1972, pp. 141-8.

———, *Francis Xavier: His Life and Times*, translated by M. Joseph Costelloe, Rome, 1973.

———, *Orientalia*, Roma, 1963.

———, *Die Zeitgenössichen Quellen zur Geschichte Portugiesisch-Asiens und seiner Nachbarländer zur Zeit des Hl. Franz Xaver, 1538-1552*, Leipzig, 1962.

Schurhammer, Georg and Voretzsch, E.A., *Ceylon zur Zeit des Konigs Bhûvaneka Bahu und Franz Xavers, 1539-1552*, vol. I, Leipzig, 1928.

Segal, J.B., *A History of the Jews of Cochin*, London, 1993.

———, 'White and Black Jews at Cochin, the Story of a Controversy', in *Journal of the Royal Asiatic Society of Great Britain and Ireland*, 2, 1983.

Sergio, Antonio, *Obras Completas de Antonio Sergio: Introdução Geografico-Sociologica a Historia de Portugal*, critical edition guided by Castelo Branco Chaves, Vitorino Magalhães Godinho, Rui Gracio and Joel Serrão, Lisboa, 1976.

Serrão, Joel (ed.), *Dicionário de História de Portugal*, 4 vols., Lisbon, 1963-71.

Serrão, Joaquim Verissimo, *Historia de Portugal*, vols. 3-5, Lisboa, 1978.

———, *O Reinado de D. Antonio, Prior do Crato*, vol. I (1580-1582), Coimbra, 1956.

Shillington, V.M. and A.V. Wallis, *The Commercial Relations of England and Portugal*, London, 1907.

Silva Correia, Alberto C. Germano da, 'Os franceses na colonização portuguêsa da India', in *Studia*, Lisbon, 4, July 1959, pp. 7-105.

Silva, Jose Gentil da, 'Alegação a favor da Companhia Portuguesa da India Oriental', in *XIII Congresso Luso-Espanhol para o progresso das Ciencias*, vol. VIII, Porto, 1950, pp. 465-537.

———, *Strategie des affaires a Lisbonne entre 1595 et 1607. Letres marchandes des Rodrigues d'Evora et Veiga*, Paris, 1956.

———, 'Une image de l'Estado da India au debut du XVIIe siecle et ses enseignements', in *Arquivos do Centro Cultural Portugues*, vol. IV, no.1, 1972, Paris, 1972, pp. 253-67.

Silva, L.A. Rebello da, *Memória sôbre a população e a Agricultura de Portugal*, Lisbon, 1868.

Silva, Richard Chandra da, 'The Portuguese East India Company 1628-1633', in *Luso-Brazilian Review*, II-2, 1974, pp. 152-205.

Silveira, Luis da, *Ensaio de Iconografia das Cidades Portuguesas do Ultramar*, vol. III, Lisboa: (no year of publication).

Simkin, C.G.F., *The Traditional Trade of Asia*, London, 1968.

S'Jacob, H.K., *De Nederlanders in Kerala, 1663-1701, De Memories en instructies betreffende het commandement Malabar van der Verenigde Ost Indische Compagnieë*, The Hague, 1976.

Sousa, Alfredo Botelho de, *Subsidios para a Historia Militar Maritima da India*, Lisboa, 1930.

Sousa, D. Antonio Caetano de, *Historia Genealogica da Casa Real Portuguesa*, vol. VII, Coimbra, 1949.

Sousa, Luis de, *Annaes de El Rei Dom João Terceiro*, Lisboa, 1844.

Souza, Teotonio R.de, *Medieval Goa. A Socio-Economic History*, New Delhi, 1979.

Souza, Teotonio R de, 'Portuguese Fiscal Administration and Monetary System', in Teotonio R.de Souza (ed.), *Goa Through the Ages*, vol. II, *An Economic History*, New Delhi, 1990, pp. 213-26.

Steensgaard, Niels, 'Asian Trade and the World Economy from the 15th to the 18th Centuries', in Teotonio R. de Souza (ed.), *Indo-Portuguese History: Old Issues, New Questions*, New Delhi, 1985, pp. 225-35.

———, *Carracks, Caravans and Companies: The Structural Crisis in the European-Asian Trade in the Early Seventeenth Century*, Kopenhaven, 1973.

Stein, Burton, 'Integration of the Agrarian System of South India', in *Land Control and Social Structure in Indian History*, edited by Robert Eric Frykenberg, New Delhi, 1979, pp. 175-216.

———, *The New Cambridge History of India* , vols. 1-2, Vijayanagara, New Delhi, 1989.

Stella, Aldo, 'La Crisi economica veneziana della seconda meta del secolo XVI', in *Archivo Veneto*, Series 5, LVIII, 1962.

Subrahmanyam, Sanjay, 'Aspects of State Formation in South India and South East Asia, 1500-1650', in *Indian Economic and Social History Review*, 23/4, 1986, pp. 357-77.

———, 'A Augsburger in Asia Portuguesa: Further Light on the Commercial World of Ferdinand Cron 1587-1624', in Roderich Ptak and Dietmar Rothermund (eds.), *Emporia, Commodities and Entrepreneurs in Asian Maritime Trade, c. 1400-1750*, Stuttgart, 1991.

———, 'Cochin in Decline, 1600-1650: Myth and Manipulation in the Estado da India', in *Portuguese Asia: Aspects in History and Economic History (Sixteenth and*

Seventeenth Centuries), edited by Roderich Ptak, Stuttgart, 1987, pp. 59-85.
———, *Improvising Empire: Portuguese Trade and Settlement in the Bay of Bengal, 1500-1700*, New Delhi, 1990.
———, 'Notes on the Sixteenth Century Bengal Trade', in *Indian Economic and Social History Review*, 24/3, 1987.
———, *The Political Economy of Commerce: Southern India, 1500-1650*, New York, 1990.
———, *The Portuguese Empire in Asia 1500-1700: A Political and Economic History*, London, 1993.
———, 'Precious Metal Flows and Prices in Western and Southern India: 1500-1570. Some Comparative and Conjunctural Aspects', in Sanjay Subrahmanyam (ed.), *Money and the Market in India 1100-1700*, Delhi, 1994, pp. 186-218.
———, 'The Tail Wags the Dog or some Aspects of the External Relations of the Estado da India, 1570-1600', in *Moyen Orient and Ocean Indien, XVIe-XIXe. S*, 5, Paris, 1988.
Sykes, Percy, *A History of Exploration from the Earliest Times to the Present Day*, New York, 1961.
Tavares, Luis C. Nozes, *O Infante D.Henrique e os Descobrimentos*, Braga, 1960.
Tavim, Jose Alberto Rodrigues da Silva, 'From Setubal to the Sublime Porte: The Wanderings of Jacome de Olivares, New Christian and Merchant of Cochin (1540-1571)', in *Santa Barbara Portuguese Studies*, vol. II, edited by Sanjay Subrahmanyam and Kenneth McPherson, Center for Portuguese Studies at the University of California, California, 1995.
Tavim, Alberto Rodrigues da Silva, 'Os Judeus e a Expansão Portuguesa na India durante o Seculo XVI. O Examplo de Isaac do Cairo: Espião, Língua e Judeu de Cochim de Cima', in *Arquivos do Centro Cultural Calouste Gulbenkian*, vol. XXXIII, Lisboa, 1994.
———, 'Outras Gentes em Outras Routas: Judeus e Cristãos-novos de Cochim - Entre Santa Cruz de Cochim e Mattancherry, entre O Imperio Portugues e o Medio Oriente', *A Paper presented in Seminario Internacional de Historia Indo-Portuguesa-Angra do Heroismo*, Açores: 7-11 de Junho de 1996.
Terpstra, H., 'De nederlandsche Voorcompagnieén'; *Geschiedenis van Nederlandsch Indié*, II, Amsterdam, 1938.
Thaliath, Jonas, *The Synod of Diamper*, Rome, 1958.
Thampuran, Ramesan, *Gosri Rajavamsavali: Genealogy of Cochin Royal Family*, Cochin, 1989.
Thomaz, Luis Filipe, 'A Crise de 1565-1575 na Historia do Estado da India', in *Mare Liberum*, 9 July 1995.
———, *De Ceuta a Timor*, Lisboa, 1994.
———, 'Diogo Pereira, O Malabar', in *Mare Liberum*, 5, 1993.
———, 'Estrutura Politica e Administrativa do Estado da India no século XVI', *II Seminario Internacional de Historia Indo-Portuguesa-Actas*, Lisboa, 1985, pp. 511-40.
Thomaz, Luis Filipe, 'Expansão Portuguesa e Expansão Europeia reflexões em Torno da génese dos Descobrimentos', in *Studia*, 47, Lisboa, 1989, pp. 371-415.
Thomaz, Luis Filipe, 'L 'idee imperiale Manueline', in *Découverte Le Portugal et l'Europe*, Paris, 1990, pp. 35-103.
———, 'Malaka et ses Communautes marchandes au tournant du 16e siecle', in Denys Lombard et Jean Aubin (eds.) *Marchands et Hommes d'affaires Asiatiques dans l'Ocean Indien et la Mer de China 13e-20e siécles*, Paris, 1988.
———, 'Les Portugais dans les Mers de l'Archipel au XVIe siecle', in *Archipel*, 18, 1979, pp. 105-25.
———, 'Portuguese Control on the Arabian Sea and the Bay of Bengal—a Comparative

Study', A Paper presented in the Conference on Bay of Bengal, New Delhi, Dec. 1994.

———, *Os Portugueses em Malacca, 1511-1580. Dissertação de Licenciatura (inedita)*, Faculdade de Letras, Universidade de Lisboa, 2 vols. (I-texto: II-documentação), Lisboa, 1964.

———, 'The Portuguese in the Seas of the Archipelago during the 16th Century', in *Archipel*, 18, 1984.

———, *A Viagem de Antonio Correia a Pegu em 1519*, Lisboa, 1975.

Timberg, Thomas A. (ed.), *Jews in India*, Delhi, 1986.

Tisserant, Eugene, *Eastern Christianity in India*, translated by E.R. Hambye, Calcutta, 1957.

Ure, John, *Prince Henry the Naviagator*, London, 1977.

Usher, Abbot Paysan, *The Early History of Deposit Banking in Mediterranean Europe*, Cambridge, 1943.

Varadarajan, Lotika, 'Commodity Structure and Indian Participation in the Trade of the Southern Seas, circa Ninth to Thirteenth Centuries', in *The Indian Ocean Explorations in History, Commerce and Politics*, edited by Satish Chandra, New Delhi, 1987, pp. 100ff.

Varghese, T.C., *Agrarian Change and Economic Consequences: Land Tenures in Kerala, 1850-1960*, Calcutta, 1970.

Vasconcellos, Joaquim de, *Albrecht Dürer e a sua Influencia na Peninsula*, Coimbra, 1929.

Vasconcelos, José Augusto Amaral Frazão de, *Pilotos das navegações portuguêsas dos séculos XV e XVII*, Lisbon, 1942.

Vasukuttan, K.A., *Bhoomisastram*, vol. III, Trivandrum, 1973.

Veluppillai, T.K., *Travancore State Manual*, 4 vols., Trivandrum, 1940.

Veluthat, Kesavan, *Brahman Settlements in Kerala*, Calicut, 1978.

Venn, T.W., *Cochin-Malabar, Palms and Pageants*, Calicut, 1948.

Verlinden, Charles, 'La colonie italienne de Lisbonne et le développment de l'économie metropolitaine et coloniale portugaise' in *Studi in Onore di Armando Sapori*, Milan, 1957, pp. 617-28 .

———, 'Italian Influence in Iberian Colonization', in *Hispanic American Historical Review*, 33, 1953, pp. 199-211.

———, 'Navigateurs, marchands et colons italiens au service de la découverte et de la colonisation portugaise sous Henri le Navigateur', in *Le Moyen Âge*, 64, 1958, pp. 467-97.

Vidago, João, 'Calendario das Armadas da India, 1497-1640', in *Anais do clube Militar Naval*, vol. CV, tom. 4-6, 1975, pp. 313-33.

Wallerstein, Immanuel, 'Dutch Hegemony in the Seventeenth Century World Economy', in Maurice Aymard (ed.), *Dutch Capitalism and World Capitalism*, London, 1982.

Wee, Hermann van der, 'Structural Changes in European Long-Distance Trade and Particularly in the Re-export Trade from South to North, 1350-1750', in James D. Tracy (ed.), *The Rise of Merchant Empires. Long Distance Trade in the Early Modern World 1350-1750*, Cambridge, 1990, pp. 351-70.

———, *The Growth of the Antwerp Market and the European Economy, Fourteenth-Sixteenth Centuries*, 2 vols., Louvain, 1963.

Wegg, Jervis, *The Decline of Antwerp under Philip of Spain*, London, 1924.

Weigend, C.G., 'Some Elements in Port Geography', in *Geographical Review*, XL, VIII, April, 1958, pp. 185-200.

Weistein, Donald, *Ambassador from Venice: Pictro Pasqualigo in Lisbon, 1501*, Minneapolis, 1960.

Werner, Theodor Gustav, 'Repräsentanten der Augsburger Fugger und Nürnberger Imhoff als Urheber der wichtigsten Handschriften des Paumgärtner -Archivs über Welthandelsbräuche im spätmittelalter und am Beginn der Neuzeit', in Hermann Aubin (ed.), *Vierteljahrschrift fur sozial - und wirtschaftsgeschichte*, Band 52, Wiesbaden, 1965, pp. 1-41.

Wernham, R. (ed.), *The New Cambridge Modern History: The Counter-Reformation and Price Revolution, 1559-1600*, vol. III, Cambridge, 1968.

Wheller, James Talboys and Macmillan Michael, *European Travellers in India*, Calcutta, 1956.

Whitehouse, T., *The Historical Notices of Cochin*, Kottayam, 1859.

Whiteway, R.S, *The Rise of Portuguese Power in India, 1497-1550*, New Delhi, 1989.

Wicki, Josef, 'Duas Relações sobre a Situação da India Portuguesa nos anos de 1568 e 1569', in *Studia*, 8, Lisboa, 1961.

———, 'The Portuguese Padroado in India in the Sixteenth Century and Francis Xavier', in Hambye E.R. and H.C. Perumalil (eds.), *Christianity in India*, Alleppey, 1972.

Wiet, Gaston, 'Ein Gutachten Conrad Peutingers in Sachen der handelsgesellschaften Ende 1522', in *Zeitschrift des Historischen Vereins für Schwaben und Neuburg*, Zweiter Jahrgang, Zweites Heft, Augsburg, 1875, pp. 188-215.

Williamson, J.A., *The Age of Drake*, Oxford, 1938.

Winius, George, *The Black Legend of Portuguese India. Diogo do Couto His Contemporaries and the Soldado Pratico. A Contribution to the Study of Political Corruption in the Empires of Early Modern Europe*, New Delhi, 1985.

———, 'Jewel Trading in Portuguese India in the XVI and XVII Centuries', in *Indica*, 25-1, March 1988, pp. 15-34.

Wood, A.J.R. Russell, *A World on the Move: The Portuguese in Africa, Asia and America 1415-1808*, Manchester, 1992.

Xavier, Felipe Neri, *Memoria sôbre as Moedas cunhadas em Goa*, Nova Goa, 1866.

Ziegenbalg, B., *Ausfürliche Beschreibung der Malabarische Heidentums*, Leipzig, 1926.

Index